INTERCULTURAL AND INTERNATIONAL COMMUNICATION

Edited by
Fred L. Casmir
Pepperdine University
Seaver College

HM
258
.I52

University Press of America

Copyright © 1978 by

University Press of America, Inc.™

4710 Auth Place, S.E., Washington, D.C. 20023

ISBN: 0-8191-0603-8

Library of Congress Catalog Card Number: 78-61389

ACKNOWLEDGEMENTS

The editor expresses appreciation to all who made significant contributions of time and expertise to this book, especially: Liisa Larson, who served as special editorial assistant; JoAnne Lam and Dorothea Molle, who prepared the manuscript; Keith Curtiss, Neva Hash and Linda Nashleanas, for indexing the volume; and Rick Bugey, Victoria Mansfield, and Helen West, who coordinated and proofread the completed copy.

CONTRIBUTING AUTHORS

J. Herbert Altschull
Professor of Journalism
Indiana University

Fred L. Casmir
Professor of Communication
Pepperdine University
Seaver College

Mary Chisholm
Professor of Sociology
Duquesne University

John C. Condon, Jr.
Professor of Communication
International Christian University
Tokyo

John David Dupree
Pacific Center for Human Growth
Berkeley, California

Jerome R. Epstein
Professor of Sociology
University of Houston

Richard Fitchen
Lecturer, Politics Board
University of California at Santa Cruz
Crown College

Edmund S. Glenn
Professor of Communication
University of Delaware

Frederick A. Gruber
Lecturer in Communication Studies
Torrence College of Advanced
  Education
Australia

James E. Grunig
Associate Professor of Journalism
University of Maryland

Anthony Hanley
Associate Researcher
PEACESAT
New Zealand

L. S. Harms
Professor of Communication
University of Hawaii at Manoa

Janice C. Hepworth
Professor of Communication
University of Colorado
Division of Continuing Education

P. Terrence Hopmann, Director
Center of International Studies
University of Minnesota

Charles H. Kraft
Professor of Anthropology and
  African Studies
School for World Missions
Fuller Theological Seminary

Arthur W. Larson
Lecturer in Speech Communication
California State University at North-
  ridge

John A. Lent
Professor of Journalism
School of Communications and
  Theatre
Temple University

CONTRIBUTING AUTHORS

Charles P. Loomis
Professor of Sociology
University of Houston

James Magee
Communications Consultant
World Health Oranization
Switzerland

Joe E. Pierce
Research Associate
East-West Communication Institute
Honolulu, Hawaii

John Saltiel
Associate Professor of Sociology
Montana State University

Margaret Schneider Stacey
Lecturer in Journalism
Marquette University

Edward C. Stewart
Washington Educational Research
  Center
Washington, District of Columbia

Yasumasa Tanaka, Chairman
Department of Political Science
Gakushuin University
Tokyo, Japan

Rolf Von Eckartsberg
Professor of Sociology
Duquesne University

Joseph Woelfel
Assistant Professor of Communication
Michigan State University

Joanne Sanae Yamauchi
Associate Professor of Communica-
  tion
School of Communication
The American University

CONTENTS

PREFACE: THE ROAD AHEAD

PREFACE

EVEN A QUICK LOOK at scholarly writings in many fields indicates that Intercultural and International Communications is becoming an area of widespread and deep concern. This is the case not so much as a result of scholarly choice, but because of very practical realities in today's world which are resulting in an ever increasing number of contacts between various cultures.

These developments come after a period of time when our faith in behavioral science-methodologies, so-called scientific rigor, and statistical analyses as means of discovering whatever exists or is assumed to exist in Man and his environment has been almost unlimited. As a result, the academicians dreaded to be accused by their peers of lacking scientific rigor in their work, or making insufficient application of existing methodologies in their research. Intuition, contemplation, or philosophical inclinations were often viewed as flying in the face of the high state of development in our mechanistically, scientifically-oriented age.

Yet recent re-evaluations of this attitude may make the present period one of the least difficult moments in history as far as the study of intercultural and international communication is concerned, helping us to avoid putting a gigantic methodology cart before the tiniest horse of a subject area. William Howell tells the story of an international meeting involving American and Japanese scholars interested in human communication. In searching for a term to make adequate discussion of a specific area possible, the term "sociolinguistic relevance" was suggested. American response was predictable, centering around an immediate demand that the word be "defined." Just as predictable, was the Japanese counter-plea not to define the word, for fear that one would "kill" it. I feel a great need, therefore, to "back off," to re-evaluate, to reconsider many things which we simply assumed to be generally accepted or agreed upon. In the pages of this book some ideas will, as a result, be challenged. Others will be re-examined, and others yet replaced by more contemporary insights.

To avoid any misunderstandings, let me emphasize that I am not attacking the necessary discipline of a rigorous scientific approach, or the use of well established methodologies, *if* we have first made as certain as possible that we are indeed being both scientific and rigorous, and that we have truly developed methodologies which are applicable in our area of concern. Maybe then we can achieve the discovery of something besides those factors which our very methodologies have pre-destined us to look for.

Among other things, this appears to me to be a time for listening, observing, thinking, and comparing notes with individuals who have multi-cultural backgrounds. Maybe that can help us to avoid building another Ptolemaic model of the world, this time one which seeks to fix human experience into orbits around the thought-models of Western Man and our established natural-science methodologies.

It seems to me that nothing could be more challenging in our search for meaning, structure, order, and control over our world than the statement by an eminent scientist-philosopher:

> The old foundations of scientific thought are becoming un-intelligible. Time, space, matter . . . structure, pattern function, etc., all require reinterpretation.[1]

Whitehead indeed seems to have had the vision or insight which made it possible to see human beings and their universe as organic, metabolic structures or systems which respond to all events in an ever changing, ever continuing search for internal balance and balanced interaction.

In recent years scientist-philosophers and epistomologists have begun to question our ability to discover all existing entities or realities by means of supposedly objective scientific observations of our physical world. Interestingly, we consider the possibility that what we observe and report may not be as much the real world "out there" as it is an expression of the world "inside us." A multitude of interrelated, interacting factors may cause us to see "our" world, but not necessarily someone else's world, maybe even after we have used the instruments which we have developed to extend the use of our senses. It is at this point that our attempts at communication become of vital concern, as we strive somehow to transmit verbal and other stimuli which are intended to reproduce in other human organisms a mental model of the world similar to our own. One natural scientist makes this important point: "Natural science always presupposes man, and we are not only spectators but also participants on the stage of life."[2]

Not only Heisenberg but many other scientists now believe that what we observe is not nature itself, but rather nature as shaped or influenced by human beings and by our methods of searching, observing, questioning—and communicating.

Consider in addition to all that has been said so far, the cultural tendency of Western Man to "conquer" his environment, or the obstacles he finds in his way. Only in our extended contacts with others, especially in Eastern cultures, have we become more aware of the possibility that there may be other approaches to life. In the ecological crises of the 20th Century many of us have been forced to question our usual, traditional methods of dealing with our environment. The idea of "fitting in" or becoming a part of what is seen as a living, ever-changing, larger, or even universal system may require some dramatic changes in all of our conceptions of self, of others, and of the environment. That appears to be true whether we want to accept this point of view as our own, or simply try to understand it. However, such an approach makes possible a very different cultural-ecological mental model which considers human beings as metabolic rather than mechanical systems. Human beings can be seen as systems or organisms which take advantage of and use all available factors in their continuing striving for understanding and adaptation. If such a model is used, human beings are seen as doing more than simply producing mechanical responses to existing stimuli, or attempting to create an organized, structured world by means of mechanical feedback loops, similar to those found in cybernetic systems.

In the Western World there have been many who attempted to superimpose their concepts of existing structures on the world or universe. Whether that was the earth-centered Ptolemaic model, the static helio-centered model of a Copernicus, or the Aristotelean logical model, all of them categorized, structured and provided with models which in turn powerfully caused us to see our world, our universe in ways specified by the models. All of them eventually were found to inadequately represent the fluid, metabolic relationships of the existing universe and human beings.

Consider Aristotle's logic for a moment. Even today we tend to use his concept of opposites while categorizing our impressions of self, others, and the world as good-bad, short-long, heavy-light, and so forth. This represents a never-ending array of polar-concepts limiting our perceptions as well as our expression of what we think we have observed. For centuries, in rhetorical systems of various types, and for a shorter period of time in such social sciences as psychology, we have worked with stimulus-response models which not only tended to shape our total approach to communication, but which eventually make it evident that we were "systematically" distorting Man's communicative efforts. We looked for effective speakers, effective sources, effective means or methods of stimulating receivers in simplistic cause-effect relationships, all the time virtually ignoring any active, fluid role which all participating factors, or participating individuals might play in the total process. Eventually even our human institutions began to reflect a static, mechanistic, cybernetic impression of individual man. More than that we tended to hold on to these institutions in spite of the mounting evidence that organizations built on such a model were not adequate for our 20th Century world. More recently we began to stress that "meaning" has to be sought in the mind and experience of the receiver, while still attempting to structure rather simplistic circular-feedback, mechanistic-interaction, or cause-effect models of human communication.

Yet on the basis of contemporary knowledge, we can assume that humans have to communicate. We can also assume that since human beings are not machines but metabolic, open systems, their communicative behavior must be considered from a holistic, open-system, metabolic, cultural-ecological point of view.

Meanwhile a number of views, still fragmented, atomistic, some built upon mechanical mental models, or applying traditional approaches, continue to appear in our publications. They are often strongly influenced, by the old, well-established approaches to the study of communication, based on centuries of Aristotelean and mechanistic thinking. Yet it is important that other views are also presented in the hope that out of all of them, may come a more adequate way of seeing the communication of individuals. After all, it is not cultures which communicate, but individual human beings (who are often associated in groups), who communicate with other individuals in other cultures, in a never-ending varied, changing, individualized kaleidoscope of interaction.

We strive to control our world and ourselves within that world. Our need for a feeling of security and order often becomes so great, that we will *force* patterns, order, and structure on all human endeavors, whether they fit or not. We need to challenge each pattern, make each inadequate frozen structure come alive in a new process of thought which requires more than memorizing old categories. We need to add, subtract, discard, accept, keeping the holistic, metabolic, open-system in mind. In that process we may also discover some of the excitement that comes with a truly interdisciplinary approach.

As a fairly specific starting point for our study together, we could try the following: Let us counteract the tendency to study Intercultural and International Communication in an attempt to discover what WE can DO to THEM with WHAT under which CIRCUMSTANCES to get THEM to see things and do things OUR WAY. In other words, let us attempt to stop forcing our world view on others for the sake of making our own thought-model of the world supreme and secure. Secondly, we need to overcome the temptation to simply fall back into patterns of thought which lead us to discover differences or opposites, quietly assuming all the time that the cultural system with which we are familiar must of necessity also adequately structure the world for others. We need to become aware of self and others as open rather than closed systems. Only then may we attempt to discover any valid *patterns* of cultural heredity which have interacted to produce the fluid, cultural characteristics which result from interaction with other human beings and the environment.

At such a level of searching we may become capable of looking for more than *equivalencies* in other cultures or languages, making simple comparisons, or categorizing parallels which use our own cultural categories as the "natural" standard. Instead we can begin to look for more than surface reassurances that all human beings see things and think about things as we do. We may even avoid making the "discovery" of similarities or differences our primary aim. We may overcome the common belief that objects simply exist and that these objects should, therefore, be thought about, and communicated about in the same way by anyone observing them.

Thus, any human being becomes more than a mechanical receiver in our mental model. He or she becomes instead an interpreter, or a filtering system, interacting with the total environment as an individual, open system, who is influenced in his or her observations by others in the culture and by the language they share. Most people see objects, and their languages represent special ways of looking at these objects and of interpreting them. We need to discover how human beings interpret, arrange, split up or lump together, observed entities in their environment. Not because these are correct or incorrect ways of reacting to the environment, but because they serve as indicators which help us to understand human beings, while avoiding a study of their environments as if they were really quite separate from communicative behavior.

For the deepest understanding of others it appears necessary to immerse oneself as a metabolic, open system in another culture, to draw one's life, as it were, from the cultural source. Only in that way would it appear possible that we learn to understand its underlying philosophy, or a culture's way of seeing the world.

For most of us, however, such an intense involvement is not possible from a standpoint of the time or effort involved, nor it is necessarily needed. Many of our encounters are short-term, part of a much larger experience involving many human beings in many cultures and settings. As a result, rather than deep immersion in the existing culture of one or more of the participants, we have to devise or develop patterns or skills of interaction which allow us to build momentary, or short-lived, communication subcultures. These provide a basis for accomplishing through mutual arrangements, understandings, and agreements the limited goals we more commonly need to reach.

We have more questions than answers concerning human communication at this point in time, but as has been suggested, the way in which we formulate our questions could have a decisive influence on the answers which we may eventually develop. It does appear that in human communicative behavior we have a subject for study which cannot be based on a thought-model of consistent, invariable human behavior in space and time. Thus a transactional approach may *remind* us that distinctive human features cannot be adequately considered if we see humans only as physical beings. Or we may be reminded by others that the involvement of human senses in communication is important, as is the involvement of the individual's ego. Certainly many other variables have been and can be considered, but they all serve to remind us to be tentative in our approach, eclectic, and centered on the individual human communicator as we work towards our eventual conceptualization of Intercultural and International Communication.

Malibu, California　　　　　　　　　　　Fred L. Casmir
July 4, 1978
fls

FOOTNOTES

[1] Alfred North Whitehead, *Science and the Modern World.* New York: Cambridge University Press, 1933, p. 21.

[2] Werner Heisenberg, "The Representation of Nature in Contemporary Physics." *Current*, June 1960, p. 59.

I

1

I

A THEORETICAL FRAMEWORK
FOR THE STUDY OF
INTERCULTURAL AND INTERNATIONAL COMMUNICATION

IN THE FOLLOWING pages we present relatively brief summaries of *some* theoretical considerations developed in a variety of areas related to the study of intercultural and international communication. A specific attempt is made to stress a holistic, or General Systems view. This is coupled with a critical reevaluation of natural-science methodologies as they are applied to the study of human interaction.

There is at present no theory of human communication. For the purposes of this book we will consider communication not merely as an "overlaid" function, or some useful technique which can at will be turned on or off by human beings, but rather as our most fundamental tool or means for survival. No growth, development, interaction, continuation of human efforts, or development of new efforts is possible without communication. Even the basic metabolic, biological, or neurological survival-processes of human beings are dependent on internal and external communication to counteract entropy in a constant exchange with the environment.

There is no possibility at this point in time of settling the issue of whether or not natural-science methodologies will provide us with an adequate understanding of human behavior. Nor will an attempt be made in this book to stress either logical or teleological approaches to the study of human communication to the exclusion of opposing points of view. All I am interested in doing at this point is to suggest that the student of human communicative interaction on the intercultural and international level needs to understand and be familiar with the approaches, systems, and findings of scholars in a variety of fields to undergird his own specific, focused search for better understanding.

2

A THEORETICAL FRAMEWORK FOR THE STUDY OF
INTERCULTURAL AND INTERNATIONAL COMMUNICATION

There is an attempt made in this book to specifically deal with *communication*. While using insights from various disciplines, the writers clearly focus on communication as the central effort of man to structure, control, and create his environment, while recognizing that human beings at the same time are influenced by that environment not merely in a circular or stimulus-response pattern, but as active partners to an intricate, highly complex *process* of communication. This process is seen as never ending, always changing, dynamic, although for a specific emphasis or study it is often "frozen" for closer inspection, and then defined in some specific, limited, purposeful way. These specific instances of communication, or communications, have indeed led to some theoretical formulations which, however, have shown little transferability, or generalizability, providing little help in the overall development of a communication-theory. Thus we have accomplished very little up to now in identifying deep structures, or communication codes existing in human beings from the moment of birth, or even before. The question of what we bring into this world and what we receive by direct impact of our environment has been debated hotly, and for a long time. Neurobiologists and neurophysiologists in an increasing number of studies indicate that we bring neurological equipment into this world which makes us *active partners* in interactional processes with our environment. This equipment allows us to receive, evaluate, reject, and use whatever our environment, society, and culture provide in a highly selective, individualized way in response to some underlying, inherent code of survival. This code appears to enable us to develop both important individual components and common features which in some way are applicable to human interaction anywhere. These observable expression-forms or communication-patterns based on our internal survival codes appear to be influenced in their specific formation by primary and other groups within our own culture, which have fairly consistent and early influences on us.

Even this brief discussion indicates that neither is it necessary for the student of intercultural or international communication to "invent the wheel over and over again," nor does that seem particularly desirable. Instead, we are attempting in this book to

3

provide a reminder of the fact that much has been done already by others to provide us with a launching-platform for the specific applications of such insights to the fields of study with which this book is concerned. What can be only a suggestion here needs to become a continued search by students of international and intercultural communication for the broadest possible understanding of relevant background information.

This section also seeks to avoid something which has been a bane of much of the past research in intercultural and international communication. *Episodic,* highly limited, but often interesting and informative reports of culture-specific ways of dealing with such matters as food, time, sex, family relations, and age have unfortunately done little to allow broader, generally applicable, or generalizable insights. The two major purposes of this first section thus are to stress *communication* and to attempt to do more than provide a number of culture-specific instances in the vague hope that they will eventually form some discernable pattern resulting in a generally applicable theory of intercultural and international communication.

Gruber's challenge to empirical methods is directed towards some specific areas, centering around the concept of a "natural language." However, his more general challenge to our use of empirical methods goes far beyond the specific examples he cites. Hepworth further develops this theme by relating her own challenges to a broad scope of methodologies and other factors, considering the applicability and transferability of various methodologies as they relate to cultural barriers. How *practical* theoretical considerations can be is clearly shown by Grunig as he indicates the need for the development of a General Systems view in both the planning and in action relating to the development of nations. His chapter represents a clearly defined rationale for an approach advocated throughout this book, considering not only the component parts of human communication, but also their interaction within systems defined and structured by human beings for their own use and the use of others. There exists also a considerable and continuing concern with statistical, empirical approaches which many of us hope will make possible valid, reliable research and eventually the prediction and control of human behavior, in keeping with long-held convictions concerning the use of natural science methodologies. One such imaginative attempt, representative of many others, is the General Linear Model proposed by Woefel and Saltiel. It is little more than an introduction to the use of such methodologies, but, depending on the inclinations of both teachers and students using this book, it can be expanded to consideration of many other, traditional, empirical approaches developed and used in the social sciences. Since this book pays great attention to the intentional aspects of human communication, Fitchen's summary of transactional analysis as it relates to intercultural and international communication allows us to briefly consider the fact that communication, finally and always, is something in which individual human beings engage, even if they represent nations or states, and even if they meet in groups. By way of summarizing the major concerns in this section of the book, Larson continues the emphasis on integrating a variety of approaches and reviewing a large number of applicable studies pointing to the relationship of factors in individuals to communication styles and interaction.

One very important aspect of all human communication efforts in contemporary society deals with the use of technology and mass communication media. Theoretical background for the use and influence of these media is provided by Tanaka, while Harms and Richstad remind us of the fact that even if the technological aspects are readily understood, or carefully considered, human communication also implies value systems, as well as complex ethical and cultural problems. Many feel a need, therefore, to provide codes or regulations to assure future development and survival under a comprehensive statement of the human right to communicate. Agencies throughout the world have struggled for some time with the perplexing problems of use and application of communication technologies. This can serve to remind all of us that the mere understanding of mechanical aspects of communication does not automatically lead to an adequate understanding of other aspects of communication such as ethics, aesthetics, values, and belief systems which may be as necessary to our survival as human beings as are the basic biological aspects of our existence. Casmir provides a summary discussion of some underlying assumptions about communication, human beings, and the processes involved in inter-cultural and international communication, leading to a practical basis or even methodology for human interaction in these settings.

In the long run all methodologies, technologies, and theories re-lating to human communication must meet the ultimate test: Do they contribute to the understanding and the ultimate purpose of human communication, namely to help assure the survival of human beings as creatures which are not merely comparable to other living beings in our world, but who are increasingly being recognized as *unique* living beings?

Frederic A. Gruber:

Why Empirical Methods Cannot Apply in Communication Research: The Case Against Behaviorism [1]

Introduction

Adequate theories of communication, including intercultural and international communication, must include accounts of underlying natural languages without which the communication could not take place.[2] While other perhaps equally crucial matters must also be contained in theories of communication (gesture, situation and occasion variables, etc.) a theory of communication incompatible with the facts of natural language could not accurately be judged complete or adequate. This position is philosophical. It asserts what a subject matter —— communications —— ought and ought not include. Consequently, this position is not arguable from a basis of fact alone. So, rather than argue perspective; consider the following assumption:

No communication theory can be adequate if it cannot, in principle, account for natural language.

If this assumption is entertained, worthwhile arguments can be, and have been constructed to show what an adequate theory of communication would have to be like were we to have one. Conversely, a number of theoretical and philosophical positions can be eliminated. These are positions which, because of their basic structure are incompatible with the facts of natural language. Among the approaches eliminated on this basis is behavioral psychology. The reasons for eliminating behavioral psychology as a contributor to communication theory cast doubt on the applicability of the empirical method of science. This does not imply that more applicable methods of science ought ignore empirical consequences; rather, that appropriate epistemologies cannot be based on objective observables. [3]

Behavior, Associationism, and a Problem in Taxonomy

Behavior theory, having been used extensively in summarizing simple relationships between "stimulation" and "response" in other species, was extended to more complex actions; most importantly, to language behavior. Consequently, we have seen many attempts to characterize human language in simple stimulus–response terms.

The founder of behaviorism, John B. Watson, stated the goal of behavior theory, ". . . to be able, given the stimulus, to predict the response —— or, seeing the reaction take place to state what the stimulus is that has called out the reaction."[4] The program of behaviorism has not substantially changed. Not so long ago, a former President of the American Psychological Association, Charles E. Osgood, echoed the same position, saying, "Behavior theory . . . operates to generate the lawful relations we observe among and between stimuli and responses."[5]

This goal cannot be realized. There are at least three lines of argument which demonstrate the futility of approaching language from a behavioral model: (1) Behaviorism is vague and where it is precise, it is tautological. (2) Language is not behavior. (3) Behavior theories do not work when applied to language. Each of these failings of behavior theory will be discussed.

It is necessary in behavior theories that the universe of behavior be parsed into distinct and discrete categories: (1) stimuli, (2) responses. It does not matter much how these categories are subdivided or represented; whether they are noted as S, s, R, r, R_x, r_m, etc., or related by boxes, arrows, lines, chains, or other devices. There must be some kind of independently identifiable stimuli and responses. No amount of modifying or patching can alter this basic assumption.

But, stimuli and responses are not nominitive concepts. We cannot generate lawful relations among and between entities we cannot lawfully recognize. We must, for example, decide if any

8

physical occurrence to which the organism is capable of reacting is to be called a stimulus on a given occasion, or only one to which the organism in fact reacts. Similarly, we must decide whether any part of the behavior is to be called a response, or only one connected with the stimuli in lawful ways.

In order to make the first distinction, that is, whether or not an organism reacts to a stimulus, we must decide of what a reaction consists. To borrow Gregory Bateson's example, [6] suppose I receive a letter from my mother-in-law today which beseeches me to reply at some future date. It will be difficult to determine if my mother-in-law's mandate (not the letter itself) is a stimulus or not unless I do, in fact, reply. On the other hand, my mother-in-law may write me again because I have not answered her first letter. Thus, for her, the absence of stimulation may serve as stimulation.

If we decide that a stimulus has not occurred unless the organism actually reacts, we have merely shifted the decision to whether all the behavior of an organism is to be considered the reaction, or only a part of the behavior. If we decide it will be all the behavior of an organism, it will be impossible to distinguish any lawful relationship between such vague and inclusive behaviors and the multitude of events we wish to call stimuli. We have, by virtue of making this decision, eliminated the possibility of making the distinctions necessary for establishing lawful relations; especially when we fail to establish limits on temporal aspects of the behavior.

Suppose we instead chose only portions of behavior. Now we must decide which parts are to be called the response. Since choosing any part at random is, in terms of lawful relations, equivalent to choosing all parts, we must make our choice on some *a priori* basis. However, to do so means our definitions of stimuli and responses are not independent, but are connected by an *a priori* choice. That is, we must identify stimuli and responses by the relations to each other. But, to assert this renders stimuli and responses extraneous to the search for lawful relations.

Alternately, if we decide that a stimulus has occurred whether or not the organism reacts, so long as the organism is capable of reacting to the stimulus, we are faced with the awesome task of determining the momentary capabilities of the organism. Assuming we can accomplish this feat, we are still faced with the difficulty of deciding just what part of the organism's behavior is related lawfully to which stimulus the organism is capable of reacting to at the moment. Here again we are faced with the necessity of choosing our relations on some *a priori* basis.

Thus, the notions of stimulus and response can be used only to reflect lawful relations already assigned and can be of no use whatever in discovering or generating such relations.

Suppose we could render the notions of stimulus and response independently distinct and discrete. What then? Implicit in this choice of terms as well as in the goals of behaviorism as stated by Watson is the allegation that a stimulus will always precede a response. The only matter left in completing a coherent theory is a mechanism by which stimulus and response are related. Behaviorism chose a single device: association.

The notion of association has been evident in explanations of human behavior at least since Aristotle's *De Memoria et Reminiscentia* [8] though it received more complete treatment in works by Thomas Hobbes[9] and John Stuart Mill.[10] What became known as the "doctrine of associations" states that when two or more objects are observed to have a common property or often appear together, a mental bond will be formed connecting those two or more objects. Specification of the sorts of common properties which have been observed to create such bonds constitutes a body of what has been known as the "laws of association." Enumeration of the laws of association includes recency, primacy, similarity, contrast, contiguity in space and time, frequency, vividness, and many more.[11] While most philosophical writings on associationism concern themselves with the association of non–observables (e.g., ideas, images, feelings, etc.) modern empiricists have rejected such notions and applied only a selected few of the laws of association to observable occurrences.[12]

Most prominent in behavior theory is association by contiguity. According to James Deese, "The law of contiguity, so far as I know, has never been doubted as the cornerstone of the associative process."[13] It is hard to imagine and perhaps impossible to cite a behavior theory which is not associationistic.

Three characteristics are essential to all behavior theories:

I.   A basic vocabulary of two categories: S, R

II.   A single relating mechanism: Association.

III.   A time—order limitation: S precedes R.

By examination, it can be seen that only three parsimonious notational combinations are possible. All three have been adopted. In historical order, they are:

A.   Classical conditioning.[14] Fig. (1)

B.   Operant (instrumental) conditioning.[15] Fig. (2)

C.   Mediation theories.[16] Fig. (3)

Classical Conditioning

Classical conditioning (also called Pavlovian and respondent conditioning) is one of the *a priori* mechanisms used by behaviorists to calculate with stimuli and responses. According to classical conditioning theory, an unconditioned stimulus (UCS) is given as eliciting a response (R). Contiguity of the conditioned stimulus (CS) with the unconditioned stimulus (UCS) is the condition necessary for increasing the CS—R relation, while the exercise of the CS—R without the contiguity of the UCS weakens the relation.

In Pavlov's classical experiment, the UCS was the presence of food powder in a dog's mouth. The R was the act of the dog's salivating. The CS was the ringing of a bell in contiguity with the introduction of food powder. Thus, the dog came to salivate at the ringing of the bell.[17]

If, as Watson,[18] Staats,[19] and Osgood[20] as well as other psychologists maintain, we come to associate certain words with outside stimulus events, then our "natural" reactions to the stimulus events will become conditioned to these words. There are several practical problems in this approach.

Imagine you have learned the word "hot" in this fashion. We could say the UCS would be the presence of heat. The unlearned R may be the sensation of heat, the opening of pores of the skin, perspiration, etc. The sound sequence "hot" would comprise the CS, which in the presence of the UCS will strengthen the relation between the CS and the R.

Now let us imagine that you were lost in the arctic. Logically, having a lifetime of conditioning to the word "hot" which now brings forth responses such as feeling warm, etc., you sit down on the

11

nearest cake of ice and begin repeating the word "hot." As a good behaviorist, you realize that two possibilities occur: (1) you would feel and act warm, or (2) the word "hot" would loose meaning for you and eventually come to mean "cold."

The trouble is, it doesn't work. Behavior theory does not make a distinction between meaning and reference, which has for so long been recognized as crucial by philosophers of language.[21] "Tricky Dick" and the Thirty–Seventh President of the United States of America may refer to the same person, but they do not mean the same thing.

Moreover, classical conditioning requires multiple repetitions of a word (or other linguistic unit) in order that the CS–R bonds be strengthened. Yet, as any mother of a normal toddler will tell you, this was not required for her youngster to acquire some of his more colorful expressions. One–trial learning may not be possible in behavior theory, but it certainly seems to happen.[22]

Pavlov observed that two other principles also operate in the classical conditioning situation.

First, although conditioning appears to take place when a paired UCS and CS relationship is repeated, this process does not seem to extend further. If a previously conditioned CS is now paired with a new CS in the same manner, conditioning does not readily occur. In Pavlov's experiment, new conditioning does not readily take place when a new stimulus, say, a word, is paired with the ringing of the bell. A third order, for example, the pairing of a second word with the first, simply does not occur.[23] There is effectively no higher–order conditioning. A consequence of these findings is that new words of an abstract nature cannot be paired to further abstract words. Hence, classical conditioning has little power to account for abstract terms by its own empirical criteria.

Second, in order that classical conditioning occur, the CS must occur temporally just before or simultaneous to the occurrence of the UCS. The ringing of the bell in Pavlov's classical experiment had to be concurrent with the introduction of food powder, or slightly prior. When a CS occurs after a UCS, no conditioning takes place, a finding which has been repeatedly confirmed. There is no "backward" conditioning.[24]

So far the arguments have centered around words. We can also consider groups of words such as the phrase and the sentence.

O.H. Mowrer in his Presidential Address before the American Psychological Association forwarded the posit that the sentence is a conditioning device.

> . . . the sentence is, pre—eminently, a *conditioning device*, and that its chief effect is to produce new associations, new learning, just as any other paired presentation of stimuli may do. This position is congruent with the traditional notion that predication is the essense of language and may indicate, perhaps more precisely than purely linguistic research has done, the basic nature of this phenomenon.[25]

Let us borrow Mowrer's example sentence, "Tom is a thief." According to Mowrer, this sentence would cause a "transferring (of) meanings from *sign to sign* within a given person, within a given mind." "Thief," according to Mowrer, ". . . is a sort of 'unconditioned stimulus' (which when) . . . we create a situation from which we, as psychologists, can predict a fairly definite result. On the basis of the familiar principle of conditioning, we would expect that some of the reaction evoked by the sign, 'thief' would get shifted to the first sign, 'Tom' so that Charles, the hearer of the sentence would thereafter respond to the word 'Tom' somewhat as he had previously responded to the word, 'thief.' "[26] Figure (4).

While this explanation of the psychological function of a sentence may have initial appeal, it cannot apply equally to the sentences.

1. A thief is Tom.
2. Is Tom a thief?
3. Tom is not a thief,
4. Pope Paul is a thief.
5. Your mother is a platypus.

Although it is almost plausible to ascribe transfer of "meaning" from "thief" to "Tom," it violates basic conditioning principles to contend the reverse as in sentence (1), which is also an acceptable English sentence, for this constitutes backward conditioning. Another exaggerated extension of basic conditioning principles is, that in order to view the sentence as a conditioning device, it must be

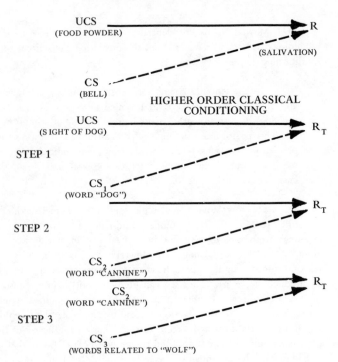

Figure 1. Classical Conditioning. An Unconditioned Stimulus (UCS) elicits a response (R). Contiguity of the UCS with a Conditioned Stimulus (CS) is an associative condition necessary for strengthening the CS-R relation. Exercise of the CS-R without the contiguous association weakens the CS-R relation. In Pavolov's experiments, the UCS was food powder in the dog's mouth. The R was the dog's resulting salivation and the CS was the sound of a bell ringing. The notion of higher order classical conditioning simply repeats this process by treating a previously conditioned CS as an UCS. Thus, in the above figure words, "related to wolf" come to draw forth whatever (total) (R_T) responses a subject may have previously had to the sight of dogs.

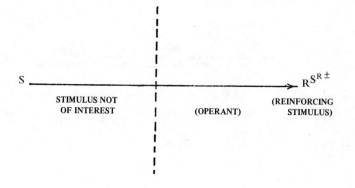

Figure 2. Instrumental or Operant Conditioning. A stimulus (S) which is assumed to have been present, but is of no immediate interest, elicits a Response (R) or "operant." If the operant is followed by a reinforcing stimulus ($S^{R\pm}$) its strength (probably of occurrence) is increased. The associative bond forms between the operant and the reinforcing stimulus.

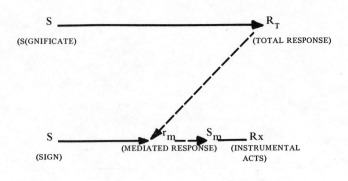

Figure 3. A Mediation Theory. Meaning and reference are distinguished as separate stimuli; the significate or referential stimuli and the sign, or "meaning" stimuli. The significate stimuli elicits a total response to that object or event in the environment. At the same time the sign stimuli elicits in the organism an intermediate response (r_m) which becomes associated with some fractional part (not all) of the total response to the significate. The mediated response also serves to elicit a mediated stimulus, or itself serves as an intermediate stimulus which elicits whatever acts "take account" of the sign stimulus. Thus, a response to a sign need not be the same as that to a significate, but the sign will "take account" of the significate. Of course, the sign and the significate presentations must, again, meet the associative conditions in presentation, e.g., contiguity, etc. The mediate stage is not directly observable, but inferable and there is no specification in the theory as to exactly which part or parts of the total response become associated with the mediated response.

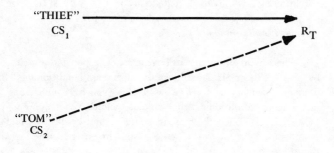

Figure 4. Classical conditioning applied to simple sentence structures.

(After Mowrer, 1954)

a device to accomplish higher-order conditioning with frequent recourse to single-trial learning. Nor can the paradigm account for a lack of belief in the predication (sentences 4 and 5) and sentential forms which are not matters of simple positive predication (sentences 2 and 3). Moreover, this analysis cannot account for simple syntactic transformations.

There seems to be no alternative but to conclude that classical conditioning is wholly inadequate to account for natural language.

Operant Conditioning

The second alternative arrangement of the essential principles of behavior theory is instrumental (operant) conditioning. B.F. Skinner's primary concern is with this type of conditioning. In instrumental conditioning, the stimulus conditions which are said to be sufficient to elicit the gross responses cannot be specified and are considered irrelevant to the process. Most important is the fact that the responses are emitted and that the emitted responses cause ensuing consequences. Skinner calls this operant behavior. He is convinced that most human behavior, including language, is of this type.[27]

The basic laws of operant conditioning are: (1) If an operant is followed by the presentation of a reinforcing stimulus (S^{R+}), its strength is increased, and (2) if an operant is not followed by a reinforcing stimulus, its strength is decreased. If it happens that the reinforcing stimulus occurs only when certain stimulus conditions are present, then it is said that the operant is a discriminated operant. However, the stimulus conditions are not said to elicit the discriminant operant. The stimulus conditions, then, are considered as necessary, but not sufficient conditions for a discriminated operant to occur. The focus is on the operant itself.

It is apparent that a key notion of operant conditioning is that of the reinforcer. In *Behavior of Organisms*, Skinner defines reinforcement.

The operation of reinforcement is defined as the presentation of a certain kind of stimulus in a temporal relation with either a stimulus or a response. A reinforcing stimulus is defined as such by its power to produce the resulting change [in strength]. There is no circularity about this: some stimuli are found to produce the change, others not, and they are classified as reinforcing and non—reinforcing accordingly.[28]

Skinner's definition of reinforcement is a tautology, his claims of non—circulatory notwithstanding. In order to identify a reinforcer, we must appeal to a preceding change in response strength. In order to predict a change in response strength, we must appeal to a reinforcer.

Skinner is not alone among learning theorists in defining reinforcement circularly. Mowrer,[29] Ferster,[30] Goldiamond[31] and many others subscribe to this view. Staats, for example, defines a reinforcer as:

> When certain stimuli closely follow a certain behavior they increase the probability of that behavior occurring again in the future. Stimuli that serve this function are called positive reinforcers.[32]

Since there exist only two basic categories of volcabulary in behavior theory, it is no wonder that they must be defined in terms of each other. The only alternative, it would seem, would be to introduce additional terms. In fact, this is what had been done earlier by theorists such as Hull[33] and Tolman[34] who spoke of "rewards" and "punishments" thereby evading some of the problems of circularity in definition. However, this alternative made theoretical predictability dependent upon the original assignment of terms.

When is candy not a reinforcer (or reward)? When you suffer stomach distress? If you are on a diet? If you are diabetic? If you have eaten too much already? If you expected one—thousand dollars instead? If you dislike that kind of candy? To make an accurate prediction involves information not included in behavior theory, but which is probably more predictive than that available in conditioning terms.

Definitional problems can sometimes be solved by examining the use of a term in context. Noam Chomsky cites more than a dozen of Skinner's uses of the term and concludes, " . . . it can be seen that the notion of reinforcement has totally lost whatever objective meaning it may ever have had."[35]

Here are a few examples of Skinner's use of the term "reinforcement."

> A man talks to himself . . . . because of the reinforcement he receives.[36]
>
> Thinking is "behaving" which automatically affects behavior and is reinforcing because it does so.[37]
>
> Care in problem solving and rationalization are automatically self–reinforcing.[38]
>
> We can also reinforce someone by emitting verbal behavior as such.[39]
>
> . . . by not emitting verbal behavior . . .[40]
>
> . . . by acting appropriately on some future occasion.[41]
>
> The writer is reinforced by the fact that his verbal behavior may reach over centuries or to thousands of listeners or readers at the same time. The writer may not be reinforced often or immediately, but his net reinforcement may be great.[42]
>
> . . . to describe circumstances which would be reinforcing if they were to occur . . .[43]
>
> . . . to avoid repetition.[44]
>
> . . . to "hear" his own name though in fact it was not mentioned . . .[45]

Chomsky observes that reinforcing stimuli for Skinner are peculiar in that they can increase the strength of behavior although no behavior may have been emitted to be strengthened, the reinforcing stimulus never impinged on the organism, and the reinforcement never existed, but was only hoped for.[46]

According to the instrumental conditioning paradigm, the organism emits gross behavior which is gradually shaped by application of careful reinforcements. In the case of language, it is presumed that vocalizations of the infant are gradually shaped by reinforcement into phonemes, words, phrases, etc., until functional language emerges. Language for the behaviorist is essentially normative verbal behavior.[47] However, cases of congenital aphonia, (children born without the physical ability to speak) show that these youngsters learn to understand their native language in spite of the handicap.[48] Since they have emitted no speech, what was reinforced? It is also a commonplace among speech pathologists and linguists that children understand more language than they employ in speech. In order of acquisition comprehension precedes production.* How can we account for this differential ability since it represents learning in the absence of overt responses?

Learning theorists claim it is necessary for the language community to carefully arrange and apply appropriate reinforcements. Yet, it is most unlikely that the average child receives such careful differential reinforcements for his language behavior. It is even less likely, as Chomsky points out, that the immigrant child who learns a second language in the streets receives the necessary contingent reinforcements.[49] Yet, these children learn the language to which they are exposed with little difficulty while their parents often do not.

Moreover, for all normal speakers of a language there are innumerable sentences we have never uttered and therefore could have received no reinforcement for speaking them. Yet, we may speak them with our next breath. For example, "The triceratops rambled aimlessly in the briar," is a new sentence for me, as far as I know.

But, there is an accumulation of experimental data alleged to demonstrate the efficacy of operant conditioning. Since these experiments have been conducted on many species and on many different tasks, it is superficially reasonable to make the kind of generalization Skinner does.

> . . . recent advances in the analysis of behavior permit us to approach it with a certain optimism. New experimental techniques and fresh formulations have revealed a new level of order and precision. The basic processes and relations which give verbal behavior its special characteristics are now fairly well understood. Much of the experimental work responsible for this advance has been carried out on other species, but the results have proved to be surprisingly free of species restriction. Recent work has shown that the methods can be extended to human behavior without serious modification.[50]

* See notation following footnote[81].

21

Greenspoon, echoing the same optimism, states:

> . . . it should be possible to work with verbal behavior in much the same way that experimenters have worked with the behavior of rats, pigeons, etc. It should also be possible to investigate the same kinds of variables that have been investigated with the non—verbal behavior of humans and infra—humans.[51]

According to these predictions, we would expect the principles of instrumental conditioning would hold true for at least the most simple forms of verbal behavior.

To test this hypothesis, many verbal conditioning studies have been conducted. Verbal conditioning studies are those in which an examiner sets out to change the performance of a certain preselected class of verbal behavior (e.g., "human" nouns, plural nouns, color words, etc.) by the systematic utilization of reinforcement. In a typical verbal conditioning experiment, the subjects are asked to say whatever words come into their head. The experimenter then reinforces those words produced by the subject which fit into the preselected class. Usually, the reinforcement consists of a positive response such as the words, "good," "um hmmn," "yes," by the experimenter. The total number of words produced and the number of the words produced which belong to the reinforced class are carefully counted. Evidence for the effectiveness of verbal conditioning is a rise in the number of words in the selected class produced by the subjects. This is what, in fact, most such experiments report.[52] A typical plotting of such data appears in Figure (5).

While this might superficially seem like clear evidence of verbal conditioning, the matter is not that simple. We might ask in such a case, "What is the subject really learning?" Many behaviorists would say the subjects are simply being "conditioned" without their knowledge to produce the specified class of words, just as they would say a rat learns without being aware to press a lever by being reinforced for so doing by a food pellet.[53]

However, there is a more complex, but alternative viewpoint. We may contend the rat presses the lever because he has become aware that doing so will produce food. However, we cannot ask the rat. We can ask human subjects.

This latter procedure has been applied to verbal conditioning experiments by asking subjects what they think of the experiment periodically, say after every tenth word they produce.[54] An appraisal of what the subjects write can tell the experimenter if and when the subjects became consciously aware of what the experimenter wanted in the way of words produced.

When the subjects' performance is plotted, it is found that only those subjects who became aware, that is, who figured out what the experimenter wanted, in fact learned anything. Those subjects who never became aware never increased their production of the specified class of words. A plotting of the data for these experiments is characterized in Figure (6).

Further, careful experiments of this latter type have shown the subjects who became aware increased their production of the specified class of words immediately after they gained awareness.[55]

Thus, the apparent success with verbal conditioning is only an artifact of what we might call "awareness." Awareness does not fit into an instrumental conditioning schema. Even the most simple of conditioning experiments seem unable to demonstrate the usefulness of learning theory in analysis of language.

Mediation Theories

These objections appear not to have daunted some psychologists. Charles Osgood in his article, "Behavior Theory and the Social Sciences," reviews a few of the objections to a learning theory model of language and concludes,

. . . the single stage S–R model is incapable of handling *symbolic* processes, which are so characteristic of human behavior. The reader should keep in mind, however, that in pointing out these insufficiencies of the S–R model, I am not claiming that its basic principles are thereby invalid –– to the contrary, in dealing with the symbolic process, at least, the same general principles will be assumed to operate. [56]

23

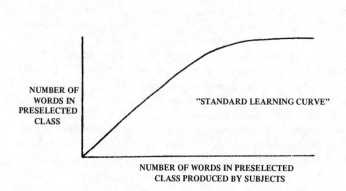

Figure 5. A typical plotting of data in studies of verbal operant conditioning. The plots approximate the "standard learning curve" quite closely. See text.

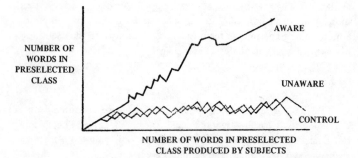

Figure 6. Awareness in verbal conditioning. (After Speilberger and DeNike, 1966.) When subjects are asked if they are aware of the intent of an experimenter in verbal operant conditioning experiment and the data for the "aware" subjects and the "unaware" subjects are plotted separately, it is found that no learning occurs in unaware subjects as compared to control subjects who were "reinforced" randomly.

24

To accommodate these principles of classical and instrumental conditioning to language, Osgood[57] proceeds as Hull[58] had done before him, to introduce an additional stage in the middle of ("mediate") the S–R chain. This additional stage Osgood calls a "representational mediation process," which is similar to the "disposition" theory of language forwarded by Charles Morris.[59]

However, Osgood does not apply his two–stage theory to problems of syntax and sentence relatedness. (The fact that we see definite relationships between otherwise identical sentences expressed in a different tense, mood, etc.) which were a primary reason for the admitted downfall of the single stage S–R models.

Although the additional, intervening variable does not alleviate the problems of higher–order or backward conditioning, it does prevent prediction of an anticipated response. It is this inability to predict which renders experimentation difficult. This is probably why the Osgood[60] paradigms have not generated much empirical research into the mediation process. Recognizing some of these problems, in 1963, Osgood opined: "Can our psychological theories incorporate and render comprehensible the way human beings understand and create sentences? If not, then our theories are at best insufficient and at worst erroneous."[61]

This remark is prefatory to Osgood's adandonment of the two–stage mediation model in favor of a three–stage model which he attempts to apply to sentences with the supplement of the essentially statistical Markov process.

Since sentences have a way of proceding sequentially (or from left to right on the printed page), it seems intuitively reasonable that each succeeding word should be probabilistically dependent upon the preceding words, and hence a Markov–type sentence generating machine should be sufficient. The probabilities at each transition point would depend upon the machine's previous experience . . .[62]

What Osgood seems to have overlooked in the probabilistic model is that probability must be considered an *effect* and not a *cause* of behavior. It is absurd to say that I will probably do something because the probability is that I will do it. Such a statement is tautological and has no explanatory power whatever.

Even if it were possible to determine such probabilities, which it is not since the language has an infinite set of sentences possible, we might well ask "Probabilities of what?" On one level, Osgood asserts that it would be the probabilities of words within a form—class or, as he puts it, a "word form pool."[63]

Should we attempt to use a "word form pool" we should expect each word in a given class of forms (i.e., proper nouns, pronouns, etc.) to function in the same manner in every grammatical sentence. If they do not, we can either assert that the unruly word either belongs to more than one class, or, that the specific class in question must be subdivided. Unfortunately, attempts to make such classification schemes have resulted in failure because most words simply belong in too many classes.[64] A few theorists even believe that ultimate refinement of this proposal would result in every word being the only word in its own class!

To appreciate the difficulties, compare the function of the words "easy" and "eager" in the following sentences:

6.   John is easy to please.
7.   John is eager to please.
8.   It is easy to please John.
9.   *It is eager to please John.

Were both words to be in the same form—class, they would have to function the same way in every context. It is obvious that they don't. Few, if any, words do under similar kinds of examination. Further consider:

10.   She put her coat on.
11.   He put her coat on.
12.   She put her coat on herself.
13.   *He put her coat on herself.

The problem for behaviorism, and possibly for empiricism in general, is that in order to account for facts such as these, some abstract, non—observable mechanism is required. That is precisely what behavior theory prevents in its anti—mentalist thrust.[65] To restate the difficulty, accurate accounts of human language require more than a single level of analysis and simple surface taxonomic means cannot work as they remain on an observable (behavioral) level.[66] If you stop to consider that there are an infinite set of sentences in any natural language (in principle, there is no longest sentence) it immediately follows that no matter how many classes you divide sentences into, the result will still be infinite.[67] Infinity divided by any number (except itself) is still infinity. Consequently, no taxonomic means including various forms of descriptive linguistics such as those of Leonard Bloomfield[68] and Charles Hockett,[69] as well as behavior and information theories [70] have the capacity to account for many forms of human activities, including natural language.

Some General Arguments

I believe a fundamental error is rooted deeply in empiricism and has been correctly isolated by the eminent philosopher, Willard Van Orman Quine. He points out that empiricism has been subject to two ill—founded dogmas:

> One is the belief in some fundamental cleavage between truths which are *analytic,* or grounded in meanings independently of matters of fact, and truths which are *synthetic,* or grounded in fact. The other dogma is reductionism: the belief that each meaningful statement is equivalent to some logical construct upon terms which refer to immediate experience.[71]

Consider, then the following essential facts about natural languages:

I.   The same physical signal (stimulus) can have two or more separate meanings on every basic level of analysis:

A.   Phonological: /kæts/ (plural), /kæts/ (possessive).

B.   Lexical: homophones such as "to," "too," "two," and in multiple meanings; "dog" can be a canine or a fixture on the deck of a ship.

C.   Syntactic: As in ambiguous sentences, e.g., "Flying planes can be dangerous." "The shooting of the hunters was awful." Also in ambiguity of segmentation, e.g., "The good candy came anyways," "The good can decay many ways." And, "Gal, amant de la Reine, ala (tour magnanime)." "Galamment de l'arene de la Tour Magne, a Nimes."[72]

II.   Different physical signals (stimuli) can have the same meaning on every basic level of analysis:

A. Phonological: plural status can be indicated by /s/, /Iz/, /In/, /∅/, etc. As in "cats," "notches," "oxen," "deer," etc.

B. Lexical: As in synonymy, e.g., "dog" and "canine," "bachelor" and "unmarried man."

C. Syntactic: As in certain transformations, e.g., "Mary loves John." "John is loved by Mary." And in paraphrase.

These facts about natural language seem to be universal. And there is good reason to speculate the same principles apply to many other behaviors and perceptual activities as well.[73]

But the most difficult and inclusive attack on behaviorism as it applies to natural language is found in a series of formal proofs that no theories founded on the essential principles of behavior theory (1–2) can account for natural language, no matter how elaborated or extended.[74]

These proofs show that if associative principles are rules defined over the terminal (surface) vocabulary of a theory and that if any description of behavior based on associations must be a possible description of the actual behavior, then natural language cannot be described.[75]

Central to these proofs and allied demonstrations is the observation that natural languages have "nesting" characteristics; that is, one element of a language can be "nested" or "embedded" within another. For example, consider the following two sentences:

14. The man you met yesterday.

15. John went home.

Any native speaker–hearer of English will recognize (14) and (15) can be combined to form:

16. John, the man you met yesterday, went home.

Note that this single, simple example represents an indefinitely large number of grammatical sentences in English that have nesting characteristics. Additional examples abound in "if–then" and "either–or" constructions.

Generally, no behavior which can "build from the middle" (a fact of language Osgood seems to have overlooked) can be described by any method which limits itself by addressing the behavior in terms of symbols immediately reflecting that behavior. The simplest way possible to account for nesting involves abstract elements which are neither an S, nor an R, i.e., which are not in the terminal vocabulary, regardless of the symbols used.

28

To rephrase it, natural languages and many non–language behaviors as well, cannot be represented by finite state mechanisms, including associations, statistical formulations, and Markov chains. In short, if you think you can go ahead and try. But, there's a formal proof you will be wasting your time.

This does not mean to say these simple mechanisms fail to handle any aspect of language at all. To the contrary, stochastic mechanisms can account for a number of sentence and behavior types. But these mechanisms are, formally speaking, special cases of more powerful and interesting mechanisms, just as Newtonian physics is a special and limited case of relativity theory. As Sol Saporta aptly put it, "Anything you can do with one hand tied behind your back, you can do with both hands free." [76]

Conclusion and Prospectus

There seems to be little of natural language and possibly of any other kind of human action that behavior theories can handle. I do not believe that these and other related criticisms can be dismissed casually as B.F. Skinner has done recently.[77] Although several attempts have been made at answering a few of these criticisms, none have found fault with the formal proofs or satisfied the serious contentions.[78]

It is irresponsible in view of the facts which now abound in the literature for the informed scholar to continue applications of behavior theory or descriptive linguistics to language and language–like behaviors. It behooves the conscientious scholar to either abandon these approaches or to reply to each fundamental criticism. To do less is to act irresponsibly.

What alternatives are these?

Just as John B. Watson's empirically–oriented behaviorism was in opposition and a healthy alternative to the array of imaginary constructs and notions forwarded by his rivals E.B. Titchner and William James and constituted a "revolution" in psychology; we are now experiencing a more cautious and hopefully, a more profitable counter–revolution spearheaded by Noam Chomsky and his colleagues from MIT.

29

They propose a revival of rationalist thought with its corresponding focus on the nature of mind through determination of abstract, unobservable mechanisms which can, in principle, account for the nature of language and thought. As it has always been, this is an ambitious enterprise. But, the counter—revolution is proceeding with some caution.

Early rationalism as applied to psychology and linguistics omitted certain crucial aspects of methodology. Because rationalism as a method of science is not based on observables, but on intuition and inference it can easily be seen how theorists of this bent tended to construct elaborate and essentially unchecked theories. There seemed at the time to be no reliable way to hold the academic imagination in check. Fortunately, today we are aware of a number of mandatory techniques which have this capacity.[79]

Rationalism received its fullest expression from a series of continental European mathematicians, for here was a technique of handling purely abstract entities without capriciousness. That technique is the rigor of pure logic: formalism. The position is well expressed by William Rozeboom:

> . . . formal methodology is merely the story of the scientist's verbal or conceptual techniques; and any researcher who feels that the unexamined language habits he picked up at his mother's knee are adequate to see him through the most complex scientific investigations is living at about the same level of reality as the high school pitching star who is sure he would be a valuable asset in the current major league pennant race. Moreover, where is the necessary methodology going to get done if not in close association with actual scientific problems? If the researcher sometimes feels that the dicta of philosophers of science are frequently oversimplified, excessively restrictive, and of little relevance to his own work, he has only himself to blame for making no attempt to clarify just what his conceptual procedures really are.[80]

Thus, were we to have an adequate theory of communication, we know it would not be based on observables. It would not be empirically-oriented. It would not be behavioral or even primarily descriptive. It would be of a rationalist nature. It would be power-

30

ful enough to account for nesting and embedding operations and the transforming of one string of symbols into another. It would be explicit and permit little or no vagueness and ambiguity in application. It must be formal.

Our communication theories must precisely and faithfully account for *all* of the human actions for which they are devised. They must be faithful to the empirical *consequences* of their abstract calculations.

It is therefore our obligation to address ourselves to the development of rationalist thought and the rigors of the attendant methods if we hope to be able to meet the challenges which are ours, for ultimately international and intercultural communication is concerned with man understanding man.

Considering an antithesis can be illustrative. Modern military cryptographic experts have devised an almost foolproof method of ensuring their secret messages cannot be understood by enemy interceptors. Imagine you are given a single wire and all the elaborate electronic and computer facilities you might wish. You are told that through this wire is being transmitted secret messages you must decode. We are aware from legends of the Second World War, most codes are breakable. But, further suppose that flowing across this wire are transmissions from one computer to another. Now the task becomes more difficult. Yet it is still possible provided you can make some reasonable estimate as to the kind of computers and computer programs originating the signals. Of course this has also occurred to those who have originated the messages; hence, the electronic machines in use are designed specifically to be peculiar in essential respects. And as an added precaution, they change their own internal electrical and mechanical functions according to prearranged, but randomly selected conditions. Now the messages are virtually impossible to decode and interception is not feared.

The principle underlying this exercise is that we can learn to understand each other only to the degree that we are mentally alike. There are universals of language and culture because we inherit similar mental endowment. Mutual understanding naturally progresses as identity is discovered. And the identities are not necessarily physical, but in the kinds of operations prohibited or permitted. A tube–type computer and transistor model could perform identical functions and yet look very different just as two individuals could learn to play the same game such as chess from instruction books expressed in different languages and perspectives. The universalities which are important are abstract in nature.

Yet, scholars often treat the rigors of formal abstraction as a tedious undertaking destined only to lead them away from the essential humanism which motivates.

Rationalist methodology largely concerns itself with constructs which are not claimed to have existing counterparts. Most concepts dealt with by mathematicians are convenient fictions engaged in for the purpose of better understanding abstract relationships.

Rationalist linguistics similarly holds promise of helping us better appreciate in new and more comprehensive ways our common humanity. There is no intrinsic intent in rationalist methods which place as a goal better prediction, control or manipulation of men as the empirical techniques require under the rubric of "validity." Rationalism does attempt a deeper and more appreciative understanding of mankind, even though attention is directed at imaginary and admittedly non–existent constructs. Noun phrases, transformations, and vocalics as well as the other devices weilded by linguists are not envisioned as existing in the same sense as your liver. They are a shorthand for the abstract capabilities we, as users of a language, must have in order to communicate as we do.

Languages, cultures, and nations are, after all, mental events even though each will have its own distinctive physical, empirical consequences. But an artifact is no more a culture than a sound wave is a speech.

The essence of international and intercultural communications is the interaction and transformation of mental events and the subsequent emergence of new understandings. To comprehend aspects of this subject we must therefore concern ourselves with entities in the mental domains which do not behave according to the laws of physics as we know them. To meet the challenges ahead we must be precise and responsible in our treatment of the non–existent. In the words of Hermann Hesse from his Nobel Prize winning novel *Magister Ludi*:

> . . . . then in certain cases and for irresponsible men it
> may be that non–existent things can be described more

easily and with less responsibility in words than the existent, and therefore the reverse applies for pious and scholarly historians: for nothing destroys description so much as words, and yet there is nothing more necessary than to place before the eyes of men certain things the existence of which is neither provable nor probable, but which, for this very reason, pious and scholarly men treat to a certain extent as existent in order that they may be led a step further towards their being and their becoming.[81]

FOOTNOTES

[1] An earlier version of this paper was presented to the Speech Communication Association 59th Annual Meeting in New York City, November 10, 1973.

I am indebted to Richard Martin, Robert Scott, Gerald Siegel, David Smith and others for their valuable comments on earlier versions of this paper. I am especially indebted to James J. Jenkins for having pointed out much of the material contained in this paper and having helped me to appreciate its ramifications. Of course, I alone am responsible for the selection and presentation of material in this paper; a fact I trust will be understood by those who would differ.

[2] "Adequacy" here is used as an abbreviated form for "explanatory adequacy" in the sense of Noam Chomsky, *Syntactic Structures* (The Hague, Netherlands, 1957), pp. 30-47 and *Aspects of the Theory of Syntax* (Cambridge, Mass., 1965), pp. 25-27, 30-38, 59-62, and elsewhere.

[3] By "objective observables" I mean sense—data external to the perceiving organism. We can, of course, observe certain internal events as well, e.g., a ringing in our ears, nausea, hunger, and much intuitive and introspective information. I believe it reasonable to assert that "John observed a pain in his toe." It is less reasonable to say that "Sam observed that John had a pain in his toe," for it is not the pain that Sam is observing, but John's reaction to the pain. Rather, "Sam inferred that John had a pain in his toe on the basis of John's observable behavior."

[4] John B. Watson, *Behaviorism* (Chicago, 1924), p. 18.

[5] Charles E. Osgood, "Behavior Theory and the Social Sciences," *Behavioral Science*,I., (1956), p. 169.

[6] This example was used by Gregory Bateson in an unpublished lecture, "Man and His Environment," at the University of Hawaii in Honolulu in 1967.

[7] Watson, *loc. cit.*

[8] Aristotle, *De Memoria et Reminiscentia*, from *Parva Naturalia*, trans. W.A. Hammond as *Aristotle's Psychology*, (New York, 1902), pp. 12ff.

[9] Thomas Hobbes, *Humaine Nature: or the Fundamental Elements of Policie*, (London, 1650), pp. 84ff. It is interesting to note that Hobbes was a contemporary of Rene Descartes and attempted to reduce the content of the mind to sense-experience as against Descartes' dualism as did his follower John Locke, who is probably more noted as associationistic.

[10] John Stuart Mill, *System of Logic, Ratiocinative and Inductive*, (London, 1843), bk. vi, chapter 4.

[11] See, B.R. Bugelski, *The Psychology of Learning*, (New York, 1956), ch. 11, for a recent itemization.

[12] See, Leo Postman, "Association and Performance in the Analysis of Verbal Learning," in Theodore Dixon and David Horton, eds., *Verbal Behavior and General Behavior Theory*, (Englewood Cliffs, 1968), pp. 550-571, but cf., James Deese, "Association and Memory," also in Dixon and Horton, pp. 97-108.

[13] Deese, p. 98.

[14] As exemplified in Watson, *Behaviorism*, passim., and Ivan P. Pavlov, *Conditioned Reflexes*, (London, 1927), passim.

[15] As exemplified in B.F. Skinner, *The Behavior of Organisms*, (New York, 1938), passim., *Science and Human Behavior,* (New York, 1953), passim., *Verbal Behavior,* (New York, 1957), passim., and elsewhere.

[16] As exemplified in O. Hobart Mowrer, "The Psychologist Looks at Language," *American Psychologist*, IX, (1954), pp. 660-694, Charles E. Osgood, "Behavior Theory and the Social Sciences," *Behavioral Science*, I, (1956), pp. 167-185, "On Understanding and Creating Sentences," *American Psychologist*, XVIII, (1963), pp. 735-751, and elsewhere.

[17] Pavlov, *Reflexes*, but, interestingly, the dog made no attempt to eat the bell.

[18] Watson, pp. 224-256.

[19] Arthur W. Staats, *Complex Human Behavior*, (New York, 1964), ch. 4ff.

[20] Osgood, "Behavior Theory," pp. 179ff.

[21] See, Leonard Linsky, ed., *Semantics and the Philosophy of Language: A Collection of Readings*, (Urbana, Ill., 1952), passim.

[22] W.K. Estes, "Learning Theory and the New 'Mental Chemistry,' " *Psychological Review*, LXVII, (1960), p. 216ff., and Benton J. Underwood and Geoffrey Keppel, "One—Trial Learning?" *Journal of Verbal Learning and Verbal Behavior*, I, (1962), pp. 11-12.

[23] "Higher order" conditioning was first investigated by J.P. Frolov, *Pavlov and His School: The Theory of Conditioned Reflexes*, (New York, 1937), a student of Pavlov's and also pursued by G. Finch and E. Culler, "Higher Order Conditioning with Constant Motivation," *American Journal of Psychology*, XLVI, (1934), pp. 596-602, who, in animal experiments, showed that "second-order" conditioning was possible, but of less response strength. Response strength in "third—order" conditioning was so weak as to be judged non—existent by Pavlov in his own observations. The current status of higher—order conditioning is muddied. Claims tend to support one's theoretical investment. Definitive experiments with humans have been elusive. My position is that natural language calls for a far higher order of conditioning than has been experimentally demonstrated in satisfactory experiments. Moreover, the whole conditioning approach seems extraneous to general language analysis.

[24] Pavlov, *Reflexes*, Clark L. Hull, *Principles of Behavior*, (New York, 1934), W.F. Grether, "Pseudo—Conditioning Without Paired Stimulation Encountered in Attempted Backward Conditioning," *Journal of Comparative Psychology*, XLII, (1938), pp. 91-96, Bugelski, *Learning*, pp. 128-131., W.N. Dember and James J. Jenkins, *General Psychology: Modeling Behavior and Experience*, (Englewood Cliffs, N.J., 1970), pp. 317-318, 331-332.

[25] Mowrer, "The Psychologist," p. 13.

[26] *Ibid.*, pp. 11-12.

[27] For example, Skinner, *Behavior*, passim., and *Verbal Behavior*, passim.

[28] Skinner, p. 62. More directly, in *Science and Human Behavior*, (New York, 1953), Skinner says, " . . . the only defining characteristic of a reinforcing stimulus is that it reinforces." (p. 72). To this he adds, "There is nothing circular about classifying events in terms of their effects; the criterion is [sic] both empirical and objective. It would be circular, however, if we went on to assert that a given event strengthens an operant *because*, it is reinforcing." (p. 73 italics is original) This is a denial of the principle of causation, which has, in fact, been asserted by Skinner's colleague, P.W. Bridgeman, in *The Way Things Are*, (New York, 1959), which I find peculiar for men who speak of "controlling behavior," and "consequences." It seems we can take a choice between behaviorism being based upon either tautologies or contradictions. A third possibility is to assert the universe is essentially random. But, this is antithetical to scientific enterprise which Skinner also espouses.

[29] O. Hobart Mowrer, "On the Dual Nature of Learning –– A Reinterpretation of 'Conditioning' and 'Problem Solving,' " *Harvard Education Review*, XVII, (1947), pp. 106-107, 147.

[30] Charles B. Ferster, "Classification of Behavioral Pathology," in Leonard Krasner and Leonard P. Ullman, eds., *Research in Behavior Modification: New Developments and Implications*, (New York, 1967), pp. 10-13.

[31] Israel Goldiamond, "Stuttering and Fluency as Manipulable Operant Response Classes," in *Ibid.*, p. 109.

[32] Staats, p. 47.

[33] Hull, passim., esp. chs. 1-3.

[34] E.C. Tolman, *Purposive Behavior in Animals and Men*, (New York, 1932), passim.

[35] Noam Chomsky, "Review of *Verbal Behavior* by B.F. Skinner," *Language*, XXXV, (1959), p. 48.

[36] Skinner, *Verbal Behavior*, p. 163.

[37] *Ibid.*, p. 438.

[38] *Ibid.*, p. 442.

[39] *Ibid.*, p. 167.

[40] *Ibid.*, p. 199.

[41] *Ibid.*, p. 152.

[42] *Ibid.*, p. 206.

[43] *Ibid.*, p. 165.

[44] *Ibid.*, p. 222.

[45] *Ibid.,* p. 259.

[46] Chomsky, *loc. cit.*

[47] For example, Ferster, "Classification," says, "The English language is similarly a set of customs maintained by explicit contingencies applied by a community of individuals, all of whom will react only to particular stimuli." (p. 11.) Such unfounded statements are fundamental to the behavioral enterprise and encompass not only language but culture, society, national behavior, etc. Skinner's most recent restatement of this position is in his *Beyond Freedom and Dignity* (New York, 1971), which has also been reviewed by Chomsky, "The Case Against B.F. Skinner," *The New York Review of Books*, XVII, no. 11, December 30, 1971, pp. 18-24.

[48] E. Lenneberg, "Understanding Language Without Ability to Speak: A Case Report," *Journal of Abnormal and Social Psychology*, LXV (1962), pp. 155-159.

[49] Chomsky, "Review," p. 50.

[50] Skinner, *Verbal Behavior*, p. 3.

[51] J. Greenspoon, "The Reinforcing Effect of Two Spoken Sounds on the Frequency of Two Responses," *American Journal of Psychology*, LXVIII, (1965), p. 107.

[52] For example, D. E. Dulaney, "Hypotheses and Habits in Verbal 'Operant Conditioning,' " *Journal of Abnormal and Social Psychology*, LXIII, (1961), pp. 251-263, C.W. Eriksen, "Unconscious Process," in M.R. Jones, ed., *Nebraska Symposium on Motivation*, (Lincoln, Nebraska, 1958), pp. 169-228, L. Postman and J.M. Sassenrath, "The Automatic Action of Verbal Rewards and Punishments," *Journal of Genetic Psychology,* LXV, (1961), pp. 109-136.

[53] For example, J. Greenspoon, "Verbal Conditioning and Clinical Psychology," in A.J. Bachrach, ed., *Experimental Foundations of Clinical Psychology*, (New York, 1962), pp. 510-553, L. Krasner, "Studies of the Conditioning of Verbal Behavior," *Psychological Bulletin*, LV, (1958), pp. 148-170, K. Salzinger, "Experimental Manipulation of Verbal Behavior: A Review," *Journal of Genetic Psychology*, LI, (1959), pp. 65-94.

[54] L.D. DeNike, ''The Temporal Relationship Between Awareness and Performance in Verbal Conditioning," *Journal of*

Experimental Psychology, LXVIII, (1964), pp. 521-529, C.D. Speilberger and L.D. DeNike, "Verbal Operant Conditioning," *Psychological Review*, LXXIII, (1966), pp. 306-326.

[55] Speilberger and DeNike, *Ibid.*, p. 315ff.

[56] Charles E. Osgood, "Behavior Theory and the Social Sciences," *Behavioral Science*, I, (1956), p. 177.

[57] Osgood, *loc. cit.,* and elsewhere.

[58] Hull, *op. cit.,* and elsewhere.

[59] Charles Morris, "Foundations of the Theory of Signs," vol. I, Bk. 2, in Otto Neurath, ed., *International Encyclopaedia of Unified Science*, (Chicago, 1938).

[60] Osgood, *Method and Theory in Experimental Psychology*, (New York, 1953), "Behavior Theory," *op. cit.,* and "On Understanding and Creating Sentences," *American Psychologist*, XVIII, (1963), pp. 735-751.

[61] Osgood, "On Understanding," p. 735. Original underlining omitted.

[62] Osgood, *loc. cit.*

[63] Osgood, "On Understanding," p. 741ff.

[64] For example, James J. Jenkins, "Mediation Theory and Grammatical Behavior," in S. Rosenberg, ed., *Directions in Psycholinguistics*, (New York, 1965), and J.J. Jenkins and D.S. Palermo, "Mediation Process and the Acquisition of Linguistic Structure," in U. Bellugi and R.W. Brown, eds., *The Acquisition of Language. Monographs of the Society for Research Child Development*, XXIX, (1964), pp. 79-92.

[65] See, J.J. Katz, "Mentalism in Linguistics," *Language*, XL, (1964), pp. 124-137.

[66] See, for example, Noam Chomsky, *Language and Mind*, (New York, 1968), T.G. Bever, J.A. Fodor, and M. Garrett, "A Formal Limit of Associationism," in Dixon and Horton, op. cit., pp. 582-585, J.A. Fodor, "Could Meaning be an r_m?" *Journal of Verbal Learning and Verbal Behavior* , IV, (1965), pp. 73-81.

[67] Chomsky, *Syntactic Structures* , and *Aspects.*

[68] L. Bloomfield, *Language*, (New York, 1933).

[69] Charles A. Hockett, *A Course in Modern Linguistics*, (New York, 1958).

[70] C.E. Shannon and W. Weaver, *The Mathematical Theory of Communication*, (Urbana, Illinois, 1949).

[71] W.V.O. Quine, *From a Logical Point of View*, (New York, 1953), p. 20.

[72] The examples of ambiguity in segmentation come from Chomsky and G.A. Miller, "Introduction to the Formal Analysis of Natural Languages," in R.D. Luce, R.R. Bush, and E. Galanter, eds., *Handbook of Mathematical Psychology*, vol. 2, (New York, 1963), p. 280. The English example was first used by Miller, "Speech and Communication," *Journal of the Accoustical Society of America*, XXX, (1958), pp. 397-398. The ambiguous sentence examples are, I believe, originally from Chomsky, but have become standard examples in generative linguistics in the past decade as has the "easy—eager" sentence example in (8) and (9).

[73] See, W. Kohler, *Gestalt Psychology*, (New York, 1929), K.S. Lashley, "The Problem of Serial Order in Behavior," in L.A. Jefress, ed., *Cerebral Mechanisms in Behavior*, The Hixon Symposium, (New York, 1951), and Quine, esp. chs. 1, 3, 4.

[74] See, Chomsky and Miller, "Formal Analysis," Chomsky, "Formal Properties of Grammars," in R.D. Luce, et. al., pp. 323-418, and Bever, et. al., "A Formal Limit."

[75] Bever, et. al., *Ibid.*, p. 583.

[76] Quoted in Bever, et. al., *Ibid.*, p. 585.

[77] Skinner, "On 'Having' a Poem," *Saturday Review*, July 15, 1972. His remarks, in part, are: "Let me tell you about Chomsky. I published *Verbal Behavior* in 1957. In 1958 I received a fifty—five page typewritten review by someone I had never heard of named Noam Chomsky. I read half a dozen pages, saw it missed the point of my book, and went no further. In 1959 I received a reprint from the journal *Language* It was the review I had already seen, now reduced to thirty-two pages of type, and again I put it aside. But then, of course, Chomsky's star began to rise. Generative grammar became the thing —— and a very big thing it seemed to be. Linguists have always managed to make their discoveries earthshaking. In one decade everything seems to hinge on semantics, in another decade on the analysis of the phoneme. In the sixties it was grammar and syntax, and Chomsky's review began to be widely cited and reprinted and became, in fact, much better known than my book.

Eventually, the question was asked, why I had not answered Chomsky. My reasons, I am afraid, show a lack of character. In the first place I should have had to read the review, and I found its tone distasteful. It was not really a review of my book but what Chomsky took, erroneously, to be my position . . . No doubt I was shirking a responsibility in not replying to Chomsky, and I am glad a reply was supplied in 1970 by Kenneth MacCorquodale in the *Journal of the Experimental Analysis of Behavior.*

. . . " . . . Chomsky was later invited to give the John Locke Lectures at Oxford. I was at Cambridge University at the time, and the BBC thought it would be interesting if we were to discuss our differences on television. I don't know what excuse Chomsky gave, but I agreed to participate if the moderator could guarantee equal time. I suggested that we use chess clocks. My clock would be running when I was talking and Chomsky's when he was talking and in that way I planned to have the last fifteen or twenty minutes to myself. The BBC thought that my suggestion would not make for a very interesting program."

One wonders how, without reading, the contents of a review can be judged.

[78] See, E. Crothers and P. Suppes, *Experiments in Second—Language Learning*, (New York, 1967), ch. 1, Kenneth MacCorquodale, "On Chomsky's 'Review of Skinner's *Verbal Behavior*,' " *Journal of the Experimental Analysis of Behavior*, XIII, (1970), pp. 83-99, Alan Paivio, *Imagery and Verbal Process*, (New York, 1971), pp. 393-431, Skinner, "On 'Having,' " *loc. cit.*, Arthur W. Staats, "Linguistic—Mentalistic Theory Versus an Explanatory S—R Learning Theory of Language Development," in Dan I. Slobin, ed., *The Ontogenesis of Grammar*, (New York, 1971), pp. 103-152.

[79] For example, Chomsky, *Syntatctic Structures* and *Aspects, op. cit.*, and Noam Chomsky and Morris Halle, *The Sound Pattern of English*, (New York, 1968).

[80] W.W. Rozeboom, "Formal Analysis and the Language of Behavior Theory," in H. Feigl and G. Maxwell, eds., *Current Issues in the Philosophy of Science*, (New York, 1961), p. 473.

[81] Herman Hesse, *Magister Ludi (The Bead Game)*, trans. Mer - vyn Savill, (New York, 1949), p. 13.

* This paper was originally written in 1964. It was revised in 1973. Since that time I have become aware of certain instances in which production may precede comprehension. See Keeney, T. and J. Wolfe, "The Acquisition of Agreement in English," *Journal of Verbal Learning and Verbal Behavior,* 1972, II, 698-705, and de Villiens, J.G. and P.A., "Development of the Use of Word Order in Comprehension," *Journal of Psycholinguistic Research,* 1973, 2, 331-341. These results, however, will not invalidate the general principle stated above. In addition, for readers who think events in psycholinguistics have outdated the position and that I am flogging dead horses, see Koestier, Arthur, *The Ghost in the Machine* (London, 1967), Appendix II, "On Not Flogging Dead Horses," pp 349-353.

Janice C. Hepworth:

Some Pre-Empirical Considerations for Cross-Cultural Attitude Measurements and Persuasive Communications

———

PERSUASION is generally thought of as the means by which behavior is changed or reinforced. In spite of the simplicity of the general purpose of persuasion, there is no universal formula to fit scientific criteria so that the results of a persuasive effort can be predicted each time. Replications of American–designed experiments in foreign cultures indicate that, in general, more pre–empirical studies must precede experimentation. Test equivalence in design, content, scoring and interpretation has not been adequately studied.

It is quite possible that persuasion can alter or reinforce behavior, but experimental designs often constrain the observations of alterations or reinforcement of behavior to the time limits prescribed in a particular experiment. How do we know, for example, that behavior response to a persuasive communication may not occur over time —— the limits of which have not been satisfactorily investigated in our own culture. The time variable in foreign cultures remains largely unexplored. Persuasive appeals in foreign cultures often involve goals of long term, massive and permanent changes in behavior. Generalizing from the results of controlled laboratory or sample population experiments of the American kind to foreign populations requires an inferential leap that is not justified at this stage in cross-cultural research. More pre-empirical study of the instruments used in cross-cultural attitude and personality measurement must be conducted. In addition, more field work is necessary to collect and assess ethnographic data from foreign cultures in which experiments are to be conducted. Finally, after instruments for testing have been validated for cross-cultural use, and after a target culture has been studied, experimentation can proceed and the information gained can be utilized by the persuader to maximize his success.

If one assumes that persuasive appeals are directed to attitudes, then the level of observation is no longer concrete or explicit. Copious literature has grown out of the investigation of persuasion and attitude change and the unsatisfactory conclusion of all the research is that the "relationship between concepts of attitude and persuasion remain relatively ambiguous."[1] The reciprocity of persuasion and behavior is equally ambiguous.

Rownow and Robinson[2] believe an attitude is made up of three components: affect, cognition and behavior. Of the three, overt behavior is the only measurable component. Very often overt behavior is diametrically opposed to feelings or beliefs so there is no assurance that an understanding of an individual or group attitudes can predict behavior or that behavior is an accurate indicator of feelings and beliefs. Triandis has been concerned with the weak relationship between attitudes and behavior and suggests a model to increase the predictive power of an attitude index:

> Behavior is a function of (a) behavioral intentions, (b) norms, and (c) habits. Behavioral intentions are, in turn, a function of (d) affect toward the object of action, (e) norms and roles, and (f) cognitions about the attitude object, including expectations of reinforcement for behaving in a particular way toward it. It should be noted that norms, according to this model, make both a direct and indirect contribution to the determination of behavior. Furthermore, according to this model, attitudes will not be found to be related to behavior unless the other variables of the model are kept constant, which is rarely the case in studies reporting nonrelationships. Finally, when only the cognitive or affective components of attitudes are measured, the relationship between attitudes and behavior will be indirect, and therefore weak.[3]

Perhaps persuasion must expand its base of investigation and assess intentions, norms, roles and habits of a target population. The complex nature of social constraints on attitudes, such as language, class, occupation, have been largely ignored. There is no scientific formula to gain access to man's mind, but an investigator may edge closer to what is actually going on if he accounts for some external influences. In a communicative sense, feelings and beliefs that are verbally expressed pass through a filter of social constraints so that what is expressed survives as a communicated message. Responses to a Likert type scale are essentially communicated messages which have been filtered through individual and social restraints.

If an attitude is defined as a "conceptual bridge between an individual's psychological states and his overt behavior,"[4] there is no way to retrieve or quantify a conceptual bridge. Bettinghaus' definition is unassailable, but there is no way to operationalize the definition.

Perhaps an attitude does not exist as a subjective phenomenon. Instead, an attitude may be a stop-point on a behavior continuum of an individual. The choice in stop-point reflects the choice of an investigator who through the means of a survey or questionnaire requires a linguistic expression of an arbitrarily chosen point. A behavior continuum may be represented in the following way.

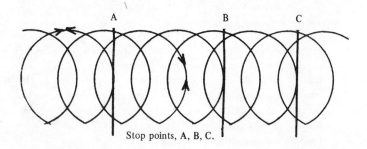

Stop points, A, B, C.

The spiral diagram represents the cluster configuration (loops and connecting links) of concept formation, so that behavior depends on past as well as anticipated events. The context of situation, for experimental purposes, is chosen by the investigator rather than the subject so that a stop-point on the continuum marks an externally conceived concept to which a subject must respond. A subject in an experimental situation is often required to verbalize a feeling or belief that has only random, if any, relation to his evolving cognitive continuum. There are cognitions common to a culture or population that can be used as focal or stop-points. These cognitions can be elicited through testing after the cognitive modes of a particular culture are understood by an investigator. A solution to the ambiguous and often unreliable nature of attitude surveys that employ a criterion type test (made up of items taken from statistical data usually collected in one culture) is suggested in the present inquiry. The recommendation may not solve the problem of how to validate attitude surveys in cross-cultural research, but does suggest a more reliable planning stage.

The following inquiry is concerned with the generality of American and western-designed attitude measures and persuasive communication techniques. Cross-cultural studies have been collected to assess the reliability of extending American and western-designed testing procedures to cross-cultural environments. The inquiry is divided into three sections, each of which is thought to have a profound influence on the success or failure of persuasive communication: (1) Equivalence in Cross-Cultural Attitude and Behavior Studies, (2) Influence of Language on Attitudes, Personality and Behavior, and (3) Influence of Culture on Attitudes and Behavior.

Equivalence in Cross-Cultural Attitude and Behavior Studies

Whenever a theory is stated certain assumptions are implicit. The theory has withstood the test of observation and experimentation and either achieved confirmation in an incremental sense or in an absolute sense. [5] There is little hope at this stage of observation and experimentation in persuasion studies that we can talk about an absolute confirmation of a persuasive theory, but we can talk about incremental confirmation; that is, observed instances in which behavior has been reinforced or changed because of a persuasive appeal. Dissonance Theory claims universal validity for all men and yet one recent use of Dissonance Theory in a Chinese culture challenges its validity. Paul Hiniker concludes in his Chinese study that Dissonance Theory may need "sharper specification and definition of the rules of psychological implication that are basic to it, with an eye to the empirical conditions, especially cultural, under which they hold."[6]

In cross-cultural contexts, theories of persuasion may be further tested for incremental confirmation so that we may edge closer to some kind of absolute confirmation of a theory of persuasion. In cross-cultural contexts the field for testing persuasion theories has been greatly expanded, but so has the latitude of interpretation. After problems in test design, interpretation is the problem that plagues the experimenter in cross-cultural studies of attitudes, behavior and persuasive techniques. The problems of design and interpretation can be minimized if and when more rigorous attention is paid to the planning of cross-cultural research. The question for cross-cultural research can be stated in the following way: Can a persuasion theory be made operational in other cultures without altering the logic of the theory? Przeworski and Teune believe "cross-national analysis requires research procedures that involve caution in order to yield validity in a more differentiated setting."[7]

If a theory is to be tested cross-culturally, certain adaptations in the testing of a theory must be made; that is, the test of the theory must fit the culture. The extent of adaptation to bring about a fit is the most worrisome task in cross-cultural research. "The critical problem," according to Przeworski and Teune "is that of identifying "equivalent" phenomena and analyzing the relationships between them in an "equivalent" fashion."[8] The caution is eminently clear while the practical application or actual doing is less clear. In cross-cultural testing the criteria selected are ultimately the choice of an investigator. There is no short cut to the requirement that an investigator must have at least an ethnographer's knowledge of the culture in which he conducts research. Suppose the same attitude survey concerning poverty is submitted to individuals in India and Japan. Do the items of this survey measure attitudes in an identical or equivalent (local definitions of variables) manner in both cultures? Are the indicators of poverty the same in both cultures? Any persuasive appeal to alleviate poverty in India through some innovation such as increased and improved rice production should ideally be based on observations of attitudes concerning poverty. However, the instrument for attitude measurement may not yield very valid results if, in fact, the instrument is the same one used in western cultures. On a cognitive level, poverty may be differently categorized in Indian languages. According to Frijda and Jahoda, "Different cultures use different category systems to describe similar phenomena."[9] Because content variables rarely exist in comparable places across cultures, it seems useless to pursue a cross-cultural study with the expectation that these variables will be manifest in the same way (verbal description) or for the same reasons. The substance of cognitions are manifest in a variety of symbolic systems of which language is only one system. A more useful approach requires an investigation of the structure which "refers to the systematic way in which aspects of content are organized and interrelated."[10] Description of a culture is not an end result but rather a pre-empirical requirement. Przeworski and Teune make this point quite clear in the following way:

> In scientific research the goal is not description . . . but rather a set of statements concerning relationships between or among variables. In addition to classifying, ranking, or scoring specific units on economic productivity, technological development, or some attitude such as "achievement," the relationships between these phenomena are examined. Thus productivity would be related to technology, or to attitudes, or to the social structure, or to a combination of these factors.[11]

A review of experiments on self-esteem in various cultures demonstrates the ethnocentric assumption that self-esteem can be elicited by one unmodified measure. Peter Collett takes issue with studies such as the one by Smart and Smart[12] who replicated a western-designed self-esteem questionnaire study among Indian children in Delhi and compared the data with the results of the previous study among American children. The only concession to culture in the Smart and Smart study was a translation of the questionnaire. The results of the questionnaire presumes "that the

range of statements available to Americans was equally appropriate
for Indian subjects,"[13] and that "the meanings of these statements
were the same in America and India, and hence that the choice of a
statement was indicative of the same orientation in both cultures."[14]
Evidence of differing meaning systems in cross-cultural semantic
studies challenges the assumptions and results of the Smart and
Smart study. Tanaka's [15] study revealed some very real differences
in semantic systems of different languages which requires much more
study than has been attempted to date.

Collett developed a set of criteria for cross-cultural studies of
self-esteem which includes cultural concessions and is worth
including because of its possible use in other attitude surveys:

1. Subjects' descriptions of themselves or ideals should not be
constrained by too few options, and where these options are
limited they should be equally so for all cultures being
compared. 2. Salient criteria should be selected for each
culture. 3. To control for varying distances between self and
referents, self-other studies should employ peer-comparisons.
4. Studies of the content of self-esteem confront problems of
equating meanings, and must therefore involve careful
cross-cultural operationalization of meaning categories or be
abandoned in favor of studies of structural aspects of self
esteem.[16]

Collett conducted an experiment to measure the self-esteem of Arabs
and Englishmen and to test the general observation that Arabs have
an inflated self-esteem. A first experiment determined the "extent to
which Arabs and Englishmen esteem themselves relative to their
personal ideals."[17] Subjects were given a pile of cards each of which
contained an English adjective from which a selection was required
to describe a personal idea. Other adjectives could be written in on
blank cards. The one immediate criticism of the experiment is that
Collett used English as the medium for response. Even though all
subjects were conversant in English, the presumption that the same
words generate the same expectations for bilinguals is questionable.
Paul Kolers' experiment on the information processing of bilingual

subjects indicates that "words referring to concrete, manipulable objects were more likely to elicit similar responses in the bilingual person's two languages than abstract words."[18] The implication for Collett's experiment is that as words become more abstract or refer to feelings, a bilingual comes to have different expectations for each of paired words. For example, love and liebe, although dictionary translations of the same thing, do not necessarily mean the same thing to a bilingual German-English speaker. Although the question of language is pertinent to Collett's experiment, the above comments will be expanded upon in the second section of this inquiry. For the time it is useful to assume caution when reading the results of an experiment among bilinguals which utilizes an affect meaning system of one language.

From the first experiment Collett took twenty-two words most frequently selected as descriptive of the ideal-self among English and Arab subjects. These words were rated by subjects in a second experiment designed to elicit peer comparisons. Each word had ten vertical circles. The top circle carried a value of ten while the other circles represented decreasing values to the lowest which had a score of one. The subject's choice among the ten circles for each word represented his perception of "how many of his class-mates had more and how many had less of that quality than himself."[19] Results of the experiment confirmed the general expectation that Arabs have a more inflated self-esteem than Englishmen.

There is a personality trait not accounted for in Collett's experiment. Englishmen may not report a covert sense of self-esteem. This reluctance may be part of cultural learning and/or a model English personality trait. In addition to the above shortcomings of Collett's experiment, comparison of the goals and results of the experiment reveals a serious disparity. In some introductory remarks Collett says that his paper "will argue that the requirements for an idiographic science are more easily fulfilled by attention to structural rather than content variables."[20] His experiment is not without content variables for the very design assumes a common meaning system.

Cross-cultural experimentation has polarized some other investigators on what constitutes an appropriate test. The use of translated American-devised tests has been challenged on the grounds that items of the original may not measure the same thing in a foreign culture. Leonard Gordon[21] argues convincingly that construct tests are more valid than criterion tests. The latter tests are devised without prior theorizing and include items gained from statistical data from the culture in which the test originated. Construct tests require prior theorizing; that is, a phenomenon such as self-esteem or respect for authority is measured by appropriate items. A construct test is built through the following steps or process:

1. A construct (theory) is developed that reflects what is to be measured.
2. Test items are devised to measure the construct.
3. Items are pre-tested against the construct among groups of subjects expected to differ in performance.
4. As a result of pre-tests an investigator can gauge whether or not the chosen items reflect the construct. If not the items or the construct must be modified.
5. The next step is to translate the test for cross-cultural use. The translation must be tested and "we must next ascertain that corresponding constructs are measured in the two cultures."[22]
6. Finally the translated construct must be validated. "If it is found to measure construct X adequately in the second culture, we may then proceed with cross-cultural comparisons."[23]

The above process of arriving at a construct and items for measurement cannot be omitted in planning tests in foreign cultures. The above criteria must be met if a theory is to be validated through cross-cultural testing. The one caution that Berrien[24] proposed is that the test does not become too culture-free so that similarities are found when in fact they do not exist. For example, an overlapping technique was considered by Berrien.

If items on a test for a construct are elicited for two cultures without making cultural concessions in items, the array of indicators might fall between A–C for culture X and between B–D for culture Y. The B–C overlap represents the commonality or the comparable portion between cultures X and Y. If, however, the items on a test were culture-free or represent comparable sampling items, then Berrien feels the responses would cluster in a common range B–C and further distort the "strength of the construct within each culture,"[25] especially as A and D spread further apart.

The problem of how to set up a test to measure personality, attitudes, values or beliefs in a cross-cultural context has permeated all the social sciences. Anthropology[26] has developed another terminology which tags the same problem. An etic construct (theory) is said to be universal or culture-free while testable items are referred to as emic or culture-bound. In this framework an etic construct guides observation and indicators of an etic construct in a target culture must be emically defined. The best operational definition of this concept is found in Osgood's Semantic Differential[27] wherein activity, evaluation and potency represent etic constructs arrived at in much the same way that Gordon proposed in the six step sequence. Incidence of activity, potency and evaluation in a cross-cultural sampling are arrived at by eliciting emic or locally defined items that reflect the construct.

Level and content are the two features of a cross-cultural measure that must be comparable. Level represents these individuals who support an item while content refers to the meaning of the test items. In diagrammatic way level of cultures I and II are represented by Gordon[28] in the following way:

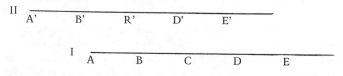

If an item "C" in culture II cannot be comparably translated then the item can be replaced but "the new item should be at or near the projected level for the old item in the second culture."[29]

In another figure, Gordon[30] represents the content of indicators for culture I and II in the following way:

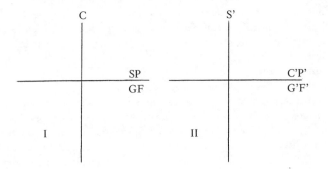

Sociability is the construct under observation in this diagram. The letters stand for the following indicators: "   "Wants to be with people" (P), "likes social gatherings" (G), "strikes up conversation with strangers" (S), and "finds it easy to make friends" (F).[31] These indicators fall on the same factor for cultures I and II; however "strikes up conversations with strangers" (S) may relate to an orthogonal factor "unconventionality," while "frequents cafes" (C') may reflect sociability."[32] In this case (C') could replace (S') in order to maintain the comparability of construct in the two cultures. The kind of substitution recommended in the above diagram requires great care and the amount of substitution should be minimal. However, concessions to cultures should not be avoided when comparability demands they be considered.

One way to approach equivalence in cross-cultural studies is to go back to the old way of eliciting a taxonomy of a subject group or culture. Studies of folk taxonomies suggest a method for eliciting and analyzing a group's classification system. A folk taxonomy "is the grouping of entities in terms of the category labels given to them by the culture, rather than by the observer's common sense or scientific knowledge."[33] Although folk taxonomies have been studied by linguists, a new surge of activity in the same direction has been labeled ethnoscience. Ethnoscientific methods are used to explore the "system of knowledge and cognition typical of a given culture."[34] A projective technique is the most useful means to elicit a taxonomy for it avoids predisposing subjects to perceive in prescribed ways and allows them to make manifest their own cognitions and conceptualizations. Test equivalence in design and content might be better served if attention is given to these pre-empirical considerations.

Available ways of measuring attitudes, values, beliefs or personality traits in a cross-cultural study have not been exhausted in the foregoing discussion. The discussion has concentrated upon some major areas of concern: how to develop and ensure a theory of cross-cultural validity and how to confirm or disconfirm a construct through rigorous attention to item selection. All of the above considerations can be called the pre-empirical groundwork to actual testing, scoring and interpretation of results in cross-cultural research. Study of a target culture may reveal the cognitive modes of that culture; that is, how a culture thinks about and expresses certain ideas or subjects of concern. If an attitude assessment of a population or culture is attempted through tests, surveys or questionnaires, then a construct must be developed and the items chosen for response must reflect the construct or goal of the investigation in a target culture. Pre-empirical study of a foreign culture may reveal that a construct is not comparably expressed across cultures. Self-esteem may be verbally expressed in one culture (the base culture or origin of test) and non-verbally expressed in a foreign culture. Symbolic systems for expression of a construct may not be comparable. A structural analysis of the communication system of a foreign culture would reveal how responses to a construct might be elicited. In this case, a construct may be tested cross-culturally, but the instrument must be made to fit non-verbal responses in the foreign culture.

A persuasive campaign to change a situation or condition in a foreign culture as well as our own culture should be preceded by some measurement of attitudes, values, beliefs or personality traits which will then direct the persuader to achieve optimal success. In this case the target population provides the indicators of the construct rather than the outside investigator.

Influence of Language on Attitudes, Personality and Behavior

The influence of language on attitudes, personality and behavior
revives an old question, but one of eminent importance in
cross-cultural studies. At least from the eighteenth century, scholars
have argued the possible effects of language on cognition, while
Benjamin Whorf, in the twentieth century, made the most convincing
argument for linguistic determinism. Thinking, according to Whorf

> will be found to be FUNDAMENTALLY DIFFERENT for
> individuals whose languages are of fundamentally different
> types. Just as cultural facts are only culturally determined, not
> biologically determined, so linguistic facts, which are likewise
> cultural, and include the linguistic element of thought, are only
> linguistically determined.[35]

The Osgood Semantic Differential was devised to refute the
Whorf-Sapir hypothesis, but current use of the Semantic Differential
questions its universal validity. Denmark et. al.[36] conducted a study
among freshmen students in New York City colleges. The subjects
were divided into three groups: white middle class, black middle class
and black lower class. Six scales of the semantic differential referred
to education (for example, group discussion, studying, learning, etc.)
while the remaining two scales related to self-perception (real self
and ideal self). The results of the test indicate that even in one
culture with a common language, although different dialects,
responses are varied. According to the authors, there may be a white
middle class bias to Osgood's factor loadings explained in the
following way:

> The white subjects' factor structure closely resembles that
> specified by Osgood. However, the differences in factor
> structure between the two groups of black subjects, as well as
> the differences between both of these groups and the white
> subjects, raised questions as to whether Osgood's semantic space
> can be applied to ALL groups.[37]

Translated attitude and personality measures, without
concession to cultural category systems, would produce rather

inaccurate scoring and interpretation, if one believes language influences an individual's thought. Collett argued that an investigator cannot assume questionnaire statements on self-esteem are equally appropriate for American children (original version) and for Indian children (translated version). On the problem of semantic equivalence in cross-cultural studies of self-esteem, Collett concludes that "an inability to fulfill the requirements of semantic equivalence has rendered cross-cultural studies of content unsatisfactory."[38]

The influence of language on attitudes, personality and behavior has not been adequately investigated and the Whorfian hypothesis has not been permanently discredited. A study by Michael Ryan proposed to test the validity of the hypothesis by measuring Canadian "Bilingual Attitudes Towards Authority."[39]

For the purposes of the study an attitude is defined as "responses on a Likert-type scale."[40] Language is carefully defined by the author as a social, emotional and cognitive system that integrates a language community. A corollary to Ryan's idea of the function of language proposes that the social attitudes of French speakers should differ from the social attitudes of English speakers "as their respective attitudes serve to integrate them into differing social, familial, occupational, and, in some cases, religious patterns."[41] For the experiment, subjects were chosen from summer session at various Canadian universities and all subjects were only part-time students otherwise having full-time occupations. Each student responded to a twenty-four item Likert type scale to measure "three affective dimensions of attitudes towards authority: attitudes of hostility, attitudes of acceptance, and attitudes of anxiety."[42] Two developmental questionnaires followed — the second of which contained selected items from the first. An example of an item from the second questionnaire follows:[43]

1. I am speechless around law officers.
   a) hostile
   b) accepting
   c) anxious
   d) neutral

The results of the study indicate that bilingual attitudes towards authority differed from unilingual attitudes in the following respects:

> Significant differences between these groups appear on attitudes of anxiety towards authority although none appear on attitudes of hostility and acceptance towards authority. More specifically, attitudes of anxiety held by bilinguals differ significantly from the attitudes of anxiety held by French Canadians but not from the attitudes of anxiety held by English Canadians.[44]

Several reasons can be suggested for the correlation between the bilingual and English unilingual attitude structure. The author found that of the 29 bilinguals, 24 spoke French as a first language. The acculturation of the bilingual into the English speaking community and the adoption of attitudes consistent with the unilingual English speaker may account for the lack of significance that Ryan noted between these two language groups. It is possible that occupations in which the bilinguals were involved placed greater stress and prestige on the use of English and in fact the occupations may have required the use of English. The author did not examine the language requirements of the occupations of the bilinguals which may have yielded pertinent information on the reasons for the correlation between bilingual and English speakers on the anxiety dimension.

Still another measure of bilingual (French and English) attitudes was made by George Larimer[45] in order to test the generality of western findings. Using a latitude of acceptance and rejection scale, 340 male French and English speaking Canadians responded to nine statements ranging from pro-French to Anti-French. An example of a pro-French statement follows: "The preservation of French Canada, its language and culture, is absolutely essential from all points of view for the good of the country."[46] A second part of the experiment exposed a selected number of subjects to propaganda speeches rated and labeled on an attitude of acceptance-rejection scale. The French speeches were translated and both sets of speeches were presented in slightly altered order. Subjects were required to rate the personalities (traits such as height-taille, leadership-qualité de chef, etc.) of the writers of the tape recorded messages. The results of the experiments confirmed Sherif, Sherif and Nebergall's contention that "derogation of a communicator and his message —— far from being an 'alternative' to attitude change —— occurs when the communication is within the latitude of rejection."[47]

The usefulness of this kind of experiment to successful persuasive communication is unquestionable. A persuasive message should be construed so that it does not fall within the latitude of rejection on a social judgment continuum. A persuasive communicator who has first surveyed the range of acceptance and rejection of a population can better predict attitudes toward a message and can in fact alter his message if he suspects it will fall in the rejection range. The obvious benefits of assessing attitudes of a population before a persuasive message is introduced should not only increase interest in attitude surveys as a pre-empirical source of information of a target population, but also enable a communicator to couch his message in an acceptable form. However, Larimer's study does not assess the effect of language on subject response which seems to indicate a serious flaw in his experiment —— especially since his experiment was designed to elicit responses from two language groups. As a result, there is no way to separate and analyze the responses of the two language groups. Although it may be predictable that French speakers will respond positively to pro-French statements, it is not certain how English speakers will respond to pro and anti-French statements. For this reason Larimer's experiment as a bilingual measure of attitudes is unsatisfactory.

Two other bilingual studies are included because they offer pertinent information on the effects of language on thought. Eliza Botha[48] conducted a study of the effects of bilingualism or values. Three language groups were represented in her Capetown, South Africa speakers, English speakers and bilinguals. The testing instrument was Dennis' Uses Test which requires answers to questions "concerned with the utility of objects, people, and events."[49] An interesting aspect of this experiment is that the author is an Afrikaans-English bilingual. Eight value categories were established in which to fit answers: for example, religious, esthetic, etc. The result of the experiment confirmed her hypothesis that "when no marked difference exists in instrumental value or status attached to the two languages of a bilingual, differences in value systems as expressed in the two languages may exist, but significant differences are fewer than have been obtained in a situation in which the second language carried particular social rewards."[50] This hypothesis may have been of use to Ryan in his Canadian study since he was unable to assess the reasons for the lack of significance between the bilingual and English response to the anxiety dimension.

Finally, the last bilingual study on attitudes considered in this inquiry is one conducted by Joshua Fishman. Fishman's subjects were selected among members of a Puerto Rican Youth Organization in New York City. According to Fishman, the study

> seeks to determine whether commitment items show any greater relationship to pertinent language behavior criteria than do more traditional dispositional or role playing language use and language attitude items.[51]

The results of the experiment indicate that commitment items on the questionnaire are factorially separate from "attitudinal and other self-report items,"[52] and that commitment items were more closely related to the criterion behavior (attendance at a Program of Puerto Rican songs, dances, recitation, etc.) than were attitudinal or other self-report items,"[53] In summary, Fishman suggests that "language behaviors and attitudes toward language"[54] may have a more significant relationship in subcultures where commitment to a language is higher than in the population at large.

The effect of language on attitude and behavior has not been conclusively proved or disproved. However, the several studies considered in this section suggest that the amount or intensity of effect can vary among language populations. When two languages represent politically polarized populations such as French and English Canadians, the attitude structure of a bilingual may be volatile depending on the social situation and context. A bilingual Canadian may manifest one set of attitudes in one social situation such as at home and another set during working hours. Weinreich has referred to this phenomenon as the result of a code switching paradigm.[55] Social demands on a bilingual individual will determine the interaction of the two codes.

Individuals of subcultures may have high commitment to their primary language because of the social and emotional integration it provides. Fishman's findings may be appropriately extended to subculture language use in foreign cultures.

A language does provide a category system and cross-cultural testing for correspondence among category systems is inadequate. Folk taxonomies for some primitive languages do exist, but for languages that serve a technologically complex culture, taxonomies only exist for parts of the culture: for example, subcultures and social class dialects in America. Translated attitude and personality instruments may overlook the unique features of a category system and for this reason the appropriateness of translated instruments is questionable. One aspect of the relationship between language and attitudes derives from the certainty that language serves different purposes in different cultures and that it may also serve similar purposes among cultures in different ways.

An attitude structure cannot be without linguistic influence. The extent or amount of influence of language on attitudes can only be determined, if at all, through a very careful item and construct adjustment in pre-empirical investigations. Cross-cultural studies must make cultural concessions in order to make cross-cultural attitude measurements valid, but the amount and kind of adjustment must be determined in each testing situation.

Influence of Culture on Attitudes and Behavior

Differences among cultures in response to persuasive communication have been noticed in several cross-cultural experiments. In general, more study on personality and persuasibility as a cultural phenomenon is needed. Godwin Chu[56] replicated the Janis and Field[57] experiment in Taiwan to determine whether or not differences in core values between American and Chinese students cause the latter to be more persuasible by mass media messages. Chu used a translated version of the Janis and Field procedure with slight modifications in some items and deletions of other items but he employed the same indicators of persuasibility as the original instrument: such as "lack of self-esteem and richness of fantasy"[58] on which positive correlations were expected and "interpersonal aggressiveness and neurotic defensiveness"[59] for which negative correlations were expected. Among Chinese boys a correlation occurred between persuasibility and "test anxiety and hyper-aggressiveness,"[60] which was contrary to expectations. In general, Chinese students were found to be more persuasible than American students, but Chu suggests that persuasibility may be "part of an integrated personality structure."[61]

An investigation of modal personalities of American and Chinese students suggests that a greater understanding of the whole cultural personality structure must be reached before valid cross-cultural measurements of personality can be made.

Paul Hiniker suggests testing two theories as explanations of "Chinese reaction to Forced Compliance."[62] More specifically Hiniker explored answers to the question: "What is the attitudinal effect on Chinese of making a public statement contrary to private opinion under inducement of an authority figure?"[63] In order to understand Chinese attitudes to forced compliance, Hiniker first examined the characterological theory which builds a modal personality from responses to three self-report items: "conception of self; relation to authority; and ways of dealing with primary conflicts."[64] Dissonance Theory was used by the author as an alternative explanation of Chinese reaction to forced compliance. An impressive corpus of literature confirms the claims of Dissonance Theory in American experiments while Chinese responses in Hiniker's experiment indicate a need for either making modifications in the theory or in the testing procedures. The author notes some cultural bias in Dissonance Theory, particularly in the "follows from"[65] phrase. According to Festinger, "two cognitive elements are in dissonant relation, if the obverse of one element follows from the other."[66] This condition was not met in the expected way in the Chinese experiment.

Hiniker's experiment was carried out in a precise and overall commendable manner. It is one of the most thorough pieces of empirical research reported in cross-cultural studies. The results of the experiment, according to the author, indicate that for Chinese subjects, the increased inducement produces increased compliance; but that neither increased inducement nor consequent increased compliance has any observable effect on internalized attitudes under the conditions tested.[67]

Instead of treating the results of the experiment as disconfirmation of Dissonance Theory, cross-cultural experimentation might serve to refine the theory to ensure its universal validity.

Godwin Chu noticed an excessive amount of test anxiety among his Chinese subjects which may be attributed to the novelty of testing among students in Taiwan. Testing among university students is a western tradition which is not usually met with opposition or reluctance. However, individuals from other cultures may not be as willing to submit to tests which may be interpreted as an "unwarranted invation of their privacy."[68] McGinnies encountered this kind of reaction among Japanese students during his study of attitude change. A modal personality component of privacy was noticed among the Japanese students in that testing was considered an infringement on their privacy and in fact the students requested that their names not appear on the questionnaires.

Other problems thwarted McGinnies' experimental plans. Students at Japanese Universities are not compelled to attend class so that class attendance is sporatic and lateness to class is also an accepted condition. For these reasons, it was difficult to conduct an experiment using a class as a subject group. Relationships between professors and students are formal which is consistent with the formal structure of interpersonal relations in Japan.

The purpose of McGinnies' study was to elicit student attitudes on three subjects: "a) the Cold War; b) the Cuban situation; and c) nuclear-powered submarine visits."[69] The persuasive communications used were pro and con arguments for each issue which were collected from speeches and newspaper editorials.

The knottiest problem concerned the translation of the attitude scales. The problem of translation, as mentioned earlier, is not easily solved where an American-designed test is used in translated form as

61

the instrument. The language consultants, according to McGinnies, "almost invariably disagreed over the proper translations of both the attitude scales and the persuasive communications."[70] The Japanese translators used a "hard" style of written Japanese rather than a "soft" style and the Japanese psychologists concurred with the choice. However, the experimenters thought the "soft" style was more appropriate, but the Japanese opinion prevailed.

One of the most interesting results of the experiment was a partial confirmation of the greater impact of written over oral persuasive communications among Japanese students. This finding suggests that the Japanese language may be a visual language. Other languages might be investigated to determine the relative effectiveness of oral and written communication.

McGinnies' experiments among Japanese students do not offer conclusions, but do suggest areas for further study. For example, the one-sided versus the two-sided persuasive communication was tested and the experimenters found some evidence to support the latter. Japanese students seem to resist the hard-sell approach of the one-sided argument. The resistance may have little to do with the fairness of presenting both side of an issue, but may be traceable to a Japanese personality trait.

Modal personality structures of foreign subjects may be inaccurately manipulated by American-designed tests. Knowledge of a modal personality structure can be useful to the cross-cultural researcher. Testing in foreign cultures for confirmation of theories such as Dissonance Theory may require alterations in procedures as well as value judgments on results. If results of tests for Dissonance Theory in a foreign culture do not match results of an American subject group, an experimenter may choose one of two alternatives: (1) He may simply assume Dissonance Theory does not work in the foreign culture, or (2) He may, if knowledgeable in the foreign culture, review the procedure of the original test and make alterations in procedure and interpretation to fit the foreign culture. After a cultural fit of the test has been assured, then he may assess the results of the test. The validity of cross-cultural research depends heavily on the second alternative. Experimenters should maximize their efforts to assure equivalence in cross-cultural experimentation.

Conclusion

Equivalence in cross-cultural attitude and behavior measurement is a problem for continued research. The literature on equivalence suggests there may not be a universal formula, but that equivalence in measurement must be worked out in each case. Gordon[71] describes a useful procedure for arriving at a construct and items to reflect a construct. His procedure calls for a cultural fit of each test. Translation of an American-designed instrument is not a short-cut to cross-cultural research nor is a translated test a reliable indicator of attitudes and behavior in a foreign culture. Knowledge of cross-cultural testing measures goes beyond the testing device and, in fact, requires the experimenter to be an ethnographer of the culture in which he conducts experiments.

Language seems to have an effect on attitudes, personality and behavior, but the experimenter must determine the intensity of effect in each experimental case. A political-economic system that polarizes language groups does intensify the effect of language on attitudes and behavior. Subcultures seem to have a higher commitment to their natural languages than a population at large.

Environmental and cultural factors affect attitudes and behavior but the extent and kind of influence must be determined in each case. Behavioral variables have different weights in different cultures. Modal personality studies of foreign cultures reveal idiosyncratic traits which may cause subjects to respond to American-designed tests in unexpected ways. Some of the unexpectedness can be eliminated by pre-empirical studies of target cultures. Tests used to assess attitudes, personality and behavior must be culturally appropriate.

Whether the goal of cross-cultural research is a comparative study or a single culture innovation and change study, attitudes and behavior of the target culture(s) should be subjects of pre-empirical study. After attitudes and behaviors of a target culture have been studied and assessed persuasive techniques can be recommended. These techniques may vary widely from culture to culture. If the goal of a persuasive communication experiment is one of making response comparisons among cultures, the researcher may simply want to compare responses to a specific kind of persuasion or persuasive technique. If the goal of a persuasive communication is to alter behavior in a foreign culture, the choice of the most workable technique is imperative to ensure success.

Cross-cultural persuasive communication study is not a simple extension of American-researched behavioral science to foreign cultures. Much more pre-empirical study of foreign cultures is necessary before valid comparisons can be made and before persuasive techniques can be recommended for use in foreign cultures.

FOOTNOTES

[1] Thomas D. Beisecker and Don W. Parson, "Introduction," in *The Process of Social Influence*, ed. Thomas D. Beisecker and Don W. Parson (Englewood Cliffs, New Jersey: Prentice-Hall, Inc., 1972), p. 2.

[2] Ralph L. Rosnow and Edward J. Robinson, "Introduction," in *Experiments in Persuasion*, ed. Ralph L. Rosnow and Edward J. Robinson (New York: Academic Press, 1957), xvi.

[3] Harry C. Triandis, Roy S. Malpass, and Andrew R. Davidson, "Cross-Cultural Psychology," in *Biennial Review of Anthropology 1971*, ed. Bernard J. Siegel (Stanford, California: Stanford University Press, 1972), p. 33.

[4] Erwin P. Bettinghaus, *Persuasive Communication* (New York: Holt, Rinehart and Winston, Inc., 1968), p. 22.

[5] Wesley C. Salmon, "Confirmation," *Scientific American* (May, 1973), pp. 75-83.

[6] Paul J. Hiniker, "Chinese Reactions to Forced Compliance: Dissonance Reduction or National Character," *The Journal of Social Psychology*, 77 (1969), p. 173.

[7] Adam Przeworski and Henry Teune, "Equivalence in Cross-National Research," *Public Opinion Quarterly*, (Winter, 1966-67), p. 552.

[8] *Ibid.*, p. 553.

[9] N. Frijda and G. Jahoda, "On the Scope and Methods of Cross-Cultural Research," in *Cross-Cultural Studies*, ed. D.R. Price-Williams (Baltimore, Maryland: Penguin Books, 1970), p. 37.

[10] Peter Collett, "Structure and Content in Cross-Cultural Studies of Self-Esteem," *International Journal of Psychology* 7, 3 (1972), p. 170.

[11] Przeworski and Teune, p. 554.

[12] M.S. Smart and R.C. Smart, "Self-Esteem and Social-Personal Orientation of Indian 12- and 18-year-olds," *Psychological Reports*, 27 (1970), p. 107-115.

[13] Collett, p. 171.

[14] *Ibid.*

[15] Yasumasa Tanaka, "Cross-Cultural Compatibility of the Affective Meaning Systems (Measured by Means of Multilingual Semantic Differentials)," *Journal of Social Issues,* XXIII, 1(1967), pp. 27-46.

[16] Collett, p. 173.

[17] *Ibid.*

[18] Paul A. Kolers, "Bilingualism and Information Processing," *Scientific American* (March, 1968), p. 82.

[19] Collett, p. 176.

[20] *Ibid.,* p. 169.

[21] Leonard V. Gordon, "Comments on "Cross-Cultural Equivalence of Personality Measures," *The Journal of Social Psychology,* 75 (1968), pp. 11-19.

[22] *Ibid.,* p. 13.

[23] *Ibid.*

[24] F.K. Berrien, "Cross-Cultural Equivalance of Personality Measures," *The Journal of Social Psychology,* 75 (1968), pp. 3-9.

[25] *Ibid.,* p. 5.

[26] See William C. Sturtevant, "Studies in Ethnoscience," in *Transcultural Studies in Cognition,* ed. A. Kimball Romney and Roy Goodwin D'Andrade (Menasha, Wisconsin: American Anthropological Association, 1964), pp. 99-125.

[27] Charles E. Osgood, "Semantic Differential Technique in the Comparative Study of Cultures," in *Transcultural Studies in Cognition . . .,* pp. 171-200.

[28] Gordon, p. 15.

[29] *Ibid.,* p. 14.

[30] *Ibid.,* p. 15.

[31] *Ibid.*

[32] *Ibid.*

[33] Madeleine Mathiot, "Noun Classes and Folk Taxonomy in Papago," in *Language in Culture and Society,* ed. Dell Hymes (New York: Harper & Row, 1964), p. 156.

[34] Sturtevant, p. 99.

[35] Benjamin Lee Whorf, "A Linguistic Consideration of Thinking in Primitive Communities," in *Language, Thought & Reality,* ed. John B. Carrol (Cambridge, Massachusetts: The M.I.T. Press, 1956), footnote p. 67.

[36] Florence L. Denmark, Ethel J. Shirk and Robert T. Riley, "The Effect of Ethnic & Social Class Variables on Semantic Differential Performance," *The Journal of Social Psychology*, 86 (1972), pp. 3-9.

[37] *Ibid.,* p. 9

[38] Collett, p. 170.

[39] Michael G. Ryan, "Bilingual Attitudes Towards Authority: A Canadian Study," Reprint of a paper presented to the International & Intercultural Division Speech Communication Association, (December 27-30, 1972), pp. 14.

[40] *Ibid.,* p. 1.

[41] *Ibid.,* p. 3.

[42] *Ibid.,* p. 6.

[43] *Ibid.,* p. 7.

[44] *Ibid.,* p. 9.

[45] George S. Larimer, "Social Judgment Approach to the Investigation of French and English Canadian Attitudes," *Public Opinion Quarterly,* 32 (Summer, 1968), pp. 281-286.

[46] *Ibid.,* p. 283.

[47] *Ibid.,* p. 286.

[48] Eliza Botha, "The Effect of Language on Values Expressed by Bilinguals," *The Journal of Social Psychology*, 80 (1970), pp. 143-145.

[49] *Ibid.,* p. 144.

[50] *Ibid.,* p. 145.

[51] Joshua A. Fishman, "Bilingual Attitudes and Behaviors," *Language Science,* (April, 1969), p. 5.

[52] *Ibid.,* p. 8.

[53] *Ibid.*

[54] *Ibid.*

[55] Uriel Weinreich, "Mechanisms and Structural Causes of Interferences," in *Psycholinguistics*, ed. Sol Saporta (New York: Holt, Rinehart and Winston, 1961), p. 381.

[56] Godwin C. Chu, "Culture, Personality, and Persuasibility," *Sociometry*, 29, 2 (June, 1966), pp. 169-174.

[57] Irving L. Janis and Peter B. Field, "A Behavioral Assessment of Persuasibility: Consistency of Individual Differences,"

Sociometry, 19, 4(December, 1956), pp. 241-259.

[58] Chu, p. 172.

[59] *Ibid.,* p. 173.

[60] *Ibid.*

[61] *Ibid.*

[62] Paul J. Hiniker, "Chinese Reactions to Forced Compliance: Dissonance Reduction or National Character," *The Journal of Social Psychology,* 77 (1969), pp. 157-175.

[63] *Ibid.,* p. 157.

[64] *Ibid.,* p. 158.

[65] *Ibid.,* p. 159.

[66] *Ibid.*

[67] *Ibid.,* p. 175.

[68] Elliot McGinnies, "Cross-Cultural Investigation of Some Factors in Persuasion and Attitude Change," (College Park, Maryland: Institute for Behavioral Research), August 1963, p. 5.

[69] *Ibid.,* p. 11.

[70] *Ibid.,* p. 16.

[71] Gordon, pp. 11-19.

BIBLIOGRAPHY

Beisecker, Thomas D. and Don W. Parson, "Introduction." In *The Process of Social Influence.* Eds. Thomas D. Beisecker and Don W. Parson. Englewood Cliffs, New Jersey, 1972.

Berrien, F.K. "Cross-Cultural Equivalence of Personality Measures." *The Journal of Social Psychology*, 75 (1968), pp. 3-9.

Bettinghaus, Erwin P. *Persuasive Communication.* New York: Holt, Rinehart and Winston, Inc., 1968.

Botha, Elize. "The Effect of Language on Values Expressed by Bilinguals." *The Journal of Social Psychology*, 80 (1970), pp. 143-145.

Chu, Godwin C. "Culture, Personality, and Persuasibility." *Sociometry*, 29, 2(June 1966), pp. 169-174.

Collet, Peter. "Structure and Content in Cross-Cultural Studies of Self-Esteem." *International Journal of Psychology*, 7, 3 (1972), pp. 169-179.

Denmark, Florence L., Ethel J. Shirk, and Robert T. Riley. "The Effect of Ethnic and Social Class Variables on Semantic Differential Performance." *The Journal of Social Psychology*, 86 (1972), pp. 3-9.

Fishman, Joshua A. "Bilingual Attitudes and Behaviors." *Language Sciences* (April, 1969), pp. 5-9.

Frijda, N. and G. Jahoda. "On the Scope and Methods of Cross-Cultural Research." In *Cross-Cultural Studies.* Ed. D.R. Price-Williams. Baltimore, Maryland: Penguin Books, 1970.

Gordon, Leonard V. "Comments on "Cross-Cultural Equivalence of Personality Measures"." *The Journal of Social Psychology*, 75 (1968), pp. 11-19.

Hiniker, Paul J. "Chinese Reactions to Forced Compliance: Dissonance Reduction or National Character." *The Journal of Social Psychology*, 77 (1969), pp. 157-175.

Janis, Irving L. and Peter B. Field. "A Behavioral Assessment of Persuasibility: Consistency of Individual Differences," *Sociometry*, 19, 4 (December, 1956), pp. 241-259.

Kolars, Paul A. "Bilingualism and Information Processing." *Scientific American* (March, 1968), pp. 78-87.

Larimer, George S. "Social Judgment Approach to the Investigation of French and English Canadian Attitudes." *Public Opinion Quarterly*, 32 (Summer, 1968), pp. 281-286.

McGinnies, Elliot. "Cross-Cultural Investigation of Some Factors in Persuasion and Attitude Change." College Park, Maryland: Institute for Behavioral Research, August 1963. Distributed by National Technique Information Service: U.S. Department of Commerce.

Osgood, Charles E. "Semantic Differential Technique in the Comparative Study of Cultures." In *Transcultural Studies in Cognition*. Eds. A. Kimball Romney and Roy Goodwin D'Andrade. Menasha, Wisconsin: American Anthropological Association, 1964.

Przeworski, Adam and Henry Teune. "Equivalence in Cross-National Research." *Public Opinion Quarterly* (Winter, 1966-67), pp. 551-568.

Rosnow, Ralph L. and Edward J. Robinson. *Experiments in Persuasion.* New York: Academic Press, 1957.

Ryan, Michael G. "Bilingual Attitudes Towards Authority: A Canadian Study." Reprint of a paper presented to the International and Intercultural Division, Speech Communication Association (December 27-30, 1972), p. 14.

Salmon, Wesley C. "Confirmation." *Scientific American*, (May 1973), pp. 75-83.

Smart, M.S. and R.C. Smart. "Self-Esteem and Social-Personal Orientation of Indian 12- and 18-year-olds." *Psychological Reports*, 27 (1970), 107-115.

Sturtevant, William C. "Studies in Ethnoscience." In *Transcultural Studies in Cognition*. Ed. A. Kimball Romney and Roy Goodwin D'Andrade. Menasha, Wisconsin: American Anthropological Association, 1964.

Tanaka, Yasumasa. "Cross-Cultural Compatibility of the Affective Meaning Systems (Measured by Means of Multilingual Semantic Differentials)." *Journal of Social Issues*, XXIII, 1 (1967), pp. 27-46.

Triandis, Harry C., Roy S. Malpass, and Andrew R. Davidson. "Cross-Cultural Psychology." In *Biennial Review of*

Anthropology 1971. Ed. Bernard J. Siegel. Stanford, California:
Stanford University Press, 1972.

Weinreich, Uriel. "Mechanisms and Structural Causes of
Interferences." In *Psycholinguistics*. Ed. Sol Saporta. New
York: Holt, Rinehart and Winston, 1961.

Whorf, Benjamin Lee. "A Linguistic Consideration of Thinking in
Primitive Communities." In *Language, Thought & Reality*. Ed.
John B. Carrol. Cambridge, Massachusetts: the M.I.T. Press,
1956.

James E. Grunig:

A General Systems Theory
of Communication, Poverty, and Underdevelopment

AMERICANS have long been concerned with the fate of the disadvantaged and the poverty stricken. Social scientists have reflected this concern by studying means of stimulating individual and social changes that would improve the lot of the disadvantaged. Communication scholars have been at the forefront of this research, since communication generally has been assumed to be a necessary if not sufficient condition for change.

Rural sociologists were the first to study planned change in an effort to stimulate the diffusion of innovations in rural communities.[1] Other social action studies concerned charity drives, school bond issues, and hospital construction, among others.[2] During the late 1950's and the 1960's researchers placed great emphasis on finding means of using communication to stimulate change in underdeveloped countries. And with the Great Society came concern for domestic anti—poverty efforts.

Communications researchers have attacked problems of poverty and underdevelopment using such theoretical concepts as the relationship of mass media development to national development, the diffusion of innovations, freedom of the press in developing countries, media usage by the poor, empathy, modern values, modernizing attitudes, cultural change and restrictions, literacy, achievement motivation, rising expectations, want/get ratios, the two—step flow, opinion leaders, traditional and transitional individuals, and numbers of theater seats and radios.

If, however, the most important test of any social science theory is its ability to prescribe solutions to practical problems, then few, if any, of these concepts could be said to have contributed much to a theory of communication and development. If we as researchers ask a simple question, the rationale for this conclusion should be obvious: What would we tell a professional communicator or government official in Colombia, India, Afghanistan, or a low—income region in the United States to do if he wanted to improve communications with poor people.

Ilchman and Uphoff make a similar point about political science theory as it applies to developing countries. They ask what a political scientist could have told Colonel Gowon when he became president of Nigeria in 1966:[3]

> Colonel Gowon would have found small consolation in the assurance that advancing differentiation would probably usher in a new Nigeria eventually marked by achievement, universalistic and affectively neutral norms, and functionally specific institutions. Nor would it have helped him to be told that "transitional" periods are difficult and unavoidable. What he needs was assistance in shaping productive, constructive policies of the sort normally employed by statesmen.

Research on the relationship of communication and underdevelopment is at a standstill because theorists have assumed for too long that messages can be given to traditional individuals that will change those individuals to make them more modern. These researchers assumed further that modern individuals can change the political, social, or economic system to make it more modern also.

Unfortunately, however, individuals in nearly every underdeveloped country or region of a country are bound in by restrictive system structures which they as individuals are powerless to change. Even if communication could endow them with more modern attitudes, the structure would not allow them to change their behavior or more importantly to change the system.

Change in system structure rather than individual change, then, is the essence of economic development. Yet it is structural change that communication directed at individuals is almost powerless to effect. What kind of communication theory, then, is necessary if we are to understand the relationship of communication to poverty and development? Obviously, it should concern how communication can bring about structural change. And since individuals alone seldom change a structure, the unit of analysis for this research should be systems which encompass and affect individuals –– including formal communication organizations, the mass media, pressure groups, and communities.

Two Competing Paradigms

In the early years of research on communications and development, a single paradigm tended to dominate the field. That paradigm had its origin in Lerner's classic study of communication and modernization in the Middle East.[4] In brief, Lerner found that individual mass media exposure gave the individual an empathic personality which in turn was associated with participation in the social and political system. But, importantly, in Lerner's model of change, urbanization and literacy are antecedent conditions to mass media exposure.

Lerner's model has also been adopted by Rogers[5] and many other communications researchers, including some who have applied the concepts to research in underdeveloped areas of the United States.[6]

This predominant paradigm can perhaps be characterized by a simple statement, that communication causes change. Research e r s subscribing to this paradigm have spent years correlating mass media exposure and other individual communication behaviors with various indices of individual modernization and national development. Most of the findings have been purely descriptive, and many –– for example, Lerner's –– basically tautological. For example, it helps little to learn that a lower–order concept (media development) correlates highly with a higher–order concept (national development) which at the same time subsumes the lower order concept.

Lerner found urbanization to be the antecedent condition for the other elements of his model –– literacy, media exposure, empathy, and participation. What he failed to recognize is that the urbanization variable, more than anything else, probably indicated the extent to which an individual was a part of the economic elite of the country, an elite which in most underdeveloped countries has almost exclusive access to education, the media, and the political system. Thus, Lerner was not describing a dynamic process, he was describing a static status quo. If we take his model to its logical conclusion, we could say that moving impoverished people to cities would lead to modernization. As experience in U.S. and Latin American cities shows, that prescription clearly does not work.

The most important problem with this predominant paradigm —— from a scientific point-of-view, is that it has produced little true theory, theory being distinguished from what Brown calls an empirical generalization.[7] A theory exists, according to Brown, when the question of "why" an observed phenomenon occurs can be answered in terms of increasingly more abstract concepts which apply to many situations. It is because of the absence of such abstract theory that communications researchers have a difficult time turning their descriptive findings into prescriptive advice for professional communicators.

In contrast to the predominant communication paradigm, however, it is possible to interpret most of the existing literature on communication and development in precisely the opposite fashion. Communication does not cause change. Change creates the need for communication. This simple cause—effect reversal has been the basis of a new paradigm developed by the author and others. Essentially this paradigm holds that structural change must come first and that communication then enlarges and supports the consequences of that change by making more and more individuals aware of new opportunities.

The results of several studies have supported this hypothesized relationship between communication and development. During two years of research in Colombia, this author conducted two studies relating communication behavior to decision situations of large landowners (latifundistas)[8] and then of peasants (minifundistas).[9] In both studies a set of decision concepts was used to predict information seeking. The concepts are based on two dimensions, the openness of the individual and the openness of the structure.

Figure 1.   The decision-situation model defined as four
typologies.

		Structure	
		Open	Closed
Individual	Open	Problem Solving	Constrained Decision
	Closed	Routine Habit	Fatalism

As Figure 1 illustrates, the model holds that individuals will
seek information when they perceive a problem (the individual is
open). To have a problem simply means that the individual
recognizes that he has a choice between alternatives. Secondly, the
model predicts that individuals will seek information only about
alternatives which are feasible within their situation or environment.
The combinations of these two dimensions yields four types of
decision situations and/or decision modes.

Problem solving is a type of decision situation in which the
individual recognizes that alternatives are present and therefore that
a problem exists. Alternatives are also available within the structure.
The individual in this situation is rational. He weighs alternatives and
chooses among them. Volition, or perceived volition, in making a
choice exists. Because the individual evaluates alternatives,
information is useful to him, and information seeking and giving are
important aspects of problem solving. This is the only decision mode
which is "modern" in nature.

Constrained decision is characterized by physical or structural
blocks within the system which rule out all but one alternative or a
limited range of alternatives. The individual has little perceived
volition, even though he recognizes alternatives that are excluded by
constraints in his situation. Because alternatives are constrained,
information seeking will be low, although information about
excluded alternatives will not be avoided.[10]

Routine habit is characterized by a close–minded individual in
an open structure. This individual considers only a habitual
alternative. His cognitive process is rigid, and his information seeking

is negligible and directed only toward messages which reinforce his habitual alternative. He readily gives information, however, when his alternative is threatened.

In *fatalism*, the individual neither recognizes a problem nor has alternatives available within his structure. He feels that he has no control over his environment and he has lost interest in controlling it. For these reasons, he is not an information seeker.

Some readers may object that these decision modes are too idealized and like most typologies, too inflexible (i.e., there may be middle points between them). This is a valid criticism and for this reason, some may prefer to interpret the decision modes as discrete points on two continuous scales (Figure 2).

Figure 2.   The decision-situation model defined as points on two continuous axes.

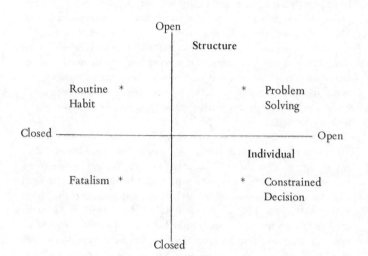

Because this model was receiver—oriented and predicted communication behavior rather than the effects of messages, it seemed perfectly suited to test the hypothesis that change creates the need for communication. To apply the model in the Colombian studies, Q factor analysis of survey data (correlation and factoring of people rather than of variables) was used to develop six types of large landowners and six types of peasants. Then analysis included three types of variables: (1) pre—cognitive variables, to indicate the opportunity structure and individual differences, (2) cognitive variables, the decision modes and communication variables, and (3) post—cognitive variables, consequences of cognition such as income, adoption of technology, and productivity (which become pre—cognitive variables in a continuous process).

In these two studies, the decision modes were measured through a series of factual and projective questions. The factual questions came immediately after questions which determined each respondent's use of markets, transportation, technology, etc. At this point, the respondent was asked why he chose the alternative he did. The projective questions came later in the interview when the respondent was asked what he would do in several hypothetical situations ranging from crop failure to finding employment off the farm. Each response was coded as one of the decision modes. Each respondent then received an overall percentage score for each mode based on the relationship with the total number of decisions which he was questioned about.

The resulting Q—typologies showed that the type of decision mode and the resulting communication behavior depended to a large extent on the structure of the situation. For the large landowners, routine habit became less common as the typologies moved from traditional to modern (Table 1). But importantly, the most traditional types had large amounts of land and could make extremely high incomes from routine habit behavior —— they had no need for the problem solving mode. The problem solvers were renters, the foreign born (Germans and Japanese), those with less land, and new entrepreneurs in a frontier region. In all cases, they had to make problem solving decisions to attain what they considered sufficient income.

The minifundistas became more characterized by problem solving and less characterized by the other decision modes as the structure offered more opportunities (Table 2). In both studies, the problem solvers were characterized by information seeking and exposure to a variety of information sources. The major exception was that the most traditional latifundista type was most exposed to newspapers — no doubt because of the status quo orientation of Colombian news media. The communication variables also correlated with the decision modes as expected. (Tables 3 and 4).

Table 1.   Relative importance of four decision variables in determining six Q-typologies of Colombian Latifundistas.

	Type of Decision[a] (Z-scores[b])			
	Problem Solving	Routine Habit	Constrained Decision	Ignorant Habit
Type 1 (Most entrepreneurial)	1.39	−1.49	−0.29	−0.91
Type 2	0.45	−1.73	−0.13	−1.18
Type 3	1.10	0.36	−0.33	−0 15
Type 4	0.44	−1.05	0.75	−0.73
Type 5	−1.39	1.66	0.68	1.31
Type 6 (Least entrepreneurial)	−2.19	2.48	0.04	1.58

[a] At the time of this study, ignorant habit was conceptualized separately from constrained decision. Fatalism was not found for latifundistas.

[b] Factor scores of variables on types of people. In a standard normal distribution, about 68% of the Z-scores fall between −1 and +1, 95% between −2 and +2, and 99% between −3 and +3. The mean is zero, standard deviation one.

Table 2. Relative Importance of five decision variables in determining six Q-typologies of Colombian minifundistas.

	Type of Decision[a] (Z-scores[b])				
	Problem Solving	Routine Habit	Constrained Decision	Ignorant Habit	Fatalism
Type 1 (Most entrepreneurial)	1.75	−1.24	−1.80	−1.90	−0.99
Type 2	0.62	−0.87	0.55	−0.57	−0.61
Type 3	0.00	−1.14	1.41	−0.23	−0.47
Type 4	−0.92	−0.50	−0.26	2.07	0.40
Type 5	−1.89	1.21	1.94	1.20	1.77
Type 6 (Least entrepreneurial)	−1.23	3.32	0.12	0.68	0.94

[a]At the time of this study, ignorant habit was conceptualized
separately from constrained decision.

[b]Factor scores of variables on types of people. In a standard
normal distribution, about 68% of the Z-scores fall between
−1 and +1, 95% between −2 and +2, and 99% between −3
and +3. The mean is zero, standard deviation one.

Table 3. Correlations of four decision variables with eight
communication variables for a sample of Colombian
latifundistas.

	Problem Solving	Routine Habit	Constrained Decision	Ignorant Habit
Information seeking	.38	−.45	.16	−.23
Perception of usefulness of information	.53	−.53	.10	−.38
Newspaper exposure	−.05	.12	.06	.10
Agricultural magazine exposure	.30	−.24	−.02	−.16
Authoritative sources	.45	−.45	−.01	−.11
Commercial sources	.27	−.29	.02	−.16
Peer sources	.21	−.29	.18	−.18
Private sources	.10	−.19	.14	−.02

At the .05 level, all correlations greater than .21 are significant.

Table 4. Correlations of five decision variables with twelve communication variables for a sample of Colombian minifundistas.

Information seeking	.37	−.34	−.06	−.14	−.23
Perceived Usefulness of information	.25	−.26	.05	−.04	−.41
Newspaper exposure	.24	−.12	−.14	−.08	−.16
El Campesino exposure	.06	−.10	.08	−.08	−.11
Exposure to agricultural radio programs	.14	−.19	−.08	−.05	.09
Authoritative sources	.46	−.23	−.23	−.28	−.19
Commercial sources	.15	−.12	−.01	−.10	−.12
Peer sources	.22	−.32	−.02	.09	−.22
Situational relevance of content	.45	−.19	−.25	−.31	−.14
Market information	.44	−.26	−.25	−.17	−.22
Technical assistance with credit	.45	−.19	−.32	−.31	−.14

At the .05 level, all correlations greater than .20 are significant.

Table 5. An R factor entitled "problem solving" derived
from a sample of Columbian minifundistas.

	Factor Loading
Problem solving decision behavior	.711
Adoption	.547
Level of aspiration	.527
Achievement motivation	.521
Authoritative information sources	.514
Information seeking	.509
Situational relevance of information content	.480
Input scarcity[a]	.478
Market information	.465
Technical assistance with credit	.450
Literacy	.447
Perceived usefulness of information	.416
Cosmopoliteness	.405
Economic rationality decision criterion	.348
Peer information sources	.304
Commercial information sources	.187
Off-farm income	.185
Social-Psychological values decision criterion	-.153
Work days lost for sickness	-.214
Risk and uncertainty decision criterion	-.245
Anomie	-.267
Tenure and title	-.279
Percent income of total costs[a]	-.360
Land taxes	-.382
Percent income of variable costs[a]	-.383
Age	-.384
Miscellaneous decision criteria	-.495
Ignorant habit decision behavior	-.504
Fatalism decision behavior	-.508
Routine habit decision behavior	-.516
Subjectivity of land to productive limitations.	-.524

[a] Input scarcity generally represented how many modern
inputs were utilized; if they were used, they were perceived
as scarce. Thus it was related to adoption and the rest of
the factor. The percentage income variables were likewise
negatively related to income and to capital use.

Table 6. An R Factor entitled "problem solving" derived from a sample of Columbian latifundistas.

	Factor Loading
Adoption	.770
Problem solving decision behavior	.613
Information seeking	.557
Salary of farm manager	.556
Level of education	.535
Economic rationality decision criterion	.525
Market used (degree of control	.525
Magazine exposure	.521
Authoritative information sources	.521
Intensity of land use	.510
Perceived usefulness of information	.506
Quality of farm manager	.499
Land value	.485
Fixed costs per land unit	.478
Peer information sources	.467
Number of transportation alternatives	.466
Voluntary organization memberships	.463
Modernity of transportation methods	.418
Responsibility given to farm manager	.414
Cosmopoliteness	.410
Productivity per land unit	.400
Variable costs per land unit	.398
Man-days labor per land unit	.395
Commercial information sources	.393
Private information sources	.381
Transportation information content	.345
Labor problems	.327
Political efficacy	.309
Labor cost per man-day	.272
Education in agriculture	.267
Political connections	.225
Labor productivity	-.111
Family size	-.218
Ignorant habit decision behavior	-.279
Medical services	-.346
Amount of land	-.311
Traditional social value	-.410
Age	-.420
No decision criterion	-.434
Ownership of land	-.452
Management ease decision criterion	-.458
Routine habit decision behavior	-.658

Another significant aspect of the study was an R factor that emerged in each of the two studies, a factor which in both cases could be called the problem—solving factor (Tables 5 and 6). This factor confirmed the conceptualization of problem solving and in addition appeared to subsume the traditional social psychological variables associated with modernity, adoption, aspiration level, achievement motivation, economic rationality, cosmopoliteness, and literacy. Empathy also loaded positively, although not highly, on the factor (there was, however, difficulty with the measure used for empathy).

Studies by several other researchers can also be cited to support the change—communication paradigm. For example, Fett measured the degree to which peasant farmers in Brazil sought various types of market information.[11] He found that peasants sought information about crops for which several alternative markets existed. They did not seek information when the market structure was closed.

In a study in Afghanistan, Whiting found that structural factors, lack of supplies of new technology and lack of finances, were more important reasons for not adopting new technology than was attitudinal resistance.[12] He also concluded, "Since media exposure was very low and characterological modernity surprisingly high it seems clear that mass media are not *necessary* conditions for characterological modernity."[13]

Likewise, Sultana Krippendorff used historical analysis to show that the mass media in India resisted religious change and supported the status quo when British missionaries entered the country.[14] Marceau, similarly, showed that social conflicts in French communities prevented communication messages from bringing change:[15]

> Conflicts mean that instead of clear guidance for action, confusing messages are sent out concerning innovations of all kinds . . . . There will be conflicts over the aims, means, and results of social, economic, and political change and the desirability of even technical innovations, conflicts which will be reflected in the messages mass media, "experts," and ordinary individuals receive and transmit.

In a study of road building projects in 31 Colombian communities, Felstehausen concluded that:[16]

> . . . . information and technology were available to the operational level, a conclusion attested to by the fact that local groups often undertook and completed road projects without outside technical assistance. The principal obstacle did not appear to be information. Rather, the rules, rewards, and sanctions of the system were organized in such a way that they did not foster the desired action.

What these studies show is that system control is by far the most common communication function in underdeveloped countries, a function which cybernetic theorists have traditionally viewed as the major purpose of communication in a system. We might go so far as to say that it is "natural" for communication to maintain the system, unnatural for it to change the system.

This conclusion sharpens our theoretical perspective on the relationship of communication to development. But the conclusion is a sobering one for a communication researcher because it means that the only thing he can recommend to a professional communicator is to wait for change to occur so that he can then communicate information about new opportunities created by structural change. But change is unlikely to occur because social and economic elites control the system and have little desire to change it except when change improves their own situation.

Development Communication as an Organizational Activity

Few communication researchers have recognized an important attribute that all communications designed to stimulate economic development have in common. They are, almost without exception, produced by a member of a formal organization, be it an agricultural extension agency, land reform agency, economic development agency, a mass medium, or an anti—poverty or community action agency.

These organizations are themselves social systems with roles, norms, values, and communication channels that influence the professional communicator. Quite frequently that organization is a system with norms and roles that diverge from those of the clientele system. Rarely, then, is the communicator capable of being the disinterested, empathic individual which he must be to provide low—income people with information which is situationally relevant.

This fact explains to a large extent why pro—development and anti—poverty messages have so little effect. They are communicated by individuals who perceive their role to be preserving the system and controlling its low—income members rather than of changing the system. Along these lines, this author's research in Colombia showed that a key structural block cutting off opportunities was the inability (or unwillingess) of social action agencies and the mass media to produce information situationally relevant to the clientele. Opportunities became unbearable risks to these individuals because of the absence of relevant information.

The media and action agencies could not provide needed information because they were staffed by individuals from upper—and upper—middle class primary reference groups, groups with a vested interest in the status quo, a different set of values from those of the clientele, and an inability to empathize with the clientele. Community studies by Haney[17] and Drake,[18] both in Colombia, documented this elite domination of social action agencies. Felstehausen has also compiled a good deal of evidence showing elite domination of Colombian communities.[19]

Although the evidence presented thus far about the nature of organization to low—income clientele communication has come from research in an underdeveloped country, the same situation is by no means rare in the United States. Several years ago, Janowitz and Delany showed that administrators in upper levels of a public bureaucracy had more knowledge of the perspectives of the general citizenry and its voluntary organizations than they did of their clientele.[20] The opposite was true for lower—level bureaucrats. Given the common finding that upward communication in an organization is biased in favor of the superior's expectations, we could conclude that the information that flows to top administrators does not adequately reflect client needs.

Lipsky's study of "street—level bureaucrats" shows that the clientele does not serve as a primary reference group for policemen, welfare workers, lower court judges and teachers. It is not that street—level bureaucrats are unresponsive, he concluded. It is that they are "responsive to constellations of reference groups which have excluded client—centered interests."[21]

In a review of the literature on communication by the urban poor, Greenberg and Dervin concluded that few low—income individuals mention the "caretaker" (minister, case worker, teacher, or lawyer) as a primary source of information.[22] The reason:[23]

> The professional caretaker and the establishment to which he is attached are often viewed with suspicion and hostility. It is believed that the social service agencies simply attempt to get their clients to adjust to the status quo. The law, police, and government agencies are viewed as exploiters of the low—income community.

Miller et. al., have concluded that social action agencies "cream the poor," i.e., choose to serve only the best—off of the low—income clientele. "Persons who make and administer organizational policy select and process applicants on the basis of how they fit their own and the organization's needs and outlook."[24]

In a participant—observation study of three Pennsylvania cities, Pollitt found that business interests dominated community action committees and generally thwarted community action programs.[25] He explained the process as a group of "haves" looking down on the "have—nots" as children struggling to be like themselves. Thus, they held the belief that the poor could not manage their lives but needed help in doing so.

In a study of the suburban Washington, D.C. community of Montgomery County, Maryland, this author found that community decision makers could communicate more readily with middle—class opponents of low—income housing and understand the opponents' demands on the political system better than they could communicate with and understand poor people.[25] Thus, the demands of the opponents could be serviced more easily than those of the proponents.

If the needs of the poor are recognized, they are often avoided through an organizational action which Baratz and Bachrach call a "non—decision":[27]

> . . . . a decision that results in suppression or thwarting of a latent or manifest challenge to the values or interests of the decision—maker. To be more nearly explicit, nondecision—making is a means by which benefits and privileges in the community can be suffocated before they are even voiced; or kept covert; or killed before they gain access to the relevant decision—making areas; or, failing all these things, maimed or destroyed in the decision—implementing stage of the policy process.

Baratz and Bachrach used a case study of black organizations in Baltimore to demonstrate the existence of nondecisions. Prior to 1965:[28]

> The channel of communicators was one—way, not two-way, *from* the agencies *to* the poor. Indeed, the agencies were a potent instrument for stifling grievances, in that "uncooperative" and "undeserving" clients could be, and probably were, denied service (force) or threatened with its denial (power). Nor were there other avenues for the poor to air their grievances and gain redress. The poor had no access to the newspapers or radio and TV stations, and the news media apparently saw no point in becoming self—appointed champions of the down—trodden.

In 1966 and 1967, according to Baratz and Bachrach, black leaders used conflict to gain access to "key centers of decision making." But nondecisions kept them from success:[29]

> Nondecisions on behalf of the white majority in the city reinforced the bias against the black poor. The latter's potential adversaries —— landlords, employers, bureaucrats, politicians —— often found it in their own interest to avoid being drawn

into conflict, relying instead for protection of their interests upon established institutions and procedures.

Only when blacks gained "power resources" were they able to effectively counter competing political groups:[30]

> . . . federal anti—poverty programs backed with federal funds and federal endorsement of the principles of maximum feasible participation have played a central role in the black drive for political access.

Stone found a similar nondecision making process in a study of Atlanta's urban renewal program:[31]

> In the formulation and implementation of policy, officials are most responsive to those group spokesmen regarded as reasonable, community—minded and trustworthy. Consequently, an advantage, especially in early involvement in policy planning, accrues to those who are known at City Hall and who can be dealt with in personal and informal terms. A group spokesman not part of the established order thus faces a dilemma. If there is no protest, no open display of power, then he may be ignored. If there is protest, then he runs the risk of being regarded as irresponsible.

A Theory of Inter—System Communication

Thus far, it has been shown that social action organizations and the mass media have difficulty communicating with low—income people because individuals in these organizations share the values of reference groups other than the clientele. Within a community, communication inputs (information) are more readily understood and less easily ignored when they come from these reference groups than when they come from low—income people. And frequently no information at all comes from the low—income clientele. As a result, pro—development information fits squarely into the status quo of the predominant system and seldom changes that system.

The next step is to show in theoretical terms why communication between social systems or subsystems with competing norms and values is so difficult and then to derive conclusions to show how to facilitate such communication.

Westley has theorized in general systems concepts that communication has the same functions at all system levels — — individual, interpersonal, group, and societal.[32] Cognitive balance theories hold that messages either change attitudes or are rejected or distorted by the attitudes. Westley believes the norms and values of a social system serve much the same functions as attitudes:[33]

> Information from outside the system keeps it (the system) informed as to changes requiring adjustment, and such information often is carried by public communication channels. But this information must be processed to test for its congruence with existing states; if hopelessly incongruent, it will be modified to make a mutual adjustment to the existing culture.

In other words, communication has two functions, in all systems: (1) to maintain consensus or (2) to seek a new consensus. According to Westley, the roles which constitute a social system are interdependent, so that a change in one role necessitates a change in the entire system. Thus, information which contradicts existing values must either change the system or be rejected or distorted. He adds that public communications media most often serve the consensus—seeking function, interpersonal channels t h e consensus—maintaining function.

These functions can perhaps most accurately be called the "social change" (system change) and "status quo" (system control) functions of communication. These concepts subsume Lasswell's three functions of communication: (1) surveillance of the environment, (2) correlation of parts of society to the environment, and (3) transmission of the social heritage between generations.[34] Schramm called these three functions the watchman decision—maker, and teacher functions.[35] To me, the surveillance function is the social change function, the correlation and transmission functions, the status quo function. The correlation function maintains a status quo in the present, the transmission function extends it into the future.

Thayer conceptualized two basic functions of communication: (1) adaptation —— when we are "communicated–to" by our environment "to adapt to it and maneuver our way through it" (i.e., the social change function) and (2) maintenance —— when we "communicate–to some living aspect of the environment (such as a person) in such a way that we establish, maintain, exploit, or alter the relationship of that person to us" (i.e., the status quo function).[36]

Thayer's description of these functions adds one important element to the theory being developed here. That is, communication takes the form of information giving when the status quo is threatened, information seeking when social change takes place.

The concept of the opinion leader fits well with this formulation, especially as re–conceptualized by Bostian and Westley.[37] Information from outside the system flows to the opinion leader. Followers seek information from the opinion leader because they expect him to have such information. He in turn is motivated to seek information from outside the system because he knows followers expect him to be informed —— i.e., social change information has utility for him.[38] But he transmits information, not influence (although possession of information can make him influential in another sense). He is influenced mutually by other members of the system, and his function is to translate social change information to make it congruent with the values of the system (the status quo function). In other words, the role of the opinion leader is more that of maintaining the prevailing opinion by filtering incoming information than that of changing opinions of system members.

Early sociologists (e.g. Cooley[39]) thought that the consensus in a system would inevitably be completely determined in a democratic fashion. But certain individuals or groups have more authority and power than others. Consensus is developed through bargaining and trading, but only those with power resources have anything to bargain and trade. Hence consensus is generally skewed in the direction of those with the most power. This is especially true in a formal organization where a "dominant coalition" has varying degrees of power.[40] Communication is often a means of consolidating power between those with similar problems, so information seldom flows to and from those with no power. It might be added, however, that the ability to communicate can be a source of power.

Given these functions of communication within a system, the next step is to conceptualize the nature of communication between two systems (or subsystems). Since any one system is a subsystem in a progressively larger suprasystem, inter–system communication should take place much like interpersonal communication. Information flows easily between systems which have similar status quo values but only with difficulty between those with different status quo values. The amount of power one system possesses vis–a–vis another also determines the extent to which it is "communicated–to" by other systems.

In a community, for example, component systems, such as the poor, which share few problems with other subsystems and which have little power generally would have difficulty making communication inputs to the community decision process. If social action agencies and the mass media reflect the status quo of the larger community system, then they will have difficulty communicating with a clientele which does not reflect the status quo. To use other terms, the needs of the dissonant group will be subjected to a nondecision.

Toward Effective Extra–Organizational Communication

The theory constructed above shows the inherent difficulty of communication between conflicting systems. That theory explains well the inability of most formal organizations to communicate with their clientele. In Colombia, information produced by most communication organizations such as the mass media and extension agencies did not even articulate alternatives for individuals who were in an open structure. Even problem solvers and information seekers could not obtain situationally relevant messages. Fett obtained similar results in a content analysis of the agricultural pages of several Brazilian newspapers. "Of the 725 items coded," he reported, "only 64 had high situational relevance."[41]

As a result of the difficulty of communicating between systems, organizations typically audit the success of their external communication by determining the number of clients whom they have persuaded to accept their services (which generally requires acceptance of the agencies' value systems). In essence, they audit communication success in terms of the status quo function of communication, in Thayer's terms, the extent to which the communication "establishes, maintains, exploits, or alters the relationship of that person to us."[42]

Instead, pro–development organizations should determine the success of their communication effort by the extent to which incoming communication brings about the social change function for the organization as a system. We need to measure the extent to which the organization understands the clientele's view of what the situation is and what constraints are included in the situation. In instances when the clientele does not itself understand its situation, we need to measure the extent to which the organization can think through the clientele's situation from the standpoint of the problems and constraints of the clientele, and then bring in new information which would help clients become aware of the reasons there are constraints and to evaluate the consequences of individual actions to solve problems and collective activities to eliminate constraints.

Research has shown that low–income individuals will use information which they can understand in terms of their experience and situation. In a Venezuelan study, Mathiason found that the mass media gave people attributes (facts) about objects in their situation, but did not tell them how to organize and utilize these facts. He concluded:[43]

> . . . . the mass media, rather than dealing with attributes (our classical conception of news), could deal in modes of discrimination. They could teach . . . how individuals do and/or can cope with situations. They could show, not the big picture nor the view from the institution, but rather the picture from the viewpoint of the individual who is trying to cope . . .

In a sense the parables in the New Testament are a demonstration of how people should organize reality. It seems certain that this technique placed in a mass communication medium had great effect for many centuries in altering people's way of structuring reality, leading to rapid social change.

Brown found in research in Chile that if content is relevant even printed messages can reach illiterates.[44] This occurred through "dependent literacy" in which a literate family member or friend read to the illiterate.

Communication is most effective when it results from what Thayer calls a symbiotic or synergetic relationship.[45] This means that both the organization and its clientele must learn from each other. But it would appear logically necessary for the organization to learn from its clientele before the clientele can effectively learn from the organization. In Boulding's terms: "The incoming messages only modify the outgoing messages as they succeed in modifying the image."[46]

To be able to think through the recipient's situation requires a set of theoretical concepts which allow the professional communicator to empathize with his audience and to seek information from that audience. The decision–situation model conceptualized above has worked well for that purpose. In the Colombian studies, for example, the model made it possible to outline the information needs of the types of peasants and large landowners even when those individuals were not aware of the needs.

The model tells a communicator that if he knows his clients are problem solvers he can expect them to seek information relevant to their problem orientation (their most important perceived problems). If they face a constrained decision, they will seek little information unless the information tells them how to remove the constraints.[47] If they are in a routine habit or fatalism situation, communication will do little, and a drastic change in their situation must come before the communicator can communicate with them. For example, taking away most of a Colombian *latifundista's* land would provide this drastic change in his situation.

In summary, professional communicators should seek information from their audiences so that they in turn can give relevant information to these audiences.[48] In this regard, then, an important task for communication researchers is to study means of improving the information seeking capabilities of professional communicators who deal with low–income people. Merely changing the abilities of individual communicators, however, will not change the formal organizations for which they work. To understand the impact of the organization on its members, it is possible to use the decision model which up to this point has been used to predict the communication behavior of client individuals to also predict the communication behavior of the formal organization sending this message.

Chaffee and McLeod's coorientation paradigm provides a framework for this analysis.[49] With the co-orientation paradigm, a theorist stops looking at sources, messages, media and receivers and starts looking at the communication dialogue between two individuals or systems. If we apply this framework to the decision–situation model, we begin to look at combinations of decision modes in coorientation situations. These combinations also explain clearly the nature of intersystem communication as it was conceptualized above.

Of the ten possible combinations of the four decision situations, only the combination of two problem solvers facing the same problem would seem to allow for symbiotic communication and success in achieving accuracy, understanding, or agreement, the dependent variables in Chaffee and McLeod's paradigm.[50]

On the other hand, two individuals in a routine habit situation could communicate with and reinforce one another only if they are attached to the same alternative. Two individuals facing a constrained decision could communicate about a common constraint or could share frustrations about being constrained. It is also feasible that a problem solver could communicate with any individual in one of the other three situations to the extent of achieving accuracy (being able to predict the cognitions of the other person). But this accuracy would be one–sided, i.e., the other persons would not seek information from the problem solver. In none of the other combinations could communication occur with any degree of success, and it is probably these combinations which most often characterize intersystem communication.

In terms of these combinations, most Colombian mass media and organizations sponsoring development programs would seem to fall into the routine habit category while most low—income individuals in that country most often face constrained decisions. That combination of routine habit and constrained decision is a situation in which successful communication would seldom occur. A system in a routine habit situation seeks only information which reinforces its status quo and gives information supporting its status quo. The system in constrained decision communicates little except about means to eliminate the constraint. This combination of routine habit organizations and constrained decision clients seems to explain the Colombian situation perfectly as well as most situations in which a formal organization communicates with a low—income clientele.

Thus to be able to place empathic professional communicators in problem—solving pro—development organizations, communication researchers and other social scientists must find means of jolting organizations out of a routine habit mode so that they can seek information from poor individuals. Organizations must be problem solvers if they are to isolate and articulate the constraints on poor people and to organize these individuals to bring pressure on the political and economic system to eliminate these constraints.

Communication Procedures for Emergent Systems

In a recent paper, Carter defined one purpose of communication as the bridging of gaps necessary to bring about an emergent system.[51] An emergent system, in contrast with a given system, does not now exist but for various reasons it might be desirable to bring that system into existence.[52]

If we contrast an emergent system with a given system it becomes evident that the social change and status quo functions of communication for a system are really the effect of communication on individual elements that constitute a given system. For a system to continue to exist, it must control the individuals within it, i.e., reinforce its values and norms. Systems resist messages which might change their constituent elements (subsystems), because changing these elements would by definition of a system change the system as a whole.

If, however, an individual who is constrained in a given system can communicate with individuals in other given systems who are facing similar constraints, then they should be able to interact in order to bring about an emergent system with new rules and institutions. Creating emergent systems then would seem to be the essence of development.

Carter says communication researchers should search for procedures which are effective in bridging gaps in emergent systems. Thus, communication researchers should search for organizational and institutional structures and staffing patterns which have been and/or could result in communication procedures effective in creating collectivities which in turn can pressure for change. Although we may most often think of emergent systems in terms of constrained low—income people, we also should search for procedures through which professionals constrained in different organizations can communicate with one another in order to change the routine habit organizations for which they work.

The effect of emergent system communication generally will not be a change in the structure of given systems. Rather its effect will be to create an awareness by some individuals that other individuals share common problems and that as a collectivity they could apply influence to bring about structural change (at which point conventional given system communication would take over and reinforce the change).

Organizations are important units of analysis for the study of emergent systems because emergent systems are almost always collectivities, and collectivities are seldom stable and have few power resources unless they are formally organized. In particular, it is important to study the structure of these organizations because organizational structure generally restricts or enhances the behavior of individuals within the organization more than the attitudes of these individuals.[53] Organizational structure is an especially important predictor of information seeking and giving of individuals within the organization.

Another important task, then, for the communication researcher should be to determine the kinds of organizational structure that will best facilitate empathy, learning, and communication with low—income people. The best method for such research would be either case study or comparative analysis of pro—development organizations which are problem solvers and which have been successful in bringing constrained individuals together.

Some examples might be peasant unions in some Latin American countries, the Catholic Church in Brazil and Chile, a variety of organizations in Communist countries, or civil rights organizations in the United States. Also, if one could find a successful agrarian reform agency or community development agency, its structure and communication procedures would merit study. Likewise, there should be mass media which have been successful in bringing about emergent systems in some countries of the world.

A recent case study by this author of a community development agency in a Maryland suburb of Washington, D.C. with a substantial low—income segment, illustrates one kind of individual—role relationship that in this case facilitated communication between the organization and a low—income clientele.[54] The agency was formed by the county primarily to seek and administer federal antipoverty funds. We had expected that communication within the organization would flow most readily between individuals who shared the same conception of the most important social problem which the agency should solve (in line with the decision—situation model). We had also expected that community aides working daily with the clientele would have the greatest understanding of the clientele and that this understanding would be less complete higher in the organization.

Neither of these hypothesis was supported by the data. Nearly all individuals interviewed from the organization could accurately predict the views of the clientele. Within the organization, communication flowed as frequently between individuals with different problem conceptions as between those with the same conceptions.

Significantly, however, there was a good deal of difference between blacks and whites in the organization. Blacks felt more congruent with the low—income clientele. Both saw the social problem in terms of symptoms —— poor housing, poor services.

Whites understood the problem conception of the clientele, but saw the problem differently themselves — in terms of underlying causes, employment difficulties of the poor. Blacks also communicated more often with the clientele, believed themselves members of lower SES levels, and lived in subdivisions with a substantial low—income component. Nevertheless, within the organization communication took place as often as between races as within races.

The important structural relationship was the planned or unplanned mixture of races in interacting roles throughout the organization. Blacks were found at all levels, and the top administrator was a black. Whites were concentrated in administrative positions, but some were also found at lower levels. When individuals with different reference group attachments were mixed throughout the organization, all members were subjected to communication inputs representing reference groups of the poor.[55] As a result, the low—income clientele was able to use the organization to bring pressure upon other county agencies to service their problem needs.

At this point, however, we must turn to perhaps the most difficult research question of all. Suppose we do find effective organizational structures and communication procedures for developing emergent systems. How do we plant and nurture this promising organization within the larger and generally alien suprasystem of most communities or countries? Perhaps only the study of application of power and conflict will provide the answer.

Even if this final question is not answered, however, we will have discovered means of arousing the consciousness of constrained individuals to the existence of the constraints. And at least we will have useful advice to give when professional communicators, government officials, and pro—development organizations ask us how to improve communications with poor people.

FOOTNOTES

*James E. Grunig is an associate professor in the College of Journalism, University of Maryland

[1] See, for example, Herbert F. Lionberger, *Adoption of New Ideas and Practices* (Ames: Iowa State University Press, 1960); Everett M. Rogers and F. Floyd Shoemaker, *Communication of Innovations*, 2nd ed., (New York: The Free Press, 1971).

[2] Erwin P. Bettinghaus, *Persuasive Communication* (New York: Holt, Rinehart and Winston, 1968), ch. 11.

[3] Warren F. Ilchman and Norman Thomas Uphoff, *The Political Economy of Change* (Berkeley: University of California Press, 1971), pp. 9-10.

[4] Daniel Lerner, *The Passing of Traditional Society* (New York: The Free Press, 1958).

[5] Everett M. Rogers with Lynne Svenning, *Modernization Among Peasants: The Impact of Communication* (New York: The Free Press, 1969).

[6] For example, Lowndes F. Stephens, "Media Exposure and Modernization Among the Appalachian Poor," *Journalism Quarterly* 49 (Summer 1972): pp. 247-257; Michael E. Bishop and Pamela A. McMartin, "Toward a Socio–Psychological Definition of Transitional Persons," Paper presented to the Association for Education in Journalism, Carbondale, Ill., August 1972.

[7] Robert Brown, *Explanation in Social Science* (Chicago: Aldine Publishing Co., 1963).

[8] James E. Grunig, "Information and Decision Making in Economic Development," *Journalism Quarterly* 46 (Autumn 1969): pp. 565-575.

[9] James E. Grunig, "Communication and the Economic Decision Making Processes of Colombian Peasants," *Economic Development and Cultural Change* 19 (July 1971): pp. 580-597.

[10] When these studies were conducted, the conceptualization of the decision model included a fifth decision situation called ignorant habit. Its only distinction from constrained decision was that the structural block came from the individual's lack of intellectual or

educational capacity needed to cope with a particular situation. When the model was reconceptualized in matrix terms, this decision type was equated with constrained decision.

[11] John H. Fett, "Infrastructural Factors and Information Search," Paper presented to the Association for Education in Journalism, Carbondale, Ill., August 1972.

[12] Gordon C. Whiting, "Individual Innovativeness and Agricultural Development: The Afghan Case," Paper presented to the Rural Sociological Society, Denver, August 1971.

[13] Gordon C. Whiting, "The Development Role of Mass Media in Afghanistan," Paper presented to the Association for Education in Journalism, Colombia, S. Car., August 1971.

[14] Sultana Krippendorff, "A Sociological Approach to Mass Media Development in India," Paper presented to the Association for Education in Journalism, Carbondale, Ill., August 1972.

[15] F. Jane Marceau, "Communication and Development: A Reconsideration," *Public Opinion Quarterly* 36 (Summer 1972): pp. 235-245.

[16] Herman Felstehausen, "Conceptual Limits of Development Communications Theory," *Sociologia Ruralis* 13 (1973): pp. 39-54.

[17] Emil B. Haney, Jr., "The Economic Reorganization of Minifundia in a Highland Community of Colombia," Ph.D. Dissertation, University of Wisconsin, Madison, 1969.

[18] George F. Drake, "Elites and Voluntary Organizations: A Study of Community Power in Manizales," Ph.D. Dissertation, University of Wisconsin, 1971.

[19] Felstehausen, *op. cit.*

[20] Morris Janowitz and William Delany, "The Bureaucrat and the Public: A Study of Informational Perspectives," *Administrative Science Quarterly* 2 (1957): pp. 141-162.

[21] Michael Lipsky, "Toward a Theory of Street—Level Bureaucracy," Paper presented to the American Political Science Association, New York, 1969.

[22] Bradley S. Greenberg and Brenda Dervin, *Use of the Mass Media by the Urban Poor* (New York: Praeger Special Studies, (1970).

[23] *Ibid*, p. 100.

[24] S.M. Miller, Pamela Roby and Alwine A. do Vos van

Steenwijk, "Creaming the Poor," *Transaction* (June 1970): pp. 39-45.

[25] Michael Pollitt, Ph.D. Dissertation, Pennsylvania State University, 1972.

[26] James E. Grunig, "Communication in Community Decisions on the Problems of the Poor," *Journal of Communication* 22 (March 1972): pp. 5-25.

[27] Morton B. Baratz and Peter Bachrach, *Power and Poverty: Theory and Practice* (New York: Oxford University Press, 1970), p. 44.

[28] *Ibid*, pp. 69-70.

[29] *Ibid*, p. 80.

[30] *Ibid*, p. 102.

[31] Clarence N. Stone, "Overt and Latent Issues in the Urban Renewal Program of Atlanta: A Response to the Pluralist Critique of Non—Decisionmaking," Paper presented to the American Political Science Association, New York, 1969.

[32] Bruce H. Westley, "The Functions of Public Communication in the Process of Social Change," Paper prepared for the AID—Michigan State University Seminar on Communication and Change, East Lansing, April 1966; "Communication Theory and General Systems Theory: Implications for Planned Change," *Public Opinion Quarterly* 34 (1970): p. 446; "Communication and Social Change," *American Behavioral Scientist* 14 (1971): pp. 719-743.

[33] Westley, "Communication and Social Change," *Op. cit.,* p. 738.

[34] Harold D. Lasswell, "The Structure and Function of Communication in Society," in Wilbur Schramm (ed.) *Mass Communications*, 2nd ed. (Urbana: University of Illinois Press, 1960), pp. 117-130.

[35] Wilbur Schramm, *Mass Media and National Development* (Stanford: Stanford University Press, 1964.)

[36] Lee Thayer, *Communication and Communication Systems* (Homewood, Ill.: Richard D. Irwin, 1968), p. 33.

[37] Lloyd R. Bostian, "The Two—Step Flow Theory: Cross—Cultural Implications," *Journalism Quarterly* 47 (1970): pp. 109-117; Westley, "The Functions of Public Communication in the Process of Social Change," *Op. cit.*

[38] For an example of the effect of communicatory utility see Charles K. Atkin, "Anticipated Communication and Mass Media Information—Seeking," *Public Opinion Quarterly* (1972): pp. 188-199.

[39] Charles H. Cooley, *Human Organization* (New York: Charles Scribers Sons, 1929).

[40] James E. Thompson, *Organizations in Action* (New York: McGraw—Hill, 1967), p. 143.

[41] John H. Fett, "Content and Situational Relevance of Agricultural News in Brazilian Papers," *Journalism Quarterly* 49 (1972): pp. 505-511.

[42] Thayer, *Op. cit.*, p. 33.

[43] John R. Mathiason, "Communication Patterns and Powerlessness among Urban Poor: Toward the Use of Mass Communications for Rapid Social Change," Paper presented to the Association for Education in Journalism, Washington, D.C., August 1970.

[44] Marion R. Brown, "Communication and Agricultural Development: A Field Experiment," *Journalism Quarterly* 47 (1970): pp. 725-734.

[45] Thayer, *Op. cit.*, p. 82.

[46] Kenneth E. Boulding, *The Image* (Ann Arbor: University of Michigan Press, 1956), p. 28.

[47] Felstehausen says much the same thing: "Seen thus, relevant information for development is that which contributes new institutional roles and relationships." *Op. cit.*, p. 49.

[48] See also Hans C. Groot, "A Diachronic Communication Construct for Information Systems in Development," Paper presented to the International Communication Association, Phoenix, April 1971.

[49] Jack M. McLeod and Steven H. Chaffee, "Interpersonal Approaches to Communication Research," *American Behavioral Scientist* 16 (1973): pp. 469-500.

[50] Such a relationship was found in the study of community decision making in a suburban county of Washington, D.C. by Grunig, "Communication in Community Decisions on the Problems of the Poor," *Op. cit.*

[51] Richard F. Carter, "A General Systems Theory of Systems in General," Paper presented to the Far West Region Meeting, Society for General Systems Research, Portland, Ore., September 1972.

[52] Engineers also consider one of their most challenging problems to be that of defining a desired system and then building the necessary structure to achieve that system.

[53] For the structural approach to organizations see Charles Perrow, *Organizational Analysis: A Sociological View* (Belmont, Calif.: Brooks/Cole Publishing Co., 1970).

[54] James E. Grunig, "Communication in a Community Development Agency," *Journal of Communication,* 24 (1974): 40-46.

[55] This result is similar to Guetzkow's conclusion that, "The greater the extent to which an external environment provides multiple bases for the orientation of communication, the greater the differentiation of perceptions within the organization. Harold Guetzkow, "Communications in Organizations," in James G. March (ed.) *Handbook of Organizations* (Chicago: Rand McNally, 1965), pp. 534-573.

Joseph Woelfel and John Saltiel:

Cognitive Processes as Motions in a Multidimensional Space:
A General Linear Model*

THE EFFECTS of communication on the formation and change of attitudes has consistently attracted the attention of psychologists and communication researchers over the years, and is very likely one of the most carefully studied topics in the social science literature. While potentially powerful theories asserting curvilinear[1] relationships among key information (message) variables and attitude change have found some measure of empirical support (Hovland, *et. al.*, 1957; Sherif & Hovland, 1961; Sherif, *et. al.*, 1965; Sherif & Sherif, 1967; McLaughlin & Sharman, 1972) it is clear that most theories (and the analytic procedures used in researching them) assume a linear model, and treat departures from linearity as special cases requiring further explanation. Such a model assumes that attitudes (or other cognitive components) are some linear aggregate of some finite set of variables. Mathematically the general linear model takes the form of the familiar linear regression polynomial:

$$(1) \quad A = a + b_1 x_1 + b_2 x_2 + \ldots + b_n x_n = a + \sum_{i=i}^{n} b_i x_i$$

Where A = the dependent attitude

a = the y intercept for the vector of the polynomial

b_i= coefficients or weights indicating the relative net effectiveness of each of the variables (messages) x_i in effecting changes in the attitude A

x_i= the variables (usually information-flow variables) assumed to exert causal influence over attitude formation and change.

In addition to its widespread use, there are several substantial reasons for a close analysis of the general linear model. First, although expressly curvilinear models show theoretical promise, none has shown impressively better empirical results overall than simple linear models (Bochner & Insko, 1966).

In general, empirical results show that statistically significant curvilinear effects are not frequently noted (Bochner & Insko, 1966; Aronson, *et. al.*, 1963; Bergin, 1962; Fisher & Lubin, 1958; Freedman, 1964; Goldberg, 1954; Helsen, Blake & Mouten, 1958; Howland & Pritzker, 1957; Rosenbaum & Franc, 1960; Tuddenham, 1958; Zimbardo, 1960). When found, curvilinear relationships between change advocated and change effected are found usually for messages sent by low or medium credibility sources (Bergin, 1962; Bochner & Insko, 1966; Aronson, *et. al.*, 1963; Freedman, 1964; Insko, Murashima & Sayadaian, 1966). Under special circumstances, however, clearcut curvilinear and even non-monotone relations of some substance ("boomerang effect") are noted (Cohen, 1962; Ablesen & Miller, 1967; Berscheid, 1966; Kelley & Volkhard, 1952; Mann, 1965). In spite of their infrequent appearance, these negative effects remain troublesome, and most investigators would probably agree that fully satisfactory explanations have not yet been made (Insko, 1967).

A second reason for closer scrutiny of the general linear model is the fact that linear aggregation models, even in their simplest forms, are frequently very successful empirically, particularly in real life (non-experimental) settings. Using a simple linear model, Woelfel & Haller (1970) account for 64% of the variance in high school students' educational aspirations, principally on the strength of the *average educational expectations* of their "significant others;" Mettlin (1970) replicated these results on a second sample with equal success. Woelfel & Hernandez (1970) account for 86% of the variance in marijuana use using a linear model, and nearly equivalent levels of success are recorded for attitudes toward French Canadian Separatism (Woelfel, *et. al.*, 1974), cigarette smoking (Mettlin, 1973), and the extent to which children view television as "real" as opposed to fantasy (Reeves, 1974). Even though there may be situations in which the linear model fails, nonetheless its general utility in everyday life is clear from these findings.

Still a third reason for examination of the linear model is the fact that it implies a theoretical model which is very parsimonious in its basic form, yet which can be expanded easily to encompass very complex empirical phenomena. With this in mind, this article will present one theory (sometimes called "Force Aggregation Theory," or FAT) based on the linear model, and assess its status in the light of available evidence.

I.   The Theoretical Model

The simplest linear theory that could be posited to explain the joint effects of a set of messages $x_1, x_2, \ldots x_n$, on an attitude a would be one which assumed each message had an effect equal to each other message and that no other variables had substantial effects. This formulation[2], as shown in equation (2) below, stipulates that the resulting attitude a should equal the arithmetic mean of all messages:

$$(2) \quad a = \frac{1}{n} x_1 + \frac{1}{n} x_2 + \ldots + \frac{1}{n} x_n = \sum_{i=i}^{n} \frac{x_i}{n}$$

It follows immediately from (2) that this simple theory is a "balance" theory, since, for any mean $\bar{x}$,

$$(3) \quad \sum_{i=i}^{n} (x_i - \bar{x}) = 0; \text{ and hence } \sum_{i=i}^{n} (x_i - a) = 0$$

If each message x_i is construed as a "force" which "pulls" the attitude one way or another, expression (3) shows that the mean constitutes that point at which such forces sum to zero or "balance."[3] Simple though it is, this theory suggests a continuously-scaled least-squares balance point, which is a considerably more powerful mathematical model than the discrete graph-theoretic representations of many balance formulations (Newcomb, Heider, Osgood, Tannebaum & Suci, et. al.).

Given equation (2), it is possible to derive the expression for the value of the new attitude a_2 given the receipt of new information by the individual as

$$(4) \quad a_2 = \frac{n_1 a_1 + n_m m}{n_1 + n_m}$$

Where a_2 = the new attitude

a_1 = the old attitude

n_1 = the number of messages out of which the old attitude was formed

m = the average value of the messages received about the attitude over the time interval $t_1 - t_2$

n_m = the number of messages about the attitude received during the interval $t_1 - t_2$

More informative is the same equation solved for the amount of change in the attitude $(a_2 - a_1)$ given the receipt of the new messages:

$$(5) \quad a_2 - a_1 = \frac{n_m (m - a_1)}{n_m + n_1}$$

Equation (5) is graphic, in that it shows clearly that three factors are causally related to attitude change according to this theory: (1) n_m, or the number of new messages, (2) n_1, or the number of old messages out of which the original attitude is composed, and (3) $(m - a_1)$, or the amount of discrepancy between the old attitude and the mean position advocated by the new messages. More precisely, the amount of attitude change is directly related to the product of the average discrepancy between incoming information and the old attitude (average change advocated) and the number of such messages, and inversely related to the sum of the number of messages out of which the change message and the original attitude is composed.[4]

The role of n_m, or the number of new messages with which the old attitude is impacted, seems clear and has been a fundamental principle of contemporary advertizing, political campaigning and other large-scale persuasive activities, and its role in attitude change is generally confirmed in the laboratory (Sherif, 1935; Asch, 1951). The role of n_1, that is, the number of messages out of which the original attitude was formed, has been explored systematically in at least one study (Saltiel & Woelfel, 1974). Briefly, using a two-stage least squares path analytic procedure on panel data from 126 high school students, these researchers found changes in overall value positions of the students over a six-month interval were inversely related to a reliable measure of the amount of communication the students had had about those values prior to the onset of the research. They found further (as the theory predicts) that changes over the interval were not related to the stress the students reported experiencing, the students' own reports of the strength and certainty with which they held their attitudes about the topics, or the strength and certainty the "significant others" of the students reported holding about the information they had originally transmitted to the students about the attitudes in question (Saltiel & Woelfel, 1974).

The effects of the third of these variables, $(m-a_1)$ or the average change advocated, on $a_2 - a_1$ (the amount of change observed) has been very carefully studied by many investigators. Experimental work has shown consistently that these two variables are related, that they appear to be linearly related when the change message is delivered by high credibility sources (although the definition of credibility is not precise), but non-linear and even sometimes non-monotone in the case of low credibility sources (see Roloff, 1974). Plausible hypothetical explanations for this latter ("boomerang") finding have been offered by the non-linear social judgment theory (Hovland, et. al., 1957; Sherif & Hovland, 1961, Sherif, et. al., 1965; Sherif & Sherif, 1967; McLaughlin & Sharmon, 1972), and by the frequently but not universally found tendency to derrogate the source of the message (Bergin, 1962) and the message itself (Bochner & Insko, 1966). Data do not support any of these explanations unambiguously, however, and boomerang effect remains troublesome to the attitude change researcher (Ablesen & Miller, 1967).

II.   Scaling Models

Even in this relatively simple form, the linear model has a fair record of predictive accuracy. Before elaborating the model further, however, it seems wise to consider the scaling procedures available for use with the theory, particularly since the scaling requirements of this mathematical model are severe, calling in the ideal case for continuous ratio scaling as a prerequisite.

Early formulations of this theory (Woelfel & Haller, 1970; Mettlin, 1970) attempted to circumvent this problem by utilizing rate-like dependent variables such as *educational aspirations* (measured in years of school a student expects to attain). Later studies explicitly utilize *rates of behavior* as dependent variables, like frequency of attendance at French Canadian Separatist rallies and demonstrations (Woelfel, *et. al.*, 1974) and rate of marijuana use (Woelfel & Hernandez, 1970).

While fairly successful in explaining the phenomena they address, these studies reveal difficulties which suggest even more elaborate scaling procedures, as well as some mathematical elaborations in the linear model developed so far.

First, while a surprising number of theoretically and substantively important phenomena may be expressed as rates, not all variables may be so conceived, and this limits the generality of the model. Secondly, while the linear model anticipates that identical messages from different sources may be differentially forceful,[5] both the separatism study (Woelfel, *et. al.*) and the marijuana use study (Woelfel & Hernandez) find that, controlling for the content of the message, messages sent interpersonally have very substantial effects over attitudes, while messages sent via mass media generally have very tiny effects, even though sample sizes are quite large in some cases (over 400 in the separatism study). Not only is such an outcome unanticipated by the theory, but it clearly contradicts equation (5), unless one is willing to assume media messages are nearly totally massless, which is unlikely.

Woelfel & Hernandez present an alternative explanation. They speculate rather that the implicit assumption of the typical unidimensionally scaled studies that all forces are expressed completely along the vector of the dependent variable is unrealistic. They theorize instead that the attitude change process may be construed as a multidimensional space in which every message x_1 exerts a force given by u_i $(a_1 - x_i)$ is the discrepancy between the position advocated by the message and the position held by the receiver. They further hypothesize, however, that this force is exerted at an angle α to the dependent attitude vector, which they interpret as the "relevance" of the message.

Taking advantage of the fact that the relative net effectiveness of any two messages is given in the multiple regression equation by the ratios of their respective slopes, and further that the angle α

between the vector of the message and the vector of the dependent variable is given by the arc cosine of the correlation coefficient (Woelfel, 1973), these authors estimate the inertial masses of messages from the several media.[6] These preliminary estimates show the masses of the media messages are roughly equivalent to those of interpersonal messages, but that the angles between media message vectors and the dependent variable are significantly close to 90°. (While the mass of messages from movies was estimated as between three and four times as great as that of interpersonal messages, for example, the angle included between the movie message vector and the dependent attitude vector was greater than 89°. Clearly whatever effects these messages might have cannot be exerted along the dependent variable vector, since they are nearly orthogonal to it.)

While the Woelfel and Hernandez paper provides some evidence for a multi-dimensional representation of the attitude change process, they do not provide a procedure for obtaining such a space, and use correlational techniques to estimate the appropriate angles between vectors taken two at a time. Procedures for multi-dimensional attitude scaling are well known in the psychometric literature, however, and are rapidly gaining currency in the communication literature. (Torgersen, 1958; Shephard, Romney & Nerlove, 1972; Woelfel, 1973, 1974a, 1974b; Woelfel & Barnett, 1974; Serota, 1974; Barnett, 1974; McLaughlin & Sharmon, 1972).

These techniques begin by assuming that the process of perceiving and identifying any "object" is basically a process of differentiation wherein the individual learns to discriminate the stimuli which are the mechanism of the perception of the object from other stimuli representing other objects on the basis of their dissimilarities with regard to certain underlying attributes (Torgersen, 1958). Thus, for example, one identifies a yellow ball as different from a red ball because she or he recognizes them to be dissimilar by a certain amount in terms of the attribute *color*. Although in the example given the two objects presumably differ only in color, it is most frequently the case that objects differ with regard to *many* attributes at once. Two *persons*, for example, may differ in regard to the attributes *sex, age, height,* and so on through many attributes. The *aggregate* of all these dissimilarities can be taken as a measure of the *overall difference* or dissimilarity of these two persons.

Dissimilarities among cognitive objects may be represented by a continuous numbering system such that two objects considered to be completely identical are assigned a paired dissimilarity score or distance score of zero (0), and objects of increasing dissimilarity are represented by numbers of increasing value. Assuming that the definition of an object or concept is constituted by the pattern of its relationship to other objects, the definition of any object may be represented by a 1 x n vector where s_{11} represents the distance or

$$s_{11}, s_{12}, s_{13}, \cdots s_{1n}$$

dissimilarity of object 1 from itself (thus $s_{11} = 0$ by definition), s_{12} represents the distance or dissimilarity between objects 1 and 2, and s_{1n} represents the distance between the 1st and the nth objects. Similarly, the second object may be represented by a second vector

$$s_{21}, s_{22}, s_{23}, \cdots s_{2n}$$

and the definition of any set of concepts or objects may therefore be represented in terms of the matrix

$$
\begin{matrix}
s_{11}, & s_{12}, & \cdots & s_{1n} \\
s_{21}, & s_{22}, & \cdots & s_{2n} \\
\cdot & \cdot & & \cdot \\
\cdot & \cdot & & \cdot \\
s_{n1}, & s_{n2}, & \cdots & s_{nn}
\end{matrix}
$$

where any entry s_{ij} represents the dissimilarity or distance between i and j.

Once these dissimilarities have been estimated,[7] the matrix will represent the pattern of differences among the stimuli across whatever attributes the respondent (or sample members in the aggregate case) perceive the stimuli to differ. While this matrix S contains an immense amount of information about the interrelationships among the stimuli scaled therein, much of this information (like the attributes along which the respondent(s) see the stimuli differing) is in latent form, and, furthermore, the matrix is usually large and unweildy. Fortunately, techniques for the recovery of this latent information which also generally reduce the size and complexity of the matrix have been well developed, particularly since the early work of Torgersen. (See especially Young & Householder, 1938; Torgersen, 1967, 1968; Shephard, Romney & Nerlove, 1972; Woelfel, 1974; Barnett, 1974; Woelfel & Barnett, 1974; Serota, 1974). While many variants of these multidimensional scaling techniques (MDS) have been developed (Torgersen, 1958; Shephard, 1962, 1966; Kruskal, 1964; Young & Torgersen, 1967; Guttman, 1968; Lingoes, 1972; Carroll & Chang, 1970; Woelfel, 1972), all existing variants may be classified into two types depending on the rigor of the scaling assumptions required. When the matrix of dissimilarities can be trusted to be equi-interval and reliable (as is the case given the direct quantitative pair-comparison estimates suggested in Woelfel, 1974a, b), then "metric" techniques are appropriate and techniques defined by Young & Householder (1938) and elaborated by Torgersen (1958) are utilized. Specifically, the dissimilarities matrix D is converted to a scaler product matrix $^8B^*$, which is then factored by any standard factor analytic procedure like principal components analysis or jacobi. The result is a spatial coordinate system represented in an m x r matrix R, where m = the number of objects or stimuli represented in S; $r \leqslant m-1$, orthogonal dimensions of the space and where any entry of R_{jk} represents the coordinate value of the jth concept or stimulus on the kth dimension. This matrix has the strong mathematical property that

$$s_{ij} = \sum_{k=1}^{r} (R_{ik} - R_{jk})^2$$

That is, the matrix R and the matrix R are exactly equivalent; R does not in any way distort the relationships defined in S. (See Woelfel, 1974).

When the data in the matrix S are poorly measured, the "nonmetric" procedures are typically applied. These differ from metric procedures only in that the matrix R is estimated by an iterative procedure which produces a configuration constrained to fit only the *ordering* of the dissimilarities in R; R is then related monotonically to the matrix R, which is a weaker mathematical assumption than that of metric procedure. (Shephard, 1962, 1966; Kruskal, 1964; Young, 1972).

Regardless of whether metric or non-metric procedures are utilized (although metric procedures seem clearly preferable for time-series or process models like the one implied in the present case) the result may be seen as an r dimensional space in which a set of *m* objects are arrayed such that the distances between any two objects corresponds (exactly or monotonically, as the procedures are respectively metric or non-metric) to their distances in the data. When these data consist of perceptions of dissimilarities among objects, the definition of each object or stimulus within the domain of objects or stimuli scaled is given wholly by its location in the space; i.e., vis-a-vis all other objects arrayed in the space. Changes in the definition of any object may be represented as movement of the object in the space relative to the other objects. This is exactly the kind of multidimensional representation called for by the Woelfel-Hernandez findings.

How this may be made relevant to the attitude change process is illustrated in Figure One.

Figure One.

NOT CREDIBLE

X

BAD

X

GOOD

X

CREDIBLE

X

114

Figure One represents a hypothetical two-dimensional plot of the cognitive structure[9] of an individual (or set of individuals) including: 1) a definition (given in the space, of course, wholly by its location relative to the other objects in the space) of the source of a message, like a medium or a person, 2) a definition of "own position," i.e., the position of the receiver vis-a-vis the source, the position advocated and other concepts, like good-bad, etc., 3) a definition of the *position advocated*, and 4) a definition, vis-a-vis the other concepts, of the concepts "good," "bad," "credible" and "not credible."

(B) Assume these are arrayed as in Fig. 1, and assume the source (S) has sent to the receiver (R) a message suggesting (R) adopt S's own position, (P). Following FAT theory (and entirely consistent with dissonance theory and other balance formulations), this message generates a set of forces which may be described as follows: By saying, "you should adopt position P," the source sets up forces toward the convergence of R and P (remember P's location in the space represents R's definition of P prior to the message) which are represented by the dotted vectors a and b. Similarly, by suggesting that P's position is his or her own, S is arguing that R has erroneously defined P and S as non-coincident, and sets up further forces for the convergence of P and S on each other represented by the dotted vectors c and d. Furthermore, since the message clearly implies that R should move closer to S, forces for convergence of these concepts on each other are set up, and are represented by the dotted vectors e and f. The resulting vectors (solid lines 1, 2, and 3) represent the resolution of these forces according to the mathematical model explicit in the linear model.

While this illustration represents the main variables in the theoretical model quite graphically, several questions still require clarification. First, this representation introduces into the discussion the concept of "force" as an explicit variable. Specifically it hypothesizes three main forces, F_{ab} (the force for the convergence of [R] and [P] on each other), F_{cd} (the force for the convergence of [P] and [S] on each other), and F_{eg} (the force for the convergence of [S] and [R] on each other). Since nothing is implied in the message given in this example other than that each pair of concepts should converge on each other (and following standard theoretical practice in physics), each of these forces has been divided such that $F_{ab} = F_a + F_b$ where $/F_a/ = /F_b/$; $F_{cd} = F_c + F_d$ where $/F_c/ = /F_d/$; and $F_{eg} = F_e + F_g$, $/F_e/ = /F_g/$. A fundamental question still open, however, is how the forces F_{ab}, F_{cd} and F_{eg} are to be estimated. Perhaps the simplest hypothesis would suggest that the force for the convergence of any two objects on each other is proportional to the distance between them, since this seems initially to be consonant with the notion that the amount of change effected (CE) is proportional to the amount of change advocated (CA). Following from this assumption, and since (in this hypothetical case) the distances between all pairs of concepts are roughly equal (i.e., $d_{pr} \cong d_{ps} \cong d_{rs}$) then $FAB \cong FCD \cong FEG$; further, $F_a = F_b = F_c = F_d = F_e = F_g$, and the resulting force vectors are given by (1), (2), and (3) in Figure One.

Even should this hypothesis prove correct, we should still not expect the *changes* in the cognitive structure pictured to conform exactly to these force vectors, since the theory (see particularly equation (5) above) expects change to follow not only from message factors (i.e., amount of change advocated) but from characteristics of the concepts as well. Specifically, equation (5) requires that attitudes resist forces toward change by a function of N or the *number of messages* out of which the old conception was composed. Following the example of physicists, this quality of the attitude which resists acceleration is defined here formally as the *inertial mass* of the concept. Inertial mass, therefore, is operationally defined in equation (5) as proportional to N. Such a formulation, in fact, is in the spirit of less precise equivalent concepts like "embeddedness," (Sherif, 1961). At this early stage of theorizing, it would be apt to suggest, perhaps, that the *acceleration* of the concept through the space will be roughly proportional to the force to which it is exposed and inversely proportional to its inertial mass.[10]

If we assume for convenience that all inertial masses in Figure One are equal[11] (i.e., $m_s = m_p = m_r$), then the distances moved after one unit of time will be proportional to the force vectors (1), (2), and (3). Sensibly, these vectors predict a convergence of all three concepts, S, P, and R, if the interaction continues without limit.

This seems intuitively sensible (and corresponds with most —— but not all —— empirical evidence), yet note some interesting anomalies: Assuming that the concepts good-bad, credible-not credible are arrayed in the space as shown, then the result of all these motions would be a *decrease* in source credibility, but the source would move somewhat closer to both *"good"* and *"bad."* Clearly, attempts to measure *this* phenomenon on unidimensional scales would result in unpredictable outcomes, probably substantial increases in unreliability of measure. This would explain the mixed results in source derogation very parsimoniously, without requiring additional theoretical premises.

Of course, *where* in the space all these concepts are located is an empirical matter; if, for example, "credible" and "not credible" were *reversed*, then the result of the situation would be an *increase* in the credibility of the source. This possibility may have been overlooked because of the implicit assumption that all changes advocated would be viewed by receivers as undesirable changes,[12] and this in turn probably follows from the empirically unsupported but widely held notion that people themselves take the position they think "best" in some sense.

Even in this crude form, the multidimensional representation of the general linear model can be seen to account for a great deal of what is known about attitude change. Still, it should be made clear that the combination of inertial masses, forces and coordinate values of concepts in the space necessary to predict negative attitude change, that is change in a direction opposite that advocated ("boomerang effect"), does not seem to correspond to the conditions under which "boomerang effect" is usually observed under the assumption that force for change is directly proportional to change advocated. Figure Two depicts the two general cases in which the general linear model and the assumption that force is proportional to amount of change advocated predicts boomerang effect.

Assuming that the force generated toward attitude changes is proportional to the amount of change advocated, clearly the forces F_{rs} in (1) and $F_{s^1 p^1}$ in (2) are larger than the respective forces F_{pr} in (1) and $F_{r^1 p^1}$ in (2). Given the pattern of masses indicated, resultant motions will be proportional to the vectors a, b, c, and $a^1 b^1 c^1$ in Figure Two. The result of these motions will be an

Figure 2. Conditions under which the direct linear model predicts negative attitude change.

$$1 \qquad P_h \xrightarrow{u} R_1 \xrightarrow{b} \qquad\qquad \xleftarrow{c} S_h$$
$$2 \qquad R^1{}_h \xrightarrow{a^1} P_1 \xrightarrow{b^1} \qquad\qquad \xleftarrow{c^1} S^1{}_h$$

P = position advocated in message a,b,c,a^1,b^1,c^1, = distances
R = receiver of message   travelled in one unit of time
S = source of message
subscripting = mass of conception: h = high; l = low

absolute *increase* in the distances s_{PR} and s_{P1R1}, i.e., a net movement *away* from the position advocated, or boomerang effect.

As suggested earlier, these conditions do not generally conform to those in which boomerang effect is observed, particularly since they imply greatest boomerang effect when the smallest changes are advocated, and negative effects are most frequently notes when large changes are advocated. While these speculations are hardly conclusive, still the failure of the linear model under these specifications to predict a known outcome is sufficient reason to explore alternative formulations.

The beginnings of such a formulation may be found in the fact that the pattern of movement predicted in Figure Two is a consequence not of the linear form of the model, but of the substantive hypothesis that the *amount of force* toward change is directly proportional to the amount of change advocated. This assumption, coupled with the pattern of masses indicated in Figure Two, leads to the pattern of motion implied in the vectors a, b, c, a^1, b^1, and c^1. This assumption seemed plausible since the *amount of change effected* is generally found to be proportional to the *amount of change advocated*, and it seems a very reasonable assumption that the amount of change effected should be proportional to the force for change created by the message. While this may be plausible, it need not be the case, however, that the amount of change effected should be proportional to the *instantaneous* force generated by the message. To understand why this is the case, it is necessary to introduce *time* as an explicit variable in the attitude change process. Figure Three represents two parallel attitude-change situations.

Figure Three. Change Effected by Change Advocated for Small
(Case 1) and Large (Case 2) Advocated Changes

1   R ————————————→ P

2   R' ————————————————————→ P'

In the first of these cases, only a relatively small attitude change is implied. In the second, considerably more change is advocated. Rather than assuming that the process of attitude change takes place instantaneously, we assume that delivery of the change message (R should adopt position P) sets up a process of change which takes place over time (t), and which continues until the equilibrium point predicted by equation (5) is reached. Given that the inertial masses of the concepts involved are in the order $m_p = m_p 1$; $m_r = m_r 1$, equation five predicts the total change $\Delta R^1 P^1$ will be larger than DRP. What equation (5) *does not predict*, however, is the length of time it will take for the changes $\Delta R^1 P^1$ and ΔRP to take place. A plausible assumption might be that the *rate of change*, rather than the *amount of change*, is proportional to the force generated by the change message. Under this assumption, Figure Four shows that the total changes of attitude might well be in the order $F_{PR} > F_{p1R1}$, giving $\dfrac{\Delta PR}{\Delta t} > \dfrac{\Delta P^1 R^1}{\Delta t}$, and still result in $\Delta P^1 R^1 > \Delta PR$ as long as the interval Δt is made larger without limit. Thus, as Figure Four shows, if $\Delta t < 9$, $\Delta PR > \Delta P^1 R^1$, but where $\Delta t > 9$, $\Delta PR < \Delta P^1 R^1$, since ΔPR approaches its maximum (6 units in Fig. 4) as Δt approaches 4, and $\Delta P^1 R^1$ approaches 6 only as Δt approaches 9. After 9 units of time have passed, however, $\Delta P^1 R^1$ continues to increase until it reaches its maximum of 11 at $\Delta t = 15$.

The point of this discussion is to show that the assumption (given in equation 5) that amount of change is directly proportional to amount of change advocated can be maintained even though it is also assumed that the amount of *force* for attitude change is *inversely* proportioned to the amount of change advocated. Not only is such a view possible, but it fits available evidence closely enough to warrant further careful investigation.

First of all, this inverse linear model predicts negative influence or boomerang effect under conditions like those in which it is usually observed, as Figure Five illustrates:

Figure Five.　Conditions of negative influence (boomerang effect) as predicted by the inverse linear model.

1　　$R_h \xrightarrow{\ a\ }$　　　　$P_1 \xrightarrow{\ b\ }$　$\xleftarrow{\ c\ } S_h$

2　　$P^1_h \xrightarrow{\ a^1\ }$　　　$R^1_1 \xrightarrow{\ b^1\ }$　$\xleftarrow{\ c^1\ } S^1_h$

R = receiver　　　　　　　　Subscripting:
P = position advocated　　　　h = high mass
S = source　　　　　　　　　l = low mass

The inverse linear model quite clearly predicts that the forces toward convergence will be in the order
$$F_{sp} > F_{pr} > F_{sr} \ \text{and} \ F_{r^1s^1} > F_{r^1p^1} > F_{p^1s^1}$$

Given that the patterns of masses are as shown in Figure 5, resultant movements are given by the vectors a, b, c, d, a^1, b^1, c^1, and d^1. When $b > a$ and $b^1 > a^1$, the result will be a net *increase* in the distances S_{rp} and $S_{p^1r^1}$, or boomerang. Of the two cases, the first seems most likely empirically, in that it represents a large change advocated by a source whose position is also viewed as extreme, and further assumes the receiver's conception of his or her own position and the position of the source to be stable (high mass). The result (which is quite consistent with most dissonance formulations) predicted by the theory is a redefinition of the position advocated as even further from the receiver's own, even though the overall result of the change attempt is a change of the receiver's position in the direction advocated. Although not every relationship implicated in Figure Five has been examined empirically, it is the case that boomerang effect is noted when large changes are advocated

(Bochner & Insko; Ableson, *et. al.,* Aronson, *et. al.*) and when the receiver's own position is massive ("embedded").

Very little is known empirically about the second case, but boomerang effect does not seem implausible under these conditions, since it represents the case in which a receiver whose own position on an issue is tentative receives a message from a source whose position the receiver firmly perceives to be very discrepant from the position advocated by the same source. This situation would seem very likely to generate disbelief in the receiver, and should be expected to yield significant message derogation (Bochner & Insko). Under these circumstances, negative influence or boomerang effect seems plausible, as the inverse linear model predicts.

In the light of evidence currently available it is difficult to assess the relative fit of the direct and inverse linear models to the data. First, although the inverse linear model seems to fit the pattern of "boomerang" effects observed somewhat better than the direct linear model (and about as well as non-linear models hypothesized), the data are not unambiguous in their support. Secondly, it follows from Figures 3 through 5 and the attendant discussion that both models predict the same outcome (i.e., that amount of changee effected will be linearly proportional to the amount of change advocated) when the interval of time (Δt) elapsed between delivery of the change message and measurement of its effects is greater than the interval of time required for the smallest of the changes advocated to take place. Data from an unpublished study by Woelfel & Walker tend to indicate that the interval of time needed for changes generated in a laboratory induced low-mass attitude was less than five minutes, but studies by Walster (1964) and Roloff (1974) show changes still occur respectively 90 minutes and several days after the change stimulus when the masses of attitudes are higher. Roloff's data further show that the correlations between changes advocated and changes effected vary about as predicted by the inverse linear model when the interval from stimulus to measurement is varied (Roloff, 1974). Several studies (McGuire, 1969) have indicated that attitudes move back toward their original positions after they have changed when measured later ("sleeper effect"), and these findings plausibly support the notion of an "equilibrium point" beyond which further change is inhibited, an occurrence anticipated by equation (5) and necessary to allow the inverse linear model to account for the pattern of available data.

None of these studies, however, consider the multidimensional representation of the attitude change process. Here only fragmentary initial data are available. Barnett (1974) has shown that aggregate metric multidimensional configurations show sufficient stability (reliability) over time to provide a stable measurement system for these processes, and further shows this stability increases monotonically with sample size. Gilham (1972) has shown that accelerations of concepts measured in metric multidimensional spaces are correlated with changes in measures of information received over a time interval, and Gilham & Woelfel (1974) have shown that the orderings of masses of objects in a multidimensional space estimated by equations drawn from the theory are constant across time periods. Although these early researchers are very enxouraging, all share the limitations of early efforts, and process analysis of multidimensional attitude representations over time are very rare.

III.   Discussion

In order to discuss these issues in proper perspective it is essential to make emphatic the extent to which the reasoning outlined in this paper is tentative. First, although a considerable array of carefully observed data have been brought to bear on the predictive capacity of the general linear theory and its two respective formulations treated here, the overwhelming bulk of these data were observed in studies intended for other purposes, and the hazards of such secondary analyses are well known. Secondly, the embryonic status of multidimensional scaling algorithms and their attendant computer software, along with the primitive state of the hypotheses deriveable from the theory at present has required considerable mathematical ingenuity among those investigators who have attempted multidimensional process models.[13] Even so, these studies reveal many compromises resulting from such restrictions.

Given these limitations, however, several tentative conclusions seem warranted. First, the general form of the linear model seems about as effective a theoretical model of attitude change as has yet been posited. Within this linear model, two alternative forms may be distinguished: 1) A direct model based on the assumption that force for change is proportional to amount of change advocated, and 2) an inverse model, which assumes that force for change is inversely proportional to the amount of change advocated. Comparison of these models requires an explicit examination of the role of time in the attitude change process, and such a consideration makes useful the specification of concepts borrowed from dynamics like *velocity, acceleration, force,* and *mass.* Although tentative, currently available data will support a theory which suggests that these variables are related in a way at least roughly analogous to their relation in physics, particularly when these concepts are combined in a metric multidimensional distance model of cognitive structure and process. While it would be rash to suggest such a model adequately represents the process of attitude change, it is clear that currently available data are consistent with such a view, and further investigations of this dynamic model represent potentially fruitful grounds for future research.

FOOTNOTES

[1] While the question of linear vs. curvilinear relationships among variables is a real question, the characterization of *theories* as linear or non-linear is often ill-considered. We call this theory linear because it considers the *new attitude* to be a linear combination of the old attitude plus message effects, but many curvilinear relationships among other variables are also predicted by this formulation, as the following pages will show.

[2] This model assumes a continuous ratio scale metric as a precondition. Techniques for providing such variables and their measures are outlined in Section II of this chapter.

[3] It can easily be shown that expression (3), as well as the results that follow, apply equally to those *more complex models* which assume each message to be of *differential effectiveness.* To do so it is sufficient to show that

$$\sum_{i=1}^{n} (b_i x_i = a) = 0 \quad \text{when } a = \sum_{i=1}^{n} \frac{b_i x_i}{n}$$

This follows directly from the property of closure under multiplication, which implies that $b_i x_i = x_i 1$, where $x_i 1$ is a scaler;

thus $\sum_{i=1}^{n} \dfrac{x_i 1}{n} = a$, and therefore $\sum_{i=1}^{n} (x_{i^1} - a) = 0$, which is equivalent to (3).

[4] Interestingly, even though derived from the general linear model, equation (5) argues for a 3-way interaction among n_1, n_m and m-a_1. Empirically this equation can be estimated by an ordinary least squares regression equation of the form

$$\text{Log } /a_2 - a_1/ = B_1 \log/m - a_1/ + B_2 \log n_m +$$

$$B_3 \text{Log}(n_m + n^1) + B_4 \text{ Log } U$$

where U is the residual error term. This equation, of course, anticipates non-linear relations among the variables (cf. note 1).

[5] See note (3) above.

[6] The dependent variable in the Woelfel-Hernandez study is frequency of use of marijuana. Woelfel & Hernandez do not imply these results hold for any dependent variable, but rather are specific to this one.

[7] Numerous procedures for establishing numerical estimates of the distances among cognitive objects have been developed. See particularly Torgersen, 1958; Miller & Nicely, 1955; Shephard, 1962. Techniques which provide continuous ratio scale measurement implicit in the theory described here are described in Woelfel, 1973, 1974a, 1974b; Barnett , 1974; Serota, 1974.

[8] Traditionally this matrix is double centered to yield an origin on the centroid of the distribution of the objects or stimuli. The exact transformation for any cell b^*_{ij} is given by

$$\left[b^*_{ij} = 1/2 \quad \frac{\sum_{i=1}^{n} d^2_{ij}}{n} + \frac{\sum_{j=1}^{n} d^2_{ij}}{n} - \frac{\sum_{i=1}^{n} \sum_{i=1}^{n} d_{ij}^2}{n^2} - d_{ij}^2 \right]$$

[9] This configuration can be obtained by metric procedures applied to an aggregate matrix of direct quantitative pair-comparison dissimilarities estimates averaged over a large number of people. See Woelfel, 1974a; Serota, 1974.

[10] While this formulation may sound unduly similar to Newtonian physical notions, it should be recalled that it fits the data about as well as any other.

[11] This assumption is solely for simplicity of illustration, and calculations involving unequal and non-constant masses and forces are straightforward.

[12] In fact, most experimental studies of attitude change have attempted to induce attitude changes unfavorable to the subjects. Ableson & Miller (1967), for example, induce "boomerang" effect by exposing naive subjects to personal insult; Cohen (1962) mobilized large scale apparatus to lower subjects' self-esteem; Aronson, Carlesmith & Turner (1963) advocate higher tuitions to student subjects; etc. Curiously, Fisher & Lubin (1958) who advocate essentially *judgmental* changes (e.g., the *number of paratroopers* in a photograph) do not observe source derogation.

[13] Many of these technical problems have been reduced by computer software specifically designed to deal with process models of metric multidimensional scaling (Serota, 1974). Copies of this program (Galileo I) are available on request from the author.

BIBLIOGRAPHY

Ableson, Robert P. and James C. Miller, "Negative Persuasion via Personal Insult," *Journal of Experimental Social Psychology*, vol. 3, pp. 321-333, 1967.

Aronson, Elliot, Judith Turner and J. Merrill Carlesmith, "Communicator Credibility and Communication Discrepancy as Determinants of Opinion Change," *Journal of Abnormal and Social Psychology*, vol. 67, 1, pp. 31-36, 1963.

Barnett, George A., "Social System Himopholy as a Function of Communication," International Communications Association Annual Meetings, New Orleans, 1974.

Bergin, A.E., "The Effect of Dissonant Persuasive Communications Upon Changes in a Self-Referring Attitude," *Journal of Personality*, vol. 30, pp. 423-438, 1962.

Berscheid, Ellen, "Opinion Change and Communicator-Communicatee Similarity and Dissimilarity," *Journal of Personality and Social Psychology*, vol. 4, pp. 670-680.

Bochner, Stephen and C. Insko, "Communicator Discrepancy and Opinion Change," *Journal of Personality and Social Psychology*, vol. 4, 6, pp. 614-621, 1966.

Carrol, J.D., and J.H. Chang, "Analysis of Individual Differences in Multidimensional Scaling Via an N-way Generalization of 'Eckart-Young' Decomposition," *Psychometricka*, 35, pp. 283-319, 1970.

Cohen, A.R., "A Dissonance Analysis of the Boomerang Effect," *Journal of Personality*, vol. 30, pp. 75-88, 1962.

Fisher, Seymour and Ardie Lubin, "Distance as a Determinant of Influence in a Two-Person Interaction Situation," *Journal of Abnormal and Social Psychology*, vol. 56, pp. 230-238, 1958.

Freedman, Jonathan, "Involvement, Discrepancy, and Change," *Journal of Abnormal and Social Psychology*, vol. 69, 3, 290-295.

Gillham, James R., "The Aggregation of Shared Information in a Sociology Department," unpublished Ph.D. dissertation, Urbana: University of Illinois, 1972.

Gillham, James, and Joseph Woelfel, "A Sociological Illustration of Construct Explication using multi-dimensional scaling." Central States Sociological Association Annual Meetings, Windsor, Ontario, 1974.

Goldberg, Solomon, "Three Situational Determinants of Conformity to Social Norms," *Journal of Abnormal and Social Psychology*, vol. 49, pp. 325-329, 1954.

Guttman, L.A., "A General Nonmetric Technique for Finding the Smallest Coordinate Space for a Configuration of Points," *Psychometrika*, 33, pp. 469-506, 1968.

Helson, Harry, Robert Blake and Jane Mouton, "An Experimental Investigation of the Effectiveness of the 'Big Lie' in Shifting Attitudes," *Journal of Social Psychology* vol. 48, pp. 51-60, 1958.

Hovland, Carl, O.J. Harvey and Muzafer Shevif, "Assimilation and Contrast Effects in Reactions to Communication and Attitude Change," *Journal of Abnormal and Social Psychology,* vol. 55, pp. 244-252, 1958.

Hovland, Carl and Henry Pritzker, "Extent of Opinion Change as a Function of Amount of Change Advocated," *Journal of Abnormal and Social Psychology,* vol. 25, pp. 393-411, 1957.

Insko, Chester, *Theories of Attitude Change,* New York: Appleton–Century–Crofts, 1967.

Insko, Chester, Fusako Murashima and Mirza Sayadaian, "Communicator Discrepancy, Stimulus Ambiguity and Influence," *Journal of Personality,* vol. 34, pp. 262-274, 1966.

Kelley, H.H. and E.H. Volkhart, "The Resistance to Change of Group-Anchored Attitudes," *American Sociological Review,* 17, pp. 453-465, 1952.

Kruskal, J.B., "Multidimensional Scaling by Optimizing Goodness of Fit to a Non-metric Hypothesis," *Psychometrika,* 29, pp. 1-27a, 1964.

Kruskal, J.B., "Nonmetric Multidimensional Scaling: A Numerical Method," *Psychometrika,* 29, pp. 115-129b, 1964.

Lingoes, James C., "A General Survey of the Guttman-Lingoes Nonmetric Program Series," in Roger Shephard, A. Kimball Romney and Sara Beth Nerlove, eds.: *Multidimensional Scaling: Theory and Applications in the Behavioral Sciences,* New York: Seminar Press, 1972.

Mann, L., "The Effects of Emotional Role Playing on Smoking Attitudes and Habits," unpublished doctoral dissertation, Yale University, 1965.

McGuire, William J., "The Nature of Attitudes and Attitude Change," in Gardner Lindzey and Elliot Aronson, eds., *Hardbook of Social Psychology,* Reading, Massachusetts, 1954, vol. 3.

McLaughlin, Margaret, and Heather Sharman, "A Scalor Distance Model for the Measurement of Latitudes of Acceptance, Rejection and Noncommitment," *Speech Monographics,* vol. 39, 4, pp. 302-305, 1972.

Mettlin, Curt, "Assessing the Effects of Interpersonal Influence in the Attitude Formation Process," unpublished Ph.D. dissertation, Urbana: University of Illinois, 1970.

Mettlin, Curt, "Smoking as Behavior: Applying a Social Psychological Theory," *Journal of Health and Social Behavior*, no. 14, pp. 144-152, 1973.

Reeves, Byron, "Predicting the Perceived Reality of Television Among Elementary School Children," unpublished M.A. thesis, East Lansing: Michigan State University, 1974.

Roloff, Michael E., "An Application of Linear Force Aggregation Theory to the Relationship between the Amount of Change Advocated in a Message and the Amount of Attitude Change Obtained."

Rosenbaum, Milton and Douglas Franc, "Opinion Change as a Function of External Commitment and Amount of Discrepancy from the Opinion of Another," *Journal of Abnormal and Social Psychology,* vol. 61, 1, pp. 15-20, 1960.

Saltiel, John, and Joseph Woelfel, "Accumulated Information as a Basis for Attitude Stability," *Human Communication Research,* (forthcoming), 1974.

Serota, Kim B., "Metric Multidimensional Scaling and Communication: Theory and Implementation," unpublished M.S. thesis, East Lansing: Michigan State University, 1974.

Shephard, Roger, "Metric Structures in Ordinal Data," *Journal of Mathematical Psychology*, 3, pp. 287-315, 1966.

Shephard, Roger, "The Analysis of Proximities: Multidimensional Scaling with an Unknown Distance Function." *I Psychometrika*, 27, pp. 125-140(a), 1962.

Shephard, Roger, "The Analysis of Proximities: Multidimensional Scaling with an Unknown Distance Function." *II Psychometrika*, 27, pp. 219-246(b).

Shephard, Roger, A. Kimball Romney, and Sara Beth Nerlove, "Multidimensional Scaling: Theory and Applications in the Behavioral Sciences," New York: Seminar Press, 1972.

Sherif, Muzafer and Carl Hovland, *Social Judgment*, New Haven: Yale University Press, 1961.

Sherif, C., Muzafer Sherif and Robert Nebergall, *Attitude and Attitude Change: the Social Judgment-Involvement Approach*, Philadelphia: W.B. Saunders, 1965.

Torgersen, Warren S., *Theory and Method of Scaling*, New York: Wiley, 1958.

Tuddenham, Read, "The Influence of Distorted Group Norm Upon Individual Judgment," *Journal of Psychology*, vol. 46, pp. 227-241, 1958.

Walster, Elaine, "The Temporal Sequence of Post-Decisional Processes," in Leon Festinger's (ed.) *Conflict, Decision and Dissonance,* Stanford: Stanford University Press, pp. 112-127, 1964.

Woelfel, Joseph, "A Theory of Occupational Choice," in J. Steven Picou and Robert Campbell's (eds.) *Career Patterns of Minority Youth* (forthcoming), 1974.

Woelfel, Joseph, "Multivariate Analysis as Spatial Representations of Distances," American Sociological Association Annual Meetings, New York, N.Y., 1973.

Woelfel, Joseph, "Procedures for the Precise Measurement of Cultural Processes," unpublished manuscript, (mimeo), 1974.

Woelfel, Joseph and George Barnett, "A Paradigm for Mass Communication Research," International Communication Association Annual Meeting, New Orleans, 1974.

Woelfel, Joseph and A.O. Haller, "Significant Others, the Self-Reflexive Act, and the Attitude Formation Process," *American Sociological Review,* 1971.

Woelfel, Joseph and Donald Hernandez, "Media and Interpersonal Influence on Attitude Formation and Change," unpublished manuscript, (mimeo), 1970.

Woelfel, Joseph, John Woelfel, James Gillham and Thomas McPhail, "Political Radicalization as a Communication Process," *Communication Research,* forthcoming vol. 1, no. 3.

Young, Forrest W., "A Model for Polynomial Conjoint Analysis Algorithms," in Roger Shephard, A. Kimball Romney, and Sara Beth Nerlove, eds., *Multidimensional Scaling: Theory and Applications in the Behavioral Sciences,* New York: Seminar Press, 1972.

Young, Forrest W., and Warren S. Torgersen, "TORSCA: A FORTRAN IV program for Shephard-Kruskal multidimensional scaling analysis," *Behavioral Science,* 12, p. 498, 1967.

Young G., and A.S. Householder, "Discussion of a Set of Points in Terms of Their Mutual Distance," *Psychometrika,* 3, pp. 19-22, 1938.

Zimbardo, Philip, "Involvement and Communication Discrepancy as Determinants of Opinion Conformity," *Journal of Abnormal and Social Psychology*, vol. 60, 1, pp. 86-94.

Richard Fitchen:

Transactional Analysis of Intercultural Communication

PRESENT interest in the study of intercultural communication was stimulated perhaps by the almost global phenomenon of domestic cultural conflicts in the 1960's and by an increasing use of international channels of communication. This interest is reflected by the publication of several books on intercultural communication.[1] Many writers consider that intercultural communication occurs for the most part as a consequence of social and technological change, but that it also occurs to some extent as a result of an aspiration to communicate. It is probably some combination of aspiration and change that inclines persons to undertake intercultural communication, since in general people are predisposed to communicate within their own cultures.

The primary focus here is communication between cultures rather than culture itself; so, to take a simple definition, culture may be regarded as a preference for certain patterns of communicative behavior.[2] Insofar as there is cross-cultural variation in such things as language, kinesics, art forms, belief systems, patterns of personality reinforcement, and proxemics, there are inevitably special conditions of intercultural communication.

Sometimes it is useful to analyze intercultural communication in terms of an intentional process of communication, perhaps viewing normal communication in each culture as parallel processes. Analysis can begin with demonstrating the existence in different cultures of corresponding points in the respective communication processes, and it may seek to describe generalizable means of constructing bridges for communication between such points. For example, if two persons from different cultures are not inhibited by their cultures from communicating with one another and they are motivated to communicate, they then require a medium to bridge their cultural differences. One of them may learn the native language of the other, or they may employ a contact language or a translator or rely on non-verbal communication. The choice of medium depends both on the ramifications that follow from each choice and on the resources for communication the two persons have at their disposal, but most significant in determining both the disposition of resources and the gravity of different ramifications is the object or reason for their communication. If the object is crucial, every resource will be thrown in and there will be great interest in knowing all the possible ramifications.

The object of communication might be defined in economic, social, political or psychological terms, but the process approach tends to subordinate communication as an activity to this object. Frequently though, more comes out of intercultural communication than can be planned ahead of time, as is suggested by the familiar observation that studying a foreign people involves learning two cultures —— theirs and your own. The point is that significant changes in the manner of communicating interculturally can come from communication itself, quite apart from the original object held in mind by the communicators. In practical terms, the communication experience itself transforms the communicators and hence also the resources for communication they will use. These are transactional communication experiences.

Some examples of this kind of experience appear in the phenomena of stylistic shifting described with simultaneous linguistic and social definition by Joos.[3] Suppose A and B are strangers to one another and they therefore use a formal style of language to communicate. Normally they will speak very properly and will not interrupt one another. Then, perhaps without either A or B being certain why, their communication changes and becomes more casual. Both A and B elide the formal flourishes, use slang expressions (i.e., language that is currently in vogue), and interrupt one another easily. Both A and B realize they feel differently about one another and that they are using a different style of language. They would agree that their relationship has changed from formal to informal or casual. They are aware of the linguistic and social changes between them, and in terms of the present discussion these changes altogether add up to a transactional change in their relationship. As communicators they are not immediately interested in what caused the transaction, although they are competent to give information pertaining to such causes to someone observing them.

A transaction happens *to* the communicators, whereas it happens *for* an observer. A transaction is an event in which there is simultaneous change in a communicator, the phenomena (including other communicators) encountered by the communicator, and what is symbolized or known about these encounters.[4] All that is apparent to the observer is an event in his field, a perceived change in the relationship between two objects in his view. But he can theorize that if the change he has perceived may be defined as a transaction between communicators A and B for example, they are in a relationship of communication interchange. The interchange relationship means that the communicators' experiences are interrelated and mutually adaptive. The change in what A has encountered is connected with the change in B and the change in what B has encountered is connected with the change in A.

Intercultural transactions involve a mutual activity of creating and adjusting communication behavior. Culture as a preference for particular patterns of behavior shapes both the impressive and expressive dimensions of each communicator's experience, while at the same time the communicators have an existential capability to produce some modifications of their cultures. In a phenomenological sense, they encounter one another by becoming mutually involved by means of their communication. Each communicator gains awareness of the other and of himself through his activity of communication.[5] So the basic source of action is identified here with the communicators rather than with any object or goal that might originally motivate communication.

It is possible to imagine communication between A and B in terms of some sort of intercultural hybrid or ad hoc symbol system that is not apparent to a would-be observer, particularly if the relationship between A and B is one of communication interchange. Phenomenologically the symbol system used by them may not be immediately apparent to an onlooker without the potential bias of his own cultural perception. It may even be so foreign or so subtle to him as to be literally invisible. Lacking the presence of immediately recognizable symbols, a potential observer waits for some significant event of intercultural communication to arrest his attention and focus his perception. What is perceived in this event is a change in the behaviors of A and B, which appears to be interrelated change. The transactional event is the phenomenon that attracts the onlooker's attention, and if he treats the phenomenon as a *case* his role of observation follows.

Since the observer cannot directly view the symbol system of communication between A and B without introducing his own bias, he can conceptualize its presence as necessary for interchange between them and then proceed by evidentiary steps to confirm its presence by means of his direct access to A and B. The symbol system may be called "X", to minimize any bias in naming it. Even though X is outside his phenomenal field, the observer does require information about it in order to verify that the theoretical transaction has actually taken place between A and B. And beyond that he needs information about X in order to define variables of interchange between A and B, which are required for his subsequent comparison of different cases.

Upon assuming the role of observation to inquire about X, the observer must take into account the changes his presence as observer makes in transactions between A and B. (Of course nothing prevents A or B from performing observation of their own respective activities, but they cannot logically be in an interchange relationship and at the same time simply be observing each other.) The observer wishes to avoid touching off further transactions between himself and them since this would tend to cut him off from X. Two things help him to control the effect of his presence. He has made a preliminary observation of the relationship existing between A and B before his presence necessarily becomes significant to them, which provides him with a reference pattern. And his communication with each of the transactants follows rather than precedes the event of their transaction, so that his appearance is likely to be less interruptive than if he approached them individually beforehand.

The unit of analysis proposed here can be identified as an ABX system, consisting of a communication dyad in a triadic universe of data. ABX is not being treated as an objective system, as it has been for other purposes by Newcomb;[6] but rather it is regarded as phenomenal for an observer. Seeking indications of interrelated experience between the communicators changes the nature of ABX as a data system, since the observer can only confirm this kind of interrelationship in terms of non-inferential information about X that A and B alone can supply. If the observer can identify an X based on separate reports by A and B about their interchange, and if there is correlation between A's and B's separate reports of A's change in behavior and between their reports of B's change of behavior, the observer has a means of defining variables in relation to X and with separate cases he can cross-check them in relation to each other.

These variables fall into two interdependent categories, which may be labelled tentatively as instrumental and volitional. The two categories include matters which arise in sociolinguistics and social psychology respectively. A and B are able to define certain limits in their transaction, according to where it began and where it stopped. With reference to the terminal limit, they may report a deficiency of similar instruments with which to communicate or a deficiency of willingness to use instruments which were similar and available. In actual practice these two variable categories are interdependent. This interdependency is taken into account by the transactional case study approach, as anticipated by Pride.[7]

Transactional analysis of intercultural communication offers a means of integrating linguistic and sociological factors, which are generally treated as separate in other approaches.

Up to this point the observer has performed analytic steps of inference and evidence. The remaining step is interpretation or evaluation. For this the observer compares different cases, so as to appraise the persistence of variables defined in each of them. Persistent variables identified under this power of observation would bear importantly on the success or failure of goal-oriented intercultural communication.

The transactional approach has been discussed here in terms of cases where the communicators are individuals. But it also applies to situations of communication involving more than two persons, up to and including the level that Michael Prosser calls "intercommunication among peoples." For example, transactional interchange probably applies to nation-building integration under charismatic leadership. Such transactions presumably occur also in communication between nations, though in such cases the critical variables include law and politics as well as culture.

FOOTNOTES

[1] L.S. Harms, *Intercultural Communication* (New York: Harper, 1973); Michael Prosser, ed., *Intercommunication Among Nations and Peoples* (New York: Harper, 1973); A.L. Smith, *Transracial Communication* (Englewood Cliffs, N.J.: Prentice–Hall, 1973); Larry Samovar and Richard Porter, eds., *Intercultural Communication; A Reader* (Belmont, Ca.: Wadsworth, 1972), which has appeared in revised edition.

[2] Edward T. Hall defines culture in terms of communication in *The Silent Language* (1959) and in *The Hidden Dimension* (1966); also see Karl Deutsch, *Nationalism and Social Communication*, 2nd ed. (1966).

[3] Martin Joos, *The Five Clocks* (New York: Harcourt, 1967).

[4] Henry Kariel, closing correspondence to the "Transactionalism Net," 1973.

[5] Maurice Merleau-Ponty, *Phenomenology of Perception*, translated from French by Colin Smith (New York: Humanities, 1962), p. 178.

[6] Theodore M. Newcomb, "An Approach to the Study of Communicative Acts," *Psychological Review*, LX (1953), pp. 393-404.

[7] J.B. Pride, "Customs and Cases of Verbal Behavior," in *Social Anthropology and Language*, ed. Edwin Ardener (Tavistock, 1971).

Arthur W. Larson:

Apperceptual Style and Intercultural/Interpersonal [*]
Communication

Introduction

TO PARAPHRASE Gerald R. Miller (292), research in the field of speech communication is not phenomenal. In lamenting that discipline's "environmental-phenomenal schizophrenia," Miller embraces a key notion advanced by psychologists interested in individual differences in perception. His distinction between "Information 1" (environmental cues in their objective form) and "Information 2" (these cues as selected and interpreted) and his admonition that researchers habitually manipulate the former, ignoring or assuming the subjects' phenomenal states, add up to a problem identified by an eminent perceptual psychologist. George S. Klein (227) recently made the important observation that perceptual psychologists and personality theorists have, for a number of years, gravitated toward the assumption of "autochthoneity" (uniform perception) of the stimulus field. Accordingly, acknowledgement of consistent individual differences in modes and styles of sensory perception is a comparatively recent occurrence, as is the study of correlated personality, intellectual, and physiological characteristics. In order to avoid this problem, DeRidder (99) chose to use the term "apperception," meaning an organism's dynamically meaningful interpretation of a perception. It is DeRidder's view that apperceptual distortions of perceptual impressions are a function of personality type. The implications of this problem for communication theorists are suggested by Miller: " . . . means for determining the available fund of Information 2 must be developed, and generalizations concerning ways in which differences in Information 2 affect the processing of Information 1 must be sought" (p. 56). For an example of the problem, Miller points to source credibility research:

> "One reason for this paucity of knowledge can be found in the relative lack of attention paid to the role of Information 2 in shaping perceptions of credibility. While we would all admit that . . . credibility is in the eye of the receiver, typical research procedures approach the problem almost entirely in terms of Information 1 inputs" (p. 58).

To illustrate the type of theorizing which might lead to research addressing this problem, Miller speculates: "It seems possible that . . . perceptual differences may apply to communication sources, that some message recipients may make sharp distinctions between high and low credible sources, while others may not" (p. 59).

Fortunately, our field is not so devoid of the phenomenal" orientation as Miller would have us believe. Among other trends, there is a modest, though growing, interest in personality variables in explaining variation in communication behavior. For example, Burgoon (59) states that:

> " . . . it seemed logical to a number of communication theorists that one should be able to predict a person's response to a message based on a particular personality trait. Indeed, a considerable amount of time and effort has been devoted to determining the relationships between certain personality traits and persuasibility. The findings may be of use to a source since they provide some insights into the nature of the decoding process" (p. 64).

Cronkite (82) contends that knowledge of personality differences should facilitate communication. Those lending support to this position include Bettinghaus (36), McCroskey and Wheeless (265), Tubbs and Moss (414), Wenburg and Wilmot (431), and Hart, Friedrich, and Brooks (186). Among the more popular personality variables are self-esteem, authoritarianism, dogmatism, aggressiveness, tolerance for ambiguity, locus of control, and Machiavellianism.

Nevertheless, while communication scholars have broadened our understanding of strategies both characteristic of and appropriate to individuals possessing these various traits, at least two critical issues are usually left unaddressed: (1) how one can identify these personality characteristics in receivers, and (2) how much variance within domains of communicative behavior these personality characteristics account for.

Designing receiver-appropriate strategies presupposes awareness of relevant receiver attributes; however, some of the least identifiable attributes may be personality characteristics. Holtzman (194) claims that: "Even though in experimental studies some personality traits apparently determine part of what the listener contributes to communication outcomes, the significance of these traits for understanding audiences is quite limited" (p. 60). His reasoning is quite clear: " . . . the personalities of speakers' audiences are not discernible enough for application" (p. 63). Cronkite's recent book (82) joins several others in illustrating this oversight. In his chapter entitled "The Role of Personality" he discusses a number of personality characteristics in terms of communication strategies symptomatic of and adjustive to them. After covering authoritarianism, dogmatism, self-esteem, security, need for achievement, need for affiliation, and aggressiveness, respectively, with no clues whatsoever as to how these traits could be reliably identified in individuals, he finally mentions, with reference to Machiavellianism, that "such persons are easier to identify than some of those previously discussed" (p. 111). For all that he has told us, Cronkite may have more accurately penned: "such persons are conceivably identifiable in stark contrast to those previously mentioned." This is doubtless not the same Cronkite who six years earlier (83) had advised: " . . . it is only occasionally that the communicator finds himself in a group with identifiable personality types" (p. 124). For the moment it seems that continued speculation concerning the imprint of personality differences on communication behavior might best be preceded by rigorous attempts to access the identifiability of such receiver characteristics.

While the first question concerns the usability of information regarding receiver personality characteristics, the second question addresses the relative significance of that information. Few would doubt the wisdom of assigning variables which account for variation of little magnitude low priority. It was Cronkite's (83) opinion that personality variables deserve such a status. In his words " . . . these variables do not seem to account for any considerable proportion of the variance . . ." (p. 124). While this assertion is ripe for scientific investigation, it fails to confront an equally fundamental issue: within how large a domain of communicative behavior do certain personality variables account for variance? Given the typically myopic perspective of many communication theorists, whose starting point for research is a narrow domain of communicative behavior from which they reason to the variables which might account for variation within it, this judgment is understandable. Seldom do we encounter reasoning from the personality variable to those domains within which it might account for variance. Few, if any, attempts have been made to assess the overall explanatory power of such a variable across a broad spectrum of behaviors. If a personality variable is capable of explaining a small portion of variation within, for instance, each of a large number of source/message domains (e.g., perception of source credibility, organization of message, delivery style, language intensity, use of evidence, etc.), thus generating numerous differential strategies, is it not as worthy of study as a second variable which accounts only for the bulk of variance in one source/message domain? Is not their total explanatory power roughly equivalent? While King (224) argues that this approach would constitute more theory-proving than theory-testing, he nevertheless would concede that it is imperative if we are to discover which variables and underlying theoretical formulations are worth including in research patterned after the more traditional approach. Hence, a second criterion for assessing the importance of personality attributes to communication theory is the "range" as well as magnitude of variance explained.

In this chapter, I will introduce an individual difference variable, and its cluster of correlates, which may have the potential of meeting the aforementioned criteria. The central construct, field dependence-independence, falls under the rubric of what I term *apperceptual style*. Because what is at issue is the self-consistent approach a person brings with him to an array of situations, the concept of style is appropriate; and because the style cuts across cultural, perceptual, physiological, intellectual, and personality boundaries and constitutes the dynamically meaningful way of sorting, processing and reacting to environmental cues, I speak of it as apperceptual. This chapter has three major divisions: (1) a review of research relating to systematic individual and cultural differences in the perceptual style field dependence-independence and a summary of the subsequent theory of psychological differentiation; (2) a review of research concerning the physiological, personality, and intellectual correlates of field dependence-independence; and (3) an overview of some of the pragmatic, theoretical, and methodological issues raised by psychological differentiation theory for the fields of intercultural and interpersonal communication studies.

I

To describe the nature of field dependence-independence a brief history of the laboratory work of Herman A. Witkin and his colleagues is in order. Numerous, more or less comprehensive, summaries are available elsewhere (e.g., 449, 454, 455, 457, 459, 460, 462, 465); this section relies on that of Witkin, Moore, Goodenough, and Cox (464).[1]

Their earliest work concerned the issue of how people locate the upright in space (447, 448, 450, 456). They observed that perception of the vertical was a function of two types of information — visual-environmental and internal-proprioceptive cues. Ordinarily these reference standards are consistent and complement each other to give us a quick, accurate sense of the vertical. What they did in their experiments was eliminate the complex visual world and substitute a simpler, more manipulable visual surround; at the same time they separated the visual and bodily standards.

In one experimental situation, employing what has been called the Tilting-Chair-Tilting-Room (TCTR) or Body Adjustment Test (BAT), the subject was blind-folded and then seated in a chair within a small room. Both the chair and the room could be independently positioned by the experimenter to vary to any desired degree from (or to conform to) true vertical. After both the chair and the room were brought to prepared tilted settings, the unblindfolded subject, looking straight forward, was instructed to tell the experimenter, who gradually adjusted the chair, when his body was perfectly upright. Witkin and his colleagues (462) found a wide range of individual responses to this task. At one extreme, there were people who, in order to perceive their bodies as upright, required that they be fully aligned with the surrounding tilted room, even with the room as far as 35 degrees off true vertical. At the other extreme were people who, regardless of the positioning of the room, were able to place their bodies close to upright. They seemed able to apprehend the body as an entity discrete from the surrounding visual field, thus freeing proprioceptive cues to play their role in the judgment of verticality.

In another experimental situation, this time involving the Rod-and-Frame Test (RFT), the blindfolded subject was lead into a completely dark room and seated. In front of the subject was a luminous square frame and a luminous rod pivoted at its center. Both the rod and the frame could be independently tilted by the experimenter either clockwise or counter-clockwise from true vertical. After both the rod and frame were brought to prepared settings, the then unblindfolded subject was instructed to tell the experimenter, who gradually rotated the rod, when it was perfectly upright. Again, a wide range of individual differences emerged. As expected, at one extreme were subjects who consistently aligned the rod with the frame, even with the frame far off of true vertical, seemingly unaware of proprioceptive cues to the contrary. At the other end of this performance continuum were subjects who had the rod placed more or less at true vertical, regardless of the positioning of the frame. Witkin and his colleagues suggested that these persons were able to apprehend the rod as an entity discrete from the prevailing visual frame of reference, again freeing internal, bodily cues to influence perception of the upright.

A third task involved the Embedded Figures Test (EFT), Witkin's (447) version of the Gottschaldt Hidden Figures Test. In this situation the subject was shown a simple geometric shape on the left; it was then removed and he was shown a corresponding complex geometric figure on the right, with the directive to locate the simple figure within it. The complex figure "used up" the lines of the simple figure in its various subwholes, so that the simple figure no longer appeared, at first glance, to be there. Described in these terms, the similarity between this task and the other two space-orientation situations became apparent. Here, too, the subject was given an item — a simple figure rather than a rod or the body — which was contained within a complex, organized[2] field — now a complex design rather than a frame or room — and, once more, was told to "disembed" the item from its surrounding visual framework. Again, marked individual differences in proficiency at this task were observed. For people at one extreme, the simple figure resisted disembedding and was not located in the allotted time, whereas for people at the other extreme the simple figure quickly emerged (as if "popping off" the printed page).

These three perceptual tasks were taken, collectively, as indicators of the extent to which a person's perception of an item was influenced by its surrounding, organized field. Scores on these tests, expressed in terms of deviation in degrees from the true vertical for the BAT and RFT and number of seconds elapsed before the simple figure is located for the EFT, gave evidence of self-consistency in performance across tests. Those subjects whose perception of the verticality of body was influenced by the positioning of the room strongly tended to align the rod with the frame and have difficulty locating the simple figure.

As should be evident from the above account, the common denominator underlying individual differences in performance on these tasks is ability to perceive part of a field as discrete from the surrounding field as a whole, rather than as embedded in the field. Consequently, those who performed well on the tasks were termed "field independent" (their perception of an item being independent of its organized context); those performing poorly were termed "field dependent." It must be emphasized that this individual difference falls along a continuum — it is in no way implied that there are "two types of people" (other than those above and those below average in performance on the criterion measures).

Subsequent research has revealed that people are likely to be quite stable in their preferred mode of perceiving, both over time and across sensory modalities. Numerous longitudinal studies have been conducted and they point to the marked, relative stability of this perceptual style (18, 111, 129, 288, 326, 415, 418, 451, 461, 465). While over time people tend to gradually improve in their ability to disregard the prevailing, organized field when attempting to focus on an item embedded within it, *relative* to a peer group their perceptual style remains fairly constant. This stability is also evidenced by the failure of significant "life changes" to induce alteration. Evidence regarding the effect of various experimental manipulations on short-term fluctuations in perceptual style is mixed, some indicating marked, temporary changes (153, 216, 260, 263, 268, 321, 343, 370, 371, 386), others showing no effect (172, 215, 233, 335). This kind of self-consistency has also been found to extend across tasks involving sensory modalities other than those featured in the three tasks reviewed above —— including, for example, an auditory embedded figures test, where a single tune must be located in a complex melody, and a tactile embedded figures test, where, with eyes closed, a felt-out simple figure, with raised contours, must be located in a complex design (8, 132, 438, 458, 459).

Subsequent to laboratory investigations of individual differences in this perceptual style, the research team headed by Witkin sought its theoretical description and explanation. Largely relying upon the comparative-developmental framework of Heinz Werner (435), they developed, for descriptive purposes, the theory of psychological differentiation. Before we look into this theory, it is instructive to briefly touch upon a few of Werner's key notions.

Werner conceived of all development as following two major trends, toward greater differentiation and increased hierarchical integration. According to Werner, primitive, developmentally-early behavior is marked by its global, diffuse, and unarticulated nature. Different areas of activity emerge as parts of an amorphous whole and evolve toward greater differentiation of function. At higher levels of differentiation, all psychological phenomena —— perceiving, thinking, learning, feeling, and language behavior —— become more discrete and include structured subordinate components. By hierarchic integration Werner was referring to the relationships between operations belonging to different levels of functioning. In a state of hierarchic integration, operations characteristic of lower levels of functioning are subordinated to those of higher levels. Primitive operations can be inhibited yet used in service of more mature operations. And, according to Werner, the higher the level of differentation, the greater the hierarchic integration. Thus highly differentiated persons have greater latitude of regression to lower levels of functioning than do less differentiated persons, enabling the former to approach novel, uncertain situations with a larger response repertoire.

The central construct of the theory put forth by Witkin, et. al. (459) is psychological differentiation. The debt to Werner is immediately apparent in their definition of the broader concept of differentiation: " . . . the complexity of a system's structure. A less differentiated system is in a relatively homogeneous structural state; a more differentiated system in a relatively heterogeneous state . . . " (p. 9). Increased differentiation implies increased specialization or separation of psychological functions (e.g., thinking from acting, perceiving from feeling). Furthermore, in a highly differentiated state:

> "Specific reactions are apt to occur in response to specific stimuli as opposed to diffuse reaction to any of a variety of stimuli. Parts of the perceptual field are experienced as discrete rather than fused with their background. Impulses are channelized, contrasting with the easy 'spilling over' characteristic of the relatively undifferentiated state" (p. 10).

Finally, it is important to note that progress toward greater differentiation during development involves the person as a whole, rather than proceeding discretely in separate domains. Hence, a tendency toward more or less differentiation of functioning in one domain tends to "go along" with a similar tendency in other domains, making for self-consistency. This description makes apparent their version of the basic difference between field independent and field dependent perceivers. The former, having a more differentiated perceptual style, are viewed as being more psychologically differentiated than the latter.

Having reviewed the standard theoretical description of field dependent-independent perceptual styles, what remains to be considered are various explanations for the phenomenon. Witkin and Berry (457) offer a taxonomy of four "antecedent factors": socialization, social tightness, ecological adaptation, and biological effects.

Most of the research concerning the role of socialization in the development of this apperceptual style focuses on patterns of mother-child interaction.[3] A number of studies, including several cross-cultural investigations reviewed by Witkin (445) and Witkin and Berry (457), have generally found a clear positive relationship between the cognitive styles of children and of their mothers (10, 78, 117, 118, 160, 217, 311, 365, 425). These studies reported both the types of mother-child interactions which contribute to the development of a particular style and the impressions of those interactions held by the child. At one end of a continuum of "child-rearing styles," corresponding to the development of field dependent apperceptual style, Witkin posits "growth constriction" (449). This style features, among other behaviors, demand for adherence to parental authority, encouragement of reliance on others (especially the mother), restriction of exploration and stifling of curiosity, negative reinforcement, lack of emphasis on achievement, absence of explanations for behavior, and inarticulate verbalization. And this "smothering" style can be observed in the very earliest mother-child interactions —— field dependent mothers being less differentiated in their response to the child's anxiety and less differentiated in the general handling of infants (454). These descriptions closely parallel those of Hess and Shipman (191), in their portrait of the "status-oriented" child-rearing style, as well as Abrams and Neubauer's (1) characterization of the upbringing of "person-oriented" (vis-a-vis "thing-oriented") children.[4] At the other end of this continuum, that which corresponds with the development of field independent functioning, is what Witkin terms the "growth nurturing" style. Among the typical behaviors noticed here are the encouragement of self-reliance, supportive interaction with the child, positive reinforcement of curiosity, achievement striving, separation from mother (446), leniency, and more articulate verbalization.

A second factor contributing to the development of apperceptual style is social tightness. According to Witkin and Berry (457), this construct encompasses both social conformity and sociocultural stratification; hence, it "relates to the degree of hierarchical structure among sociocultural elements in a society" (p. 15). In anthropological literature, societies which assign people to many different roles, elaborately organized, are labelled "tight," whereas those with minimal role differentiation and a less elaborate hierarchy are referred to as "loose" (327). Witkin and Berry explain further:

> "In tight societies . . . there is a high level of pressure of various kinds placed on the individual to conform; social control surrounds him. In the loose societies, there are few such pressures, allowing self-control to operate. In a sense, the tight society maintains a continuous socialization of the individual, in contrast to the loose society which sets him more on his own way" (p. 15).

Consistent with this formulation is Berry's (31) theory that field independent societies can be differentiated from field dependent ones on the basis of: (1) family structure (nuclear versus extended, respectively), (2) social structure (egalitarian-atomistic versus hierarchical-stratified), and (3) social relations patterns (reserved-fragmented versus mutual dependence-integrated). Given the large number of studies, to be reviewed in section two, which have linked the field dependence end of the continuum with relatively high social conformity and sense of fused identity, some effect of the social tightness factor on apperceptual style is indicated.

Ecological adaptation, the third antecedent factor, refers to the "characteristic relationship between man and the land he occupies" (457, p. 15). Berry (30, 33) offers the ecological contrasts between "hunters and gatherers" and "agriculturalists and pastoralists" in order to highlight the distinction between ways of apperceptual coping. He reasons that the ecological demands confronting persons pursuing a hunting or gathering subsistence life style require disembedding perceptual abilities, both to locate food and safely to return home. These demands, for Berry, go hand in hand with self-reliance socialization, and loose social pressure. According to cross-cultural field investigations conducted by Berry and others, "low food accumulating societies" indeed tend toward greater field independence, and "high food accumulating societies" are usually more field dependent (31).

A final group of contributing variables are classified as biological effects. Many studies in this general area have centered on hereditary and/or nutritional factors. One research team, headed by Broverman, maintains that perceptual style is largely a function of hormone balance —— a predominance of androgen leading to field independent functioning, a predominance of estrogen causing field dependent behavior (55, 56, 108, 225, 273, 467). Dawson's independent investigations have led him to postulate an interaction between hormone balance and socialization (90, 91, 92). Another body of research, which includes comparisons between identical and fraternal twins, supports the supposition that there is a gene or group of genes contributing to field dependence-independence on the X chromosome (166, 392, 401, 416). Theoretically, adaptive selection, prompted by, among other events, changing ecological circumstances, has altered the balance between "pools" of "field-dependent-fostering" and "field-independent-fostering alleles," through mutation (457). Further support for the hereditary hypothesis is garnered from studies involving the observation of neonates (232, 422). These investigators have observed patterns of infant behavior which reveal substantial and consistent individual differences corresponding to field dependent-independent apperceptual styles. Given the observed differences in socialization, summarized above, there is some question concerning the extent to which the child's basic nature at birth dictates the feedback the child provides the mother in the interactive process. Finally, the role of nutrition is supported in the researches of both Dawson and Berry. Low protein availability, a characteristic of high food accumulating societies and a precursor of androgen reduction, is found to be associated with field dependence and vice versa (457).

In closing, it should be noted that in Berry's (31) clustering of the four factors considered to be antecedent to the development of psychological differentiation he reviews research relating to the interrelationships of these factors, if some of those correlations are not already apparent. For example, hunting and gathering societies tend to be loose and have socialization practices which emphasize independence, achievement, and self-reliance, whereas agricultural and pastoral societies tend to be tight and emphasize responsibility and obedience (e.g., 17, 274). A summary depiction of consistent relationships among these factors and of their correspondence to field dependent-independent apperceptual style is reproduced from Witkin and Berry (457, p. 17), as Figure 1.

ANTECEDENT FACTORS	CLUSTERING AT POLES OF DIMENSION	
Ecology	Migratory hunters and gatherers ⟷	Sedentary agriculturalists and pastoralists
Social pressure	"Loose" social pressure and authority ⟷	"Tight" social pressure and authority
Socialization	Independence, self-reliance, and achievement emphasized ⟶	Responsibility, obedience emphasized
Biological	(A) Protein intake adequate; no androgen reduction ⟷	Protein intake inadequate; androgen reduction
	(B) Genetic selection for differentiation	Genetic selection against differentiation
Behavioral	Higher differentiation ⟷	Lower differentiation

Figure 1. Clustering of four factors considered to be antecedent to development of psychological differentiation.

II.

In this section some of the major physiological, personality, and intellectual correlates of field dependence-independence will be explicated. Only those which are relevant to the formulation of specific communication hypothesis will be included.

Physiological Correlates

For apperceptual style, the role of the human brain and nervous system in information processing are of paramount interest. If we can isolate certain differential, psychophysical processes which correspond to apperceptual functioning then we are closer to, among other things, both an understanding of the nature of psychological differentiation and of individual differences in communication style. Research delving into the so-called "split-brain" phenomenon promises to help provide that understanding.

Individual Differences in Extent of Brain Lateralization

One way of viewing psychological differentiation is as a function of cerebral development. What helps distinguish man from lower mammals is not only the complexity of his brain; it is also that his mental functions are capable of lateralization. Lower mammals almost universally behave as if their two hemispheres were one; damage to or removal of one hemisphere normally leaves their behavior unaffected. Though humans differ in the extent to which mental functions tend to reside in one hemisphere or the other, all human brains exhibit the developmental advance of bifurcated information processing to some degree. Countless studies involving observation of patients with damage to or surgical removal of one of the hemispheres reveal at least temporary loss of one or more functions, be they speech, mathematical ability, memory of faces, or other abilities. This lateralization of functions represents greater cerebral differentiation because it enables the skills to become more articulated and less "competitive" with one another for control over decision-making behavior. The reasoning and evidence for these conclusions will become apparent as we review some of the findings which grew out of the original "split-brain" experiments.

Sperry (391), Gazzaniga (151), and others, in the early 1960's, conducted numerous experiments with "commissurotomized" patients. In order to remove the physical manifestations of intractable epilepsy in these persons, the corpus callosum underwent surgical section, thus eliminating what was subsequently discovered to be the communication bridge between the right and the left hemispheres. Observed differences in postoperative behavior lead to investigations of the functional abilities of the two hemispheres — experiments usually involving the unilateral visual, haptic, or aural presentation of tasks and comparison of the relative performances of the two hemispheres. These studies were later supplemented by those involving simultaneous measurement, in normal persons, of EEG wave patterns over both hemispheres under various task conditions. These experiments revealed nonsynchronous alpha and beta wave activity, demonstrating that for most tasks one hemisphere is usually active while the other is at a state of rest. Taken together with research concerning the effects of hemisphere-specific damage, these studies helped refine our models of human information processing. It is now generally agreed that the left and right hemispheres, respectively, tend to specialize in, among other functions: (1) logical-analytic operations vis-a-vis synthetic-gestalt processing (47, 149, 303, 304), (2) verbal processing (the left having near exclusive jurisdiction over propositional, reflective speech) vis-a-vis nonverbal-visuospatial processing (such as recognition of faces) (27, 58, 73, 148, 149, 151, 152, 250, 293, 394, 469), (3) temporal sequencing vis-a-vis simultaneous awareness (249), and (4) secondary (conscious) vis-a-vis primary (subconscious) process (148). Bogen (46) summarized a number of seemingly parallel dichotomies coined by scientists attempting to make an overall, "lowest common denominator" distinction between the relative proficiencies of the two hemispheres, and then proposed his own fundamental distinction: the left specializing in "propositional" thought, the right in "appositional" thought. He next (47) amassed evidence pointing to the existence of individual and cultural differences in what he termed the "appositional/propositional (A/P) ratio." According to Bogen, et. al., some people seem to prefer left hemisphere ways of coping, others seem habituated, more or less, to right hemisphere coping styles.

A recent off-shoot of lateralization research has focused upon the correspondence of individual differences in apperceptual style to individual differences in degree of brain lateralization. Examining the relationship between field dependence-independence and various known properties of the two hemispheres, Berent and colleagues (23, 24, 25, 26, 27, 28) concluded that field independent persons may be more adept than field dependent persons at tasks which involve left hemispheric functioning. As we shall see, a more accurate way of describing this performance superiority may be that the skills required for success on these tasks are more clearly lateralized in field independent persons than in field dependent persons. The obverse, that field dependents are more adept at right hemisphere skills, was not found; rather, field dependent persons appear to be less cerebrally lateralized (67, 92, 131, 333, 362, 376). This means that, in field dependents, mental functions are less completely partialled out between (are more shared by) the two hemispheres, and may well mean that field dependent persons consequently suffer less articulated skill development in *both* hemisphers. Why? Palmer (318) offers evidence that the greater the differentiation of mental functions the greater the tendency toward lateralization. Case and Globerson (67) offer a plausible rationale: the more differentiated the person's skills, the more competition there will be for "central computing space," and lateralization reduces this competition by creating more function-specific computing space (cf. 370, p. 1233). In this vein, Bogen (45) summoned evidence that, as a given function becomes progressively more active in one hemisphere, it becomes steadily more inhibited in the other. Could it be that this reciprocal inhibition accompanying lateralization of functions occurs in order to reduce competition for central computing space in each hemisphere? If so, then degree of lateralization can reasonably be equated with level of psychological differentiation and attendant level of discrete functioning.

Some behavioral manifestations of individual differences in extent of lateralization are illustrated in a study by Meskin and Singer (287). They asked both field dependent and field independent subjects questions requiring reflection and observed subsequent face-looking behavior. When attempting to answer, field dependent subjects looked away from the experimenter far more often than did field independent subjects. The researchers concurred with Singer, et. al. (385) that, whereas field dependents need to glance away in order to "clear channel space," field independents are capable of "gating out" the face by relying on some central inhibitory mechanism. Certainly relevant here is a study by Shipman, et. al. (372). They concluded from their observations that field dependents may have to "work harder" to block out external stimuli when trying to process information internally. Other, indirect evidence of the link between level of psychological differentiation and extent of lateralization is found at the juncture of two separate lines of investigation: one finding reading problems to be associated with field dependence (66, 400, 441), the other observing an association between reading problems and incomplete lateralization (185). Perhaps poor readers, in the school environment, have greater difficulty "gating out" social cues when trying to focus on the reading task. Also, Abrams and Neubauer (1) contend that "thing orientation" (vis-a-vis "person orientation") represents greater cognitive development and is accompanied by more complete cerebral dominance (recall that the socialization of "thing oriented" children closely resembles that of field independent children).

According to the present view, then, field independents not only possess more differentiated cognitive structures, but are able to function, at any given moment, in a more operationally discrete fashion. For them, disparate functions may not as often "interfere" with each other. All that remains to be discussed is evidence that field independents, being more completely lateralized, are more capable of "higher level" functioning.

It is interesting to note Galin's (148) equation of degree of lateralization with "cognitive style," for much of the research testing the relative abilities of field dependent and field independent persons falls under the rubric of cognitive styles. Witkin, in coining this term, explained that a person's relative level of differentiation is the "style" he brings with him to any situation and that style is "cognitive" because it cuts across both perceptual and intellectual activities (465). Further, he proposed the distinction between "analytic" and "global" cognitive styles. In his words:

"Perception may be considered articulated, in contrast to global, if the person is able to perceive items as discrete from background when the field is structured (analysis), and to impose structure on a field, and so perceive it as organized, when the field has relatively little inherent structure (structuring)" (454, pp. 688-9).

Among the large number of studies finding field independents to be superior at analytic functioning are: those finding field independents to use less global, more differentiated psychological defenses (201, 361, 383, 451; see however 417); those finding field independent persons relatively more articulated in pain reactivity (404) and stimulus differentiation (101); those finding field independents relatively more analytic in perceptual concept formation (124), attribution of causality (19), categorization of environment (174, 176, 218), reasoning about speed (122), sentence disambiguation ability (246), observational clarity (320), general reasoning ability (241), complex learning situations (42, 95, 168), and conservation of substance (145, 307); and those finding field independent people to be higher in "need to be analytical" (128). From these studies it seems plausible to conclude that lateralization may "free" higher functions from the influence of primitive, developmentally early functions by segregating them, respectively, between the dominant and non-dominant hemispheres (cf. 148).

On the basis of the above discussion, the following postulates and corollaries are derived:

Postulate 1: Field independent persons have greater ability and preference than field dependent persons to cope in an analytic fashion.
Corollary 1a: Field independent persons have greater ability and preference than field dependent persons to cope with unstructured (uncertain, ambiguous) circumstances.
Corollary 1b: Field independent persons have less need than field dependent persons to rely on other people in attempting

to cope with unstructured circumstances.

Corollary 1c: Field independent persons are less likely than field dependent persons to perceive other people as possessing information or skills useful for helping them cope with unstructured circumstances.

Corollary 1d: Field independent persons are less likely than field dependent persons to leave an unstructured situation "as is."

Postulate 2: Field independent persons are better able than field dependent persons to "gate out" informational cues that are irrelevant to the task of coping with ambiguous circumstances.

Postulate 3: The reaction of field dependent persons to external stimuli is more functionally global; the reaction of field independent persons more functionally discrete.

Individual Differences in Automatic Functioning

Scientists have devoted considerable attention to the question of individual differences in autonomic nervous system (ANS) behavior. For instance, the work of Wenger (432, 433, 434) lead him to conclude that people differ substantially in overall level of arousal, some habituated to a relatively hypermetabolic state, others to a relatively hypometabolic state. Along similar lines, Lacey (235, 236) documented the existence of another dimension of differential ANS behavior. He encountered people, at one extreme, whose level of arousal fluctuated widely over time and, at the other extreme, people whose level of arousal remained fairly stable. Of particular interest here is the body of research which put to test the differentiation hypothesis by comparing various aspects of ANS functioning in field dependent and field independent subjects.

In the section of his general reviews concerning the field dependence-arousal relationship, Long (257, 258) summarized a group of studies which supported apparently contradictory conclusions: (1) that arousal, by constricting the perceptual field/range of sensory inputs, altered performance in the direction of greater field independence, and (2) that relatively higher arousal was a characteristic of field dependent persons. Failing in his initial attempt at resolving this "inconsistency" (257), Long (258) chose to rely on that of Witkin and Oltman (465). These authors focus on the adaptiveness of the autonomic nervous system to the situation, as it is interpreted by the individual. Adaptation is a response to perceived agents in the environment which upset homeostasis ("stressors") (367); hence, field independent ANS functioning may be characterized as more "stressor-specific" —— that is, under those conditions in which arousal may be considered an appropriate response, necessary for increased alertness and vigilance, field independent subjects may exhibit the increased arousal level reported by many researchers (79, 112, 140, 159, 183, 189). By the same token, in circumstances not considered to threaten homeostasis, field independents may exhibit the lower overall ANS activation found by other researchers (41, 200, 269, 332, 341, 377, 381). One rationale for the "stressor-specificity" distinction between field independent and field dependent ANS functioning follows from their differential perceptual abilities. Given the greater discrimination ability of the former, they may be sooner able to focus on cues salient to the task at hand, and may thus be less needful of an autonomic "head start." For example, there is ample evidence that field independents pick up on "danger cues" much more rapidly than do field dependents (15, 16, 162, 181, 290, 312). Viewing the relatively hypermetabolic state of field dependent persons as a state of readiness, Silverman and colleagues conclude that these people may characteristically be more on guard in order to compensate for poorer perceptual ability (375, 379). This formulation is consistent with Witkin and Oltman's (465) hypothesis that field dependents experience a "spilling over" of autonomic response to innocuous stimuli and have less "situation-appropriate" differentiation in autonomic arousal. It may help clarify various depictions of field dependent ANS as being relatively less sensitive or differentiated (40, 79, 134, 135, 137).[5]

Another important distinction between field dependent and field independent ANS reactivity is proposed by Silverman, et. al. (380). They observe that uncertain or ambiguous situations cause greater relative arousal in field dependent subjects, whereas highly structured situations induce relatively greater arousal in field independent subjects. Their conclusion is buttressed by other research which found field dependents more disrupted by isolation

(87, 277, 299, 378, 381) and novel situations (472), as well as studies which reveal that field independents are both more able and willing to provide structure to unstructured cirumstances (57, 142, 228, 231, 296, 302, 344, 364, 395). Perhaps field independents are more aroused by highly structured situations because they prefer to structure their own environment, whereas field dependent people are more aroused by ambiguity because they, being less analytically disposed, are less able to cope with such circumstances.

On the basis of the above discussion the following postulates and corollaries are derived:

Postulate 4: Field independent persons experience a lower overall level of autonomic arousal than do field dependent persons.

Given Hebb's (188) theory that there exist for individuals "optimum arousal levels," below which they experience boredom and above which they feel stressful, and Shelly's (368) refinement, that optimum arousal level is, for a given individual, a direct function of the stressfulness of his life circumstances:

Corollary 4a: Field independent persons have a lower "optimum arousal level" than do field dependent persons.
Corollary 4b: Field independent persons feel a need for less arousing life circumstances than do field dependent persons.
Postulate 5a: Field independent persons are less aroused by unstructured situations than are field dependent persons.
Postulate 5b: Field independent persons are more aroused by structured situations than are field dependent persons.

Given the tenants of dominant response theory (arousal heightening one's dominant response):

Corollary 5a: The more unstructured the situation for field dependent persons the more they will tend to rely on other persons to help resolve the ambiguity, whereas
Corollary 5b: The more structured the situation for field

independent persons the more they will eschew the help of others in attempting to overcome structure.

Personality Correlates

When we shift to the realm of personality correlates of field dependence-independence the self-consistency of this style across areas of apperceptual functioning becomes all the more apparent. The personality characteristics to be discussed at some length include sense of identity, reliance on external social referents, and interpersonal orientation. Also to be touched upon are activity/passivity, emotional control, and reflection/impulsivity.

Individual Differences in Sense of Identity

There are many indicators that field dependents tend to possess a sense of fused identity, whereas field independents perceive their identity as separate. One certainly might expect this to be the case given the more differentiated cognitive structure of field independent persons; it would not seem unreasonable to assume that differentiation of environmental cues corresponds with differentiation in self-perception. Before proceeding to some of the indicators of individual differences in this area, a fuller explication of the sense of identity concept is in order. Witkin (444) provides one of the more cogent delineations:

> "A sense of separate identity entails the existence of stable internal frames of reference for self-definition and for viewing, interpreting and reacting to the world. It implies a self experienced as segregated and structured. The capacity to establish and, within limits, maintain attitudes, judgments, sentiments without continuous reference to external standards, and in face of contradictory expressions from others, may be considered presumptive evidence of a developed sense of separate identity. On the other hand, ready and continuing use of external frames of references for definition of one's feelings, attitudes, needs would be suggestive of a poorly developed sense

of separate identity" (pp. 252-3).

Witkin and Goodenough (460) put this distinction in slightly different terms:

> "One of the main features of psychological differentiation is segregation of the self from non-self. Self-nonself segregation means that boundaries have been formed between inner and outer; particular attributes are identified as one's own and recognized to be distinct from those of others. It means as well that what lies within and constitutes the self is articulated. Differences in degree of self-nonself segregation lead to differences in the extent to which the self, or alternatively, the field outside is likely to be used as a referent for behavior" (p. 2).

This general difference between field dependent and field independent persons also has been expressed in a variety of other ways.

The initial studies concerning sense of identity grew out of observed individual differences in TAT response style (459, 462). This measurement technique was soon supplemented by the Draw-a-Person (DAP) test, from which the "articulation of body concept" variable emerged. This relatively stable (129) continuum refers to, among other things, the perceived permeability of body boundaries, overall differentiation in perception of the body, the articulateness in experience of both the surface and interior of the body, and the degree to which the body is perceived as discrete from the surrounding socio-environmental context, all as reflected in human figure drawings. Though there is some question whether the criterion measures of field dependence and the DAP test load on similar factors (3, 7, 459), there is little disagreement that field independent persons are more articulated than field dependent persons in their conception of the body (3, 75, 110, 126, 129, 156, 301, 378, 402; see however 387). Illustrating this fundamental difference, Lewis (251) found that field independent people have a more "individuated" self, whereas field dependents tend to merge more with the surround. Her rationale was that whereas the former experienced more guilt and outer-directed hostility (guilt being "self-contained"), the latter experienced more shame and inner-directed hostility (shame involving "permeable body boundaries"). In a similar vein, Taylor (407), through observation of hallucinatory and delusional psychotics, found field dependents to possess more "permeable ego boundaries." And Witkin, et. al. (463) offered indirect evidence of such differences in sense of identity. In their observations of depressives (who were relatively more field dependent), they found them to possess a "weak self" which attaches readily to others and takes on the "coloration" of the environment.

Another class of studies indicative of field dependent-independent differences in sense of identity are those addressing external orientation. The distinction made here is not the same as that made by Rotter (356). His "internal" and "external" loci of control refer, respectively, to whether an individual perceives control over his fortune to rest within or without himself. While this personality characteristic would appear derivable from the theory of psychological differentiation, internals being field independent, externals field dependent, a host of studies have found no correlation (43, 44, 74, 94, 245, 271, 310, 356, 366, 398).[6] The distinction rendered here is the extent to which external stimuli are salient to, or are perceived as impinging upon, the individual. In the general sense of this distinction, the research of Goldstein (158) led him to conclude that field independents are less "externally reliant." Also David and Glicksman (89) found strength in the conclusion that field dependents possess a more outer-directed frame of reference. Two related studies by Bell (22) and Doyle (109), found field dependence-independence to be associated with Riesman's (347) inner-other directedness dichotomy. Goodenough (163) summarized studies which, in tandem, support a view of field dependents as more repressive of externally stressful material. Haer (180) reported that field dependents' external orientation may be responsible for their more frequent altered states of consciousness accompanying "sensory overload." Finally, Campbell and Douglas (63) found field dependent children to be more pessimistic than field independents in

face of threatened frustration (perhaps viewing external events as
more encapsulating).

Aside from differences in articulation of body concept and
external orientation, there are other indications that field
independents have the more developed sense of separate identity.
Studying the "twinning reaction," Winestine (443) discovered that
field dependent twins experienced themselves more an integral part
of the twinship, as opposed to as individuals, than did their
counterparts. Investigating patterns of patient-therapist interaction,
Pollack and Kiev (334) surmised that, for field dependents, their
social roles are not defined as distinct from the roles of those with
whom they interact. Martin and Toomey (282) found field
independents more capable of putting themselves in the place of
another (empathy), attributing this difference to their better
developed sense of separate identity. Locascio and Snyder (256)
hypothesized that paranoids, who project their own system of ideas
upon the world in a highly selective fashion (to particular people),
would tend to be more field independent. Their experimental results
were supportive. Using the term "interpersonal differentiation,"
Rhodes, et. al. (346) posited a continuum coextending with level of
psychological differentiation. By no means exhausting the studies in
this area, I conclude with the recent investigation reported by
Steingart, et. al. (396). They found field independent persons unique
in their treatment of monologues as if they were dialogues. These
results seem to indicate the presense of receiver-orientation in field
independents, and the relative absense of sender-receiver
differentiation on the part of field dependent persons.

*Individual Differences in Extent of Reliance on External Social
Referents*

A second fundamental, distinguishing personality characteristic
is extent of reliance upon external social referents. The intitial
expectation was that field dependent persons generally rely more on
external social referents in defining their attitudes and opinions, in
making self-evaluations, and in arriving at decisions than do field
independent persons. Much of the early research seemed to support

this hypothesis. However, a review inclusive of recent research on the question lead Witkin and Goodenough (460) to amend this view. They concluded:

> "In general, the evidence suggests that field-dependent people make more use of information provided by another when the situation is ambiguous and the other is seen as a source of information that will help remove the ambiguity; field-independent people seem to function with a greater degree of separateness from others under such conditions. On the other hand, when the situation is well structured or when there is reason to believe that the other is not a useful source of information for resolving the ambiguity, field-dependent and field-independent people are no different in their response to external social referents. Furthermore, there is little evidence that field-dependent people are emotionally dependent or that they seek approval or attention from others" (p. 4).

The first qualification, ambiguity, would seem to refer to, among other circumstances, events promulgating self-evaluation and uncertain task situations. Studies in either or both of these settings have revealed differences in extent of reliance on external social referents between field dependent and field independent subjects.

If one were to grant the assumption that the impetus for self-evaluation is perceived, potential discrepancy, in one or more respects, between real self and ideal self, then it is this perception which may cause the feeling of ambiguity. There is ample experimental evidence indicating that field dependents (vis-a-vis field independents) cope with this ambiguity by seeking relevant information from other people. For instance, Sousa-Poza, et. al. (390) found that field dependents engage in more self-disclosure than do field independents. This result was, in part, predicted on the basis that the former attach greater salience to "significant others" (who, according to Jourard, inform the discloser through confirmation of his "authenticity"). This finding also emerged in studies by Taylor and Oberlander (406) and Berry and Annis (34) and is supported in studies involving frequency of self-disclosing statements by patients in therapy (170, 389), by interviewees during an interview (243), and in written stories (208). A more obvious instance of reliance on others in this circumstance is reported by Greene (169). Among other findings, he observed that field independents exhibited more (and field dependents less) "distancing" when given *positive* feedback. The impetus for self-evaluation may have been, in this weight control situation, subjects' perceptions of potential discrepancies between ideal and real competence. And this ambiguity of task competence may have lead field dependents to move closer to others giving positive feedback, field independents resenting the intrusion on their right to structure their own self-definition. A number of studies have found field dependents to be more sensitive to external criticism (116, 130, 139, 230, 340). In an experiment conducted by Gates (150), field dependents displayed more anxiety in the interview-with-no-feedback condition. Such subjects verbalized a greater need to know how the interviewer felt about their performance. Similar results were obtained in studies by DeGroot (97) and Freedman, et. al. (146). Further corroboration is furnished by Rudin and Stagner's (358) oft-noted report. They found that, across situations, field independent subjects experienced more stable self-evaluations, indicating the relative salience of external sources to the outcome of self-evaluation in field dependent persons.[7] A few studies tend toward the conclusion that field dependents are more aware of themselves as objects of perception, that is, "objectively self-aware" in Duval and Wicklund's (115) parlance (243, 437). Finally, Linton and Graham (255) published evidence that field dependent people rely more on others for self-definition. it seems clear that, in one class of ambiguous situations, those which give rise to efforts at self-evaluation, field dependents turn more toward others for relevant information.

A second type of ambiguous circumstance is the uncertain task. Finding himself in this setting, the field dependent also appears to rely more on the information of other people. The earliest work in this area is that of Linton (12, 254). She found that level of psychological differentiation was significantly related to a confederate's effect on judgment of movement in an autokinetic situation. In their review of such research, Witkin and Goodenough

(460) concur that: "Most of these studies have confirmed Linton's conclusion that field dependent subjects are particularly apt to make use of the opinion of other people with whom they are involved in a group interaction" (p. 5) (see e.g., 50, 51, 317, 354, 355). Those studies failing to substantiate this conclusion have generally involved other than direct interaction with actual (or bogus) group members (see 32, 93, 94, 204, 252, 289). A number of studies, falling under the heading of conformity research, and usually employing some variant of the Asch-type procedure (certainly an ambiguous task), find field dependents to be more yielding to the judgments of others (210, 297, 374, 388, 393, 466). "Need succorance" is a construct meaning reliance on others for helpful information. It is hardly surprising that research should confirm its correspondence with field dependence-independence. Alexander and Gudeman (4) and Gruenfeld and Arbuthnot (174) offer evidence that field dependents are above average in "help seeking" behavior. Block (41), in his inquiry in the lie detector setting, noticed a greater seeking of reassurance from others on the part of field dependent subjects. In an investigation involving the E effect, field dependent persons were found to be significantly more conforming to experimenter expectancy (267). This result was predicted on the supposition that field dependents, being less able to cope with ambiguity, would look more to the experimenter for helpful clues. Other studies, using children as subjects, found field dependents to more likely engage in "help-seeking" verbal and nonverbal (e.g., glancing) behaviors (223, 330).

A second condition delimits the information-seeking behavior of field dependent persons: the perceived likelihood that other people possess information useful for reading ambiguity. When field dependent people feel more confident in their own judgments than in the judgments of those around them, they are unlikely to engage in such information-seeking behavior. This prediction received some confirmation in a study by Mausner and Graham (284). When instructed, in pairs, to openly assess the rate of flicker of a flashing light, half the partners led to believe that they were performing poorly, corresponding partners convinced they were performing well, field dependent "poor performers" altered their judgments so that they were more in line with those of their partners than did field independent "poor performers." Interestingly, field dependent "good performers" were less influenced by their partners' judgments than were field independent "good performers." It may be that field independents, when in the presence of others, adjust to ambiguous situations with little consideration of their relative competence at the task. Relevant here are studies testing field dependent-independent differences in paper-and-pencil attitude change response to arguments attributed to "authoritative" sources. Most have found field dependents no more persuasible under these conditions (53, 76, 104, 143, 154, 198, 212, 234, 238, 264, 289, 384). While one would expect field dependents to perceive themselves as relatively less competent than an authority on any given topic, and, therefore, take more account than field independent persons of the information furnished by the authority, it is doubtful that the differences would manifest itself in other than social situations perceived as real-to-life. The same would go for paper-and-pencil measures of authoritarianism. Studies concerning the correlation between level of psychological differentiation and the tendency to yield to the judgment of a perceived authority figure have produced understandably mixed results (70, 335, 401). If further persuasibility research were to involve real-to-life persuasive messages, the difference between field dependents and field independents in tendency to align attitudes with those of authoritative sources might more clearly emerge. Finally, a study by Kendon and Cook (222) seems particularly applicable here. Subjects were instructed to "get acquainted" with another subject in an observation room. They were informed that some aspect(s) of their behavior would be observed, but were given no specifics. Contrary to hypothesis, field independent subjects exhibited higher "percentage gaze while speaking" than field dependent subjects, indicating that the former looked more at their conversational partners while speaking. While one would normally expect the uncertainty of the initial interaction situation (29) to cause field dependent subjects to be more visually attentive to their conversational partners (whose nonverbal cues would help reduce some of the ambiguity), perhaps the ambiguity of the experimental situation was overriding. If the ambiguity most stressful to subjects concerned the degree to and criteria with which they were being "evaluated" (certainly a plausible conclusion given the probable salience to them of the experimental situation relative to a chance acquaintance finding himself in similar circumstances), then their conversational partners would not likely be viewed as sources possessing useful information. This would predict equivalent "percentage gaze while speaking." What would account for the higher percentage observed of field independents? Again, if subjects were preoccupied with uncertainty regarding the motivations of the observers, and, hence, were trying to reduce uncertainty via internal processing (reasoning, guessing, etc.), then field independents might have been better able to gaze while speaking, by virtue of their hypothesized superior ability to "gate out" the face while thinking (cf. 287).[8]

The conclusion, that field dependents are dependent only when they find themselves in the presence of others who are perceived as likely to possess information useful for the resolution of ambiguity, is bolstered by studies which find field dependents not to be generally dependent on others (21, 105, 121, 138, 167, 428). Also, there is little evidence that field dependents are generally more approval-seeking as measured by tendency to give socially-desirable responses on questionnaires (80, 128, 157, 240, 264, 409; see however 325, 351, 439). Nor are field dependents generally more responsive to extrinsic awards in learning situations (163).

The above provide bases for the following postulates and corollaries:

Postulate 6: In ambiguous circumstances, field dependent persons are more likely to engage in external (social) information processing than are field independent persons, provided that information is perceived as useful.

Corollary 6a: In uncertain situations, field dependent persons are more likely than field independent persons to over-estimate the qualifications of those perceived as possessing useful information.

Corollary 6b: In uncertain situations, field dependents are more likely to resolve experienced dissonance by complying with the requests of those perceived as possessing useful information, whereas field independents are more likely to resolve experienced dissonance through internal, analytic processing (e.g., counterargumentation, source deprecation).

Postulate 7: Field dependent persons experience themselves as relatively more an integral part of an external surround than do field independent persons.

Corollary 7a: Field independent persons are less likely than field dependent persons to be attentive to cues external to them.

Corollary 7b: Field dependent persons are less likely than field independents to possess attitudes that are at variance with those of persons in their social surround.

Corollary 7c: In group decision-making situations, field independent persons are more likely than field dependent persons to feel individually responsible for the group outcome.

Postulate 8: A feeling of uncertainty is more easily induced in field dependent persons than in field independent persons.

Postulate 9: Field dependents are more accustomed than are field independents to a state of objective self-awareness.

Individual Differences in Interpersonal Orientation

The greater use by field dependent people of external referents implies not only a greater felt need on their part for information in the persons of more knowledgeable others, it also suggests that field dependents are more adept at directly or indirectly procuring informational assistance from other people. It follows that, in order to assure direct access to other people when needed, field dependents must characteristically behave in a socially facilitative fashion. It also follows that, for field dependents to maintain indirect access to information emanating from other people, they must be habitually attentive to social cues. Neither of these behavioral prerequisites appear as applicable to field independents. These conclusions are suggestive of a third personality difference between field independents and field dependents: the former appear to be more intrapersonally oriented, the latter more interpersonally oriented. Preferring to word the two poles on this continuum "interpersonal" and "impersonal," Witkin and Goodenough (460) nevertheless concur with this rationale for the postulated correlation:

"To the extent that field-dependent people tend to seek
information from external sources as an aid in structuring their
experiences, we may expect them to gravitate toward situations
where such information is available. As with selective attention
to social aspects of the environment, the favoring of personal
situations over impersonal ones may be seen as helpful in
obtaining information from others. The evidence . . . is clear in
demonstrating that field-dependent persons show a strong
interest in people, prefer to be physically close to others, are
emotionally open and favor real-life situations which will bring
them into contact with people; in contrast, field-independent
persons are less interested in people, show both physical and
psychological distancing from others and favor impersonal
situations" (p. 24).

This overview of "still another psychological domain . . .
encompassed by differentiation theory" is reminiscent of Jackson's
(203) observation that resistance to field forces in perceptual
situations is significantly correlated with resistance to social field
forces. The following review will be divided roughly along the lines
of the two prerequisites postulated above: those studies relevant to
socially facilitative behavior and those investigating salience of social
cues.

The tendency of field dependent persons to behave in a more
socially facilitative manner has been tested in a wide variety of
settings. Marcus, et. al. (275, 276, 430) found field dependents to be
more convergent in their temporal speech patterns, indicating a more
accommodating verbal style. Oltman, et. al. (314) observed greater
anticipated and actual success at conflict resolution as a function of
the prevalence of field dependence among group members. Perhaps
one reason is the greater assumption of socio-emotional (vis-a-vis task
oriented) roles on the part of field dependents (360). Bard (11), in
his study tapping preferences for individual and team sports, found
field dependents to prefer the latter while field independents
preferred the former. This finding was replicated in a study by
Barrell and Trippe (13). Coates, et. al. (71) found field dependent
children to have a greater preference for social, as opposed to

nonsocial, play (see however 81). In a similar study, Nadeau (300) found field independent boys to prefer more solitary play. A not inconsiderable group of investigations witnessed the tendency of field dependent persons to be less willing to openly display hostility toward others (69, 98, 463), despite their equivalent likelihood of experiencing hostile feelings toward others (166, 240). Supportive evidence may be found in research concerning defense mechanism preference. These reports found field dependents to have a greater affinity for "turning-against-self" whereas field independents are more accustomed to "turning-against-object" (48, 106, 155). An additional indication of this tendency is Goldstone's (161) finding that field independents committed more negative acts in a small group situation. However, when it comes to positive evaluations of others, field dependents appear more willing to so engage (103, 136, 226, 275). There is evidence that field dependents may also be more fearful of the loss of "needed others" (464), better able to perform given interpersonal tasks (244), more desireous of being physically (170, 193, 209, 413)[9] and emotionally (6, 436) close to others, and less isolated and anti-social (35, 393). Also of interest are studies, reviewed by Witkin, et. al. (464) which point to "people orientation" in the educational-vocational interests and aptitudes of field dependent persons. Studies in this area found their counterparts to be more interested and skilled in analytical, nonsocial fields (e.g., 14, 38, 86, 100, 195, 199, 211, 285, 315, 328, 331, 337, 352, 353, 473). Another insight into the relative proclivities of field dependent and field independent persons to embark upon socially facilitative endeavors is provided by ratings (both by self and others). Witkin and Goodenough (460) offer this juxtaposition on the basis of available studies:

> "Among the descriptors of relatively field-dependent persons . . . are: like being with others, sociable, gregarious, affiliation oriented, socially outgoing, prefer interpersonal and group to intrapersonal circumstances, seek relations with others, show participativeness, show need for friendship, interested in people, want to help others, have a concern for people, have wide acquaintanceship, know many people and are known to many people. A contrasting set of descriptors of relatively

field-independent persons has included: prefer solitary activities, individualistic, cold and distant in relations with others, aloof, never feel like embracing the whole world, not interested in humanitarian activities, highly cathect intellectual activities, value cognitive pursuits, concerned with philosophical problems, concerned with ideas and principles rather than people, task oriented, have work-oriented values such as efficiency, control, competence, excelling" (pp. 24-5).

Finally, there is evidence that field dependents are generally more successful at meeting this first prerequisite for maintaining access to others. Research indicates not only that field dependents view themselves as more popular (125), but that they are both better known by more people (314) and better liked by others (102, 297, 314).

The second prerequisite, recall, is habitual attentiveness to social cues. The modifier "habitual" is used here to imply that the attentiveness remains even when social cues seem to be peripheral to the central exigency. Salience of social cues has been experimentally operationalized in several ways. One of the more popular has been to compare field dependent and field independent subjects in terms of attraction to verbal messages with social vis-a-vis nonsocial content (120, 140, 141, 156, 219). These studies found field dependent persons more incidentally attracted to social content. Two related projects (119, 139), which failed to arrive at these results, were not testing incidental attention to social content, however, and therefore did not address the issue of cue salience. Other investigations have found field dependents to be better able to identify warmth in other people (429), superior at nondeliberate memory of peoples' names (314), and more disrupted by a mismatch between verbal and nonverbal (social) message components (169). Recently, Birnbaum (39) asked subjects to verbalize what they recalled feeling or noticing in an immediately preceding experimental session. Field dependent subjects recalled more social aspects, whereas field independents reported more task-related aspects of the experience. Perhaps the most oft-used cue-salience paradigm has been face perception. Field dependent people appear more likely to look at the faces of other people (230, 306, 357, 463); they also seem to be superior at incidental memory of faces (2, 9, 85, 288). Not inconsistent with this indicant of differential social cue salience are studies which report the superiority of field dependents to disappear when subjects are specifically directed to remember faces (5, 298).

Given the large number of studies, the high frequency of replication, and the breadth of operational definitions, the tentative, overall conclusion that field dependents tend to be more interpersonally oriented than field independents appears to be a fairly safe one; hence, the following postulate and corollaries:

> *Postulate 10:* Field dependent persons are more interpersonally oriented, field independent persons more intrapersonally oriented.
>
> *Corollary 10a:* Field dependent persons habitually behave in a more socially-facilitative fashion than do field independent persons.
>
> *Corollary 10b:* Field dependent persons are more habitually attentive to incidental social cues than are field independent persons.

Other Personality Characteristics

Among the myriad other personality correlates of field dependence-independence, three appear to be potentially relevant here: activity/passivity, emotional control, and reflexivity/reflectivity.

A number of studies tend to support a view of the relatively field independent person as possessing an aggressive, active coping style. Witkin (452, 462) found such persons to exhibit more initiative and greater activity in contradistinction to the characteristically passive stance of field dependent persons (see however 242). These findings are corroborated in subsequent studies reported by DuPreez (114), Svinicki, et. al (403), Stansell, et. al. (393), Gruenfeld and Arbuthnot (174), Young (468), Ladkin, et. al. (237), and Goodenough (163).

As for emotional control, the available evidence seems to indicate that field dependents possess more integrated emotional and intellectual structures. That is, field dependents appear to be more attentive to emotional information (294), less able to separate content or idea from affect (35, 201, 295), and less able to control (repress) emotion (3, 75, 305). Witkin, et. al. (459) characterized field independents as "emotionally hard." Consistent with these findings is research showing females (who are relatively more field dependent) to be more emotionally "prototypic" (382), more receptive of emotionally intuitive cues and experiencing more personal feelings (382), and more accurate in the judgment of emotion (436). The recent work of Janov and Holden (207), purporting to demonstrate, among other things, an inverse relationship between ability to intellectualize and access to feelings, as well as the role of lateralization in emotional repression, is consonant with this view of field dependence-independence.

Available research points toward the relative reflexivity (impulsivity) of field dependent persons and the corresponding reflectivity of field independent persons. Haronian and Sugarman (184) support the latter conclusion in their finding that field independents manifest more "conscious control over experience." Safer (360) found field independents to engage in more interpretive behavior in small groups. Weiss, et. al. (426) found such individuals to possess more "impulse control." And finally, working with children, Campbell and associates (62, 63, 64) and Massari (283) report field dependents to be more impulsive and their counterparts more reflective.

Consequently, these postulates are derived:

Postulate 11: Field independent persons manifest a more active coping style than do field dependent persons.

Postulate 12: Field dependent persons are more attentive and responsive to affective cues than are field independent persons.

Postulate 13: Field independent persons are more likely than field dependent persons to reflect before making a decision.

The Issue of Intelligence

A final correlate of field dependence-independence is intelligence. This has led critics of Witkin's differentiation theory to conclude that his construct may not be theoretically or pragmatically useful (e.g., 54, 470, 471). Along these lines, Dubois and Cohen (113) claim that intelligence may be a better unitary construct for consistencies among individual differences across diverse areas of cognitive functioning.[10] Witkin responded by reiterating the results of studies which anticipated this objection. His own integration (459) had revealed that field dependence-independence correlated only with those intelligence subtests (e.g., the so-called Wechsler Analytic Triad) which loaded on a visual disembedding factor — thus yielding an overall, though lower-order, correlation with general intelligence. In fact, Witkin and colleagues consider these intelligence subtests to collectively constitute a measure of field dependence-independence. Subsequent research has tended to support this view (87, 124, 165). This issue is not entirely so clear-cut, however, given Dubois and Cohen's unique finding of a significant correlation between general intelligence and field dependence-independence using intelligence tests which did not tap disembedding or spatial factors.[11]

III

In this final section some of the pragmatic, theoretical, and methodological implications of differentiation theory for intercultural and interpersonal communication studies will be discussed. It is important to recall at this point the two criteria outlined in the introduction. An individual difference variable is of importance to communication theory only if: (1) the relative presence of the trait can be identified in individual communicators and groups, and (2) the variable accounts for sufficient variance across a range of communication domains.

The major pragmatic issue is the extent to which the relative field dependence or field independence of receivers can be reliably estimated. A number of readily observable characteristics of such receivers already have been mentioned. For example, if one were to encounter a relatively socially active person or group, then all other things being equal, the safer assumption would be that field dependent-appropriate communication strategies would be in order. In addition to these indicators, an equally extensive body of research is suggestive of others. It is generally agreed that males tend to be more field independent than females (20, 37, 48, 49, 182, 192, 216, 229, 253, 286, 306, 316, 319, 322, 342, 349, 350, 386, 401, 453, 457, 464). Older adults tend to be more field dependent than younger adults (8, 77, 279, 280, 363, 411, 457). There is also modest evidence that Blacks (316, 329) and Chicanos (339) are relatively more field dependent, as are persons of lower socio-economic status (68, 130, 175, 177, 239, 345, 350; see however 214) and urban background (309, 345). Finally, a large body of research, reviewed by Witkin (445) and Witkin and Berry (457), has identified specific cross-cultural differences along this dimension. In the absence of studies specifically designed to assess the identifiability of receiver apperceptual style, available evidence suggests that field dependence-independence is fairly estimable. The first criterion may already have been met. To illustrate some of the theoretical implications of differentiation theory for communication, this section will focus on three broad areas: (1) the concept of communication style, (2) communication domains falling under the rubric of attitude change, and (3) other selected interpersonal communication domains.

While the notion of communication style is not new to our field (cf. 308), systematic attempts to elucidate the theoretical underpinnings of any particular communication style are few and far between. The present report constitutes a germinal effort which, hopefully, may one day generate a model for such endeavors. Piggybacking the notion of apperceptual style, communication style refers to the characteristic manner of interacting which an individual brings to any given situation. This style helps determine the preferred content, form, and modality of that interaction. A person or group's communication style can also be viewed as a relatively stable characteristic, thus making for self-consistency across a broad array of communication situations. The remainder of this section will speak in terms of field dependent-independent communication styles, proposing specific theoretical hypotheses which appear to follow from postulates (P) and corollaries (C) derived from differentiation theory and research.

Both source and message attributes constitute key concerns for those attempting to induce attitude change. Before proceeding to the formation of hypotheses subsumed within each of these categoreis, it is important to consider them together.

Communication theorists typically draw a clear-cut distinction between the source and the message. Do all receivers make a similar juxtaposition, separating the message from its context — the source? Assuming that the criterion measures of field dependence-independence tap disembedding ability, then might we predict that field independent receivers are better able, when they consider it appropriate, to separate message from source? And given the postulated preference of field independents for internal-analytic processing, then would not such persons more often, consciously or subconsciously, consider this separation appropriate? Harvey, Hunt and Schroder (187) posited the notion of source-message orientation to help explain differences in attitude change. For Kelman and Eagly (221), source and "content" orientations are essentially the motivational bases of attitude change — identification mediating the former, and internalization the latter. McDavid (266) went so far as to treat these orientations as levels of a personality variable. He defined source-message orientation as the individual's dispositional tendency to respond to interpersonal communications in terms of either the source or the message of the communication. And two more recent studies (291, 397) have attempted further refinements. In view of the considerably more extensive theoretical groundwork underlying the field dependence-independence construct and the apparent ability of differentiation theory to explain and predict individual differences in source and message orientation (cf. Pl, 2, 6, 7, 10), would McDavid's proposed personality variable be more appropriately subsumed within Witkin's construct? The findings of at least one study provide direct evidence of the relative source-orientation of field dependent persons and vice versa (52).

Moving now to the source component of persuasive communication, we will focus mainly on those factors contributing to the perception of source credibility. In their recent review, Cronkite and Liska (84) reminded us that the various factors of source valence differ not only across topics and situations, but across audiences as well. Is it likely that relatively field dependent and field independent groups differ here? Most factor analytic studies of source credibility find the construct to break down into a limited number of substantive dimensions —— usually two to four. Among these principal factors, those which may as well be labelled "competence" and "attractiveness" usually emerge. "Expertise" and "authoritativeness" correspond with the former; "sociability" and "dynamism" with the latter (cf. 190). There are preliminary indications that field independents are more likely to look for competence in a source when judging his credibility, whereas for field dependents attractiveness is more likely to be salient overall. Schimek (361) found field independents to rely more on "objective factors" and "reliable expert opinion" than field dependents. Gruenfeld (173) hypothesized that field independents would assign more importance to the competence of a "Least Preferred Co-worker," whereas field dependents would view sociability as more salient. His experimental results confirmed this hypothesis. The superior "face-gating" ability of field independents, as well as their relative impersonal, task orientation, would also lend credence to this view. To the extent that field independents are indeed relatively more "message-oriented," then McDavid's (266) conclusion, that source-oriented people are those "who attend primarily to their relationship with other people" whereas those who attend primarily to the source's credentials in the topic area at hand are classified as "message-oriented," adds further support. Finally, if most persuasive communication situations are perceived as ambiguous (inducing dissonance), then the tendency of field dependents to rely on others under such circumstances is relevant here.

As a corollary to the above speculations, perhaps the differential analytic and interpersonal skills of such persons renders them less critical of source characteristics which are less salient to them. According to this reasoning, field dependents, for example, would be more inclined to assume the possession of appropriate credentials by a source. Fleshler, et. al. (143) indeed found field dependent raters to evaluate speakers as more "qualified" than did field independent raters. Perhaps the same would be true of attractiveness ratings by field independent audiences.

Because of the obvious spillover of certain source attributes into delivery of the message, further speculations regarding delivery will be discussed here. At least two studies, contrasting dynamic and conversational delivery, found differences in delivery intensity to not affect attitude change (196, 324). This may have been due to unrepresentative subject samples. Pearce and Brommel (324) propose that subsequent studies "should determine the effects of delivery style on message effectiveness with audiences other than college undergraduates . . . [It] would seem that various social subgroups would develop different stereotypes associated with various styles of delivery" (pp. 305-6). There are at least two reasons why field dependents and field independents might comprise useful comparative subject samples. First, if dynamic delivery is more rich in social cues than conversational delivery, then it should be more preferred by field dependent persons (cf. C10b, P12). Second, assuming that dynamic delivery is more arousing than its counterpart, then it should likewise be less appropriate to relatively field independent auditors (cf. P4, C4ab). Aside from intensity of delivery, there is also the question of extemporaneity. The respective strengths of the manuscript and extemporaneous presentation are accuracy and audience involvement. It should be quite clear that field independents may be more likely to prefer the former, field dependents the latter.

The use of evidence certainly moderates judgments about the source. It has long been assumed that the more rigorous the evidentiary documentation the higher the source credibility (by virtue of augmented authoritativeness). However, Fleshler, et. al. (143) found field dependents and field independents to differ in their evaluations of vaguely versus clearly documented sources of information. Apparently, field dependent persons are not as likely to demand evidentiary rigor.

A final variable conceptually linked to source is homophily/heterophily. Do field dependents and field independents differ in the importance they assign to source/receiver similarity? Would such persons differ in their susceptibility to speaker attempts at "identification"? It seems plausible that, for the same reasons field dependents are hypothesized to be relatively more source oriented, field dependents would be more influencible in homophilous circumstances than should field independents. The obverse should obtain for relatively heterophilous circumstances (cf. P7). Brilhart's (53) finding that field dependent persons are more subject to congruity effects provides some corroboration.

Differentiation theory would also predict individual differences in susceptibility to certain message strategies. These variables are arranged along familiar content/form lines.

A first content variable is suggested by Janis and Hovland (206):

> "In the content of many communications one finds appeals which explicitly promise social approval or threaten social disapproval from a given reference group. Responsiveness to these social incentives partly depends upon the degree to which the person is motivated to be affiliated with the reference group. Personality differences may also give rise to differences in responsiveness to social appeals concerning group consensus and related social incentives" (p. 9).

Such social appeals may be more effective with field dependent audiences, assuming these audiences perceive the situation to be uncertain and perceive the reference group appealed from as possessing helpful information. Another variable, emotional/logical appeals, seems a likely candidate for field dependent-independent comparison. Studies assessing the relative effectiveness (for inducing attitude change) of emotional and logical appeals found either no difference (427) or that emotional appeals have greater impact (123). Available research warrants the tentative conclusion that field dependents are more persuaded by emotional and field independents by logical appeals. For example, Keiser (220) found the latter better able to overcome a verbal context, i.e., to isolate, analyze, and compare parts of discourse — certainly prerequisites for attending and processing logical appeals. Brilhart (53) lends weight to this prediction in her finding that field dependents are less able to perceive logical fallacy (see also 12). Greene's (169) finding that field dependents are the more disturbed by mismatches between the verbal and nonverbal components of the source/message, along with evidence regarding their greater social cue attentiveness and less emotional control, supports the conclusion that field dependents are likely to possess more of the skills essential to attending and processing emotional appeals. Therefore, Janis and Hovland's (206) suspicion that individual differences affect the degree to which a person would be influenced by rational or logical types of argument seems justifiable. A third type of appeal is humor. At least two studies (261, 278) found humor to not affect overall persuasiveness. Clearly, humor is socially facilitative; to the extent that it might increase perceived homophily, would not humor be an enhancer of persuasibility in field dependents? Perhaps the findings to date are an artifact of unrepresentative samples, and, with field dependent-independence as a moderator variable, distinct differences might emerge. Finally, we come to fear appeals. McGuire (270) argues that the higher the chronic anxiety level of the receiver, the less appeals to fear may be optimal. This conjecture is in line with Leventhal's (248) conclusion that low fear appeals are appropriate for those receivers who consider themselves relatively vulnerable to threat. All of this should be at least vaguely reminiscent of earlier descriptions of field dependent autonomic functioning (cf. P4). Accordingly, field independencts should be relatively more persuaded by moderate fear appeals overall.

Communication theorists have singled out many form characteristics of the message. The initial form variable to be considered here is organization —— that is, the extent to which the message is constructed as a unitary whole and proceeds in a coherent, temporal sequence. Are receivers different in their perceptions of the presence and/or necessity of structural sophistication in messages? The superior ability of field independents to provide structure to unstructured material and their relative preference to impose such structure respectively suggest that organizational schemes are least necessary for field independent receivers and that field independent persons would be more inclined to underestimate the presence of organizational structure (given their likely tendency to rearrange already organized material). On the other hand, the disposition of field dependents to leave a stimulus configuration "as is", suggests that, when confronted with such an audience, source concern for message organization is likely to reap a higher payoff. Another important form variable is sidedness of message. Studies by Lumsdaine and Janis (262) and Paulson (323) found one-sided and two-sided message strategies to be of equal effectiveness. However, Hovland, et. al. (196) detected an intelligence interaction effect. It is now generally agreed that one-sided messages are preferred both when inoculation is perceived as having low success-potential and when counter-argumentation is not expected to be forthcoming. A study by Wilner (440) fuels speculation that field independent receivers would be more capable of counter-arguing as well as more successful inoculees. Wilner discovered that field independents have more complex styles of attitude expression, that they can produce more reasons for a given attitude, and that they know more opposition arguments. It is therefore predicted that two-sided messages are more appropriate if receivers are relatively field independent. The decision to make one's conclusion explicit or implicit is also of consequence. A number of studies found explcit conclusions more effective overall (133, 179, 197, 272). However, Thislethwaite and Kamenetsky (408) noted that those few subjects who did succeed in arriving at the implicit conclusion were more persuaded. For several reasons it appears probable that field independent receivers would be more favorably predisposed to implicit conclusions than would field dependent receivers. The greater analytic capabilities of the former, coupled with their preference for imposing structure in ambiguous circumstances, should render them more likely to favor drawing their own conclusions. The next form variable is conclusion placement. Should it be situated at the beginning or end of the message (assuming that it is explicitly stated)? If one wishes to forestall counter-argument, it might be wise to state the conclusions last for relatively field independent audiences; and, given Wilner's (440) finding that field dependent subjects are quicker to state their own conclusion and are less willing to remain attentive to a relatively complex question, conclusion first might work better for field dependent receivers. Wilner's results are also consistent with the hypothesis that anti-climactic argument placement should be more appropriate for field dependent receivers (cf. 413). Incidentally, Wilner reported a related finding that field dependents usually gave their own best reason first. Yet another variable is message repetition. Available research suggests that persuasive messages should be comparatively more repetitive for field dependent receivers for reasons of comprehension (96) and identification (336, 348).

Applicability of the differentiation hypothesis to communication theory may extend to other intercultural and interpersonal communication domains as well. For example, in the realm of small group communication field dependence-independence may account for some of the variance in decision behavior, Armed with the prediction that field dependent persons will more often submerge themselves within a group (having a less articulated body concept, a weaker sense of separate identity, being more conforming and sensitive to social cues), Wallach, et. al. (424) confirmed the hypothesis that less psychologically differentiated groups engage in riskier decision making. They reasoned that, in group situations, field dependents are more likely to experience a lower sense of individual responsibility. Also, numerous studies, previously reviewed, point out the relative task-orientation of field independents and the corresponding social-orientation of field dependents. Festinger, et. al. (131) surmise that there are two classes of needs which group membership satisfy: (1) needs which require the singling out of the individual, and (2) needs whose satisfaction require being fused with the group. It seems likely that individuals high in psychological differentiation might more often perceive group association as satisfying the former needs, and vice versa. As for the role of argument in group decision, Burstein, et. al (60) found, using psychology students as subjects, that persuasive argumentation better explained group-induced shifts in individual choice than interpersonal comparison, Had they used a more heterogenous sample, or, better yet, employed field dependence-independence as a moderator variable, perhaps different results might have emerged (cf. C6b).

Witkin's theory may, in addition, predict individual differences in, among other things, initial interaction behavior and relational communication (cf. 29), nonverbal communication behavior (cf. 146, 147, 369, 405), the mediation of interpersonal attraction (103, 144, 205, 464), classroom communication behavior (338, 339, 455, 464), communication modality preferences (400, 441), and verbalization style (107, 208, 373).

Because the preceding discussion barely scratches the surface in unearthing communication hypotheses which appear to follow from differentiation theory, it should be clear that Witkin's construct has the potential of meeting the second criterion posed at the beginning of this chapter. If field dependence-independence accounts for variation across a broad range of communication domains then we may well begin the task of constructing a theory of cultural and/or personal communication style.

The sole methodological issue to be discussed here is one which directly addresses the significance issue. Most of the research concerning this variable has involved relatively homogenous groups of subjects. The literature is replete with ex post facto lamentations that perhaps true field dependent persons or groups were not included and that the subjects compared may have fallen from the middle to the field independent end of the "real world" distribution. Hence, many, if not most, of the statistical findings may be quite conservative. Conclusions regarding variance explained, drawn from correlation coefficients or strength of association tests, are likely, under these circumstances, to understate the impact of this individual difference variable. What is often encountered in this body of research is relatively greater maximization of systematic variance for the *active* (manipulable), independent variables, and less maximization of systematic variance for such *attribute*, independent variables as field dependence-independence. Perhaps this occurs because of the difficulty entailed in securing relatively heterogeneous subject samples. The study by Fleshler, et. al. (143) is a case in point. Their three-way analysis of variance, involving the active variables message documentation and source authoritativeness and the attribute variable field dependence-independence, found the former two variables to account for the bulk of variance explained. However, the nature of the levels of these variables may have considerably biased the results. It was not surprising that application of a strength of association test to their data revealed little explained variance associated with the individual difference variable. Future research can produce meaningful results only by testing more heterogeneous subject samples.

FOOTNOTES

[1] The present review does not include certain methodological issues, such as construct validity, reliability, etc. Such reviews are available elsewhere (7, 171, 247, 257, 258, 419, 420, 421, 423, 470, 471). Research seems to indicate acceptable construct validity and reliability. However, these issues are far from being definitively resolved.

[2] The distinction "organized" is vital, given evidence that these tasks tap a dimension other than simple distraction (213, 359).

[3] A few studies have confirmed the role of peer reinforcement as well (66, 202).

[4] This latter similarity is consonant with Ramirez and Castaneda's (339) observation that field dependent children learn animate material more easily than do field independent children.

[5] Because the relationship between physiological measures of overall anxiety and paper-and-pencil indices of "manifest" or "trait" anxiety is not known to this author, it is difficult to assess the importance of several studies which purport to refute this view of field dependent-independent autonomic functioning (61, 88, 259).

[6] However, the RFT, BAT, EFT testing situations, and the nature of the locus of control measure, may obscure an actual relationship. Tobacyk, et. al. (410) offer the view that "adjustment" (to preceived discrepancy between ideal and real self) moderates the field dependence-locus of control relationship. Discrepancy, either short-term (e.g., due to perceived RFT, BAT, or EFT performance) or longer-term (in one or more salient areas), may induce dissonance which is resolved in normally internal field independent persons by temporarily shifting to the external end of Rotter's paper-and-pencil continuum, thus converting a significant correlation to zero-order.

[7] Relabelling Rudin and Stagner's "stable self-definition" "transituational consistency," Campus (65) failed to find any difference between field dependent and field independent subjects in this dimension, and suggested that Witkin's sense of separate identity notion needed refinement. Witkin and Goodenough (460) have since offered that refinement, by reviewing a large number of studies which collectively suggest that field dependents rely on external frames of reference mainly in ambiguous circumstances. Since it is quite possible that the "situations" confronting field dependent and field independent subjects in Campus' study were largely unambiguous or certain (structured), her failure to replicate Rubin and Stagner's finding of individual differences in "transituational consistency" may be quite understandable.

[8] Kendon and Cook do not report the nature of the initial interactions that took place. They may well have been fairly automatic or ritualistic, and, therefore, might not have interfered overly with the hypothesized "background" internalizing.

[9] Evans (127), Guardo (178), and Wineman (442) failed to find this relationship. However, they employed mere representations of people or questionnaires involving "projected use of interpersonal distance."

[10] Should this prove to be the case, then a systematic theoretical explication of the role of intelligence in communicative behavior, conceptually similar to the present attempt, may be in order.

[11] See Witkin, et. al. (464) for a fuller explication of this issue.

NOTE: All numbers appearing in brackets throughout the Larson chapter refer to references appearing in an extensive appendix beginning on page 763. These references are provided in an attempt to give an overview of the existing, rich literature dealing with the individual aspects of human communication as they relate to our study of intercultural and international communication.

Yasumasa Tanaka:

Proliferating Technology and the Structure of Information-Space

---

Exploding Information for What

TO MANY contemporary Japanese, the concept of "Information-oriented Society," or "Knowledge-intensive Society," connotes a strong realization that they have reached a new stage of industrial development which is often called the "post-industrial" stage. This concept is a unique cross-product of both an earlier conception of "informationalization" which originally referred to the wide use of digital computers in Japanese society in the 1960's, and the theory of post-industrial society presented by a number of futurists in America and Japan at about the same time. It is maintained that an "information-oriented society" differs from any preceding stage of industrial society in that "information" is now as highly valued as energy and raw materials to constitute a base for the economic and industrial development of the nation.

In 1972, a study group organized by the Japanese Ministry of Posts and Telecommunications, working on the census of information distribution, published a very unique report entitled *Is Information Exploding?*[1] The purpose of this research was to provide basic statistics concerning production and consumption of information in Japanese society. Using the information theory, a·mathematical theory of communication, this group attempted to "estimate" the total amount of information generated in both the mass and personal communication systems in society and the total amount of information consumed by the public.

The working-group engineers used the "Bit" (binary digit) information measure[2] as the single uniform unit of *communication capacity,* in order to make the amounts of information transmitted and consumed compatible. A standard unit of communication capacity is needed because signals which convey information vary in forms (visual, audio, linguistic, or their combinations) from one communication system to another. By using this single standard measure, they estimated mathematically the total amount of information generated and distributed. They also estimated the total amount of information consumed by the public, by taking into consideration physiological and cognitive limitations of humans who receive information. When they compared the two estimates of generation and transmission of information and of consumption of information, they did indeed come up with an intriguing result. They took the 10-year period from 1960 to 1970, for example, and subsequently found that information supply increased by almost 400% during this period, whereas consumption increased only by 140%. It was clearly seen that the information industry at large is capable of multiplying their facilities, information processing and transmission apparata, thus bringing about exponential increase in the volume of information production and transmission. But such abundant information did not seem to be effectively consumed by the receiving public, probably because of limitations in time, chances of exposure, and the cognitive capacity of individual humans. The study showed that there is in fact an information explosion in Japanese society, but it also suggested that the Japanese are still incapable of coping with it, both physically and psychologically.

It is also worth mentioning that the same working group has developed a measure known as an "index of information orientation," which indicates quantitatively the degree of information orientation in a society. The index is comprised of four composite factors — that is, *the amount of information, the information equipment, the communication subjects,* and *a coefficient of information,* and each "factor" is constructed in the following way: First, the *amount of information* is actually represented by five discrete variables — i.e., the amount of mail sent per capita, the number of telephone calls made per capita, the number of newspapers circulated per 100 inhabitants, the number of books published over 10,000 inhabitants, and the population density. The second factor, *information equipment,* consists of three variables, such as the number of telephones, and color and black-and-white TV sets per 100 inhabitants, and the number of digital computers per 10,000 inhabitants. The third factor, the *communication subjects,* are measured by two variables, the ratio of the tertiary-industry workers in total working population and the number of university and college students per 100 inhabitants. The fourth and the last factor, a *coefficient of information,* is derived from a single scale — i.e., the ratio of miscellaneous expenditures in total personal consumption.

The index of information orientation can be used in various ways and has proved its tremendous usefulness. For examples, in the *White Paper on Communications for 1975,* published by the Ministry of Posts and Telecommunications in 1976, the growth of information orientation in Japanese society was clearly shown by this index.[3] For an 8-year period from 1965 to 1973, the figures of this index increased at an average annual ratio of 10% each year, which is almost equivalent to the increase in the net GNP of Japan for the same period. Japan's information orientation thus clearly appears to be rapid and real, has almost doubled for the past eight years. Hence, we do not have any reason to believe that any sudden "dip" in this trend will occur as we approach the next decade.

Using the same index, it is also possible to make cross-national comparisons. For instance, the *1975 White Paper* also reported that in a 5-nation comparison involving Japan, the U.S.A., England, France, and West Germany, Japan was found to rank at the bottom of the composite scale with an index score of 100, while she ran up to the second in 1975 with an index score of 242, next only to the U.S.A. — another indication that Japan's growth in information orientation has been fast and remarkable for the past eight years. Table 1 shown below displays summary statistics comparing the relative degree of growth of these five developed nations. It can be clearly seen that in 1965 the United States is a lone "information" super-state, very far ahead of the rest; when Japan was at the bottom of the scale with an index score of 100, the United States was on top with 242, followed by England whose index score was 117, while in 1975 the United States was again on top with a score of 531, followed by Japan with only 242. The gap between the leader and the runner-up appears insurmountable.

Table 1. Indices of Information Orientation: A Five-Nation
Comparison

Country	Year	Indices of Information Orientation
Japan	1965	[100]
	1973	221
U.S.A.	1965	242
	1973	531
England	1965	117
	1973	209
France	1965	110
	1973	210
West Germany	1965	104
	1973	211

Quoted from the *White Paper on Communications for 1975,* pp. 30-31.

Turning now to problems of a more domestic nature, the question arises as to which of the four factors previously mentioned — *the amount of information, the information equipment, the communication subjects, and the coefficient of information* — has contributed most significantly to the emergence and growth of an information-oriented society in Japan. Once again, the relevant data can be found in the *1975 White Paper.* It is reported that, for the 4-year period from 1970 to 1974, information orientation in Japanese society has significantly increased from a factor of 100 to 122. It was also noted that more than 70% of the increase was accounted for by a single factor, *information equipment,* which includes telephones, TV sets, and computers. *Communication subjects* (the tertiary-industry workers and students), *amount of information* (mail, telephone calls, newspapers and books, population density), the *coefficient of information* (miscellaneous expenditures) has contributed to the increase by only 19%, 5% and 3%, respectively.

On the basis of these statistics, it appears that the rapid growth of the information-oriented society in Japan has been made possible almost exclusively by the tremendous increase in the number of telephones, TV sets, and computers, and while the contribution of the remaining three factors is also present, it is only nominal. It appears clear that "equipment" hardware dominates in Japanese information-oriented society. And so we may understand the reason behind the substantial expansion as well as gigantic buildup of these three information-producing and information-transmitting electronic media in Japan. It is also noteworthy that this trend is not unique to this country, but appears throughout the world. The same trend can clearly be found in the United States, England, France, and West Germany.

In summary, we have thus far seen two separate phenomena in contemporary Japanese society. First, we noted that there is a clear tendency for more information to be generated and transmitted in society than can be effectively consumed by the people. Secondly, we also observed that the significant growth of information orientation in Japan is attributable to the rapid increase of what is termed *information equipment* –– telephones, TV's and computers. It can be generally stated, therefore, that the growth of an information-oriented society in Japan is attributable in the main to the growth of what may be termed the "information industry"–the manufacturers of various *electronic* information equipment.

So far so good. Internationally, Japan is the first runner-up, second only to the U.S.A., with respect to its information orientation. Domestically, Japan is an information-rich and information-affluent society in which a gigantic amount of information is produced to give the people abundant opportunities for the wider use as well as a greater choice of information. Thus far, we have received every blessing of the progress in information engineering and large capital investment in the information industry. A rosy image of the maturing information-oriented society appears true and real, until we realize that we know very little about the impact of information technology upon the populace, or how it affects the people's minds. In other words, we have accumulated fairly satisfactory, quantitative knowledge by means of statistical analyses or economic predictions about what an information-oriented society is and will be like in the future. We have come to realize, however, that "subjective" or "human" aspects of information orientation are still to be explored. For example, we do not know how the abundance of information is related to amelioration of the quality of life in an information-affluent society. We do not know whether or how both freedom and equality can be maintained in a "democratic" information-rich society, if we are to avoid the institution of discrimination between the *information-rich* and the *information-poor* classes. In this connection, we do not know, either, whether an information-rich society is merely a linear extention of materialism upon which most capitalistic societies have been built.

These are difficult questions to answer, since no ready-made answer seems available. But they are a true challenge to the social and behavioral scientists interested in the interface between technology and society. In the following sections, the present writer will attempt to deal with some "subjective" or "humanistic" aspects of "information-processing" by taking the proliferating nuclear technology as an example.

Subjective Culture and an Information-Space for Nuclear Power

Culture has been defined as the man-made part of human environment,[4] and divided into two distinct subsystems: *objective* culture and *subjective* culture. The distinction between the two "cultures" is derived from the observed interaction between humans and their environment. By definition, *objective* culture is comprised of artifacts and technology that produces them (e.g., tools, habitations, modes of transport, paintings, buildings, and so on) and observable human activities (e.g., behavioral norms, interpersonal roles, child-rearing practices, institutional structures, social and legal prescriptions, etc.). *Subjective* culture, on the other hand, consists of human cognitive processes (e.g., values, stereotypes, attitudes, feelings, motivations, beliefs, and most generally, meanings).[5]

This distinction between *objective* and *subjective* cultures seems to correspond to what has been referred to as "material" and "non-material" traits by anthropologists, and further to parallel a distinction made by Ward Goodenough:[6]

"We have . . . two kinds of culture: culture 1, the
recurring patterns which characterize a community as a
homeostatic system, and culture 2, people's standards for
perceiving, judging, and acting. Culture 1, moreover, is an
artifact or product of the human use of culture 2 . . .
(I)ndividuals can be said to possess culture 2 but not culture 1,
which is the property of a community as a social-ecological
system."

Historically, over time and space, societies have striven to create
an environment that provides safety and satisfaction for the people
in them. With respect to the degree of dependence of society upon
culture, however, all individuals begin to learn in their subjective
culture. They learn, for instance, what is safe, and how safe is safe
enough. They also learn what "signs" represent safety (or danger) by
what linguists and psychologists call the symbolic process. When they
encounter dangerous objects or signs, they learn how to avoid them.
Thus it is in this subjective-culture domain where individuals
gradually learn to perceive and construct a complicated environment
in such a way that their fears can be reduced. Fear of destruction by
natural forces, for instance, is one of the major determinants that
accounts for the psychological need to visualize and construct a
world in which one can feel secure —— a world in which one can
expect a longer life span, better health, and greater happiness.

In the subjective culture of many highly industrialized societies,
science and technology have been perceived as a valuable means by
which these societies can achieve material wealth, national strength
and personal happiness. It should be recognized that both science
and technology have indeed served to reduce excessive labor and a
number of human miseries, such as illness and poverty, thereby
making the world a safer place to live in. Since the early 1960's,
however, there has been a growing awareness in these highly
industrial societies that both mass production and the consumption
of goods and services, which have hitherto symbolized the prestige of
advanced nations, do not always bring about an appropriate
improvement in values —— that is, a commensurate increase in the
happiness of the people. On the contrary, both mass production and
consumption have been found to cause new nuisances, such as safety

and health hazards, complicated environmental disruptions, mental health problems, infringement on the right of privacy, and pathological changes in society. It now seems clear that in most advanced nations the fundamental value of science and technology to society is being seriously questioned. With the expansion of techno-scientific systems, negative side effects which detract from economic and social benefits, have thus come to receive more public attention.

It should be recalled here that technology and science, be they primitive or advanced, are products of the human use of subjective culture. This re-examination of the value and role of science and technology to society seems to suggest that some basic changes are taking place in the subjective culture of advanced nations, such as the United States and Japan. In the subjective culture of these countries, the psycho-historical pendulum of societal values seems to be swinging to the opposite direction after having reached the extreme end of the pole —— that is, changes in the unquestioned faith in science and technology first occur in the value orientation in the minds of the people.

In this connection, it is worth noting that the newly emerged interface of technology and society has become the subject of scientific investigation by social and behavioral scientists. Referring to the role of social and behavioral scientists in what has been known as the nuclear power controversy, the psychiatrist Pahner, for example, observes the following:[7]

> The task of the socio-behavioral scientist is to provide continuing information and insights regarding the impact of technology on man's health and well-being. It may even be that he will have to assume a more active role in confronting those aspects of the technological environment that threaten individual and societal well-being.

The nuclear power controversy is an ongoing public debate between those who promote and those who oppose nuclear power with regard to a number of techno-societal issues, such as safety standards, health hazards, economic rentability, risks related to accidents, and so forth, which are "controversial" in the sense that the conflicting interpretations of assumptions, facts, theories, and the likely future consequences of nuclear development are debated by the opposing parties. It cuts across national and cultural boundaries —— it goes on in the United States, Japan, West Germany, France and Sweden. It also cuts across societal strata within a society —— it involves conflicts among professional scientists and technocrats, businessmen and economists, and the public at large, male and female, young and old. And, as Haefle observes, it has gradually become clear that the nuclear power debate "embeds into the sociosphere," which means that the nuclear power issue is no longer a problem of pure technology and science but it has become a serious socio-political issue of the day.[8]

Both the proliferation and the societal adoption of nuclear technology seem to bring about a number of non-technological problems. For example, it has been pointed out that risk-benefit analysis, a rational means of examining the balance between risks and benefits accruing from introduction of new technology, is more often than not so superficial and over-optimistic about long-term consequences of the use of atomic power, that it fosters criticism and opposition even among potential supporters of atomic power. It often seems true that the potential perils of large-scale man-made systems (such as wars, governments, big businesses, dictatorships, technology, etc.) are neglected in these risk-benefit analyses, making their results appear either too rosy to be true or too unrealistic to believe. As one behavioral scientist remarked, "such a rational probabilistic assessment of risk in an issue as apparently anxiety-provoking as the nuclear energy debate does not necessarily reduce public concern . . . (T)he risk-benefit methodology fails to consider conceptual differences in how risks are perceived by the public and by those compiling such statistics."[9]

Keeping this basic realization of differences in perception in mind, an extensive interdisciplinary investigation was carried out under the direction of the present writer, between 1975 and 1977 both in Tokyo and at a nuclear-power-plant site which is hereafter anonymously called Town-H, in order to examine the interface of technology and society in atomic power development. The basic purpose of this research was two-fold: (1) to examine the socio-political dynamics of the opposition to atomic power, and (2)

Table 2. Major Hypotheses Derived from the Notion of "Information-Space"

Major Hypothesis -formulation	Major Approaches
1. Intensity of fear of nuclear power plants as a function of the distance from a nuclear power plant	a. Communication research in general
2. Frequency and modes of exposure to nuclear power plants and related cognitive events	b. Quantitative social psychological experimentation
3. The structure of communication systems which transmit information concerning nuclear power plants and related cognitive events	c. General semantics and rhetoric
4. Effects of communication concerning nuclear power plants and related cognitive events	

to learn if there is a consistency of attitudes held by the Japanese toward atomic power and related cognitive events.

What is termed the "structure of 'information-space' regarding nuclear matters" is most relevant to the above-mentioned problems, for it deals with the psycho-social dynamics of attitude formation and change as the result of various types of communication concerning nuclear matters. The notion of an "information-space" which is now in wide use in Japan among proponents of an information-oriented and knowledge-intensive society, is *four-dimensional* in the sense that it is a space for production, transmission, distribution, storage, and retrieval of information by men over *time* and *space*. In abstraction, an information-space can be considered as the integral whole of what might be called "information experience" of all kinds accumulated in a society as well as the individuals in it. A conversation is a form of information experience, as is reading, watching or listening, and so are war, revolution, famine, and an atom bomb, which is experienced either directly or indirectly via signs and symbols. In other words, an information-space is considered to contain information, various hardware and software information systems dealing with information, and, above all, *people's emotions either synchronically or diachronically evoked by information.* Therefore, a nation and a culture may have its own unique "information-space," and so may a community and individuals.

Using this notion of "information-space," the following hypotheses were formulated in our research, as shown in Table 2:

(1) Intensity of fear of nuclear power plants may vary as a function of the distance from an atomic power plant,

(2) Frequency and modes of exposure to nuclear power plants as cognitive objects and other related cognitive events may affect attitudes toward atomic power,

(3) The structure of communication systems which transmit information concerning atomic power plants and related cognitive events may affect attitudes toward atomic power.

In order to test these hypotheses, the actual field research was carried out in Tokyo in January, 1976, and in Town-H in November of the same year. Tokyo which is both highly urbanized and highly knowledge-intensive was selected as a "control" location, while two considerations dictated the selection of Town-H —— that an atomic power plant has already been in operation and that no violent opposition to the atomic power plant has occurred in the town. Regardless of the absence of violent opposition, however, it was predicted that a high level of anxiety might be present toward the atomic power plant located nearby, even if such anxiety might not always be explicit. A two-stage stratified sampling method was used uniformly in both locations and a total of 514 samples in Tokyo and 871 samples in Town-H constituted the respondents in our field research.

In connection with the Town-H survey, the distance factor was taken into account as one of the major variables in the present research —— the distance from the atomic power plant in operation. Consequently, the whole target area was divided into three areas differing in distance from the atomic power plant in question in the following way:

Area 1 = Town-H itself where an atomic power plant is in
operation (N=319)

Area 2 = The four towns ajoining Area 1 (N=320)

Area 3 = The towns and villages outside Area 2 (hence outside
Area 1 as well) and within 25km from the atomic power
plant (N=232)

All data for both Tokyo and Town-H were collected by using
the interview method on the basis of a prepared questionnaire.
Despite the highly technical and controversial nature of the
questions, rejection rates were extremely low –– about 8% in Tokyo
and about 2% in Town-H.

Attitudinal Differentiation as a Function of Distance

First, the obtained data was submitted to a kind of multivariate
analysis derived by Chikio Hayashi and known among Japanese social
and behavioral scientist as Hayashi's Quantification Analysis
Category III.[10] The method is similar to factor analysis with respect
to its purpose but unique in that it is in principle applicable to survey
data for which normality can not be assumed. It must be recalled
that the factor analytic method can be applied only to that data
produced by interval scales. On the other hand, Hayashi's method
can be applied to data produced by nominal scales.

Using this method, all the survey data variables were put into a
hyperplane and two orthogonal "axes" were found to be most
salient, each accounting for a large amount of the variance. The first
axis may be identified as relating to "COGNITION" for it is defined
by those question-category variables which are primarily concerned
with the amount and the content of "knowledge" possessed by the
respondents concerning nuclear matters, while the second axis may
be identifiable as "ACCEPTANCE," for it is defined by those
question-category variables which are directly related to affective
evaluation and hence acceptance of nuclear power plants and related
events. Basically, the same results appeared in the Tokyo data as
well.

Thus, we have an indication that "COGNITION" and
affect-laden "ACCEPTANCE" are the two most salient dimensions in
judging nuclear power plants and other associated nuclear matters.

FIGURE 1. Allocation of "Marker" Question Categories in a Two-Dimensional, Cognition-Acceptance Space for the Town-H

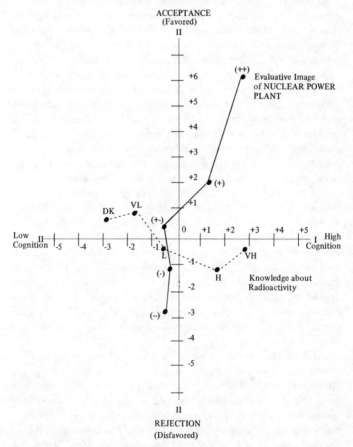

Note: These (++) (+) (+-) (-) (--) signs indicate *very safe and pleasant, slightly safe and pleasant, neutral, slightly dangerous and unpleasant,* and *very dangerous and unpleasant,* respectevely. VH, H, L, VL, and DK mean *very high, high, low,* and *very low* cognition, and *Don't Know,* respectively.

However, this is not necessarily a novel discovery, for these results are consistent with the contemporary attitude theory in that, it is assumed, attitudes consist of three components — i.e., *cognitive, affective* and *conative.*[11] In compliance with this attitude theory, two "marker" question-categories had already been included in the questionnaire for both Tokyo and Town-H — that is, the ratings of NUCLEAR POWER PLANT on Semantic Differential *evaluative* scales (*pleasant-unpleasant* and *safe-dangerous*), for the *affect,*[12] and the question-item concerning the amount of objective knowledge about radioactivity, for the *cognition.* When analyzed by the multivariate method, these two "markers" were expected to produce a clue useful for both interpreting and naming the extracted axes. The relative relations of these two "marker" variables to the respective axes are displayed in Figure 1, by allocating each question category in the two-dimensional space defined by both axes. It is clearly seen that the first axis, "COGNITION," is in fact defined by the varying degrees of "KNOWLEDGE ABOUT RADIOACTIVITY," whereas the second axis, ACCEPTANCE, is defined by the "EVALUATIVE IMAGE OF NUCLEAR POWER PLANT" which varies from very *safe and pleasant* to very *dangerous and unpleasant.* We have thus obtained two independent axes of COGNITION and ACCEPTANCE, and this suggests that there is no mutually dependent relation between the two — that is, *contrary to common-sense speculation, knowing more about atomic power plants and other nuclear matters had nothing to do with their acceptance.*

In this conjunction, we are also interested in knowing how the distance factor may affect the attitudes. It can be speculated that the "information-space" of Area 1 — that is, the town where a nuclear power plant is in operation — should be saturated with both direct and indirect "information experience" concerning the nuclear power plant and hence "cognition" in Area 1 should be higher than that in Areas 2 and 3, and in Tokyo. In other words, it is likely that "cognition" should interact with distance. On the other hand, the interaction between "acceptance" and distance seems to be more complex, probably contingent upon the nature of each specific question category. In order to examine the two-way interaction of distance with both "cognition" and "acceptance," Figure 2 was constructed on the basis of a separate quantification analysis for each location.

Figure 2. Distance from a Nuclear Power Plant and Attitudinal Differentiation

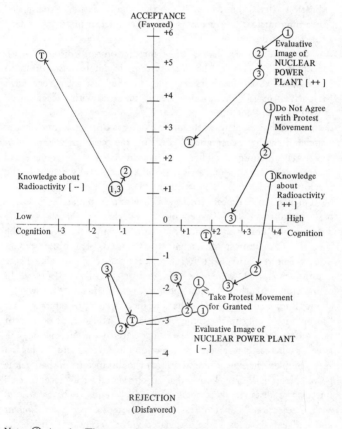

Note: ① Area 1 (The town where a nuclear power plant is in operation)
② Area 2 (The four towns adjoining to Area 1)
③ Area 3 (The towns and villages outside Area 2 and within 25km of a nuclear power plant)
T Tokyo

First, it seems clear in Figure 2 that the distance does indeed interact with "cognition" in nearly every case. Within each question category, Area 1 is almost always found to be closer to the positive end of the first axis, COGNITION, whereas Tokyo is nearly always found to be closer to the negative end of the same axis —— a clear indication that "knowledge" or the "information experience" concerning nuclear power plants and other nuclear matters is indeed a function of distance.

On the other hand, the interaction of distance with "acceptance" seems to be less systematic, more susceptible to case-by-case variation. For example, in the case of "Very High Evaluative Image," the distance clearly interacts with "acceptance" as well as with "cognition" —— that is, the shorter the distance from the nuclear power plant is, the more closely is this (*very good*) image associated with "acceptance." But in the case of "Very Low Evaluative Image," the interaction between distance and "acceptance" is not seen as clearly and systematically as was in the previous case. Next, the attitude, "Do not agree with Protest Movements," also appears to show a clear and systematic interaction between distance and "acceptance" —— that is, the shorter the distance, the closer the association with "acceptance," while in the case of "Take Protest Movements for Granted," the distance does not seem to interact with "acceptance" at all. These question-categories were not included in the Tokyo survey. In connection with the question category, *very sufficient* "Knowledge about Radioactivity" [++], the distance seems to interact with "acceptance" only in the three Town-H groups. Here, possession of very sufficient knowledge is clearly associated with "acceptance" in Area 1, whereas it is related to "rejection" in Areas 2 and 3. This is a very complex three-way interaction. If the distance from the nuclear power plants is short, "knowledge" is correlated with "acceptance." But as the distance increase, "knowledge" tends to be associated with "rejection." In contrast, possession of *very insufficient* knowledge [- -] tends to be associated with "acceptance" in all the "distance" groups. In both *very sufficient* [++] and *very insufficient* [- -] cases, Tokyo, which, both in reality and in terms of cognitive information experience, is most distant from the nuclear power plant site, tends to perceive the nuclear power plant more favorably than all the three Town-H groups.

All these observations seem to indicate that distance does interact with "cognition" in these cases. On the other hand, the interaction between distance and "acceptance" is more complex, and there is probably no linear relation between the two. This can be clearly seen in Figure 2. Note that, for "acceptance," the two "highest-category-score" question-items are the *very good* "Evaluative Image of a Nuclear Power Plant [++]" of the Area-1 group and the *very insufficient* "Knowledge about Radioactivity [- -]" of the Tokyo group. In other words, it appears as though maximum acceptance could be obtained *both* in the group *closest* to the nuclear power plant if it has an extremely good image of the nuclear power plant *and* in the group geographically and psychologically *remotest* from the nuclear power plant if it has very little knowledge of the nuclear matters!

Predicting the Acceptance of Atomic Power

The same data obtained from the Town-H research was also submitted to Hayashi's *Quantification Analysis Category-II analysis*.[13] This method is similar to *multiple regression analysis* but differs in that it is applicable to survey data. Like multiple regression analysis, this method can be used to predict a dependent variable called "external criterion" from various independent variables. In our case, the question variable, *"How do you feel about the atomic power plant in Town-H?"*, and its response categories "very much satisfied," "satisfied," "unsatisfied," and "very much unsatisfied," etc., were used as "external criterion" to predict "acceptance" and "opposition" from other psychological and non-psychological variables. The results of this analysis are shown in Table 3.

Partial correlation in the table shows the degree of contribution to which each variable discriminates between "acceptance" and "opposition," and the ten most salient variables are shown in order of degree of such contribution. In this connection, the attitude toward "safety control performance of nuclear power plants" was found to be the best predictor of either "acceptance" or "rejection" of atomic power plants. If the respondents feel the safety control performance" is *satisfactory,* they tend to "accept" nuclear power

Table 3. Ten Most Salient Attitudinal Variables Contributing to Nuclear Power Plant Acceptance

Question Items	Partial Correlations	Acceptance	Rejection
1. Safety control performance of nuclear power plants	.26	satisfactory	unsatisfactory
2. Examination of safety measures by nuclear power plants	.18	satisfactory	unsatisfactory
3. Actual distance from nuclear power plants	.18	Area 3	Area 1 and 2
4. Preferred means of electric power generation in 10 years from now	.15	hydro-steam-nuclear hydro-steam	hydro-steam-solar-geothermal
5. Political party identification	.12	New Liberal Club, Social Democratic Party, Komeito	Japan Socialist Party Liberal Democratic Party
6. Liability in case of an accident	.12	vis major	local governments, or electric companies
7. Choice between industrial development and conservation of Nature	.11	industrial development	conservation of Nature

Table 3 Cont'd. Ten Most Salient Attitudinal Variables Contributing to Nuclear Power Plant Acceptance

Question Items	Partial Correlations	Acceptance	Rejection
8. Exposure to nuclear power plants	.10	have already seen nuclear power plants	do not want to see nuclear power plants
9. Major supply of electricity in Japan	.09	steam or nuclear	hydro
10. Previous knowledge of solar and geothermal energy applicable for electric power generation	.09	yes	no

plants, while if they see the same as unsatisfactory, they tend to "reject" nuclear power plants. In this analysis, it is remarkable to note that the two best predictors are those "psychological" variables both relating to "*safety*" of atomic power plant facilities, followed by "*distance*" from the actual atomic power plant (this can be expected from the preceeding analysis), the perception of "preferred means of future electric power generation" and the "political party identification." It is particularly interesting to note that opponents of atomic power feel the option of "hydro-steam-solar-geothermal" energy to be most desirable. This option made by residents of a small town in Japan seems to be consistent with the current world-wide argument that more effort should be made to develop solar and geothermal energy instead of atomic power. It is also worth noting that political party identification also affects "acceptance-rejection" discrimination. Strange as it may seem, supporters of both the conservative Liberal Democratic Party (LDP) now in power and one of its strongest oppositions, the Japanese Socialist Party (JSP) are against atomic power, probably because they both have many vested interests in the community and hence their *status-quo* orientation is high despite obvious ideological differences.

Finally, Table 4 shows the same analysis made with regard to exposure to communication media. It can be clearly seen in the table that, in Area 1, exposure and non-exposure to the communication media do not discriminate between "*acceptance*" or "*rejection*" of the atomic power plant by the respondents. In Area 1, there is a tendency for both the readers of the electric company's P.R. bulletin and the newspapers to be even more inclined toward opposition than are non-readers. However, this seems to be a phenomenon unique only to Area 1, because in Areas 2 and 3, exposure to communication media in most cases tends to be associated with more favorable attitudes. One way of explaining these complicated phenomena is that opposition in Area 1 reads the bulletin and newspapers because of its strong motives to oppose. It needs information to oppose the atomic power plant. The foregoing analysis clearly shows that the communication media do in fact supply needed information to the opposition.

Table 4. Nuclear Acceptance and Communications Exposure

	Town P.R. bulletin		Electric Co. P.R. bulletin		Newspaper		TV		Total
	Yes	No	Yes	No	Yes	No	Yes	No	
Area 1	−.29	−.30	−.32	−.26	−.37	−.25	−.30	−.29	−.29
Area 2	−.12	−.15	+.19	−.32	−.14	−.14	−.17	−.12	−.14
Area 3	−	−	+.89	+.51	+.61	+.57	+.61	+.57	+.60

Note: Figures are in mean category scores concerning "Acceptance" and "Rejection." Minus (−) and plus (+) signs indicate *rejection* and *acceptance* of nuclear power plants, respectively.

It must be recalled at this point that Marshall McLuhan once stated that "the medium is the message."[14] The most powerful medium in the present case is the nuclear power plant itself, as it emits fear-evoking "signals" in the everyday information experience among the Area-1 residents. Those Area-1 residents are constantly exposed to "the message" signifying the potential danger of accidents, for any man-made system is fallible no matter how negligibly small the probability of a lethal hazard may be. It is quite natural, therefore, that these people feel as if they are sitting on the top of a sleeping volcano. If these people were to be converted, it would not be through words, but by the "deeds" of the nuclear power plant itself, which are to be accumulated over a considerable length of time –– such as continued safe operation without accident for twenty years. Yet, this would conversely increase the probability of actual accident.

On the basis of our findings, it appears safe to conclude that the role of communications media in nuclear matters is limited. Communication media are certainly extremely useful as a source of information. They might also be able to change the attitude of "bystanders," such as the populace in Area 3, in a more favorable direction. But it is questionable whether they can psychologically reduce the intensity of opposition among those committed to opposition –– that is, those who are constantly exposed to the nuclear power plant itself and determined to oppose.

Summary and Conclusions

First, Japan's position as an advanced information-oriented society was examined by means of a statistical operation termed "the index of information orientation." This index developed by a group of Japanese engineers takes into account (1) *amount of information,* (2) *Information equipment,* (3) *communication subjects,* and (4) *a coefficient of information,* and is considered to represent quantitatively the degree of information orientation in a society at large. Using this composite index, Japan was compared with the U.S.A., England, France and West Germany with respect to the relative degree of information orientation. For an 8-year period from 1965 to 1973, Japan's information orientation was found to have progressed very rapidly from the bottom ranks to a position second only to the U.S.A., although the gap between the U.S.A. and Japan still appeared insurmountable in 1973. The major reason for this rapid progress in information orientation appears to have been the tremendous increase in *information equipment* — i.e., the number of telephones, TV sets and computers. While the contribution of *communication subjects, amount of information* and *the coefficient of information* was present, it was only nominal. It was also pointed out that more information is generated and disseminated in Japanese society than can be effectively consumed by the people. It is apparent that there is a tendency for information overproduction. This can be taken as the logical consequence of the rapid increase in information equipment. Information orientation, then, can be regarded as nothing more than a component of the man-made environment — that is, the product of what is termed *subjective culture.*

Turning now to the second problem area, the problems of nuclear technology proliferation were discussed, based upon an empirical study carried out in Japan. Whether or how the Japanese may accept atomic power plants in Japan was briefly illustrated as an example of the interface between technology and society — or that between objective and subjective cultures. A unique communication variable termed "information-space" was taken into account in this analysis. With respect to attitude organization, the result of a multivariate analysis clearly showed both "cognition" and affect-laden "acceptance" as being the most salient, and mutually independent dimensions of attitudes regarding nuclear matters, as might be expected from the attitude theory. It seems appropriate to state that the information experience of respondents is indeed multi-dimensional, defined by *time* and *space* and by *psychological* factors such as *cognition* and *affect.*

As for the problem of space, the distance from the atomic power plant was found to discriminate between "acceptance" and "rejection" of the atomic power plant. The shorter the distance from the atomic power plant, the stronger opposition tends to become. No matter how implicitly the threat may be felt, fears are evoked by the presence of the atomic power plant itself in those living close to it. Also related to the distance factor is exposure to communication media. It was found that exposure and non-exposure do not clearly distinguish between "acceptance" and "rejection" of the atomic power plant in Areas 1 and 2, while exposure is apparently correlated with "acceptance" in Area 3. Particularly in Area 1 which is most closely located to the atomic power plant site, a greater exposure to the electric company's P.R. bulletin and newspapers tends to be more closely associated with opposition. This unexpected finding suggests that while persuasive communications to promote the public acceptance do in fact reach the audience, both in favor and in opposition, it does not change opposition's attitude in a favorable direction, but it serves to give "information" to the opposition. The opposition needs information, so it reads more bulletins and newspapers. With this condition, persuasive communications cannot be effective; communications cannot exert much influence upon those who are committed to opposition.

In summary, what was described here is a brief illustration of an information-space in which complex interactions among *time, space* and *humans* take place. We have come to realize that information involves all kinds of perceptual input to humans, such as linguistic and non-linguistic signs and symbols, and things themselves, as the vehicle of information. But how information is perceived, understood, or interpreted, is dependent upon the structure of the information-space. It is hoped that this illustration also served for the understanding of the complex interface between technology (objective culture) and the humans (subjective culture) who produce it.

On the whole, it is symbolic that the United States is about a decade ahead of Japan with respect to the degree of information orientation. The United States is both a material-rich and information-rich society. It is also a dynamic society. But many serious problems still remain in the United States. Polls show that only a small portion of the populace at large are interested in domestic politics and international affairs. Statistics also tells us that crime rates are going up, and there is even a new type of crime — computer crimes committed by some irresponsible computer technicians. The economy is slowing down while the environmentalists are determined to oppose atomic power. Hundreds and thousands of Ph.D.'s are out of jobs. One might ask whether this is the future shape of post-industrial, information-oriented society.

What is an information-oriented society? Thus, we have come back to the beginning of a circle. It was shown in the beginning of this report that an information-oriented society is a type of society in which *information equipment* dominates. It is a man-made, machine society. As an extention of highly industrialized society, it has all the attributes of a materialistic society which is excessively oriented toward technology and quantity rather than toward humanity and quality. It should be recalled that the term "information" itself has come to be used as an engineering term (certainly not a poetical term) and at the same time connotes quantity grammatically through its function as a material noun: i.e., an uncountable mass of matter. *Information* theory in fact is a mathematical theory of communication which deals exclusively with calculating the amount of information transmitted. It by no means takes into account the *content* nor the *meaning* of information.

With respect to the content and meaning of information, it is obvious, for example, that there is a great difference between ACTUALLY SITTING ON THE TOP OF A SLEEPING VOLCANO and simply reading about it in a book or in the newspaper. These two are entirely different information experiences, both in cognition and in affect. To put it in another way, actually *sitting on the top of a sleeping volcano* could have a real "active" effect on one's existence — i.e., should the volcano erupt, such information would motivate one to rapid action. However, merely reading about the act, or about such an eruption, has no tangible effect upon one's concrete experience — i.e., one merely accepts the fact "passively." Hence, when considering the risks of an information-abundant society, the nature of the information itself should be taken into account. "Passive" information does not merely have a neutral, "narcotizing" effect on its receiver but it has a "negative" affect on his cognitive space, for it prevents the registration of "active" information on this space — information which the receiver can actually use in his immediate environment and which would accordingly have some effect on his existence and the existence of those around him.

Information disseminated by the electric companies controlling the nuclear power plants is immediately related to this problem. The electric companies intend such information to be "passive information" which will "narcotize" the receiver into inaction. And yet, it is received as "active" information by opponents of the nuclear power plants residing in the immediate vicinity of the plants. Hence the best possible active strategy that the electric companies could take would be to disseminate "passive" information about everything *except* nuclear power in the vicinity of the power plants. For example, if the nearby residents were concerned with a forthcoming local festival or a performance of popular singers, they would have neither time nor energy to protest against the power plant.

A society rich in "passive" information is a society in which the passive symbolic experience is in fact dominant, and it will become a weak, vulnerable society, because the people will become incapable of coping with real matters and handling real situations effectively. Information may be abundant, but it is only "active" information which activates people to action. The potential risk of a society rich in "passive" information has already been suggested in what is known as the "narcotizing dysfunction" hypothesis which was first presented by Paul Lazarsfeld and Robert Merton almost three decades ago.[15] This hypothesis states that if individuals are over-exposed to communication, they tend to be satisfied with their "passive" substitute experience, be alienated from reality, and become incapable of taking action toward important social issues. We should note that this hypothesis is concerned solely with what is here referred to as "passive" information — i.e., information which has no relation to the people's actual existence. "Active" information, however, can motivate the people and effect a tangible change in their lives and the lives of those around them.

The Japanese have much to learn from the American experience with respect to both the blessings and the miseries of an information-oriented society, its advantages as well as disadvantages. At the same time, both Americans and the Japanese have many problems in common — to fight against poverty and illness, to promote the human rights, and above all, to strive for the greatest happiness of the greatest number. Hence, it should be clear that information sources and content should be oriented more towards such critical problems facing mankind, and in such a way that can maximize response on the part of the receiver, and at the same time the dissemination of "passive" information should be discouraged for the good of all.

FOOTNOTES

[1] Ministry of Posts and Telecommunications, 1972, *Is Information Exploding? (Jōhō wa bakuhatsu shite iruka).* A Ministry of Posts and Telecommunications Report, Tokyo, Japan, (text in Japanese).

[2] Shannon, C.E., 1949, "The Mathematical Theory of Communication," in C.E. Shannon and W.Weaver, *The Mathematical Theory of Communication,* Urbana, Ill.: University of Illinois Press.

[3] Ministry of Posts and Telecommunications, 1976, *The White Paper on Communications for 1975 (Shōwa 50 nendoban, Tsūshin Hakusho),* Tokyo, Ministry of Finance Printing Office, (text in Japanese).

[4] Herskovitz, M.J., 1955, *Cultural Anthropology,* New York: Knopf.

[5] Osgood, C.E., May, W.H., and Miron, M.S., 1975, *Cross-Cultural Universals of Affective Meaning,* Urbana, Ill.: University of Illinois Press.

[6] Goodenough, W., 1961, "Comments on Cultural Evolution," *Daedalus,* 90; pp. 521-528.

[7] Pahner, P.D., 1976, *A Psychological Perspective of the Nuclear Energy Controversy,* RM-76-67, Laxemburg, Austria: International Institute for Applied System Analysis.

[8] Haefle, W., 1974, *Hypotheticality and the New Challenges: The Pathfinder Role of Nuclear Energy,* Minerva, 10(3), pp. 302-322.

[9] Pahner, op. cit.

[10] Hayashi, C., and Suzuki, T., 1975, "Quantitative Approach to a Cross-Societal Research: A Comparative Study of Japanese Character, I & II," *Annals of the Institute of Statistical Mathematics,* (Tokyo), 26(3): pp. 455-516 and 27(1): pp. 1-32.

[11] McGuire, W.J., 1969, "The Nature of Attitudes and Attitude Change," in G. Linzey and E. Aronson, eds., *The Handbook of Social Psychology,* second edition, vol. 3, pp. 136-314.

[12] Osgood, C.E., Suci, G.J., and Tannenbaum, P.H., 1957, *The Measurement of Meaning,* Urbana, Ill.: University of Illinois Press.

[13] Hayashi, C., 1952, "On the Prediction of Phenomena from Qualitative Data and the Quantification of Qualitative Data from the Mathematico-Statistical Point of View," *Annals of the Institute of Statistical Mathematics* (Tokyo), 3(2): 69-98. Also, Hayashi, C., 1954, "Multi-dimensional Quantification —— With the Applications to Analysis of Social Phenomena," *Annals of the Institute of Stat -*

istical Mathematics, 5(2): 121-143.

[14] McLuhan, M., 1965, *Understanding Media: The Extensions of Man,* New York: McGraw-Hill.

[15] Lazarsfeld, P.H., and Merton, R.K., 1949, "Mass Communication, Popular Taste and Organized Social Action," in W. Schramm, ed., *Mass Communications,* Urbana, Ill.: University of Illinois Press, pp. 459-480.

L.S. Harms and Jim Richstad:

The Right to Communicate: Status of the Concept

———

THE CONCEPT of the Right to Communicate evolves and expands as a consequence of several interrelated factors. Among these are the possibilities inherent in the new communication technologies, an awareness of global interdependence, the policy questions surrounding concerns for *information imbalance* and *cultural imperialism*, the basic paradigmatic shift from conceptualizing communication as a one-way and linear process to a two-way or multi-way and interactive process, and the insistence on participatory communication. These are among the factors that stimulate the growth of the Right to Communicate concept.

While it is an idea of the early 1970's, the roots of the Right to Communicate are deeply embedded in the human communication history which we all share and which is reflected in our most treasured secular and sacred documents. The basic distinctions between monolog and dialog were well understood, for example, by the time of Socrates. Many of the specific rights of communication have long and rich histories in many parts of the world. All of this past heritage from around the world is encompassed by the modern and future looking Right to Communicate, but there is more.

In fact, so many specific aspects of the Right to Communicate are so familiar to so many people that it is easy, at first, to overlook the important new dimensions inherent in the concept. A first question often posed is how the Right to Communicate differs from Article 19 of the Universal Declaration of Human Rights (1948). Another question asked is whether the Right to Communicate is, or can only be, a collection of familiar rights —— such as rights relating to information, assembly and association, speech and press, privacy, and so forth, as they are found in various national constitutions.[1] On the international level, a question often asked is whether the Right to Communicate goes, or can be expected to go, beyond the controversial *free flow of information* formulation, and whether the most that can be expected is a slightly better balance in the flow of information among nations. Questions about the relationship between the Right and communication policy, or participation are also frequently posed. We shall deal with these questions and a number of related ones in this discussion of the Right to Communicate.

The Right to Communicate as a distinctive concept was first enunciated by Jean d'Arcy in a 1969 article in the European journal, *EBU Review*. The article, "Direct Satellite Broadcasting and the Right to Communicate," provided an early worldview of the meaning of the global communication revolution, and of the need for new social and political concepts to harmonize technological capabilities with human information and communication needs.

Soon after this now classic statement, a series of intensive studies in Canada developed some hard and practical parameters for the Right to Communicate, in an effort to meet Canadian needs. Other work soon followed and enlarged, expanded, enriched, and clarified what was meant, and what could be meant, by the Right to Communicate.

A number of important conceptual attempts and perceptions, as well as involvement in the Right to Communicate, came about in the first half of the 1970's. These include the International Institute of Communications (IIC) meetings in Nicosia in 1973, Mexico City in 1974, and Cologne in 1975. The Right to Communicate was introduced, discussed, shaped, described and evaluated in these meetings. Other milestones in the early 1970's were the emergence in UNESCO of the Right to Communicate concepts, leading to a study resolution and other continuing activity. UNESCO communication officials saw in the concept a way to bridge what was becoming a polarization between the concept of free flow of information and national control of communication, a possibility of keeping the debate open.

In an earlier work we described the emergence of the Right to Communicate in three overlapping stages.[2] First, the pioneer stage, where individuals and institutions were essentially working on pieces of the concept by themselves, with little contact with each other.

This stage includes the d'Arcy 1969 paper, the Canadian studies, and the new paradigm-work in Honolulu. Second, there were organizing activities, when individuals, professionals and scholars, started regular contacts with each other. At that point the Right to Communicate was increasingly recognized at conferences and seminars, and it was beginning to be taken seriously. Third, the present stage or the development of projects designed to fully explore and expand the concept, to apply it in a multi-cultural context, to seek new methodologies necessary for research into the rich questions inherent in the Right to Communicate as, for example, the work underway in Australia.[3]

In the remainder of this chapter we will develop some foundations for the concept, discuss an emerging right to participate, discuss the link with communication policy, suggest topics for further study and dialog, and report on the current status of the concept.

Foundations of the Concept

The authors are attempting to explore the intellectual foundations of the Right to Communicate —— to examine the components of the right, and to identify where they developed, as well as to try to give a full answer to the question of why the Right to Communicate is different. We hope also, during our account of the intellectual development of the idea, to give a deep sense of what the Right to Communicate can mean for humankind. We realize this brief history is partial, incomplete and fragmentary, representing some of the first insights rather than the final ones. The Right to Communicate is an emerging and evolving concept, which must be kept flexible because of the immensity of human differences. The intellectual constructs of the Right to Communicate, as they emerged from the different activities over the past half dozen years, can be traced in an attempt to show why it represents a new and exciting concept for communication, one that opens a context for *all* humans, one that is based on human communication needs, and one that recognizes present and future technology.

As we discuss the developments and move into the more organized, global aspects of the Right to Communicate, there seem to emerge three general views of human beings and their relations to society and to communication. These views, expanded later in this chapter, are the traditional Western view of Freedom-of-Expression, the Soviet-Socialist view, and an increasingly coherent Third-World view. All these views contribute elements to what could emerge as a multi-cultural Right to Communicate, and all restrict in some sense its development. On the basis of these ideas, we would like to move to an examination of the 1969 d'Arcy paper.

D'Arcy initiated and focused much of the subsequent work on the Right to Communicate in his 1969 paper.[4] He accurately predicted "the time will come when the Universal Declaration of Human Rights will have to encompass a more extensive right than man's right to information, first laid down 21 years ago in Article 19. This is the right of man to communicate." Further, he established the role of the new communication technologies in this transformation, particularly that of direct-broadcast satellite.

The ideas contained in the 1969 paper have grown broader and deeper over the years, and still contain much of what is meant by the original concept: The Right to Communicate. D'Arcy immediately moved from the concept of freedom of information to the Right to Communicate, as something needed to shape policy and the future developments of communication. He saw the new technologies, broadcasting satellites, computers, videotape recorders, and wire distribution of sounds and images, as bringing new capacities for the exchange of information into a context of *scarcity of communication possibilities*. He saw information liberation in the new technologies, and the need for a broader, new concept of social policy, in other words, the Right to Communicate. "The instruments of communication," d'Arcy wrote, "still seem to be something quite separate from ourselves and we go on delegating their use to magicians, even if we do complain about them." D'Arcy saw it as a time to break down the mental barriers of the past, and to construct a communication-rich future. Thus he believed that the new technologies cannot be contained within the concepts of an Article 19, or similar guidelines and laws; new ones are needed, within a broader Right-to-Communicate-framework. D'Arcy did not specify what he meant by a Right to Communicate; but he did place the concept in the context of technology and global interdependence, as well as the growing possibilities of information-abundance. While much of the world will remain in an information-scarce condition for some time, a global view is likely to evolve requiring us to prepare for future information-abundance.

The Canadian Telecommission Studies of the early 1970's explored many of the basic principles of a Right to Communicate.[5] They included such important concepts as the need for communication to satisfy spiritual as well as material requirements, and that new technologies should offer greater access to information as well as wider participation in community affairs. Some explicit statements on what the Right to Communicate meant were compiled in a remarkable paragraph of *Instant World*:

> The rights to hear and be heard, to inform and to be informed, together may be regarded as the essential components of a 'right to communicate.' . . . the realization of a 'right to communicate' is a desirable objective for a democratic society, so that each individual may know he is entitled to be informed and to be heard, regardless of where he may live or work or travel in his own country. The people of Canada — as a body and as individuals — are therefore entitled to demand access to efficient telecommunications services on a non-discriminatory basis and at a reasonable price.

Here are clear intellectual foundations for a two-way process of communication; to hear and to be heard, to inform and to be informed — and for the concept of equity in the use of communication resources. Obviously stressed is the concept of vesting communication rights in both the individual and society.

Later in the same source is a classic statement: "If it be accepted that there is a 'right to communicate,' all Canadians are entitled to it." Tomo Martelanc recently translated this statement into global terms.[6]

One of the most enduring themes of *Instant World* and of the Right to Communicate, is that people should have equitable access to information and, more broadly, to appropriate communication resources. Participants in the studies actually considered a " 'right to communicate' as a fundamental objective of Canadian society." A further significant attribute were the safeguards against invasions of privacy mentioned in the same book.

Taken together, *Instant World* and the Telecommission Studies provide the first extensive examination of the importance of the

217

Right to Communicate and some of the means to make such a right meaningful. Henry Hindley tells us that the participants were aware of and impressed by the 1969 d'Arcy paper.

Out of the context of *Instant World* came Canadian concern over communication policies that would put such concepts into effect. The use of communication satellites to provide village-service in the north of Canada, for example, linking Indians and Eskimos who previously were out of the communication process with the existing system, is a clear implementation of some of the concepts included in the Right to Communicate. Another implementation on the international scale are policies which were developed to preserve the *Canadianess* of the country's mass media system, to avoid domination by the communication flow from the United States. These practical applications of the theoretical concepts of access to communication resources offer some means to test the original concepts. The Canadian experience is still evolving and exploring parameters of the Right to Communicate, but it offers examples of applications not only on the national but also on the subnational and transnational levels.

Another important conceptual statement relating to the Right to Communicate was made by Harold Lasswell in a Honolulu speech in 1972 on "The Future of World Communication: Quality and Style of Life."[7] Lasswell presented two models of human organization: the Oligarchic Model and the Participatory Model. Both relate quite directly to communication patterns and processes that would be found in different social organizations. In the power-oriented Oligarchic Model, Lasswell said communication was "used to indoctrinate and distract," while the "intermediate, resource parsimonious technology" of the Participatory Model lead to the use of communication to "provide attention opportunities that generate and re-edit common maps of man's past, present and future and strengthen a universal and differentiated sense of identity and common interest." Lasswell, in many ways, was also contrasting the mass media type of one-way communication with the multi-way, non-linear mode of communication, allowing for wider participation of various people on their own terms. He also indicated a clear distinction between vertical and horizontal communication systems. While these points were not fully developed in the Lasswell paper, they are important, particularly since they come from the man who developed a classic communication paradigm which has been so influential in research over the past forty-five years.

Further foundations for the Right to Communicate grew from a series of experimental seminars on that right, conducted since 1973 at the University of Hawaii by the authors. These seminars used contrasting approaches which still provide a framework to the Right to Communicate discussions. An urge to be more concrete in conceptualization was particularly noticed among students, who wanted clear parameters to work with. The intellectual content of the seminars developed the linkages between communication needs, technology and policy, and the relationship of communication rights to other human rights. The immense difficulties of where the right was vested, in the individual or the community, were somewhat resolved by saying it had to be vested in both, for different reasons. The question of whether the Right to Communicate had to have the force of law behind it, or whether we are talking about moral precepts or guides, was never fully resolved. Some contributors felt enforceable rights were the only meaningful ones, and we should forget about the rest. Other participants felt the discussion, the statements, the examination of the alternatives in the Right to Communicate debate was a positive force, and that it was too early in the process to stress enforceable rights within a multicultural context. The great problems of developing a multicultural concept were examined, and for many seminar hours a deep feeling of despair seemed to take hold, since it seemed so unlikely that the different human societies around the world, and the sub-societies within them, could ever come to an agreement on such a topic as the Right to Communicate. Out of the working papers and documents for the seminar grew a comprehensive collection of essential first papers on the Right to Communicate, and these were used later as background materials for a collection of essays, which were recently put together in one volume.[8]

Perhaps the most significant effort coming out of Hawaii resulted in a proto-type draft-resolution and justification-paper in the fall of 1974, when E. Lloyd Sommerlad was at the East-West Center in Honolulu, and conferred with the authors. Sommerlad felt that it would be useful to initiate a discussion in UNESCO. His suggestions resulted in a two-page statement highlighting the key elements of the

Right to Communicate as they were then understood by the authors of this chapter.

Our statement began with a note that communication is a basic human process, in local communities as well as in the global community. Article 19 of the Universal Declaration of Human Rights was cited:

> Everyone has the right to freedom of opinion and expression; this right includes freedom to hold opinions without interference and to seek, receive and impart information and ideas through any media and regardless of frontiers.

Article 19, strong and comprehensive for its era, was found increasingly unsuitable as we attempt to cope with rapid technological changes, and with widespread distribution of interactive capabilities never before possible, as well as other practical applications of the "free flow" policy. While many aspects of a general Right to Communicate were recognized in some societies by some groups of people, a comprehensive, universal, multicultural conceptualization of communication rights did not exist. The initial statement of justification covered several of the basic constructs of the Right to Communicate.

> In the communication era, the communication resources of man should be grounded in a *two-way, interactive, participatory* process. The world is being flooded with information useful to people, but that information needs to be organized, localized, individualized, easily and inexpensively available and responsive to human needs. And with a high degree of access comes concern about rights of privacy. Three special concerns of the communication era are the right of privacy, cultural preservation and diversity, and information overload. With wide access to vast quantities of information, there will be a need to balance the flow of information to avoid the extremes of both overload and scarcity, and to balance the sending and receiving of information.

The draft resolution stressed these themes, with emphasis on communication technology development, global interdependence, the earlier work by UNESCO on freedom of expression and association as well as cultural choices and freedom, and it related the development of communication-policy-science to the Right to Communicate. In all instances communication continued to be viewed as a two-way, interactive, participatory human process.

From Honolulu, the draft-resolution and justification-paper were carried to the annual meeting of the International Institute of Communications in Mexico City for two intense evening meetings that tested the Right to Communicate in an international setting. IIC in 1973 had introduced the concept of a Right to Communicate at its meeting in Nicosia, perhaps the first time an international communication group of professionals and scholars paid serious attention to its development. In many ways, the 1973 meeting set the stage for the intensive Mexico City debates in 1974.

A major challenge in Mexico City to the Right to Communicate idea came in the form of questioning the "free flow" concept, and a concern that the Right to Communicate was just another name for the "free flow" idea.[9] Some members of the working-group intensely opposed the "free flow" idea, as originally embedded in Article 19, because they said it meant a one-way flow of information, from the developed to the developing countries, and that the flow was controlled by the developed countries to their advantage. To some of the participants, "free flow" meant nothing but "information imperialism." It soon became evident, as Daniel Lerner was to remark at a 1976 conference, that the phrase "free flow" is so emotionally loaded that we need to retire it and find a replacement. While many observers from many regions of the world have acknowledged that the concept of "free flow," in the abstract, is theoretically sound, the international communication flow has never been a "free flow," but rather an imbalanced "one-way flow." A similar imbalance pattern can, of course, also develop within any one nation.

To make international communication equitable, concerns for *balance, access to communication resources, cultural integrity* and others need to be considered with the same urgency as *free flow*. The Right to Communicate at its core is an attempt to widen the parameters of communication to account in a serious way for these legitimate concerns. The Mexico City discussions were a difficult intellectual and multicultural test, and depth was added to the original concept of a Right to Communicate. From Mexico City, the Right to Communicate discussions moved to UNESCO headquarters in Paris, and continued in Sweden, where a formal resolution on the Right to Communicate was prepared for the November 1974 meeting of UNESCO.

The Swedish resolution was introduced during the UNESCO General Conference by Minister Bertil Zachrisson, with a stress on the role of the Right to Communicate in a democratic society and for participation in that society. He said:

> In education, science and culture, the right to communicate is essential. This right is indispensable in order to accord people their democratic rights and make it possible for everyone to exercise democratic control, and to grant all members of society participation in its development. The will of the people cannot be effectively expressed without a free public discussion and open communication.[10]

The resolution referred to the Universal Declaration of Human Rights, the Charter of the United Nations, and then said that "communication is the foundation of all social organization," and that "human communication must be an interactive participatory process." The insistence that communication *must* be an interactive participatory process was a stronger statement than had been made before. The problems of access and control were noted, along with the promises of communication abundance. Other points concern "the plurality and equality of cultures and the potential now existing for all groups and individuals in society to give full expression to their cultural values." The emergence of a science of communication as well as the need for planning of communication resources were recognized, as was the point that "all individuals should have equal opportunities to participate actively in the means of communication." The resolution asked the Director-General "to study and define the right to communicate." The right of participation in the communication process was strengthened by an amendment submitted by the Netherlands, which added the phrase, "ways and means by which active participation in the communication process may be possible."

Thus the resolution which was passed contained not only the
call for a study and definition of the Right to Communicate but also
urged investigation into ways that humans could participate actively
in that communication process. This addition to the UNESCO study
plan gave a practical-application direction to the
Right-to-Communicate-discussions, and helped to guide research
proposals in UNESCO and elsewhere.

Gunnar Naesselund, director of the UNESCO Department of
Free Flow of Information and Development of Communication,
interpreted the resolution as a turning away from what had become
an increasingly sterile discussion on freedom of information.[11]
Naesselund said the Right to Communicate and active participation
provide a chance to put aside the increasingly stylized debate on
freedom of the press and freedom of information and "to see in the
right to communicate the pattern of access and participation and of
dialogue, or even a multilogue which will enrich not only individuals
but also States in their relations with the outer world." He also saw
in the resolution and study a chance for "a better balance between
the rights of States and of individuals."

The UNESCO study surveyed member countries and
professional organizations, seeking to identify components of the
right, as they applied to nations, individuals and media institutions.
In all, more than forty specific components were identified in the
UNESCO survey, with priority listings for individual rights, rights of
nations, and media-institution concerns.

In the cover letter to media organizations prepared in
Sommerlad's office, two new foundations to the Right to
Communicate were put forward.[12] The first related to the new
international economic order, and stressed that the "social aspect is
at least as crucial as the economic aspect." The related concept is one
that has been shown over and over in studies and applications of the
use of communication in such national development programs as
agriculture, education, public health and, particularly, population.
The letter notes that "the human being is at the center of the
development process. This leads to a recognition that development
cannot take place without popular participation, involvement and
motivation. The implications for communication are obvious." A
subsequent UNESCO report, 19C/93, was approved at the November
1976 General Conference in Nairobi.

During the two years between the UNESCO General Conferences, several important events took place in Sri Lanka, in Cologne, and in Honolulu, which contributed further to the development of the Right to Communicate. The first major discussion of the Right to Communicate after the Swedish resolution was passed in UNESCO in November 1974, was held in Sri Lanka in April 1975 under the auspices of the Asian Mass Communication Research and Information Center. The announcement for the AMIC meeting noted that "The concept of the 'Right to Communicate' has provoked a great deal of interest among the international communication fraternity . . . " and in his keynote paper, AMIC Secretary-General Y.V.L. Rao stated:

> It seems to me that the first question we need to find answers to is: What has happened since 1948 that has brought about almost a total turn-around in our approach to the grandiose intentions in the field of flow of information? What is it that has gradually but perhaps inescapably led us to question all over again premises upon which the whole edifice had been built? Why is it that the same UN agency which had successfully established agreements to facilitate the free flow of information around the world, today finds it necessary to go through the whole exercise again and initiate studies to look into more or less the same question all over again under a different phrase: "The Right to Communicate?"

The AMIC conference was focused on Information Imbalance in Asia, and the Right was discussed informally from time to time during the week in relation to the information imbalance problem.

In a special two-hour session on the final day of the AMIC conference, several panelists made some pointed and useful observations. For instance, Rosihan Anwar said, "Dialogue on the Right to Communicate could shift the concern in some Asian countries from the technology to the substance of communication." Anwar discussed the implications of concentration on up/down versus down/up communication in a country. A.F. Kalimullah of Pakistan added that the problem of defining a multicultural Right to Communicate is bound to be a difficult one. He pointed out that "If I claim a right for myself, I must be prepared to concede it to others." He felt that out of a beginning such as this a "two-way traffic" will develop into a "mutual understanding." Kalimullah noted that "The right to communicate becomes relevant as we seek to treat all humans as one family." Anwar and Kalimullah, and the other members of the panel, raised many of the same questions and voiced many of the same concerns that had been expressed elsewhere in the world.

The AMIC panelists in Sri Lanka recognized the difficulties, the problems, the hard realities that would have to be dealt with if a Right to Communicate were to evolve. Nonetheless, a "healthy optimism," as one observer put it, seemed to pervade the discussions.

The IIC conference in September 1975 at Cologne followed by a few months the AMIC conference in Sri Lanka. Working Committee IV, in a series of meetings over four days, discussed four papers that had been prepared as background and then turned to the task of describing the Right to Communicate.[13] The description developed by that thirty-person, multicultural, diverse group is repeated in its entirety below.

> Everyone has the right to communicate. It is a basic human need and is the foundation of all social organization. It belongs to individuals and communities, between and among each other. This right has been long recognized internationally and the exercise of it needs constantly to evolve and expand. Taking account of changes in society and developments in technology, adequate resources —— human, economic and technological —— should be made available to all mankind for fulfillment of the need for interactive participatory communication and implementation of that right.

This descriptive statement is very rich and not only includes many of the essential ideas from the earlier discussions but also begins to organize them.

At the close of the Cologne meeting, it was becoming clear that the descriptive statement also pointed the way to an important next step. Both Professor Tomo Martelanc and Professor Aldo Armando Cocca strongly encouraged the authors to collect a body of original thinking on the Right to Communicate concept. Jean d'Arcy gave his support to the idea, and thus the plan for a volume of original essays was a direct outgrowth of the Cologne meeting.[14]

From the d'Arcy paper in 1969, it has been apparent that a major influence of the Right to Communicate concept will be on communication policy. It now appears that influence will be widely felt not only at the national level but also at the sub-national and international levels, as has been evident in Canada. This influence was also evident during a week-long conference conducted at the East-West Center in Honolulu in April 1976, on the topic of Fair Communication Policy.

This Honolulu conference reviewed the main concerns over the international flow of communication as now practiced, and particularly the concerns over the impact of such communication (relating to cultural imperialism issues), and the means of control of such flow. Over and over again, the discussion came back to the point that the essential locus of change in international communication rests with national communication policies. It is through policy development at the national level that the benefits of international communication without the detrimental aspects of one-way flow and other familiar complaints can be achieved. Sommerlad took the assignment of relating the development of "free-flow" to the "free-and-balanced-flow" concept, examining the role the Right to Communicate could play in such concerns.[16]

Today, an examination of the Right to Communicate leads to the observation that *the* Universal Right to Communicate is differentiated from *a* specific communication right, or a set of communication rights. Further discussion and study can be expected to clarify the dimensions of a four-level concept somewhat like the one presented below:

1. *Universal Right to Communicate*: A comprehensive, multicultural, culture-fair and general human right that serves to clarify values and illuminate long-range communication goals. It provides a framework for examination of any specific right or a set of specific rights.

2. *Specific Communication Rights*: A set or collection of rights capable of being defined and acted upon in terms of policy. The set may add new rights, or fuse two old ones, and so on. A specific communication right has privileges and responsibilities, or guarantees and obligations, etc. associated with it.

3. *Communication Issues*: Clusters of related problems and questions under discussion, typically encompassing two or more specific rights and sometimes two rights in opposition: a right to inform plus a right to be informed; or, a right to be informed and a right to privacy.

4. *Communication Environment*: In the sociocultural context, human communicators react to or sense changes in the communication environment such as the structural and other problems that have generated "balance in communication flow" issues.

Obviously, further study and discussions will reshape and refine this preliminary outline, and at this early stage there will be apparent overlapping.

Participation and the Right to Communicate

We are now ready to relate the Right to Communicate to "active participation in the communication process" and discuss ways and means by which participation can become possible in communication environments. UNESCO Resolution 4.121 links active participation and the Right to Communicate. A key phrase from Article 19, "to seek, receive, and impart information," provides a starting point for the examination of that linkage.

The one-way mass communication systems that have prevailed since Article 19 was drafted in 1948, have generated a number of imbalances. While many persons and communities have a right to receive certain kinds of information, they have been given only a limited right to seek information, and very little opportunity to impart information. In practice, Article 19 is most often a "receive only" right. As one participant remarked at the Cologne discussions, "from the perspective of the Seventies, Article 19 now appears technologically naive." A quest for active participation in the communication process emphasizes the *impart* dimension of Article 19. Quite obviously, a mass medium is not formally organized to permit more than a few persons or groups to impart information. Thus, a receive-impart imbalance is built into the basic communication structure in many communities of the world.

As the receive-impart imbalance comes under examination, it becomes apparent that opportunities to *seek* information are also severely constrained by current mass media structures. Most persons are able to seek certain types of information from family and friends and from local groups. But they are unable to seek other kinds of information, say, on matters of health, beyond that which has already been imparted (and often imported) through existing, established channels. Whole nations, not just individuals, may be affected in much the same way. In practice, seeking information is often limited to an operation such as changing from one radio station to another with alternatives being even more limited in information scarce societies. More generally, the opportunities to seek information are often discussed under the term "access to sources of information." Thus, access to the ways and means of communication are closely related to and probably inseparable from active participation in the communication process. A series of interrelated questions arise when the "seek, receive, and impart" phrase is examined from an expanded view of human communication.

There are obvious limits to participatory communication. Everyone cannot participate in every communication act, or there would be no communication beyond the Tower of Babel. Given that, what are the practical limits to participatory communication? We will consider that question in two parts. First, we have to assume that all of the people do not *want* to participate on all of the issues all of the time, and certainly not in the same manner or by the same means. Christopher Kolade put it in quite practical terms at a July 1976 conference at Stanford University, when he said that in many societies of the world, people are not used to participation, they do not expect to participate, and they even do not want to participate. This certainly raises the problem of forcing participation on people that really do not want it, or who are not prepared for it. In the extreme, this should not put us in the position of requiring people to exercise their Right to Communicate, whether they want to or not.

Second, there are physical, technological, economic, political and other limitations on participatory communication rights. It is too easy to condemn mass media because they are one-way, generally non-participatory means or systems of communication. Talking theoretically about the right of the audience to participate in a radio or television station programming, for example, is one thing, the practical problems of making such participation a reality are immense. As a result, the question soon becomes: How does a medium serving an audience of hundreds, thousands, or even millions, operate on a participatory basis? While admitting that a participatory element can and is being built in, it can never be one equally shared by all members of a possible audience. Another limiting factor is cost. We are finding in the United States, for example, that it is not inexpensive to provide information for people. For instance, if enough people ask a local government for information, cost can rapidly become a major problem. Public administration journals in the U.S. regularly examine this situation from a very practical view. It becomes readily apparent that no government can provide unlimited access to information, even while acknowledging that the right of one should be the right of all. This is an old problem and it is certainly not limited to access to information. Technologically, there are also limits to available channels of communication. One prominent example of technological limitations is the burst of Citizen Band radio activity in the United States. This extremely popular form of communication, which in many ways provides an ideal individual communication system, is overwhelming the available capacity by its popularity. Too many people want to use the limited number of channels at the same time, and there are presently inadequate rules for making the process orderly. Thus a point has been reached where the use of CB in a place like Los Angeles becomes maddening for serious communicators. There will probably never be enough capacity, despite technological, professional advances ahead, for everyone to have the kind of access to media that may be desired in highly developed nations. It is also obvious that culturally and politically, some societies view participation as a traditional matter, controlled by prescribed rules that simply do not permit everyone equal participation at all times. In fact, it is a rare society which would provide that right and opportunity.[17]

So, the full possibilities of participation in communication are really not known. Human beings are still exploring the question, and they probably always will be. Participatory communication, like the Right to Communicate, is an evolving and expanding concept. We are far from knowing what the end will be, or if we ever will know where that concept leads us, but we do know that participatory communication supplies human communication needs in a way that the contemporary mass media do not.

In the past, the role of communication in human society was often seen as an attempt to inform and influence people. It is now more generally accepted that communication should be understood as a process of social interaction through a balanced exchange of information and experience. In recent years, the traditional "persuasional" concept of communication has become a subject for debate. Communication now is not seen as a process in which one talks and one listens, for instance, but rather where all participants talk and all listen, in a serious, seeking way, and with a possibility for change based on the content of the interaction. As a growing emphasis has been placed on participation in the media, there has been a call for wider choice of materials, with the choices increasingly being made by individual consumers, rather than by a production organization. There is even a concern that many individuals within the media are not sufficiently involved in the program planning or in the production process. This shift in perception implies a predominance of dialog over monolog. The aim is to achieve a system of horizontal communication based upon an equitable distribution for sending as well as receiving messages, thus enabling individuals to become more fully communicators, as we use the term today. Such a system is seen as functioning with and alongside mass media systems. Individual participation in communication through the mass media may at the present time be possible in only a very limited way. What is important is that both present and future technological possibilities for participation should become increasingly important points of focus in order to broaden individual participation in various ways.

Based on this discussion of participation, a fundamental and basic claim is here put forward: The human right to participate. Viewed as a right, there appear to be both old and new components to the concept. For instance, the right to participate appears to encompass part of a prior right of association and assembly, in the sense that active participation requires communicative interaction. But it also encompasses a part of the earlier right to culture, and requires *transceiver* rather than mere transmitter-receiver-technologies. Taken together, the components of a right to participate suggest a pattern of emphasis on the "right to seek, receive and impart information" that was not apparent in 1948 and not well understood even in 1970.

Within the broad framework of a Right to Communicate, a specific right to participate can be examined closely and its major dimensions can be outlined. Further, it can be seen in its relationship to other rights, such as a right to privacy, or a right to be informed. A current Pacific-wide satellite communication demonstration illustrated many of these points. The Pan Pacific Education and Communication Experiments by Satellite (PEACESAT) is an international educational experiment involving institutions in twelve nations of the Pacific Basin.[18] All are linked by communication satellite for information sharing. The purpose is to experiment with the application of available communications technology as well as new methods of operation especially designed for health, education, and community services. Attention in this effort is focused on interaction among societies and requirements for social developments. The project began in 1969, and the experimental system has operated regularly since April 1971.

The PEACESAT system is a new arrangement of communications technology that is extremely flexible, permitting conferencing among many locations over great distances. Needs are met and purposes served for which existing communication systems were not designed. In the system, the National Aeronautics and Space Administration's ATS-1 satellite is the central relay point linking small ground terminals which are located according to the purposes and operations of various social services. These terminals, which can be set up quickly, are designed for two-way communication. When associated with related equipment, communication may be by voice, teletype, wired blackboard, computer, and still pictures. TV motion pictures are not included because of the extremely high costs involved, and the project's emphasis on two-way communication from all locations. The system-users prepare all exchanges, there is virtually no "software," and *dialog dominates*. Local institutions arrange for capital and operating costs of the terminals, which are licensed by local national authorities. The application of the satellite, used in this way to support social services, has great international potential. It can provide immediate access to information- and experience-sources for the less-developed areas of the world, while providing for direct dialog between developed and developing countries on mutually agreeable terms. At the same time, it can make worldwide contributions to the advancement of science, the strengthening of culture, an increased flow of information, and more effective health, education, and community services. It can accomplish all this as has been demonstrated, without the kind of negative effects inherent in the term "communication imperialism." There are, of course, other forms of regional communication exchanges which contain their own lessons in working out specific aspects of the general Right to Communicate.

The Links to Communication Policy

An important impact of the multicultural and global Right to Communicate would be on the area of communication policy. This observation has been made repeatedly at UNESCO and in various international and national professional groups. In the past quarter-century, the policy sciences have come into being and policy research organizations have been formed in many countries, universities offer advanced academic programs in the policy sciences, and specialized journals and books are being published. It has been noted that "policy studies in all countries suffer from an extreme scarcity of persons who are qualified to engage in policy research on complex issues."[19] Apparently, at least in some countries, there exists a demand for the services of the policy scientist.

In a major review article, Lazarsfeld examines the "policy science movement."[20] He notes that the self-assigned task of the policy scientist includes "reassessment of a problem's goals" and the view that he represents a "new type of professional," one who "cannot be expected to contribute to general knowledge of specific academic disciplines." The concern of the policy scientist is with "making recommendations that are acceptable to his sponsors." Lazarsfeld further observes that the policy scientist in his research style usually emphasizes a "systems approach," expresses an interest in "futurism," and identifies with "interdisciplinarity." Further, he is more likely to use available macrosociological data than generate microsociological data on the work he does. After a quarter-century, the policy sciences are unfolding, evolving rapidly, or emerging, and, specific new policy sciences are developing. Of particular interest to this particular effort is the "emergence" of a communication policy science.

At this stage, a communication policy science appears to be developing with little direct contact with the formal body of policy theory. While a healthy independence from past traditions can be viewed as a positive factor, nonetheless it seems there is much to be learned from the policy sciences approach in general, and from other more advanced, specific policy science disciplines. As a guide to a series of studies sponsored by UNESCO, communication policies were described in the following words:

> Communication policies are sets of principles and norms established to guide the behavior of communication systems. They are shaped over time in the context of society's general approach to communication and to the media. Emanating from political ideologies, the social and economic conditions of the country and the values on which they are based, they strive to relate these to the real needs for and the prospective opportunities of communication.
>
> Communication policies exist in every society, though they may sometimes be latent and disjointed, rather than clearly articulated and harmonized. They may be very general, in the nature of desirable goals and principles, or they may be more specific and practically binding. They may exist or be formulated at many levels. They may be incorporated in the constitution or legislation of a country; in overall national policies, in the guidelines for individual administrations, in professional codes of ethics as well as in the constitutions and operational rules of particular communication institutions.[21]

Somewhat more succinctly, another UNESCO document states:

> Communication policies are sets of principles and norms established to guide the behavior of communication systems.

Their orientation is fundamental and long-range, although they may have operational implications of short-range significance. They are shaped in the context of society's general approach to communication. Emanating from political ideologies, the social and economic conditions of the country and the values on which they are based, they strive to relate these to the real needs and prospective opportunities of "communication."[22]

At this time, several points of similarity between the general policy sciences approach and the specific-communication-policy-science should be pointed out. Both draw heavily on system theory. Both stress interdisciplinary activity. Both express an interest in long-range goals and futurism. Both are still undergoing the rapid rate of change associated with the early stages of development.

In the basic research and the applied studies that are just now becoming available, the distinctions by Lasswell between the *policy process* and the *intelligence needs of policy* are again evident.[23] For convenience, the term *research* will be restricted to "research on the policy process," while the term *studies* will be restricted to "studies of the intelligence needs of policy."

From the outset, it has been apparent that interaction, interchange and participation were at the core of the Right to Communicate concept. In a recent paper, Sommerlad made a similar point:

> The right to communicate is not just a new name for the free flow of information. It has much wider dimensions. It takes two to communicate and the essential new ingredient in the "right" is the idea of dialogue, inter-action, exchange, response, sharing, a two-way flow with mutual respect. While the central idea in free flow is the *dissemination* of information, the essence of communication is *interchange*[24]

Or, to place the idea in a slightly different framework, the new "ingredient" in the Right is not merely one step beyond the "two-step flow;" what is required is to take enough steps backward to reach a new starting point, and then to take the first steps on a new and very different path. The Right to communicate is part of an attempt to discuss and study what human communication ought to be, present and future. In this way, it resembles the other Human Rights, and the central concerns are moral, ethical and cultural. In fact, the idea that the Right would grow out of and take its basic shape from extensive multicultural dialog and interchange, dialog in which very many people participate, is in harmony with the new "ingredients" of the Right itself. Process and content are in harmony. The concept is not only multicultural, it is also multilevel, and at this early stage of its development, it is quite complex. The levels, discussed earlier, are four: Universal Right to Communicate; Specific Communication Rights; Communication Issues ; Communication Environment. The first two levels are, of course, most closely associated with the concept, but the Issues- and Environment-levels are also essential to understanding the scope of the concept.

The Universal-Right-to-Communicate-level is comprehensive and multicultural, a whole of an idea that is and will remain larger than the sum of its parts. It evolves and expands as a result of study and dialog and experience, and as is true of most important concepts, it will have periods of consistency and stability, when it embodies a consensus, and it will undergo substantial change when it does not. It thus is part of our world-culture which draws from and contributes to many local cultures, and is enriched by them. If a "supranational" world-communication-theory were developed it would correspond to this level. If this policy were widely regarded not only as fair, but as the best possible, then the Right and World Policy might become indistinguishable. However, even at present, international and national communication policy efforts can draw from the body of understanding about the role of communication in society, which is embodied in a Universal Right to Communicate.

The specific Communication Rights level corresponds more directly to what is commonly regarded as the domain of communication policy. As specific rights are examined more closely, it becomes evident that they are at present and in most places subject to regulations by law and policy. For example, information rights are usually surrounded by a body of communication policy, thus the emergence of a right to participate raises a number of important but difficult policy questions. When policies regarding different specific communication rights develop independently and come into conflict, then it may be useful to view the policy concerns from the Universal-level in order to seek resolution of the conflict.

In any community, a variety of communication issues are under discussion at some level at any time. Many of these issues are talked out or replaced by others, but some become policy issues of enduring concern. Usually, such issues become linked to prior discussions of specific communication rights. If the issue is a fundamental one, such as access or participation, the policy issue may evolve into a communication right and require further adjustment at the Universal Right to Communicate level, a complicated, multi-level process that seems to be underway at this time. Changes in the basic Communication Environment can be expected from time to time. The development of "distance free" satellites is one example, and the gradual discovery of the multiple interconnectability of transceiver technology a second, and, of course, the appreciation of the role in communication of and necessity of cultural diversity probably is the most subtle, pervasive and important environmental change of all. A few of these changes become communication issues and, in turn, some of these lead to communication policy changes.

In a time of rapid change across the entire area of human communication, the evolving conceptual framework of the Right to Communicate comes into contact at many points with the formulation of a body of communication policy. To the extent that sub-national, national and international policies recognize Human Rights, to that extent at least, the Right to Communicate is relevant to communication policy.

Status of the Concept

Today, the Right to Communicate concept does not rival the precision of an atomic clock, nor is it ever likely to do so. But the broad outline or "skeleton" of the Right is becoming clear, and the work underway can fill in that outline in the next decades. Altogether, the concept now appears both more important and more complex than had been anticipated.

The concept does evolve and expand, and in still unexpected ways. Obviously, it benefited from the clear statement by Jean d'Arcy in 1969 and from the subsequent pioneering Telecommission Studies in Canada under the leadership of Henry Hindley. The forward looking resolution introduced into the UNESCO General Conference in 1974 by Sweden placed the concept, with the timely assistance of Tomo Martelanc and others, on the international agenda. UNESCO has prepared a document for its 19th General Conference proposing a series of studies and conferences to be scheduled over the next several years, IIC at its past five annual meetings has contributed significantly to the growth of the concept. During the past year, the authors have assembled twenty original essays on the Right to Communicate—from eighteen different countries by twenty-two authors including, for instance, Aldo Cocca, Boris Firsov, Henry Hindley, Hidetoshi Kato, Asok Mitra, Ithiel de Sola Pool, Astrid Susanto, Luis Neltran, Y. V. Lakshamana Rao, Ali Shummo, and Henry Cassirer. There are many other activities, but the ones cited do illustrate the range of persons and institutions contributing to the evolution and expansion of this multicultural concept.

The importance of developing the Right to Communicate from a multicultural perspective has been stressed over and over again. This is a major source of the difficulty in coming up with a simple or quick definition of the Right to Communicate. In the past, definitions have usually developed within the framework provided by a single culture. The great intricacies of culture and communication are well known, and must be fairly reflected in any consideration of the Right to Communicate.

Beyond culture are other contexts which shape communication systems and behavior. While many such contexts can be outlined, one in particular seems to be important in the Right to Communicate. It is based on the contrasting views of what can be called the Western "free flow" concept, the Soviet-Socialist national-security concept, and a mixed concept in the Third World with concerns such as political and social integrity as it relates to international communication, and national unity as it relates to domestic communication.

The Western view of "free flow" of communication and the Soviet-Socialist view of security were brought together in the 1975 Conference on Security and Cooperation in Europe, the Helsinki agreements, with differing interpretations. It is not our purpose here to examine these contrasting views in detail, much has already been done on that, but rather to note that there are different bases from which each proceeds, and then to note that there are also different and more diffuse concerns in the Third World. All three approaches are provocative, and force attention to different dimensions of the Right to Communicate. How these three approaches can be reconciled we do not know yet, but it is hoped that the Right to Communicate framework will be large enough and will be kept open long enough to let full and rich interaction develop. This is one of the critical concerns for development of the Right to Communicate.

FOOTNOTES

[1] See any compendium of UN instruments and national constitutions.

[2] See the Preface and the final paper by L.S. Harms, Jim Richstad and Kathleen A. Kie, eds., *Right to Communicate: Collected Papers,* Honolulu: Social Sciences and Linguistics Institute; distributed by the University Press of Hawaii, 1977, pp. 126.

[3] See *Telecom 2000* published by the National Telecommunications Planning Branch, Telecom Australia, 199 William Street, Melbourne 3000.

[4] First published in *EBU Review*, 118(1969): 14-18. Reprinted in Note 2 above.

[5] See whole of *Instant World*, Ottawa: Information Canada, 1971. Selected excerpts reprinted in Note 2 above.

[6] See the Foreword in Note 2 above.

[7] See Harold Lasswell publication of this title in the East-West Communication Institute lecture series, paper No. 4.

[8] See the volume referred to in Note 2 above.

[9] See the report in *Intermedia*, vol. 2, no. 3, 1974.

[10] See the full text of Zachrisson's intervention in Note 2 above.

[11] See *Intermedia*, vol. 2, no. 5, 1975.

[12] Major sections of these materials are included in the final paper prepared by the editors of the volume referred to in Note 2 above.

[13] See the IIC conference documents for the 1975 Cologne conference. Selected documents on Right to Communicate from that conference are included in volume referred to in Note 2 above.

[14] See L. S. Harms and Jim Richstad, eds., *Evolving Perspectives on the Right to Communicate*, Honolulu: East-West Communication Institute; distributed by the University Press of Hawaii, 1977, pp. 285.

[15] See Jim Richstad, ed., *New Perspectives in International Communication*, Honolulu: East-West Communication Institute, 1977, pp. 241.

[16] See paper by E. Lloyd Sommerlad titled: "Free Flow of Information, Balance, and the Right to Communicate" in Note 15 above.

[17] See, for instance, the discussion papers in *Policy Dialog on the Right of Everyone in Hawaii to Communicate*, Honolulu: Social Sciences and Linguistics Institute, June 1976, edited by L.S. Harms, Jim Richstad, Bruce Barnes, and Kathleen A. Kie for a variety of viewpoints on participation.

[18] See various papers and reports by John Bystrom, Director of the PEACESAT Project, University of Hawaii, Honolulu. See also the *Communication inthe Pacific,* edited by Daniel Lerner and Jim Richstad and published at The East-West Communication Institute, 1976.

[19] See Y. Dror, "Prolegma to Policy Sciences," *Policy Sciences*, 1(1970), pp. 135-150.

[20] The article by Paul Lazarsfeld appeared in *Policy Sciences*, 6(1975), pp. 211-222.

[21] Taken from the Introduction of the UNESCO volume on "Communication Policies in . . . "

[22] From the UNESCO document titled: "COM/MD/24," Paris, 1 December 1972, p. 8.

[23] Two papers by Harold Lasswell, one of special importance:

"The Policy Orientation," in D. Lerner and H. Lasswell, eds., *Policy Sciences*, Stanford: University Press, 1951; and "The Emerging Conception of Policy Sciences," *Policy Sciences*, 1(1970), pp. 3-14.

[24] From the Sommerlad paper referred to in Note 16 above.

Fred L. Casmir:

A Multicultural Perspective of Human Communication

I AM DEFINING human beings as open, biological, metabolic systems in this chapter, which views communication as the major human survival tool. Any approach which limits or hampers the innate, metabolic human ability to adapt, in order to maximize the chances for survival through communication, I consider to be dangerous. Suggested instead is a methodology to develop *situationally* a communication *sub-culture*, to facilitate individual contributions and adaptations, rather than the use of methodologies, organizations or systems, based on fitting participants into preconceived structures. Development of a matrix for interaction thus becomes a result of maximized individual development and adaptation rather than submerging or forcing the individual into some definitional group, system, or organization. This basic principle is here specifically applied to the area of international and intercultural communication while recognising that it could be also applied to other areas of human communication. However, since a variety of difficulties are commonly presumed by non-experts or -scholars to result when representatives of different cultures or nations interact, a study of these areas of human interaction may provide more readily accepted insights which can also be related to other areas. Some of my basic assumptions underlying the specific factors discussed in this chapter are:

> Communication is the basic survival mechanism of human beings, both internally and externally. Without the ability to communicate we lose, on the biological-metabolic level our very lives, and on the cultural, social, symbolic, interpersonal,

and aesthetic levels we lose our distinctly human features, although we may continue to survive biologically.

Communication is thus seen not merely as a cultural or social attribute of human beings but as our most basic mechanism or tool for existence.

Communication is significantly identified with the receiver. That is, so called reality in all instances is a matter of interpretation. Communication can be viewed on one level as purposive, that is directed towards someone or something with a specific purpose in mind. It can also be considered, on another level, as a constant internal and external process, based on the evaluation of anything the human organism perceives, interprets, and interrelates, whether that be another organism, an object, or an event. I believe that combination of *both* these approaches is fundamental to the study of human communication.

It is my contention (as also argued in another context) that human communication should be considered on two levels. One relates to the observation and interpretation of the purposeful, fluidly constructed systems in our environment, devised to meet situationally specific communicative needs. The second, deeper level, relates to the biologic-metabolic, creative, generative mechanisms or codes within us, which result in the discovery and use of basic communication rules. These rules then are interpreted situationally, culturally, and socially in an infinite variety of ways and result in the identification and use of the system. I believe that our methodologies and studies can suffer if the vital differences between these two levels are not adequately considered.[1]

In attempting to determine generally applicable communication norms, students of human communication in the past have heavily relied upon methodologies which were devised for the discovery of natural laws, and which therefore, primarily relied upon the approaches used by the natural sciences. Against the background of a changing emphasis and the development of a pluralistic approach to methodologies in the social sciences, this chapter takes also into consideration a variety of other bases, which have been carefully outlined by Monge and Cushman, among others.[2]

Monge indicates that the approach of the behaviorists, basing their work on a laws-perspective and strict causal-relations, is challenged today by the views of the anti-Positivists, idealists, or teleologically-oriented students who in their finalist approaches use more than the patterns required by the natural sciences in their attempts to rationally interpret reality.[3] Monge also argues that in the past students of human communication have, in their insistence on purposive, pro-active, and choice-oriented theories actually worked much more consistently within a teleogical framework. At the same time they have often claimed, probably because of the assumed inherent values of the natural-sciences-approach, that their work has been basically behavioral.[4]

For the purpose of this chapter two basic approaches have been combined: Human communication is interactional, generative, creative, it is the product of generative mechanisms, as outlined by Madden and others in their studies on causality.[5] Commonly observed and described regularities in human communicative interaction, however, are not the result of factors in the natural order of things, but they are the result of systems constructed by human beings to demonstrate the results of such underlying codes and rules in specific situations. Usually, they do not sufficiently take into account the possibility of deep-structures, or innate codes in human beings similar to or equivalent to biological codes.

Useful in describing many human interactions is some sort of a structure, or system of interrelations within an environment, which can be identified or defined.[6] Systems should not be perceived as being a part of the natural order of things but rather as created structures which are fluid and situationally idenfiable.[7] Cushman sees the main component parts in the identification and study of systems as: a set of objects or events; a set of relationships; and a calculus or operation for manipulating or drawing conclusions from the systems as we attempt to make our findings about specific systems more generally applicable.[8] Systems-theorists, generally agree that these are overlaid models, not actual discoveries of natural systems. Thus it becomes evident that the general-systems-approach does little to identify what causes the development of systems or the underlying rules which may determine their coming into existence. Marlowe defines systems as " . . . a unique whole of interacting and interdependent parts, containing people and things, whose effectiveness is the degree to which planned-for goals are achieved within the environment."[9] Schein adds some important dimensions when he sees a system as something which imports elements from the environment, converts them, and exports them back to the environment. This is basically the description of an open metabolic system, such as a human being.[10] Elsewhere, I have indicated my own stipulation, that the basic human (physiologically- and neurologically-based) survival mechanism underlying all rules of human communicative behavior is probably a metabolic, interactional function which seeks through constant interaction, internally and externally, to preserve a basic, individual equilibrium by means of a variety of communicative processes.[11] Change, according to Schein, comes about through perceived inconsistencies, or the perception of an imbalance.

A concern with rules as one aspect of underlying factors in human behavior has been recently developed, as another means of gaining a more complete understanding of human communication.[12] Strictly causal-connections under this perspective are no longer thought to be sufficient, rather, teleological approaches requiring consideration both of the intentional level and past experience, as well as the surface or outward activities resulting from these underlying factors, are considered to be more adequate. With Cushman, I would accept the necessity of consensually shared, GENERATIVE rules underlying observable instances or systems. His four propositions appear to be an excellent starting point for the factors relating to intercultural communication later on considered in this chapter:

1. That conjoint, combined and associated action is characteristic of human behavior.

2. That the transfer of symbolic information facilitates conjoint, combined and associated behavior.

3. That the transfer of symbolic information requires the interaction of sources, messages, and receivers guided and governed by communication rules.

4. That communication rules form general and specific patterns which provide the ground for a fruitful exploration and description of particular communicative transaction.[13]

A pluralistic methodology is suggested which does not confuse the systems-level or rules-level with the discovery of anything which may lead to identification of factors which are a part of any inherent, innate, or creative-generative mechanism in human beings on the level of the natural order of things. To put it in Koestler's words, we should not confuse the matrix and the code.[14]

The basic concern of this chapter is that we develop thought-models which consciously allow for the development of situations in which codes (and not merely preconceived systems) can become active, generative forces, PRIOR to any attempt to create a formal system or systems of human interaction based on rule identification. The model I have in mind resembles one provided for us in neurological development (since I believe that the eventual theory, or model of human communication which we will find most adequate, will be biologically-neurologically oriented), "progressive individualism within a totally integrated matrix, and not progressive integration of primarily individuated units."[15] This explanation for the growth of motor neurons as they prepare for later contacts with not yet existing muscles, may serve as a model for human interaction. Such a communication matrix, eventually defined or discovered by interacting human beings, can encourage meaningful and highly productive, creative, progressive individualism through "metabolic" adaptation. Any attempt at merely integrating individual units into some sort of culturally, functionally, sociologically or otherwise pre-determined system, on the other hand, can lead to breakdowns or the insufficient use of the available creative-generative aspects of human interaction at the "code-level," especially when it is done across or between cultures.

Marlowe makes clear that in human interaction all partners want to maximize their personal benefits, but they are also willing to develop and accept rules to "stabilize the social order" in order to get at least something out of the interaction.[16] It is at this level that human communication provides the mechanisms, or tools for working out both individual and group (or cultural and social) needs. I agree with those social scientists who state that our survival depends on interaction with others, as well as adequate interaction within our individual, internal physiological-neurological systems. Mutual influence may make us both human, and *effective* human beings.[17] Without such interaction both individuals and societies would eventually collapse because our most important survival ability, our adaptive, creative-interactional communication would be severely disturbed. As Marlowe points out, "Affiliation is a means of survival. Affiliation means a close connection and relationships, and it implies a desire for such an association to exist . . ."[18] Our judgments and perceptions are modified by interaction with others. Indeed our motives change, based on the adaptive-interactional rules of human behavior stipulated to underlie our communicative interactions.

Dissonance-theories, balance-theories, and others have fairly consistently described what happens when our dynamic state of equilibrium is challenged or disturbed, but they have not adequately addressed themselves to the underlying codes or mechanisms which bring about feelings of imbalance.[19] All seem to agree on the necessity for mutually supporting cognitions, emotions and actions, however. Within cultures and societies, over time, agreements are "worked out." In most intercultural or international communication situations however, because of time and other pressures a "compromise-model" is usually introduced which attempts to *arbitrarily* combine what some dominant individuals or leaders judge to be the most acceptable component parts of all involved views. At other times, the dominant power of one or more of the participants may be used to force others to accept his concepts, rules, or models of an acceptable balance. It is my contention that since, as Marlowe indicates, we are suggestible, persuasible, and conforming in the presence of others, it should be a conscious part of our interactional patterns to provide opportunities for imitation, attachment, and interdependence worked out within the immediate setting, rather than introducing them as preconceived factors brought to situations by one or more of the partners.[20] I agree with Larsen that the situational structure is all important in human communicative interaction,[21] and with Walker and Heyns that "Conformity and non-conformity are instrumental acts, means to ends, ways of achieving goals to satisfy needs . . . always involving movement or change."[22]

Association with systems which are well known to us, or which we have previously discovered and used within one culture or society, (usually our own), readily can lead us to communicative interactions with others based on apparently logical structures. These may, however, appear quite different or less logical to our partners in interaction if they come from a different cultural background. To avoid such problems, and considering the bases relating to systems, rules, and the nature of human communication as a culturally shaped survival function discussed in this chapter, a different approach is proposed.

First, I would like to outline the basic problem as I have identified it in my personal experiences as well as in those of many others. One challenge posed by the thought-model proposed here is whether or not it is adequate to consider communication primarily from the standpoints of "conflict–resolution," "argumentation," "confrontation," "rhetoric," "sender–receiver," "communication-equals-agreement" and similar perspectives, some of them very popular or "common sense" approaches, typical of Western or American cultures. These appear indeed frequently to be based more on Western cultural training and observed systems, than the processes we might identify if we broke away from our own traditional systems and categories, and considered those developed in other cultures and societies.

I personally agree with those who indicate that the only real communicative confrontation or interaction which humans can experience has to take place with other individual human beings, even when we associate in groups. My own belief that communicative interaction is the most basic survival mechanism used by human beings, is indicated by the following question:

> Is it possible to identify any human interaction, structure, organization or even culture which is not entirely dependent upon communication for its existence, maintenance, and continuation? (In addition, communication between individuals, in my experience, is the only way in which human institutions, including cultures, can be established and maintained.)

Howell represents a common reaction when he speaks of the "workable boundaries to communication," and defines communication as anything one does to influence others.[23]

However, I perceive problems with any approach which sees the "use" of communication primarily as an attempt to influence others. I see this approach as *one*, conscious, aspect of the overall survival-role which communication plays in human life. It is true that purposeful things are above the threshold of awareness, lending themselves more readily to analysis and revision, as Howell has indicated. But it appears equally true that these analyses and revisions eventually depend on much deeper and broader, underlying human mechanism, such as codes, rules, or biological-neurological mechanisms which I have stipulated earlier, because overtly and culturally, identifiable human communication systems are shaped by them.

Some specific approaches to multicultural communication resulting from the thought-model suggested here can now be mentioned. The first major premise I developed earlier, concerns the possibility of studying human communicational processes through the use of models which closely resemble those of biological, metabolic, survival functions, or the neuro-physiological developmental-patterns of the human body.[24] The progressive, individualism within a totally integrated matrix discussed earlier, may lead us to develop a more successful, or efficient model for *individual* communication, and one which may result in a different basis for the development and study of *larger communicative structures*, matrixes, organizations or institutions, including nations and cultures, because we start with consideration of the individual and his needs. I assume here that any approach to human communication will be strongly, or perhaps entirely, influenced by the underlying philosophy we bring to it. Thus, if we study communication within the framework of repetitive-mechanical, law-governed concepts, we are likely to develop different insights than if we use an open, biological, metabolic, fluid, process-oriented approach.

It appears to me to be a significant problem that closed, mechanical systems tend to *occupy* or *take over* territory, because by definition they do not interact with their environment or adapt to it in the same way as an open system, resulting in eventual imbalance or disintegration. In other words, mechanical systems tend not to fit in, they do not *discover* their places, rather they occupy any given space. On the other hand, open, metabolic systems, make use of their survival-function or -ability to adapt, through import and export of factors in their environment. Thus they can more readily *fit-in,* become *ecological partners, discover their place*, with a minimum of disruptive or destructive conquest and confrontation. Models of structures, institutions, organizations, and even cultures from a Western perspective have tended to be mechanical, closed, institutionally-oriented. In the long run, these models have frequently been *control-* or *dominance*-pyramid-shaped models. I have tried to indicate in an earlier section of this book that the use of models based on closed, mechanical systems may create significant problems for human survival because they can stifle the innate, creative, generative mechanism in human beings, as open systems.

I propose, therefore, that we conceive of systems or institutions as *extensions* of human beings, rather than of human beings as parts or extensions of organizations or groups. This thought-model results in the consideration of all institutions as *human* structures, as reflections of their human component parts, rather than endowing organizations with super-human qualities, often causing us to maintain them at all costs, even if they become destructive of the very beings who develop them. Rather than forcing models (which may be more in line with the maintenance of dominance-oriented-theories or -concepts), on communicative processes, I suggest that we combine the insights of many fields and areas of human study to determine what most adequately can serve human beings as a thought-model or approach to communicative interaction, based on our very nature as biological, metabolic, open systems, and thus serve human survival.

To suit such an approach, a specific procedural framework, or system, is suggested here. Even as two nations may attempt to find a kind of *third realm,* a kind of *neutral* meeting place, to provide one basis for the settlement of international conflicts, we can benefit from the development of a similar concept in international and intercultural, or multicultural, communication. Thus we move away from the study of established, identified individual component parts, or even systems, identified *within participating cultures or nations,* to a model which focuses on the situational, interactional, communication *processes* between individuals from various nations, or cultures. I view this process as the conscious establishment of a *third* or *alternative realm*, a situational, supportive *subculture*. I am advocating the conscious development of a multi-cultural systems-construct applicable to specific communicative interaction. It appears to me that this would allow us to see the communication *process* more readily as something different from, or consisting of more than its original component parts. It becomes something based upon and contributed to by *both* original and new factor-combinations, a kind of *situational subculture* developed through the interaction of its members. The approach discussed here may prevent us from assuming that we can understand common communicative-process-functions by studying the original, individual culture and national-compound parts of any communication system in their pristine states. It forces us, *in each instance*, to start with a basically new, situational, systems-model for what may be a significantly different situation, created by the interaction of all contributing parts. It can also prevent the unwarranted and seductive conclusion that we have discovered the underlying *rules of the total game,* rather than gaining some limited, specific insights.

It is assumed that methodologies or systems used in one culture, including those relating to human communication, do not automatically have comparable meanings in other cultures. The basic change in thought and approach suggested here, would require that in the area of multicultural communication we indicate our awareness of the fact that any communication situation consists of parts of all participating cultures, in turn helping to generate a new or different system. This approach may also provide scholar and communicator alike with a basis for avoiding the temptation of simply falling back into his own, best-known, cultural patterns by forcing us into creating an *alternative realm* of communication. This generative interaction, in a situation perceived to be essentially new or different, may, rather than requiring the defense of an existing system or its defeat, make it possible to overcome the alienation or the threats most individuals experience, when they are forced to submit to what they perceive to be a strange culture (or its representatives), for the sake of *getting along*, or for the sake of *communicating*. This latter concept frequently is equated with *agreement.*[25]

The mere existence of the model of this *alternative realm*, or *alternative system*, for those participating in the international or intercultural situation does not create a new basis of interaction by itself. I am suggesting, however, that it might allow participants to interact meaningfully because they see themselves as being individually associated in the situational *structuring* of the actual communication situation. Thus participants can help to develop a common (and meaningful-to-them) system, with a minimum of assumed or real threats resulting from a situation which is perceived as making any one culture or nation the criterion for the human interaction in which participants are engaged.[26]

I stipulated earlier that communication takes place in any situation if there is cognition, and if any kind of meaning is assigned by the participants. It may, however, not result in the cooperative conflict-resolving kind of communication which we tend to consider desirable in Western culture when we use the term communication. Relating all this to international and intercultural communication, I am saying that only when communication becomes a *mutually* beneficial, not a subversive, destructive, or overpowering situation can we have optimum, positive success as a result of international and intercultural, or multi-cultural interaction. Already existing cultural patterns, forming part of any communication situation and forced on others, may very well result in frictions making it impossible to settle disputes, or to accomplish necessary tasks.

What I am suggesting to overcome this problem is a specific phase in multi-cultural communication which is *not dominated* by the already existing parts of the situation. Instead it should be marked by an attempt to make the deep, generative mechanisms of human communication processes function more effectively by allowing creative interaction on all levels. This should result in such an adjustment of human beings as biological, metabolic systems, that a situational *territory of mutuality* is created which can make later task-orientations more beneficial. Whether this territory provides for deep immersion or a more temporary adjustment should be a feature of the actual process of communication, rather than some arbitrary, or absolute standard which has been predetermined. General-Systems theorists suggest that we should not develop any approach to multicultural communication which is merely based on the understanding of parts, but also on their functions as they interact in the systems, and their functioning in specific situations.[27]

The system suggested here, is based on a definite, initial effort to develop what I have called *mutuality* within an *alternative realm* or setting, rather than a jockeying for positions while attempting to persuade others to see *our* side of the issue. This may make it possible to create less offensive bases for interaction, because we do not start by requiring someone to move to our side, nor do we begin by *coercing* others in a variety of physical and intellectual ways. Important to such an approach (both in practice and in model- or theory-construction) would also be the willingness of participants to first understand themselves, their own background, needs, or even their lack of awareness or naivete. It requires a kind of growing together in an area or phase that some might describe as *neutral*, but which I see more as a state of readiness, going beyond that which would be available if we merely *mixed* already existing and available component parts. What is suggested is that participants need to develop a new, or different communication situation *together*, by helping their social-communicative-survival metabolism to adjust first. Communication thus is seen not merely as a service-function, or as a superimposed methodology for accomplishing other things, but as an expression of human beings engaged in a mutually beneficial, supportive process.

In a way then the *alternative realm* is a conscious, probably limited-in-time creation of a *sub-culture* for the purpose of accomplishing certain tasks based on communicative interaction. Communication becomes a major sub-culture-tool used by all participants for *fitting* into a pattern which somehow has to make sense to individuals in that sub-culture, as it contributes to their feelings of homeostasis. Some of these communicative associations may be *deep* because they have a great *utility*. Others can be easily shed, if we see new needs develop. The use of the *alternative realm* thus taks cognizance of the fact that regardless of what culture or nation an individual belongs to, he still interprets and uses his culture in individual ways. The *alternative realm* assists in making personal interpretations of culture consonant with other concepts held by other individuals. In the long run, that is always accomplished by using, hiding or applying what is available, according to some internal code or set of *rules* which makes sense to individual human beings.

Culture is defined here as all common features developed and accepted by individuals for their *own purposes* as well as *common* goals, within a given setting. The *alternative communication subculture*, suggested here forms the basis of a proposed multicultural communication model. Culture is not defined as an idealized concept of *absolute sameness* or highly developed *similarity*. Because, whatever similarities are stressed, whatever sameness there is seen in members of the same culture, frequently is only the result of some preconceived concept which has been developed to indicate the unity of some group. Culture can thus become a construct altogether too easily *discovered* by those who look for it as related to the system-constructs they bring to it, and used for their own, prejudiced purposes.

Culture is a system for structuring the environment and responses to it, for purposes of explanation, understanding, use, control and social interaction by people. As was indicated earlier, culture thus can become a formal institution, or an institutionalized concept, used by individuals who are interested in uniting or controlling individuals by using perceived similarities for their own purposes. However, over time human beings tend to preserve those factors which a community of individuals has somehow judged valid to their *personal* human survival needs. Others are rejected or overturned, because they were not judged to be thus valid. Since this approach appears to be commonly used by individuals over long periods of time within existing or developing cultures to optimize their survival chances, the question can be asked: Why not use a similar approach of *cultural development*, in a very similar way for the purpose of developing the proposed or *alternative* realm, as a *sub-culture* for communication, but in a shorter period of time? I am not suggesting the development of another static state, or another limited definition of culture which freezes the underlying concept. Much rather, it appears clear to me that both culture and communication, because of their close relationship, are continually changing, inventing and reinventing, creating and recreating their component parts on the basis of underlying, generative codes and rules, rather than merely on the surface, or the systems-level discussed earlier.

Another basic concept developed in this paper is that it is impossible to find the answers we seek on the basis of any *one*, culturally-based, systems-theory. For instance, it is becoming evident that we have exhausted the utility of mechanical sender-receiver models, and that we have to look at interpersonal communication as generative, situational interaction. The contact of individuals has to be seen from the standpoint of surface, systematized component parts as well as the underlying codes and rules which are brought to it, making each event unique. What has been stressed here is that communication is a joint venture to which its participants contribute, each at his own level, according to his own perceptions and needs, but all of them making up the total situation. As a result, everything that is done or said by any individual in that situation does modify what others say and do. Having understood that factor, it becomes clear that *deviation from any established or preconceived norm of multi-cultural interaction is a usual rather than an exceptional thing.* Moreover, as a result, normative generalizations cannot be meaningfully applied to all individual instances. In any situation people shape each other's perceptions and thus their overall interaction. Meanings discovered or ascribed are unique to the moment, continuously *generated* by those who participate in the communicative event. Give-and-take between participants in these situations may finally result in a kind of common ground, or matrix, but understanding depends on internal corrective adjustments of the usual interpretations which a culture or subculture has prepared an individual to *discover.*

Any instance of multicultural communication would appear to require an intent, a need, or set toward some direction, response, or the seeking of context. If this is not in some part a *mutual* interactional feature of the communication process, many problems and confrontations develop. However, if or when such *mutuality* does exist, we tend to say that effective intercultural and international, or multi-cultural, communication results, and that we are witnessing successful attempts to actively go beyond what would routinely or *normally* happen within any *one* culture, or without that mutuality.

What I have tried to outline in this chapter can be briefly summarized. A major problem in studying international and intercultural, or multi-cultural, communication, arises from the assumption that existing systems, structures, theories, or choices in one (usually our own) culture will produce very similar communicative frameworks or systems in another culture. This idea is often the result of the unproven assumption, that "after all, human beings, underneath it all, are really all the same." In effect, frequently it does not concern itself with individual human beings and their interactions, but rather with the interpretation of systems stipulated by various observers, and dealt with as if they were part of the natural order of things. As a result, we often end up on a merry chase with predetermined results. We may become victims of our desire to discover commonality or universality, instead of being comfortable with individuality or variety as a possible basis for human communication. Earlier approaches may very well have guided our thinking to such an extent that we simply look for methodologies and structures which will produce *the same meaning* in other cultures. What we have referred to as communication thus often requires *submission* by one or more of the participating cultures (or their representatives) rather than *mutuality*, which leads to adaptation, understanding, interaction, interdependence, or a feeling of meaningful participation, if not equality, by all.

FOOTNOTES

[1] Fred L. Casmir, "Integrating Theoretical Constructs in Human Communication," an unpublished paper presented to the Annual Convention of the Communication Association of the Pacific, Kobe, Japan, June, 1976.

[2] Peter R. Monge, "Alternative Theoretical Bases for the Study of Human Communication: The Systems Perspective," a paper presented at the Annual Convention of the Speech Communication Association, Houston, Texas, December 1975; and Donald P. Cushman, "Alternative Theoretical Bases for the Study of Human Communication: The Rules Perspective," a paper presented at the Annual Convention of the Speech Communication Association, Houston, Texas, December, 1975.

[3] Monge, p. 14.

[4] Monge, p. 15.

[5] Edward H. Madden, "A Third View of Causality," *The Review of Metaphysics*, 23 (1969), pp. 67-84.

[6] Ervin E. Lazzlo, *The Systems View of the World* (New York: Braziller, 1972), p. 20. See also, Cushman, p. 5.

[7] Cushman, p. 5.

[8] Cushman, p. 4.

[9] Leigh Marlowe, *Social Psychology*; Boston: Holbrook Press, Inc., 1975, p. 305.

[10] Edgar H. Schein, "Changing Top Management Values Through Action Research," a paper presented at the 81st Annual Convention of the American Psychological Association, 1973. As quoted by Marlowe, p. 306.

[11] Casmir, pp. 19, 20.

[12] Cushman, 6 ff.

[13] Cushman, p. 14.

[14] Arthur Koestler, *The Act of Creation*; New York: The MacMillan Company, 1964, pp. 40, 38.

[15] G.E. Coghill, "The Structural Basis of the Integration of Behavior," in: *Proceedings of the National Academy of Sciences*, 16(1930), p. 637.

[16] Marlowe, p. 305.

[17] Marlowe, p. 207.

[18] Marlowe, p. 122.

[19] James T. Tedeschi, Barry R. Schlenker, Thomas V. Bonoma, "Cognitive Dissonance: Private Ratiocination or Public Spectacle," *American Psychologist*, 26(1971), p. 8; and Leon Festinger, *A Theory of Cognitive Dissonance*, Stanford, California: Stanford University Press, 1957.

[20] Marlowe, p. 89.

[21] Knud S. Larsen, Don Coleman, Jim Forbes, Robert Johnson, "Is the Subject's Personality or the Experimental Situation a Better Predictor of a Subject's Willingness to Administer Shock to a Victim?" *Journal of Personality and Social Psychology*, 22 (1972), p. 3.

[22] Edward L. Walker, Roger W. Heyns, *An Anatomy of Conformity*, Belmont, California: Brooks/Cole, 1967, p. 5.

[23] William S. Howell is Professor of Speech-Communication at the University of Minnesota. In a series of exchanges in the form of letters and discussions at various national, professional meetings, these ideas were expressed by him.

[24] Coghill. See also Koestler, p. 415 ff.

[25] Consider the discussion of "two-story-culture" in L. Stanley

Harms, *International Communication*, New York: Harper & Row, 1973.

[26] Harms, Chapter 3.

[27] Monge, pp. 4-12.

II

II

INTERCULTURAL COMMUNICATION

THERE have been a number of attempts to categorize types of human communication. Because of varied interests and the nature of the academic world in the United States, very few such definitions have been fully acceptable to everyone, and most of them have been the subject of long debates and sometimes vigorous disagreements.

I shall not attempt to add to that confusing array of definitions. For our purposes, it will suffice to indicate that the following chapters will deal with a number of aspects relating to interaction between people who have different cultural backgrounds. Culture under those circumstances refers to the values, experiences, precepts and other lasting factors which have been transmitted by human beings through generations, or certainly over a period of time involving more than one generation, because they were considered to be of some value in the maintenance of human society and the survival of its individual members. It is not my intention to claim that such factors, summarized here under the term culture, are necessarily clearly understood or recognized as cultural factors by individuals who are members of a cultural group. As a matter of fact, it has been consistently pointed out that the only thing more difficult than understanding another culture may be understanding one's own culture on a level which makes the purposeful, planned sharing of its concepts and values easy. People, in other words, frequently have trouble identifying what are the *major* component parts of their own culture if they are asked to do so, and they may have even greater trouble listing all the *smaller* component parts of their cultural heritage. As a result, most of our learning about other cultures results from painstaking and long-range observation of what others say and do, or formally structure, record and transmit in some

fashion. In addition, in that kind of study the cultural background of
the observer can interfere with his observations, frequently resulting
in misinterpretations.

In any case, it is evident that it is neither easy to report on one's
own culture nor is it easy to adequately observe another culture.
Much of the problem results simply from the dynamic nature of
man, the dynamic communication of human beings, the constantly
changing nature of the total human process and the human
communication process. This must be coupled with the fact that
what we summarize as culture is always used, interpreted, or rejected
by individual human beings in keeping with their personal survival
needs. Cultural consistencies thus may be no more than statistical
averages compiled by an observer, for which we may have difficulty
finding specific examples in the daily lives of members of the given
culture. On the other hand, culture-specifics identified by an
observer may also be very consistent and persistent factors which
tend to be modified only slightly by individual members of a cultural
group. What I am warning against is the attempt to oversimplify,
when in effect we are ignoring the need for situational, individual
evaluations; observations; or interpretations; that is, for flexibility in
applying what we may have learned.

Our assumption in the past has been that culture is a major
factor, or possibly *the* major factor, in much of human
communication. At present, our earlier overemphasis tends to be
modified by what I consider to be a more adequate point of view,
namely that culture is *one* factor, and often an important one.
However, it is also a factor which is or can be significantly modified
by individual human beings when their own needs demand it. Such a
modification in application of cultural norms does not necessarily
mean that we discard a specific cultural value or concept for all
times.

Different scholars have seen a need to identify types of
interaction between members of different cultures by different terms
such as "cross-cultural" or "inter-cultural." The common feature in
the use of all these terms appears to be an awareness that human
beings are put into positions where they have to go beyond, or cross
lines of cultural demarcation, cultural barriers, or cultural lines of

separation in order to accomplish their purposes. That could be the case with a missionary who desires to share a religious message with a member of another culture, possibly even in a different nation/state. Or it could be illustrated by the desire of a white businessman in American society to interact successfully, in accordance with whatever definition of success is relevant to him, with a member of a minority culture in his own nation. Whenever differences in important value systems or concept structures are transmitted by one group to another group, we often face an intercultural or cross-cultural communication challenge. Let me mention here just in passing that because of our own "conflict-solution" or "problem-solution" orientation in American society we tend to approach such communication situations as problems or challenges which need to be "solved." Seldom, if ever, does it occur to us, or do we include in our thinking the possibility that such intercultural or cross-cultural situations could enhance communication or make it richer and more meaningful. Differences, real or perceived, are seen as barriers. Similarity or sameness, on the other hand, is seen as desirable. That appears to be the case notwithstanding the fact that one of our cultural values can be identified as a concern with individuality, uniqueness, or non-conformity. Here, as in many other areas, our expectations may very well lead us to discover agreement with our preconceived points of view, rather than discovery of what "may really be out there."

A large number of items relating to intercultural communication could have been considered in the following chapters, but of necessity we had to limit our considerations to a few vital areas. However, the authors of the following chapters have made an attempt not merely to come up with episodic, or highly specific examples, but to deal as well with underlying structures, complete systems, or at least with more generalizable concepts which can be used in a number of specific ways as the necessity arises. The reader is thus urged to read beyond the specific examples and search for principles or general considerations which may be developed into applicable systems in a variety of ways.

Stewart provides a sweeping review of disciplines and scholars which can be of great help in our study. Whether or not the reader concludes that intercultural and international communication are separate academic fields or disciplines, or merely specific emphases within some larger field of human endeavor, is up to the reader. Individual preferences, specific situational needs, our own backgrounds, insecurities, or methods of classification will result in different conclusions. Agreeing with General Semanticists, I would urge the reader to avoid looking at our areas of emphasis in the hope of discovering an absolute, already existing reality. I don't really know what intercultural communication IS, or what international communication IS. Rather, I am willing to deal with specific definitions provided by various authors and scholars and see how they fit into their own General, Systems thinking not merely to search for existing systems on the level of natural laws, but to flexibly structure, evaluate, and use such systems depending on specific situational, interactional needs.

To make that point, a discussion of the relatively new field of sociology and its interests in the communicative interaction of human beings is followed by a chapter dealing with speech communication in the forms of speaking and writing. Both sociology and speech communication thus provide bases on which we can study the relationship of long-standing principles to our specific emphasis on the relationship of culture to human communication. Loomis, Epstein, and Condon thus build a bridge from the broader theoretical bases provided in the first section of this book to intercultural communication as a specific area of interest. Kraft addresses himself to value systems which are often considered to be vital in understanding our functioning as human beings, and Glenn develops basic intercultural models which find their specific application in political interaction. Chisholm and von Eckartsberg provide a reminder of the fact that whatever innate bases there are for human communication, it is also a process which can be improved through learning, through interaction, and through the total socialization process in which human beings are involved. Thus, moving from theoretical bases to practical application, these authors help in devising specific educational models which can assist us in improving communication or overcoming difficulties. Yamauchi, on the other hand, develops age as one among a number of possible factors such as sex, race, etc., to indicate how such fairly readily identifiable features of individual human beings, become bases for norms and standards of interaction in human society.

Much more could obviously be included in this study of the intercultural aspects of human communication. However, as in the case of all introductions to a subject matter, I hope these samples will serve as means for whetting our appetite as we attempt to discover more and more facets of the everchanging kaleidoscope of human communication.

Edward C. Stewart

Outline of Intercultural Communication

Intercultural communication is called a *field* for simplicity in writing. This area of communication is so loosely structured that some writers deny to it the status of a field in any formal sense. (Howell, 1976) The ambiguous theoretical structure reflects the status of both major concepts, *communication* and *culture*, which have stoutly resisted formal definitions in the social sciences.

Concepts in intercultural communication generally "sensitize"; they "convey a sense of reference and orientation grasped through personal experience."[1] Although formal concepts exist, they are not the significant features of the field. It is premature and may be irrelevant for intercultural communication to construct formal theories, test hypotheses and verify postulates following the traditional canons of the sciences. Crystallization of terms now would probably dampen development. Furthermore, loose theoretical structure can be expected in areas of the social sciences which do not abide solely, if at all, by models, principles and terms derived from the study of the physical sciences.

For these two reasons, and others as well, the *Outline* proposes competence as the frame for formal definition of theoretical terms. The cluster of concepts filed under theory attracts research, stimulates thought and sustains vigor in the field. Intercultural communication impinges upon the humanities and the arts and derives from them, as well as from veins of social sciences. The *Outline* draws boundaries for the field, selects topics, provides a review of theories of intercultural communication, scans the empirical accomplishments and inches into the future. Even as a map it must exclude some views and must adopt a system of projection. Thus it is inevitable that distortions appear; some views are omitted, and both a direction and a position emerge in the *Outline*.

I. Basic Concepts

A.   Paradox of Communication

Writers in the field of information and communication theory refer to the paradox that communication is concerned with what is shared, but if senders and receivers share too much, there is no need for communication. The need arises because something is not shared, cannot be foreseen and must be conveyed. It is this unknown element that is an essential part of communication.[2] Having mentioned the paradox, most writers move on to consider the shared aspects of communication and neglect the non-shared. The paradox of communication, and the stress on the shared qualities, reveals the pervasiveness of the principle of similarity in communication.

1.   Similarity Principle

The concept of similarity has often been used in psychology and philosophy, but seldom has it received the treatment of theory. Writing of the problem of similarity quantification, Gregson observes the

> . . . sheer paucity of psychological theorizing on similarity before the 1950's is due, apparently, to the subject being defined as inherently intractable by some philosophers, and being made a prior issue in symbolic logic by others. If a psychologist were to do experiments on similarity, he had either to do that which had been defined away, or to refuse to be outfaced by the elaborate formal rigor of the logical analysis.[3]

Attneave drew attention to the neglect of the measurement of similarity and to the resulting confusion caused in areas of psychology (1950). He was concerned with the precision of quantification unlike Wallach (1958), who gives a qualitative analysis suggesting four ways of defining psychological similarity[4]. These are common environmental properties, common responses, closeness of neural traces, and, fourth, assignment of items to a common category.[5] Gregson, in his *Psychometrics of Similarity* provides the most thorough treatment of similarity, although it is well to note that he writes from the perspective of measurement and quantification. (1975)

More recently, Tversky has turned his attention to the subject of "features of similarity." His opening paragraph places the role of similarity in the field of psychology:

> Similarity plays a fundamental role in theories of knowledge and behavior. It serves as an organizing principle by which individuals classify objects, form concepts, and make generalizations. Indeed, the concept of a similarity is ubiquitous in psychological theory. It underlies the accounts of stimulus and response generalization in learning, it is employed to explain errors in memory and pattern recognition, and it is central to the analysis of connotative meaning.[6]

Tversky develops a model of similarity in which objects are represented as collections of features. The similarity between objects is expressed as a combination of features which they share in common and those which are distinctive to each object. In less rigorous language, the simultaneous attention given to similarities and differences of the objects implies a *contrast model.*

> The contrast model expresses similarity between objects as a weighted difference of the measures of their common and distinctive features, thereby allowing for a variety of similarity relations over the same domain. (Tversky, 1977.)[7]

In the contrast model, both likeness and difference are used to express similarity, which loses its status of uniqueness in the paradox of communication. For Tversky, differences gain a berth alongside similarities.

B.   Similarities in Communication

Researchers in the field of interpersonal attraction, who examine the psychological bases for social interaction, generally conclude that attraction is positively influenced by personality similarities. (Byrne and Griffitt, 1973) The research has usually been conducted with American subjects, but a recent study systematically extends the finding to other cultures, and concludes that there is a ubiquitous relationship between attitude similarity and attraction. (Byrne, 1971)

Descriptions of behavior or of attitude which fall into the dichotomy of either similar or different are too sweeping to serve empirical purposes. It is clear that a general psychological theory, at *some* level of abstraction, shall contain behavioral laws independent of cultural backgrounds, and hence based on similarities. The more widely that an "attribute set" is defined, the more likely is similarity discovered.[8] There are universals of human behavior, such as in basic processes. In learning, for example, food serves an identical function of reinforcer. Specific details differ: the effectiveness of "chocolate" or "whale fat" varies from society to society.[9] The argument for similarity frequently associates similarities of biology and environment with transcultural properties of behavior, which view in turn launches the proposition:

> Our supposition is that the response to attitudes is based on common learning experiences which stresses the desirability of being logical and correct in perceiving the world as others do.[10]

These conditions and conclusions are general, lack operational definitions and specify little outside the context of the experimental studies in which the alternative responses of subjects are limited. These are the conditions for collecting responses on the basis of similarity, since it has been shown that strong situational variables will obscure the role of individual differences.[11] In unscrambling the effects of similarity and difference, it is essential to stress the interaction between dualities of personality and the situation and the great difficulty of attributing determination of behavior to global qualities or traits of personality. (Mischel, 1973)

The field of personal attraction has recently provided a forum for increasing the differentiation of the psychological and social bases underlying the processes of communication. Mettee and Riskind show that under circumstances of competition, the defeated prefer to lose at the hands of those who are different, not similar (1973). Fromkin (1973) reviews a body of research in which the general categories of similarity and differences are refined. He reports, for instance, that when facts are at issue, people are attracted to others who are different, but when values are in question, people choose others who are similar. In these observations we find the start of a useful analysis of similarities and of differences.

A second area of research which is relevant to our inquiry is the field of diffusion of innovation. At the social level, theory has provided the context for the development of ideas of *homophily* and *heterophily*, referring respectively to similarity and differences. The concept of homophily, similarity, apparently originated with Tarde (Tarde, 1903), who stated that social relations are closer among people who are similar in occupation and education. The term now is used primarily in the literature on innovation, and homophily, similarity, is declared to underscore the adoption of innovations. Rogers and Shoemaker (1971) write:

> When source and receiver, share common meanings, attitudes and beliefs, and a mutual language, communication between them is likely to be effective.[12]

The quotation conveys the flavor of the position underscoring the importance of homophily. It is a position which is now undergoing modification as heterophily is discovered to underlie diffusion of innovation. Dodd reaches a similar conclusion in his study of the spread of Christianity in Ghana, focusing on a non-technological innovation (1973). He concludes that in the adoption stages of innovation, heterophily prevails, while homophily characterizes sociometric choice of opinion leaders.[13] It would seem that diffusion of innovation, by definition, involves heterophily, since innovation is a difference diffused among dissimilar people.

Although research may modify the significance of similarity, the principle is deeply entrenched in American conventional wisdom. Its strength perhaps is great enough for it to qualify as an assumption in American thought and communication. Thus the more similar two persons are, the better they should communicate, whereas differences impede communication. In some other cultures, however, differences may be assumed necessary for communication to take place, and success is not measured by agreement and conformity as it tends to be in American life.[14]

C. Differences in Communication

The need to communicate arises when senders and receivers do not share something which should be conveyed. It would appear that this difference is the core of communication, yet study of the process has normally searched for the similarities, as we have seen. It is only with intercultural communication that difference becomes the centerpiece of communication, studied in its variations throughout cultures.

The incisive insight about differences suggests that, first, "difference" is an abstract matter, and, secondly, it is in its most elementary sense synonymous with the word "idea."[15] The conclusion begins with an observation about:

> . . . an important contrast between most of the pathways of information inside the body and most of the pathways outside it.[16]

The distinction is straightforward and the usual one made: external-internal, exterior-interior, substance-mind, etc. In the external world, "effects" in general are brought about by concrete conditions or events which can be classified as impact, force and energy exchanges.[17] When energy from the external world impinges upon receptor organs leading to the mind, there is transformation of energy. In the internal world, in the mind, the flow of energy and the production of effects observe principles different from the cause and effects of the world of substance, where events are caused by forces and impacts and in which there are no differences.

270

In the internal world of mind it is differences which bring about "effects," if the word is still appropriate.[18] Following Bateson closely, Adams claims that:

> To speak of dissimilarities or differences places us squarely within the mentalistic structural realm. We must assume that the world about us is made up of things that vary in similitude and, further, that our powers of observation are not entirely misleading in telling us that two horses are more alike than are a horse and a ladder. But we also have good indications that where we draw the line between similarity and dissimilarity depends greatly on our own experience and that it is always a *relative* boundary.[19]

It is Bateson, the anthropologist, who has stressed most clearly the keen insight that differences are the stuff of the mental world. Abundant anthropological information was accumulated during the 1920's and the 1930's to test out theories of basic human nature. By the end of this period, enough evidence was in hand to verify the plasticity and variation of man's behavior. (Byrne, 1971) In the field of psychology the study of differences languished. Psychologists did not generally exploit the information collected by anthropologists, so that the literature on differences was slight in comparison to that on similarity. Since World War II, the interest of anthropologists shifted toward similarities among cultures, which enabled psychologists to test out the validity of their theories.[20] (The same postwar period, nevertheless, provided the frame for the psychology of human differences (Tyler, 1956), a minor trend running against the current.)

The popularity of similarity is suspect when considered from a systematic point of view and particularly if we accept Bateson's insight. To perceive a likeness is bound up with a difference; to note a similarity must imply recognition of a difference, a divergence from sameness. It may be better to consider perception or the expectation of communication to rest on anticipated differences. If a difference is not noted, then the judgment of sameness is made in the sense of a residue. Hanson appears to propose such an idea: "There are

271

alternative ways of determining whether two particles are identical, but the answer is always the same: they are completely identical unless they are obviously different."[21] The germ of the idea is there that the perception of difference is at least as fundamental as that of similarity.

From the laboratory in the area of judging sounds, there is the discovery that judgments of sameness of sounds and of difference of sounds are not equivalent obverse aspects of a unitary judgmental process such as two sides of the same coin. Subjects take longer to decide that two tones are the same than that two tones are different. (Bindra, 1965) At the perceptual and judgmental level there exists a difference between perceiving and judging same and different, with difference apparently the easier and preferred response. Building on this psychological process, there may well exist a general "mental set" to find similarities versus meeting differences. It is on this issue of differences, either naturally or by acquisition, that intercultural communication rests its claim for identity. The concept of differences may be approached by building theory on dimensions ("diversified sameness") rather than on categories. Furthermore, contrasts may replace comparisons as tools of thinking. Finally, static concepts may yield to dialectical processes.

D. Theory of Competence

Two issues have been broached which deserve mention before we develop the underpinnings of competence theory in communication and culture. The first issue was the reference to concepts in the field of intercultural communication, which were described as "sensitizing." The looseness of the description invites a firmer definition, but one that preserves the essential quality of sensitizing concepts, evocation of the experience of the communicator. This quality leads to a search for a theoretical position closely aligned with applications.

The second issue, which like the first will serve as preconception, is the concept of differences and the distinction made between internal and external worlds. The statement readily brings to mind the analysis of Chomsky, who distinguished between theories of competence and theories of performance (1960). The suggestion emerges that competence should reside in the internal world while performance should take its place in the external. But before reaching this conclusion, it is necessary to demonstrate how competence theories contribute to the understanding of communication and culture. We will address the question by characterizing the features of theories and concepts which benefit from competence theories, using language as an example, and then arguing by analogy, that similar conclusions apply to both communication and culture.

Perhaps the most interesting feature of a language, English for example, is the infinite capacity of a speaker to produce original utterances which have never been said before; yet each is understood and clearly classified as English. On the one side, we have a code of the language, which can be defined, and its specific features identified. On the other side, there are the productions of the language. Experience tells us that any speaker has the competence to regale us with entirely original utterances, which he has never learned specifically and which therefore cannot be treated as verbal habits. The speaker has created; he has produced an innovation in language.

This dilemma of language led Chomsky to develop his theories of competence and of performance. Language, and we will argue by analogy communication and culture, represents concepts which can be given finite expressions, but these concepts are Janus figures with a second face turned toward behavior. This perspective has no vanishing point, while the first face exists within a finite space of the mind. The production of behavior is infinite, and no formal definition can encompass its possibilities. This domain of behavior and theories about it are what is meant by *performance*.[22]

The inability of perception, or we might say of the ability to categorize and bring order, and particularly to set the boundaries on performance, leads to the search for some structure of process, for a model which can be used to at least approximate the plenitude of human productions. With the use of imagination, intuition and fantasy people are able to respond to what was not observed[23] and build a more nearly perfect world, orderly and dependable. Perceivers make discriminations among classes of stimuli that resist analysis and must be called by sensitizing terms of aesthetic, good continuation, etc.[24]

Theory must handle these complexities. First it is necessary to point out that performance is linked to what is happening in the internal world; these are not separate realms enjoying independent sovereignty. They are formally linked so that we can describe the internal correspondence as a mental or cognitive representation of the external world of objects and the environment for performance.[25] Competence theory is about mental representation of information about the perceptual and behavioral worlds. [26]

It is important to retain a difference between competence theory and cognitive processes theories. The two are not the same. When we refer to competence theory, we talk about the mental representation of specific routines of perception on one side, and of performance on the other. The representation is spare, built with parsimony; it governs performance. It is clearly a part of the mental representations of the cognitive processes, but competence does not trap the rich complexity which quivers the cognitive processes. Thus we may speak of a tier of theories of decreasing specificity and simplicity: cognitive, competence and performance.[27]

Returning to competence theories, there are two conditions to be met for membership. The first is that belongingness cannot be specified by any finite list of elementary sensory properties, nor by logical combinations of elementary properties alone. Membership is a matter of *recursive definitions*.[28] The features of the definition include aspects which we have already mentioned, and in addition a pattern for definitions in which instances of a concept are analyzed into finite features; and representation of a concept also yields a finite set of parts or features. Finally, descriptions must be procedural, and on this point, Pylyshyn quotes Humboldt's famous phrase: "Infinite product by finite means."[29]

The mental representation which we have assigned to competence theory is generative, yielding recursive definitions and procedural descriptions. These ideas are clear, although sometimes controversial in linguistics. By analogy we argue that the competence model is appropriate in communication. This identifies the core of competence in communication as processes and structures in the brain, the mental representation of communicative perceptions and behavior. Definition of communication specifies components and functions.

By analogy it is possible to treat culture as competence theory. The concept can be reduced to component parts, functions can be defined, and in all respects, the conditions for competence can be met. This strategy also reflects conventional wisdom. For instance, when assessing a traveler's adjustment to another society, we may refer to his *cultural competence*. It is possible to identify the actions and the *performance* on which our evaluation is based.

In the field of intercultural communication and for this *Outline*, the concept of *subjective culture* is used. Cultural refers to mental representations, and this meaning indicates a second theoretical interpretation of culture, which would complement our treatment of communication as competence. In this second sense, subjective culture would serve as the background of cognitive processes for communication competence.

In conclusion, selections of competence, cognitive or even of performance theories, reflect strategic choices. Competence is the most useful view of communication, while either competence or cognitive processes mediate the meaning of culture. These choices are summarized in Figure 1.

Figure 1. Tier of Theories

Cognitive Theories	Psychological Cognitive Processes	Subjective Cultural Processes
Competence Theories	Cultural Competence	Communication Competence
Performance Theories	Actions	Behavior

II. Theory of Communication

Theory in communication draws concepts and procedures from information theory, linguistics, social psychology, semiotics, perception, technology, psychology, philosophy, sociology, aesthetics and language. The *Outline* avoids a roll call of the sciences and arts; instead it turns to each to extricate the principles, concepts and contents which seem relevant for intercultural communication.

One guide is to determine the process and structure of communication and to identify those principles, laws and methods which characterize communication as an idependent field. Efforts along this direction, such as those grounded in information theory, symbolism, or in some other model, do not present a coherent and comprehensive theory of communication. Thus this section contains "chunks" or empirical problems treated at a systematic and theoretical level.

A. Core Theory of Communication

The mathematical theory of communication provides a precise set of concepts and during the ensuing twenty years has yielded an impressive body of empirical data. Concepts drawn from the mathematical theory have been widely applied in practice and in other fields, inappropriately nevertheless. The core meaning of the mathematical concepts has been lost in the transformation so that what the man in the street means by information and communication has perfectly indifferent relationship to the mathematical concepts developed in information and communication theory.

Although the vocabulary of the mathematical theory is retained, social psychology, psychology, linguistics and symbolic processes are employed to provide both theory and an empirical body of facts to communication. This practice contributes to interdisciplinary efforts and raises the question of the core theory of "communication." What are the theories and bodies of facts which make a unique contribution to communication and set the field apart from others?

Smith edited *Communication and Culture* (1966), Dance collected original essays in *Human Communication Theory* (1967), Pool and others edited *Handbook of Communication* (1973), and innumerable other books and articles have been written to present theories and views of communication. Nevertheless a comprehensive and definitive view of a separate field has not appeared. Core theory can perhaps be approached by drawing from each relevant area the key ideas which contribute to communication.

Information and communication theories provide the central idea that communication means that a communicator selects a message (information) drawn from a universe of possible alternatives like selection of a card from a deck of cards. All the alternatives are known or determinable so that communication occurs within a domain of determinable factors, and it can be quantified. This key idea provides much of the special quality easily recognized in information theory. Using terminology developed by Black (1972), the mathematical theory can be said to employ selected information and ignore substantive information -- or what the layman would call *meaning*. To bridge this gap, the concept of semantic information has been developed (Black, 1972), and although it too fails to attain meaning, semantic information introduces the area of linguistics, which has taken such spectacular strides in recent years. The chief contribution of linguistics from the point of view of communication is that it presents an analysis of the code, the language which is deeply enmeshed in undetermined ways with communication. The field also provides methods and empirical bodies of data which are extremely useful -- but eventually do not define a core theory.

The work with generative grammars has raised the very interesting question of universals in language. (Chomsky, 1957) In some way, it is asserted that cognitive processes underlie and are expressed through all languages, thus the Whorfian hypothesis, that language governs thought, is turned on its head: language flows from thought. Whatever the case may be, there is a close connection between thinking and language. It would appear natural for psychology to make contributions to language and to communication by drawing upon samplings from learning, motivation, perception, personality, cognition, small groups and psycholinguistics. The clarity and precision of the mathematical definitions, quantified and based on process, are overwhelmed by onslaughts of facts, perspectives and theories. The only areas passed over by psychology are picked up by sociology and anthropology.

The title of Hulett's article, "A Symbolic Interactionist Model of Human Communication" (1966), recalls the emphasis on acts and on the setting where communication takes place. A second focus in this tradition, frequently identified with Duncan (1967), stresses symbols and symbolic processes, with the result that communication acquires a deeper level or perhaps a second level of meaning. The symbol suggests a link with the society, history and perhaps even myth for the selection and transmission of messages in a contrast to the cognitive depth implanted in psychology and projected by deep structures of language. Beyond the stress on symbols, communication has been given the very general and pervasive definition which identified it with the fabric of society itself. (Pye, 1963) These broad uses raise the legitimate question of the core of the theory of communication.

B. *Components of Communication*

The process of communication is made up of eight components, according to the analysis of Hymes (1973).
1. Code
The first component, *code*, must be shared, or it must be similar to some significant degree, for the process of communication to take place. An example of a code is represented by language (English is a code), but there are non-verbal codes as well, for example, music, visual stimuli, kinesics. The term *semiotics* has been applied to refer to all codes, verbal and non-verbal.[30]
   a. Verbal Codes - language
A code is a set or a system of symbols which are combined according to rules or procedures. Words or vocabulary compose one set of elements of verbal codes, while the rules and procedures of combination are the grammar or syntax. Other codes are also composed of elements and the rules for combining. In addition to these two aspects of codes, there is a third which refers to the relationship between the code and its users. This aspect is usually handled in terms of meaning, function, or application, or of some combination of these concepts.

The elements of the code were said to be symbols which are intentional representations standing for something else. The search for a symbol can continue one more step, to reach the sign which represents it. Thus *tree* is a symbol at one level, but the visual pattern which makes up the word is a sign, or the relationship between trees and other words in grammatical arrangement refers to signs but not to symbols. The relationship between the sign and its object of reference introduces the symbol. This distinction between what may be termed manifest meaning, the sign and latent meaning, is an important one, which will recur, since it provides a means of separating variant from invariant factors in language.

The field of linguistics was galvanized by the publication of Chomsky (1957), who precipitated a renewed search for universals of human cognitive processes, or cognitions, which underlie all languages. These deep structures of the mind are transformed into surfaces or spoken and written language. This view of thought and of languages gives rise to the terms generative and transformational grammars, which are the rules connecting the deep structures and surfaces of language.

Verbal codes of language serve many functions. One of these is that of meaning, which some linguists have associated with semantics, assigning it more stress than has Chomsky. This direction in linguistics is known as generative semantics, and in a non-technical perspective topics such as word taboos and sacred words establish a connection between semantics and social and personal control of actions.

b. Patterns of Codes

Some writers emphasize variations of communication which occur in communicative events. Such an approach (Hymes, 1973) leads to efforts to develop frames of reference rather than theories of communication. The parameters of situations, or of events, become systematic aspects of theory, and in a sense there are codes which are applicable for specific events rather than for general communication.

2. Content or Topic of Communication

Communication involves the transmission of a message, and the material in it can be defined as the *content* or *topic*. As with the code, analysis of content yields both elements and structure. *Content analysis* is an effective method of research in communication which can be taken far beyond the simple distinction made here. (Holsti, 1968)

3. Participants in Communication

The customary analysis of the participants to sender and receiver should not obscure the assumption that communication is a process. (Analysis of receiver and sender provides the entry into intercultural communication and hence will be elaborated under III. Cultural differences will be defined as properties of the sender and the receiver.) An important focus for analysis is the disparity between the sender and the receiver in the process of communication: the receiver listens for a "sound," but the sender emits "words." Thus the sender and the receiver do not obtain a symmetrical relationship with the process of communication. To send and to receive are not the same. Whatever attributes are employed to define the sender and the receiver should take stock of their asymmetries to each other. They may differ with respect to reality or illusion. What is real for one may be illusionary for the other, but whatever their type, attributes may be differently distributed for different groups of senders or receivers. A third consideration involves the accessibility or the visibility of the attributes, and closely related is the quality of how comprehensible it is in respect to communication and the compatibility between sending and receiving. The degree to which attributes of senders and receivers are accepted, desired, feared, avoided, obviously influences the process of communication. A final factor refers to the congruence which may exist among the values of senders and receivers.

4. Form or Shape of Messages

Selections made by a sender of code and content represent his style, patterns or arrangements of the message. When these are selected for persuasion and considered in the context of speech and philosophy, we speak of *rhetoric*. The form of a message raises the significant issue of level of communication. Two levels can be distinguished at the outset: overt and covert; or manifest and latent; or meaningful and perceptual levels.

In the area of the arts, music, painting and sculpture, the perceptual aspects of form in sound and vision are systematically linked to the overt meaning of the "message." This perceptual aspect receives treatment as the "code" of aesthetics.

Drawing on painting to illustrate, communication may be considered at two levels simultaneously with three possible relationships existing between the two levels. In the first, the painterly qualities of a painting (color, design, brightness, etc.) communicate the same or similar message as the content of the painting. The two levels may on the other hand communicate contrasting messages, or the relationship between the two may be ambiguous. (A similar analysis can be conducted to establish the relationship between verbal messages and paralanguage, kinesics, etc.)

5. Channels of Communication

The means by which messages are transmitted, considered from the perspective of senders and receivers, are the senses of vision, audition, touch, pain, kinesthesis, temperature, smell and taste. If the message is transmitted by *one* of these, it spreads to others in the brain of the receiver and is thus decoded and stored with imagery from more than one channel. The combination of vision and audition in television provides the most obvious multiple channels of communication, but there is the important example of perception itself in both vision and audition combining with the content or the symbols of the message to provide content as well as form in the message. An example which makes the point is *onomatopoeia*, in which the sound as well as the word conveys meaning. Sounds may arouse imagery in other sensory modalities and then give rise to *synesthesia*, which may be defined as an image in one sensory modality which simultaneously registers an image in another sensory modality, associating colors with musical sounds, for example.

Interactions between concepts and sensory images introduce an additional complexity in the sphere of multiple channels of communication. Numbers are sometimes perceived with qualities of colors and forms ["2 is flatter, rectangular, whitish in color, sometimes almost gray"].[31] Some persons perceive number series distributed in regular geometrical spaces, sometimes in three dimensions, called *number forms.*

6. Setting or Context of Communication

Messages are sent and received against a background of distractions, irrelevancies and secondary communications. All of these factors -- which do not define the event of communication -- comprise its setting or the context.

7. Event of Communication

The context suggests a look at the central activity in communication which develops around a *role* and *event.* The doctor or the salesman represents roles, highly structured, and displays action in events such as emergencies for the doctor, or the front-door sales pitch for the saleman. Patterns of communication can be described as largely determined by the structures of the events. Salient human activities, such as eating, supply the focus for specialized roles and for event-structures. Public speaking is another example of salient activity which provides occasions for generating the force to suggest *events* as the units of analysis for communication. Hymes (1973), among other writers, has drawn attention to the necessity of analyzing communication in the totality of its occurrence, and Barker (1968), in psychology, analyzes the ecological variables of behavior to piece together events in which communication takes place.

These seven components (eight if senders and receivers are separated) furnish the most complete list, which is never finished. We will add one more dimension.

8. Temporal Dimension

Communication is a process which must occur in time. Hall distinguishes three stages, assigning to the first and the third significance for intercultural communication. The stage of foreshadowing, *adumbration,* precedes the peak phase. The final phase is the termination and is critical for feedback. (Hall, 1973)

Time introduces a second variable which is important for communication. To process messages, encode and decode, takes time; communication occurs in time, which should be interjected into the analysis to account for the effects of perception, thinking and learning.

Jones (1976) develops a theory of perception and attention within the context of auditory pattern research including speech sequences. She concludes that time is part of the definition of stimulus structure.[32] The rhythmic theory developed offers a framework for understanding diverse phenomena, and from the point of view of communication, establishes time as part of structure.

C. Function of Communication

For Hymes (1973), the conditions of communication, such as purposes, feedback and the capabilities of senders and receivers, comprise selectors of functions of communication. These can be assembled around the various components. For analytical convenience, the receiver and the sender are separated, even though communication is a process. The list of functions is given by key words, each one linked with the component which the function primarily serves:

1. Metalinguistic (Code)

    This function refers to communication about the system used in communication, its analysis and development. Inquiry reveals a broad function which unfolds the connections between language and communication, and leads to the underlying structure imputed to the world, to values and to patterns of thinking themselves. The participants are also implicated by this function through learning and perception.

2. Referential (Content)

    This establishes references and identification of meaning and topic; it is the traditional imparting of knowledge and information with presumed neutrality, and provides the aspect of communication which is most amenable to treatment by information theory.

3. Expressive (Sender)

    This function encroaches on the emotional spheres and associates with attitudes.

4. Directive (Receiver)

This focus leads to the function of persuasions and rhetoric in the traditional sense. A concentrated focus attains subtleties of direction translated into motivation and needs of the receiver.

5. Aesthetic (Form)

Hymes (1973) calls this function "poetic," and in an analytical vein, he talks about proof-reading, emendations, mimicry and editing. A different view calls attention to the pervasiveness of mental categories in perception, not to speak of thinking, so that the classification of perception influences what is perceived. Numbers refer to class or category assignments and not to enumeration of concrete items. Despite these abstractions, there remains a stubborn, unrelenting, concrete world which provides anchors, and when it is communicated with vivid reference to the categories to which it belongs, poetry springs forth as fusion of concrete perception and abstraction. Poetry in this sense, which is style and not substance, seems to score the apprehension of meaning.

6. Phatic (Channel)

This function refers to contact maintained among participants by means of the channel of communication; its purpose is to unite, to affirm cohesion and to stress the belonging and the affiliation of individuals to each other.

7. Contextual (Setting)

By this function, the message is amplified or softened; other messages are separated or are perceived to modify the central message. Secondary messages may be verbal or nonverbal.

8. Metacommunicative (Event)

This function parallels the function for code with the distinction that the reference is to the event, such as, "This is a recording." On a broader scope, metacommunication may refer to communication in general, and hence approach replacing all the other components as it nears identity with action (behavior) and with performance theory.

9. Individuates (Time)

Esoteric time appears to have at least two functions in the domain of communication. Individuates first refers to the reception of a message by registering it in the reserves of the individual, those of memory and experience, processes which can be systematically considered as aspects of long-term memory, storage and synthesis of perception and experience, and of learning. Turning to communicative events, time primes individuation through a frame for communication, which divides one phase from another and projects messages into a temporal frame which is broader than sending-receiving relationships. Communicative time flows in rhythm different from those of individuals and measures social, cultural and historical meaning. Appeal to communicative time "individuates" communication with its social-cultural-historical meaning in a manner analogous to the personal "individuation" of a message by the marks of memory and experience.

D. *Concepts of Communication*

1. Structural Concepts — Information Theory

Influence on communication has flowed from information theory during the last twenty-five years as the ideas of Wiener, Shannon, Weaver and others penetrated the technical areas of communication dealing with symbols. Hymes (1964, 1967) writes that only Bateson and Levy-Strauss treat communication theory in social anthropology. Hall mentions information theory (1973), while in psychology and in speech communication, reference is more frequent. Conventional wisdom has absorbed information theory, but has not digested it. Its concepts have scarcely affected communication theory. Hymes observes that models of information theory depend upon information of past events,[33] a condition which is not realistic in the study of language and linguistics. In interpersonal processes in general, the "interpersonal history" of participants in communication is difficult to determine, and it is even more difficult to establish its influence in a given communication event. Thus application of information theory concepts is likely to restrict inquiry to identifiable stimuli in the immediate environment. (Rosenberg and Cohen, 1966) The theory of *adaptation level* systemmatically encompasses what the past brings to the present situation (Helson, 1964), but it has not been extensively applied to stamp the communication of participants with the marks of past history. The limited treatment of communication within the frame of adaptation level stresses contextual effects on communication. (Manis, 1971) For visual perception, Black (1972) gives a penetrating analysis of the concept of *information*.

The work of Deutsch represents an enlightened and enthusiastic attempt to work with the concepts from information theory. (Deutsch, 1966) The book begins with a general analysis of models for society and politics, and then proceeds to examine a cybernetic model in communication and control. Deutsch ranges widely and releases a cascade of insights and analysis. it should be noted, nevertheless, that he aims primarily for the mass media and for political discourse and not so much for interpersonal communication.

Apart from specific and precise application, information theory advances general ideas which appear critical, even though they may not receive quantitative treatment. The concept of information defines a universe of potential information as well as what is communicated. Thus the content of a message transmitted points to information suppressed, not sent, which can be inferred by appeal to the total domain of information from which the message was drawn. The idea of suppressed information can be broadened to include implicit assumptions in communication.

The logic of information theory may be extended for comparisons with other systems of logic. Berlo (1960) provides a good basic discussion. His stress on the indirection and negative method of *inductive inference* resembles the idea of suppressed information and occurs in the context of statistical theory and *stochastic models*. (Naroll and Cohen, 1973)

Distinctions important to this issue in communication are found in historical and philosophical treatments. (Von Wright, 1971)

The logic of suppression of information is clearly established for information theory and statistical inferences, but it is not so clear when the code of communication is nonverbal, as in the visual arts. (For instance, does a picture implicitly suppress other visual images?) The improbability of the distribution of pictorial elements in a picture seems to suggest an aesthetics found in principles different from the suppression of information, or the negative method of inductive inference. The conclusion remains tentative; it is engaged in some form in the writing of Arnheim (1969), Child (1969), Gombrich (1972a, 1972b) and Kennedy (1974).

Communication logic, as we have discussed it, is primarily associated with qualities of the message, and parallel to this topic, there are tacit understandings which cement social exchanges. This area of *ethno-logic* or "social logic" is the province staked out by ethnomethodology. (Garfinkel, 1967) In these studies the implicit expectations, verbal and nonverbal, composing common sense social reality are revealed.

2. Structural Concepts - Linguistics

Smith (1966) identifies three scientific approaches to the theory of human communication; the third is linguistics, or in his words, "linguistic anthropology." (The other two are mathematical theory and social psychology.) The same volume of communication and culture organizes the substantive selections according to the threefold breakout familiar in linguistics: *syntax, semantics,* and *pragmatics.* The identical analysis appears in the title of a review of linguistics theory. (Silverstein, 1972)

Within the three categories, analysis of structural concepts can proceed to fine gradation of microstructure, found in volumes such as that of Saporta (1961), a book of readings, or the treatment by Slobin of psycholinguistics (1971). Durbin reviews linguistic anthropology (1972), while Johnson-Laird accomplishes a similar task for experimental psycho-linguistics (1974). A comprehensive review of psycholinguistics which ranges into adjacent areas is given by Miller and McNeil (1969). Bauman and Sherzer (1975) cover the field of ethnography of speaking, and Rubin looks at the study of sociolinguistics (1973).

3. Structural Concepts – Mechanical, Games and Computer Models of Communication

This category is offered to collect a variety of approaches to communication which are not easily classified as processes and which by and large omit change. Mechanical models are intended to include efforts to discover simple principles around which communication can be draped. The issues of mechanical models and of models in general are brilliantly covered by Deutsch (1966).

Games and computer representatives of communication are generally static in concept. They have been applied to the simulation of memory. (Frijda, 1972) Programs have been constructed for thinking (Simon, 1969; Feigenbaum and Feldman, 1963), for problem solving (Newell and Simon, 1972) and for many other fields (Buchler and Nutini, 1969).

4. Structural Concepts – Physiological Principles

Treatments of communication conducted from the perspective of physiology generally fail to satisfy. There are cogent reasons for making the effort, since physiology should provide theoretical variables for communciation and introduce objectivity. It should establish limits for research and theory which will assist in ordering the field of communication by bringing in experimentation methods and data. Seldom have these objectives been realized despite a renewed interest in the physical limits of communication associated with the work of Chomsky and colleagues. Developmental studies in the tradition of Piaget and of Gessel should be reviewed for their implication to communication. Similarly, cross-cultural studies of development and clinical studies of brain and neural function as affected by disease and injury – under both natural and laboratory conditions – should be examined. Language studies can be expected to be prominent.

There is a line of investigation in the field of vision beginning with Hartline, proceeding to Kuffler, Hubel, Wiesel and to others. (Stent, 1972; Zusne, 1970) It particularly deserves investigation for its promise of applications to communication. This line of experimentation has successfully begun the analysis of how light is transformed into a mental response; it begins with impingement at the retina and ends with cortical representation. There are three levels of abstraction within the cells of the retina which compose the nervous system of the receptive fields of various animals.[34] These levels of abstraction involve selectivity and supression of information according to specific principles of *cytoarchitecture*, confronting the physiologist with an unexpected degree of analysis and resolution in the mammalian retina. At each level only certain information "registers" and is "coded" and passed on to the next level.

The differentiated levels of cytoarchitecture parallel the agreement among workers in communication that exchanges occur at several levels simultaneously and the corollary belief that despairs of an exhaustive analysis of communication from a single perspective. These general trends of communication are referred to by Stent , who claims that these findings on the nature of nervous communication "have some important general implications, in that they lend physiological support to the latter-day philosophical view that has come to be known as 'structuralism.' "[35] Stent goes on to assert that structuralism represents the overthrow of positivism (behaviorism in psychology) and the recognition "that information about the world enters the mind not as raw data but as highly abstract structures that are the result of a preconscious set of step-by-step transformation of the sensory input."[36] In a similar vein, it should be noted that there is a general compatibility between structuralism and recent work in neurophysiology, particularly the concept of consciousness advanced by Sperry (1969).

Research in the field of binocular perception has produced findings which provide a model for intercultural differences, even though the research was done in a monocultural setting. Using pictures, diagrams, and computer system generated stereograms, Ross showed that when different stimuli are presented at about the same time to the two eyes, the observers' responses

> . . . reveal some critical faculty in the visual system that is capable of making decisions and of rejecting information, apparently on aesthetic grounds . . .[37] It appears there are records of visual input that can be consulted before anything at all is seen in order to determine the proper framework for perception . . .[38] What we see is an interpretation of the external world, ordered within a framework the visual system imposed because of the attitude it adopts. In other words, we adopt a perceptual attitude in order to comprehend the world.[39]

The last statement by Ross establishes the possibility that the framework imposed by the visual system leaves a cultural imprint. Using the same methodology of binocular perception, Bagby showed the effect of culture (1957) although the early work did not have the sophistication of the experiments of Ross.

Examination of these principles and processes with an application of them to communication should yield instructive theories and data. Physiology should be scanned in particular for guides to the resolution of the difference between concreteness and abstraction and between particular and universal features of language. A final knotty problem which may be illuminated by physiology is the ancient problem of two-term, three-term or n-term logic. All of these problems, which involve a binary view to serve as a frame of reference, have received impetus from the developing literature on the two hemispheres of the brain, and on the identification of two or more states of consciousness. (Nebes, 1974; Ornstein, 1973) The "duality" of human existence, so often assumed in conventional wisdom, seems interpretable according to the left and the right hemispheres of the brain. Work in this field suggests that different aspects of communication can be traced back to one or the other hemisphere. This recent work provides a physiological model for exposition of past observation concepts and theories based on dualities. In addition, the brain research poses a physiological model for the concept of complementarity, namely that the experience of one hemisphere cannot be exhaustively and perfectly represented to the other hemisphere. The non-verbal understanding of the right cannot be adequately understood by the verbal left hemisphere. Complementarity is suggested for the brain, and the same principle can be extended to levels of analysis in communication, such as interpersonal communication versus communication between nations. The concept appears to cast understanding on past problems, although its use in the social sciences is unusual. The socio-scientific climate is more likely to search for a unified set of explanations, regardless of level of analysis, and therefore to overlook the potential application of complementarity to communication.

5. Functional Explanation and Principles

Communication was defined as a process, and a pursuit of this view leads easily to imagining communication as a flow of events in time. Earlier events prepare a mold for shaping later events and thus fashion a function or a purpose of some kind. In communication theory, the purpose may be general, such as adaptation or survival. Functional positions in theory frequently include some principle of explanation, such as *balance* or *congruity*. Principles with the contemporary sound of communication would be *feedback* and *negative homeostasis*.

Classification of theories or of models occasionally becomes arbitrary. Some examples do not fall neatly into one or another category. Deutsch speaks of structural-functional analysis in which function refers to the pursuit of some value or goal. Even more generally, it may refer to maintenance of the system.[40]

The concepts of process and of function extend in time, suggesting a temporal analysis of communication. Such a diachronic perspective leads to the study of sequence effects, which become particularly important in persuasion and in the use of visual images.

6. Empirical Areas

A great deal of research has been conducted outside general theories of communication, in many cases inspired by specific problems or by a body of empirical findings. The field of disonance theory is an example.

E. Processing and Encoding-Decoding of Messages

Encoding and decoding messages are the mental operations of the sender and receiver in communication. The two phases differ, but both can be described as the *mind*. Work in understanding its operations has flourished in recent years. Fixing a steady gaze on communication, Deutsch analyzes mind, listing nine different operations. These are selecting, abstracting, communicating, sorting, subdividing, recalling, recombining, critically recognizing, and reapplying items of information. A list of seven operations is given earlier in the same book.[41] This provocative view may be simplified by centering the issue on perception and psychology more than on the operations which the mind may possess to complement technical operations in communication. It is possible to identify perception, encoding, storage, retrieval and steering or governance, and thus reduce the phases to five.

1. Perception

Incredible quantities of information impinge upon the sensory organs. It has been estimated that the human eye can respond to 7,500,000 separate stimuli. No observer has the capacity even to remotely approach this number of separate color sensations. The impingement of the external world is severely limited by processes of attention and selection, which can be collected under the title perception -- a process which is far more complex, and hence difficult to define, than it appears to be at first sight. The external world never enters the mind through the sensory receptors to form a point-for-point representation. Some trace, some imprint of the external world, however, does enter the mind, for it is clear that perception and

experience are not self-locked; the individual is sensitive to
some environment, even if it is selective and abstract.

2.   Encoding and Acquisition

The world of perception exists in continuities in which one
color shades into another, shape dissolves into shape and sounds
melt into other sounds. Although discontinuities may exist in
nature, those that register on the brain are transformations
imposed by the neural system on natural continuities. The
process of selecting and suppressing, of accentuating or
smoothing incoming stimuli eventually produces discontinuities
of how the world is represented in the mind. This observation
leads to the conclusion that a patch of red is seen as a color
which is red, and a white oak is seen as an example which can
be placed under the concept of trees with spreading limbs and
grey, flaked bark. Perception is general. When the observer
appeals to the concreteness of a perception, he refers to a
category in the mind filled with examples. He does not discover
a *white oak*.

The field of perception and of cognitive processes which
fall into the area of acquisition or encoding is complex and
technical. It will suffice to call attention to this mushrooming
field of research as one phase in the process of perception-
thinking-memory-learning.

3.   Storage

Once a complex experience is encoded and stored as a
white oak, it remains accessible to change. Its form becomes
more regular, its bark probably whiter, the foliage greener in the
store of memory than in the view of perception. Systematic
changes take place in storage naturally and also from the impact
of individual notions and specific events in the life history of
the individual. Responses in communication may be given to
these storage aspects of images and not to the acquired one.

4.   Retrieval

The past is neither mechanically stored nor automatically
retrieved. When an experience is encoded and then stored, it
must be associated with a cue or a rule for retrieving it. The
white oak may be recalled under the concept *tree* for some

persons, while others may be able to retrieve it more readily under the concept of *oak;* others may recall it as a name for a region of a city. Whatever the case may be, since the white oak itself is not stored, only a trace, it is retrieved by indication of the category under which it is filled; that is the retrieval rule.

5.   Steering and Governance

The relationship between what is stored in the mind, retrieved, and what is effective in steering and governing behavior is not at all clear. There are indications that visual images endure, return readily, but are bound to the store and do not steer action. Verbal commands, on the other hand, seem more difficult to store and retrieve, but once they are released, they steer and govern.

III. Cultural Aspects

A.   *Core Theory of Culture*

For our purposes, culture is defined as aspects of subjective culture (Triandis, 1972), perceptions of the individual shared with only some others belonging to the same collectivity, which govern behavior. The perception's function as predispositions can be identified as values, systems of reasoning and other cognitive attributes shared by the members of the collectivity and not shared generally by members of other collectivities. The definition of culture sensitizes and can be treated as either competence or cognitive process theory.

A second definition of culture is given as the ambience or the system of predispositions derived from statistical variables of population and demography which are shared by its members. This perspective discards the point of view of the individual and implies a different set of cause and effect relationship at the level of population. Although the collectivity which determines the cultural factors is clearly defined, it is a statistical community which obscures the relationship between membership in the community and the cultural factors identified as attributes of the individual. The two levels of references introduce *complementarity* between the two definitions. Explanation of an educational system cannot be completely represented in terms of the qualities, needs, and purposes of any one student attending that educational system.

The analysis and description of a cultural system has proceeded from the outside point of vantage, *etic*, or from the inside view of a member of the culture, the *emic* approach. (Lounsbury, 1955) The etic approach will be related to stress on identifying cultural universals, qualities shared by all men, and the emic will stress cultural specific items.

For those involved with intercultural communication, it is critical to note that some human qualities are universal, others are shared with some persons, but not with everyone; and there are some qualities which are unique to each individual. Intercultural communication is concerned with the middle case, cultural differences.

B. *Components of Culture*

Some anthropologists insist that *culture* is a unit and that it must be considered as a total system. This is the position attributed to structuralists, for instance. (Maranda, 1972) Others might adopt a different unit for culture, as we will, to use culture as a filter for the process of communication. We are interested in a cultural unit which adequately explicates the process of communication. This choice of unit already courts difficulties. Not all cultures hold the same regard and esteem for communication as western and American societies. Selecting the units of culture from the point of view of utility for communication becomes a crude exercise from the cultural point of view, but there seems to be no recourse short of an extended treatment of both communication and of culture, an enterprise which lies far beyond the scope of the *Outline*.

1. Components of Culture

Cultural anthropologists have considered for some time the appropriate definition of the culture-bearing unit and appear to agree that the unit transcends the individual. Naroll summarizes the past work in defining the culture-bearing unit and proposes the *cultunit,* which is a collectivity defined in terms of language and territorial contiguity; and when there is sufficient authoritative political structure transcending the local community, Naroll includes the criterion of political organization.[42]

Adoption of Naroll's cultunit implies that no one person in a society will carry all aspects of the culture. For example, cultural features about shopping in American society will be more intensely distributed among women than among men; knowledge of music and use of computers will be more familiar to youth than to middle-aged persons. Thus no one informant is able to "produce" his culture in the sense that Naroll defines the cultunit. Although we may speak of culture as transcending the individual, the assumption does not detain us from defining all aspects of culture as they might be carried by the individual in his head, as *internal cognitive form.* This is an essential point for the position adopted in this *Outline* of communication at the interpersonal level. *All cultural items must be defined in reference to a potential cultural bearer.*

2. Quantum of the Culture

The cultural unit expresses the view of the student of cultures and communication. We turn now to alternatives for the unit of the culture as perceived by members of a society themselves. Appeal to informants in the culture may fail. They may disagree among themselves, and some people claim they do not know who they are. The people of Gyem area of the Gabor district of Gabon say that they do not know whether they are Fang or Ntumu.[43] Many Americans are reluctant to identify themselves as members of American culture and prefer to perceive themselves as individuals. These two examples interject into the discussion the need for interpretation of empirical results, instead of accepting them at face value, to determine the quantum of the culture used by its members.

The uncertainty of Americans with their own cultural identity supplies a basis for the inference that the *individual* is the *quantum* in American culture. Conventional wisdom in psychology, epistemology, logic and even language adapts to

296

this cultural assumption. In other cultures the quantum may coincide with a set of roles, a group of some sort, family, clan, caste or some other collectivity and in that sense the cultural quantum would more nearly approximate the anthropologist's cultunit than it does with the American's individualism.

3. Cultural Interface

For our purposes, culture refers to attributes of the individual and thereby poses the problem of the relationship between the quantum and the cultural system as a totality. The interface, the juncture between the individual and the society, may be described as a cultural placenta. On one side of the placenta, American society places the full range of individual experience, and on the other, the total cultural system. The cultural placenta does not establish structure but supplies the juncture and the limits of the interface. For Americans, the scope of the interface between the culture and the individual ranges over the full gamut of experience. The individual, however, is permitted some latitude in conforming to cultural norms. They are diffuse and the individual usually chooses from more than one alternative. For Americans, it turns out that the style, primarily the informality and the indirection of coming to terms with cultural prescriptions, is the important feature for dominant, middle-class culture. Persuasion, guidance and perhaps governance of behavior are accepted, but are not the explicit rule. Imperious directives are disdained.

The cultural interface suggested for dominant American culture is not found in all societies. The interface will be different. On one side of the cultural placenta only a brief range of the individual's experience may lead to the culture, but within that range, complete conformity may be required to the community or to the family or to some other aspect of cultural life which is defined to be critical. Once the responsibilities, duties and privileges have been exercised in these areas, the individual may experience a freedom of action which startles many Americans who have noticed the conformity in the critical areas. This second model of the cultural interface does not exhaust alternatives, and for the moment, passes over the tone and quality of sympathy, empathy and trust, which characterize the interface between the individual and his culture.

4. Meaning of Communication

Communication considered as a component of culture must be analyzed in a cross-cultural context, since it has different meanings from society to society. Several assumptions are normally made by Americans which are not made in all other socieities. Any study or work in communication must adapt to the implicit assumptions and usages found in various societies.

It has often been remarked that in American culture communication is usually treated as a surface phenomenon. To exchange information summarizes the general belief and also shows the affinity in American culture between conventional ideas of communication and communication theory which cluster around the concept of information. Americans, as a cultural practice, tend to minimize symbolic and implicative meanings of communication and rivet their attention on what was said and secondly how it was said.

A second set of conventional beliefs is that communication encourages participation, reduces conflict and enhances resolution of interpersonal problems. These beliefs contribute to a high evaluation of the process of communication in American life and propound the idea that to communicate means to receive compliance with the message. Thus when people disagree, an implicit judgment is made that they have not communicated. It is assumed that communication means agreement and perhaps it is this implicit assumption in American life which has placed the study and use of communication on such a high pinnacle. It is apparent that these views of communication are not universal.

C. Functions of Culture

Culture is a broad concept which has been used to encompass a way of life ever since Tyler's famous definition in 1874. Voget quotes it as follows:

> Culture or Civilization, taken in its wide ethnographic sense, is that complex whole which includes knowledge, belief, act, morals, law, custom, and any other capabilities and habits acquired by man as a member of society.[44]

The wide sense of meaning is still present, although usually refined for more specific application. The variations and the evolution of cultures can be interpreted as the construction of social realities in an objective world which is impartial to human needs and desires. Culture is the source of meaning which is interposed between perception of a senseless world and actions designed to delay the world's entropic march. Man's products in the sciences, arts and technology are created to relieve the objectivity and the randomness of the world he lives in. The function of culture in its broadest sense is to craft meaning from the natural world and shape its objectivity into the form and the reference which engages human feelings.

Both concepts of communication and culture were described as competence theories. The designation is a matter of choice. Our focus on intercultural communication, however, leads us to treat communication as nearer to application and performance. Communication then is analyzed as competence theory, and culture is treated as the cognitive process serving as the background of communication. The term *subjective culture,* used in the literature of cross-cultural psychology, refers to the inner experience, and it is precisely what we are talking about.

We can now define the function of culture in intercultural communication more precisely: culture is an analytical tool for assessing communication, selecting strategies and evaluating results. Culture serves as a filter for communication.

D.   Concepts of Culture for Communication

In this *Outline* we shall mention one theory in cultural anthropology, *world view,* which should be broad enough to encompass any position from which an anthropology of communication might be developed. The task is one for the future, since

> An anthropology of communication does not exist. My apology for discussing it is a belief that it can exist, and that there are signs of its coming into being.[45]

Kearney proposes seven universal cognitive categories to serve as the skeleton of any functional world view: self, other, relationship, classification, space, time, and causality. (Kearney, 1976) It is clear that a world view theory has much room for almost any position which falls within the scope of cognitions. A clearly significant book in this field, with implications for intercultural communications is *Natural Symbols* (Douglas, 1973). Douglas bases her inquiry on the work of Bernstein (1964), showing the relationship between language usages and social forms. Going beyond the sociolinguistic formulation, Douglas unfolds the hypothesis that social forms in a society give rise to the beliefs and attidudes held by members of the group. In other words, "the fundamental attitudes to spirit and matter" are governed by the social life of the members of the society.[46]

The implications of the approach of Douglas are clear. The mature individual's cosmology, what Douglas calls "fundamental attitudes to spirit and matter," is shaped by the process of socialization which is mediated by the social forms of the society. Thus the person's basic beliefs derive from how that individual is raised, praised and admonished by parent and authority figures. On the question of what comes first, cosmology or social forms, Douglas comes out on the side of social forms:

> . . . the social relations of men provide the prototype for the logical relations between things, then, whenever this prototype falls into a common pattern, there should be something common to be discerned in the system of symbols it uses.[47]

Later on Douglas hedges a bit on social determinism, but the central idea remains unmoved: world views are generated by socialization. Two interpretations of this provocative theme bring it in line with another main stream of thought. If we introduce the idea of *activity,* which is not crucial to the theory but certainly seems appropriate and compatible, and, secondly, consider world view to mean mental products in the sense of the results of any activity, then we can conclude that the Douglas theme is very similar, in the aspects we have discussed, to the world outlook of Marx.[48] The similarity is with how the world view is attained and not with the features of the mental products.

What we infer from Douglas is more explicit in Marx. Cole and Scribner describe it thus:

> The central idea . . . is that man's nature evolves as man works to transform Nature. The sweep of this concept—that both subject and object, man and his product, arise from a unitary process of activity -- can best be grasped by an understanding of what Marx meant by *production.* Marx used the term to refer not only to the making of material products but to mental products as well (law, religion, metaphysics, and so on): similarly, *productive activity* encompasses not only manual but mental labor -- labor in its broadest sense.[49]

Russian psychologists, Vygotsky and Luria in particular, conducted research within a general Marxist perspective. In their works they developed the concept of *functional systems,* which Cole and Scribner discuss as *functional cognitive systems.* [50] These are operating processes integrating theoretical and practical activities, and resemble what we have called competence theories. Although Cole and Scribner do not provide analysis and examples of the functional cognitive systems, decision-making seems to be a candidate. An example comes from Luria, who observed that scientists investigating the psychological laws of perception assumed that they were independent of social practices and remained unchanged over the course of social history.

> In the last few decades, however, the development of psychology undermined these naturalistic notions about the relative simplicity and immediacy of perception. The evidence gathered suggests that perception is a complex process involving complex orienting activity, a probabilistic structure, an analysis

and synthesis of perceived features, and a *decision-making process*. [51] (Italics ours)

The quotation is taken from an important source, Luria's report on the field work done in the remoter parts of European Russia and in the Siberian North East in 1931-32. The Soviet Union mounted a program during this period to eliminate illiteracy and to collectivize the economy. Luria seized the opportunity to

. . . observe how decisively all these reforms effected not only a broadening of outlook but also radical changes in the structure of cognitive processes. [52]

In his book, Luria reports data which support the three basic ideas of the position: social historical development of higher cognitive processes, the social determinism causing their changes, and the role of activity. He writes a paragraph that can be used to summarize his position as well as the process aspect which we inferred about Douglas's theory.

The way in which the historically established forms of human mental life correlate with reality has come to depend more and more on complex social practices. The tools that human beings in society use to manipulate that environment, as well as the products of previous generations which help shape the mind of the growing child, also affect these mental forms. In his development, the child's first social relations and his first exposure to a linguistic system (of special significance) determine the forms of his mental activity. All these environmental factors are decisive for the sociohistorical development of consciousness. New motives for action appear under extremely complex patterns of social practices. Thus are created new problems, new modes of behavior, new methods of taking in information, and new systems of reflecting reality. [53]

1. Approaches and Positions
    Componential analysis is a technique borrowed from linguistics and applied to uncover a native speaker's cognitive

processes. The analysis sets up a semantic duality, representing a conceptual one, and establishes the simplest and most direct connection between the polarities. Although the interest in componential analysis has declined, the basic tenets of the point of view (Goodenough, 1956) lead in the same directions as intercultural communication.

The conceptual approach of componential analysis fits into the broader frame of structuralism in anthropology, a movement primarily identified with Levy–Strauss. Theory stresses structure in distinction to functions and synchronic instead of diachronic analyses. The structuralist pursues a basic form, "the structure," in myth, in customs or even in actions. Transformational analysis simplifies empirical multiplicity to attain the pattern of the structuralist; or the reverse, the structuralist begins with patterns which are transformed into empirical hypotheses. (Maranda, 1972)

In the field of psychology, Piaget can be said to belong within the general program of structuralism. His work has been attractive to the field of intercultural communication, since the abstractions of his theories easily cross cultural boundaries to participate in cross-cultural comparisons. In addition, Piaget incorporates levels in attainment of cognitive structures, which is a feature attractive to researchers working in the cross-cultural area. (Piaget, 1969)

Another approach in psychology which has received attention in cross-cultural research is the analysis of motivation in hierarchies by Maslow (1943). Although the stress on motivation is a product of the west and particularly of American society, the idea of levels and stages is attractive and provides room for accommodating to variation within a culture and between cultures. More so than other workers in the field, F. Kluckhohn has emphasized the necessity of accommodating to cultural variations and considering them in the analysis of cultures. Her five value-orientations are highly abstract and cross-cultural in application. Data are collected empirically, bridging a yawning chasm between the particular and the universal. (Kluckhohn and Strodtbeck, 1961)

2. Values

Values refer to conceptions of the desirable. More formally, values may be said to be *optative*. The concept in one form or another has been often used to describe and analyze cultures and cultural differences. F. Kluckhohn uses five value-orientations to describe cultures. (Kluckhohn, 1961) C. Kluckhohn has provided a comprehensive treatment of values (1951). One of the first social scientists to apply the concept of values is Robin Williams in his original volume of *The American Society*. The third edition continues the exposition of values (1970). A sophisticated analysis and application of values is the volume edited by Baier and Rescher, *Values and the Future* (1969).

3. Role

Important behavior for communication occurs in a social context. The concept of *role* is a valuable analytical tool for analysis. It represents a social and behavioral extension of the preceding concepts, since roles can be partly analyzed as role expectation containing core values.

Roles also provide an entry into a huge literature on small groups, reference groups and interpersonal interactions. (Biddle and Thomas, 1966) One area which needs more research is the empirical analyses of roles which will contribute to the construction of a grammar of roles.

4. Event

Trait theories of personality or theoretical approaches of cultural personality which fail to link the individual with the conditions under which actions take place are likely to show serious limitations. It is becoming increasingly clear that people show more variability in behavior than has been previously accommodated by theoreticians. The concept of the event and event-structures are analytical tools to overcome past deficiencies. The levels of values, role and events are probably needed in a triadic application effectively to analyze cultural behavior. Only a few social scientists pay attention to events: Hymes in linguistics (1973); the anthropologist Frake has provided a classical example of an event (1964); and the ecological psychology of Barker can be construed to investigate event structures. The most extensive analysis of events is Goffman's *Frame-Analysis* (1974), although the investigation is generally restricted to the American scene with only a sprinkling of observations and examples from other societies.

In the intercultural field, it is Cole and Scribner who have discussed communication events in research,[54] while Cole has developed our concept of events as *situation variation.*[55]

E. Processes of the Individual Affected by Culture

1. Perception

The term *perception* has been used freely in cross-cultural studies so that we have in our hands a concept drained of meaning. Tajfel (1969) suggests useful distinctions which should assist in assessing the role of culture in perception. Social and cultural factors in perception should satisfy four conditions. First, the factors should be directly tied to sensory information, received at the time the individual responds. The response itself should be relatively independent and not occur on a chain of complex and abstract inferences. Three, the response should not involve a choice among alternatives; instead, four, the perceiver should have available the possibility of a correct response concerning the relevant attribute of the stimulus.

As we have already seen, many psychologists agree with Luria that perception does involve higher cognitive processes such as decision-making, attitudes, etc. Thus the concept *perception* is frequently used to apply with essentially the same meaning as "subjective" or "inner" experience, and becomes indistinguishable from *cognition, imagery* or *symbolism.* (Singer, 1976) To investigate the cultural influence on perception, it is necessary to detect a cultural factor associated with a stimulus which meets the four criteria. If we examine stimuli perfectly based on sensory perception, we deal with *sensation* rather than perception, and conclude that there are no cultural influences present. (Triandis, 1964)

Active research of preceding years yields a modest body of findings suggesting that culture influences perception. Perhaps the best known perceptual area is that of illusions. Segall,

Campbell and Herskovits (1963) were able to show that people in different parts of the world perceive geometrical illusions (the Muller-Lyer is one) differently. The original findings have been revised by later research (Pollack, 1970), and although the status of the difference is not entirely clear, it is probably appropriate to conclude that the geometrical illusions carry a residue of cultural influence.

Color perception has received a great deal of attention in cross-cultural research. Berlin and Kay (1969) conducted a comprehensive study of color terms in a large number of languages. When Bornstein investigated variance in color-naming systems among different societies, he discovered a regular geographic patterning of color-naming confusion. People near the equator and living at high altitudes adapt to ultraviolet components of sunlight and may experience ocular deposits of xanthrophyll, which results in depression of sensitivity to the blue end of the light spectrum.[57] The perceptual result is the lack of differentiation of colors in the blue-green range.

Bornstein's research and Pollack's (1970) on the geometrical illusion have a common ground; both advance a physiological basis for perceptual responses which have often been attributed to cultural differences. With color confusion, the physiological layer of the explanation represents an adaptation to environmental conditions, a conclusion which mediates differences of perceptual responses by means of environmental conditions.

In the past it is clear that cross-cultural research has been too eager to attribute differences in perception to cultural differences. To the degree that the physical stimuli are ambiguous and to the degree that Tajfel's four conditions are violated, cultural influences intrude into perception and cognitive processes. Meanwhile processes of sensation and objective perception demarcate the grounds for universal human qualities. The most lucid account of the subject is perhaps that of Cole and Scribner in *Culture and Thought* (1974), while for incisiveness, the reader should turn to the formidable review by Tajfel, "Social and Cultural Factors in Perception." (1969)

2. Patterns of Thinking

The ways in which people reason are critical for communication, particularly since most people lack insight of various patterns of thinking, including their own. The subject has interested philosophers since antiquity, and for the field of speech-communication, when attention is directed toward intercultural communication, Aristotle's rhetoric receives review. More recently, some psychologists, linguists and experimental psychologists have devoted attention to patterns of thinking.

Cole and colleagues have done some of the best research in the field of cross-cultural psychology in the area of patterns of thinking. The distillate of their field research and a summary of the experimental literature are given in *Culture and Thought* (1974), the book we have already had repeated occasions to cite.

The field work of Cole and colleagues was done primarily in Liberia and in the United States. Regarding patterns of thinking, we have already seen that their research and a review of the literature lead them to adopt the concept of functional cognitive system. Much of their work is an attack on theories of cognitive process which assigns certain capacities of thinking to members of one society and different capacities to members of another. An example would be the capacity for abstract thought in one society and its absence in another, or the prevalence of "primitive mentality." Cole and colleagues work with the concept of process rather than capacity, and assume that processes are universal for all people. Differences from society to society should be sought for with functional cognitive systems.

There is a second area in patterns of thinking which has emerged in intercultural communication. With a background in linguistics and semantics, and influenced by anthropologists and the political scientist Pribram, Glenn has developed a schemata for the analysis of patterns of thinking. (Glenn, 1966)

3. Assumptions

The surface content of any message rides over a deep, implicit and silent sea of assumptions. (Some may call them preconceptions.) The features of styles of thinking, the quantum of a culture, certain values and other cognitive elements may be so deeply entrenched in the consciousness of a communicator that they are considered natural, normal and universal. Deviations from the assumptions are generally misunderstood and evoke negative emotions. Assumptions may be treated as suppressed information in communication theory. Practically speaking, people do not talk about assumptions, while values, lying closer to the surface, may become subjects of conversation.

F. *Alternative Definitions of Culture*

Although the definition of subjective culture seems to be appropriate for intercultural communication, the view neglects the bonds which exist among people who compose the same cultural group. This problem has come up, but the precedent for adopting a Darwinian level of definition is so strong that alternatives to subjective culture deserve brief mention.

Culture may be defined at the level of institutions and precipitate a search for societal universals in the areas of economics, politics, religion, education and the family. Treatment of these subjects can be found in sources such as *Handbook of Social and Cultural Anthropology* (1973).

The culture of technology has received much attention from social scientists, as the values underlying technology and science have been investigated in the United States, Japan and other countries. Historical studies have plotted changes in values at the opening of the industrial revolution in England in the nineteenth century. (Baier and Rescher, 1969)

The quality of life under the impact of technology in urban centers has been examined with psychologists pinpointing information overload, while others have focused on problems of urbanization. Some observers foresee the development of universal cultural forms based on technology and urban patterns.

A new field of futurology has emerged as a discipline and as a target of concern for conventional wisdom. The fledgling field has experienced an early Waterloo as researchers and experimenters dissect rational predictive systems to reveal their irrational uses in the hands of planners and futurologists. Kahneman and Tversky's "On the Psychology of Prediction" (1973) demonstrated that heuristics of probabilistic judgment led to "biases that are large, persistent, and serious in their implications for decision making."[58]

The United States is the site of the majority of intercultural communication research and training. It is inevitable that the values of the society will leave their mark on the field. Yet the suitability of American values for the future has been questioned. As an alternative, both contemporary conditions and those of the preceding past are investigated to discover the forms and patterns of change in technology, information systems, communication, social norms and in other areas as well. Contemporary insights, particularly social ones, have been used to reinterpret history, while culture and knowledge are increasingly cast into historical and evolutionary molds.

IV. Intercultural Communication

The two preceding sections, communication and culture, have been organized along similar lines. In this section the theory of communication is combined with cultural components to produce the variations in communication caused by the cultures of the sender-receiver. The core problem examined is communication across cultural boundaries.

A. Core Theory

For intercultural communication, difference supplies the key concept for theory. Analysis incurs the risk of either triviality or empty abstractions, since the significances of cultural differences, levels of analysis and of abstractions are critical issues which have been dismissed by the simple treatment of similarity and difference in both theory and practice. This conclusion is reflected in a review of studies of attitude change. The authors conclude that

> . . . irrelevant similarities have little effect on attitudes and that certain dissimilarities (particularly membership-group dissimilarities) contribute to attitude change in that they lead to perceptions of competence, fairness, prestige, etc. Attitudinal similarity seemed clearly related to attraction but the previously

alleged effects of attraction on attitude change were questioned.[59]

The analysis of difference in communication can be distinguished by reference to an experimental study conducted to establish the optimal amount of difference or similarity in effective communication. The results were that moderate differences produce the most effective communication. (Alpert, Anderson, 1973)

The problem of what existing cultural systems should be used to serve as reference cultures in the study of intercultural communication has to be settled. The choices may be determined by the cultural background of writers; it may be chosen on some other basis which is judged significant, such as politics, economics, or the choice of cultures may be arbitrary and made on a basis of convenience.

The use of componential analysis as a method suggests employing *contrast cultures* as the vehicles for content. These are artificial cultures derived from analyses of cultures by means of a finite set of dimensions selected to give adequate and objective coverage to any culture (Stewart, 1969) An American, Japanese or Mayan cultural group can be summarized on the dimensions. The end positions on the dimensions are arbitrarily designated *contrast cultures*, and give the frame of reference for analysis of the effect of cultural differences on communication. The logic of contrast cultures may be compared with the reasoning of ideal models and with the logic of generative grammars in language.

B.   *Critical Components of Intercultural Communication*

The components of communication should reflect the differences of contrast cultures. For practical purposes, certain of the components of culture represent more critical differences in communication. A combination of critical components from communication and from culture yields nine empirical areas, as follows:

1.   Language and Thinking

Language is a human product, while thinking is a process. They combine in the Whorfian hypothesis as mirror images. Here they are treated in the same section because of their natural association with the code of communication. The

Whorfian hypothesis, however, serves to introduce several important issues for language and thinking into the the the cultural context. Since there is a multiple connection between thinking and language, the hypothesis can never be either completely accepted or not accepted. It is useful to consider the Whorfian hypothesis in the context of recent physiological work on the two hemispheres of the brain. The integration of language and thought is more likely to represent the functions of the left hemisphere, while the hypothesis is more perilously applied to the right hemisphere for English and most western languages. Both the physiology of the brain and the hypothesis interject useful means of looking at communication by classifying both individual and cultures according to the degree to which their cognitive structures correspond with Whorf's hypothesis.

Leaving aside the Whorf hypothesis, the functions of language differ from culture to culture, and the differences might be examined from the point of view of their features. It is clear that certain languages have expanded the potential for coding certain kinds of experiences better than others, and that these qualities of language should be amenable to representation in terms of the components and the functions of communication. The work of Bernstein (1964) analyzing *elaborated* and *restricted* codes in English is one of the best examples.

Recent work in the field of psycholinguistics deserves to be examined for its implications in intercultural communication. The concept of lexical markings (Clark, 1969), which identifies negative and positive aspects of adjectives, for example, brings to language psychological and emotional dimensions which the intercultural communicator should be aware of.

The second major topic in this section is patterns of thinking, which comprises one of the most important areas for intercultural communication, since most communicators assume a universal pattern and do not have an insight into the various patterns in cultures. There are several issues in this area which frequently crop up. The dichotomy is a strong shaper of conceptualization in some patterns of thinking with a tendency to stress the end positions. In other patterns the dichotomy is much less obvious and there is a tendency for thinking to occur in middle ranges rather than to move toward extremes. Meanwhile, thinking can be described as seeking a level of abstraction ranging from particularistic to a universal level. This is one of the fundamental issues discussed by a number of writers in the field and has provided the point of departure for several theories. (Glenn, 1966)

Patterns of thinking has practical application despite the subject's abstract features. Activities of evaluation and rules of evidence which prevail in any society are closely allied to systems of thought and bring to the topic a flavor of pragmatism at the concrete level of the conventional wisdom of communication.

2.   Values

Values can be correlated with the content of cultures and hence fit into our scheme with the content of communication and with the referential function. The analysis of values in cultures has been extensive; what is needed at the present is research to differentiate more important from less important values of intercultural communication. The first step entails development of a scheme for analysis and describing values. Kluckhohn's scheme has been very influential in the development of the value analysis of contrast cultures which fall into clusters of values combined into the components of self perception, perception of the world, motivation, social relations and activity. (Stewart, 1969) The values in the area of social relations, those referring to problems of role identification, equality and forms of social interaction seem to be the most pragmatic values, while the cluster of values around the perception of self promise the greatest potential for theory.

3.   Interfaces in Communication

The rapport existing between the sender and the receiver during communication can be treated as structure and called the *communication interface*. The concept is important for intercultural communication, since the features of the interface lie largely below awareness and are composed of hazy intuitions, rules of thumb and emotional impression. In a different cultural setting, communicators may find that a kind of interface prevails which is different from the one they are accustomed to.

a. Two Interfaces

Among Americans the interface commonly used in communication has been called *sympathy*. (Stewart, 1976) To explain how sympathy functions, we can imagine a communicator reasoning as follows:

> I feel good about how I am going through; therefore we must be communicating. Since I feel good about it, the others too must be satisfied just like I am about the interaction.

Sympathy should be an effective interface if senders and receivers share a great deal in common and if they resemble each other. Under these circumstances, use of one's own perceptions and feelings as a barometer for those of others should be valid. When differences exist, as in intercultural communication, then sympathy misleads, producing miscommunication.

Under conditions of cultural difference, *empathy* is the better interface. It does not assume similarities among communicators to the degree of sympathy. Instead communicators must establish a common domain of activity and share congruent objectives in their communication. Success rides the crest of attainment of objectives, while the identities of communicators are held in reserve to direct communication but not to judge its success or failure. (Stewart, 1976)

b. Emotional Expressiveness

The analysis of communication as interfaces is a cognitive task which bypasses emotional aspects of sympathy and empathy. Nevertheless competence to understand the emotional responses of the self and others is perhaps one of the critical areas of intercultural communication. The topic has received much talk and little investigation. The most significant contribution in psychology is being made by Ekman and his colleagues. (Ekman and Friesen, 1975) (Ekman, 1972) This body of research investigates the universality of human emotions and elucidates how their expression is governed by cultural rules of display. Cultural influences are primarily found in managing emotions, and with this conclusion we discover a competence theory of emotions.

c. Interpersonal Knowledge

It does not lie within the scope of the *Outline* to review the field of interpersonal knowledge. Our purpose is to put a finger on a subject which the traditional sciences ignore.

The field of interpersonal communication is well established, but when the communicator asks about the sender and receiver, he must turn to the behavioral sciences for answers to questions asked in the languages of the realm of the logical-experimental sciences.[60] Yet there is a body of belief about human beings within the range of conventional wisdom in education, management, human relations, and folk beliefs of human growth and development. Some writers straddle the area between the logical-experimental sciences and the beliefs of conventional wisdom, but only a very few have attempted to develop the twilight area, usually arguing that the sciences do not observe their own canons in collecting and integrating empirical knowledge. Nevertheless, scientists cling to the belief of the sole validity of their methods and ignore that all men, including themselves, develop rules of thumb, intuitions and display intentional knowledge of other people and of the world.

Blackburn argues that

. . . logical-experimental structure of science that has evolved since Galileo's lifetime is magnificent.[61]

It is incomplete, nevertheless, lacking the "aesthetic" perception which provides an intuitive and concrete comprehension of complex systems. Blackburn contrasts the intellectual knowledge of the sciences with the epistemology of direct sensuous experience, which is qualified by

. . . subjectivity, and respect for intuition —— especially intuitive knowledge based on a "naive" openness to nature and to other people. [62]

314

The main argument of the article centers on the need for direct sensuous experience in science and that its products are complementary to those attained pursuing an intellectual-logical approach. The knowledge attained by one is not reducible into the knowledge attained by the other.

Much influenced by the counterculture of the 1960's, Blackburn is content to rest his case on general observations. Polanyi (1968) looks at "knowing" and knowledge in depth. He defines five indeterminacies in the sciences and proposes a new source of Knowledge: *tacit knowing* (Polanyi, 1968). Personal knowledge is developed through an active process which is anchored to perception and which reposes on a different conceptual base from the sciences as they are assumed to be. Polanyi goes so far as to claim that science can be regarded as an extension of perception.[63] Tacit knowing involves the knower, who links particulars of perception into an integrated focal meaning.[64]

The complexity of the subject defies brief treatment, but we can conclude that Polanyi, and there are others, attack the logical-experimental basis of the sciences and argue for a kind of knowledge based on intuition, aesthetic or some other undetermined basis. These positions are usually seen as complementary to the sciences, rather than contradictory. Phenomenology, ethnomethodology, as well as the anslyses of Blackburn and Polanyi, map a slippery subject reaching back to find a precedent in the western world in the discoveries of Vico (1668-1744), the Italian philosopher whose ideas were essentially lost to the modern world until recently, when they have emerged into contemporary consciousness.

Vico identified four types of knowledge in his theory of epistemology. (Bergin and Fisch, 1969) The fourth, which received no special name but is usually associated with *verstehen*, postulates a personal kind of knowledge reached through *fantasia* (i.e., imagination), and derived from the mental ruminations of inner historical experiences. It incorporates the intentional awareness of the person as an actor; the source of knowledge originates from those internal relationships and interconnections between thought and action, observations, theory, motivations, practice.[65] Vico's ideas, interpreted by Berlin, appear to develop what we have called a competence theory of interpersonal knowledge. It is clear that Vico believes that this kind of knowledge is generated in interpersonal relations; it has social origins. Berlin writes:

> We perceive and act in terms of responses to our questionings, which themselves are conditioned by our institutional life, but we do not generate the answer freely, "out of whole cloth." The answers to our questions are not arbitrarily invented by us, but their shape is determined by the nature of the questions: selection is a creative art. In this respect Vico is the ancestor of those who . . . stress the role played in men's experience by their own transforming acts, individual or collective; . . . he is opposed to the claims of rigorous determinists, positivists, philosophical realists and materialists, or psychologists, sociologists and philosophers of science with a mechanistic bias, and the like.[66]

The thought of Vico has just recently returned to the West. Perhaps Vico is the originator for Westerners of the personal knowledge which has been the hallmark of Eastern thought since antiquity. (Northrup, 1953) With the growing awareness that the prolegomenon of rationality of western science has fallen short of capturing even the western mind,[67] the precedents of Vico and the current work on personal and interpersonal knowledge will yield a synthesis between East and West in the realm of knowledge, whether it is recognized as such or not.

d. Interpersonal Behavior

An analysis of interpersonal behavior can be expected to develop performance theories, which should correspond with competence theories. Movement from one level to the next, however, requires a theoretical leap over the gap which exists between the two areas. The lack of correspondences between competence and performance can be recognized in the debates between academicians and practitioners, each establishing territoriality in separate preserves.

A major problem with performance is found with the ambiguity of behavior. When we consider an act as *effect*, it is usually possible to infer numerous *causes* to explain its happening. The uncertainty which connects cause and effect renders the activity of predicting perilous. (No wonder that in some societies forecasting the future is considered madness and vies with supernatural power.)

A significant approach to the solution of the problem is offered in *social exchange theory*. Foa (1971) describes the exchange of resources among people necessary to their well-being. He distinguishes material resources, which have traditionally been the concern of economists, from more subtle resources investigated by psychologists and sociologists. Empirical investigations establish six classes of resources: love, services, goals, money, information and status. The classes represent ranges orderly plotted on a two dimensional surface based on two coordinates: concreteness versus symbolism and particularism versus universalism.[68]

The range of resources, according to the two dimensions, tells us a great deal about the values attached to the kinds of exchange that take place among people. For instance, it matters a great deal from whom we receive love (particularistic value), but money is more likely to retain its value (universalistic), regardless of the conditions and participants in the exchange.[69]

Foa's social exchange theory is a contribution toward bridging the gap between cognitive theories (competence) and performance theories (behavior). For intercultural communication, much development is still needed, since there is little research investigating cross-cultural variations. Triandis has taken Foa's social exchange theory and combined it with other traditions in social psychology to construct a theory which can be described as a competence theory. He also provides an analysis of the process of training in preparation for life and work in another culture. With this step, Triandis moves closer to an integrating theory with power to generate rules for cross-cultural performance. (Triandis, 1975)

4. Orientation to Action

The components of communication identify the fourth component, the receiver, and the related function, directive.

This context serves to draw attention to *decision-making* and *problem-solving*. In American society these two strategies in thinking are presumed to be universal. In fact, they are not. Decision-making and problem-solving are functional cognitive systems in the sense used by Cole and Scribner (1974) and *competence theories* in our usage.

5. Forms, Principles and Representation

The complex component of *form* and function (aesthetic) interjects concepts which can be mentioned only as issues. They refer to principle representation and transformation, and also to methods. The first one is the idea of *simulation* as a method of communication and also as a principle in epistemology. Closely allied to this observation, Maranda observes that structuralism obeys the principle of the metaphor rather than a system of representation. (Maranda, 1972) One can add to these two "as if" strategies and games which have been employed in the social sciences. All of these strategies in the social sciences and in education merit careful study for applicability in intercultural situations.

These questions should be examined in the context of the principles of representation in the arts. The question to be asked is what is the relationship between the art product and the object of its representations, whether naturalistic, abstract or symbolic? An answer to this question for the arts should illuminate the various forms available for synthesizing the concrete and the abstract.

In his provocative *A Poetic for Sociology*, Brown (1977) asserts that *cognitive aesthetics* provides a theoretical base for sociology and in a wider sense for the sciences. The theory can be seen as a development of the issues suggested above in the discussions of interpersonal knowledge. Brown agrees with Vico that metaphors are meant to convey intelligible meanings. He employs it as the central concept in the *Poetic*. The metaphor is an imaginative strategy to reach the inner meaning of things. Brown refers to it as originative mental synthesis and claims that it is a unifying presupposition.[70] In this view, Brown resembles Polanyi as well as Vico.

318

Perhaps enough has been said to indicate that Brown presents a point of view annihilating the distinction between subjective-objective and internal-external. Cognitive aesthetics is a logic with the problematic of representation rather than definition. This point of view presumes to stand as a logic for both the sciences and the humanities, and comes closer to patterns of thought in the East than those in the West.

6. Trust

We have looked at sympathy and empathy as two potential models for interfaces between senders and receivers. In the concept of *trust* we turn to important literature which is too vast and complex a topic to be defined here. Trust should be treated at the personal level and also at the institutional and organizational levels.

7. Private and Public Rules

Cultural styles of communication essentially define topics and styles of exchanges according to event-structures and roles. Definition of topics of conversation, for example, which are appropriate to certain events, would contribute to intercultural communication.

The area of ethnography of speaking seems to be particularly important for the subject of private and public rules. By these we mean transformation of competence theory into performance. Under functions of communication we have provided an analysis which moves toward the appropriate competence theory. We should note that subsequent work in the area of ethnography of speaking has led to modifications of the original framework. The reformulation is coded as *SPEAKING: Setting* or scene; *Participants* or personnel; *Ends*, including goals, purposes and outcomes; *Act*, characteristic of both form and content of what is said; *Key* (tone, manner, or spirit in which act is done); *Instrumentalities* or channel and code; *Norms* of interaction and interpretation; *Genre* or categories of speech, acts and events. (Hymes, 1972)

8. Reserve of Meaning

Effective communication often requires that the sender amplify the basic message so that its meaning is clearly received.

To do this, we can speak of the sender appealing to reserves of meaning which are instructive for the receiver. Thus for some persons, their cultural background encourages that messages be amplified within a diachronic frame of reference; the sender employs a historical rhetoric. American reserves of meaning typically stress synchronic –– or contemporary –– economic and technical factors. In contrast to it, there is the symbolic reserve of meaning which is so attractive in some other cultures. Science, and some cultures as well, cultivates an abstract reserve of meaning. This and other possible reserves of meaning carry important implications in sustained communication in writing or in spoken exchanges.

9. Competence Theory of Implied-Observer Agent

This final critical issue for intercultural communication is selected to illustrate a factor in thought which can be assigned to functional cognitive systems, to a competence theory, and in a loose way, it is associated with individuating function in communication. The connection with time, the ninth component of communication, is more remote.

The concept of the implied observer agent (IOA) refers to a quality in American thinking in which language, thinking and values tend to point toward an individual who functions as an observer or as an agent. The language which requires an agent, *it, to rain,* illustrates the concept. The working of the IOA can be seen in patterns of thinking, methods of working and of communication, such as decision-making and problem-solving, which represent organizations of information from a specific point of view, an IOA.

C. *Functions of Communication*

The process of communication is valued in American society and in those disciplines in which the study of it has been developed during the last twenty-five years. The application of communication in these natural settings involves assumptions and values derived from the culture which are mistakenly attached to communication. The results may be desirable until the models and practices of communication are carried to another society and imposed in a setting with prevailing assumptions and values different from those in the original setting. Under new circumstances, as found with intercultural communication, it is necessary to analyze the functions of communication to determine their application and determine the relative emphasis placed on each. The analysis of components, content and functions given in the sections above should prove adequate to the task of evaluating communication in a variety of cultural settings.

D. Concepts of Communication

In previous sections, "concepts" has referred to models for analyzing content, values under culture, for instance. Under this section, the "concepts" from communication and culture combine to yield three general problems, each one an indication of aspects of communication, often neglected, which will vary from society to society.

Much of the thinking and work in communication assumes an exchange between the sender and the receiver. The presence, or the absence, of others should make a difference in communication, and its effect might well vary in different societies. A second aspect of the presence of others, *apopathetic behavior*, occurs when intermediaries participate in communication. Here the cultural differences are known. Americans prefer direct communication, avoid intermediaries, and when they are needed, as interpreters, for example, they act as window panes. In other societies, intermediaries in communication may be preferred.

The discussion of information theory mentioned the idea that choice of information implies other potential information not selected. "To communicate" implies "not to communicate" alternative messages. These are not neutral and this *null logic* prevails at more conventional levels of communication. Americans typically assume that an attribute given to A means the same attribute denied to B. There is a competitive factor in American communication which is not found in all other societies.

Null logic in communication puts a premium on conducting exchanges, and failure to do so communicates negatively. Silence is also negative and so is non-participation. Under these conditions, the right "not to communicate" is difficult to preserve. In societies where this constellation of factors is not found, the right is easier to maintain.

E. Processes in Intercultural Communication

Processes in intercultural communication are similar to those in communication. The subject is raised to summarize the role of assumptions in communication and to suggest a few empirical areas which are particularly important.

Thinking and reasoning are "mental" operations, essentially lacking in content. To think is to combine ideas, images or other content items into some form. The invisible workings of thought seem so natural to members of a culture that a pattern of thinking functions as an assumption, deep, implicit and silent, unrecognized by the thinker. Forms of thought —— dialectics, apocalyptic or revolutionary mode —— rules of evaluation, and principles of association and other conceptualizations of the process of assumptions can become formidable obstacles in intercultural communication.

Change and its expectations is a cultural curiosity which functions as an assumption in American society. Needless to say, the need for change and the assumption of its unrivaled benefits do not occur in all societies. It is associated with orientation to the future, values of doing, belief in the primacy of consequences as a guide to action, and with other cultural factors in American society.

Language often reveals assumptive processes in a culture which may impede intercultural communication. One of the best investigated areas is the semantics of socialism (White, 1966), with the results of the study showing that the language used to describe socialism conveys greater differences of views than the values held by samples of persons in various nations.

There is an additional area which deserves mention in passing: the cultural differences associated with the sense of space and place. Ideas of "spatial" imperatives, territorialism and proxemics come up in this context, which is often considered with patterns of time, a subject raised earlier in this *Outline*.

V. Applications and Training

The field of intercultural communication arose from the need of practitioners to cope with and work in a strange culture. Since the early days, researchers and practitioners alike have stayed in close touch with applications in the field. In the academic world, the discipline of speech and communication has led in interest in intercultural communication. It is in these departments that is found the greatest density of courses in intercultural communication. The three "textbooks" on intercultural communication — Harms (1973), Condon and Yousef (1975) and Sitaram (1976) — have been written by authors in speech communication. Perhaps it is the nature of the field, assisted by the eclecticism of speech communication, which has produced in its first wave of introductions and foundations a broad and gentle sweep of issues. Analytical probes found in the readers are usually written by linguists, psychologists and others from the traditional disciplines. The Condon and Yousef *Introduction* (1975) has a broad coverage and tackles some complex issues, i.e., epistemic structures. Within the same book, the reader finds anecdotes and down-to-earth issues in keeping with the applied nature of intercultural communication. A major work in intercultural communication is still to be written.

The main area of application for intercultural communication has been in the field of training, which is the major thrust of this section. Before turning to training, we wish to mention two other areas which have received some influences from intercultural, or which should benefit from an intercultural perspective.

The first one of these is persuasion and influencing. It is a vast topic with important work on attitude change, presenting two sides of an argument, attribution theory, dissonance theory, frames of reference, psychological manipulations, propaganda and suscepti- bility to influence. The list could be lengthened considerably, since the topics mentioned barely scratch the surface of empirical areas which deserve intercultural analysis but have received very little, if any.

A second area of application has received attention from people in communication: it is the area of diffusion of innovation. How one goes about bringing change in another society would seem to reside in the middle of the field of intercultural communication. Yet there has been a surprising lack of sophistication in cultural sensitivity in diffusion of innovation. It is only very recently that the cultural problem has begun to emerge in the round. (Rogers, 1976)

A.   Training

Although we have labelled this section "Training," we have in mind the fields of education and orientation as well as training. Courses in intercultural communication, preparation of Peace Corps volunteers for service abroad, the orientation of businessmen to work abroad — all these activities conducted for the purpose of preparing people to live and work in another culture fall within our subject. It is in this area of application that intercultural communication has found the most application. It is seldom that the insights from the study of different cultures have been used in either planning or decision-making.

For the sake of convenience, we shall refer to all receivers of communication as "students" and to all activities of preparation as "training." The goal of these activities is to bring about changes in the students which will make them more effective in the other culture.

Nine objectives can be identified for training, each one referring to a change in the student. There is a correspondence between the objective on one side, and content, functions and methods of training on the other. A better fit can also be found between the objectives and applications of training in behavior. A great deal of training strategy invokes working with the correspondence to attain maximal training effects.

1.   To inform

Informing is primarily concerned with imparting specific objective facts which the student will use to select information or responses from alternatives he already possesses. Briefings are activities based primarily on informing.

2.   To orient

The content of training to attain this objective tends to be more general than for informing, and the training effect should contribute to the student, guiding his choices because of the training.

3. To identify (to recognize)

The student acquires generalizations and concepts in training which modify his perception of events and guides his performance in a general sense.

4. To know

Attainment of the objective *to know* implies greater rigor in the content of training, more abstract content which must be imparted through methods to guide performance to a degree that will affect responses of others to the student.

5. To understand

The content of training contains sensitizing cultural concepts which are imparted for the purpose of steering performance in all aspects of the student's experiences, and of steering ways of interacting with others.

6. To empathize

This level involves changes in cultural self-perception as well as acquisition of emotional and cognitive factors which govern performance. The change brought about is in the person of the student; thus to empathize is an objective in education for intercultural communication.

7. To adapt

The change brought about in the student prepares him to govern his performance and his emotions in working and in living with others from another culture. The content of training includes diagnostic abstractions which prepare the student for future changes in his perception and behavior in another culture.

8. To adopt

The essential difference between this level and the preceding one is that the student trains to adopt a changed way of perceiving and behaving so that he is able to change the social and performance activities in another culture for which he is trained. His perceptions and performances are steered by the training effect for the purpose of changing others.

9.   To integrate

The objective, to integrate, is directed to bring about an emotional and perceptual change in the student which will govern his actions and perceptions to a degree of severance from his actions and emotions prior to training. The student integrates with a changed set of persons and circumstances as someone going to another society to become a permanent member of it.

B.   *Issues in Training*

Training and applications in the cross-cultural areas have not received systematic treatment. Perhaps the pioneering effort to regulate training was carried out for the Peace Corps. (Wight, 1969) Orientation programs have been covered by Brislin and Pedersen in their book (1976). The great bulge in training programs, however, is probably with Peace Corps, other government agencies, and then business. Feldman (1976) has reviewed the government programs.

None of the current sources on training –– and there are many informal papers and materials circulating –– provides a systematized look at training. In this section we refrain from making an exhaustive expansion of the objectives of training, and instead briefly note some selected issues which typically come up in training activities.

1.   Cultural Self-awareness

Some trainers insist that learning about another culture is not enough, that students who are going to another society must also develop some awareness of themselves as cultural beings. The implied assumption in this belief is that cultural problems invariably involve an interaction between two cultures, not merely the problems arising with the differences of the society to which the students are going.

Cultural self-awareness raises the additional issue of how effective it is to train for cultural self-awareness to increase the efficiency of performance in another culture.

2.   Training for Communication Interfaces

It would seem that training given around the concepts of communication interfaces would be extremely important. Yet little if anything has been done in this area. We know very little about the emotional consequences of using sympathy or empathy, of the consequences of holding given views of personal knowledge, etc. Very little effort seems to be devoted to the investigation of the conditions needed for creating trust. Finally there is little attention given to issues of defensive mechanisms, including projection and introjection, with the exception of some work in this area around the phenomenon of culture shock.

3. Cultural Adaptation

To some degree, training to facilitate adaptation means that responses of the student are modified to fit into a different cultural system. The attainment of the objective raises questions of ethical issues in requesting that students adapt to other cultural systems. If the ethics can be resolved, we are still faced with questions of choice. If changes in the behavior of the student are needs for adaptation, what aspects of the student's behavioral repertoire, or what attitudes and values, require change?

This difficult question can be followed with another which is equally difficult. If a choice has to be made about what is to be changed, what is the basis of the choice? Effectiveness of cross-cultural performance or minimal interference with the student's attitudes or values? The problem of training raises delicate issues regarding effectiveness and ethical choices.

4. Strategies in Training

The trainer has available a battery of approaches and of methods for training. Experience of trainers has developed guidelines.

a. What is learned?

One of the issues in training which would have considerable influence for strategies is the question of exactly what are the expected outcomes of training procedures. The issue may be posed as a question. Does the training impart new ways for the student, or does it provide coding for retrieving old patterns in new combinations and for different events?

The technical vocabulary of the psychologist provides a contribution to the analysis of the question. For instance, is the student asked to learn a new response to an old stimulus, or an old response to a new stimulus? The problem may be one of situational generalization, or the contextualizing of a response.

b. "Insular Communication"

Training methods such as human relations tend to facilitate learning similarities across cultures. Yet it would seem that the brunt of training should address itself to the differences. This raises the question of how to introduce differences and how to work with cultural contrasts in a training program. What are the effective strategies and methods of training? Whatever there are, and there are some, they tend to oppose the *insular communication* which can develop within a well-knit group.

c. The Use of Contrasts

Training should minimize the use of dichotomies and introduce genuine alternatives for cross-cultural perception, evaluation and performance. This implies the introduction of analysis of the student's own culture, the culture to which he is going, and also a third culture. If the idea is accepted as a strategy to avoid stereotypes, or even 'the refinement of stereotypes, severe challenges are thrown at the trainer.

d. Special Effects in Visual Modality

The visual image is ambiguous in meaning and hence strongly dependent on past experience and knowledge of the perceiver. It must be particularly effective under conditions of cultural differences, since it appeals to universal qualities of people, their ability to respond to the visual code. As a contrast, the spoken or written language in cross-cultural communication involves adoption of the other system entirely by the student, since language as a code entails much more invariance than the image. It would seem that the "variance" of the image would be particularly useful in education in the field of intercultural communication serving as a projector for personal and cultural predispositions. The visual image is excellent for arousal, problematical for expression, but lacks statements without the expectations of the perceiver. With images, the disparity between the sender and the receiver is maximized: what is intended by the sender is only very generally received with accuracy. It is possible that various persons, and cultures as well, become specialists in certain aspects of visual messages because their invariance is small, and that the variance becomes diagnostic of the culture or the individual. These comments support the contention that the visual modality has a special significance for intercultural communication.

e. Using the Mass Media

This is an important and interesting topic viewed from the point of view of definition of senders and receivers, and from the difficulty of analyzing exactly how changes are brought about in attitudes or behavior by the mass media. Evidence suggests that the mass media contribute more to awareness than to action.

VI. Theoretical Summary

Much of the impetus behind the *Outline* has been an intent to examine the field of intercultural communication to determine its unique contribution, if any, to the field of communication. For purposes of directness and simplicity, the theoretical underpinnings of the entire effort were kept to a minimum in Section I. To attain the original purpose of the *Outline*, a thorough and systematic examination of basic concepts seems necessary. This final section is intended to serve as an index of selected topics which should be developed in a full-fledged work in intercultural communication. Coverage of theoretical topics is not complete.

A.   Communication and the Principle of Similarity

Gathering evidence suggests that research must go beyond the simple distinction between similarity and difference and begin to isolate similarities of senders and receivers that are necessary for communication and those that are not. It is becoming increasingly important to revise the simple notion of similarity as the basic principle of communication and of information. Theory would benefit from a systematic application of similarity to the dimensions of time and a systematic investigation of the effects on communication of repetition and sequences in time ("diachronic effects").

Turning to the dimension of space, "synchronic" issues of symmetry and redundancy and their effect on communication deserve further study, particularly as they are transformed into elements of order, pattern and structure. Repetition can contribute to structure as controlled redundancy.

B. Communication and the Principle of Difference

Randomness, choice and entropy are important concepts in communication theory which subsist on similarity. Future research faces the task of developing metatheory in intercultural communication around differences and uniqueness and placing it in the context of existing concepts and theories. In the *Outline* we accepted the notion that difference is an idea.

Communication theories were developed as theories of competence governing theories of performance. Culture was then treated as either competence or as a cognitive process theory serving as background for communication, as a field articulated as differences. In this way we constructed a tier of theories, reserving for the applications of communication, theories of performance considered as interpersonal behavior.

The schemata of theoretical positions gave us convenient niches for several ideas, such as functional cognitive systems and decision-making. Central to communication, to decision-making, and to our approach in the *Outline* is the concept of *choice*. It is a strategem for avoiding explanations of difference: *choice* enjoys a provocative epistemology and an uncertain status in theory, at least according to its usage.

Choice can be treated as metatheory, and with its first kin *preference*, it is a powerful concept that lies outside ordinary causal systems. The two concepts raise questions of cause and effect in communication theory and introduce one of the least understood problems in communication: the relationship, including the causal one, between content of a message, its effect on the receiver's predispositions (attitudes, values, etc.) and its effect on behavior. The examination of *choice* and *preference* as favorite underpinnings of American psychology identifies a concept with a thread running through the sections of the *Outline*. This thread begins with the source of behavior, the provenance, buried in the agent of *choice* and *preference*. Thus there is a necessary stress on qualities of the agent as the origin of his actions. The thread from section to section would provide the following sequence of topics: (1) epistemology of *choice*, and *choice* as difference; (2) theory of *choice* in communication; (3) stress on certain functions of communication, such as referential, and cultural differences regarding the sources of behavior; (4) specific effects attained by intercultural communication, i.e., sender functioning on the basis of *choice*, but receiver on the basis of role; (5) personal involvement of student in training.

FOOTNOTES

[1] K.R. Williams, *The Journal of Communication,* 1973, p. 243.

[2] J.R. Pierce, "Communication," *Scientific American*, 1972, p. 36.

[3] Robert A.M. Gregson, *Psychometrics of Similarity* New York: Academic Press, 1975, pp. 27-8.

[4] M. Wallach, "On Psychological Similarity," *Psychological Review*, 1958, p. 104.

[5] *Ibid.,* p. 105-6.

[6] A. Tversky, "Features of Similarity," *Psychological Review* 1977, p. 327.

[7] *Ibid.,* p. 352.

[8] Robert Gregson, 1975, pp. 11-12.

[9] D. Byrne, "The Ubiquitous Relationship: Attitude Similarity and Attraction," *Human Relations*, 1971, p. 201.

[10] *Ibid.*, p. 205.

[11] W. Mischel, "Toward A Cognitive Social Learning Reconceptualization of Personality," *Psychological Review,* 1973, p. 276.

[12] E.M. Rogers and F. F. Shoemaker, *Communication and Innovation*, New York: Free Press, 1971, p. 201.

[13] C.H. Dodd, "Homophily and Heterophily in Diffusion of Innovators: A Cross-cultural Analysis in an African Setting," paper presented at the Speech Communication Association Convention, New York, November, 1973, p. 8.

[14] E.C. Stewart, "Cultural Sensitivities in Counseling," in P. Pedersen, W. J. Lonner and J.G. Draguns, eds., *Counseling Across Cultures.* Honolulu: The University of Hawaii Press, 1976, p. 102.

[15] Gregory Bateson, *Steps to an Ecology of Mind,* New York: Ballantine Books, 1972, pp. 452-453.

[16] *Ibid.,* p. 453.

[17] *Ibid.,* p. 452.

[18] *Ibid.,* pp. 452, 456.

[19] Richard N. Adams, *Energy and Structure*, Austin, Texas: University of Texas Press, 1975.

[20] D. Byrne, 1971, p. 201.

[21] N.R. Hanson, *Pattern of Discovery*, Cambridge: Cambridge University Press, 1958, p. 133.

[22] Z.W. Pylyshyn, "Competence and Psychological Reality," *American Psychologist,* 1972, p. 546.

[23] *Ibid.,* p. 547.

[24] *Ibid.,* p. 549.

[25] *Ibid.,* p. 548.

[26] *Ibid.,* p. 548.

[27] *Ibid.,* pp. 550-551.

[28] *Ibid.,* pp. 549-550.

[29] *Ibid.,* p. 549.

[30] T.A. Sebeok, *Approaches to Semiotics,* The Hague: Mouton, 1964, p. 5.

[31] A.R. Luria, *The Mind of a Mnemonist,* New York: Basic Books, 1968, p. 26.

[32] Mari R. Jones, "Time, Our Lost Dimension: Toward A New Theory of Perception, Attention & Memory," *Psychological Review* 1976, p. 353.

[33] D. Hymes, "The Anthropology of Communication," in F.E.X. Dance, ed., *Human Communication Theory,* New York: Holt, Rinehart and Winston, 1967, p. 8.

[34] L. Zusne, *Visual Perception of Form,* New York: Academic Press, 1970, pp. 97-103.

[35] G.S. Stent, "Cellular Communication, *Scientific American* September, 1972, pp. 50-51.

[36] *Ibid.,* p. 50.

[37] J.Ross, "The Resources of Binocular Perception," *Scientific American,* 1976, p. 81.

[38] *Ibid.,* p. 85.

[39] *Ibid.,* p.86.

[40] K.W. Deutsch, *The Nerve of Government,* New York: Free Press, 1966, p. 47.

[41] *Ibid.,* pp. 85-86.

[42] R. Naroll, "The Culture-bearing Unit in Cross-Cultural Surveys," *Handbook of Method in Cultural Anthropology,* New York: Columbia University Press, 1973, p. 732.

[43] *Ibid.,* p. 730.

[44] F.W. Voget, "History of Cultural Anthropology," *Handbook of Social and Cultural Anthropology,* Chicago: Rand McNally, 1973, p. 44.

[45] Hymes, 1967, p. 1.

[46] Mary Douglas, *Natural Symbols,* New York: Vintage Books, Random House, 1973, p. 18.

[47] *Ibid.,* pp. 11-12.

[48] M. Cole and S. Scribner, *Culture and Thought,* New York: John Wiley and Sons, 1974, pp. 30-31.

[49] *Ibid.,* p. 30.

[50] *Ibid.,* pp. 31, 192-194.

[51] A.R. Luria, *Cognitive Development: Its Culture and Social Foundations,* Cambridge, Massachusetts: Harvard University Press, 1976, p. 20.

[52] *Ibid.,* p. V.

[53] *Ibid.,* p. 9.

[54] Cole and Scribner, 1974, pp. 178-188.

[55] M. Cole, "An Ethnographic Psychology of Condition," *Cross-cultural Perspectives on Learning,* New York: John Wiley & Sons, 1975, pp. 171-174.

[56] H. Tajfel, "Social and Cultural Factors in Perception," in G. Lindzey and E. Aronson, eds., *The Handbook of Social Psychology,* second edition, volume three. Reading, Massachusetts: Addison-Wesley, 1969, p. 321.

[57] M.H. Bornstein, "Color Vision & Color Naming: A Psychophysiological Hypothesis of Cultural Difference," *Psychological Bulletin,* 1973, p. 280.

[58] P. Slovic, B. Fischhoff, S. Lichtenstein, "Behavioral Decision Theory," in M.R. Rosenzweig and L.W. Porter, eds., *Annual Review of Psychology,* vol. 28, Palo Alto, California: Annual Reviews, Inc., 1977, p. 14.

[59] H.W. Simons, N.N. Berkowitz, and R.J. Moyer, "Similarity, Credibility, and Attitude Change: A Review and a Theory," *Psychological Bulletin,* 1970, p. 13.

[60] T.R. Blackburn, "Sensuous Intellectual Complementarity in Science," *Science,* 1971, 172, p. 1003.

[61] *Ibid.,* p. 1003.

[62] *Ibid.,* p. 1003.

[63] M. Polanyi, "Logic and Psychology," *American Psychologist* 1968, p. 28.

[64] *Ibid.*, pp. 30-31.

[65] I. Berlin, *Vico and Herder*, New York: Vintage Books, Random House, 1976, pp. 107-108.

[66] *Ibid.*, p. 109.

[67] K.R. Pelletier and C. Garfield, *Consciousness East and West*, New York: Harper Colophon Books, Harper & Row, 1976, pp. 6-9.

[68] U.G. Foa, "Interpersonal and Economic Resources," *Science*, 1971, pp. 345-349.

[69] *Ibid.*, p. 346.

[70] R.H. Brown, *A Poetic For Sociology*, London: Cambridge University Press, 1977, pp. 144-145.

BIBLIOGRAPHY

Adams, Richard N. *Energy and Structure*. Austin, Texas: University of Texas Press, 1975.

Alpert, M.I., and Anderson, W.T., Jr. "Optimal Heterophily and Communication Effectiveness: Some Empirical Findings." *The Journal of Communication*, 1973, 23, pp. 328-343.

Arnheim, R. *Visual Thinking*. Berkeley, California: University of California Press, 1969.

Attneave, F. "Dimensions of Similarity." *American Journal of Psychology*, 1950, 63, pp. 516-556.

Bagby, James W. "Dominance in Binocular Rivalry in Mexico and the United States." *Journal of Abnormal and Social Psychology*, 1957, 54, pp. 331-334.

Baier, K., and Rescher, N., eds. *Values and the Future*. New York: The Free Press, 1969.

Barker, R. G. *Ecological Psychology*. Stanford, California: Stanford University Press, 1968.

Bateson, Gregory. *Steps to an Ecology of Mind*. New York: Ballantine Books, 1972.

Bauman, Richard, and Sherzer, Joel. "The Ethnography of Speaking." In B.J. Siegel, A.R. Beals, and S.A. Tyler, eds., *Annual Review of Anthropology*. Vol. 4. Palo Alto, California: Annual Reviews, Inc., 1975.

Bergin, T.G., and Fisch, M.H. *The New Science of Giambattista Vico*. (Rev. translation of 3rd ed.). Ithaca: Cornell University Press, 1969.

Berlin, B., and Kay, P. *Basic Color Terms*. Berkeley, California: University of California Press, 1969.

Berlin, I. *Vico and Herder*. New York: Vintage Books, Random House, 1976.

Berlo, D.K. *The Process of Communication*. New York: Holt, Rinehart and Winston, 1960.

Bernstein, B. "Elaborated and Restricted Codes: Their Social Origins and Some Consequences." *American Anthropologist*, 1964, vol. 6, no. 6, part 2, Special Publication, "The Ethnography of Communication," pp. 55-69.

Biddle, B.J., and Thomas, E.J., eds. *Role Theory: Concept and Research.* New York: John Wiley and Sons, 1966.

Bindra, D., Williams, J.A., and Wise, J.S. "Judgments of Sameness and Difference: Experiments on Decision Time." *Science,* 1965, 150, pp. 1625-1627.

Black, M. "How Do Pictures Represent?" In E.H. Gombrich, J. Hochberg and M. Black, eds., *Art, Perception, and Reality.* Baltimore: The Johns Hopkins University Press, 1972.

Blackburn, T.R. "Sensuous Intellectual Complementarity in Science," *Science,* 1971, 172, pp. 1003-1007.

Blumer, H. *Symbolic Interactionism: Perspective and Method.* Englewood Cliffs, New Jersey: Prentice–Hall, 1969.

Bornstein, M.H. "Color Vision and Color Naming: A Psychophysiological Hypothesis of Cultural Difference." *Psychological Bulletin,* 1973, 80, pp. 257-285.

Brislin, R.W., and Pedersen, P. *Cross-Cultural Orientation Programs.* New York: Gardner Press, 1976.

Brown, R.H. *A Poetic for Sociology.* London: Cambridge University Press, 1977.

Buchler, I.R., and Nutini, H.G., eds. *Game Theory in the Behavioral Sciences.* Pittsburgh: University of Pittsburgh Press, 1969.

Byrne, D. "The Ubiquitous Relationship: Attitude Similarity and Attraction." *Human Relations,* 1971, 24, pp. 201-207.

Byrne, D., and Griffit, W. "Interpersonal Attraction." In P.H. Mussen and M.R. Rosenzweig, eds., *Annual Review of Psychology,* 1973, p. 24.

Child, I.L. "Esthetics." In G. Lindzey and E. Aronson, eds., *The Handbook of Social Psychology.* Vol. 3. Reading, Massachusetts: Addison-Wesley, 1969, pp. 853-916.

Chomsky, N. *Syntactic Structures.* The Hague: Mouton, 1957.

Clark, H.H. "Linguistic Processes in Deductive Reasoning." *Psychological Review,* 1969, 76, 4, pp. 387-404.

Cole, M. "An Ethnographic Psychology of Cognition." In R.W. Brislin, S. Bochner and W.J. Lonner, eds., *Cross-Cultural Perspectives on Learning.* New York: John Wiley and Sons, 1975.

Cole, M., Gay, J., Glick, J.A., and Sharp, D.W. *The Cultural Context of Learning and Thinking.* New York: Basic Books, 1971.

Cole, M., and Scribner, S. *Culture and Thought*. New York: John Wiley and Sons, 1974.

Condon, J.C., and Yousef, F. *An Introduction to Intercultural Communication*. New York: The Bobbs-Merrill Company, 1975.

Dance, F.E.X. *Human Communication Theory*. New York: Holt, Rinehart and Winston, 1967.

Deutsch, K.W. *The Nerves of Government*. New York: Free Press, 1966.

Dodd, C.H. "Homophily and Heterophily in Diffusion of Innovations: A Cross-Cultural Analysis in an African Setting." Paper presented at the Speech Communication Association convention. New York, November 1973.

Douglas, Mary. *Natural Symbols*. New York: Vintage Books, Random House, 1973.

Duncan, H.D. Short bibliography of works on symbolic analysis that relate form to social content. In F.E.X. Dance, ed., *Human Communication Theory*. New York: Holt, Rinehart and Winston, 1967.

Durbin, M.A. "Linguistic Models in Anthropology." In B.J. Siegel, A.R. Beals, and S.A. Tyler, eds., *Annual Review of Anthropology*. Vol. 1, Palo Alto, California: Annual Reviews, Inc. 1972.

Ekman, P., and Friesen, W.V. *Unmasking the Face*. Englewood Cliffs, New Jersey: Prentice-Hall, 1975.

Ekman, P., Friesen, W.V., and Ellsworth, P. *Emotion in the Human Face*. New York: Pergamon Press, 1972.

Feigenbaum, E.A., and Feldman, J., eds. *Computers and Thought*. New York: McGraw-Hill, 1963.

Feldman, M.J. A Survey of International Cross-Cultural Training sponsored by the Federal Government during the period December 1968–September 1975. Unpublished Dissertation. The School of Education, The George Washington University, Washington, D.C., 1976.

Foa, U.G. "Interpersonal and Economic Resources." *Science*, 1971, 171, pp. 345-351.

Frake, Charles O. "How to Ask for a Drink in Subanun." *American Anthropologist*, 1964, vol. 66, no. 6, part 2, Special Publication, The Ethnography of Communication, pp. 127-132.

Frijda, N.H. "Simulation of Human Long-term Memory." *Psychological Bulletin*, 1972, 77, 1, pp. 1-31.

Fromkin, H.L. *The Psychology of Uniqueness: Avoidance of Similarity and Seeking of Differentness*. Paper no. 438, Institute of Research in the Behavioral, Economic, and Management Sciences, West Lafayette, Indiana: Krannert Graduate School of Industrial Administration, Purdue University, 1973.

Fromkin, H.L. "Some New Meaning for Interpersonal Similarity." Paper presented at the American Psychological Association convention. Montreal, September 1973.

Garfinkel, H. *Studies in Ethnomethodology*. Englewood Cliffs, New Jersey: Prentice-Hall, 1967.

Glenn, E.S. "Meaning and Behavior: Communication and Culture." *Journal of Communication*, 1966, 16, pp. 248-272.

Goffman, E. *Frame Analysis*. Cambridge, Massachusetts: Harvard University Press, 1974.

Gombrich, E.H. "The Mask and the Face: The Perception of Physiognomic Likeness in Life and Art." In E.H. Gombrich, J. Hochberg and M. Black, eds., *Art, Perception, and Reality*. Baltimore: The Johns Hopkins University Press, 1972.

Gombrich, E.H. "The Visual Image." *Scientific American*, 1972, 227, pp. 82-96.

Goodenough, W.H. "Componential Analysis and the Study of Meaning." *Language*, 32, pp. 195-216.

Gregson, Robert A.M. *Psychometrics of Similarity*. New York: Academic Press, 1975.

Hall, E.T. "Adumbration as a Feature of Intercultural Communication." In M.H. Prosser, ed., *Intercommunication Among Nations and Peoples*. New York: Harper and Row, 1973.

Hanson, N.R. *Patterns of Discovery*. Cambridge: Cambridge University Press, 1958.

Harms, L.S. *Intercultural Communication*. New York: Harper and Row, 1973.

Helson, H. *Adaption—Level Theory*. New York: Harper and Row, 1964.

Holsti, O.R. "Content Analysis." In G. Lindzey and E. Aronson, eds., *The Handbook of Social Psychology*, 2nd edition, vol. 2,

Reading, Massachusetts: Addison—Wesley, 1968.

Honigmann, J.J., ed. *Handbook of Social and Cultural Anthropology*. Chicago: Rand McNally, 1973.

Howell, W.S. "A Model for the Study of Intercultural Communication." Unpublished manuscript, University of Minnesota, 1976.

Hulett, J.E., Jr. "A Symbolic Interactionist Model of Human Communication." *Communication Review*, 1966, 14, p.1.

Hymes, D. "Models of the Interaction of Language and Social Life." In J.J. Gumperz and D. Hymes, eds., *Directions in Sociolinguistics*. New York: Holt, Rinehart and Winston, 1972.

Hymes, D. "Toward Ethnographies of Communication." In M.H. Prosser, ed., *Intercommunication Among Nations and Peoples*. New York: Harper and Row, 1973.

Jaffe, H.L.C. "Syntactic Structure in the Visual Arts." In G. Kepes, ed., *Structure in Art and in Science*. New York: George Braziller, 1965.

Johnson—Laird, P.N. "Psycholinguistics." In P.H. Mussen and M.R. Rosenzweig, eds., *Annual Review of Psychology*, vol. 25, Palo Alto, California: Annual Reviews, Inc., 1974.

Jones, Mari R. "Time, Our Lost Dimension: Toward a New Theory of Perception, Attention, and Memory." *Psychological Review*, 1976, 83, pp. 323-355.

Kahneman, D., and Tversky, A. "On the Psychology of Prediction." *Psychological Review*, 1973, 80, pp. 237-251.

Kearney, Michael. *World View*. New York: Holt, Rinehart and Winston, 1976.

Kennedy, J.M. *A Psychology of Picture Perception*. San Francisco: Jossey-Bass, 1974.

Kluckhohn, C., et. al. "Values and Value-Orientation in the Theory of Action." In T. Parsons and E. Shils, eds., *Toward A General Theory of Action*. Cambridge: Harvard University Press, 1951.

Kluckhohn, F., and Strodtbeck, F. *Variations in Value Orientation*. New York: Row, Peterson, 1961.

Lounsbury, F.G. "The Varieties of Meaning." *Georgetown University Monograph Series on Language and Linguistics*, 1955, 8, pp. 158-164.

Luria, A.R. *The Mind of a Mnemonist*. New York: Basic Books, 1968.

Luria, A.R. *Cognitive Development: Its Cultural and Social Foundations*. Cambridge, Massachusetts: Harvard University Press, 1976.

Manis, M. "Context Effects in Communication: Determinants of Verbal Output and Referential Decoding." In M.H. Appley, ed., *Adaptation-Level Theory*. New York: Academic Press, 1971.

Maranda, P. "Structuralism in Cultural Anthropology." In B.J. Siegel, A.R. Beals and S.A. Tyler, eds., *Annual Review of Anthropology*. Vol. 1. Palo Alto, California: Annual Reviews, Inc., 1972.

Maslow, A.H. "A Theory of Human Motivation." *Psychological Review*, 1943, 50, pp. 370-396.

Mettee, D.R., and Riskind, J. "When Ability Dissimilarity is a Blessing: Liking for Others Who Defeat Us Decisively." Paper presented at the American Psychological Association convention. Montreal, September 1973.

Miller, G.A., and McNeill, D. "Psycholinguistics." In G. Lindzey and E. Aronson, eds., *The Handbook of Social Psychology*. Vol. 3. Reading, Massachusetts: Addison—Wesley, 1969.

Mischel, W. "Toward a Cognitive Social Learning Reconceptualization of Personality." *Psychological Review*, 1973, 80, 4, pp. 252-283.

Naroll, R., and Cohen, R., eds. *A Handbook of Method in Cultural Anthropology*. New York: Columbia University Press, 1973.

Naroll, R. "The Culture—Bearing Unit in Cross—Cultural Surveys." In R. Naroll and R. Cohen, eds., *Handbook of Method in Cultural Anthropology*. New York: Columbia University Press, 1973.

Nebes, R.D. "Hemispheric Specialization in Commissurotomized Man." *Psychological Bulletin*, 1974, 81, pp. 1-14.

Newell, A., and Simon, H.A. *Human Problem Solving*. Englewood Cliffs, New Jersey: Prentice—Hall, 1972.

Northrop, F.S.C. *The Meeting of East and West*. New York: Macmillan, 1953.

Ornstein, R.E., ed. *The Nature of Human Consciousness*. New York: Viking Press, 1973.

Pelletier, K.R., and Garfield, C. *Consciousness East and West*. New York: Harper Colophon Books, Harper and Row, 1976.

Piaget, J. *The Mechanisms of Perception*. New York: Basic Books, 1969.

Pierce, J.R. "Communication." *Scientific American*, 1972, 227, pp. 31-41.

Polanyi, M. "Logic and Psychology." *American Psychologist*, 1968, 23, pp. 27-43.

Pollack, R.H. "Muller—Lyer Illusion: Effect of Age, Lightness Contrast and Hue." *Science*, 1970, 170, pp. 93–94.

Pool, I., Schramm, W., Frey, F., Maccoby, N., and Parker, E.B., eds. *Handbook of Communication*. Chicago: Rand McNally College Publishing Company, 1973.

Pye, L.W., ed. *Communications and Political Development*. Princeton, New Jersey: Princeton University Press, 1963.

Pylyshyn, Z.W. "Competence and Psychological Reality." *American Psychologist*, 1972, 27, pp. 546-552.

Reichenbach, H. *Atom and Cosmos*. New York: George Braziller, 1933.

Rogers, E.M., ed. *Communication and Development*. Beverly Hills, California: Sage Publications, 1976.

Rogers, E.M., and Shoemaker, F.F. *Communication and Innovation*. New York: Free Press, 1971.

Rosenberg, S., and Cohen, B.D. "Referential Processes of Speakers and Listeners." *Psychological Review*, 1966, 73, pp. 208-231.

Ross, J. "The Resources of Binocular Perception." *Scientific American*, 1976, 234, pp. 80-86.

Rubin, J. "Sociolinguistics." In J.J. Honigmann, ed., *Handbook of Social and Cultural Anthropology*. Chicago: Rand McNally, 1973.

Saporta, S., ed. *Psycholinguistics: A Book of Readings*. New York: Holt, Rinehart and Winston, 1961.

Sebeok, T.A. *Approaches to Semiotics*. The Hague: Mouton, 1964.

Segall, M.H., Campbell, D.T., and Herskovits, M.J. "Cultural Differences in the Perception of Geometric Illusions." *Science*, 1963, 139, pp. 769-771.

Silverstein, M. "Linguistic Theory: Syntax, Semantics, Pragmatics." In B.J. Siegel, A.R. Beals and S.A. Tyler, eds., *Annual Review of Anthropology*. Vol. 1. Palo Alto, California: Annual Reviews, Inc., 1972.

Simon, H.A. *The Sciences of the Artificial*. Cambridge: Massachusetts Institute of Technology Press, 1969.

Simons, H.W., Berkowitz, N.N., and Moyer, R.J. "Similarity, Credibility, and Attitude Change: A Review and A Theory." *Psychological Bulletin*, 1970, 73, pp. 1-16.

Singer, M.R. "Culture: A Perceptual Approach." In L.A. Samovar and R.E. Porter, eds., *Intercultural Communication: A Reader*. Belmont, California: Wadsworth Publishing Company, 1976.

Sitaram, K.S., and Cogdell, R.T. *Foundations of Intercultural Communication*. Columbus, Ohio: Charles E. Merrill Publishing Co., 1976.

Slobin, D.I. *Psycholinguistics*. Glenview, Ill.: Scott Foresman, 1976.

Slovic, P., Fischhoff, B., and Lichtenstein, S. "Behavioral Decision Theory." In M.R. Rosenzweig and L.W. Porter, eds., *Annual Review of Psychology*. Vol. 28. Palo Alto, California: Annual Reviews, Inc., 1977.

Smith, A.G., ed. *Communication and Culture*. New York: Holt, Rinehart and Winston, 1966.

Sperry, R.W. "A Modified Concept of Consciousness." *Psychological Review*, 1969, 76, pp. 532-536.

Stent, G.S. "Cellular Communication." *Scientific American*, September 1972, 227, 3, pp. 42-51.

Stewart, E.C. "Cultural Sensitivities in Counseling." In P. Pedersen, W. J. Lonner and J.G. Draguns, eds., *Counseling Across Cultures*. Honolulu: The University Press of Hawaii, 1976.

Stewart, E.C., Danielian, J., and Foster, R.J. *Simulating Intercultural Communication Through Role Playing*. Alexandria, Virginia: Human Resources Research Office, The George Washington University, 1969.

Tajfel, H. "Social and Cultural Factors in Perception." In G. Lindzey and E. Aronson, eds., *The Handbook of Social Psychology*, 2nd edition, vol. 3. Reading, Massachusetts: Addison–Wesley, 1969.

Tarde, G. *The Laws of Imitation*. New York: Holt, 1903.

Triandis, H.C. "Cultural Influences Upon Perception." In L. Berkowitz, ed., *Advances in Experimental Social Psychology*, vol. 1. New York: Academic Press, 1964.

Triandis, H.C. *The Analysis of Subjective Culture*. New York: John Wiley and Sons, 1972.

Triandis, H.C. "Culture Training, Cognitive Complexity and Interpersonal Attitudes." In R.W. Brislin, S. Bochner and W.J. Lonner, eds. *Cross—Cultural Perspectives on Learning*. New York: John Wiley and Sons, 1975.

Tversky, A. "Features of Similarity." *Psychological Review*, 1977, 84, pp. 327-352.

Tyler, L.E. *The Psychology of Human Differences*. 2nd edition. New York: Appleton—Century—Crofts, Inc., 1956.

Voget, F.W. "History of Cultural Anthropology." In J. J. Honigmann, ed., *Handbook of Social and Cultural Anthropology*. Chicago: Rand McNally, 1973.

von Wright, G.H. *Explanation and Understanding*. Ithaca, New York: Cornell University Press, 1971.

Wallach, M. "On Psychological Similarity." *Psychological Review*, 1958, 65, pp. 103-116.

White, R.K. "Images in the Context of International Conflict: Soviet Perceptions of the U.S. and the U.S.S.R." In H.C. Kelman, ed., *International Behavior*. New York: Holt, Rinehart and Winston, 1966.

Wight, A. (Project Director). *Cross—Cultural Training: A Draft Handbook*. Estes Park, Colorado: Center for Research and Education, 1969.

Williams, K.R. "Reflections on a Human Science of Communication." *The Journal of Communication*, 1973, 23, pp. 239-250.

Williams, R.M., Jr. *American Society*. 3rd edition. New York: Knopf, 1970.

Zusne, L. *Visual Perception of Form*. New York: Academic Press, 1970.

Charles P. Loomis and Jerome R. Epstein:

Transcending Cultural and Social Boundaries Through Communication

---

In the Beginning of Sociology, Communication had a Place

AUGUSTE Comte, who gave Sociology its name stressed the importance of language which furnished the vessel by which preceding generations reached the present and by which present learning is stored for the future. Language also, according to Comte, binds us to our fellows and without a common language there could be no social order, no consensus, no solidarity.[1] Moderns who talk about doing "their thing" may be informed by one of the earliest texts in the field of sociology by Robert E. Park and Ernest W. Burgess, in which we read: "In human, as distinguished from animal, society common life is based on a common speech . . . The same 'thing' has a different meaning for the naive person and the sophisticated person, for the child and the philosopher . . . The ecclesiastic, the artist, the mystic, the scientist, the Philistine, the Bohemian, represent more or less different 'universes of discourse.' Even social workers occupy universes of discourse not mutually intelligible."[2] Practically all studies in comparative sociology, especially those of inter-group and international relations, demonstrate the very great importance of communication. A series of recent studies of actual and desired relations between Americans and Mexicans indicated that nothing was more important in creating "good relations" between these citizens of two nations than a high volume of interaction, communication and contact. This supports the thesis common in American sociology that "the more frequently persons interact with one another, the stronger their sentiments of friendship for one another are apt to be."[3]

Conversely it has long been recognized that where a serious conflict of interest exists between two parties, an increase in communication may serve to accentuate the differences, thus heightening rather than reducing tensions.

It has not only been the emphasis which sociology has placed on communication itself, but the great stress placed upon its opposite, isolation, which has served to drive home to us the tremendous importance of communication, especially in personality development. Thus the early and very important text in sociology mentioned above carries a dramatic account of feral man and a bibliography on the subject. This is prefaced by the question: "What would the results be if children born with a normal organism and given food and light sufficient to sustain life were deprived of the usual advantage of human intercourse?"[4] Then the authors relate the sad stories of those who were denied meaningful interaction with others: the story of Caspar Hauser, the Hungarian peasant boy reared in strict seclusion, about whom thousands of articles have been written; the stories of the Hessian Boy, the Irish Boy, the Lithuanian Boys, the Girl of Cranenburg, Clemens of Overdyke, the Wolf Children of India, and others. In this same early sociology text Helen Keller in her own words reports on "the most important day I remember in all my life" when her teacher, Anne Mansfield Sullivan, began linking Miss Keller's two lives, the one of a deaf and mute childhood which lasted seven years to those years in which, liberated from her handicap, she became a famous inspirational figure. The place of isolation in what began then to be called "social distance" was mentioned in several contexts in this early text. Since, as we shall argue below, human nature can only come into existence as the growing individual takes and gives messages, isolation, social distance and any impediment to communication is of great importance to sociologists.

The basic nature of social distance as measured and studied by Robert Park[5] and Emory Bogardus[6] almost half a century ago (on a scale which bears the latter's name) is directly related to isolation resulting from lack of social participation and identity. Characterized as measuring the "degree of sympathetic understanding" that actors feel or would feel between themselves and members of other groups in such roles as neighbor, citizen, family member or club or work group participant, and growing out of the significance of interaction for the development of the self and for social existence, this scale has been followed by more recent measures of communication potential and behavior. Such sociological concepts as status incongruence and status consistency have been developed. An easy to understand example is the situation common in restaurants where the waitress must give orders to the cook who outranks her. The status incongruence created by this work-flow is sometimes reduced by having the orders come in over high barriers or through small windows in order to "take some of the curse off the incongruence . . ."[7]

Definitions, Fundamental Units and Intended Scope

We define communication as the process by which information, decisions and directives are transmitted among actors and the ways in which knowledge, opinions, and attitudes are formed or modified by interaction. [8] Interaction, the core datum of sociology, has been defined as "any event by which one party tangibly influences the overt actions or state of mind of the other."[9] As will be emphasized in the present chapter it is reciprocal and interdependent activity, designated as having the quality of complementarity or double contingency.[10] Communication is, therefore, central to the interests of sociologists. Since it verges on tautology to say that human "social" phenomena are cases of "*interaction* between two or more human beings conceived as 'persons,' 'organisms,' 'selves,' or 'actors,' "[11] it may be well to note here that our subject is not simplistic or something to be treated only as common sense knowledge. Although we do not have space to elaborate the variations in the conceptions of what is subject and what is object as treated by such writers as Descartes, Kant, Hume, Hegel, Marx, G.H. Mead and Max Weber, the mere fact that such writers have given careful consideration to the topic should testify to the complicated history of our subject.

To cope with the myriad approaches to communication found in sociology in a brief space is, of course, impossible except in the most general terms. Since social and cultural boundaries are blurred and the size of the entities involved ranges from the minute to the immense, we will emphasize those conceptualizations which are relatively free of parochial bonds. Whether international

347

communication takes place at the lowest level of informal interaction between two citizens or in the form of artistic exchange or in official communiques between governments, it is subject to analysis according to the same broad principles which govern exchanges between groups both smaller and larger and which may well be less formally defined. Communication is founded on shared meanings and since in an exact sense it is unlikely that any two people attribute precisely the same meaning to any communication we take the position that the problems of inter-cultural communication are merely an amplification of the problems attendant to any form of intercourse. Thus we will focus on broad theoretical orientations in sociology with the thought that they can be applied in any field of interest concerned with communication.

We will offer a few examples of the type of consideration and level of generalization prevalent among those in sociology for whom communication is but one of many significant facets of social existence. In contrast we will also offer highly abbreviated versions of several theories of society which have communication as their core. Beyond these variations in views of communication itself, an example will also be given to illustrate how different conceptualizations of other facets of society are in turn reflected in the treatment of communication. Also we will indicate some ways in which considerations advanced by the sociology of knowledge can be relevant to the study of communication along with other general remarks. We shall terminate the discussion with the senior author's Processually Articulated System Model (PASM) as this features communication.

Communication in Broad Context

The modern sociologist in his study of man in a social context attempts to make behavior in general the object, with biological, psychological, social and cultural components. Out of this approach grew the most significant effort in inter-disciplinary research resulting in the publication, among others, of *Toward a General Theory of Social Action*.[1][2] Among the many kinds of inputs, the cultural component alone encompasses such unique creations of man as language, science, philosophy, religion, the fine arts, ethics, law, technology, economics and politics. In the quest for comprehension of the complex interrelation and interpenetration of the various components, no sociological equivalent of the Rosetta Stone has been found, no Newton or Einstein has emerged. Consequently theories finding primacy in each of the components have been advanced with combinations and permutations so numerous and varied as to resist cogent classification.

Not surprisingly then we find that communication as above defined, is also accorded widely divergent treatment and emphasis. Still, the salient feature of communication is its pervasive character. So inextricably is it interwoven into the social fabric that each elemental facet of social structures can be examined with at least an implicit recognition of its existence. However, as one views the theories of many eminent sociologists one is faced with an interesting anomaly. While each readily recognizes the essential nature of communication there is often all too little effort made to discover *how* communication *per se* takes place. Thus Talcott Parsons specifies that "disruption of the communication system of a society is ultimately just as dangerous as disruption of its system of order . . . [and] a social system . . . is not possible without language . . ."[13] More recently he writes about "specialized 'languages,' such as money, power, and influence."[14] Obviously it will be many years before the functions of all these, and other languages such as those used in computers, will be understood cross-culturally and between and among disciplines.

For Kingsley Davis communication is the core of civilization, the keystone of civilization.[15] Howard P. Becker considers communication to be the essence of sociation and observes that enculturation begins at an early age. With Jean Piaget and others he differentiates phases of development, maintaining that what he calls sociation and/or dissociation can develop only later after the child makes self-and-other differentiation in role playing, perhaps after age three.[16] Alvin A. Gouldner, an organizational theorist, feels the essence of an organization is found in the quality, extent, and control of communication. Robin M. Williams, Jr. sees the role of communication as the integration of interaction.

For Sorokin communication takes various forms. It can have a hierarchical base, horizontal (within class), vertical (between classes) and intermediate (blurred). He also states that "upper-middle-urban

groups" have more efficient communication than others. We shall
have occasion to mention Sorokin again below but here it may be
noted that few sociologists have treated either sociology or
communication so broadly either in their temporal or spatial
dimensions. For Sorokin the social system and the chief concern of
sociologists is the superorganic world. This world "is equivalent to
mind in all its clearly developed manifestations" and embraces all the
cultural components mentioned earlier. Although found mainly in
the interaction of human beings and in the products of such
interaction, its rudiments can be observed outside the human species
in such phenomena as "reflexes and instincts; sensations, fe e l ings
and emotions; traces of reproductive imagination; elementary
association of images; and rudimentary ability to learn by
experience."[17] For Sorokin "vehicles" play an extremely important
part in communication. Through vehicles, both in physical forms
such as telegraph apparatus and in symbolic form such as codes, ideas
and meaning are communicated. One of his important conclusions
was that vehicles condition behavior and mental states. Roads dictate
direction of traffic and fetishization of vehicles generally may lead to
their becoming sacred.

Taking a different vantage point, Gouldner infers that some
forms of communication (rules) are more functional for those in
higher positions, while Williams stresses the role of equalitarian
symbols in cushioning and minimizing class differences. Williams is
here touching on a concept postulated by Robert Merton who
conceives "visibility" as the degree to which norms and
role-performance are observable throughout a structure. Merton
expresses in several instances the difficulties which can arise in
communication. He examines the manner in which norms and values,
in contrast to actual behavior, are more readily transmitted to
non-members of a group. Consequent distortions are used to explain
why new and marginal members may "over-conform" sometimes
assuming saint-like behavior. He also treats the difficulty of the
unorganized expressing their feelings to the power elite, and the use
of propaganda and the problems which arise from improper emphasis
on symbols. The above mentioned difficulty in transmitting actual
behavior can lead to what Williams characterizes as an inability to
reconcile the real and the ideal, and the consequent development of
the cynical or revolutionary outlook. In more general terms all of

these problems recall Parsons' absolute belief that communication cannot exist where common meaning of symbols is not present. Without necessarily contradicting Parsons, Williams notes the use of common symbols with meanings so amorphous that they can be all things to all men. A related phenomenon is probed by Homans and Gouldner who note the increased difficulty encountered with the increase in distance, especially social distance.

Sociologists For Whom Communication is ALL Important

As Homans selected his four key concepts; namely, interaction, sentiment, activity and norm when writing in *The Human Group* he considered using the term *communication* but opted for *interaction* instead, because he wanted to deal not with content of messages but "the sheer fact, aside from content or process of transmission, that one person has communicated with another."[18] Homans in this respect differs greatly from the symbolic interactionists in sociology to whom we now turn. That large group of sociologists who think of themselves as symbolic interactionists make communication in most of its aspects a central concern.

Herbert Blumer defined symbolic interaction as the process by which individuals relate to their own minds or the minds of others; the process, in which individuals take account of such things as their own of their fellows' motives, desires, needs, ends, knowledge, etc.[19] Symbolic interactionism traces its intellectual heritage through the pragmatic philosophers, John Dewey and William James and the work of such sociologists as Florian Znaniecki, W.I. Thomas, Robert Park, Charles Cooley, and particularly George Herbert Mead. Related ideas may also be found in work as disparate as that of George Simmel, Sigmund Freud and Martin Buber. This school of thought views man as an innovative symbol user and creator; he is man, the communicator, or in the term of Ernst Cassirer, *animal symbolicum*. It is precisely this facility with symbols which distinguishes man from other biological organisms. Communication is the carrier of culture, the means by which man is able to transcend time and space. Moreover, the groups in which man is arrayed are dependent upon and pervaded by complex symbolic processes.

George H. Mead argued that the mind and self arise in man who is both the product and the creator of society. The sequence in which this occurs can only take place through the medium of language. Non-verbal communication (behavior) must have meaning for a child if language describing that behavior is to have meaning to him. Once meaning is established, language makes it possible to replace behavior with ideas, and having the idea, the child can think about it, thus acquiring mind as he acquires language. Mead further posits that a child learns not only the names of objects but the attitudes and emotions with which his teacher (e.g. parent) views those objects. At that point the child enters the realm of shared social meanings and he learns not only to share attitudes about external objects but about himself as well. In this manner, the self emerges.

As a self-conscious individual, through becoming an object unto himself, the child evaluates and controls himself, responding to his own behavior. The whole process is facilitated by a child's role playing in games and fantasy. "A child plays at being a mother, at being a teacher, at being a policeman; that is, it is taking different roles."[20] This introspective view is a matter of reflection made possible by the child's capacity to take the role of the "other." Certain "others" will have more influence and are called "significant" others. Moreover, in playing multiple person games with rules the child must take the role of the "generalized other." For Mead the maturation process of the child reaches the final stage as the individual takes the role of the "generalized other."[21] At this later stage of development the child can take on not just a series of roles of individual others, but of a social group as a whole, including governing norms and values. At this point he is responding to a "generalized other," defined by Mead as "The organized community or social group which gives to the individual his unity of self . . ."[22]

> "To stress the essentially social nature of the self may seem to imply that the self is completely determined by the internalized attitudes of others. This is not so . . . Nevertheless, his behavior has a large element of freedom and spontaneity. The demands of the social situation pose a problem to the acting individual, but there is considerable leeway in how he meets the problem. Furthermore, the individual can never predict precisely what his response in a given situation will be . . .

Mead called the acting self the "I." The "me," on the other hand, is that part of the self that is an organization of the internalized attitudes of others. The "I" represents the self insofar as it is free, has initiative, novelty and uniqueness. The "me" represents the conventional part of the self. The "I" responds to the "me" and takes it into account, but it is not identical with it.

There may be varying amounts of "I" and "me" in behavior. In impulsive behavior, the "me" is absent; in Freudian language, the "I" is not being censored by the "me." The over-institutionalized individual is over-determined by his "me." In more normal circumstances, the individual responds to a situation in its social aspects but does so with some regard for his own unique capacities and needs. The most gratifying experiences are those in which the demands of the "me" or of the social situation —— permit the expression and realize the potentialities of the "I".

In primitive society, the individual self is more completely determined than in civilized societies by the "me," that is, by the particular social groups to which the individual belongs. Primitive society offers much less scope for the "I." Indeed, the development of civilization is largely dependent upon the progressive social liberation of the individual self. The "I" is the innovator, the source of new ideas and energy to initiate social change."[2][3]

The emphasis we have given to the distinction between the "I" and the "me" is reaction to the frequent failure of some modern-day sociologists to preserve that distinction. Many of Mead's ideas have received broad acceptance, and while many have incorporated some version of his concepts on interaction, role and self, some of those more influenced by the importance of structure, function and system have muted the degree of freedom accorded the "I" by Mead, even while retaining the original terminology.

As Mead and his followers developed a theory of society based on a creative man using complex symbols, the behaviorists were developing a view of circumscribed man whose complex social behavior could be explained in terms of communicative mechanisms shared with animals. Experimenting extensively with pigeons and other animals, the behaviorists have produced a highly psychological view of a mechanistic society heavily reliant on concepts such as reward and punishment. Each communication is for them a part of the conditioning process, and if all the conditioning factors were known it would allow the accurate prediction of the response to future stimuli, man being incapable of countermanding his programming. Though such research is not without merit, we would agree with Anselm Strauss and Alfred Lindesmith, among many, that there have been unduly broad theoretical conclusions drawn from these studies of low level interaction.

Many behaviorists consider themselves, in general, as followers of Ivan Pavlov and his work on the conditioned response. It is instructive to repeat Lindesmith and Strauss' quotation of Pavlov himself, as he clearly demonstrates his belief in the exclusively human nature of some forms of communication.

> "When the development of the animal world reached the stage of man, an extremely important addition was made to the mechanisms of nervous activity. In the animal, reality is signalized almost exclusively by stimulations and the traces they leave in the cerebral hemispheres, which come directly to the special cells of the visual, auditory, or other receptors of the organisms. This is what we too possess as impressions, sensations, and notions of the world around us, both the natural and the social — with the exception of the words heard or seen. This is the first system of signals of reality common to man and animals. But speech constitutes a second signaling system of reality which is peculiarly ours, being the signal of those first signals . . . It is precisely speech that has made us human . . .
>
> In the final analysis, all complex relations in man have passed into the second signaling system. Verbal and abstract thinking has been elaborated in us. The second signaling system is the most constant and ancient regulator of human relations. But there is nothing of the kind in animals. Their entire higher

nervous activity, with its supreme manifestations, is included in the first signal system. In man the second signal system acts on the first signal system in two ways: in the first place by inhibition which is greatly developed in it, (and) . . . in the second place by its positive activity . . . Such relations cannot exist in animals."[24]

Rather than focus on either the symbolic interactionists or behaviorists in their treatment of aspects of communication, an attempt to integrate all levels of interaction is today being made by the adherents of information theory in which sociologists are involved. This line of thought strives to extend the highly interpersonal focus of symbolic interactionism to an all encompassing synthesis of the biological, psychological, social and cultural aspects of life into a totally integrated system with communication as its base. Thus Orrin Klapp[25] posits man as being inherently encoded with a strain for order, even as homeostasis is encoded in other biological organisms. Life is a communication process, the aim of which is to defeat disorder. Man innately seeks to live in harmony with the environment and his fellow man. Even as fish instinctively spawn, man instinctively seeks his version of order, and like the fish he too is constantly confronted with disorder.

Using computer terminology, the sociologist using this approach to information theory visualizes society as a complex network of feedback and control loops which provide the information at both natural and symbolic levels which must be encoded if man is to adapt to defeat disorder. But there are limits to the amount of information a system can assimilate. Consequently there must be a constant opening and closing of the system to available input. Closure is not viewed as a setback to progress, only as a necessary balancing of the system against disorganizing communication and information overload.

Man is viewed as a builder and grower through cooperative effort with his own kind, he is fitted by heredity and learning to produce relevant signals. Enduring patterns and networks of communication constitute social systems, and collective symbolic memory, culture. Disorder is met in the efforts of others to build and grow. Information output now provides the means to control or negotiate and closure provides the haven of the ingroups (family, church, ethnic group, etc.) if the input is too threatening. Without the supportive ingroup to fall back on in times of stress, man succumbs to disorder.

Our interpretation of modern interactionist theory will not coincide at every point with every information theorist, but it is representative. What is generally shared by information theorists, especially those of the symbolic interactionist stripe and others who particularly focus on communication, and perhaps even a majority of sociologists, is a view of society which emphasizes both the integrating, equilibrating and/or consensual aspects and conflict.

The viability of information- and communication-theory for the development of integration in its various forms has been the central research focus of many social scientists. Karl W. Deutsch[26] maintains that the formation of a 'community' by the people of a nation or other unit depends on the degree to which they have a common language and culture for fidelity in communication and are mobilized as the sole input by communication. Most sociologists doubt the efficacy of communication in producing such "generalized others" and/or communities.[27] Neither do they believe as do some conflict theorists, that it is the chief engine agent of progress. As Cooley and Gouldner correctly observed, "The more one thinks of it the more he will see that conflict and cooperation are not separable things, but phases of one process which always involves something of both . . ."[28] "Awareness of self is sharpened by increasing social differentiation and by conflict with others; conversely, social differentiation and conflict are necessary conditions for a heightened sense of self."[29] This is especially true in differentiated and non-primitive societies where there is no single, all-powerful "generalized other," but rather competing others. Obviously both integration and conflict are most important for institution building and self-fulfillment.

Erving Goffman,[30] one of the most influential writers in the Meadian symbolic interactionism tradition, stresses the discrepancies between the self-image which the actor presents to others in the interactive process and his basic private attitudes and concerns. Although most symbolic interactionists do not pose as conflict theorists they usually place great importance upon conflict in the development and maintenance of the self. Also, despite arguments to the contrary, Talcott Parsons' use of the concept double contingency, to summarize the reciprocal nature of self-development, is very close to this school. His writings[31] on conflict seem not to be read by the conflict sociologists, who single him out as a non-conflict oriented sociologist, in part because of his emphasis on integration.

Polarization in Sociology

Polarization has arisen between a growing number of sociologists who identify themselves as conflict theorists, and those sociologists of whom the former claim to be opponents. Usually the conflict theorist identifies more with various sub-groups of a society or nation rather than with the whole. Integrationists stress society and sometimes humanity as a whole and such values as ends and norms while those who call themselves conflict theorists give primacy to such subgroups of the whole society as the "proletariat" or various ethnic and racial groups. Marxist conflict theorists, of course, envision a classless society in the future, emerging from the proletariat.

Among modern sociologists, perhaps Ralf Dahrendorf of Germany and Karl Marx may be chosen to represent the conflict theorists. Although Marx died too soon to name any present-day sociologists as opponents, his contempt for August Comte's thought in some respects is no different from the later reactions by Dahrendorf and other conflict theorists as they identify Talcott Parsons, Robert K. Merton, their students, and others like them as "integrationists." Most conflict sociologists name Emile Durkheim as one among the earlier sociologists whom they oppose because he, in their belief, over-emphasized integration or cohesion, calling them crucial phenomena in human life.

In over-simplified terms, we may state that the conflict theorist analyzes such processes as communication in terms of their relation to coercion, resulting exploitation, and possible liberation from these conditions. In a symbolically consistent manner words themselves become weapons to them, with biting sarcasm and wrathful scorn hurled at opponents. A much quoted passage from Marx states that when there is more than one possible outcome for a given action, or there "is an antimony . . . force decides," and "force is the midwife of every old society pregnant with a new one."[32] More recently Dahrendorf, reaching back to the thinking of earlier times, praised

Plato's *Thrasymachus* for claiming that "justice is nothing but the utility of the stronger . . . [that] every ruler gives the laws for his own uses . . ."[33] Writing in *The German Ideology*, Marx and Engels stressed the importance of communication and language as these relate to consciousness: "Language is as old as consciousness; language is practical consciousness, as it exists for other men, and for . . . me . . . Language like consciousness arises only from need, the necessity, of intercourse with other men . . ."[34] Prior to the emergence of their Utopian classless society, Marxists believed integration can only be attained when "false consciousness" is eliminated, and "true conscious" comes from "the practical activity of making revolution."[35] At the same time, "the existence of revolutionary ideas, in a particular age presupposes the existence of a revolutionary class."[36]

It is often the conflict theorist's self-imposed duty to make those who are coerced and exploited conscious of their condition so they will act to bring about change. Meaningful communication for them is thus related to the development of this sense of awareness, this impetus to action. Latter-day Marxists and their conceptions of class, determinism, the significance of the economic structure and the like, vary, of course, as much as the proponents of any current major school of thought. Their variations on the theme are more sophisticated, and it would be unfair to hoist them collectively on Marx's petard just as it would be unfair to attack today's positivists only on the basis of statements by Comte. Still, strong similarities among Marxists do exist and the heavy emphasis on flux, power and conflict remains.

As previously noted, Talcott Parsons has been heavily involved with information theory for some time. For him, communication between and among actors is the core of sociology. "When symbolic systems which can mediate communication have emerged we may speak of the beginnings of a 'culture' which becomes part of the action systems of the relevant actors."[37] A shared symbolic system which functions in interaction is a "cultural tradition." To have such a tradition requires integration because "even the most elementary communication [requires] some degree of conformity to the 'conventions' of the symbolic system."[38] Thus, the common understanding of the meaning of money and other forms of "language" in non-primitive societies is often used by Parsons to illustrate how agreement on 'conventions' is necessary. Durkheim maintained that "when society is strongly integrated, it holds individuals under its control,"[39] and that people who live in integrated societies are less subject to frustrations and manifestations of unhappiness such as high rates of egoistic and anomic suicide. Parsons goes to some length to explain how ritual reduces emotional tension by providing a situation in which wishes and strains can be "acted out" symbolically.[40] Labor unions are held to protect the worker by "symbolizing his anxieties and other sentiments . . . reinforcing his self-respect and confidence."[41] For him, as with Ferdinand Toennies, labor unions had a latent function for the worker of strengthening his identity and providing an interaction arena in which alienation was reduced. Emile Durkheim advocated the workers' syndicate for this purpose.

For Parsons, new symbols of sentiment communication are brought into being by the creative artist whom he views as being a "direct parallel to the . . . scientist and philosopher,"[42] who creates beliefs. Communication for integrative functions involves moral considerations. The moral-evaluative meaning of objects in a given society can skew effective communication. Thus, Parsons notes that the ideological differences between the Western and Communist powers as they are represented in the U.N., pose a communication impasse because of different beliefs concerning what the U.N., in fact, is.[43] He has noted that common commitment to an erroneous belief is more facilitative of communication and integration than the situation characterized by one party in interaction having corrected a false belief and a second party persisting in believing that the original is still true. Conflict sociologists maintain that those of a Parsonian bent lay inordinate stress on the importance of the rules of the game or the norms and value orientations of actors, and emphasize integration and cohesion as the cement which makes group life possible. Thus, according to conflict theorists, the concern with communication of non-conflict theorists focuses on its role in the muting of "dysfunctions," via pattern maintenance, and tension management. Conflict oriented critics contend that such a stance results in an uncritical posture which tends to be strongly supportive of the status quo.

Communication and Sociology of Knowledge and General Remarks

Students of the sociology of knowledge maintain that group affiliations and pertinent cultures of the groups involved affect the communication of the subject (the initiator of the message) and also the object (the recipient), and that conscious or unconscious assumptions about the nature of man and his relation to society also affect communication.[44] We would suggest that concern for such considerations has at least a three-fold significance.

First, it enhances the ability to make a more objective, realistic evaluation of existing work. The conflict-consensus schism is only one of a multitude of examples that might have been selected. Though we feel it to be a particularly critical issue, the differential effects of other theoretical orientations could as readily have been observed. Second, researchers in the future can accept an obligation to provide along with their work a specification of the assumptions, as best they can determine them, under which they operate. Not only will this enhance the reader's ability to put the material into perspective, but the required self-examination might increase the objectivity of the researcher.

Finally, the meaning of the communications which become the object of study may be better revealed through this examination of the sociocultural pressures and antecedents which impinge upon the communicator. Our concern with the intentions and purposes of the subject is at variance with those symbolic interactionists who seek meaning only in the response of the object of communication. We contest such an orientation only to the extent that it excludes other methods of analysis.

Communication as related to the sociology of knowledge is given emphasis by Robert Bellah who joins Kenneth Burke [45] in stating that "language does not merely reflect or communicate social and psychological realities. Rather, language contains within itself a 'principle of perfection' which operates relatively independently of other factors . . . Once the terms *king, society,* and *god* come into existence . . . [there is available] the logical possibility that someone will ask what a perfect king, society or god is . . ."[46] Such a contention means that anyone using language is not value-free, but it does not mean objectivity in social or any other science is any more a myth than perfection is a myth. For the scientist following his norms for achieving truth, the ideal of perfection contrary to some Marxists, need not be mere epiphenomena. "Perfection" as an ideal may influence the quest for truth and justice as well as power. In any case we hope to have made the point that communication and the sociology of knowledge are mutually relevant.

Communication as a Systems Problem

The study of communication may be approached in many ways. We may consider the isolated actor such as Kasper Hauser, Helen Keller or others; the development of personality and "human nature" in terms of symbolic interaction and role playing; the importance and also the limitation of behavioristic approaches to the study of communication; modern information theory with attention on the actor inherently encoded with a strain and need for order; the importance of conflict versus integration theory in communication; or the importance of position for the subject and/or object in communication as related to what one knows or how cognitive mapping takes place in the sociology of knowledge. At the same time, system theory can provide a means for noting common elements and processes and making comparisons. A systems approach is presented in Table 1 which gives the essence of what the senior author has called the Processually Articulated Systems Model (PASM).[47] Wilbert E. Moore metaphorized about the PAS model: It "made a notable advance by inviting in . . . the strangers [process and change] to put the house on rollers and permit it to move, while furnishing the interior with flexible and movable partitions and occasionally discordant inhabitants."[48] The processes which "permit . . . [the system to move] include the master processes; "namely, communication, (with which we have been and shall continue to be concerned), boundary maintenance, system linkage, institutionalization, socialization, and social control. Also each element on the right of Figure 1 is articulated by an elementary process found on the left. Thus (1) belief (knowledge) is articulated by cognitive mapping and validation; (2) sentiment by a) tension management and b) communication of sentiment; (3) end or goal by a) goal attaining activity and b) comcomitant "latent" activity as process; (4) norm by evaluation; (5) rank by a) evaluation of actors

Table 1

Elements, Processes and Conditions of Action of Social Systems
The Processually Articulated Structural (PAS) Model*

Processes (Elemental)	Social Action Categories	Elements
1) Cognitive mapping and validation	Knowing	Belief (Knowledge)
2) Tension management and	Feeling	Sentiment
(a) Communication of sentiment		
(b)		
3) Goal attaining activity and	Achieving	End, goal, or objective
(a)		
(b) Concomitant "latent" activity process		
4) Evaluation	Norming, Standardizing, Patterning	Norm
5) Status-role performance †	Dividing the functions	Status-role (position)
6) (a) Evaluation of actors and	Ranking	Rank
(b) Allocation of status-role		
7) (a) Decision making and	Controlling	Power
(b) Initiation of action		
8) Application of sanctions	Sanctioning	Sanction
9) Utilization of facilities	Facilitating	Facility
Comprehensive or Master Processes		
(1) Communication	(3) Systemic linkage	(5) Socialization
(2) Boundary maintenance	(4) Institutionalization	(6) Social control

Cont'd

Cont'd

Table 1

Elements, Processes and Conditions of Action of Social Systems
The Processually Articulated Structural (PAS) Model*

Conditions of Social action
(1) Territoriality   (2) Size   (3) Time

*For a more detailed version of this figure see Figure 1 in Charles P. Loomis, *Social Systems*, *op. cit.*, p. 8. For the relation of the above concepts to the Gemeinschaft-Gesellschaft continuum see *Ibid.*, pp. 61ff.

†Status-role, alone of the concepts, includes both element and process.

and b) allocation of status roles; (6) status-role as a position by status-role as performance; (7) power by a) decision-making and b) its initiation into action; (8) sanction by application of sanctions; and (9) facilities by application of facilities.

In system analysis it is important to note that as actors communicate or articulate a system through these and other processes, there are *conditions* or factors which by definition are not under the control of the actors. Two conditions which are universally present are *time* and *space*.

Communication Restraints Illustrated in System Analysis

The Old Order Amish community in Lancaster County, Pennsylvania, an interaction and communication arena familiar to the senior author, may provide a means of illustrating the application of system analysis to communication. No other group known to the authors has retained social and cultural traits originating and/or existant in the late Middle Ages so successfully in the heart of an industrial civilization. It affords a prime example of the resistance to change through control of communication. A system analysis has been presented elsewhere in considerable detail.[49] Here our purpose is merely to illustrate the nature of communication through an example, so the treatment will be relatively brief. We shall first consider conditions of space or territoriality and time.

Territoriality —— The 33 church districts, including around 7,000 people whose interactions constitute the social system to be described, is located in an area or space of approximately 150 square miles. Since the use of all forms of travel, other than foot or horse-drawn buggy, is for most purposes taboo, geography has a special meaning for the Amish. Similar sects in other counties which have adopted the automobile have almost overnight "moved out of the neighborhood." So great is the desire to maintain boundaries that land in the center of the settlement has a higher value, other things equal, than land on the periphery with exposure to the "gay" world. The settlement is small and dense, and many "swarmings" to other parts of the country have resulted in new settlements.

Time –– For the Amish, time as a condition uncontrollable by man, is reflected in their conceptions of eternity and concern that each should accomplish as much good as possible before he dies. Frequent prayers and weekly sermons continually remind each person that earthly existence is brief and not important at all, except for attaining salvation in eternity.

Elements and Elementary Processes

Knowing

Belief (Knowledge as an element) –– A belief is any proposition about the universe which is thought to be true. The Amish believe that each individual is responsible for his own salvation in after life and that the Amish are a chosen people. Like other Protestant groups, the Old Order Amish believe in the supremacy of the Bible and the necessity of living and worshipping as prescribed by the Bible, as they themselves interpret it. Likewise the Amish believe no salvation can be communicated through sacraments mediated by formally trained or ordained priests.

Cognitive mapping and validation as process. What is true and what false is to be determined by the Bible. Whether an agricultural or living practice will make more money or reduce effort is of less importance than what is communicated by the Scriptures from reading and listening to sermons. Many Amish farmers claim, and some believe, that the use of tractors which are forbidden by the norms, would decrease profit. These beliefs are rather surprising and contrary to fact, a state of affairs which indicates that the process of cognitive mapping is capable of neglecting some pieces of evidence and overemphasizing others in validating, and thus making usable the fund of available knowledge. These are, of course, important considerations for both the sociology of knowledge and communi - cation.

Feeling

Sentiment as an element. Whereas beliefs embody thoughts, sentiments embody feelings about the world. An Amishman feels reverence, awe, and holiness in the conduct of religious services, but he also feels piety as he works the fields, tends the livestock and the crops, sells his wares, and converts his savings into capital gains.

Tension management as process. Among the Amish various rites of passage are operative at potentially tension-laden points of the family cycle. The baptismal ceremony, for example, inducts young people into the fellowship of the church from ages 16 to 18 up to 20, for those who give evidence of "true conversion." Rites of intensification, such as family and community prayer, are examples of communication which regularly accompany crises such as impending legislation threatening their way of life. Institutionalized methods of dealing with the deviant reduce the tensions of "not knowing what to do" when someone has driven a forbidden automobile, or has indulged in a too short haircut.

Communication of sentiment as process. Tabooing of paintings, family pictures, radio, and other means of mass communication and of self expression, leaves the process of communication of sentiment almost entirely to personal precept and example. The cultivation of sentiment, of feeling "different," is probably assisted by the true horror tales in the widely owned *Martyr's Mirror*, a book, which communicates the in-group feelings of a persecuted people. In times of crisis, cliques and family groups in dozens of kitchens, discussing, praying, and lending support to one another, are commonplace.

Achieving

End, goal, or objective as an element. Eternal life is the highest goal of the Amishman. The families strive to increase yields, incomes, and success in farming, although these are secondary goals.

Goal attaining, and concomitant "latent" activity as process. Whether the Amishman, or the member of any other religious system, attains the goal of salvation can, of course, never be proven or disproven. However, when all Amishmen are motivated toward this goal by becoming active in particular ways, their unified activity is palpable in the greater society. The processes comprised of all this unified activity are called "latent" because their consequences are unintended and unrecognized. Thus, as thrift, industry, and careful stewardship became activities which give proof of goodness, the average income and property values of these farmers became for a period the highest in the nation.

Norming —— Standardizing ——– Patterning

Norm as an element. The rules which prescribe what is socially acceptable or unacceptable are the norms of the social system. The most highly visible norms among the Amish are those of grooming and dress which hark back to bygone periods: beards, long hair, and many other features differentiating them from others. The taboo on use of electricity from generators for lights, telephones, and anything else places great restrictions on modern communication. Only farming or farm-related occupations are permissible, and most of the norms support the injunction from the Bible for separation from the world and non-conformity to it.

Evaluation as a process. Evaluation is the process through which varying positive and negative priorities or values are assigned to concepts, objects, actors, or collectivities, or to events and activities, past, present, or future. A most crucial evaluation is made by the congregation as a whole each time that it must deliberate on reported moral shortcomings of members. Whether a practice such as an electric fence or a telephone in an outhouse is moral or not, or whether the group must consider leaving the country, as other similar groups have done to seek freedom, requires evaluation.

Dividing the Functions

Status-role as a unit incorporating both element and process. The two-term unity, status-role, contains the concepts status, a structural element implying position and the term, role, a functional process. Both determine what is to be expected from an incumbent. Among the most important differentiated status-roles in Amish society are those related to sex and age with sharp differentiation in grooming, clothing and actual behavior. For example, at marriage the smooth-shaved face of the youth becomes the bearded face of the man who assumes the new status-role of head of a household. His open buggy used during courting days is replaced by the closed family-style buggy. As noted below under socialization, role playing and consequently personality development is limited to the repertoire of positions among Amishmen. A "generalized other" will therefore not be the equivalent of a "gay" community for any but those exposed to "gay" society.

Ranking

Rank as an element. Rank or standing includes the value an actor has for the system in which the rank is accorded. Few groups are more equalitarian in ideology but success in farming, church duties, leadership, and age are important rank-giving qualities among the Amish. Young people often line up by age to march into church service and in Lancaster County, of the 16 bishops the five oldest are the most important. These characteristics will serve to illustrate the characteristics of rank among the Amish.

Evaluation of actors and allocation of status-roles as process. The community gives high evaluation to the successful Amish farmer who demonstrates qualities of church leadership. Honor and high standing are accorded to those whose lives exemplify godliness, humility, and "full fellowship." This is exemplified by the rank accorded to those whose farming enterprises have been so successful that their houses are large enough to hold 200 or more persons in church meetings.

The achievement-ascription process by which the status-role of minister is allocated must serve as a single example of that process. All baptized members of the congregation participate and any man who receives as many as three votes is entered as candidate for the selection ceremony. Bibles of similar outward appearance are placed on a table, one for each candidate, by the bishops. A slip of paper hidden from view in one Bible designates that the chooser must give his life to this new post or status-role. Candidates file past the table and each picks a Bible. Through this ceremony God chooses the one who must take this great responsibility and honor. Among the Amish no status-roles are more important in communication than those of ministers, deacons, and bishops.

Controlling

Power as an element. Power is the capacity to control others. There are two major forms of control, authority and influence. Authority is the right, as determined by the social system (and built into the status-role), to control others, whereas influence is non-authoritative. Influence may rest on personal characteristics, social capital, and many other bases. In the Amish family the husband and father is the chief authority figure. The ministers, deacons, and bishops exert more control over community affairs related to the church than do ordinary members. In the family and in the community the element, power, is plainly evident as the family makes its living and the community maintains its boundaries. The father in the family controls agricultural operations and marketing. He is a patriarch, but a Gemeinschaft-like authority figure. His directives, although not as affective as the mother's solice in times of sorrow, are nonetheless affective.

Decision-making and its initiation into action as process. Decision-making is the process by which the alternatives available are reduced. Illustrating this process is the after-church session held to decide what is to be done in the case of outside threat, or to ascertain the guilt or innocence and sanctions for alleged breach of rules. The deacon repeats the charge after all unbaptized persons leave. Unanimity of decision concerning the offender is the ideal, and with few exceptions is attained. Majority vote means that the members are acting upon the recommendation of the ministers and deacons who are, it is believed, chosen by divine influence. Often the bishop is slow to arrive at a decision concerning what point of view he will espouse. Once he nods his head in approval, the opinions of the congregation are likely to coalesce in agreement. Thus, in terms of communication, "the bishop's nod" has come to be practically synonymous with ultimate decision and the execution or initiation into action follows. It goes without saying that the "bishop's nod" and the army officer's or bureau chief's order are very different.

Sanctioning

Sanction as an element. Sanctions may be defined as the rewards and penalties which through their application motivate conformity to the ends and norms. The most interesting and powerful sanction among the Amish is negative: the *Meidung*, or the practice of shunning. The *Meidung* shuts off the violator from *communication* with anyone of the congregation, his family, his friends, his neighbors. Persons subjected to it have been known to lose their memories and even to commit suicide. It is an example of communication control par excellence.

Application of sanctions as process. After evaluation and decision-making has assigned the sanction, usually amends are required in order that the sanction be lifted. The Lord's Supper and full fellowship may be refused the deviant until public repentance is made and the deviancy discontinued. Usually the family member who is being shunned must eat alone and remain apart from the rest of the family, but a certain amount of affection, especially from the mother, during the period is inevitable, although forbidden. Failure to recant may result in permanent *Meidung* and rejection from the group, and does occur.

Facilitating

Facility as an element. A facility is a means used within the system to attain the system's ends. One of the characteristics of the Amish as non-conformists is that facilities of worship and facilities of everyday life are limited. No churches or other intermediary facilities between man and God are permitted and many "wordly" things for the home and farm, used by "gay people" or non-Amish, are forbidden.

Utilization of facilities as process. Consistent with the relative unimportance of facilities as articles of worship, is the highly institionalized use of the straight backless long wooden benches which serve as congregational seats and which are moved from home to home as the place of service shifts every fortnight. Likewise there is no improvisation of use of the Bible or the *Ausbund*, the hymn book used by the Amish which is claimed to be the oldest unchanged hymnal in use. On the agricultural front the very avoidance of most normal agricultural facilities (the tractor, various forms of power-driven machinery, and others) has led to the most ingenious improvisation in the utilization of the permitted facilities.

Comprehensive or Master Processes

Communication. The radio, television, many of the other mass media, and the telephone are tabooed by the Amish. Only farm magazines, religious literature, and newspapers are generally permitted. Amishmen are trilingual, speaking a High German dialect known as Pennsylvania Dutch, Biblical High German, and English.

The High German which is used for religious purposes in sermons, singing, and reading of religious literature may have a special place in interaction, particularly with God, but intimate interaction among kin, friends, and neighbors is carried on in Pennsylvania Dutch. The communication of sentiment has been mentioned above.

Boundary maintenance. Through boundary maintenance, as members control communication, the social system retains its solidarity, identity, and interaction pattern. So much of the energy of the Amish goes into this process that it is difficult to single out illustrative items. The hypothesis has been advanced that the norms concerning communication which are most unanimously observed and obeyed, and the violation of which results in the keenest felt indignation, are those which, if violated, would result in the absorption of the "gay" culture. Thus, introduction of electricity into the houses might bring the radio and television. The introduction of the automobile would expose the traveler to the temptations of the outside world; and the discontinuance of distinctive dress and grooming would reduce the visibility of the Amishman who was attempting to dally with worldly ways.

Systemic linkage. This is the process whereby the elements of at least two social systems come to be articulated, so that in some ways they function as a single system. Whereas the processes previously discussed give primary reference to the intra-system interaction, systemic linkage involves inter-system interaction. The actors of the Old Order Amish social system attempt to minimize systemic linkages with systems other than their own, but are unable to maintain complete isolation. Compulsory school attendance laws, draft laws in time of war, various governmental agricultural programs, marketing transactions, contacts designed to improve and enlarge the knowledge of agricultural advances, and medical and legal services, are examples of almost inevitable interaction with other social systems and resultant systemic linkages. It is through this process that most of the many changes adopted by the Amish have come.

A Communication Dialectic of Change vs. Non-Change

As the Amish attempt to remain God's chosen people "not conformed to the world" and "not unequally yoked together with unbelievers" a dialectic involving the processes of boundary maintenance versus systemic linkage takes place. This is not the dialectic of some Marxists described by Sorokin as "fetishism of antinomy" or by Gurvitch as the "grave error . . . of polarization of contradictories."[50] It results from contradictions which arise when any individual or group attempts to retain identity, or in more modern terms to "do its thing," in an environment of others with different ends and norms. Amishmen own their farms in fee simple and enter the market as do other farmers. They must get health, educational, financial, governmental and other services in a highly differentiated society. Survival requires linkage despite the moral restrictions against communication with actors in the outside "gay" world.

Institutionalization. Institutionalization is the process through which human behavior is made predictable and patterned. Through this process social systems are given the elements of structure and the processes of function. As each invention or practice is either accepted or rejected as a part of the Amish life, institutionalization of relationships concerning it takes place. The comparatively static Old Order Amish social system is replete with institutionalized practices; compared with the rapidly changing world which surrounds it there are few areas of life which are not predictable and patterned. One such contingency arose over the threat of school consolidation. The Amish, who were earlier prohibited by their own norms from voting, began to vote in defense of a self-contained school system, an institution evidently evaluated more highly than that of political non-participation. Voting on this one issue is becoming institutionalized. In recent U.S. Supreme Court decisions, Amishmen have been freed from some compulsory school laws. Evidence presented in the hearings stressed the right of Amishmen to their way of life free from the threat of "gay" or non-Amish schools.

Socialization. Socialization is the process whereby the social and cultural heritage is transmitted. Amish children play mother, father, farmer, and farmer's wife. The only approved role-model for the boy is that of the farmer and for the girl, that of the farmer's wife.

Social Control. Social control is the process by which deviancy is counteracted. Most pressure among the Amish toward deviancy is toward the norms of the larger society. For this reason the processes of social control and boundary maintenance tend to merge. There are no police arrests of Amishmen by Amish officers. Controls are built into the system so that the deviant is deprived of "full fellowship" by informal procedure, if not through formal *Meidung* or other procedures.

Retrospect and Prospect

By its very nature sociology seeks to discover principles of communication which transcend cultural and social boundaries. Yet to discern these underlying uniformities, and to test the validity of such hypotheses, the meaning of communications must be sought within their sociocultural context. Attempts to bridge the chasm of cultural differentiation are confounded by the inability to study communication in anything approximating laboratory conditions. Only on rare occasions may the effects of virtually no communication be observed, as in the previously noted descriptions of extreme isolation and in the systems analysis of the Amish. In complex societies we are confronted by a seemingly endless host of variables, difficult not only to control but even to detect. Because of these and many other difficulties data are often carelessly stuffed into ill-defined categories.

The rapid growth of technology has meant increasing contact between cultures and nations which historically have lived in relative cultural and social isolation. Two people may still readily comprise a small social system but it is not unrealistic today to view all men as members of one large social system. Groups now find themselves meaningfully related to other groups with whom their only previous bond was mere spatial adjacency as inhabitants of the same planet. Each communication is not only an expression of both past and present, but a shaper of the future and as society undergoes kaleidoscopic changes and the sheer number of transmissions multiply the task of analysis becomes more difficult.

The information explosion brings not only problems but the potential for deeper understanding and a positive exchange of ideas. How to capitalize on the potential without being deluged by the misunderstandings and stoppages haunts every serious student of communication. To cope with the massive amounts of data there will be a continual increase in the use of computers. Massive data banks will continue to develop under the auspices of UNESCO and major research centers. Methodological tools like content analyses will be sharpened and a myriad of new statistical techniques brought to bear.

While we applaud the development of new methodological approaches we would remind that the results will be sterile if similar advances do not take place on a broad theoretical plane. Sterile, too, will be the output if it has not been first categorized and later analyzed with an empathetic spirit akin to Max Weber's *verstehen* (interpretive understanding) and Mead's taking the role of the other.

Further development of a trend toward interdisciplinary and international exchange and cooperation is to be encouraged particularly at a time when a variety of significant work remains untranslated, and some of that which is available remains ignored.

With the plethora of avenues available to be travelled, we think it pertinent to present the following comment by Hugh Duncan:

> "In moments of candor, scholars admit that when method a n d technique, a n d not *the problems important to an age*, are held to be the proper end of study, there is great danger of irrelevancy, or what Burke calls 'inaccuracy.' Thus, when we should by studying the rise and fall of dictators, how they stage their drama of power, what means of communication they use, where, when, and for what purpose, we select instead problems that are amenable to techniques considered 'proper' to the subject by those in power over the subject . . ."[51]

In our attempt to cover the study of communication in the sociological framework in this short space we have inevitably skimmed some exceedingly significant approaches and frames of reference and failed even to mention a multitude of others. Hopefully we have conveyed some feeling for the diverse amounts of attention and points of focus accorded the study of this ubiquitous phenomenon, the profound differential effects of various points of view and the fact that such effects are but a microcosmic expression of the complex variations encountered by the sociologist in his examination of society as a whole.

The brief synopses of the role of communication as seen from several theoretical perspectives were largely uncritical perhaps due partly to space limitations or some differences between our own orientations, but primarily because we believe that all had something significant to offer. Consistent with a conflict orientation, there is ample evidence of man's exploitation of man in today's world, and it is equally evident that a failure to mediate consensually some of the differences that exist could result in the ultimate conflict from which there is no recovery. However Utopian the goal, we are hopeful that further study will provide additional clues as to how communication can most effectively be used to combat the former and avoid the latter.

FOOTNOTES

[1] Comte stressed the importance of language, religion and division of labor as crucial components of society. See August Comte, *The Positive Philosophy*, translated and condensed by Harriet Martineau (London: Bell, 1896) vol. II, p. 292.

[2] Robert E. Park and Ernest W. Burgess, *Introduction to the Science of Sociology* (Chicago: The University of Chicago Press, 1921) pp. 763-764.

[3] For references to these studies and others like them by Zona K. Loomis, Jeanne Gullahorn and the senior author see Charles P. Loomis, "In Praise of Conflict and Its Resolution," *American Sociological Review*, 32, 6 (December, 1967) and Charles P. Loomis et al., *Linkages of Mexico and the United States* (East Lansing, Michigan: Michigan Agricultural Experiment State Research Bulletin 14, 1966.) See also John Madge, *The Origins of Scientific Sociology* (Glencoe, Ill., 1962), p. 521.

[4] Park and Burgess, *op. cit.*, p. 239. See a recent treatment of this subject and a discussion of the blighting effects of isolation on children in a nursing home, as described by Rene Spitz in Melvin L. De Fleur, William V. D'Antonio and Lois B. De Fleur, *Sociology: Man in Society* (Glenview, Ill.: Scott, Foresman & Co., 1971) pp. 143ff.

[5] Robert E. Park, "The Concept of Social Distance," *Journal of Sociology*, 8 (July-August, 1924) pp. 339-344.

[6] Emory S. Bogardus, "A Social Distance Scale," *Sociology and Social Research* 17, 1933, pp. 265-271.

[7] George C. Homans, *Social Behavior: Its Elementary Forms* (New York: Harcourt Brace and World, 1961) p. 298.

[8] Charles P. Loomis, *Social Systems — Essays on Their Persistence and Change* (Princeton, N.J.: D. Van Nostrand, 1965) p. 3.

[9] *Ibid.* p. 3. This is the well-known definition by Pitirim A. Sorokin, *Society, Culture and Personality: Their Structure and Dynamics* (New York: Harpers, 1947) p. 40.

[10] Talcott Parsons, "The Social System: A General Theory of Action," in *Toward a Unified Theory of Human Behavior*, Roy R. Grinker, ed. (New York: Basic Books, 1956) pp. 55-56. Here Parsons gives Robert R. Sears credit for the term, "double contingency" used frequently by Parsons especially in relation to symbolic interaction.

[11] Talcott Parsons, "Social Interaction," *International Encyclopedia of Social Sciences* (New York: Macmillan Co. and the Free Press, 1968) vol. 7, pp. 429ff.

[12] Talcott Parsons and Edward A. Shils, eds., *Toward a General Theory of Social Action* (Cambridge, Mass.: Harvard University Press, 1951).

[13] Talcott Parsons, *The Social System* (Glencoe, Ill.: The Free Press, 1951) pp. 33-34.

[14] Talcott Parsons, "Social Interaction," *op. cit.* p. 440.

[15] Charles P. Loomis and Zona K. Loomis, *Modern Social Theories* (Huntington, N.Y.: Kreige, 1975). Most of the references for the next paragraphs may be found by consulting the index of this volume under the name of the author involved and/or "communication."

[16] *Ibid.*, p. 639.

[17] Pitirim A. Sorokin, *op. cit.*, p. 3.

[18] George C. Homans, *The Human Group* (New York: Harcourt Brace, 1950) p. 37.

[19] After Guy E. Swanson in "Symbolic Interaction," *International Encyclopedia of Social Science, op. cit.*, vol. 7, p. 441. Also see Herbert Blumer, "Social Psychology," in E.P. Schmidt, ed. *Man and Society* (New York: Prentice Hall, 1937) pp. 144ff.

[20] George Herbert Mead, *Mind, Self and Society* (Chicago: The University of Chicago Press, 1934) p. 150.

[21] In our treatment of "Symbolic Interactionism" we have relied heavily on *Ibid*. For a different presentation by a social scientist on the way man relies on his Gemeinschaft-like or intimate groupings to prevent disorder see Paul Bohannan, "Our Two-Story Culture," *Saturday Review*, September 2, 1972.

[22] G.H. Mead, *op. cit.* p. 154.

[23] Leonard Broom and Philip Selznick, *Sociology* (Evanston, Ill.: Row Peterson and Co., 1958) p. 95.

[24] A.R. Lindesmith and A.L. Strauss, *Social Psychology* (New York: Dryden Press, 1949) p. 14.

[25] Orrin Klapp, *Models of Social Order—An Introduction to Sociological Theory* (Palo Alto, Ca.: National Press Books, 1973)

[26] Karl W. Deutsch, *Nationalism and Social Communication* (Cambridge, Mass.: M.I.T. Press, 1953). See also Paul Bohannan, *Saturday Review* September 2, 1972.

[27] Robert Cooley Angel, "Social Integration," *International Encyclopedia of Social Science, op. cit.*, vol. 7, pp. 389ff.

[28] Charles Horton Cooley, *Social Process* (Carbondale, Ill.: Southern Illinois University Press, 1966) p. 39.

[29] Alvin W. Gouldner and Helen P. Gouldner, *Modern Sociology* (New York: Harcourt Brace and World, 1962) pp. 57-60.

[30] Erving Goffman, *The Presentation of Self in Everyday Life* (Garden City, N.Y.: Doubleday, 1959).

[31] Talcott Parsons, *Essays in Sociological Theory* (Glencoe, Ill.: The Free Press, 1940) pp. 323ff.

[32] Karl Marx, *Capital —— A Critique of Political Economy*, Trans. S. Moore and E. Aveling (New York: The Modern Library, 1906) pp. 259, 824.

[33] Ralf Dahrendorf, *Pfade aus Utopie* (Muenchen: 1967) ch. 13.

[34] Karl Marx and Frederick Engels, *The German Ideology* (Moscow: Progress Publishers, 1964) pp. 41-42.

[35] *Ibid.*, p. 86, 230.

[36] *Ibid.*, p. 79.

[37] Charles P. Loomis and Zona K. Loomis, *op. cit.*, p. 413. The original appears in the *Social System, op. cit.*, p. 5.

[38] *Ibid.*, p. 413.

[39] Lewis A. Coser, *Masters of Sociological Thought* (New York: Harcourt Brace Jovanovich, Inc., 1971) p. 131, and Emile Durkheim, *Suicide* (Glencoe, Ill.: 1951) p. 209.

[40] Talcott Parsons and Neil J. Smelser, *Economy and Society* (Glencoe, Ill.: The Free Press, 1956), p. 408. See Talcott Parsons, *The Social System, op. cit.*, p. 304.

[41] See Parsons and Smelser, *op. cit.*, p. 149.

[42] Talcott Parsons, *The Social System, op. cit.*, p. 408.

[43] *Ibid.*, p. 276. Loomis and Loomis, *op. cit.*, p. 414.

[44] Karl Mannheim, *Ideology and Utopia* (New York: Harcourt Brace Jovanovich, Inc., 1936).

[45] Kenneth Burke, *The Rhetoric of Religion: Studies on Logology* (Boston: Beacon, 1961).

[46] Robert N. Bellah, "The Sociology of Religion," *International Encyclopedia of Social Sciences, op. cit.*, vol. 13, p. 412.

[47] J. Paul Leagans and Charles P. Loomis, *Behavioral Change in Agriculture — Concepts and Strategies* (Ithaca: Cornell University Press, 1971).

[48] Charles P. Loomis and Zona K. Loomis, *op. cit.*, p. xxiii.

[49] Charles P. Loomis, *Social Systems, op. cit.*, Essay 5.

[50] Charles P. Loomis, "In Praise of Conflict and Its Resolution," *op. cit.*, p. 875. See also Pitirim A. Sorokin, *Sociological Theories of Today* (New York, Harper & Row, 1966), pp. 463-469.

[51] Hugh D. Duncan, *Communication and Social Order* (New York: The Bedminster Press, 1962) p. 139.

BIBLIOGRAPHY

Berelson, Bernard, *Content Analysis in Communication Research* (Glencoe: Free Press, 1952).

Berlo, David K., *The Process of Communication* (New York: Rinehart and Winston, 1960).

Blumer, Herbert, *Symbolic Interactionism* (Englewood Cliffs: Prentice-Hall, 1969).

Borden, George A., Richard B. Gregg and Theodore C. Grove, *Speech*

Behavior and Human Interaction (Englewood Cliffs: Prentice-Hall, 1969).

Broom, Leonard and Philip Selznick, *Sociology* (Evanston, Ill.: Row Peterson and Co., 1958).

Brownfield, C.A., *Isolation: Clinical and Experimental Approaches* (New York: Random House, 1966).

Burke, Kenneth, *Language as Symbolic Action* (Berkeley: University of California Press, 1966).

Burke, Kenneth, *The Rhetoric of Religion: Studies of Logology* (Boston: Beacon, 1961).

Cassirer, Ernest, *An Essay on Man* (New Haven: Yale University Press, 1944).

Chase, Stuart with Marian Tyler Chase, *Power of Words* (New York: Harcourt Brace, 1954).

Cherry, Colin, *On Human Communication* (Cambridge, M.I.T. Press, 1966).

Cooley, Charles Horton, *Human Nature and the Social Order* (New York: Charles Scribner & Sons, 1922).

Cooley, Charles Horton, *Social Process* (New York: Charles Scribner's & Sons, 1918).

Cooley, Charles Horton, *Social Organization* (New York: Charles Scribner's & Sons, 1909).

Coser, Lewis A., *Masters of Sociological Thought* (New York: Harcourt Brace Jovanovich, Inc., 1971) and Emile Durkheim, *Suicide* (Glencoe, Ill.: 1951).

Dahrendorf, Ralf, *Pfade aus Utopie* (Muenchen: 1967).

Dance, Frank E.X., ed., *Human Communication Theory* (New York: Holt, Rinehart and Winston, 1967).

De Fleur, Melvin L. and Otto N. Larsen, *The Flow of Information* (New York: Harper, 1958).

De Fleur, Melvin L., William V. D'Antonio and Lois B. De Fleur, *Sociology: Man in Society* (Gleview, Ill.: Scott, Foresman & Co., 1971).

Deutsch, Karl W., *Nationalism and Social Communication* (Cambridge, Mass.: M.I.T. Press, 1953).

Duncan, Hugh D., *Communication and Social Order* (New York: The Bedminster Press, 1962).

Faris, Robert E.L., *Handbook of Modern Sociology* (Chicago: Rand McNally, 1964).

Flavell, John H., *The Developmental Psychology of Jean Piaget* (Princeton: D. Van Nostrand, 1963).

Fredericks, Robert, *A Sociology of Sociology* (Glencoe: Free Press, 1970).

Fromm, Erich, *The Forgotten Language* (New York: Rinehart, 1951).

Fromm, Erich, *Escape From Freedom* (New York: Farrar and Rinehart, 1941).

Fromm, Erich and Michael MacCoby, *Social Character in a Mexican Village* (Englewood Cliffs: Prentice-Hall, 1970).

Garfinkel, Harold, *Studies in Ethnomethodology* (Englewood Cliffs: Prentice-Hall, 1967).

Goffman, Erving, *Encounters* (Indianapolis: Bobbs – Merrill, 1961); *Interaction Ritual* (Garden City: Anchor Books, 1967). *The Presentation of Self in Everyday Life* (Garden City: Doubleday, 1959). *Strategic Interaction* (Philadelphia: University of Pennsylvania Press, 1969).

Hawkins, David, *The Language of Nature* (San Francisco: W.H. Freeman, 1964).

Henle, Paul, ed., *Language, Thought and Culture* (Ann Arbor: University of Michigan Press, 1958).

Hideya, Kumata, *An Inventory of Instructional Television Research* (Ann Arbor: Educational Television and Radio Center, 1956).

Hickman, C. Addison and Manford H. Kuhn, *Individuals, Groups and Economic Behavior* (New York: Dryden Press, 1956).

Homans, George C., *Social Behavior: Its Elementary Forms* (New York: Harcourt, Brace and World, 1961).

Homans, George C., *The Human Group* (New York: Harcourt Brace, 1950).

Innis, Harold A., *The Bias of Communication* (Toronto: University of Toronto Press, 1951).

Klapp, Orrin E., *Symbolic Leaders* (Chicago: Aldine, 1964).

Koshtoyants, K.S., ed., *I.P. Pavlov: Selected Works* (Moscow: Foreign Language Publications, 1955).

Lerner, Daniel and Wilbur Schramm, eds., *Communication and Change in the Developing Countries* (Honolulu: East-West Center Press, 1967).

Lindesmith, A.R. and A.L. Strauss, *Social Psychology* (New York: Dryden Press, 1949).

Loomis, Charles P., *Social Systems — Essays on Their Persistence and change* (Princeton, N.J.: D. Van Nostrand, 1965).

Loomis, Charles P. and Zona K. Loomis, *Modern Social Theories* (Huntington, N.Y.: Krieger, 1975).

MacKay, Donald M., *Information Mechanism and Meaning* (Cambridge: M.I.T., 1959).

McCall, George J. and J.L. Simmons, *Identities and Interactions* (New York: The Free Press, 1962).

Manis, Jerome G. and Bernard N. Meltzer, eds., *Symbolic Interactionism* (Boston: Allyn and Bacon, 1968).

Mannheim, Karl, *Ideology and Utopia* (New York: Harcourt Brace and Jovanovich, 1936).

Marx, Karl, *Capital — A Critique of Political Economy* trans. S. Moore and E. Aveling (New York: The Modern Library, 1906).

Marx, Karl and Frederick Engels, *The German Ideology* (Moscow: Progress Publishers, 1964).

Mead, George, *Mind, Self and Society* (Chicago: The University of Chicago Press, 1934).

Merritt, Richard and Stein Rokkan, *Comparing Nations* (New Haven: Yale University Press, 1966).

Merton, Robert K., *Social Theory and Social Structure* (Glencoe, Ill.: Free Press, 1957).

Parsons, Talcott, *Essays in Sociological Theory* (Glencoe, Ill.: The Free Press, 1940).

Parsons, Talcott, *The Social System* (New York, N.Y.: The Free Press, 1951).

Parsons, Talcott and Edward A. Shils, eds., *Toward a General Theory of Social Action* (Cambridge, Mass.: Harvard University Press, 1951).

Park, Robert E. and Ernest W. Burgess, *Introduction to the Science of Sociology* (Chicago, Ill.: The University of Chicago Press, 1921).

Rose, Arnold, ed., *Human Behavior and Social Processes* (Boston, Mass.: Houghton-Mifflin, 1962).

Roy, Predipto and Frederick B. Waisanen, *The Impact of Communication on Rural Development* (National Institute of Community Institute of Community Development, 1969).

Schelling, Thomas C., *The Strategy of Conflict* (Cambridge: Harvard University Press, 1960).

Schutz, Alfred, *On Phenomenology of Social Relations* (Glencoe, Ill.: The Free Press, 1970).

Shibutani, Tarnotsu, *Society and Personality* (Englewood Cliffs: Prentice-Hall, 1961).

Siebert, Frederick S., Theodore P. Siebert and Wilbur Schramm, *Four Theories of the Press*, (Urbana: University of Illinois Press, 1956).

Schmidt, E.P., ed., *Man and Society* (New York, N.Y.: Prentice–Hall 1937).

Sorokin, Pitirim A., *Society, Culture and Personality: Their Structure and Dynamics* (New York: Harper and Brothers, 1947).

Sorokin, Pitirim A., *Social and Cultural Dynamics* (New York, N.Y.: American Book Co., 1937).

Stein, Maurice, A.J. Vidich and D.M. White, *Identity and Anxiety* (New York, N.Y.: The Free Press, 1960).

Strauss, Anselm L., *Mirrors and Masks* (New York, N.Y.: The Free Press, 1958).

John C. Condon, Jr.:

Intercultural Communication from a
Speech Communication Perspective

IN SO—CALLED "developing nations," citizens eager for change often seek to imitate the ways of societies they consider more highly developed. In rejecting what they consider old-fashioned and provincial in their own culture, they also tend to lose much that is rich and unique. The speech-communication discipline may face an analogous problem. There is a real danger that those of us who have been especially interested in interpersonal communication across cultures may ignore much that is unique and of great potential value in the speech-communication field, by early imitating the purposes and methods of disciplines we consider less provincial and more developed. As a result, there is a risk that "a perspective from the speech-communication field" may not differ significantly from perspectives of several other disciplines. To show that this need not be the case, this writer seeks to present a point of view which reflects traditional and contemporary concerns of the speech-communication scholar in relation to communication across cultures. After briefly describing some of the characteristics of his discipline, the writer will propose a conceptual framework for a perspective consisting of four inter-related areas: language, nonverbal behavior, values, and rhetoric.

Some Characteristics of the Discipline

Speech, or speech-communication as some scholars now prefer to call their field, is among the oldest academic disciplines in the

Western World. Its focus on the speech act, be it a public speech, a discussion, or philosophical and theoretical questions pertaining to that act, is necessarily eclectic and interdisciplinary; consequently, it is one of the few fields that feels as congenial among the humanities as the social sciences. In spirit and in goals, however, the speech-communication field differs considerably from allied disciplines. Theory and research findings are important, but not more so than is sensitivity to communication, especially as it relates to a student's awareness of his own behavior and his responses to the communication of others. And, of course, skill in communication has been a central concern in this field for thousands of years. Thus, more than in subject matter, the defining characteristic of the speech-communication field has been in its attempt to maintain a balance among the three goals of information (including theory and research), self-awareness (sensitivity), and skill. In intercultural communication, the same three inseparable goals are essential. Skill in communicating across cultures, involving much more than knowledge of a second language, requires sensitivity to one's effect on others and to the influence of others on one's self, and this in turn requires information about culture and communication. For the researcher, too, the gathering of information requires sensitivity and skill. To this extent, at least, the speech-communication scholar can bring a vital, balanced perspective to the study of intercultural communication.

Some Limitations

The three-part concern described above has, to some extent, limited development in the field, particularly in its representation outside of the United States. As yet there are relatively few speech-communication scholars teaching in universities overseas, and many of them are primarily concerned with teaching basic skills rather than pursuing theoretical or comparative studies of communication across cultures.[1] In addition, the concern with sensitivity and skill has made the speech teacher in the U.S. most comfortable with immediate feelings and experiences shared among students, and thus he may be more reluctant to deal with extra-cultural data than are many of his colleagues in the social sciences. Another limitation is a characteristic American bias toward "Western" speech acts, including an emphasis on public deliberation, debate, individual rights, voting, etc., rather than private discussion which often involves intermediaries and is not easily open to analysis, interdependent or group-centered patterns of communication, consensus seeking, etc., which are characteristic of so many other societies.

There is also a division within the discipline between those who have followed the humanities tradition and those who have followed the goals and methods of the social scientists. The former, rhetorical critics, for example, are likely to examine more formal public speech texts, usually in an effort to pass critical judgment through analysis and interpretation of the speaker's apparent intentions and options. Those who have followed the social science trend are more likely to study large groupings of unidentified communicators in an effort to find regular patterns of behavior and correlations between cultural variables. As the former are more identified with the "speech" part of the discipline and the latter with the broader interpretation of "communication," we may also expect corresponding differences in perspective. Those in "speech" have emphasized the individual achievements ("the good man speaking well" — or occasionally the effective demagogue or dictator). Those in "communication," like so many of their social science colleagues, have tended to be both group and problem-oriented. Among other effects of following this second approach is to ignore, even eliminate from consideration the unique behavior of individuals, since groups, which may be surveyed and treated statistically, are preferred. Offsetting both of these divergent emphases is a common concern with "action," with relevance, and the here-and-now, which was of importance to speech scholars long before these terms became slogans for college reform. This emphasis is particularly apparent in the goals and teaching methods of the speech-communication field as compared with many others. Perhaps for this reason the field has found its present home largely in the U.S. where, popularly, theory is less valued than, and often contrasted with, "action." With a focus on intercultural communication, however, the discipline's characteristic interest in application may prove to be one of its greatest strengths.

Not the least important characteristic of speech-communication is a traditional emphasis on the spoken word as it affects human interaction. It is the primacy of the speech act which has shaped the field and which is still maintained, by many, as its unique focus. But even this emphasis has been blunted within the U.S. because of two apparently opposite reasons: "Speech" is much too broad to be called "an emphasis," or at least one that a single discipline can claim as its own; and over the past several decades "speech" seems too limited a subject for an adequate interpretation of human behavior. Across cultures, particularly as this most often means across languages, these objections remain and to them is added the need for sensitivity to other languages, a sensitivity which should be much greater than mere "fluency" in another language. Perhaps even more important is the realization that speech is not equally valued in all societies, or even consistently throughout the United States. The qualities of cogency, precision, and delivery which may be encouraged in speech communication courses in the United States may, in some other cultures, be regarded negatively. We shall say more about this later.

Many of the inconsistencies and disadvantages mentioned above could be re-interpreted as advantages. The best features of the speech perspective might be its multiple vision, its balance of historical and contemporary perspectives, its reluctance to divorce "form" from "content" (or at least its reluctance to give precedence of one over the other), and its set against static, impersonal models of communication. The student of speech-communication is not as interested in what is theoretically possible to say in a given situation or even in some statistical score of what is usually said or done within a single culture. Rather, he is interested, in classical terms, in "the available means" of affecting behavior, the capacity to use those means, and the results of selecting among those means. Viewed this way, the perspective bears some resemblance to what Irving Child has described as the characteristic of humanistic social psychology: a return to the individual as one who has real choices to make, and the study of his choices and their effects on him as well as others.[2] Man is an actor, as opposed to a re-actor who blindly conforms to laws identified by researchers.

There is another meaning of "the actor" which is familiar to persons in the speech-communication field. That is "the actor" as performer before an audience. Though in recent years theatre and interpretation courses have tended to be separated departmentally from courses in "communication" (including, now, intercultural communication), that relationship should not be lost. Indeed, the dramatic metaphor is currently salient among specialists in communication theories because of the contributions of Kenneth Burke and Erving Goffman. The relationship between that tradition and intercultural communication may be stronger, still.

Edward Hall in *Beyond Culture* indirectly offers support for the "performance" emphasis in intercultural studies when he emphasizes the need for a person outside of his own culture to be able to distinguish behaviors appropriate to that culture from his own culturally influenced behavior. This involves more than "self awareness" and more than theoretical and simplified models of how people in the host culture act. Moreover, Hall points out that one cannot move directly from a rational understanding of "variables" or "factors" of another culture to behavior.[3]

> "People don't learn to perform by combining parts which are memorized according to rules which they must think about in the course of the transaction . . . People learn in gestalts —— complete units —— which are contexted in situations and can be recalled as wholes.

Hall's observations are surely supported by the goals and methods of teaching in speech or speech-communication courses over a very long period of time.

It is the opinion of this writer that we may see emerging in the future a kind of "new Aristotelian scholarship" within a part of the intercultural communication disciplines. If so, the speech communication field seems most likely to develop it. What is meant is certainly not a "return to Aristotle," but rather the development of a multi-cultural rhetorical and communication concern which will more closely resemble Aristotelian goals (discovering the available and appropriate means of "performance" in a given situation) than the goals and approaches of, say, contemporary linguists, anthropologists or social scientists. These will be attempts to relate to persons of other cultures, rather than to conduct more abstracted studies which compare cultures. The former is an appropriately inter-cultural communication study, the latter a cross-cultural communication study. This is not to say that one is better than the other: both are needed, and each may complement the other. What should be noted, however, is that the speech - communication discipline should be best prepared to make a unique contribution of the former kind, while many disciplines —— not excluding speech communication —— can contribute survey, experimental, and theoretical cross cultural studies. Edward Stewart's development of training programs through role playing with a "contrast American" actor is one notable contribution along these lines.[4]

Courses in intercultural communication within the speech communication field have developed during recent years. It appears to this writer that most of these programs are of the "culture general" kind, which though data and personal contributions may be stated in terms of specific cultures, have as a primary goal the student's increased awareness of his or her own culturally based thoughts and actions. "Culture specific" programs, concentrating on communication between two cultures with one important goal of increasing one's understanding of a specific other culture, seem less common within the speech communication field. It seems likely that within other disciplines, such as anthropology, political science, or within an area studies program, "culture specific" intercultural communication programs might be more expected.

If this anticipated speech-communication approach is developed, it will be very much in keeping with the traditions of the fields; the discipline will remain eclectic, and borrowing will be selective but in addition, a measure of self-awareness, judgment, and performance, which is outside of the province of the sciences, will be required.

From this perspective, the author proposes a four-part approach to intercultural communication studies which seems to reflect both the sensitivities of the speech-communication scholar and the requirements of other specialists in intercultural communication. It is rather simple, hardly innovative, and certainly not exhaustive.

Language and Culture

When using the semiotic structure proposed by language philosopher Charles Morris, a tri-part framework of 'semantics'' (the relationship of symbols and their referents), "syntactics" (the relationship between symbols), and "pragmatics" (the relationship between symbols and human behavior), the speech-communication scholar is most interested in the pragmatic dimension.[5] Linguists, for the most part, have ignored the pragmatic dimension and, until recently, have also tended to ignore semantics; their concentration continues to be primarily on the syntactic dimension. Attention to language and culture relationships, however, inevitably involves all three of the dimensions.

No feature of inter-cultural communication is more apparent than that of language differences, causing us at times to forget that it is possible to have inter-cultural communication while using the same apparent languages.[6] Few "systems" within a culture are more examinable, less reactive, more consistent, and more reflective of other cultural differences than is language. Few have been studied longer and perhaps no area of study has produced such a wealth of information. However, identifying relationships between a language and the culture using that language, can be frustrating. As a result, the most obvious and interesting questions remain unanswerable. This appears to be one reason why most of today's linguists have declined to investigate such possible relationships. For speech-communication scholars the language and culture relationship would seem to be the most important subject for their study of intercultural communication. And yet, for reasons mentioned previously, most contemporary studies of speech-communication have been limited to the English language, and the majority of those to American speech. Selective borrowing from a few linguists, anthropologists or others who have pursued the language-culture relationship has done little more than raise old questions and provide some intriguing anecdotal evidence. But the anecdotal attraction is more meaningful to the novice than the scholar, and in this field especially, a little linguistic knowledge can be a dangerous thing. Moreover, the most provocative or most often quoted speculations about the relationships between language and culture seem to involve either relatively minor languages (Hopi, Eskimo, Wintu, etc.) or are made by non-linguists or non-specialists like McLuhan. The communication scholar's interest in language-culture relationships has been largely limited   to the moot question posed by Whorf and others: To what extent does our native language influence our ways of thinking and thus, by extension, the ways in which we act?[7] The General Semantics school has focused on this inquiry, more by assertion than question, but has stressed the influence of language habits of the individual more than the language system itself. Parallels between language structure and philosophical assumptions have been noted over the years; and the impossibility of rendering certain expressions of one language into *comparable* statements in certain other languages have also been popularly recognized.[8] Also of special interest are studies of a speaker's word choice which reflect his perceived relationship with the person to whom he is speaking. For example, while the person speaking English will identify himself as 'I' and the person spoken to as 'you,' the Japanese speaker has a remarkable range of pronouns for each depending upon how the speaker perceives his interpersonal relationship at the time.

Although the interests of the speech-communication scholar in language and culture relationships have been mostly limited to hypotheses associated with von Humboldt, Sapir, and Whorf, there are other topics in the realm of language and culture which deserve attention. These would include extra-symbolic functions and effects of speech in different cultures, such as using a second language for purposes of prestige or to indicate status or educational background; cultural preferences for spoken or for written language; the influence of second or third language speaking on social distance; cultural evaluations of the public speech act itself (in Japan to a great extent even today it is a liability to be considered "a good speaker"); and, the almost totally unexplored field of the communicative influence of the translator and interpreter.

There is a lack of research on the varied effects of communication involving translation. Reasons for this lack of study are many: most scholars lack sufficient competence in two languages, though team-studies reduce this problem; there is still a general disregard for language as anything other than a neutral medium for the expression of independent thought; and even the surprisingly low status of interpreters may contribute to the lack of study in this area. Reflecting and perpetuating all of these problems is the near absence of academic courses in translation and interpretation. Almost nobody, it seems, is very interested in translation, apart from a limited number of persons committed to the subject-matter of the translation, most notably Bible translators, and some literary critics. One could read thousands of studies involving interlanguage communication, including differences between the language of the researcher and the culture studied, and remain ignorant of the possible effects of the translation. Where interest is shown, it tends to be with a concern for particular words, and thus with the semantic reactions of the listeners compared with the speaker's intention, rather than with the vital interpersonal process itself.

To cite one example of the kind of study that might be undertaken, consider that most of the notable intercultural speakers are men while in some societies the majority of interpreters are women. What is the effect of hearing the voice of a foreign-language male speaker interpreted by a woman from one's own culture? Such a study, even if it showed no noticeable effect, could make a significant contribution to the entire field of intercultural communication. Not only are such studies ideally suited to the speech-communication student, they are not nearly as difficult to approach as are the more familiar but possibly unanswerable questions posed by linguistic relativism.

Language as an influence on and expression of a culture cannot be ignored in most studies of intercultural communication. That seems so obvious a statement that it should not be necessary to conclude with it, except for the fact that very few studies of intercultural communication, at least in the speech-communication field, make more than passing mention of language factors.

Nonverbal Behavior

It may seem odd that a field called "speech" would take an interest in nonverbal behavior, and yet "speech" studies have a long history of interest, albeit, a normative interest, in gestures, posture, movement, dress, etc. One reason for this interest is that the speech field traditionally has included drama, oral interpretation, and other speech "arts." However, a reaction against the performance nature of public speeches, such as the hollow "oratory" of the nineteenth century, reduced this kind of nonverbal concern until the recent surge of interest prompted by writers like Birdwhistell,[9] Hall,[10] and the spread of video technology. How to conduct and report nonverbal-research is still a difficult problem. How, even *if*, new nonverbal behaviors can be taught, is a more difficult question yet.

Probably Edward Hall deserves the most credit for generating a serious interest in the nonverbal aspects of intercultural communication, at least in speech-communication. Unfortunately, the very novelty of the awareness seems to have led many younger students and teachers of new courses in intercultural communication to emphasize the nonverbal far out of proportion to its relative importance, at least in the opinion of this writer. There are many reasons for this emphasis: availability of relevant materials; the novelty and, frequently, the dramatic appeal of many of the incidents cited; and the undeniable importance of the vast range of nonverbal behaviors. The importance of the nonverbal must not be underestimated. But it must also not be overestimated. There is an overemphasis when a student seeks to fix the blame for a lack of agreement between persons of two cultures only on the basis of the number of centimeters separating the two parties, or when he believes that interpersonal empathy will surely result if nonverbal taboos are avoided. Nevertheless, as interpersonal communication is frequently defined today, most communication is nonverbal, and most of it is outside of the awareness of the individual. For these reasons studies of nonverbal behavior, and particularly another's perception of one's own nonverbal expressiveness, must continue to occupy our attention.

While the analysis of speech texts most often has been undertaken with little regard for the physical characteristics of the speaker (a disembodied voice — often without even the voice!), nonverbal studies obviously cannot be carried out in the same way.

Nonverbal studies, in a sense, bring the person back into focus, and they also reduce the distance between the analyst and the subject: blinking, sweating, touching, etc., all of these factors must be studied close-up. What the speech-communication scholar will be most interested in, however, is not the total "cultural system" of nonverbal behavior, but the perception and effect of that behavior on a person from another culture. And here we find relatively little information.

In today's nonverbal studies the language model is dominant, for obvious and justifiable reasons.[11] But there are very important questions about nonverbal behavior which lie outside of that language-like framework, because they reside in the pragmatic rather than the syntactic dimension. These questions pertain to perceptions of nonverbal behavior and characteristics which are not learned nor controlled, such as reactions to differences in the physical appearance of some speakers from another culture. This distinction between controllable and uncontrollable behavior is important particularly in distinguishing the concerns of the speech tradition and those of many allied fields. The tradition of speech is one of possible choices an individual may make in influencing or otherwise relating to others. It is not primarily a study of rules, codes, patterns, or systems, except as these help to define choices.

With this in mind we should note that in interpersonal communication, one's conscious choices appear to be far greater in verbal behavior than in nonverbal behavior. Verbally one may argue this way or that way; when facing criticism one can defend himself, apologize, laugh it off, or change the subject. But many of our nonverbal expressions appear to be outside of our control, which is part of the appeal of nonverbal interaction in "sensitivity training" encounters, since it is difficult to lie or mask our feelings nonverbally. As noted previously, the speech tradition has discarded the teaching of facial expressions and gestures as an anachronism of the nineteenth century. "Be natural, be yourself, express yourself in a speech as you would in conversation." This is the usual contemporary advice on nonverbal behavior. Obviously, in intercultural communication this kind of "be yourself" advice may not suffice. As writers on the subject frequently point out, being yourself in another culture may sometimes lead to serious problems of mis-communication. What advice, what kind of training, is appropriate for persons going to another culture? There would seem to be problems with almost any answer, but the question remains.

The speech-communication scholar has a significant contribution to make here, for he should try to do more than provide research data on actual intercultural contacts. He must suggest choices for the individual outside of his culture. He should ask such questions as: What may be the effect of adapting to the patterns of another culture or of following your own "natural" behavior? What is the effect not only on members of the host culture but on the visitor himself? What third patterns are likely to evolve? What other expressions can be given (or, in Goffman's term, "given off") so that an extra-cultural expression is more likely to be interpreted appropriately? To what extent will the spoken language influence the corresponding nonverbal behavior?[12] These are not exactly questions of systems or of science, nor are they simply matters of technique or skill. In a detached examination of intercultural communication they may be relegated to foot-notes, appendices, out-of-role musings of the social scientist, or in class, they are saved for discussions at the end of the term. But as soon as one enters another culture, they become immediate questions which will unavoidably be answered in behavior.

Values

The concept of values and adaptation to the values of others is basic to the field of speech-communication, just as it is basic to studies of culture. As Ruesch noted, perhaps "no clear distinction can be made between communication theory, value theory, and anthropological statements about a culture."[13] The rhetorical tradition has always been concerned with values as central to the process of persuasion, so that today the beginning student in public speaking, the participant in group discussion, and the rhetorical critic are all concerned with the adaptation the speaker makes to the values of the listeners. However, for Aristotle and nearly every succeeding teacher of speech, values were intra-cultural factors. Thus Aristotle in *The Rhetoric* offers advice on the values of the young, the middle-aged, and the elderly, etc., within a society. The assumption appears to have always been that either the characteristics of such groupings were universal, or that cultural differences were irrelevant because nearly all speech-making is done within a single society. In this age the second possibility is quickly eroding. If the first is viable (paralleling the shift from the Whorfian interest in language differences to the Chomskian stress on language universals), speech-communication scholars might be able to repay anthropologists for some of what they have borrowed.

Currently some scholars in the field of speech seem most interested in those value differences which adversely affect intercultural communication. Largely ignored are those which seem irrelevant and those which actually facilitate understanding. One must assume that there are many more values which are shared across cultures than those which are significantly different, or else the prospects for any kind of understanding are dim. The shift from "values" to "value orientations," with the built-in assumption that there are variations within any culture, is a great conceptual aid here.[14] Thus a careful consideration of common values or value orientations rather than an emphasis solely on conflicting values should characterize future studies of intercultural communication.

Speech-communication is making and will continue to make a very important contribution to the study of values for at least four reasons. First, is the centrality of values in the field, a characteristic emphasis shared perhaps only by anthropology. Second, is the pragmatic view which frequently discovers value differences as the source of misunderstanding. A third reason is the common eclecticism of the theme of values and today's speech discipline. As Morris has said, the concept of values is one of the great terms in scholarship and nearly every writer in nearly every field has had something to say about values. But one might also sympathize with Wittgenstein's remark that when one begins to use the word he should begin to stutter! A fourth reason might be that because of the pervasiveness of values or value orientations, a full appraisal of value-related discourse requires the kind of extended, qualitative analysis which has characterized the humanities much more than the social sciences. Qualitative content analysis, for example, arises from the social sciences but is not very different from traditional rhetorical analysis of the speech critic.

Any serious values study brings with it obvious self-contradictions: the choice and the manner of value analyses are necessarily value influenced. To isolate "values" as one "factor" in "communication" reflects a preference in thinking among members of a rather small sub-culture. Most experimental studies of groups are likewise value-biased, not simply because they usually involve U.S. college students but because they are based on the value-assumption that "a group" is composed of strangers gathered together to interact in some way imposed from the outside. In most of the world, strangers do not simply get together for such purposes. American experimental studies of communication are likely to assume such risky or culture-bound values as verbalization (the silent member of a group is likely to be judged negatively whereas in many societies he might be regarded as the most powerful member, since his silence is seen as an expression of and contribution to his power), individualism, equal participation, and various culturally-influenced concepts of efficiency and satisfaction. With the U.S. having taken the lead in empirical studies of communication there is a very strong tendency to conduct comparable studies ("replications") outside of the United States which impose American value-biased research methods as well as U.S. definitions of the situations investigated.

Despite the reactive problem of values-research in intercultural communication, value-studies must continue to be emphasized. For one thing, many, maybe most, of the serious problems of misunderstanding across cultures will be better described by noting differences in values or value orientations than by observing conflicts in nonverbal behavior or language-related problems.

A discussion of values must take place within a context of intercultural communication and not as a part of an abstracted value system of a culture or sub-culture. One may survey ethnographies and generalize that Americans tend to value "youth" as part of a complex of values involving change, future-orientations, activity, achievement, etc. On the other hand, many other cultures tend to value "age" as part of another complex of values involving stability and temperance, orientations toward the past, ascription and experience, etc. But how do such contrasting values influence the communication between persons representing the two respective cultures? There is no simple answer, as indicated by the incredible reverence shown the most youthful of U.S. Presidents, John F. Kennedy, who appears to be even more highly esteemed in traditional, age-oriented cultures than in the youth-oriented culture of the United States. Obviously the relationship between persons from cultures with differing value orientations is not describable within a single system of values and value-adaptations, something which is very different from the case of language or even nonverbal differences. Representatives of different cultures *may* be mutually attracted because of some differences in values. But even supposing all of these factors could be examined and understood, the representative of any one culture still faces the problem of dramatizing some values associated with his culture or minimizing them in an attempt to adapt to his host culture.

Then there is the dilemma of foreign assistance personnel such as Peace Corps volunteers. Unless one adapts to a certain extent to the culture he enters, perhaps consisting of adaptations in values for the most part, he cannot be effective, but if he could adapt so totally as to become nearly identical to members of his host culture he may no longer have any special contribution to make. Even this possibility implies that a person *can* alter his own values to a desired extent. However, compared to changes in language behavior and non-verbal behavior, the alteration of one's values may be the most difficult of all.

It is clear that no single value system can encompass the communication of persons from two different cultures. It appears almost as clear that not even two distinguishable value systems can accomplish that purpose either, for no interpersonal communication act is a result of simple addition. What seems more likely is that some values of each participant will intentionally be altered, others will be inevitably altered, while many remain the same. Even this description oversimplifies the effect of interaction. It is not uncommon for persons from different cultures to attempt to so adapt to the assumed values of the other that the two pass each other and exchange positions. The North American visitor in Mexico, for example, may choose to arrive at a meeting place half an hour late to reflect and dramatize his awareness of *la hora Mexicana*, while his Mexican counterpart is prompt in order to show respect for his *yanqui* host.

Value analyses of intercultural communication are mostly likely to reveal something far more complicated than either the rigid retention of one's native culture, on which projections of intercultural contact are posited, or the complete reversal of value-related behaviors described above. Research in this area will be extremely complicated and may be far better suited to a qualitative interpretation than to the current variations of attitude studies applied to values. That is, the very awareness of cultural differences will make a difference in behavior, so that surveys of the "what would you do" type may be irrelevant. Most likely, one does not *know* what he would do, or even what he is perceived as doing.

Research in this field will have to become more inventive. Surveys which are subject to statistical analysis may not be appropriate, if for no other reason than that the number of persons interacting across cultures is too small or too diversified to make such surveys practical. Few persons who interact in cultures outside of their own, behave exactly as they would at home, but how they act may not be how they *think* they act nor how they are perceived as acting.

A person who appears to have adapted well to another culture over a period of years, may suddenly discover that he has been "mis-behaving" in certain respects and misinterpreting local behavior for many years. Where this occurs, and it would seem to be commonplace, it may be best described in the realm of values rather than in the area of language and nonverbal behavior about which the visitor is more conscious. Quite unlike learning a language, learning cultural value patterns to the point where they are integrated into behavior is not a task that can be accomplished through drills and exercises, nor is it something easily corrected or even identified. Moreover, the task always runs the risk of resembling more, in Wiener's splendid analogy, the Manichaean devil, who actively competes, changing his tactics when his method is discovered, rather than the Augustinian devil, who may be difficult to figure out but who does not suddenly change when discovered. Learning a foreign language and discovering other non-verbal codes is more comparable to playing against the Augustinian devil than is "value-learning."

As mentioned previously, the goal of many courses in intercultural communication is to make the student aware of his own "normal behavior," which means calling attention to his own culture's influences on that behavior. That appears to be a far more realistic goal than one which primarily attempt to specify the value orientations of other cultures. Even this apparently modest goal may be far too general for the student who may feel he is not really representative of the culture described. Therefore, it seems wise for teachers of speech-communication to continue to work with students as individuals, in small classes, as they teach intercultural communication. This individual attention, so traditionally distinctive of speech-communication courses, may serve anew as we turn our attention to intercultural communication.

Rhetoric and Argumentation

One assumes, almost by definition, that cultures will differ in languages, in nonverbal expressions, and in values. On the other hand, one is tempted to assume, also by definition, that "reasoning" is not subject to cultural variations, or if differences can be observed they may still be tested against some universal standards. What is a specious argument in Paris ought to be unacceptable in Cairo, what is a *non-sequitur* in Tokyo ought to be equally irrelevant in London. Unwarranted generalizations or false inferences should be recognized as such, apart from the cultures in which they arise, though we may be willing to expect greater tolerance for "fuzzy thinking" in some parts of the world than in others. Evidence, proof, organization of ideas, in short was conventionally called "argumentation," "rhetoric" or sometimes "reasoning," would at first glance appear to be culture-free. Indeed without such an assumption we might be reluctant to attempt any kind of scholarly cross-cultural study in the first place. Yet it seems that this is an ethnocentric view which experience refutes.

Our fourth area of concern, that of rhetoric or reasoning, is the most central to the traditional focus of speech-communication scholarship, and it appears that it is the least explored and possibly the most difficult of all.

Colleagues who are professional simultaneous interpreters, have pointed out that often their best interpretations from Japanese to English, or vice versa, are faithful to the original in style as well as substance, that is at the level of sentences or paragraphs. But the overall effect may fail because of differences in ways of organizing the speech, providing support or proofs, transitions, etc. In an English translation a Japanese speech may seem jumbled, often irrelevant to the topic at hand, lacking in transitions which relate crucial points, while being redundant elsewhere. Or the speech may be crowded with specifics but lacking in direction. Then again the speech may be so very abstract or generalized that it lacks even a shred of apparent support or proof. The reverse may be true for some on listening to a Japanese translation of what English speakers would regard as an excellent speech, with abstracts and specifics consistently balanced, points clearly enumerated, and the conclusion fully summarizing the talk. Such a speech, if given by a Japanese speaker, may seem insulting to the intelligence of a Japanese audience. The problem appears to be caused by something different from the points already discussed.

Professor Karl Pribram's promising little book, now over 30 years old, offered some hope of investigation into this broad subject of reasoning.[15] Glenn has added his insights,[16] as have a few scholars from other disciplines.[17] But the subject remains the least explored and described of the four categories considered in this chapter.

The language and culture speculations of the kind noted earlier are relevant but we might expect more progress if "language" were not required to bear the full burden of responsibility. Philosophy, religion, art and literary forms are obviously important, but most important are rhetorical studies. There are still very few rhetorical analyses of contemporary speaking outside of the English-speaking world. At the same time, with an expansion of the subjects of study must come a development of methods, even categories, for rhetorical analysis. It does seem that many of the classical rhetorical concepts, such as the enthymeme, which are terms shared by anthropologists as well as rhetoricians, might be resurrected for intercultural research. Though conceptually imprecise and much maligned even within the discipline, the enthymeme is one of those terms which could not only help to illuminate cultural patterns of argumentation but also help to re-unify the speech-communication field in the process. The concept's application to the unstated beliefs and values shared by the speaker and the audience marks it as a promising term. Similarly, classical concepts such as *topoi*, or contemporary rhetorical categories such as *warrants*, offer many kinds of applications in studying the reasoning of speakers of other cultures and those engaged in intercultural communication. In this kind of research, however, multicultural sensitivity is even more important than analytical constructs, and thus cooperation between scholars with mutual interests who are from different cultures is most important.

Of all of the four topics described, the study of "reasoning/rhetoric" may have to rely most on personal experience of individuals who have had long, direct encounters across cultures. Also we may have to follow the hunches and feelings of such persons further than we are accustomed to doing. The contributions of the professional interpreter and translater have already been mentioned. A related source is the journalist from one culture who writes for publications of another culture. A Japanese friend who is a reporter for a major U.S. newspaper points out that his American editors are always asking him to provide quotable material from the speeches of the Japanese Prime Minister. But, the reporter says, that for reasons rooted in the tradition of Japanese rhetoric there is rarely anything in the Prime Minister's speeches which is directly quotable. If the reporter attempts to give a direct quotation, the words will seem vague or insignificant, but if he rewrites what was said in order to convey what was *meant*, then it is not the kind of quotation the editors wanted. The scholar studying such a phenomenon must consider the political rhetoric of contemporary Japan, but he should also take note of American insistence on direct quotations. Insights from the professional experiences of persons in international law, advertising, marketing, diplomacy, the entertainment fields, etc., should provide a wealth of information about our fourth category.

The four areas, language, nonverbal behavior, values, and reasoning/rhetoric, have been discussed in the apparent order of available information, namely consciousness of cultural difference, and difficulty of adaptation, with "language" being the easiest and reasoning/rhetoric the most difficult category. In intercultural marriages, for example, many parents have confirmed that this is the order of difficulty in husband-and-wife relations as well as in their mutual decisions about the rearing of children. According to these subjects, language and most nonverbal behaviors are not such serious problems. As for values, husbands and wives often say that they simply have to cope with value differences which affect the "meaning" of marriage, such as the role expectations of husbands and wives, problems which appear impossible to bridge in child rearing, and many subjects report that they have given up trying to understand the other's way of thinking. Peace Corps volunteers, missionaries and others who attempt to make some contributions outside of their own culture also indicate that this is the order of difficulties they experience in another culture. Language difficulties may be anticipated and studied intensely even before venturing into another culture. Nonverbal and value differences must be experienced to be learned, and thus "culture shock" arises mostly in these two latter areas. The fourth area, that of reasoning/rhetoric may be so subtle that it is evidenced more through frustration and criticism than attempted adaptation.

The specialist in speech-communication may make his most singular contribution in that fourth area, since it would seem to the the traditional concern of his field. However, the speech-communication specialist must never become so specialized that he ignores the inter-relationship among the four areas, for it is in that relationship that we find our contemporary perspective.

Concluding Observations

The speech communication discipline as represented in the U.S., like any academic discipline anywhere, has its own values, language, and preferred modes of communication, too. Not surprisingly, many of these conform to the dominant values, assumptions and expressions within the United States. "Learning to communicate" means, to a great extent, learning to or trying to epitomize what one's society values. This writer believes it is very important for scholars within the field to recognize such cultural assumptions and values in their scholarship and teaching. Without such an awareness there is, at the very least, the danger of teaching culture-bound behavior as "normal" or "ideal" irrespective of cultural context.

The increase in intercultural, cross cultural, and inter-ethnic studies has already helped to bring into awareness some of these assumptions, but much more work is needed. Below is an abbreviated list of some contrasting assumptions, values, and features of "communication." These two columns should be viewed as differing in degree and in emphasis rather than as strictly dichotomous. Those on the left seem, to this writer, most characteristic of the view of communication as it is investigated and taught in the United States. Those on the right are often identified with interpersonal communication in various cultures, including Japan but also including portions of the United States. (These will be treated in more detail in a forthcoming article on "Cultural Assumptions in Theories of Interpersonal Communication.")

1. Individualistic Orientation
   a. assumption and value of independent "I" and "you"

   b. dominance of "I" over "we" in B. Bernstein's theory.[18]

1. Interdependent Orientation
   a. assumption and value of interdependence; as with Japanese pronouns, with "I" is relative to the kind of "you"

   b. dominance of "we" over "I"

2. Symmetrical relationships valued and encouraged; minimize differences in age, sex, status, host/guest roles, etc.

2. Complementary relationships are valued and encouraged; give emphasis to differences in age, sex, status, etc.

3. Verbalization (speech) is regarded as *the* means of communication

3. Verbalization (speech) is regarded as *a* means of communication

a. "elaborated codes" in Bernstein's theory are preferred

a. "Restricted codes" in Bernstein's theory are preferred

b. "low context culture" in Hall's theory[19]

b. "high context culture" in Hall's theory

c. discomfort, distrust of what is not said clearly

c. value of the unspoken; verbalizing may reduce value of what is communicated

4. Expressive emphasis
   a. speaker ("sender") focus of communication
   b. to communicate well is to express oneself well

4. Impressive emphasis
   a. perceiver focus in communication
   b. to communicate well is to understand the implicit

5. Objective values dominant
   a. separation of speaker and his opinions
   b. "objectivity" viewed as neutral, "natural"

5. Interpersonal values dominant
   a. inseparability of speaker and his opinions
   b. no objectivity;" everything contingent on interpersonal relations

6. Explicit logic, proofs
   a. lineal organization
   b. precision in word usage

6. Context-dependent logic
   a. non-lineal, associative logic
   b. words not taken at face value

7. Silence regarded as negative

   a. low tolerance of silence in discussions, conversations
   b. "silent person" viewed as weak, shy, troubled, etc.

7. Silence regarded as having many meanings, including positive
   a. expectations of silence, value of silence in some situations
   b. silence may convey meaning of strength, power

The writer concludes with the hope that the speech communication discipline may take a lead in identifying and clarifying such alternative forms which vary across cultures, but also in actively teaching them. If "assertiveness training" has a legitimate place, then across cultures so too, does "reticence training." If speaking clearly and precisely of what one means is valued in some settings, so, too, elsewhere is the ability to be indirect and to sense what is not explicit in words. And without disputing the value of an elementary course in public speaking, one might also learn to appreciate all that can be communicated through public silences.

FOOTNOTES

[1] Fred Casmir and L.S. Harms, eds., *International Studies of Speech Education Systems, Vol. I.* (Minneapolis: Burgess Publishing Co., 1970).

[2] Irving L. Child, "Toward a Humanistic Social Psychology." (Unpublished paper read at the Japan Social Psychology Association Conference, Kobe, Japan, December 9, 1972).

[3] Edward T. Hall, *Beyond Culture.* (New York: Doubleday, 1976), pp. 114-115.

[4] Edward C. Stewart, *American Cultural Patterns: A Cross-cultural Perspective.* (Pittsburgh: Regional Council for International Education, University of Pittsburgh, 1971).

[5] Charles W. Morris, *Signs, Language and Behavior,* (New York: Prentice-Hall, 1946).

[6] How to define a language is a problem. Some languages which are commonly identified as different reveal more characteristics in common than are found in some " 'dialects' of the same language." One must be especially careful of tautologies which define a language in terms of a single culture in which it is spoken.

[7] See, for example, Benjamin Lee Whorf, *Language, Thought and Reality,* with an introduction by J.B. Carroll. (Cambridge: Technology Press, 1956); Harry Hoijer, ed., *Language in Culture: Conference on the Interrelations of Language and Other Aspects of Culture.* (Chicago: University of Chicago Press, 1954); Dorothy Lee,

Freedom and Culture (Englewood Cliffs: Prentice-Hall, 1959).

[8] See Ludwig von Bertalanffy, "An Essay on the Relativity of Categories," *Philosophy of Science,* vol. 22, no. 4 (October, 1955), pp. 243-263.

[9] Ray L. Birdwhistell, *Kinesics and Context,* (Philadelphia: University of Pennsylvania Press, 1970).

[10] Edward T. Hall, *The Silent Language.* (New York: Doubleday and Co., 1959); and Edward T. Hall, *The Hidden Dimension* (New York: Doubleday and Co., 1966).

[11] See Hall's discussion in his "A System for the Notation of Proxemic Behavior," *American Anthropologist,* vol. 65, no. 5 (October, 1963), pp. 1003-26.

[12] The micro-kinesic studies of William Condon indicate that even a person's most subtle non-verbal behavior, such as blinking, is synchronized to speech; if so, this suggests that the learning of a foreign language is far more complicated and stressful than commonly thought.

[13] Jurgen Ruesch and Gregory Bateson, *Communication: Social Matrix of Psychiatry,* (New York: W.W. Norton, 1951), p. 8.

[14] See Clyde Kluckhohn, "Values and Value Orientations in the Theory of Action," in Talcott Parsons and Edward A. Shils, eds., *Toward a General Theory of Action,* (Cambridge: Harvard University Press, 1951), pp. 388-433; and, Florence Kluckhohn and Fred Strodtbeck, *Variations in Value Orientations* (Evanston: Row, Peterson, 1961), pp. 1-23.

[15] Karl Pribram, *Conflicting Patterns of Thought,* (Washington: Public Affairs Press, 1949).

[16] Edmund S. Glenn, "Semantic Difficulties in International Communication," *Etc.* 11(1954), pp. 163-180.

[17] For a survey of some of these contributions see John Condon and Fathi Yousef, *An Introduction to Intercultural Communication* (Indianapolis: Bobbs-Merrill, 1975), pp. 209-249.

[18] Basil Berstein, "Elaborated and Restricted Codes: Their Social Origins and Some Consequences," *American Anthropologist (The Ethnography of Communication) special publication,* vol. 66(1964), part 2, pp. 55-69.

[19] Edward T. Hall, *Beyond Culture, op. cit.,* pp. 74-101.

Charles H. Kraft:

Worldview in Intercultural Communication*

———

Introduction

COMMITMENT to a worldview or basic value system (often that of a religion or of some surrogate religion such as atheism, science or a political persuasion) appears to be a cultural universal (Lessa & Vogt 1965:xi). If so, we may assume that the influence of such basic concepts within the minds of people is of high importance in the process of interpersonal, intergroup and intercultural communication. It is the aim of this chapter to probe these influences for the purpose of explicating the ways in which a worldview affects intercultural communication.

If, as many contend, worldview pervasively influences every area of life, our topic is a very broad one. We will, however, have space enough to deal with but three important facets of the matter. In the first place it will be useful to deal briefly with the position and functions of worldview in culture. We will then attempt to discover what effects worldview influences have on intercultural communication in general. And, finally, we will probe the factors involved in attempts to communicate and win adherence to another worldview across a cultural boundary.

Worldview in Culture

Every social group has a worldview —— a set of more or less systematized beliefs and values in terms of which that group evaluates and attaches meaning to the reality that surrounds it.[1] Groups will vary with regard to the degree to which they are conscious of or can make explicit their worldviews. But the presence of such an integrating core at the center of their perspective on reality has been observed for every social group from the simplest to the most complex and is assumed to be a universal. Frequently, especially in non-western cultures, it is convenient to label that worldview "religion." In western cultures, however, many feel uncomfortable designating communism, atheism or scientism "religion." A religion, furthermore, is ordinarily conceived of as consisting of more than a worldview in that it includes ritual and other behavior in addition to the basic beliefs and values. It is, however, a people's worldview more than any other aspect of their culture that affects communication. It is, therefore, primarily worldview that will be dealt with here.

The worldview of a people serves a number of important functions. The first of these is an *explanatory* function. It provides for them explanations of how and why things got to be as they are and how and why they continue that way. The worldview embodies for a people, whether explicitly or implicitly, the basic assumptions concerning ultimate things on which they base their lives. If the worldview of a people conditions them to believe that the universe is operated by a number of invisible personal forces who are largely beyond man's control, this will affect both their understanding of and their response to "reality." If, however, a people's worldview explains that the universe operates by means of a large number of impersonal, cause and effect operations that, if learned by people, can be employed by them to control the universe, the attitude of these people toward "reality" will be much different.

These ideas are customarily articulated in the mythology of a people. This mythology, however, takes a variety of forms from culture to culture. In a large number of cultures one would look to their fables, proverbs, riddles, songs and other forms of folklore for overt and covert indications of their worldview. In more complex societies one finds, in addition to the folklore, printed literature that often overtly philosophizes the mythology of the people's science, religion, politics, and the like. The portion of the worldview of which people are conscious is thus often more easily observable in the various subcultures within western (i.e. Euroamerican) culture than in preliterate societies.

The worldview of a people, secondly, serves an *evaluational* and *validating* function. The basic institutions, values and goals of a society find their sanctions in the worldview of their culture or subculture. And for most of the cultures of the world the ultimate ground for these sanctions is supernatural. It is in their God or gods that most people understand their worldview and their culture as a whole to be rooted. And even when no external supernatural is postulated (as in communism and naturalistic American worldview) a sort of "internal supernatural" is generally present in the virtual deifying of such a concept as "the American way of life." Thus in our American worldview we find sanctions (supernatural or pseudo-supernatural) for such institutions as democratic government, a capitalistic economy, and monogamous marriage, for such values as scientism (with or without God), individual rights and freedoms and private property, and for such goals as world peace (on our terms), personal and national prosperity and a college education for everyone who wants one. As with regard to its explanatory function a people's worldview is not peripheral to but rather integral to every aspect of the life of a social group. All important and valued behavior, be it classified as economic, political, "scientific," social, educational or whatever is pervasively affected by the assumptions, beliefs, values, meanings and sanctions of the worldview of the group performing the behavior.

A third function served by the worldview or religious orientation of a group is to provide *psychological reinforcement* for that group. At points of anxiety or crisis in life it is to one's belief system that one turns for the encouragement to continue or the stimulus to take other action. Crisis times such as death, birth and illness, transition times such as puberty, marriage, planting and harvest, times of uncertainty, times of elation —— all tend to heighten anxiety or in some other way require adjustment between behavior and basic values. And each tends to be dealt with in a reinforcing way in accordance with the worldview of a society. Often this reinforcement takes the form of ritual or ceremony in which many people participate (e.g. funerals, harvest celebrations, initiation or graduation ceremonies). Frequently the worldview also requires individual reinforcement observances such as prayer, trance, scientific experimentation, or "thinking the matter through" for the purpose of squaring a prospective decision with one's core values. In such ways the worldview of a group provides security and support for the behavior of the group in a world that appears to be filled with capricious uncontrollable forces.

Fourthly, the worldview of a social group serves an *integrating* function. It systematizes and orders for them their perceptions of reality into an overall design. In terms of this integrated and integrating perspective, then, a people conceptualizes what reality should be like and understands and interprets the multifarious events to which they are exposed. A people's worldview "establishes and validates basic premises about the world and man's place in it; and it relates the strivings and emotions of men to them."[2]

Thus in its explanatory, evaluative, reinforcing and integrating functions worldview or religion lies at the heart of a culture, bridging the gap between the "objective" reality outside of people's heads and the culturally agreed upon perception of that reality inside their heads. Worldview formulates for the members of a social group the conceptualizations in terms of which they perceive reality. It also filters out for them most glimpses of reality that do not conform to their beliefs concerning the way that reality should be. It provides for people

. . . a system of symbols which acts to establish powerful, pervasive, and long-lasting moods and motivations in men by formulating conceptions of a general order of existence and clothing these conceptions with such an aura of factuality that the moods and motivations seem uniquely realistic.[3]

A group's worldview does not, however, completely determine the perception of all of its members at all times. Though there is characteristically a very high degree of conservatism to worldview conceptualization, there is change in this as well as all other areas of culture. People do, on occasion, perceive aspects of reality in ways that differ slightly (or even drastically) from the ways that their worldview has conditioned them to perceive of them. And such divergences in perception, especially if engaged in and reported by socially influential persons, may be accepted by other members of the social group. The result is worldview change.

Thus, over a period of time groups such as the ancient Hebrews moved from belief in many gods to a strong concept of monotheism. Likewise, have large segments of western culture moved through Renaissance, Industrial Revolution and American Frontierism from a belief in the supremacy of the Judaeo-Christian God to a belief in the actual or potential all-sufficiency of technological man.

There is, therefore, a fifth function of worldview that is of particular interest to us here, since it relates directly to the more disintegrative aspects of culture change. That function may be labeled *adaptational.* Wallace suggests that inherent in worldviews is the ability to reduce "internal structural contradictions" that occur in the process of culture change.[4] Worldviews devise means for resolving conflict and reducing cultural dissonance. That is, in circumstances of cultural distortion or disequilibrium there is a resilient quality to worldviews by means of which they reconcile hitherto apparently irreconcilable differences between the old understandings and the new in order to bring a society whose worldview has gotten out of balance back to equilibrium. If a society gets into such difficulty "it may be far easier to reinterpret values than to reorganize society."[5]

> Where mutually contradictory cognitions (including perceptions, knowledge, motives, values, and hopes) are entertained, the individual must act to reduce the dissonance. While, theoretically, he can do this by changing the real world in some respect, so as to modify the data coming in, he may also achieve the same effect by modifying his perceptions of self and of the real world in such a way that one horn of the dilemma is no longer recognized.[6]

In extreme cases this adaptation to changing perception calls for major replacement and what Wallace calls "revitalization" (dealt with later in this chapter). But short of such drastic "cultural surgery" the adaptational quality of worldviews is constantly in evidence in all sorts of culture change situations, whether these be mild or intensive.

The Effects of Worldview on Intercultural Communication

If a worldview is as central and integral to a cultural frame of reference as anthropological investigation would lead us to believe, it pervasively influences any attempt to communicate across cultural or subcultural boundaries. For it is the worldview of a culture or subculture that will specify which, if any, areas of the culture are closed to intercultural influence and which are open. And for those areas of culture specified as open, the worldview determines just how open and on what conditions.

It is convenient to summarize a representative number of the worldview factors most affecting intercultural communication in the following chart. The stance taken by the worldview of a culture with respect to each of these factors and to groupings of them greatly influences the attitudes and behavior of the society with respect to ideas that come to it from the members of another social group. A discussion of the factors follows the chart.

Factors influencing Intercultural Acceptance or Rejection of Ideas:

Factors	Hindering Acceptance	Facilitating Acceptance
1. Basic Premises of Source and Receptor Cultures	Very Different	Very Similar
2. Attitude of Receptor(s) Toward Their Own Culture	Highly Positive	Very Negative
3. Attitude of Receptor(s) Toward Source Culture	Despised	Respected
4. Openness to New Ideas	Closed	Open
5. Pace of Present Change	Slow	Rapid
6. Borrowing Tradition	Rejection	Borrow Freely

7. Morale	Proud	Demoralized
8. Self-Sufficiency	Self-Sufficient	Doubting Self-Sufficiency
9. Security	Threatened	Secure
10. Flexibility	Resistant	Adaptive
11. Advocate	Non-Prestigious	Prestigious
12. Relation of Idea to Felt Needs	Perceived as Unrelated to Felt Needs	Perceived as Filling a Felt Need
13. Fit of Idea	Discontinuous With Present Worldview	Congruent With Present Worldview

If (1) the basic premises on which the worldview of the receptor culture is based are similar to those of the communicator's culture the potential for acceptance, or at least of understanding, is increased. Understanding and acceptance are not, of course, the same thing. But, other things being equal, an increase in the ability to understand on the part of the receiving participant in an intercultural communication event will increase the possibility that he will be favorably disposed toward the idea. If, for example, one's worldview regards the addition of fertilizer to the soil as impermissible, tampering with an area of life that lies wholly within the province of God, it is unlikely that a simple recommendation that fertilizer be used will be either understood or accepted. If, however, both the recommender's worldview and that of the potential receptor accept the premise that such addition to the soil is legitimate, the arguments of the recommender are likely to be both understood and regarded as convincing.

If, though, even in spite of similar worldviews, such a recommendation were to come to the members of a social group whose (2) attitude toward their own culture was so positive that they believed that they had no need for suggestions from outside, the likelihood is that even good ideas would be rejected. Such was the case when attempts were made to innovate western (Christian) schools into Hausa (Muslim) society. The Hausas, even though they believed in and operated (Koranic) schools saw no need for what they regarded as inferior western schools promulgating an inferior western worldview. And today they find themselves competing at a disadvantage with their more thoroughly westernized countrymen of other tribes because their cultural pride led them to reject, while certain other tribes, manifesting perhaps a less positive attitude toward their own educational techniques, accepted educational innovation.

Likewise the (3) attitude of a group toward the source of would-be innovation affects the likelihood of acceptance. If a group despises the source, the likelihood of acceptance of ideas from that source is diminished — no matter how persuasively such ideas may be communicated.

Because of their worldviews certain cultures are (4) more open to cross-culturally communicated ideas than others. Western culture in general has manifested a remarkable openness to such innovation. We believe in and expect to find good ideas coming to us from cultures and subcultures other than our own — especially if we respect the source. Many cultures have, however, traditionally taken the opposite posture and have, because of their worldviews, been virtually closed to innovations advocated by outsiders.

In cultural dynamics (5) change tends to beget change. A culture that is changing rapidly tends to believe in change, and therefore, to readily accept recommendations for further change even if the recommenders are outsiders. If, further, (6) there is a tradition of borrowing in the society, the potential for acceptance is increased. If, however, the tradition is one of rejection, the potential for acceptance is decreased.

In our day, when the intensive impact of westernization is producing widespread cultural disruption the effect is frequently greater or lesser (7) demoralization on the part of the receptor culture. Such demoralization constitutes a serious morale problem resulting, frequently, in both the questioning of the (8) self-sufficiency of the core values of the culture and a predisposition to experiment with innovative approaches to a restructuring of the worldview. People cannot live without "gods." And when the old gods are called into question, they will bend every effort to discover new gods — a new, more satisfying worldview.

A.L. Kroeber documents such a happening among the Kota of the Nilgiri plateau in South India,[7] while Anthony Wallace in a truly significant treatment points to such occurrences in literally thousands of cultures throughout the course of history (Wallace 1956). In each case, cultural breakdown issuing in psychological demoralization and doubt of the sufficiency of the traditional answers to life problems has resulted in a conscious attempt on the part of certain members of the culture to reformulate or accept from an outside source a more satisfying value system around which to reconstruct their culture. The roots of most of the world's religious movements —— from Christianity to nativistic religious, political and economic movements —— are frequently, if not always, to be found in such revitalization of societies that were in some advanced state of self-doubt and demoralization. Societies in such a condition are peculiarly susceptible to intercultural communication of new worldview values.

Before this stage of cultural demoralization is reached, however, there may be an almost opposite attitude toward worldview change. If a society feels (9) threatened rather than secure in the face of intensive outside pressures toward change, it may be less, rather than more receptive to intercultural communication of new values. Such is the case with many Latin American Indian tribal groupings whose reaction to even very worthy suggestions is usually to reject them without serious consideration due to their lack of socio-psychological security.

Such cultures tend to develop (10) a highly resistant, rather than an adaptive attitude toward worldview change. American fundamentalism has been characterized by such an approach to issues such as evolution, Biblical criticism, cultural relativity and many other new ideas. Rather than considering the possibility of revising their worldview to incorporate any truth in the new ideas, fundamentalists have characteristically built their walls higher and thicker to keep themselves and their children insulated from such "anti-Christian" concepts. The result, however, is frequently the opposite of their hopes. For, one way or another, many children of fundamentalists become exposed to such ideas and end up adopting them all uncritically in more or less total reaction against their fundamentalistic worldview. A more secure and adaptive worldview will characteristically examine even initially threatening concepts and accept at least those parts of the new concepts that are easily integratable into their value system.

With regard to the (11) person who advocates a given idea, much depends upon the prestige assigned to him by the potential receptor group. The worldview of a social group will lead it to expect worthy ideas from certain types of persons but not to expect them from others. If a culture believes that the privilege of innovation belongs only to those of royal lineage, it may well require that even an outsider demonstrate his royal connections before his ideas will be taken seriously. Or, if a group expects to accept innovative ideas only from those who have demonstrated their abilities from within the cultural context of the potential receptor group, it is unlikely that a person who has not acquired such credentials will be taken seriously. For this reason certain Nigerian cultures have been very resistant to accepting agricultural innovations even from Euroamericans (whose prestige is generally high) since they have never observed these "agricultural experts" to have actually grown a superior crop (or any crop) of guinea corn.

The (12) relationship of the proposed idea to an area of felt need in the culture is clearly an important factor in its potential acceptance. All value systems have within them areas of inconsistency and/or inadequacy that are to a greater or lesser degree a part of the consciousness of the society. The wise intercultural communicator seeks to discover the questions concerning reality that the people of the society regard as beyond their ability to answer. He then attempts to communicate his message in such a way that the hearers perceive a relationship between that communication and questions that they feel to be left unanswered or poorly answered by their present worldview.

Similarly, an idea is more likely to gain acceptance if it (13) is congruent with the receptor culture's present worldview than if it is discontinuous with it. If the new can be built upon or grafted into the old rather than being introduced as unconnected or even in competition with it, the likelihood of acceptance is increased. In recognition of this fact, perceptive doctors, working among peoples whose concept of disease is that illness is always caused by personal forces, have learned to discuss germs as if they were personal rather than impersonal forces. Likewise, with respect to the acceptance or rejection of a "world religion" such as Christianity or Islam, the crucial issue is not the dedication of the advocate but whether or not the recommended changes in worldview can be fit into the conceptual framework of the receptor culture without completely remaking it.

These factors are not, of course, mutually exclusive. They frequently overlap or occur in association with each other. It is clear that a culture with a highly positive (2) self-image may also be characterized by such things as lack of respect for other cultures (3), pride (7) and self-sufficiency (8). Or it might feel itself so secure (9) that it adopts a very adaptive (10) posture toward new ideas. Nor is the list exhaustive.

It should, however, be clear by now that such worldview-based factors as these pervasively affect both the process and the results of intercultural communication. No communication takes place in a vacuum. There are always worldview-based presuppositions, beliefs, understandings, and other concepts in the minds of the participants that pervade the presentation and the reception of the communication. The personal worldviews of two persons within the same social group will differ slightly, affecting the communication process in a variety of ways. The worldview differences between members of the same social group will, however, be very small to the differences in worldview between groups. Furthermore, the smaller the number of mutually accepted presuppositions, the greater the difficulty in communicating adequately and effectively between the groups.

Intercultural Communication of Worldview/Religion

Ours is a day when the worldviews of group after group are being subjected to increasing pressure to change. Hundreds of the smaller, previously more isolated societies in the world are coming into intense contact with the naturalistic worldviews spawned within western cultures and are finding their previously satisfactory value systems unequal to the challenge. Western schools, western medicine, western philosophies of government, western economic systems, western individualism and western religion have combined to challenge traditional worldviews —— usually without adequately replacing them with new ones. And the result is, in the words of one Nigerian novelist, "things fall apart." (Achebe 1958).

For, as indicated above, a people's worldview provides for them the integrating core of their culture —— the "glue" that holds all the rest together. And when this core is challenged, called into question and/or held up to ridicule —— when it becomes obvious to the members of the society for which this ideology has provided a "place to feel at home" (Welbourn & Ogot 1966) that their perspective on reality is no longer adequate to cope with things as they are becoming —— the society is in desperate shape. In the words of Clyde Kluckhohn, "a system of beliefs, profoundly felt is unquestionably necessary to the survival of any society,"[8] including our own.

And it is an ironic fact that the most serious challenging of the traditional worldview of a great many of the peoples of the world has come from a variety of western culture that anthropologists must characterize as "profoundly irreligious."[9] For in place of a religious (supernaturalistic) worldview we have adopted a naturalistic "scientism" in combination with a political philosophy that we call "democracy" and an economic philosophy that we call "capitalism." But the fact that we settle for these very shallow substitutes for a "profoundly felt" religion that would provide for our need for "symbolic, expressive and orientative" underpinnings demonstrates impoverishment at the core of our culture. For cross-cultural studies demonstrate that in order to survive

> every culture must define its ends as well as perfect its means. The logical and symbolic expressions of the ultimate values of a civilization cannot arise directly from scientific investigation . . . A mechanistic, materialistic "science" hardly provides the orientations to the deeper problems of life that are essential for happy individuals and a healthy social order. Nor does a political philosophy such as "democracy." Men need tenets that . . . are meaningful to the viscera and the aesthetic sensibilities. They must be symbolized in rites that gratify the heart, please the ear and eye, fulfill the hunger for drama.[10]

Such improverishment seriously cripples a society. And this kind of crippling is a contemporary fact both in our own society and in other societies that, under the influence of western culture, have abandoned their religions. In both situations the way is paved for the communication of new values. For as people become discouraged and demoralized, they lose their will to go on. And

> this process of deterioration can, if not checked, lead to the death of the society. Population may fall even to the point of extinction as a result of increasing death rates and decreasing birth rates; the society may be defeated in war, invaded, its population dispersed and its customs suppressed; factional disputes may nibble away areas and segments of the population.[11]

Or there may be communicated to the disheartened society a new worldview, usually supernaturalistic in focus, around which the society rallies and rebuilds. Such "deliberate, conscious, organized efforts by members of a society to create a more satisfying culture" are termed by Wallace "revitalization movements."[12]

Thus, though many cultures in history have deteriorated to the point of "cultural death," a large number have rebounded and revitalized –– usually around a newly developed or communicated religion. Wallace holds that literally thousands of such occurrences have taken place in history, including a wide variety of nativistic, revivalistic, vitalistic, millenarian and messianic movements both outside of and within western cultures. The origins of Christianity, Islam and possibly Buddhism, as well as of a large proportion of other religious phenomena, are theorized to have been in revitalization movements.[13]

Social breakdown, therefore, provides a fertile setting for the communication of new worldview values (see factors 7, 8, & 12 on the Acceptance-Rejection Chart above). And the possibility of cultural revitalization holds out hope both to societies caught in the downward spiral toward destruction and to those who feel they have a worldview worth communicating. But how is a worldview communicated across cultures?

First of all it must be recognized, as Homer G. Barnett (1953) convincingly points out, (1) that all cultural change is at base the result of changes in ideas, (2) that all cultural changes are initiated by individuals, and (3) that, therefore, the laws of cultural change are psychological laws. "The fundamental condition is the desire or nondesire of a person or a group of persons" with respect to a given recommended change.[14]

Secondly, one must distinguish between the role in worldview change of the acceptor or innovator and that of the advocate of innovation. Though most change is recommended by persons within a culture to others within the culture, the advocate, the person who recommends a change, may come from outside the culture — that is, from another culture. The innovator, the person who actually effects the recommended change, however, is always an insider. It is therefore, the task of any outsider who advocates a change of worldview to convince someone(s) within the culture of the desirability of a change. He must win that person or those persons over to his point of view. He must effectively and winsomely communicate his message to certain acceptors within the culture who will first change their own ideas and then, hopefully, influence others within their culture to change theirs.

To effectively advocate worldview change, it is necessary to employ some very basic principles of communication. Four of these will be dealt with here. They may be labeled: (1) the frame of reference principle, (2) the credibility principle, (3) the specificity principle and (4) the discovery principle (Kraft 1973). These principles relate to each other in a kind of "nesting" manner thus:

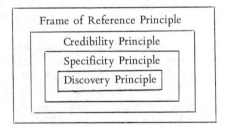

That is, if maximally effective intercultural communication is to take place, the advocate must employ first the frame of reference principle. Having established himself in those terms he then is able to employ the credibility principle and only then the specificity and discovery principles.

The frame of reference principle simply suggests that for intercultural communication of basic concepts to take place the advocate and the potential receptor must share a common frame of reference. Interculturally, this sharing will involve primarily a common understanding of cultural and linguistic categories. The categories can be those of either party but with a different outcome depending on which categories are employed.

If the advocate demands that it be his, rather than the hearer's frame of reference that provide the categories in terms of which the communication takes place, the approach may be labeled "extractionist." The attempt of the advocate, then, is to convert the receptor to his way of thinking —— to teach him to understand and look at reality in the same terms as those of the advocate. Factors 2 and 3 on the Acceptance-Rejection Chart are particularly influential whenever this approach is adopted. If, for example, the advocate's worldview holds that the physical environment is to be viewed as controllable by humans, while the receptor's worldview holds an opposite point of view, the extractionist approach attempts to convert the potential receptor to the advocate's position as pre- or co-requisite to any intercultural transaction. If, then, the culture of the advocate is highly regarded by the potential receptor, while his attitude toward his own culture is ambivalent or negative, the receptor may well agree to the advocate's demands and convert to the latter's worldview.

If, however, an "identificational" attitude is taken, it is the *receptor's* frame of reference that is adopted as that in terms of which the communication takes place. In this approach the advocate becomes familiar with the worldview of the receptor and attempts to fit his communication to the categories and felt needs of that worldview. Factors 12 and 13 on the Acceptance-Rejection Chart particularly influence this approach to the attempt to communicate worldview values across cultures. An advocate employing this approach in attempting to communicate an understanding of God as near and concerned might discover that the potential receptors feel that God has gone far away, having left man helpless and hopeless. The receptors may, however, feel very puzzled and concerned by this understanding of God. The identificational advocate, without denying the receptor's understanding, attempts to "fill in the blank" by communicating that part of his worldview that answers the receptor's felt need. By selecting those elements that most easily relate to the felt needs of the receptor society and that, therefore, most readily fit into their worldview, the advocate of worldview change seeks to lead the receptors into a value system that differs to some extent both from the worldview of the advocate and that of the receptor.

The aims of both identificationists and extractionists may be quite similar — — to lead the receptors into a worldview that the advocate judges to be more satisfying than that previously held by the receptor. Extractionism, however, requires a high degree of indoctrination and a longish period of dependence of the receptor on indoctrination in order to be effective. For the frame of reference in terms of which the communication takes place must be carefully taught. Much Christian missionary effort has adopted this approach in spite of the fact that the major changes that this approach has effected in the worldviews of receptor peoples have proved to be counter to the specifically supernaturalistic religious aims of Christianity. That is, the intercultural advocates of Christianity have typically pressed people toward a scientific, naturalistic, secularistic worldview rather than a Christian supernaturalistic focus.

The identificational approach, however, seems to be more in keeping with the approach of the early Christians. Christ himself, working on an interpersonal though not on intercultural level, seemed to start with the felt needs of his potential receptors, adopting their frame of reference as that in terms of which he operated. The Apostle Paul, then, in keeping with his principle to be Jewish when attempting to communicate with Jews and Greek when attempting to communicate interculturally with Greeks, provides a proto-typical example of an identificational approach (recorded in Acts 17). In speaking to a group of Athenian philosophers he says,

> Men of Athens! I see that in every way you are very
> religious. For as I walked through your city and looked at the

places where you worship, I found also an altar on which is written, 'To an Unknown God.' That which you worship, then, even though you do not know it, is what I now proclaim to you.[15]

Once the frame of reference is established, however, the remaining three principles here to be dealt with come into play. Within any given frame of reference predictabilities with regard to expected roles develop which combine to produce stereotypes. An outsider advocating worldview change who simply conforms to stereotyped expectations operates at a low degree of credibility, since what he says and does is so predictable in terms of the receptors's stereotype. If, however, what he says and does is not predictable in terms of the stereotypic expectations of the potential receptors, the communication value of his message and his overall credibility is increased. If, for example, the intercultural communicator of new worldview values is a missionary who simply conforms to the people's stereotype of what a missionary should act like, the communication value of his activity is slight. If, however, he acts unpredictably in terms of the stereotype, while at the same time attempting to act intelligibly within the potential receptor's frame of reference, his credibility, the communication value of his message, and the potential for its acceptance are all increased. By thus identifying with the potential receptors of worldview change and acting credibly (i.e. unpredictably in terms of the stereotype), have hundreds of missionaries and others both endeared themselves to their hearers and effectively communicated their worldviews to people all over the world.

The third of these principles of effective intercultural communication of core values relates to the specificity to human experience with which the advocate presents his message. In general, the more specific a communication is to the real life of a receptor within his frame of reference, the greater the impact of the message. Yet human commonality is apparently such that even across cultural barriers interpersonal identification is possible at many points where human experience is quite similar. An intercultural communication phrased in terms specific to the receptor's culture is, of course, more readily grasped than one phrased in terms of generalizations, since real life or true to life accounts carry greater impact than generalizations. Even life-specific accounts of events in cultures other than that of the receptor often carry great impact. This fact probably explains why, even after thousands of years, the casebook-like, life-specific accounts in the Bible and certain other religious books produce such an impact even upon cultures widely different from those of the Bible actors. Perhaps it is at this life-specific level that, even though separated by great cultural differences, "people are more alike than cultures."[16]

Though the first three of these principles all relate primarily to the activity of the advocate of worldview change, the fourth relates primarily to the potential receptor. This principle suggests that communicational effectiveness is heightened considerably if the receptor has the impression that the new information or insight has come to him via his own discovery, rather than as the result of his being told something by an outsider. The able communicator, then, seeks to lead potential receptors to the discovery of both the substance and the value of his understandings rather than to simply provide for them "prefabricated" alternatives to their present understandings.

This principle does not mean that the advocate of worldview change refrains from proclaiming his message. On the contrary, he speaks as persuasively as possible, employing the above-described principles as completely as possible but in a non-coercive manner. He recognizes that the determinative role in the communication of worldview change is that of the acceptor rather than that of the advocate. It is the acceptor-innovator alone who can make the recommended changes in his own worldview. And everything depends upon his feeling that whatever change he makes is on the basis of his own choice, rather than because of outside coercion. Discovery, then, is the process within the acceptor's mind by means of which he comes to understand the relevance to him of the communication and begins to apply the new insights to his own felt needs. Millions of members of tribal societies are in this way discovering for themselves the relevance for them of parts at least of the ideologies of world religions such as Islam and Christianity concerning which they receive communications from out-culture advocates. Such discovery not infrequently provides the kind of emotional potency necessary for the initiation of the religious revitalization movements referred to above and described by Wallace (1956).

Conclusion

In briefly surveying worldview factors in intercultural communication we first assessed the position and functions of worldview in culture. In this assessment we concluded that a people's worldview is central to their culture and that it serves at least five important functions for them. These functions have been labeled: explanatory, evaluational, reinforcing, integrating and adaptive.

Secondly, we have dealt with a list of thirteen factors characteristic of worldviews that play important parts in the intercultural acceptance or rejection of new worldview values. These factors are listed in chart form above and need not be recapitulated here.

Lastly, we have turned our attention to how intercultural communication of worldview values is most effectively carried out. We noted first the widespread fact of such communication and the destructive consequences to societies who discover that the new values that they are accepting are bankrupt, leading to demoralization and social disintegration rather than to the utopia they had hoped for. Such a process of disintegration is, however, frequently reversed by a religion-centered revitalization movement. Finally, we suggested four important principles of communication available to those who feel that they possess worldview values that they would like to communicate interculturally. These principles have been labeled the frame of reference principle, the credibility principle, the specificity principle, and the discovery principle.

FOOTNOTES

[1] See a good introductory text on anthropology for a discussion of this point. Hiebert 1976, Keesing & Keesing 1971, Bock 1968, and Beals & Hoijer 1965 are recommended.

[2] R.M. Keesing and F.M. Keesing, *New Perspectives in Cultural Anthropology* (New York: Holt, Rinehart and Winston, 1971), p. 303.

[3] C. Geertz, "Religion as a Cultural System," in Banton, M., 1966.

[4] A.F.C. Wallace, *Religion: An Anthropological View* (New York: Random House, 1966), p. 27.

[5] *Ibid.*, p. 29.

[6] *Ibid.*

[7] A.L. Kroeber, *Anthropology* (New York: Harcourt, Brace and World, 1948), pp. 503-8.

[8] C. Kluckhohn, *Mirror for Man* (New York: McGraw-Hill, 1949), p. 248.

[9] *Ibid.*

[10] *Ibid.*, pp. 248-9.

[11] A.F.C. Wallace, "Revitalization Movements," *American Anthropologist*, 58, pp. 264-81.

[12] *Ibid.*, p. 279.

[13] *Ibid.*, p. 267, p. 279.

[14] Homer G. Barnett, *Innovation: The Basis of Cultural Change* (New York: McGraw-Hill, 1953) p. 61.

[15] Acts of the Apostles, *The New Testament in Today's English Version* (New York: The American Bible Society, 1966, 1971) 17:22, 23.

[16] W. Goldschmidt, *Comparative Functionalism* (Berkeley: University of California Press, 1966) p. 134.

* A previous version of this chapter was published in *Missiology* 2:295-312, 1974, under the title *"Ideological Factors in Intercultural Communication."*

BIBLIOGRAPHY

Achebe, Chinua, *Things Fall Apart*, Heinemann, London, 1958.

Acts of the Apostles, *The New Testament in Today's English Version.* American Bible Society, New York, 1966, 1971.

Banton, M., ed., *Anthropological Approaches to the Study of Religion, ASA Monographs 3.* Tavistock, London, 1966.

Barnett, Homer G., *Innovation: The Basis of Cultural Change*, McGraw-Hill , New York, 1953.

Beals, R.L. & H. Hoijer, *An Introduction to Anthropology*, third edition, MacMillan, New York, 1965.

Berkowitz, M.I., & J.E. Johnson, *Social Scientific Studies of Religion: A Bibliography*, University of Pittsburg Press, 1967.

Bock, P.K., *Modern Cultural Anthropology*, Alfred A. Knopf, New York, 1968.

Evans-Pritchard, E.E., *Theories of Primitive Religion,* Oxford, London, 1965.

Geertz, C., "Religion as a Cultural System," in Banton, M., 1966.

Goldschmidt, W., *Comparative Functionalism,* University of California Press, Berkeley, 1966.

Hesselgrave, D.J., "Dimensions of Crosscultural Communication," *Practical Anthropology* 19: 1-12, 1972.

Hiebert, P., *Cultural Anthropology*, Philadelphia, Lippincott, 1976.

Horton, R., "The Kalabari World-View," *Africa* 32: 197-220, 1962; "African Traditional Thought and Western Science," *Africa* 37: 50-71, 155-87, 1967; "African Conversion," *Africa* 41: 85-108, 1971.

Keesing, R.M. & F.M., *New Perspectives in Cultural Anthropology*, Holt, Rinehart, Winston, New York, 1971.

Kluckhohn, C., *Mirror for Man*, McGraw-Hill, New York, 1949.

Kraft, C.H., "Christian Conversion or Cultural Conversion," *Practical Anthropology* 10: 179-87, 1963; "The Incarnation, Cross-Cultural Communication and Communication Theory," *Evangelical Missions Quarterly* 9: 277-84, 1973.

Kroeber, A.L., *Anthropology*, Harcourt, Brace & World, New York, 1948.

Lessa, W.A. & E.Z. Vogt, *Reader in Comparative Religion*, Harper & Row, New York, 1958, 1965, 1972.

Luzbetak, L.J., *The Church & Cultures,* Divine Word Publications, Techny, Illinois, 1963, 1970.

Majumdar, D.N., *Caste & Communication in an Indian Village,* Asia Publishing House, Bombay, 1958.

McCormack, W., "The Forms of Communication in Virataiva Religion," *Journal of American Folklore* 71: 325-35, 1958.

Middleton, J., ed., *Gods and Rituals,* Natural History Press, Garden City, New York, 1967.

Nida, E.A., *Message & Mission,* Harper, New York & William Carey, South Pasadena, California, 1960, 1971; *Religion Across Cultures,* Harper & Row, New York, 1968; *Communication of the Gospel in Latin America,* Centro Intercultural de Documentacion, Cuenavaca, Mexico, 1969.

Oliver, R.T., *Culture & Communication,* C.C. Thomas, Springfield, Illinois, 1962.

Reyburn, W.D., "Christianity & Ritual Communication," *Practical Anthropology* 10: 145-59, 1963.

Samovar, L.A. & R.E. Porter, *Intercultural Communication: A Reader,* Wadsworth Publishing Company, Belmont, California, 1972, 1976.

Stowe, E.M., *Communicating Reality Through Symbols,* Westminster Press, Philadelphia, 1966.

Turner, H.W., *Profile Through Preaching,* Edinburgh House Press, London, 1965.

Wallace, A.F.C., "Revitalization Movements"*American Anthropologist* 58: 264-81, 1956; *Religion: An Anthropological View,* Random House, New York, 1966.

Welbourn, F.B. & B.A. Ogot, *A Place to Feel at Home,* Oxford, London, 1966.

Wonderly, W.L. & E.A. Nida, "Cultural Differences & The Communication of Christian Values," *Practical Anthropology* 10: 241-8, 1963.

Edmund S. Glenn:

Politics: An Intercultural View

———————

THE culture of a population can be defined as the sum total of the meanings shared by that population. Although such a definition is not complete, it is sufficient to suggest that analyses of meaning can be used as partial steps in the analysis of cultures. This includes the political cultures of the populations concerned.

It must be noted at the outset that analyses of this type cannot be complete. Political behavior, and behavior in general, is determined by multiple causes. In particular, the political culture of a complex population cannot fully determine the actual political actions undertaken by the political unit encompassing such a population; for example, specific information available to the political leaders but not to the population as a whole may exercise a dominant influence in specific situations. Nevertheless the analysis of political culture (as a part of the culture in general) can lead to an understanding of an important factor in the determination of political behavior.

A Tripartite Model of Meaning

The analysis below is based on a model of analysis of meaning developed by Glenn.[1]

Linguistic meaning is conceived as determined by three divergent and mutually incompatible requirements in mutual tension among themselves. Few instances of actual expressions can be considered as pure cases; most are influenced by all three of the requirements, though to different degrees in each case. An explication of the three requirements in their purity should not be taken for the description of any particular population, but rather as the presentation of a tool for the analyst. The three requirements are presented below as the apexes of a triangle:

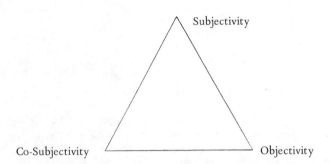

1.   *Subjectivity* stands for the need of the individual to express his personal experiences. Such experiences are ineffable in the last analysis. Thus pure subjectivity amounts to a solipsistic use of meaning, and has no communicative value. It is reasonable, however, to assume that small groups of people having shared much of the experience of their lives also share many relatively intimate meanings. Viewed in the context of the Parson—Shils pattern variables,[2] such meanings are likely to be:

   a.   Particularistic. An in-group is what comes the closest to the particularity of an individual.
   b.   Ascription-oriented. Virtues tend to be ascribed to members of the in-group, vices to members of out-groups.[3]
   c.   From the point of view of collective orientation — — self-orientation, the apex indicates deep involvement in a relatively small group. This is definitely anti-individualistic, except for a group leader endowed with sufficient charisma to be accepted by the group as its spokesman. It may be said to be collective-oriented, as long as it is understood that the collectivity involved is relatively narrow.
   d.   Diffuse. There is no need to specify precise meanings of words when those who converse share extensive experience. A word or gesture may usher in a train of shared associations. As long as the core of such associations is shared, their precise boundaries matter little and are likely not to be precisely known to the participants themselves.

e. Affective. Common belonging and loyalty to common traditions are sources of feeling and emotion, particularly when threatened from the outside.

2. *Co-subjectivity*. Co-subjectivity stands for the need of every code used in communication for the stability of the meanings of its symbols both in time and across the subjects using the code. A perfectly co-subjective situation would be one in which the meaning of symbols would never change, and would be shared identically by all possible subjects. An example of a symbolic system which comes closely to the ideal is mathematics. From the point of view of the sharing of experience, high co-subjectivity means the sharing by many subjects of many relatively inextensive portions of experience, each of which can be precisely defined to make such sharing possible.

The contrast between subjectivity and co-subjectivity is well described by Northrop[4] who notes that the wisdom of the East is transmitted by discipleship, in which master and disciple live together in a manner which makes it possible for the latter to share in the behavior of the former; in contrast the knowledge of the West is transmitted mainly by written words with precisely defined meanings.

Viewed in the context of the Parsons–Shils pattern variables, co-subjective meanings are likely to be:

a. Universalistic. The purpose of a co-subjective code is to maximize the possibility of mutual communication for the participants.
b. Achievement-oriented. Where subjectivity is lived, co-subjectivity is taught. Learning each of its portions is an achievement.
c. Collectively-oriented. The symbols constituting codes cannot be defined in isolation; each code constitutes a system, and each system of meanings constitutes a doctrine. Sharing a doctrine amounts to participating in a collectivity.
d. Specific. To be shared by many, the meaning of each symbol must be defined with precision.
e. Affectively neutral. Precise definition is antithetical to emotion.

3. *Objectivity* stands for the correspondence between concepts and referents. The latter are taken in the sense of verifiable

operations satisfying the criteria of the physical or the social sciences.

Search for objectivity implies frequent departures from symbol stability. This is particularly evident in the physical sciences: Kuhn, among others, has shown that science develops not through the accumulation of bits of knowledge but through a series of revolutions consisting in conceptual reformulations of the world—view.[5] The effect of such revolutions upon meaning is to modify the groups sharing the same objective interpretations. At the same time objective criteria of verification eliminate (at least in the ideal) the elements of randomness which characterize subjective experiences and the meanings attached to them, as well as the elements of arbitrary conventionality which are compatible with co-subjectivity.

From the point of view of the Parsons—Shils pattern variables, objectivity implies:

a. Potential universalism and effective particularism. Understanding based on scientific or operational criteria is potentially universal, since it is based on operations —— for example, experiments —— which should be identical regardless of the person performing them. However, operations (whether they be connected with scientific research or with commercial enterprises) are time consuming. As a result common understanding is likely to be restricted to common competence, and the symbolic system is likely to be subdivided into specialized jargons or codes.

b. Achievement. Even more clearly than in the case of co-subjectivity understanding is tied to competence.

c. Self-orientation. Even though the collectivity may profit from the activities of individuals or of small groups handling a portion of the objective universe, action upon objects is in the last analysis an individual affair.

d. Specificity. This point as the next one is obvious.

e. Affective neutrality.

Some Aspects of Social Organization and of Political Cultures at the Three Apexes

Once again it must be emphasized that in the quasi totality of cases, shared meanings reflect the influences of all three requirements. However, the dominance of one or another mode of thinking results in tendencies towards corresponding patterns of thought and behavior.

Subjective orientation. Communication in the subjective mode is dominated by the sharing of extensive areas of experience among the participants. This suggests either (a) relatively small communities, or (b) strongly entrenched traditions, or (c) intense common experiences sweeping through populations which may be numerous.

All three possibilities, but particularly (a) and (b) suggest that the social organization will be that of a *Gemeinschaft* rather than that of a *Gesellschaft*.[6] *Gemeinschaft* stands for a human *community* with closely shared traditions making for stereotyped behaviors immediately recognized as acceptable or not acceptable. Explicitly stated prohibitions or encouragement are unnecessary, since everybody thinks and behaves automatically according to his position within the closely knit community. Even where the population concerned is numerous, the image of the community is still that of the small group in which "there is no anonimity. Everybody is personally known to everybody else, and this in itself makes for very effective social control."[7] The world (and particularly the political world) is seen in terms of the in-group vs. out-groups, of friendships and enmities.

Gesellschaft stands for the organized *society*, ruled by law rather than by men. What the law prohibits and what it permits is specifically stated; in areas not covered by public laws, private contracts are defined in the law's image. Social control is exercised by specifically defined institutions and by the internalization of abstract values — for example of a type of honesty which applies alike to friends, foes, and those one doesn't even know. The individual is largely anonymous, except when some specific actions on his part appear as either condemnable or meritorious in the context of social rules.

The conditions described under (c) are those which favor the emergence of charismatic leadership. It should be noted that such leadership tends to strengthen the *Gemeinschaft* characteristics of societies which have reached the *Gesellschaft* stage of organization: Nazism provides a perfect example.

As it was noted above, subjective orientation in meaning and communication emphasizes the distinction between an in-group sharing the common experiences on which mutual understanding is based, and out-groups to which such experiences are alien. The mechanisms by which experience is shared are likely to be those of purely existential/historical randomness: subjective orientation implies the absence of either the co-subjective tendency to define terms broadly and rationally, or the objective tendency towards a determination of terms on the basis of observable reality. It follows that what is probably the most important trait of subjective orientation is irrationality, and in many cases even anti—rationalism.

It may be convenient to examine the possible effects of a subjective orientation towards meaning and world view depending on the size of the populations concerned. Three levels may be conveniently distinguished:

a. *Groupings smaller than the state.* This is the level of familism or tribalism, which appear as obstacles to nation building —— or rather to state building. It is also the level of the struggle within a state between a dominant ethnic or religious group and ethnic or religious minority.

The question of the viability of pluralistic societies can be examined within the context of this level. Briefly, ethnic pluralism can be tolerated if it is confined to areas which do not impinge upon the main bases of social and political solidarity. In a country such as the United States this means to a large extent that ethnic particularisms must be confined to such things as culinary preferences and folk traditions remote from the main aspects of political, juridical and economic life of the country as a whole. Particularisms extending into the main areas of common national (or state) actions will not be tolerated for long: it is perfectly acceptable for a judge of Italian descent to eat pasta, but not to follow the Philosophy of Roman Law in preference to that of English Common Law.

b. *Groupings coinciding with the state or with a potential state.* This is mainly the field of nationalism.

Nationalism does not necessarily strengthen the loyalty of the population concerned toward the "nation—state"; on the contrary, it may be subversive in respect to it. For example, in World War II most of the collaborators with the Nazis —— and thus traitors towards their own states —— were recruited from among extreme nationalists. Glenn[8] has shown that the meanings entering into the feeling of nationhood belong to the subjective mode. In contradistinction "state" is a concept tied with the theories and practices of public administration; as such it belongs to both the co-subjective and the objective modes. The two may coincide in their objects or contents, but the difference in the patterns of thought, logic, belief and behavior required by each are sufficiently great to cause antagonism, at least in the context of many political conflicts. Where such antagonism surfaces, nationalists may be willing to strengthen the influence of their subjective world view over the nationalistic world view of a state-directed public administration, even at a cost to the complex entity which we call the "nation—state."

A few examples of the psycho-logic of subjective nationalism may be to the point:

> If western Europe, international in mind and tendency, looks upon civilization as a system of ways and behavior and spiritual ideas that are humane and susceptible of universal application, the Germans understand by Kultur an intimate union between themselves and the natural forces of the Universe, whose action they alone are capable of apprehending, and as a tribal discipline designed to turn those forces into account. Fichte insisted that only the Germans know the method of realizing this intimate union . . . They, Fichte reminded them, are the 'primaeval people' (Ur—Volk) who speak the primaeval, aboriginal tongue (Ur—Sprache) which gives them contact with the forces of Nature. Therefore, German minds return more easily than those of the other nations to the instincts and concepts of the primitive world from which "the West," under the joint influences of Classical thought and of Christianity, has sought to escape. From Fichte to Hitler . . . the line runs straight.[9]

Or again:

> After the Franco—Prussian War of 1870, *Grenzboten*, the influential weekly magazine of German 'national liberals' stated: 'It is easier to accept the smooth superficiality of French civilization in spite of its inner corruption than to appreciate properly the depth of the German spirit. This has shown that in essentials Germany

can never hope to be understood by other people than those of German blood.' These words typify volumes of proto—Nazi thought in their contrast of civilization's 'superficiality' and 'corruption' with Kultur's subconscious 'depth' and 'blood.'[10]

c.   *Groupings broader than the state.* Major cultural upheavals may result in experiences common to people dispersed over very wide geographical areas. In the XIXth and XXth Centuries the impact of the Western cultures on the non—Western world resulted in widespread de—traditionalization or de—culturation. The theme of being suspended between two cultures and at home in neither of them, is extremely widespread in the literature of former colonies or dealing with former colonies.

Even though the traditional cultures from which the participants   in the experience   of partial   Westernization have become estranged are very different among themselves, de—culturation accompanied by partial acculturation to the West constitute a shared experience for many of the leaders of the Third World. Such a shared experience has led to shared political attitudes, based primarily on a resentment against the source of the cultural malaise of those concerned. This resentment tends to overtake policies dictated by more pragmatic considerations and to lead to policies based on anti-Western feelings. An expression of such political attitudes can be found in the recent history of the United Nations.

Again, a few quotations may serve as illustrations. The ones to   follow   are taken from the minutes of the Second Congress of Negro Writers and Artists, which met in Rome from March 26 to April 1, 1959, as published by *Presence Africaine.*

First, a voice of moderation:

> Our presence in Rome, as earlier our choice of the
> Sorbonne as our meeting place, has a clear meaning: a
> testimony of gratitude, an expression of respect for this
> beautiful [Western] culture . . .
> But it is no less true to say: if such are, indeed, our
> feelings, they do not suffice, they point out only one side

of the complex reality of our intellectual lives; they leave in the dark the other half, which, for being the more secret of the two, is not necessarily either the poorer or the less genuine . . .

It is that, that unclear and mysterious feeling, which will always mark the difference between our Western colleagues and us: they will never know the torment and the tearing of which we feel the bite, because they will never need to know the tension which we feel and which stems from our loyalty to our original belonging and to our ties to their culture . . .

From the Carribean to the Indian Ocean, from Sao-Paulo to Leopoldville, we have that in common . . .

This, then, is our tragedy. The tragedy of a consciousness under pressure, subject to a constant pull in two directions. Culturally French, ontologically Malgassy, my personality runs the risk of wasting its strength in this constant struggle, of being broken by the burden of a paradox, of disintegrating under the shock of my ambivalence.[11]

A more extreme expression of similar feelings can be found in the late Patrice Lamumba's protest against "the nefarious policy of assimilation and integration which has reduced Africans to the status of men without motherlands (*apatrides*)."[12]

Or again:

One of the tasks derives from the needs of our peoples to escape assimilation, to become de—Westernized so as to prevent the strangling of the spirit proper to us. This tendency towards de—Westernization, easily observable in our countries, from Madagascar to Haiti, from Timbuctu to Johannesburg, from Nigeria to Kenya, is aimed simultaneously at institutions, hierarchies, the authorities in the field of resources as well as of expression, ethnic references, and historical values. Of course, it is not for the sole pleasure of de—Westernization. We are decided to keep the gifts of the West, on the

condition of using them according to our genius and our
situations . . . [13]

The question is whether the products of a culture can be
retained without the patterns of thought which made such
products possible. In the opinion of this author, they cannot.

Polities dominated by subjective associationism are likely to be
non—aggressive culturally, but are frequently aggressive politically
(which often also means militarily). Patterns of culture based mainly
on shared traditions have in most cases little appeal to those for
whom such traditions are alien; moreover participants in the culture
often feel that only those sharing a common ancestry can really
participate in a common culture. Thus subjectivism does not seek
converts: hence its cultural non—aggressiveness.

At the same time there is little in subjectivism which can be
used as basis for conflict resolution. Subjectively oriented groupings
in conflict situations tend to take the attitude that they are totally
right and that their enemies are totally wrong. As it was pointed out
earlier, the in—group — out—group opposition is extremely strong.
Hence the political and at times military aggressiveness of
nationalisms.

It should be noted that this tendency towards violence
characterizes subjective politics not only in international but also in
domestic affairs. In the latter case aggressiveness is directed toward
domestic groups which do not share in the particular loyalties of the
subjective groups. Examples can be found in the rise of Nazism in
Germany, and in the attitudes of extreme right wing groups and also
in the New Left elsewhere. The literature tying such social
movements to subjective anti—rationalism is very rich; we might
mention Babbitt,[14] Viereck,[15] Kohn,[16] Stern,[17] Cassirer,[18]
Horowitz,[19] Lipset and Raab[20] and Glenn.[21]

Co—Subjective orientation. The subjective orientation
amounted to a tendency to restrict communication, or at least full
communication, to in—groups determined by commonality of
experience, or according to many of its practitioners by blood
kinship. Co—subjectivity amounts to attempts at broadening
communication, potentially to all mankind and practically to those
who accept a common system of thought. This orientation is derived
from the need to organize meanings into a stable system. Such a
system unavoidably amounts to the description of a world view, i.e.

the determination of a system of truth or belief, or again of a doctrine, to be shared by all the co—participants in the communicative system. In its political aspect, this amounts to the active propagation of a dogma, assumed to be potentially applicable to all of mankind.

An illustration of the difference between subjective and co—subjective attitudes may be found in the non—missionary and non—exclusive behavior of most Eastern religions, as opposed to the missionary and exclusive behavior of Christianity and of Islam. Each of these, when at the height of their influences, determined supra—political entities which maintained a large extent of inner solidarity in spite of inner divisions and disputes.

In the contemporary political world examples of supra—state dogmatic systems may be found in Marxism and in the concept of a "free world" as exemplified by the policies of John Foster Dulles. The latter named was much more ephemeral than the former, probably because the tendencies of the Western countries towards objective orientation and the tendencies of the non—Western non—Marxist countries towards subjective orientation made both of these groups of countries unwilling or unable to yield their individualities to a common dogma.

Another important characteristic of the co—subjective orientation is its unavoidable elitism. It is an elite which defines a communicative system capable of transcending the limitations of subjectivism (whether the latter be parochial tribalism or the sharing of a charismatic experience). A system capable of transcending such limitations must be codified, and only a specialized elite can watch over actual usage, to make it conform to the code.

An example dealing with a very moderate reformer, Confucius, may set the tone:

> Tseu—lu said to Confucius: 'The Lord of Wei intends to place the government in your hands. What do you consider the first thing to be done?' 'The main thing is to correct the use of titles,' answered the master. And he added: 'If the titles are not correct, words cannot conform to truth; if words do not conform to truth, the affairs (of state) have no success . . . That the Wise Man commit no error in his words, that is sufficient.' [22]

The result was the mandarinate system, probably the most successful system of intellectual elitism in history.

Where Confucius was a moderate, Plato was an extremist. The political consequence of his attempts at codifying all knowledge was the elitism of the Guardians. Even though neither the *Republic* nor the *Laws* were ever implemented, their influence on Western civilization was immense.

A more contemporary example may be to the point:

> . . . although the Cuban elite makes the decisions and dictates the time of change, it is the Cuban masses who must re—order their belief systems and their lives in the service of the revolution . . .
>
> It is this effort to create a new Cuban man, a man equal to the tasks set for him by revolutionary elite . . . that . . . is at the heart of Cuban radicalism . . . [23]

Theoretically, a co—subjective system should be monolithic. In practice, differences between the cultural conditions of countries participating in the system weaken its centripetal tendencies and make full uniformity impossible. Deviations appear, and since the system has no place for legitimate deviations, those departures from orthodoxy which cannot be repressed are labelled heresies. The Great Schism of Christianity and the present state of Russian—Chinese relations are examples. Since both heretics and outright infidels are considered embodiments of evil, with whom one should entertain relations only under the pressure of necessity, sudden reversals of alliances are to be expected. Examples may be found in the relationship between the Western and the Eastern branches of Christianity at the time of the Crusades, or closer to home in those between the Socialist and the Communist parties, or between Yugoslavia and the Soviet Union on the one hand and the Western countries on the other.

Co—subjective politics are likely to be aggressive both culturally and politically. The culture finds its expression in a dogma, and the principal duty of the state is to defend and to propagate this dogma. This results in aggressiveness at both levels.

An internal consequence of the co—subjective state of mind is a tendency towards centralization. If a set of principles is considered right, it should be implemented everywhere. Such centralization calls for the development of a strong bureaucracy, and parallel with it of a political or religious elite recruited among those having a full understanding of the dogmatic system.

Objective orientation. Subjective communication is based on the sharing of largely personal imagery, made possible by the sharing of common experiences. Co—subjectivity seeks to broaden participation in a communicative system: it defines broadly applicable symbolic relations, and it is the learning of such symbolic relations which constitutes the sharing of experience which makes communication possible. Objective orientation finds co—subjective communication insufficiently precise to deal with the technicalities involved in the solution of specific problems. This calls for a narrowing of meanings, not (as in the case of high subjectivity) through the narrowing of the human group concerned to what is allowed by shared ethnicity, but through the reduction of meanings to the description of the technicalities of actions. Thus objective orientation is derived from the need to subordinate the universality of meaning to the diversity of objective situations.[24] The diversity of human goals, coupled with the diversity of the circumstances under which such goals can be sought, leads to pragmatic attitudes in which reason is considered only as a tool for making hypotheses the values of which can be established only by success in action.

Probably the purest example of the objective orientation can be found in the free enterprise system, and also in the *ad hoc* legislation by which this system was modified where it did not perform satisfactorily. In fact, the expression "ad hoc" can be considered a leitmotiv of the objective orientation —— together with "crossing bridges when one comes to them" and "muddling through."

One of the consequences of the corresponding state of mind is decentralization: No solution is considered having universal validity; problems should be solved on the basis of the particular circumstances which define them. In the place of the single bureaucracy characteristic of the co—subjective approach, the objectives approach favors numerous mutually competing bureaucracies. In the place of an annointed elite of "guardians of truth," it favors a multiplicity of types of experts.

The impression made by the strongly objective culture of the United States on a member of the more co—subjective French culture may serve as an illustration:

There is in Russia a ruling ideology which fashions the economic and the political realities; there are in France or in Italy ideologies confronting one another. Nothing of the sort in the United States . . . One of the things which is the most disconcerting for a foreigner is the lack of something he could understand within [American] politics. The Frenchman naturally seeks to find a right and a left . . . However, at a different level, that of particular problems and of local business, political life is vigorous: the real political questions in the United States concern urban renewal, the incorporation of new suburbs, school administration . . .

From one point of view, this is tragic: no overall planning, no overall conceptualization . . . From another point of view, it is hopeful: through patience, good will, social spirit, solutions are found . . . [25]

Another illustration may be provided by American and Soviet attitudes in disarmament negotiations.

The basic American attitude in those negotiations is that only a treaty capable of controlled implementation is worth signing. As it is quite clear that the Soviets would never agree to on the spot inspection, the crucial point in most cases is to determine the extent of inspection which could be carried out at a distance. In consequence, the core of the negotiations in the eyes of Americans are feasibility studies. American delegations include numerous experts in all pertinent fields, awaiting the opportunity to examine every proposal from the technical point of view.

In contradistinction, Soviet delegations include only minimal expert staffs. The core of the negotiation in their eyes was the definition of political principles. A few quotes illustrate their attitude and their reactions to the American approach:

Indeed, we cannot seriously and effectively consider other parts and articles of the treaty before reaching agreement on principle on the basic parts of Article I, which defines the overall scope of general and complete disarmament . . . It should be clear to everyone that, before we set about agreeing on procedure, priority and methods of implementing various disarmament measures, we must settle what we understand by general and complete disarmament . . .

We propose that the discussions of technical details should be deferred until such time as we have agreed between

442

ourselves on the fundamental, basic principles that would underlie a final agreement . . . We do not intend to allow a smokescreen of technical studies to be used as a cover by those who wish to evade a solution of the political question of banning all nuclear weapons tests . . .

We are gathered here to consider a political problem. But the United States delegation is making an attempt to divert the attention of the Committee from the basic issues and is striving to get us involved in a discussion of controversies going on among scientists.[26]

Objectively oriented politics are seldom aggressive politically: except in cases where strong specific interests may be served by an expansionist attitude, they have little motivation to seek converts. They do not feel that it may be their duty towards truth (co—subjective), or their duty towards their honor (subjective) to behave aggressively. Moreover their pragmatic orientation makes them cost—conscious and capable of understanding non—zero—sum situations. However, they tend to be culturally aggressive: their ability to solve problems which others also must confront, and their ability to produce goods, tend to seduce individuals belonging to other cultures away from their subjective traditions or their co—subjective dogmas.[27]

Syntheses

All three requirements of meaning are operative at all times — — but not to the same extent. The result of their interplay is often a synthesis, a form of behavior (political or other) which can be explained by neither of the apexes taken in isolation. A few examples will be presented below.

Democracy. A form of democracy is compatible with a subjective orientation, as long as the polities concerned are small and culturally uniform. In such contexts discussion as to the course of action to follow may be opened to the entire population (or, more often, to the entire male population). The aim of the discussion is to divine the right portents dictated by tradition or by the supernatural; discussion proceeds by allusions and hints until a consensus emerges. Such a consensus is not based on pragmatic considerations; rather, it constitutes a diagnosis of the nature of the total situation. Once the sense of the community is voiced, total endorsement is required from all: opposition is construed as impious. There is no question of a majority and a minority retaining full rights to public respect. Examples may be found in the functioning of village councils in South and South—East Asia. It is, of course, questionable whether a participatory regime based on the principle of unanimity rather than on that of majority should be called democracy.

Whatever be the answer to this question, democracy and a subjective orientation appear at loggerheads in more complex societies. A subjective polity is based on shared and *often subconscious* common experiences, forming the basis of a Rousseau'ist type of general will. Outsiders are excluded —— whether they be ethnic minorities even if legally endowed with full citizenship, or natives considered as renegades —— because they have espoused different patterns of thought.

Likewise, democracy is antithetical to co—subjectivity. The point of view of the latter is that the *right* answers to all questions can be derived from the application of the proper doctrine —— as it is the case in mathematics. Within such a frame of reference weighing individual preferences is simply silly. What counts is convincing the deviants by a proper application of dialectical reasoning.

Democracy (at least in the modern and Western sense of the word) finds its source in objectivism. Since reason can serve only to establish hypotheses and the resolution of conflicting points of view can be obtained only *ex post facto* by experience, it is reasonable to let the different interested parties exercise their *influence* on the form of action which will be tried out first.[28]

Thus objective orientation provides the necessary basis for democracy. However, this basis is not sufficient: the degree of influence of the participants varies. The principle of equal and universal suffrage amounts usually to a denial of objective conditions and can be introduced only through co-subjective rationalism (or perhaps dogmatism). Interestingly enough, the countries which were the first to move in the direction of what evolved into modern democracy, were also among the last to institute universal and equalitarian suffrage: in Britain, alumni of some of the universities had the privilege of voting twice up to 1946, in Switzerland women are still largely excluded, and in the United States blacks could not vote in many states until 1965.

Thus democracy appears to be a synthesis between an objectivistic thesis and a co—subjectivistic anthithesis.

It is not, of course, fully devoid of subjectivistic elements. Living in a democratic society is an experience, and those who have shared it tend to adopt the subjective point of view that all that is democratic is holy, and all that is not democratic is evil. This is particularly true in the United States (excluding to a large extent the South which has few foreign born) as it is the only experience common to citizens of various ethnic stocks. However, subjectivistic attitudes are relatively weak in democracies; furthermore they may be further weakened by ethnic subjectivism in countries having democratic regimes but dominated by the one ethnic group or suffering from conflict between ethnic groups.[29] One of the consequences of this weakness of subjectivistic elements in democracy is the relative lack of cohesiveness of democracies in the international arena, particularly as compared with the political attitudes dominated by common co—subjective doctrines or common subjective feelings.

Political parties. The terminology surrounding political partisanship is fairly similar in countries with very different cultures. This element of commonality may be interpreted as an element of intercultural communication entering into the similar conceptualization of very different organizations.

In predominantly subjectivistic cultures (including the Old South of the United States), belonging to a party is often more of an affirmation of self—identity than of a channel for specific political action. As a matter of fact the entire approach to partisanship is diffuse and associative rather than specific and abstractive. Parties are often based on ethnic belonging (in which case membership means being *truly and faithfully* an ethnic), on family tradition, or on loyalty to a charismatic leader. The tendency to single party polities is strong.

In polities with a strong co—subjective orientation, parties are considered as channels for promoting specific ideologies. From the point of view of their number, this means either a multiplicity of parties (as many as there are ideological nuances) or a single party (once triumphant, the party which personifies truth in its own eyes suppresses those which promote error).

In polities with a strong objective orientation, parties are considered as frameworks for the working out of alliances among those willing to trade favors in order to gain some specific goals. The number of parties tends towards two umbrella organizations, often bringing together people with divergent opinions but converging interests.

International alliances. Subjectively oriented polities see alliances in the image of friendship, in which friend helps friend regardless of the particular circumstances in which aid is required. Objectively oriented polities consider alliances as contracts; these must be fulfilled regardless of affective considerations but nothing beyond contractual obligations is required from the allies.

An example of misunderstanding due to such divergent attitudes in the present state of Turkish—American relations. Turkey felt that its alliance with the United States entitled it to friendly support in the Cyprus dispute; the United States viewed this dispute as falling outside the contract of a defensive alliance against the Soviet Union, and as a nuisance which might interfere with Turkey's and Greece's ability to fulfill their contractual obligations in NATO. The result was a marked change in Turkish attitude towards the United States, which, contrarily to what was the case before the dispute, is extremely unpopular among Turks.

As for polities with a co—subjective orientation, alliances are understood as being expressions of the natural solidarity of those who share the same principles. As such they are deemed to be permanent and unlimited in their content. Alliances with non—participants in the ideology are viewed as temporary accommodations —— at best.

Form and Content

Analyses of meaning lead to hypotheses bearing on the habitual cognitive styles characteristic of given political cultures. They say nothing about the content of any particular political situation. The latter is likely to be determinant in the specific choices selected in many specific situations, particularly in those cases in which elite decision makers are relatively protected from their own public opinion. However, the cognitive forms of political cultures are likely to provide a constant background against which decision makers have to act. They also influence the perception of the assumed realities of a situation, not only on the part of the public, but also of the decision makers: no matter how professional, the latter can reach positions of power and influence only on the basis of considerable congruence between their political behavior and the political perceptions of the public.

Another point to bear in mind is that the dominance of one or another attitude towards meaning influences political rhetoric, not only at the level of propaganda but even at that of diplomatic negotiations.[30] This influence characterizes not only what is said, but also what is credible in the statements of others. The difference in basic patterns of thought between the Israeli statement that the official borders of their state make defense against aggression practically impossible, and the attitude of an Egyptian officer kneeling to kiss the soil fo the Sinai at a point where it is objectively a desert, is such as to make mutual understanding unlikely; moreover each of the parties is sufficiently convinced of the rightness of a point of view correspondings to its habitual patterns of meaning to render unlikely understanding between national leaders, even if the latter are more amenable to more balanced approaches.

FOOTNOTES

[1] Glenn, E.S., 1973, "The Symbolic Function, Particularly in Language," *Semiotica*, VIII, no. 2, pp. 97-131.

[2] Parsons, T. & E.A. Shils, eds., 1951, *Toward a General Theory of Action*, Cambridge, Mass.: Harvard.

[3] Triandis, H.C. et al., 1972, *The Analysis of Subjective Culture*, New York: Wiley.

[4] Northrop, F.S.C., 1953, *The Meeting of East and West*, New York: Macmillan.

[5] Kuhn, T.S., 1970, *The Structure of Scientific Revolutions* Chicago: University of Chicago Press.

[6] Tonnies, F., 1887, *Gemeinschaft and Gesellschaft*, Tubingen.

[7] Patai, R., 1973, *The Arab Mind*, New York: Charles Scribner's Sons, p. 78.

[8] Glenn, E.S., "The Two Faces of Nationalism," *Comparative Political Studies*, III, no. 3, pp. 347-366.

[9] Fichte's *Speeches to the German Nation*, delivered in Berlin, 1808. Quoted in H.W. Steed, "Preface," to A. Kolnai, *War Against the West*, (New York, 1938) p. 7, and in P. Viereck, 1965, *Metapolitics: The Roots of the Nazi Mind*, New York: Capricorn, p. 7

[10] Kohn, H., 1960, *The Mind of Germany,* New York: Scribner's.

[11] Rabemanjara, J., 1959, excerpt from a presentation at the Second Congress of Black Writers and Artists, March 26 to April 1,

1959, published in a special issue of *Presence Africaine*, Paris.

[12] Lumumba, P., ibid.

[13] Diop, A., ibid.

[14] Babbitt, I., 1955, *Rousseau and Romanticism*, Garden City, New York: Doubleday Anchor.

[15] Viereck, P., 1965, *Metapolitics: the Roots of the Nazi Mind*, New York: Capricorn.

[16] Kohn, H., 1960, *The Mind of Germany*, New York: Scribner's.

[17] Stern, F., 1961, *The Politics of Cultural Despair*, Garden City, N.Y.: Doubleday.

[18] Cassirer, E., 1965, *The Myth of the State*, Garden City, N.Y.: Doubleday.

[19] Horowitz, L., 1961, *Radicalism and the Revolt Against Reason*, Carbondale, Ill.: Southern Illinois University Press.

[20] Lipset, S.M. & E. Raab, 1970, *The Politics of Unreason*, New York: Harper & Row.

[21] Glenn, E.S., 1969, "New Left or New Right?" in G.R. Weaver and J.H. Weaver, eds., *The University and Revolution*, Englewood, N.J.: Prentice—Hall, pp. 99-119.

[22] Granet, M., 1950, *La Pensee Chinoise*, Paris: Albin Michel, p. 445.

[23] Fagen, R.R., 1969, *The Transformation of Political Culture in Cuba*, Stanford, Ca.: Stanford University Press, p. 2.

[24] Pribram, K., 1945, *Conflicting Patterns of Thought*, Washington, D.C.: Public Affairs Press.

[25] Domenach, M., 1958, "Le Modele Americain," Paris: *L'Esprit*.

[26] Wedge, B. and C. Muromcew, 1965, "Psychological Factors in Soviet Disarmament Negotiation," *J. of Conflict Resolution*, IX: pp. 18-36.

[27] Glenn, E.S., R.H. Johnson, P.R. Kimmel and B. Wedge, 1970, "A Cognitive Interaction Model for the Analysis of Conflict in International Relations," *J. of Conflict Resolution*, XIV: pp. 35-48.

[28] Pribram, K., op. cit.

[29] Glenn, E.S., 1970, op. cit.

[30] Wedge, B. and C. Muromcew, op. cit.

BIBLIOGRAPHY

Babbitt, I., 1955, *Rousseau and Romanticism*, Garden City, N.Y.: Doubleday Anchor.

Cassirer, E., 1965, *The Myth of the State*, Garden City, N.Y.: Doubleday Anchor.

Diop, A., 1959, *Presence Africaine*.

Domenach, J.M., 1958, "Le Modele Americain," Paris: *L'Esprit*.

Fagen, R.R., 1969, *The Transformation of the Political Culture in Cuba*, Stanford, Ca.: Stanford University Press.

Geertz, C., 1965, *The Social History of an Indonesian Town*, Cambridge, Mass.: M.I.T. Press.

Glenn, E.S., 1968, "New Left or New Right?" in G.R. Weaver and J.H. Weaver, eds., *The University and Revolution*, Edgewood Cliffs, N.J.: Prentice-Hall.

Glenn, E.S., R.H. Johnson, P.R. Kimmel and B. Wedge, 1970, "A Cognitive Interaction Model for the Analysis of Conflict in International Relations," *J. of Conflict Resolution*, XIV.

Glenn, E.S., 1970, "The Two Faces of Nationalism," *Comparative Political Studies*, III, no. 3.

Glenn, E.S., 1973, "The Symbolic Function, Particularly in Language," *Semiotica*, VIII, no. 2, pp. 97-131.

Granet, M., 1950, *La Pensee Chinoise*, Paris: Albin Michel.

Horowitz, L., 1961, *Radicalism and the Revolt Against Reason*, Carbondale, Ill.: Southern Illinois University Press.

Kohn, H., 1960, *The Mind of Germany*, New York: Scribner's.

Kuhn, T.S., 1970, *The Structure of Scientific Revolutions*, Chicago: University of Chicago.

Lipset, S.M., and E. Raab, 1970, *The Politics of Unreason*, New York: Harper and Row.

Lumumba, P., 1959, *Presence Africaine*.

Northrop, F.S.C., 1953, *The Meeting of East and West*, New York: Macmillan.

Patai, R., 1973, *The Arab Mind*, New York: Charles Scribner's Sons.

Parsons, T. and E.A. Shils, eds., 1951, *Toward a General Theory of Action*. Cambridge, Mass.: Harvard.

Pribram, K., 1945, *Conflicting Pattern of Thought*, Washington: Public Affairs Press.

Rabemannanjara, J., 1959, *Presence Africaine*.

Steed, H.W., 1938, Preface to A. Kolnai, *War Against the West*, London: V. Golanez.

Stern, F., 1961, *The Politics of Cultural Despair*, Garden City, N.Y.: Doubleday.

Tönnies, 1887, *Gemeinschaft und Gesellschaft*.

Triandis, H.C., et. al., 1972, *The Analysis of Subjective Culture*.

Viereck, P., 1965, *Metapolitics: The Roots of the Nazi Mind*, New York: Capricorn.

Wedge, B. and C. Muromcew, 1965, "Psychological Factors in Soviet Disarmament Negotiation," *J. of Conflict Resolution*, IX: pp. 18-36.

Mary Chisholm and Rolf Von Eckartsberg:

Informal–Experiential and Formal–Conceptual Learning in Cross–Cultural Education

———————

IN THE SOCIAL SCIENCES we speak of cultural education as socialization or sometimes acculturation. It is the means by which the child comes to be initiated into the ways of its culture in order to become a participant member, a citizen.

Socialization is a communication process. The parents and members of the immediate family serve as the agents which mediate the ways of a specific culture to the child. Concretely, this means that the family members show the new member how to act in different situations and what to expect. They open up a certain part of the world to the child who learns in a spontaneous and informal–experiential way through direct participation. Only later, with the mastery of language and particularly with formal schooling, does the child receive explicit formal–conceptual teaching through the study of subject-matters which thematize knowledge for him. He learns about mathematics, literature, art, politics, physics and so on. These subject matters are taught to him in a ready-made, conceptualized, disciplined manner. The explicit formal-conceptual type of learning in school is grounded in everyday praxis; i.e., upon the experiential knowledge which preceded conceptualization but which has been systematized into a specialist language that only experts in the field understand, and that appears esoteric to the "average citizen" who has an "average" degree of learning. However, in terms of their work all people are participants in a specialist language to some degree.

In our contemporary society learning is accelerated and far-ranging through media like books, movies, radio and television which put the child in touch as a spectator with a vast array of human events and a wide range of knowledge. Our culture has been called the most open in flow of information. [1] There is the greatest

451

degree of free access to information in the United States as compared to other countries. While growing up, the child thus spontaneously acquires a large stock of knowledge in both practical and theoretical terms. Psychologically this "stock of knowledge" is given as a reper- toire of activities tied to an array of situations and as a storehouse of expectations which are often stereotyped, hence typical rather than specific or based on personal familiarity. This is especially true for those areas of life with which the child has had no first- hand experience. Particularly with regard to foreign cultures and people, all of us are limited to hear-say knowledge which can be crystallized easily into prejudice; i.e., preconceived attitudes and judgments. Such attitudes can often be changed only through actual cross-cultural contact, through first-hand familiarity.

The concept of socialization refers to all those processes of learning and communication through which the child is brought into responsible citizenship. On his own or through "internalization," as we say, he comes to represent his group, its practices and its values. Socialization brings one always into an initially de-limited world-view which is held in common by a certain group of people. In the course of a person's biography he may broaden his world-view so as to include, at least partially, that of other groups and other cultures.

Speech is the primary vehicle of socialization. The child is addressed and directed by speech. As he becomes capable of using and understanding speech he gains a sense of his own identity and he begins to partake and participate in ever-widening circles of social life radiating outward from his family-home group.

Speech is an interesting phenomenon in that it is a highly complex and structured medium of communication which we are capable of using effectively without needing to understand the principles of the grammatical structure which governs our speaking. We *use* the rules; we know them implicitly in using them. This holds true also for the rules of social conduct in terms of etiquette and the assuming of various roles, the build-up of expectations and routines.[2]

We pick up this knowledge "how-to-act" and with it the rules that govern the transactions quite spontaneously and in an informal-experiential manner. Only later, on the basis of our pragmatically effective praxis, through reflective-thinking, study and scholarship do we become explicitly aware of the rules and structures. In praxis we take the rules for granted, we know them but are forgetful of them at the same time. Our knowledge regarding the rules and structures of our social life are of the same nature. We tend to take the process of socialization for granted, not to question the relativity of our place and involvement in our own society and culture. This is "the world"; this is "the way" things are done. [3] Only later do we recognize the limits of our culture experientially: through *praxis*. Through step-by-step-unfolding we learn by first-hand experience how to operate in our culture. It is important to remember that we do not need to become fully aware of this process. In the same manner that we learn to speak our "mother-tongue" so we also just "pick up" the ways of our native culture. In the give and take of dialogue we develop our speech skills spontaneously without ever formulating any formal rules about them. Later in school, in English classes, a teacher tries to explain to us these rules that we are already using. We sometimes have a difficult time understanding them in formal conceptual terms, for this is a different kind of learning. It is formal-conceptual learning, in terms of a university discipline, a science with a special language and an explicit knowledge of rules governing experience and action: *experiaction*.

As we travel and enter the context of a culture other than our own, we must learn to find and to make our way in a new world. We have to learn to speak a new language, and we often have to adopt new ways of acting in order to get along. Again, this can happen without much explicit teaching or awareness. But usually we learn more explicitly about this new culture: we take lessons in speaking the language; we study the history and art of the new country; we are taught what to pay attention to and what is important, All of this occurs against the taken-for-granted backdrop of our effective praxis-life of our home-culture. We learn the "new" by comparing and differentiating it from the "old," the familiar. Often, especially in the area of learning to speak the language and of understanding the grammar, the confrontation with a new way of living sheds light on the old and makes us explicitly aware of our old ways of living. By rebound, as it were, we experience our home-culture in a more understanding way. We reflect and are made to think about it. This is the beginning of critical and systematic, or explicit formal-conceptual learning. What we already know in a taken-for-granted manner, in praxis, is looked at again, is reviewed, is thought about and compared with the new. Through such thinking-activity knowledge becomes sharper, more differentiated; we become more aware. This is the primary aim of education: to become not only *praxis-effective* but also to become *knowledge-aware* about one's praxis, including the activities of many other persons working at different jobs, in different roles, at different scientific and scholarly disciplines in universities. The professional knowledge-makers, knowledge-gatherers and knowledge-custodians usually work in university settings. As professionals they speak the expert-languages and systematize their knowledge in formal-conceptual terms. Although they do speak about everyday-life, they do so from a great distance of abstraction in formal-conceptual expertise, which can be learned and understood only through some kind of apprenticeship. In college we get only a smattering of these diverse disciplines, offered cafeteria-style. We never achieve mastery of any one discipline nor do we learn to integrate the diversity of knowledges. The question presents itself: How do these disciplines all hang together and how can they help us to make sense of our everyday world?

Unfortunately, most American colleges do not perform this service. They do not help the student to synthesize and to integrate the knowledge that each discipline has amassed and organized. Students take "distribution requirements" prescribed like a balanced diet but little effort is made to assist in the digestion and assimilation. Specialty tests do not help toward a synthesis.

We have reached a crisis point in education in that we do not know how to bring our immense and factually detailed knowledge together again in the understanding of and by one person. Nor can we explain the development of an event or events in a given region and time-period. Our own life appears as immensely complex and fractionated, particularly our participation as citizens in public life. Through mass-media and in our role as culture-consumers, we easily loose our orientation and sense of wholeness or integration.

In view of this frightening centrifugal development of knowledge and its kaleidoscopic educational consequences, we need to find new ways to work for an integration of knowledge, for coherent understanding. Moving to and living in another cultural context is a good opportunity to become aware of the problem of cohesion of knowledge as it grows out of the need to make sense, to comprehend, to understand interrelationships in order to survive in a meaningful manner. One may choose a foreign-language culture or a different subcultural milieu within his own general culture. The more different the two ways of life are from each other, the more one can learn from the experience: *contrasts highlight the learning.*

Inter- or Cross-Cultural Education

Whether as a process of spontaneous experiential living or as a program of explicit formal – conceptual teaching and study, inter-cultural or cross-cultural education may be seen as an important undertaking that tends to lead to significant experiential and cognitive learning. We might call this a process of *learning by cultural alternation.* As we alternate from our home-culture to a foreign-culture and back again, we spontaneously compare and reflect. Through these cognitive activities there evolves a better understanding of both. The more divergent the countries are that we thus experience in cross-cultural alternation, the more dramatic the insights tend to be. In countries of similar economic development and close historical contact the differences, in spite of different languages (such as English and German) may not be so great though each culture is, in any case, unique.

When we pursue this line of thinking we realize that even within our own society of the United States of America there are many sub-cultures such as "white middle-class culture," "black-ghetto culture," "Midwest farm-country culture," "intellectual-liberal" or "The Establishment." Culture, after all, refers to the totality of ways of acting and speaking within a circumscribed group of people who have a common way of life. As nationalities, people are usually bounded within a territory. But there are also situations of overlapping cultures particularly in an open and multiplex society such as ours.

We can thus apply the concept of inter- or cross-cultural education to our own on-going situation. Part of the task of social education would be to identify the various cultural groupings and our individual membership in them with our experienced life-praxis. In formal, conceptual terms this is the task of the sociologist and the social anthropologist. They are the professional and "official" definers of social and cultural realities. Their expert knowledge gives rise to textbooks which, in turn, inform the man in the street and become the entire formal-conceptual level of schooling. We read their text-books as we study; thus, we "learn" inter- or cross-culturally. But we have seen that this is not enough and is no longer satisfying because the knowledge we gain through reading about, through "head-study" generally, is not rich and deep enough when compared to lived-in, "body-participation" experience. Immersion is more basic and persuasive than selective observation only. Immersion is the ground to which observation is directed. Inter- or cross-cultural learning gives us an opportunity to become aware of the difference between informal-experiential and formal-conceptual learning. *Immersion-praxis* is the more informal-experiential way of learning about culture which has always-already been going on before we receive formal teaching. We know the inter- or cross-cultural life-praxis in some implicit way either through personal or vicarious experience. Only on this basis does formal-conceptual learning make sense. What we study should be related to what we already know at least implicitly through our own experience. Informal-experiential and formal-conceptual learning complement one another and are in need of one another.

A Model of Inter– or Cross–Cultural Learning

A model of such inter- or cross-cultural learning has been designed within an experimental program in sociology at Duquesne University, Pittsburgh. The program was built upon the tradition of existential-phenomenology which emphasizes the central and privileged position of man as the source of all meaning and action. [4, 5, 6] According to this approach, the individual person in his own experiencing and action is the primary focus for an understanding of all human phenomena including social reality. Each person learns on the basis of his own interpretation of the meaning of any situation in which he finds himself. Thus, all of social reality is initiated and sustained by the action of individuals or collaborating groups of individuals. Each individual person is the carrier of culture and he is simultaneously responsible for creating his social world even while he is being shaped by it. Socialization is, then, a mutual exchange, both a giving and a receiving; and out of this exchange a new reality emerges. Existential-phenomenology provides the basis for a humanistic, person-centered orientation; it offers a specific methodology distinct from a natural-science point of view.

The specific methodology of existential-phenomenology is based upon description and reflective analysis of one's own inner experience of a situation. It makes explicit the *actor-perspective*: i.e., the intimate personal view of life rather than the traditional observer-perspective of the physical sciences which views all of human reality and human behavior purely from the outside, as a system of stimulus-response relationships. In sociology the schools of phenomenology from which our model was drawn are represented in the work of Alfred Schutz, Peter Berger, Peter Koestenbaum, Arthur Vidich and the school of symbolic interaction with Mead, Cooley, Blumer, Goffman —— to name only a few of the prominent workers. However, another point of view, that of *human ecology,* is likewise integrated into our basic approach.

This model emphasizes that a truly existential stance requires that one begin with the study of the *already-existing* state of affairs. A given culture, a community or any social unit, be it a family, an institution or even an individual person, always-already exists before the learner appears. Any given culture as an on-going part of a total society has already achieved a certain functional balance on a practical, lived-life level before the new-comer begins to study it explicitly, before he makes theoretical formulations or generalizations. According to this model, a student begins with what exists. He must discover the multiple patterns of dynamic interrelationships which are unique to this particular community. Within an ongoing community there are numerous patterns, really a concatenation of many contexts, which require the whole gamut of scientific disciplines for adequate understanding. An ecological approach provides a comprehensive as well as an integrative approach. This approach is capable of unifying several different aspects or levels of reality within one unitary life-phenomenon such as a given culture or subculture, and it combines several features both with regard to teaching and to learning:

> a. It combines teaching and personal discovery by focusing on a structured field-experience. The model is thus praxis-oriented and all theoretical work and reflection are based on concrete field-study and personal experience. The model

arrives at a synthesis between purely academic work and community involvement, even service. By focusing upon a specific community for study or as a learning milieu, the model is intended to bridge traditional gaps between academic learning and real-life problems.

b. The model assumes that only a genuinely co-operative learning experience between the "outsider" (researcher, learner, or whoever) and the "native" (the researched, the client, the "objects" of study) is morally justifiable. This means that students cannot stand aloof and collect data without entering the lives of the people. Furthermore, it is recognized that as one studies a given culture mutual change processes are inevitable. This is recognized from the beginning and students must be prepared to render some services to the community (host culture) for the privilege of being allowed to share in that life.

c. In its field development our approach necessitates an interdisciplinary approach. In dealing with the complexities of a living society or community we have to bring to bear specialized expertise spanning many traditional disciplines. This model, however, is interdisciplinary with the respect to a specific problem; namely, understanding the on-going life of a concretely existing culture. The community itself would dictate to what extent a given study becomes interdisciplinary by consulting with specialists such as the historian, economist, lawyer, doctor, psychiatrist, poet, theologian, who can supply needed information. This means that interdisciplinary/theoretical learning would come in only as far as each becomes relevant to increase an understanding of the phenomena under consideration. The model is not interdisciplinary just for the sake of bringing different disciplines together to discuss areas of overlap or of mutual relevance in a purely academic manner.

This model, then, combines teaching and experiential learning; it provides a link between academic work and community life; it remains in touch and responsive to all phases of the community (economy, politics, education, religion, sickness and health, recreation). As each phase of the life and culture of a particular community becomes existentially relevant to the student, various problem areas gradually emerge and these then become the focus of reflection and possible action. Sharing in any life entails natural responsibilities such as helping through work, advice, or in any other manner the specific situation may call for.

In this way, through the establishment of a field-station or a learning-center in a specific area, the student is introduced to existing situations in their total "lived-life" or "everyday-world" context. By means of systematic theorizing and the development of reflective skills, he will be enabled to enter more fully into the attitude of both informal-experiential and theoretical-formal learning. Our approach, we feel, has something to add to the traditional methodologies which we consider too segmental, too pre-structural and essentially decontextualized. Traditional approaches fail to give students an integral and comprehensive understanding of the society they study. By combining experiential methodology with an ecologic focus on the uniquely-patterned, existent urban-neighborhood-community, this model can make a contribution both to the empirical and the theoretical body of knowledge.

In the approach developed here we emphasized from the beginning a full two-way dialogue among students and faculty as co-learners, or among university representatives and community-citizens in a continuing conversation together. This is a necessary concomitant of our underlying existential-phenomenological conviction regarding the central character of "I-Thou" conversation. It is also the only justifiable attitude when we concern ourselves with the domain of the life-world and personal experience which is always unique and hence privileged knowledge to be communicated and shared only on the condition of consent and trust between partners. Such learning and the way it is shared with all participants will have evolutionary consequences, for we know that change and growth are forthcoming from any enhancement in understanding.

The model emerged as the result of a research program funded by the National Endowment for the Humanities and undertaken in Soho, an inner-city neighborhood in Pittsburgh. Graduate students who participated in the program were asked to familiarize themselves with the selected neighborhood under study by walking around in it, observing, talking to inhabitants. They learned to describe their own experiences within the neighborhood, to reflect upon them and to compare these experiences with others in a weekly seminar. Different professors from the university or representatives from the community were invited to share their expertise with members of the seminar and to direct the students in their focus on one or the other particular aspect of community study for a given week or two. Thus, the students were introduced to different methods of study as well as to various aspects of the on-going society. In each case, formal theoretical discussion could be checked or tested against the informal-experiential reality of the neighborhood.

Each student was expected to discover for himself ways of access to important information and to establish relationships with persons and with institutions connected with the neighborhood. Students were successful in varying degrees. Some established residence in the neighborhood and were able to make connections in a natural way. One student played football on a neighborhood team; another worked in a community center. Each student selected his own individual project in the neighborhood. He learned to gather data, to clarify, interpret and present his findings according to a phenomenological method or whatever other method he might find feasible for his own project. Our approach encouraged visual representations that included artistic and/or poetic imagery which could give insight toward a deeper understanding of the human dimensions of social life. Students with demonstrated skills in film-making, in photography, in the use of sound and color to convey their insights contributed to the study of sociology as an art-form rather than to sociology as a hard science.

This model of informal-experiential and formal-conceptual learning emerged from the study of an intercultural situation within the United States, a study of contrasting sub-cultures where middle-class graduate students sought to understand the on-going life of Italian-Americans within the inner-city, low-income neighborhood of SOHO. The degree of "culture-shock" encountered by students, their sense of unfamiliarity in first-hand contact with a *lived-world* within an adjacent neighborhood, was surprising. A vast difference between the primary experience of involvement within the every-day world of common-sense and the detached, abstract study within a theoretical world of formal-learning was pointed up.

If this proved true in the study of American society, a study within one's own native culture, it is likely to prove even more significant when one tries to understand a foreign culture both experientially and theoretically. The same approach and methodology described above will form the basis of an inter- or cross-cultural learning program for American students studying abroad in Basel, Switzerland.

Living in a foreign culture and participating in the ongoing flux of the daily life of a native family is a great opportunity for learning and personal growth, giving one a quite natural basis for comparisons of culture and life-style. As stated above, having to learn a new way of life in a foreign country makes explicit the process called "socialization" that we all undergo in an unconscious manner in our own development within our native country.

However, even the contrast and the newness of life in a foreign culture can quickly give way to routine and forgetfulness unless one is able to keep alert and reflective. Our embeddedness within our own culture can also blind us so that we do not see or that we distort what is present in the new. All of us are subject to this process of *habituation,* so if we want to become explicitly aware of the structure and functioning principles of our social life we need to make a systematic effort. Gaining some distance from one's usual embeddedness, such as changing one's place of residence or position or even being able to move into a totally different language and culture region, can greatly facilitate one's learning and understanding of social life in general. But this is only a first step. We believe that more is needed to enable the exchange student to gain maximum benefit from his experience.

A Proposed Model for Inter– or Cross–Cultural Learning Experience

The theoretical basis for our model is found in social psychology with emphasis on existential-phenomenological philosophy. Social psychology is a systematic way of knowing and understanding the social action and experience of an individual in his group and in his culture. As Gordon Allport used to define it, "Social psychology is concerned with understanding how the actual or implied presence of others affects our behavior." The actual or implied presence of others introduces us to social life. Groups of people, to the degree that they develop a common way of speaking intra-culturally in dialects or in special-interest group-idioms, generate their own particular styles and typical situations in their common life together. We call these variations subcultures. Nations or large populations generally form an intertwined mix of many sub-cultures and many complex forms of institutional organizations, all within the common matrix of a national language. Even if a nation such as Switzerland has within itself four language-speaking groups, within a definite geographical region one tongue will predominate. But within each tongue (language) there is further internal differentiation of vocabulary. As groups of people form and they organize themselves for specialized, co-ordinate activities related to services needed by others within a region (division of labor), the originally common speech likewise becomes specialized and differentiated. We begin to have *specialist-languages*. Depending upon our particular background, education, specialist-training each of us commands a particular vocabulary naming those people, places, things, symbols, or values which have meaning to us. These "phenomena of human meaning" then form the orbit of our social life. Each one of us has his own unique place and position within our culture.

Our proposed model presents a method by which students living in a foreign country may locate themselves within that culture. Our vehicle of approach will be the study of speech. Here we acknowledge our indebtedness to Eugen Rosenstock-Huessy and Alfred Schutz for many of the ideas expressed. When we take speech as the vehicle of approach to the discovery of one's place and function in the culture, we must learn to differentiate many forms of human speaking. Human communication governs our social life. Particular types of communication regulate particular types of interaction. Likewise, particular forms of action give rise to particular forms of expression and articulation: from silent bodily gestures to a grunt or laughter, to a musical composition, to a stock-market report, to a legal contract, to a mathematical formulation or to Einstein's equation. All domains of knowledge— the arts, the social sciences, the natural sciences, philosophy and theology -- are thus embodied in specialist-groups of people who have a particular form of language appropriate to their shared activities and their social life together. It is this special way of speaking that identifies them as specialists both to other groups and among themselves.

All of us can still talk together. We can achieve some degree of mutual understanding even though we may not be familiar with one another's specialized language. If one is to locate himself within a current cultural situation, he will need to pay attention to the kind of speaking in which he and the people close to him are involved. Speaking and acting tend to go together; they are generally appropriate to each other or at least they mutually refer to one another. Speech is involved in human action and experience.

In our research we use the term *experiaction* to indicate the unity of action and experience. A person both *experiences* (an inner process of feelings, of subjective meanings) and *acts* (outward behavior objectively observable); and each is given to awareness simultaneously as a process of active and passive conscious relating to one's situation. A situation may include things, people, and activities. As we get more deeply involved in any given situation we likewise notice more; we can distinguish better. Our language also becomes more differentiated, hence, more articulate. Shared speech among people allows others to share in a particular experiaction and in an awareness that opens up particular worlds as a constellation of situations. Each of us as individuals live in a limited world of the *concrete* and necessarily restricted but uniquely patterned *repertoire* of lived-in and lived-through situations. A repertoire means the stock of plays, operas, parts, songs, etc. that an actor is familiar with and is ready to perform; or a storehouse, a place for useful things, a repository where something acquired may be found. Each of us has such a repertoire of life-situations from which we draw and to which we add day by day.

People and situations go together in different ways. Sometimes we meet a person in only one situation, as is characteristic of many role-relationships: with a lawyer, a doctor, teacher or minister. Or we may share many or most life-situations with a partner in a very intimate way, as in marriage.

Looked at in this way, the pattern of a person's speech can reveal his situatedness within a culture in a very concrete way. His typical speaking will place him among his typical-speaking partners. His common speech makes him participate in the common life of the total community. Mass media, through mass-speaking, help to produce mass-culture. Esoteric speaking among esoteric groups helps produce esoteric awareness. Nuclear physicists speaking a "nuclear-physicese" (mathematical-physical language) produce our awareness of the world of nuclear physics.

Our speaking is continuously changing and evolving as we are changing and evolving our culture. We see culture as the totality of all experiactions of all the people involved in a language community. Some languages, such as mathematics and natural science, languages that are concerned with the materiality of our earth, are mankind's in their universality although the actual number of people involved is often very small. Much study is needed for mastery of the range and the intricacy of such languages and only a few people are gifted enough to work themselves into the forefront of specialist-speaking where new discoveries are made.

Other languages are forms of more regionally-bound experiactions -- such as folk-music -- and they are expressive of a more localized and limited number of speech-related people. Today our common language through the speaking of mass-media news allows us to stay in touch with many directions of our social world even if only in a very vague and superficial way. Alfred Schutz has given a fine description of the problem of the distribution of knowledge in social life when he differentiated three types of specialization to be found in the members of any community: that of the expert, the well-informed citizen, and the man-in-the-street.[7] Each of us at different times or in different situations may represent any one of the three types of knowledge-holding in regard to different aspects of our shared social world.

It is by means of speech-articulation that we open up for ourselves as a culture and as individuals whatever world we may inhabit, however big or little that may be: the world of an expert, of a well-informed citizen, or of the man-in-the-street. There is no limit to the possibilities of awareness which we might call a *knowing-presence* to one's own experiaction within a given situation. But individuals are limited. Each one has a limited biography and a limited situation-experience repertoire. Hence, each individual has "limited speech" when compared to the treasure-house of the accumulation of all mankind's speech throughout history. We participate in the common life only according to our share which is shaped partially by our endowment and partially by personal achievement.

Thus, in the scope of all mankind's speech, each individual occupies a delineated position. Just as one person cannot read all the books in the Library of Congress, so one man cannot know everything that is to be known. Yet when a person is creative he can help in building up further man's total speaking-power and awareness in a particular direction. Most of us tend to remain within the already constituted realm of speaking, sustaining this life and weaving new strands of our unique biographical flow of life-process, our own experiactions, into the fabric of our life-conversations and into the common cloth of our cultural heritage.

Locating oneself through speech must begin with the study of one's own situation which first must be described. These descriptions are then further studied to discover the language they utilize. The language reveals a particular flow of experiaction; and upon reflection, language also reveals the structure of understanding that binds experiactions into a coherent awareness toward thought and theory. It is speech that unites the domains of yet inarticulated life-process (to be discovered as *the root* of human experiaction) with the abstracted domains of thought and understanding, eventually of science and theory. Experiaction dawns in awareness and calls for articulation in speech. Shared speech calls us into awareness of others and of their experiaction. All speech is a highlighting of figural or thematic structures from the ground of experiaction, of everyday life.

From the situational repertoire of each student, according to our model, we ask him to call forth, to unfold and to thematize aspects of his own awareness: of people, of ideas, of values, symbols, activities, of his environment, of the extent of his natural and necessary involvement in social-institutional life in a foreign country. Each dimension of his awareness will be expressed as a specialized, systematized language. In other words, through his speech he can map out his awareness of society and culture and his own place in it.

Application in Inter– or Cross-Cultural Learning

As a means of implementing the insights expressed above, we have developed a step-by-step guided procedure as a basis for an inter- or cross-cultural learning experience for American students studying abroad. This procedure is derived from the model described above and it includes many of the same features.

We encourage the students to write their own textbooks within a shared context of readings. The readings serve to develop a conceptual language appropriate to the task of locating oneself experiactionally in one's culture. In addition to the authors mentioned before (Berger and Luckmann, THE SOCIAL CONSTRUCTION OF REALITY, and Natanson, THE JOURNEYING SELF) we would include Rosenstock—Huessy, SPEECH AND REALITY and McLuhan, UNDERSTANDING MEDIA. Their texts are "specialist speech" of the social sciences which is spoken by experts and an introduction to the formal-conceptual aspect of learning.

For a student this means that he must learn the specialist language, its particular vocabulary and usage. He comes to this task with his everyday speech which is adequate for his own everyday life but which needs to be refined and systematized for social-science purposes. The task within the classroom is, then, to learn the new language by becoming able to translate one's own everyday speech about one's own experiaction into specialist language; and vice-versa, to let the specialist language inform and refine one's everyday experiaction. Everyday speech is expressive of the level of informal-experiential learning and specialist speech relates to formal-conceptual learning.

Everyday speech relates happenings in the everyday world and in everyday life, an individual's way of living which includes the full cycle of sleep, awakening, working, eating, going to work or school, coming home in the evening, relaxing, recreating, media-watching, worshipping. The everyday world is the full round of human activities, including everything. The everyday world is matrix.

When the student goes to live in a foreign country, particularly when he enters the home-and-family life of that nation, he finds himself embedded in a new matrix. Everything in its coherent style and pervasive atmosphere is somehow different. A subtle and qualitative feeling of difference exists over and beyond the more obvious difference in spoken and written language. This difference acts as the first shock to one's consciousness giving rise to the feeling of estrangement that will initially suffuse all of one's experiactions in this "new world," this new culture, new way of life or life-style. This feeling of estrangement sometimes manifested as anxiety or uncertainty, as surprise and fascination, as bemusement and a sense of the grotesque, even the surreal, has to be seen as a gift, as a bonus for the risk of having ventured into a new land. It is the "wedge of growing awareness" which creates an openness in the otherwise taut texture of one's living matrix which has often grown small by habituation, by routine. Entering a new world demands alertness, it provokes a re-awakening and hence re-examination of the obvious, of what has been taken for granted through usage. This feeling of estrangement, of "culture shock," of "Verfremdung" — call it what you will — that happens to one as he tries to find his way in the new culture constitutes an opportunity to learn something based upon his own direct and first-hand experience. The student can look at and examine his experiactions more closely. He compares the way things are done here and the way he did them at home; he perceives the difference and can explore the reasons for differences. He will get into many questions, his own questions, that cannot rest until he finds an answer to his own satisfaction. In other words, entering into a new culture can be a very creative period in a person's life and he can learn much about society and himself, about all his relationships, if he pursues a course of serious learning and remains faithful to his own "informal experience." It seems obvious that this "strategy of self-world estrangement" is also at work in the use of psychedelic drugs by many young people today. The drug experience produces temporary alienation in that everything in one's experience changes qualitatively and offers itself under new and hitherto unsuspected aspects. Through "a trip" one's way of perceiving the world is drastically changed. Many questions arise which stimulate thoughtful reflection.

Being in a new world and recognizing that there is a total, qualitative difference in two contrasting ways of life, we try to help the student in his attempts to make sense of his experience. For help and for a language to talk about this experiencing,we go to the experts and the specialists, the social scientists. We start the students off by asking them to keep a diary or an intensive journal about their on-going life in the host country. The diary is the basic recording of each one's stream of experiaction, the informal-experiential basis of their new learning experience. The student thus puts his living into written language as best he can. Some of this may be too private to be shared which is, of course, the person's privilege. But through the diary each one gets a basic text which he uses as "data." Each description is called an "experiaction protocol."

The next phase is to teach students how to work with their protocols. They have the descriptions and now they are encouraged to reflect systemmatically on the meanings that these descriptions may have for the author himself or herself. In order to accomplish this search for meanings which are not immediately apparent but usually have been vaguely taken for granted, and also to learn by sharing one another's descriptions and another's meanings, we encourage the students to work in pairs or in small groups. They listen to each other's reports and learn how to respond with sensitivity, to question helpfully in order to bring forth the full meanings that are often latent. This is an important step in the learning process because one's own involvement often blinds him to possibilities that a partner, from a different vantage-point and with less involvement, can often more easily recognize and articulate. Much learning may occur in this way, through mutual discussion and elaboration.

Students now need to discover the inherently meaningful organization of their flow of experiaction. To accomplish this,we ask them to focus on related topics, to research various aspects of their life in a foreign culture by using their own ongoing life-processes as "data." The organizational plan includes such topics as: Situations, Perceptual presence, Motivation, Institutions, Knowledge and Media, Ideas and Values via Thought and Speech.

Situation

We begin with molar descriptive units. The student is to consider his ongoing life as a concatenation or repertoire of situations that he lives through. As a conceptual unit, "situation" allows him to investigate both the public and social definitions that structure experiactions as a *situation;* and the more personal meanings that explain how his living in situations gives expression to his own life-project. In other words, as the student examines and becomes aware of concrete "happenings" or "situations" within the native Swiss family or as part of his host culture, he learns to see them from a double perspective: the on-going, taken-for-granted definitions of his hosts and his own similar or different definitions and meanings.

We can work concretely on this problem of life's situatedness by making a representation on a map. Situations occur in physical space and time; they can be mapped out. If the student traces his activities as bodily movement through the landscape he will discover a characteristic recurrent body-movement pattern. He lives somewhere and within that homespace he goes through important recurrent situations: breakfast, lunch, dinner, conversations, letter-writing, media-watching. He goes to work or study, shopping, visiting or whatever. These situations can be identified and seen as forming the pattern of one's daily-life-round of activities. This circumscribed space is vastly extended through communication, both through conversation and media-presence, so that one's awareness of the culture around him is much greater than his bodily reach. This can be mapped also; but cognitive space is much more complicated than mere bodily presence. Mapping represents the "ecology of movement." When one examines his tracings he will find recurring patterns as well as innovations. One's life will be seen as unfolding within a repertoire of situations and people with whom one interacts in these situations.

The student can now examine the relationship of his situational repertoire to the motivational patterns which underly each situation. Again, such motivation must be discovered both from the goals of society and the goals one sets for oneself. Students are led to focus on *particular* situations: on the people and the speech-dimensions that co-constitute a situation. They begin to grasp their people-involvement as participation in different cultural sub-worlds: i.e., the world of the family, of work, of friendships, of ideas and the like To the extent that he can "speak the language," he fits into each sub-culture.

In our approach we move from experiential to conceptual learning. We emphasize that it is important to begin with the experiactions of one's own life, to try to conceptualize that and also to see its interrelationships with others and the social life at large. This also means that we want to emphasize *limits and distinctions:* what we do share in, and what we do not; what we do know and what we do not know; what we know by personal contact and what

we know only through hearsay, through media. We must become
more aware of the type and status of our knowledge. This demands
reflection indward on our own consciousness: how we co-create
our experiences by bringing to bear our expectations into situations
and perceptions; how we live in a socially and self-limited universe.

On the basis of daily protocols and systematic reflection,
students can deepen their understanding by probing the depths of
meaning to be fathomed in their participation in everyday life
situations. Dialogal collaboration with others is helpful, sometimes
indispensable. As students proceed each one finds himself involved in
the analysis of his own concepts and views, in the cognitive frames of
reference he employs whether of popular, social, ideological or
esoteric-teaching origin. They begin to see that we commonly
employ ready-made "conceptual machineries" in our interpretations
of reality; and they learn how to check out preconceived notions
against reality as it appears in their own experience or as they can
become aware of it through comparisons.

Perceptual Presence

This plan of reflective work reveals the way in which we use
language and employ concepts in our perceiving and thinking about
reality. There is an operative hierarchy of concepts: from the concrete existent that can be referred to by name, here and now, to the
abstract, universal, categorical concept that refers to a whole class of
objects or events "in general," i. e. is valid for everybody and at all
times. "Basel Railroad Station, 15th of September, 1972, 3:15 p.m."
is a concrete instance; "railroad station behavior" in general is a
much more abstract conceptualization; and "social behavior" is an
even higher order of abstraction that refers to innumerable activities
of a total populace. We have to become alerted to the way in which
we refer to particular aspects of reality so as not to get lost in empty
generalizations when we speak. To stay as closely as possible to the
concrete given of one's situation, "what you know for sure,"seems to
be the safest procedure to follow. But even with regard to that aspect
of bodily-present-reality one may be deceiving himself as to his "true
underlying motivation." Freud and Jung have made us cognizant of
the subtleties of this process, of "unconscious motivation." Hidden
goals distort our perception and thinking in the direction of

wish-fulfillment: we see what we want to see, we find what we expect to find. It seems very difficult to remain free of such protective pre-conceptions, to keep ourselves open to change and to growth, to remain faithful to the truth that reveals itself in the unfolding of one's own life and in that collaboration with others that we call society and culture. There is need for dialogue with another to help us become aware of our own blind spots.

Summary

We have expressed only some of the phenomena that can be examined fruitfully in a program of inter- or cross-cultural education. As each topic is pursued with the students, we are always concerned with discovering and appreciating the coherence and the unity of style that pervades and co-ordinates social life. Inter- or cross-cultural understanding emerges when we can compare likenesses and differences contrasting life-styles. In spite of the step-by-step procedure of writing his own self-text or intensive journal and its concomitant conceptual analysis, we regard the total learning process for the student as one of synthesis and integration. In the final analysis, of course, this work of integration must be done by the individual learner. Only he can describe and reflect upon his own situations. So the student must do the learning himself; he must write his own text. We as teachers can provide only an atmosphere and guiding direction; we can represent the available knowledge and structure of understanding. Within such a context, the student is given the opportunity to develop his understanding of culture and come to an expanded awareness of his own place and function within this social fabric.

In our work with American students within their native culture we have worked out a model and have devised a number of exercises and techniques that may serve as patterns for students when they begin to do their own research. We now seek to widen our perspective and to develop additional exercises, or refine those we have, so they may have another inter- or cross-cultural dimension. By working with American students studying abroad, we shall have direct access to other primary data of inter- or cross-cultural experiaction.

FOOTNOTES

[1] Revel, Jean Francois, *Without Marx or Jesus,* N.Y. Delta Books, 1971. It is instructive and refreshing to read how the political situation in the United States during the late 1960's appears through the perspective of a foreigner.

[2] Goffman presents us with a dramaturgical model of understanding social life. Goffman, Ervin, *Behavior in Public Places,* N.Y. Free Press, 1963.

[3] On the important issue of the social construction of reality see Berger, Peter, and Luckmann, Thomas, *The Social Construction of Reality,* Garden City, N.Y. Doubleday Anchor Book, 1967.

[4], [5], [6] Giorgi, Amedeo, *Psychology as a Human Science,* N.Y. Harper and Row, 1970. Luijpen, William, *Existential Phenomenology,* Pittsburgh, Duquesne University Press, 1963. Van Kaam, Adrian, *Existential Foundations of Psychology,* Pittsburgh, Duquesne University Press, 1966.

[7] Schutz, Alfred, *Collected Papers* Volume 2, The Hague, Martinus Nijhoff, 1964. In this volume a paper entitled, "The Well-Informed Citizen: An Essay on the Social Distribution of Knowledge," is an excellent introduction into the sociology of knowledge.

BIBLIOGRAPHY

Berger, P. and Luckmann, *The Social Construction of Reality,* Garden City, N.Y.: Doubleday Anchor Book, 1967.

Giorgi, A., *Psychology as a Human Science,* N.Y., Harper and Row, 1970.

Goffman, E., *Behavior in Public Places,* N.Y., Free Press, 1963.

Luijpen, W., *Existential Phenomenology,* Pittsburgh, Duquesne University Press, 1963.

Revel, J.F., *Without Marx or Jesus,* N.Y., Delta Book, 1971.

Schutz, A., *Collected Papers,* vol. 2, The Hague, Martinus Nijhoff, 1964.

Van Kaam, A., *Existential Foundations of Psychology,* Pittsburgh, Pennsylvania, Duquesne University Press, 1966.

Joanne Sanae Yamauchi:

The Coming of Age in Intercultural Communication

———

THE FACTORS of age and aging are often overlooked in research on intercultural communication. Yet, in every society, age serves as a fundamental aspect of social structure and interpersonal dynamics. Individuals' activities, their attitudes towards life, their interrelationships in their families and in their work, and their biological capacities are all conditioned by their position in the age structure of the particular societies in which they live.[1] Moreover, social scientists recognize the existence of specific age groups that constitute distinct subcultures with peculiar values, perceptions, and communication patterns that influence intergenerational behavior. In particular, the elderly are living longer and increasing in numbers, thereby becoming a rising, significant social force in societies.[2] Such developments suggest a significant relationship of age and communication patterns which requires closer scrutiny by communication researchers. It seems appropriate, therefore, to examine the interrelationship of age and aging to intercultural communication through an exploration of the major conceptual orientations of generational behavior, a synthesis and analysis of current empirical research on aging and communication, and a perspective on directions for future research.

Conceptual Orientations

In the study of intercultural communication, it is common practice to examine related variables that affect communication between members of different ethnic groups or of geographically diverse cultures. In considering the influence of age on intercultural communication, the researcher is confronted with the possibility of studying different age groups which comprise selected subcultures such as the youth counterculture. Moreover, the relationship of different age groups can also be examined interracially across ethnic contexts within a given culture such as the United States. And finally, the influence of age on communication can also be researched cross-culturally by comparing the communication behavior of similar age group members in one country with that of members of another society.

Probably the most commonly recognized age-related communication problem is that of the generation gap. On the popular front, such a communication breakdown between members of the youth culture and their elders seem to be taken for granted. There is still a controversy, however, among social scientists about the existence of an adolescent culture that is so distinct from their elders so as to create a *communication* gap between generations. Notions of a gap are often linked with the concept of "age-ism," a prejudice among members of one age group against those of another age group with implications of stereotyping, interpersonal distance, and conflicts of interest.

There are three generally accepted views on the problem of the generation gap. Proponents of the "great gap" position hold that there is an ever-widening gap between the generations that is often unbridgeable. Others contend that perceptions of a gap constitute a "great illusion" in that there are really more continuities than there are discontinuities between the generations. The third view on the matter is that in any generational comparisons, one will find selected areas of continuities and discontinuities. Those who advocate the first position see a social revolution along generational lines that has been extended cross-culturally and has threatened established adult social institutions. Margaret Mead explains the pulling apart as a world-wide phenomenon that is caused primarily by different experiences of each generation. On the one hand is a generation that has experienced the emergence of a world community created by many technological advances in the mass media. Revolutions in space travel, agricultural production, and medical knowledge encompass the experiential background of those born before World War II and who were also unprepared to cope with these radical changes. The younger generation, on the other hand, is familiar with satellites, wars that do not threaten annihilation, instant visual news, and population and ecological control. As children of their pioneering parents, they cannot share the memories of their elders' experiences. The two generations are therefore faced with different perceptions of the world that preclude communication.[3] Friedenberg argues further that the generation gap reflects a serious conflict of interest rather than mutual understanding. He perceives a genuine class conflict between an exploitative and dominant older generation and the youth who are only now becoming aware of what is happening to them.[4] In discussing the counterculture of youthful dissent, Rosnak sees the gap as a function of disaffected middle-class youths suffering from a malaise termed "immersiration," being caught between a permissive childhood and a demandingly conformist adulthood with no learned method of coping with a world that is essentially despised.[5]

Another group posits that the gap is essentially an illusion. They argue that between generations there are continuities that outweigh the differences. Some suggest that most adolescents and their parents do perceive a rather satisfactory relationship in terms of closeness and understanding.[6] This position also holds that generational differences are self-perpetuating. Such proponents argue that the differences among young people are often as great as differences between youth and adults.[7] There has always been gap, and whatever the perceived size of the gap today, it must be viewed within the perspective of the continuing sense of solidarity within the family, the considerable amount of traditionalism that still exists among many youths, and the extensive continuity between generations that reflects ongoing, significant parental influence.[8]

The third position is an intermediate one of selective continuity and difference. Advocates of this stance argue that student activists may be different from their parents in overt behavior but that such behavior usually reflects the logical implementation of parental values. They contend that most college students have values and norms which are considerably consistent with those of their parents;

the primary areas of difference existing in life styles, particularly with respect to use of drugs, sexual behavior, and religious practices.[9]

The "great gap" position, the "illusion" stand, and the selective continuity-difference orientation seem to represent perspectives along a continuum of generational differences and similarities. To some, these views seem not only contradictory but irreconciliable. Gerontologists, social scientists who investigate the phenomenon of aging, have proposed a set of explanatory orientations which are helpful in clarifying the seemingly contradictory views of the generation gap. Importance is placed on differentiating among three factors: (1) changes over time that are attributable to maturation or aging of individuals, (2) changes that are created by historical or period effects, and (3) contrasts reflected in characteristics that persist throughout the life span of a specific age group. In this context, there are three major ways in which the generational concept has been employed in research on aging. The *cohort* perspective of generation focuses on a macrolevel or more general analysis of the role that aging and age groups play in social change. To understand the behavioral orientations of a particular age group, then, would involve a realization that these orientations represent an interaction of (a) a particular birth cohort or group of individuals born at a particular time, and with a specific chronological or biological age, and (b) the unique socialization experience of the cohort at a common period in its psychological, biological, and social growth. Thus, at any given period, society is represented by a continuous flow of successive birth cohorts, each at a different stage of its life cycle development.[10]

The second major conceptualization of the generational construct is that of *lineage* differentiation or ranked descent within a family structure. Unlike the cohort view which focuses on chronological age dimensions of an individual's maturation, the lineage perspective directs attention to changes in the interpersonal network in which the individual is entwined. Underscored are processes of intergenerational transmission of role behaviors as the product of socialization. Thus, the focus is on interaction patterns among parents, children, and grandparents within a family unit at a microlevel of analysis and between aggregates of parents, grandparents, and children at a macrolevel of analysis. Since life cycle or lineage related roles are not correlated with chronological age, e.g. some individuals become parents at age twenty; others at thirty-five, the processes of social aging are seen through an inspection of ways in which significant social roles become the indicators of life cycle change. Such a perspective is distinctive from that of the strict cohort classification of aged phenomena.[11]

The third perspective differs from the previous two views in its focus on *generation units* or those age groups that seem to crystallize distinctive political movements or social styles. Karl Mannheim, the major prononent of this viewpoint, sees age groups as dynamic collectivities characterized by an historical consciousness, a sense of group identity that emerges from the awareness of participating in an historical event. He defines a generation unit as a component of a birth cohort or age group which has a common relationship to a political, social, economic, and cultural system and which organizes self-consciously to change that system. This perspective is useful in explaining the youth counterculture protest of the 1960's in which a peculiar combination of demographic events — a large birth cohort clashed with a general alienation from political policies and adult traditionalism — produced a generation of dissent.[12] Such an intermingling of birth-cohort categories, historical experiences, and a sense of political consciousness constitutes a more elaborate framework of generational analysis than the cohort or lineage approach to intergenerational analysis.

In reviewing the controversial views of the "great gap," "illusion," and selected continuity and difference proponents of the generation gap, the application of the cohort, lineage, and generational unit explanations becomes clear. The cohort perspective is useful in explaining the phenomenon of the "great gap" position since an overall consideration of the peculiar chronological and social occurrences affecting a particular age group can make it a generation which is generally quite distinct from another birth cohort. Furthermore, in the case of members of the counterculture, their behaviors can be explained by the generational unit perspective which views these younger members as having been influenced by a curious blend of political-social events. Those professing the illusionary nature of the generation gap are in agreement with the lineage perspective which focuses on the socialization of younger family members and the bequest of values which are adhered to through various generations of a family. Finally, the selected continuity-difference school of thought is a blend of both the generational unit and lineage perspectives in terms of pointing to value differences that are more politically and historically influenced at the macrolevel of experience and value similarities that are evident at the microlevel of family socialization patterns.

Synthesis of Generational Communication Studies

While it is important to consider all of the previously discussed explanations of generational behavior, much of the research on aging has been conducted in a more limited fashion of one-shot surveys instead of longitudinal studies across several annual spans. The result is a set of findings which serve more as a starting point than as a comprehensive set of discoveries. Related studies on the subject can be divided into areas of (1) attitudes on selected issues which are held by different generational members, (2) attitudes of another generation that are held by other generations, and (3) actual communication behavior between and among generations. Empirical research on values and attitudes held by different generations seems to reflect the continuity-difference view of the generation gap — — revealing clusters of similar and dissimilar values. Among the attitudinal studies, most of the investigations focused on a comparative look at intergenerational views on political issues. Some researchers indicated that some student activists and non-activists tend to be like their parents in their political attitudes and political behavior.[13] Unlike these findings which were based on student input from a select group of prestigious academic institutions, Pugh, in a study of students from a less prestigious university, found that (1) Democrat students with Republican parents were more likely to have participated in the antiwar demonstrations of the 1960's than Democrat students with Democrat parents, (2) student protesters perceived themselves as more politically liberal than their parents, and (3) students reporting little misunderstanding with their parents were less likely to have participated in antiwar demonstrations than those who reported a substantial generation gap. The researcher attributed these contradictory findings to the fact that these students represented a broader political spectrum with a greater likelihood of student-parent discontinuity than those students surveyed at the more prestigious universities. In this case, the generational unit hypothesis, rather than the lineage or family socialization explanation, is more accurate in identifying the influence of peer groups and campus subcultures on the political socialization of student demonstrators.[14]

More extensive studies were conducted in which responses from younger people, their parents, and their grandparents were analyzed. Results indicated intergenerational similarities on religious affiliation but differences on the marital division of household tasks, educational achievement, and family decision-making. Furthermore, additional evidence indicated more differences of opinion on sexual behavior before marriage between parents and their parents than between parents and their children.[15] Fengler found generational differences spanning three generations on such issues as the sanctity of marriage, religious values, marijuana usage, and ethnic minority group acceptance. The student generation, in general, indicated more liberal view than the parent generation; a higher proportion of parents, in turn, indicated more liberal views than the grandparents. This increasing degree of liberalism attached to particular age groups supports the cohort hypothesis that age is a contributing factor to the change in generational attitudes. Two exceptions, however, in which an increasing level of liberality was not found with an increase in age were the topics of the distribution of political and economic influence in America and a limited role for the military. In the former case, a higher proportion of students and grandparents felt that citizens were powerless and that economic well-being was unfairly distributed than the parent generation. The self-perceived powerless state of both students and grandparents suggests a situational alliance on this issue, perhaps better explained by the generational unit hypothesis regarding period and historical effects. Both students and grandparents perceived themselves as victims of societal events that did not give them commensurate political and economic rewards. With regard to limiting the role of the military, both parents and grandparents were opposed to limitation in contrast to the students who favored limiting the role of the military. This deviant case may be explained by the cohort hypothesis where the older generations experienced an ingrained dependence on and loyalty to the military through several major wars. Students, on the other hand, only experienced the "unjust" war of their present era.[16]

A recent study applied a formal cohort analysis which examined the cohort, lineage, and generational unit effects by surveying individuals in seven age groups from twenty-one to twenty-eight to a group aged sixty-nine and over during three time periods of 1952, 1960, and 1968. Results indicated that fluctuations in political alienation tended to affect all age and cohort groups similarly. All groups experienced a decrease in political alienation between 1952 and 1960 and a substantial increase in alienation between 1960 and 1968; in all instances, the level of alienation in 1968 was greater than it was in 1952. Therefore, the authors concluded that a generational unit or period-historical effect provides the most appropriate interpretation of the data.[17]

The studies reported thus far have indicated support for the age factor as an influential force in value orientations of white populations in America. Further considerations of selected ethnic minority groups indicate similar age-related differences. In a comparative study of white-black generational attitudes in Chicago, Edwards questioned Blacks and whites, ages sixteen to sixty-nine about their attitudes towards discrimination, towards members of the other race, and towards the Black Movement. Aggregate data revealed that (1) the generation gap seemed to be greater among whites than among Blacks, (2) younger Blacks and whites were more "left" or pro-Black, against discrimination due to race, and in favor of the Black Movement than were the older respondents, and (3) older whites were to the "right" of older Blacks, and younger whites were "left" of younger Blacks. The last comparison was explained by the researchers in terms of the younger Blacks having been exposed to opportunities unavailable to older Blacks, thereby creating an understandable trend to the "right" in their attitudes in contrast to those of their parents towards discrimination.[18]

Rich conducted a survey at the University of California where Blacks and whites were asked about their positions on social, moral, religious, economic and political issues. In both Black and white samples, half were under thirty years of age and the other half were over thirty. Results of the study indicated a greater similarity between Blacks and whites under thirty than between whites under thirty and whites over thirty. This generational difference did not occur with the Black sampling. Rich indicated the possible existence of a greater generational gap than a racial value orientation gap.[19]

Intergenerational value differences were also studied with one group of Asian Americans in the United States. In a study comparing generational differences in values among Caucasian Americans, Japanese Americans, and Japanese in Japan, researchers found a great similarity in the direction of intra-generational differences regardless of whether the respondents lives in Tokyo, Hawaii, or New Jersey. Daughters were less deferent, less orderly, more exhibitionistic, more succorant, less enduring, and more interested in sex than their mothers in all three locales. Sons scored lower than fathers in deference, sense of order, and endurance, and higher on sexual interest. The authors concluded that fathers and mothers in all three cultures were more similar in thinking than the parents and children in any of the three cultural settings.[20]

In a related cross-cultural study, Gutmann compared the views of young and older men on defining and managing their own experiences. Subjects in Kansas City were compared with those in several preliterate societies: Navajo, Maya of Mexico, and the Druze of Israel. In all cases, regardless of culture, the age variable was found to be a better predictor of mastery orientation. Younger men, between the age of thirty-five and forty-nine professed a more active-productive orientation focused on controlling their own destructive potential and maximizing their good, productive powers to benefit themselves and their families. Older men, aged fifty to sixty-four, displayed a more passive-receptive orientation in which they saw power which was once theirs, now resting in other hands. The oldest men, aged sixty-five and over, tended to deal with problems more projectively by confusing wish and reality through perceiving what they thought things ought to be as the way things are.[21] Cross-cultural and intercultural studies across ethnic lines tend to support the cohort hypothesis in explaining generational differences in personal and social values. It appears that across subcultures and cultures, the aging process seems to be a salient factor in influencing perceptions and attitudes.

In addition, cross-cultural research has been conducted on attitudes of individuals towards the aged in their respective societies. One study found that respondents in the United States, Great Britain, Sweden, Greece, Japan, and Puerto Rico professed many stereotyped beliefs of their aged that were predominantly negative in outlook, regardless of the country involved. American attitudes towards the aged, in light of our youth-oriented culture, were not unique, and in many instances, were more favorable than those expressed in other countries.[22]

Thus, studies in attitudinal differences among generations have produced findings that support the selected continuity-difference theory of the generation gap. When the problem is viewed in cross-cultural terms, however, research to date has indicated that there are attitudes that are more common in similarly aged groups across different cultural backgrounds than in different age groups within the same culture. The implications of attitude research are that the age factor and social maturation seem to be variables that transcend cultural lines in influencing attitude development.

The studies previously mentioned dealt with various methods of surveying attitudes of youths, the middle-aged, and in several cases, the elderly. Only a few studies have considered the relationship between the degree of accurate perceptions that an age group has of another generation. Goudy argues that because behavior is influenced by perceptions, such research is equally important in studying the problem of generational differences. When students and their parents were questioned about their own attitudes and their perceptions of the attitudes of the other generation, differences were found in attitudes between student and parent generations on such issues as leisure, the work ethic, and job considerations. Students were more positive in their attitudes toward leisure and were less likely to accept the work ethic or to consider the "good life" than their parents. When questioned about their perceptions of attitudes of the other generation, however, students and parents were able to perceive each other's positions accurately. In other words, whether or not their basic attitudes differed intergenerationally, both parent and student respondents were able to perceive accurately the responses of the other generation in an intra-familial context. The relative accuracy of perceptions indicates that if generational differences do exist, these gaps are probably recognized by the participants.[23]

A related study on intergenerational communication included a three-part survey designed to evaluate intergenerational communication in terms of: (1) shared information — the extent to which parents and students were aware of each other's histories, activities, and preferences, (2) parent-child agreement on persons with whom children would discuss specific problems, and (3) intergenerational attitudes about the content and nature of communication between them. Results indicated that parents and children who felt that they experienced more communication with each other knew more about each other. Both male and female students indicated a desire that their parents listen to them more often and not be so domineering and judgmental. The females expressed a wish that their mothers be less probing and more trustworthy of the information confided in them. The fathers felt that a lack of opportunity for communication due to limited time spent together was one of the major causes of the relatively poor communication between themselves and their sons.[24]

Perceptions of students and members of the older generation were also studied in a non-familial, macrolevel context. Researchers compared attitudes toward the town police held by students at a local university and by the older townspeople together with predictions each group had of the other group's perceptions. Results indicated that the older townspeople had a significantly more negative perception of the students' views than the students had actually professed. The students, however, seemed to possess a fairly accurate view of the townspeople's opinions of the police. This inaccuracy on the part of the townspeople was not reduced by contact with university faculty and reading about students in the local newspaper. The researchers claimed that such a cognitive gap of the townsfolk represented a misunderstanding that was an indication of the declining community-university relationship.[25] Differences in attitudes of separate generations obviously exist but in intra-familial comparisons at a microlevel of analysis, both age groups tend to perceive these differences accurately. When members of one age group are taken as a collective whole and asked to predict responses of members of another generation, however, the older members indicate some stereotyped impressions of the younger generation.

In addition to the studies of intergenerational attitudes, several investigations have explored the generational preferences for communication partners and actual communication behavior among generations. Lauer studied generational preferences for partners with whom to communicate about certain issues. He reasoned that the concept of a generation gap describes a kind of undesirable relationship between people of differing age categories. In comparison, one kind of desirable relationship is that with open communication channels. With this in mind, he argued that the generation gap might be measured through the use of sociometric choice — specifying with whom the chooser prefers to communicate. In previous studies utilizing sociometric choice, it had been shown that people select those who have qualities that are approved of by the membership of their group and which are similar to their own attitudes and values. Lauer reasoned that sociometric choice would indicate whether or not a gap exists between the chooser and the chosen and whether a communication breakdown has occurred between generations. After questioning junior high, high school, and college students, he found differences not only across subject matter but also between age categories. There was a tendency for the gap to be smallest at age fifteen, and a trend towards an increase in the gap with age. For topics dealing with a career or job, family, school, and money problems, most students preferred to talk with their parents. The largest gap occurred on the topic of sex in relation to dating. Three groups of youths emerged: those who tended to prefer peers as interactants, those who preferred adults, and those who expressed a preference for both, depending on the topic under consideration. Thus, in terms of preferred communication patterns, the Lauer study supports the notion that the gap may consist of basic value continuities with some shift in life styles.[26]

In a study that went beyond the use of sociometric choice, Wood, Yamauchi, and Bradac studied actual communication behavior between members of different generations. Interacting dyads who played a simple word game were composed of members of a younger age group between nineteen and twenty years of age and members of an older group aged thirty-five to seventy years in addition to dyads composed of interactants of similar age groups. When the younger members interacted with each other, they were able to communicate more accurately than when they communicated with older members. Likewise, older members were able to communicate more effectively with their peers than with younger subjects. In this case, data indicated significantly more effective intragenerational communication than intergenerational communication patterns.[27]

In a follow-up study with similar age groups, Yamauchi tested the effects of empathy on the communication process between generations. Dyads of similar and dissimilar age groups with high and low empathy scores interacted by playing a simple word game. Thus, there were high empathetic/similar aged dyads, high empathetic/dissimilar aged dyads, low empathetic/similar aged dyads, and low empathetic/dissimilar aged dyads who were tested. When members of different generations attempted to communicate, those with high empathy scores were able to communicate more effectively than low scorers. Despite the age differences a high level of empathetic ability seemed to enable the partners to bridge the generation gap. The ability to perceive differences in age and experiential backgrounds and the ability to place one's self in the place of another on the cognitive level enabled the high empathetic individuals, regardless of age, to communicate with other members of different generations.[28]

In addition to the previously mentioned studies that investigated interpersonal communication for the purpose of sharing information, a few studies have investigated the relationship of age to persuasive behavior —— a more conscious attempt to change attitudes and nonverbal communication —— a less conscious and more subtle form of social interaction. In studying the proxemic arrangements that dyads prefer in conversations, researchers found that American student dyads composed of male-male, female-male, and female-female partners over the age of thirty preferred a face-to-face arrangement of seating at a table. In the under-thirty dyads, male-male and male-female dyads preferred a diagonal arrangement in which each member sits on one side of a corner of a table, and the female-female dyads preferred a face-to-face arrangement. The face-to-face arrangement was hypothesized as being the more intimate of the two types of seating placements because it allowed for more psychological closeness connected with more direct eye contact.[29] This hypothesized preference for more intimacy for the above thirty group was partially supported cross-culturally by findings on interpersonal speaking distances by Heshka and Nelson. They found that in England, dyads ranging in age from nineteen to twenty-six years demonstrated a steady increase in interpersonal distancing as the ages of the partners increased. When the average age of the dyad exceeded forty, however, the interpersonal distancing began to decrease. The researchers discovered a curvilinear relationship between age and interpersonal distancing. Their explanation for the phenomenon relies on hypothesizing changes in dependency behavior with increasing maturity. In childhood and old age, there tends to be more dependency behavior on the part of these age groups, whereas during adulthood, independent behavior is encouraged and reinforced by parental norms and the person's attainment of skills to master the environment.[30]

In another area of communication that involves a more conscious attempt to influence behavior, studies in intra-cultural and cross-cultural persuasion indicated the influence of the age factor. Whittaker and Meade conducted a study in which four age groups —— fourteen years, sixteen years, nineteen years, and twenty-eight to thirty-two years —— in Brazil, Hong Kong, Lebanon, Rhodesia, Peru, and the United States were tested on their opinions on selected issues. Subjects then received a set of persuasive messages that were related to the issues to which they had responded originally, followed by a second set of persuasive appeals on the same issues but taking exactly the opposite position to those presented during the first round. The issues were varied and included topics such as the prospects for the discovery of a cure for cancer and the desirability of plankton as a food for Rhodesia. Regardless of the country involved, the authors found a consistent decline in persuasibility scores for male subjects as a function of increasing age. The same results were found for the female subjects, with the exception of the youngest age group. Thus, it appears that younger subjects, in general, are more persuasible than older subjects in all of the countries included in the survey.[31] In a related study with slightly different sets of age groups, Singh found similar results for young people in India. Subjects in two age groups, twenty to twenty-one, and twenty-two to twenty-three were given persuasive arguments for and against the nationalization of industry, trade, business,and public services followed by corresponding counter-attitudinal persuasive messages. There was a consistent decline in persuasibility scores for both sexes with increasing age. The older subjects were less persuaded to change their minds than the younger subjects.[32] Thus, studies on persuasion and nonverbal communication include additional support for the theory that the age factor plays an influential role in determining proxemic relationships and degrees of persuasibility on selected issues.

An equally important context of communication that is interrelated with the age factor is that of the mass media. A review is provided elsewhere by Atkin of (1) ways in which older people are portrayed in the media, (2) patterns of media exposure of older audience members, (3) older people's evaluations of mass media offerings, and (4) functions and gratifications of mass media exposure for the elderly. Major findings of the synthesis include the observations that the elderly spend from three to six hours in daily contact with the mass media, allocating more time to this activity than anything else except sleep. The aged are very dependent on television for entertainment and are particularly attuned to the news and information content of several media. Exposure to the mass media offers a vital link to the outside world and occasionally substitutes for direct interpersonal interaction. The author concluded that little is known about the effects of the mass media on the aged, nor is there sufficient evidence about the impact of portrayals of elderly characters on the rest of the population.[33]

In summary, it is apparent that the generation gap is not such a clearly defined result of simple differences of values which cause irreparable communication breakdowns between members of different age groups. A multi-dimensional set of cohort, lineage, and period considerations present a wider range of sources of interpretation of the generational construct. There is limited evidence that the age variable does indeed have a significant influence across cultural lines on the formation of attitudes, attitude change, and verbal and nonverbal communication behavior. Furthermore, when age-related differences are perceived, the possession of more information about the other generation and the ability to empathize with different generational members seem to help bridge the generational communication gap. When interpersonal communication is not always possible for the elderly, the mass media serve as a communication substitute. In addition, there seems to be an increased dependency on the mass media as individuals age.

Directions for Future Research

Most of the selected research findings on generational relationships reveal certain differences in attitudes and behaviors related to the maturational factor. What must be kept in mind, however, is that most of the studies previously reported constituted one-shot analyses of several age groups at a single period in time. In order to analyze a more comprehensive set of age-related data, studies of several cohorts across several decades is essential. These cohort analyses could include (1) a selection of respondents from all current cohort categories in a society, (2) stratification by appropriate socioeconomic and demographic measures, and (3) longitudinal follow-up investigations with investigations of both intra-generational differences and inter-generational differences across ethnic lines. Moreover, most of the research on the influence of age has been conducted with white college students in the middle and lower socioeconomic levels. Additional research needs an obvious focus for greater predictability on upper socioeconomic levels and ethnic populations other than just white college students. In addition to surveys of generational attitudes, empirical studies which investigate actual communication patterns of generations at both the microlevel of family interaction and the macrolevel of generational interaction might reveal more data about specific nonverbal and verbal strategies that relate to similarities and differences in values of selected generations.

In addition to the necessary methodological improvements, there are several major conceptual areas that warrant further empirical investigation. First, a more extensive look at the definition of age that extends beyond chronological, historical, and political dimensions can include (1) an individual's perception of personal age —— how old one looks and feels and appears to one's self, (2) interpersonal age —— how old one appears to others, and (3) consensual age —— the degree of agreement between the two perceptions. A study of these expanded definitions of age can supplement the more traditional conceptualizations of age and can provide additional insight into the self and other perceptions of members of different generations.[34] Secondly, the nature and extent of differences between generational cohorts is still not fully known. More systematic investigations are needed to discern the extent to which the variation of values and attitudes within a cohort compares with the variation between cohorts. Thirdly, the question of which kinds of attitudes, values, and norms exhibit the greatest variation between age groups needs to be explored. Fourth, from a cross-cultural point of view, it is important to investigate the degree to which the differences are salient in relation to ethnic variations in intergenerational communication. Finally, a wider set of considerations includes the impact of the mass media on the shaping of the attitudes of the younger and older generations. Blamed in part for intensifying the counterculture riots in the 1960's, the extent of the influence of the mass media in creating, reinforcing, and changing society's attitudes towards the elderly is still unknown. As an age group with increased longevity and larger numbers, the elderly comprise a unique cohort that seems to have the potential for gaining an unprecedented degree of social influence through movements such as the Gray Panthers. The nature and extent of their communication strategies for effecting social change warrants further study.

In summary, a case can be made for the importance of studying the age variable as a salient factor in influencing intercultural communication. A conceptual framework of viewing age-related phenomena from a cohort, lineage, and generational unit perspective has provided an initial set of research guidelines. Related investigations have indicated the influence of age on attitudes, perceptions, values, and actual communication behavior between generations across subcultural and cross-cultural boundaries. Regardless of our sexual, ethnic, socioeconomic, and regional backgrounds, the variable of age has universal application. Further comprehensive research on the specific role that age plays in human interaction will enhance our knowledge of its impact on human communication.

FOOTNOTES

[1] Pitirim A. Sorokin, "Social Differentiation," in *International Encyclopedia of the Social Sciences,* ed. David L. Sills (New York: Macmillan, 1968), pp. 406-409.

[2] Vern L. Bengston and Neal E. Cutler, "Generations and Intergenerational Relations: Perspectives on Age Groups and Social Change," in *Handbook of Aging and the Social Sciences,* ed. Robert H. Binstock and Ethel Shanas (New York: Van Nostrand Reinhold, 1976), p. 156.

[3] Margaret Mead, *Culture and Commitment: A Study of the Generation Gap* (Garden City, New York: Doubleday, 1970), pp. 6-7.

[4] Edgar A. Friedenberg, "Current Patterns of Generational Conflict," *Journal of Social Issues,* 25(1969), 21-38.

[5] Theodore Rosnak, *The Making of a Counter Culture* (Garden City, New York: Doubleday, 1969), p. 4.

[6] Vern L. Bengston, "Inter-age Perceptions and the Generation Gap," *Gerontologist*, 11(1971), 85-89.

[7] Seymour M. Lipset and E. Raab, "The Non-generation Gap," *Commentary*, 50(1970), 35-39.

[8] R. Denney, "American Youth Today: A Bigger Cast, A Wider Screen," in *The Challenge of Youth*, ed. Erik H. Erikson (Garden City, New York: Doubleday, 1965), pp. 155-179.

[9] "What Generations Are Made Of," *Trans-Action*, 7(1970), 8.

[10] Matilda White Riley, Marilyn Johnson, and Anne Foner, *Aging and Society: Vol. III, A Sociology of Age Stratification* (New York: Russell Sage Foundation, 1972), chs. 1 and 2.

[11] Ira R. Reiss, "America's Sex Standards –– How and Why They're Changing," *Trans-Action*, 5(1968), 26-32.

[12] Karl Mannheim, "The Problem of Generations," in *Essays in the Sociology of Knowledge*, ed. D. Kecskemeti (London: Routledge and Kegan Paul, 1952), pp. 276-322.

[13] Richard Flacks, "The Liberated Generation: An Exploration of the Roots of Student Protest," *Journal of Social Issues*, 23(1967), 52-72.

[14] M.D. Pugh, Joseph B. Perry, Eldon Snyder, and Elmer Spreitzer, "Participation in Anti-War Demonstrations: A Test of the Parental Continuity Hypothesis," *Sociology and Social Research*, 56(1971), 19-28.

[15] Joan Aldeous and Reuben Hill, "Social Cohesion, Lineage Type, and Intergenerational Transmission," *Social Forces*, 43 (1965), 471-482.

[16] Alfred P. Fengler and Vivian Wood, "The Generation Gap: An Analysis of Attitudes on Contemporary Issues," *Gerontologist*, 12 (1972), 124-128.

[17] Neal E. Cutler and Vern L. Bengston, "Age and Political Alienation: Maturation, Generation, and Period Effects," *Annals of the American Academy of Political and Social Science*, 415 (1974), 160-175.

[18] Ozzie L. Edwards, "Intergenerational Variation in Racial Attitudes," *Sociology and Social Research*, 57(1972), 22-31.

[19] Andrea L. Rich, *Interracial Communication* (New York: Harper and Row, 1974) pp. 115-116.

[20] F.K. Berrien, Abe Arkoff, and Shinkuro S. Iwahara, "Generation Differences in Values: Americans, Japanese-Americans, and Japanese," *Journal of Social Psychology*, 71(1967), 169-175.

[21] David Gutmann, "The Hunger of Old Men," *Trans-Action,* 9(1971), 55-66.

[22] Franklyn N. Arnoff, "Stereotypes About Aging and the Aged," *School and Society,* 88(1960), 70-71.

[23] Willis J. Goudy, "The Magical Mystery Tour: An Encounter With the Generation Gap," *Youth and Society,* 5(1973), 212-226.

[24] Ralph F. Berdie, Dorothy R. Loeffler, and John B. Roth, "Intergenerational Communication," *Journal of College Student Personnel,*[11](1970), 348-354.

[25] Kenneth R. Stamm, John E. Bowes, and Barbara J. Bowes, "Generation Gap a Communication Problem? A Coorientational Analysis," *Journalism Quarterly,* 50 (1973), 629-637.

[26] Robert H. Lauer, "The Generation Gap as Sociometric Choice," *Youth and Society,* 5(1973), 227-241.

[27] Roy V. Wood, Joanne S. Yamauchi, and James J. Bradac, "The Communication of Meaning Across Generations," *Journal of Communication,* 21 (1971), 160-169.

[28] Joanne S. Yamauchi, "The Effects of Interpersonal Decentering and Similarity on the Communication of Meaning," Ph.D. Dissertation, (1970) Northwestern University.

[29] Ann I. Tyler, Wayne L. Waag, and Clay E. George, "Determinants of the Ecology of the Dyad: The Effects of Age and Sex," *Journal of Psychology,* 81(1972), 117-120.

[30] Stanley Heshka and Yona Nelson, "Interpersonal Speaking Distance as a Function of Age, Sex, and Relationship," *Sociometry,* 35(1972), 491-498.

[31] James O. Whittaker and Robert D. Meade, "Sex and Age as Variables in Persuasibility," *Journal of Social Psychology,* 73(1967), 47-52.

[32] Udai Pratap Singh, "Sex and Age Differences in Persuasibility," *Journal of Social Psychology,* 82(1970) 269-270.

[33] Charles K. Atkin, "Mass Media and the Aging," in *Aging and Communication,* ed. Herbert J. Oyer and Jane Oyer (Baltimore: University Park Press, 1970), pp. 99-118.

[34] Robert Kastenbaum, Valerie Derbin, Paul Sabatani, and Steve Artt, "The Ages of Me," *Aging and Human Development,* 3(1972), 279-283.

BIBLIOGRAPHY

Binstock, Robert H. and Shanas, Ethel, ed. *Handbook of Aging and the Social Sciences,* New York: Van Nostrand Reinhold, 1976.

Birren, James E. and Schaie, K. Warner, ed. *Handbook of the Psychology of Aging,* New York: Van Nostrand Reinhold, 1976.

Eisenstadt, Samuel Noah. *From Generation to Generation,* New York: Free Press, 1956.

Feuer, Lewis Samuel. *The Conflict of Generations: The Character and Significance of Student Movements,* New York: Basic Books, 1969.

Gubrium, J.F. ed. *Time, Self, and Roles in Old Age,* New York: Behavioral Publications, 1976.

Keniston, Kenneth. *The Young Radicals,* New York: Harcourt, Brace and World, 1968.

Knopf, Olga. *Successful Aging: The Facts and Fallacies of Growing Old,* New Viking Press, 1975.

Oyer, Herbert J. and Oyer, Jane, ed. *Aging and Communication,* Baltimore: University Park Press, 1970.

Woodruff, Diana S. and Birren, James E. *Aging: Scientific Perspectives and Social Issues.* New York: D. Van Nostrand, 1975.

III

INTERNATIONAL COMMUNICATION

496

III

INTERNATIONAL COMMUNICATION

REFERENCES to our "shrinking world" abound. Futurists, like F.M. Esfandiary, write about the disappearance of governments and organizations which most of us have come to accept as a natural part of human existence. A great deal of turmoil within and between nations, however, seems to indicate that we may still be much closer to dreaming about a brave-new-world than we are to bringing it about in reality.

Meanwhile, technology has proven itself to be less of a positive influence than many hoped earlier in the 20th Century. With technologies have come problems of vast economic and cultural consequences. The great-leap-forward which many underdeveloped or Third World Nations tried to take with the help of radio, television, and satellites, has become a subject for heated discussions. With technology came a new, perhaps more subtle form of imperialism or colonialism. Those who controlled technological developments provided not only services to developing nations, but they also controlled the use of new technologies because of their high degree of expertise. Looking beyond the mere installation of these technological systems many people began to realize that they had a voracious appetite, that their very efficiency and complexity required continuous maintenance and input far beyond what most developing countries, and even some developed countries, could readily afford. Thus earlier, more open political-imperialism or -colonialism could turn into a subtle cultural-imperialism. A few nations, producing most of the world's entertainment and informational materials, began to become suppliers of information, ideas, and continuous images of a life-style or a world-view which was unknown to the developing countries. The resulting economic pressures exerted on governments have at times caused overextension for some nations of the world, as they tried to catch up with what had been presented as a desirable way of life, or a desirable standard of achievement, on television and in motion pictures. Because of the very nature of these media, and the compressed, oversimplified material presented on them, views of other people and nations rather than becoming more closely related to existing realities, tended to become narrower, distorted, or at least unrepresentative of the complex nature of human beings and their social structures. Thus we have witnessed an *increasing* pressure on the leaders of many nations to provide what the media have come to suggest as a reasonable standard of life.

The gap between promises made by political leaders to their people, and their actual ability to keep such promises, is widening. As a result, dissatisfaction all around the world is increasing. We appear to be living in a world of images created for us by material appearing on or in the mass media. Our ability to accept or reject the validity of these images through first-hand experience, on the other hand, is decreasing because of the complexity of our world. Thus again, distortion and dissatisfaction result as we find that many of our expectations cannot be met by the reality in which we have to exist.

Media impact has tended to create new dimensions of international interaction. Media contacts go far beyond the traditional channels between official representatives of nations in diplomatic and economic organizations, which were created and maintained earlier for the purpose of facilitating communication between nations. The final section of our book first deals with a number of the more traditional aspects of interaction between official representatives of nations, such as governmental leaders, economic experts, and diplomats. These individuals are required not merely to use their own ideas and aspirations for interaction with representatives of other nations, but they must also carefully consider official policies, standards, and national requirements which various governments have developed. However, beyond these traditional approaches we have also developed new international communication channels which may be as important, or sometimes more important, than the traditional ones. When contacts concerning the Cuban missile crisis, leading to eventual agreements between the United States and the USSR, were made through the good offices of a journalist, when Walter Cronkite and his television-newsprogram became a major conduit for the discussion of peace-efforts between Israel and Egypt, international communication took on new dimensions which had not been included in that term, or which had been considered to be less important adjuncts.

Another important consideration is the interaction between individual governmental representatives in a face-to-face encounter. The confrontations already mentioned can be extended to cover other instances, such as the war in Vietnam, and the conflicts in the Sudan or South Africa. In each of these cases, and in many others, it has been shown again and again that beyond the influence or use of the United Nations and other Super-National organizations, dramatic and bloody conflicts were resolved or modified by personal diplomacy and by the direct intervention of a few large nations. Our hopes and dreams for human interaction and cooperation may make us look to large international organizations, but reality teaches us that such organizations lend themselves more to the discussion of issues by small nations than their solution. Even today, solutions still have to be worked out in traditional ways by the large nations and through individual- or small-group-efforts. Methods, approaches, or styles tend to develop, change, or reappear, depending on the interests, background, or abilities of individuals representing their respective nations, rather than by official agreement or decree. Communication, even on the international level, thus tends to be influenced strongly by individual styles of communication.

I have touched on a variety of areas, but a large number of these vital issues could be further subdivided. Certainly they have internal, domestic, local reference-points, as well as international applications. The work of an individual like Henry Kissinger can hardly be understood only within the larger international framework of issues, it has also to be understood within the narrower focus of internal political, economic, racial, cultural, and possibly even religious issues within the United States. What I am saying here relates back to the interconnectedness of all human communication within the framework of systems we create for the purposes of meeting the needs of interacting people and groups of people everywhere.

Traditionally, not only in the United States but throughout the world, those of us concerned with international communication have begun our work in an area which used readily identifiable component parts, namely the study of human languages. Pierce addresses himself to many of these traditional concerns while using a more contemporary, expanded, view of communication, by going beyond the study of language as a vehicle, to interactional features. This theme of imbedding linguistic studies within social-frameworks or -systems, is a necessary response to situations we find as we study the actual use of languages. Pierce continues this emphasis, and expands upon it, in the second chapter of our third section. The relationship of language to culture is explored in some detail. At the same time, the focus on communicating individuals as our basis for the study of communication is continued. This emphasis is especially related to metalanguage, and the individual interpretation or attachment of meaning. Pierce contributes to our understanding by indicating that individual responses, across cultural and national boundaries, are also shaped and influenced by our cultural heritage and upbringing. Significantly then, Pierce's chapters serve as a link with what has been established in both Sections I and II. We must return, even in international communication, to the individual, his personal, individual make-up as well as his cultural background.

It is not always easy to determine exactly how or when interpersonal- or intercultural-communication turn into international-communication. But I do not intend to provide sharply defined lines of demarcation, which are established once and for all. That would be contrary to the very nature of human-communication-systems discussed throughout this book. On the other hand, Margaret Schneider Stacey provides in her chapter some insights into various categories of political communication which lend themselves to a better understanding of those patterns we have traditionally identified as international communication. Stacey gives us an overview of the complexities involved in these interactions, while helping us to clarify them by sorting out some major components or patterns.

One should also consider Stacey's patterns in relationship to Hopmann's discussion of international communication, in an area

which we have traditionally considered to be the primary
representation of international interactions: Diplomacy. Hopmann
provides direction to our continuing effort to relate individual
perspectives to organizational- and institutional-aspects of human
communication as they relate to international affairs. Considering
the many organizations within modern society, and our reliance upon
them, this effort does not negate our emphasis on the individual
within various communication-processes, but it is a realistic
extension of it. In a kind of case-study, a major experiment in
international communication, the United Nations and its agencies,
are used by Magee, to allow us to make application of many of the
concepts discussed earlier. Important historical periods in the
development and maturation of that international organization are
used to identify organizational aspects of human communication in
action.

Diplomacy has been joined by another area of increasing
concern in today's technological world, as a major area of
international communication: the Mass Media. Covering all the mass
media in a precise summary, Lent discusses their development and
current status. He provides insight into existing situations as well as
tracing their history to make us understand some of the intricate
interactions between national- and international-systems of
communication. I have already referred to the relationship of
diplomacy to mass media. It is also the basic theme of Altschull's
exploration of the dialogues carried out by governments through the
mass media. Concern has been voiced by many who consider the
influence of mass media on the lives of individuals, and the impact of
electronic and print media on the role of governments vis-a-vis their
own citizens as well as those of other nations. Propaganda is only one
of the problems mentioned as a result of the increasing availability of
mass media messages. The future shaping of moral-, religious-, and
cultural-values via the mass media is of concern to all those who
depend heavily on other nations and cultures for their supply of
media programs. An interesting attempt to meet some intercultural
and international needs is the PEACESAT experiment. Limited in
nature, it nevertheless has effectively linked representatives of many
cultures and nations in a positive, interactional

mass-communication-network, which can be explored as one answer to some of the future needs of our world. Hanley's personal experience in establishing and developing that system represents the work of many thousands of individuals who are engaged in similar efforts to link nations and people. In the final chapter of this section of the book, Dupree reminds us that the performing arts, through cultural exchange programs, have provided opportunities not only for entertainment, but for cultural insights which may go far beyond more indirect contacts. They tend to provide personal and emotional opportunities to become acquainted with the accomplishments and contributions of other people, which are often difficult to observe in official or political contacts.

Joe E. Pierce:

The Linguistic Study of International Communication*

———

LINGUISTS have been unusually remiss in their study of communication in general and international communication in particular, considering the fact that communication is the central function of language. As an example of this omission, consider the fact that Leonard Bloomfield, writing in the early 1930's, did not even print the word communication in his index in the book *Language*. In reality, he did devote considerable space to the fact that people talk to one another, but, like most linguists, he was concerned primarily with the basic vehicle or mechanism of communication, i.e. the linguistic structure, not the process. Even as late as 1972, George L. Trager, in his book, *Language and Languages*, mentions the word in only four places and nowhere does he define the process. Winfred P. Lehmann in his book *Historical Linguistics* 1962, A. Koutsoudas in *Writing Transformational Grammars*, 1966, and John T. Waterman in *Perspectives in Linguistics*, 1963, also do not mention the word in their indices at all.

Over the past three or four decades the general approach of linguistics has been to consider language as part of a total communication situation.

Language is used in a total communication situation. When a person talks, his vocal activity may be called speaking, or speech. Speech consists of language in its environment of

———————————————.

*While Pierce stresses international communication in this chapter many of the features of spoken and written communication which are of concern to linguists apply equally to intercultural differences within nations and intercultural differences between nations. (Ed.)

paralanguage. Paralanguage may be described as consisting of voice set and voice quality, and the vocalizations accompanying the language material.[1]

Since another chapter of this book, which deals with anthropology and communication, will discuss paralanguage, we shall leave the point for the moment and concentrate on the principal concern of the linguist, i.e., the structure of the language itself. Traeger's definition of language is typical of dozens that have appeared in the literature over the past century.

> Language is defined as the learned system of arbitrary vocal symbols by means of which human beings, as members of a society, interact and communicate in terms of their total culture.[2]

The definition of this phenomenon among structuralists varies somewhat from linguist to linguist, but all are similar to the one cited above. However, transformational grammarians see language as something quite different.

> I will consider a language to be a set (finite or infinite) of sentences, each finite in length and constructed out of a finite set of elements.[3]

It should be clear from the two definitions that it is very difficult to discuss what "linguists" do because their basic definitions are so different. Despite this difficulty, if we are to understand how linguistics as a science can contribute to international communication studies, we must look at the way these scholars analyze a language structure, i.e., the basic units isolated, rules of analysis, etc.

All linguists, whether explicitly stated or not, recognize a phonological level of analysis.

> Martin Joos says, "the central problem of phonetics . . .is a two-dimensional problem: (1) Segmentation: how to cut

the flow of speech into consecutive pieces for comparison with pieces of other utterances; and (2) Decomposition: how to split the flow of speech into simultaneous layers for comparison with layers of other utterances.[4]

It can easily be seen from the quote above that phonology must be approached from two points of view, i.e., the segments and the layers.

The concept of the segment as a functional unit evolved in the early twentieth century. These segments are called phonemes, and a phoneme is defined as

A minimum unit of distinctive sound feature.[5]

In recent years the label "minimum unit" has been replaced by the more descriptive, "shortest isolable segment," but the meaning is the same. For example, the English words *beet* and *peat* are identical, except for the initial consonant.

It is this difference in consonants which makes possible the correct identification of the word when it is said as a complete utterance over a telephone without contextual cues which often identify words in normal conversation.

Concerning the level of analysis which deals with the layers of phonological characteristics, Roman Jakobson says:

Nous identifions les phonemes d'une langue donnee en les decomposant en leurs caracteres phonologiques constitutifs, c'est-a-dire que nous establissons pour chaque phoneme quelles qualites l'opposent aux autres phonemes du systeme en question.[6]

The units on this level are called *distinctive features*. From the above quote one can derive a definition of a distinctive feature as a phonological quality which functions in a given language to distinguish one phoneme from another, as the phoneme distinguishes one word from another. Returning to our example of *beet* and *peat*, the initial consonants /b/ and /p/ enable a hearer to tell which word he has heard in a conversation. The secondary question then becomes, how does he tell the difference between /p/ and /b/? By a series of tests a linguist is able to determine for any given language which phonological feature enables a speaker of that language to identify a sound he has heard as a /b/ and not a /p/. In English this distinctive feature is voicing, i.e. whether the vocal chords are vibrating or not. If they are, the sound is heard as a /b/, but if they are not it is heard as a /p/, and subsequently the word is heard as *beet* and not *peat*.

> Any one language code has a finite set of distinctive features and a finite set of rules for grouping them into phonemes.[7]

This quote explains the relationship which exists between the phonemic level and the distinctive level. The distinctive features correspond to sub-atomic particles in physics, i.e. electrons, protons, etc., and the phonemes are parallel to the atom. The distinctive feature is the lowest level of analysis, and the units on the phonemic level are composed of distinctive features. A complete description of a language on the distinctive feature level of analysis consists of a list of the sound features which are distinctive for that particular language and a set of rules for combining these features into phonemes. For example, let us create a hypothetical language which utilizes only the distinctions of high versus low tongue positions for vowels, voicing and lack of voicing, stoppage of air out of the mouth and the lack thereof with the stoppage being made at the velum or at the teeth. If this were true, we would describe this language as having the distinctive features of voicing, high tongue position, stoppage, and dental articulation. Further, we would have to state any restrictive rules governing the combination of these three features, such as: stoppage cannot be combined with voicing to produce a phoneme in this language. This would mean that the language in question would not utilize such sounds as /d/ or /g/ except as variants of /t/ and /k/. Most languages have slightly over a dozen such distinctive features and a variable number of rules such as the one illustrated. A listing of these distinctive features and rules results in a complete description of the language on the distinctive feature level of analysis.

Returning briefly to the phonemic level, since it is the next higher level above that of the distinctive feature, we find that a complete description of this facet of linguistic structures consists of a listing of the phonemes and a set of rules for combining these units to form units on the next higher level of analysis. Rules are generally stated in terms of syllabic patterns, such as: Japanese has a basic syllabic pattern of CV (consonant-vowel) and a secondary syllabic pattern of CVn (consonant followed by a vowel followed by an /n/). Some languages, such as Japanese, have only two or three syllabic patterns and some, such as English, have a great variety of such sequences. However, it is my opinion that the phonemic sequences should be discussed in terms of morphemes, or the shortest stretch of speech which has a distinct meaning affixed to it, instead of a syllable. The reason for this is that syllables are very clear in some languages and almost impossible to discern in others, but all languages have identifiable morphemes. Looking at a language with a complicated set of patterns, English has morphemes which consist of a single phoneme. Consider for instance, the past tense marker /t/ as in whipped which is /hwip/ plus the past tense market /t/, a single consonant (c) phoneme, though it is written with an -ed suffix. English also has morphemes consisting of a single vowel phoneme (v) as / ɪ / in the sequence a bit, /ˌbit/. Some of the more complicated morphemic patterns are CV, VC, CVC, CCVC, CCVCC, CCV, CCCVCC, etc. In describing English, one is faced with a list of phonemes which numbers around 40, depending upon exactly which of several theoretical frameworks one is working within, and a set of rules which tell a person studying the language which vowels and which consonants can occur in which of the above positions, or slots. Significantly, sequences of phonemes form units on the next higher level of analysis, which is called morphology.

> "A morpheme can be described phonetically, since it consists of one or more phonemes, but its meaning cannot be analyzed within the scope of our science . . . The meaning of a morpheme is a semene. The linguist assumes that each semene is a constant and definite unit of meaning, different from all other meanings, including all other semenes, in the language, but he cannot go beyond this."[8]

The basic unit on the morphological level of linguistic analysis is the morpheme. This is defined as:

"the smallest meaningful elements in the utterance of a language."[9]

The problem of meaning is a difficult one to handle scientifically. Further, the definition of meaning by various scholars is very different. As an anthropological-linguist, I much prefer to define the meaning of a morpheme as the category of reality for which a given sequence of phonemes is a symbol, for instance, the collection of objects symbolized by *spoon* (cf. chapter II in this section). To use another illustration, the meaning of the word *book* is the total range of all elements for which one would utilize the morpheme *book*, and *book* is a single morpheme which is also a *word*. There are two major problems involved here, (1) different people include different items in the category *book* and (2) is the morpheme *book* in the sequence *to make book* the same as or different from *to make a book?* The general rule applied to this latter problem is that if two units have identical phonemic shape (cf. Joe E. Pierce, "Morphemes as Sequences of Phonemes," *Linguistics*, Volume 80, pp. 65-67, 1972) and an overlap in items denoted, then they should be treated as a single morpheme. The first problem is quite simple. No two people classify items in their culture or their environment in exactly the same way. This means, quite clearly, that the only type of meaning that has any validity in terms of linguistic structure is some sort of statistical treatment of the varied meanings held in the minds of the different speakers. There is currently no agreement among linguists as to how this should be handled. As a result, each treatment, if indeed the subject is treated at all, is idiosyncratic.

Morphemes come in two fundamentally different types. Traditionally this difference has been discussed in terms of whether a given morpheme is considered to be an affix or a stem. However, this difference is misleading, because whether a morpheme is a stem or an affix is irrelevant to linguistic analysis, except insofar as this difference correlates with the linguistic function of the morpheme in question. The problem here is not a major one for most European languages which are highly inflective. However, the problem becomes acute when one attempts to understand the structure of an isolating language like English or Chinese. In isolating languages the great mass of morphemes are all free forms, hence by the traditional definition all stems. Yet this sort of lumping obscures the critical functional differences between such morphemes as *book* and *to*. In most languages the former would be a stem and the latter an affix of some sort. However, in isolating languages, both are stems. The fundamental difference shows up clearly in the frequencies of usage for the lexical and grammatical morpheme (cf. Joe E. Pierce, "A Statistical Study of Grammar and Lexicon in Turkish and Sahaptin," *International Journal of American Linguistics*, Volume 29, Part 2, pp. 96-106, 1963). In an attempt to escape this problem C.F. Voegelin and others have coined the labels *major morphemes* and *minor morphemes*.

> "Parallel to the cover term 'major morpheme class' for stem classes, we use the cover term 'minor morpheme class' for affixes and operators." [10]

This is a significant step in understanding how languages operate, because the concept of the minor morpheme enables us to put such forms as in, to, at, from, with, who, into the same category as such morphemes as, -ment, -tion, -s, -en, -er. This classification is based on the function of each morpheme as a grammatical marker. The point is that major morphemes are the symbols for the things that people want to talk about, and the minor morphemes are the grammatical forms which tell us how these items relate to each other and to other aspects of reality. Consider the following English sentence.

> The smargs were glumphing over the squirzy jobe while the garnads frenzed warfully.

This statement is a perfectly correct English sentence, as far as the grammar is concerned, and any speaker of English has a very clear idea of who is doing what to what. However, one does not know what *smargs* are, what *glumphing* is, what a *jobe* is, what quality *squirzy* refers to, what *garnads* are, the meaning of the verb *frenzed* or what emotional state *warful* represents. However, you know that whatever the *smargs* are, they are performing the act of *glumphing* over the *jobe*, and that the *jobe* was *squirzy*. At the same time the *garnads* were performing the act of *frenz* and they were doing it *warfully*. The content is absent. The real point is that you cannot speak or understand a language without knowing practically all of the minor morphemes, which number only about 300 in any given language, because they come up with high frequency in any communication situation. The content, or major, morphemes are situationally determined. For example, a person can speak English all his life without hearing the word *brazier*. Some words occur in connection with cooking, some baking, some with engineering, some in the north, some in the south, etc., but the minor morphemes occur everywhere. It is totally irrelevant whether or not they are stems or affixes, and it is this irrelevant item which is eliminated by the new concepts of major and minor morphemes.

A description of a language on the morphemic level of analysis consists of a set of classes of major morphemes, such as noun, verb, adjective, etc., and a set of classes of minor morphemes, such as pronoun, prepositions, conjunctions, etc. The labels listed in the preceding sentence might give one the impression that this approach is parallel to the traditional analyses of European languages, and it clearly is not. One has to define noun in terms of the types of syntactic functions a given set of morphemes can perform, not their meaning. Definitions such as a noun is the name of a person, place or thing are really quite meaningless. Nouns in English are morphemes which can be pluralized or have the possessive suffix affixed to them. Other classes are defined in terms of the sequences into which they can and cannot be placed in real, meaningful English sentences. In addition to the sets of classes mentioned above, there are a set of rules which tell how to form grammatically correct words in that language. Both structuralists and transformationalists would agree generally with this statement, but the way representatives of the two schools would determine the classes and the way they would state the rules are very different. Here again, we see that the units on one level are combined to form units on the next higher level. This method of organizing linguistic phenomena probably reflects some sort of ordering within the human brain which makes language possible.

On the word level of analysis we have a situation parallel to that on the morpheme level. Words in one language, for instance Chinese, will consist of a single morpheme. Nearly all words in that language are single morphemes, and as a result there is little difference between the two levels. In other languages there are long and complex words, for example in Turkish, where one can find a word such as "gel-mi-yor-sunuz-mu?" which means "is it that you are not coming?", a sequence of five morphemes. Some Turkish words are as long as seventeen morphemes and only a few consist of a single morpheme. As a matter of fact, several counts have shown that the average Turkish word consist of between four and five morphemes. This means that there are four or five concepts involved in each word, whereas in English a word generally has only one or two concepts involved (cf. Joe E. Pierce, "Words vs. Morpheme Levels of Analysis in English Grammar," *Linguistics*, Volume 68, pp. 29-34, 1971).

A description of this level of analysis would consist of a set of classes of words, which may be the same or different from the sets of classes of morphemes, and a set of rules for combining words into phrases. For example, it is almost impossible to make a good case for a *morpheme* class "noun" in English as opposed to a *morpheme* class "verb," because virtually every noun can be used as a verb and virtually every verb can be used as a noun. However, when we get to the *word* level, there are great lists of derived words such as *government*, which can be used only as nouns. In that case one is on fairly safe ground when he sets up a *word* class "noun" as opposed to a *word* class "verb." These then are combined into sequences which form units on the next higher, i.e. phrase, level of analysis.

Most linguists go directly from the morpheme level to the phrase level without worrying too much about words, or at best they describe a hopelessly confused mixture of words and morphemes. Trager honors the distinction at least verbally.

> "The relations of morphemes are studied in terms of the sequences and arrangements of the morpheme complexes known as words, as these sequences and arrangements –– called phrases and clauses –– are delimited by suprasegmental (accentual) and terminal (transitional contour) patterns.[11]

Trager misses a critical point, however, in the analysis of linguistic structures. The point is that there are different parts of speech, or different classes, on the morphological and word levels of analysis.

Most practicing linguists set up a language as having nouns, verbs, etc., and almost never does one mention in print that English has a clear-cut class differentiation between nouns and verbs on the word level and not on the morphological level. Further, there are totally different rules for combining morphemes into words and words into phrases. Hence it is very confusing to describe a language without separating the two levels and giving a clear set of which classes exist on which level and stating the rules which make possible the formation of words and the rules which make possible the formation of phrases.

A complete description on the word level of analysis, as is true for the lower levels, consists of a description of a set of classes and a set of rules for combining these units or words, on the phrase level to form the basic units on that level, that is the phrases.

The following statement is typical of the general definition of syntax by linguists.

> "The analysis of constructions that involve only free forms is called *syntax*."[1][2]

The lumping of all facets of analysis above that of the bound form into a single level of analysis is the most serious handicap that linguists have inflicted upon themselves in the past century. It is perfectly clear at this stage of our knowledge that there are several different levels above that of morpheme, each of which has its own distinctive units and rules for combining these units into units on the next higher level. Each of these levels represents a fully independent system, and the nature of language is such that the analysis of any one level cannot be completed until the level immediately below it has been completed. The reason for this is that there is a great variety of acoustic features which languages utilize, but only some of them are distinctive and some are nondistinctive. One cannot fully understand the phonemic structure of a language until the free variation is sorted out and labelled as nonsignificant. Once this is done the number of variables in every utterance is greatly reduced.

One cannot understand the great range of variations in morphemes until the phonemic structure, including the morphophonemic rules, has been clarified. When that task has been accomplished, another array of variables can be discarded and need not be considered further in the analysis.

If one attempts to analyze the sentence level without having the distinctive features, phonemes, morphemes, words, phrases, and clauses clearly described, he is faced with so many variables, that it becomes absolutely hopeless to determine exactly what variables change the meaning of a given sentence. To mention some possibilities, the variable can be due to free variation on any level below it, the Markov process, or the social situation. As a result one of the great problems in linguistics is to reduce the number of variables to a point where one alteration can be demonstrated to cause a change in meaning. Then and only then is it possible to really understand what is going on in a given speech situation.

Hockett states even more clearly than do Block and Trager the traditional position on the status of morphology and syntax.

> "it is customary to regard the grammatical system of a language as composed of two subsystems. *Morphology* includes the stock of segmental morphemes, and the ways in which words are built out of them. *Syntax* includes the ways in which words, and suprasegmental morphemes, are arranged relative to each other in utterances."[13]

Each of the two subsystems mentioned by Hockett is composed of additional subsystems which are not generally recognized. For purposes of this discussion it is unnecessary to explain every level, but it is necessary for the person interested in any aspect of communication to understand that linguistic structures operate on a series of levels. Each level consists of a series of units classified into categories. In addition, there is a set of rules to indicate the manner in which the units are combined to form units on the next higher level. The meaning of the unit on the next higher level usually has something to do with the sum of the meanings of the units on the lower level, but not necessarily. In any conversation, the listener hears incoming sounds, accompanied by visual cues, and he must have enough distinctive features to identify enough phonemes to identify enough morphemes, to identify enough words to identify enough phrases, etc. He does not need all of the cues, because linguistic structures are at least 70% redundant. Between two speakers of a given language approximately 70% of the stream of speech can be blotted out with no loss of intelligibility. In other words, only about 30% of the available cues are needed to correctly identify the elements in a message sent by a transmitter.

So far, we have attempted to present the basic elements utilized in the study of languages, and given some explanation of what they mean by showing the concept of language as a structure consisting of a series of levels. It is now time to attempt to relate these items to the problems of international communication. In order to do this we must return briefly to paralinguistics, because the units on the linguistic level, with the exception of the phonological levels, are symbols for items. For example the sentence fragment, "The big old barn burner we had last year," is a symbol for something, and what it symbolizes depends on the past history of the individuals involved. It could symbolize a party for two people who had shared a wild experience the year before. It could symbolize a large racing car, if one had a different background, or a number of things. The meaning of the syntactic symbol is not the same as the sum of its many parts. Returning to chapter II of this section, which concerns the relationships between life histories of individuals and the meanings that they attach to linguistic symbols, we must recognize the fact that the meaning of any symbol on the sentence level of analysis, is a matter of relating the symbol to the past life of the individuals who are communicating. If one attempted to interpret the "barn-burner" sentence literally, he would almost certainly jump to the conclusion that we are talking about a man or a machine which was large and which went about burning barns. According to the sentence this man or machine must have been owned by the speaker and the hearer during the previous year. As a matter of fact, this is not likely to be what our hypothetical communicators are talking about, but it is exactly what a person who has learned English as a second language is likely to conclude. A frequent problem results when the receiver hears a meaningful sentence and understands something, but the meaning that he gets from the message is very different from what the speaker intended. This type of misunderstanding also occurs between native speakers, but it is multiplied many fold between speakers from different cultures, because their life-histories are so radically different.

Let us look briefly at the way this sentence would be handled in the mind of the speaker and listener in attempting to communicate ideas. First, the way a person thinks is strongly determined by the structure of his language. For example, an American is most likely to think first of when an action occurred, who did it, what he did and finally what he did it to. This is very clear when an American is attempting to learn Turkish or Japanese, because he puts words together in the usual "American" order and often comes out with meaningless sentences. One of the most difficult problems I have encountered in teaching second languages is that of getting the students to think in proper sequences so that they can put together meaningful sentences in the new language. An American, while learning Turkish, must think in a subject-object-verb order of sentence structure, but because of learned linguistic habits he thinks subject-verb- and then realizes that he has forgotten to put in the object. Even if he knows Turkish fairly well, he often has to stop, go back, and begin over again in order to get the items in each sentence in their proper Turkish order. In Japanese, the American is always putting in the subject or object of a sentence when the Japanese would leave it out entirely, and this makes the American use of Japanese sound "funny."

The brain works something like a giant computer, and the sequencing method above could be compared to the programming of a computer. Probably the grammar of any language is learned and stored in a special part of the brain, just as a program is put in a computer. The sequence in which the smaller symbols are extracted from the brain depends on the sorting procedure of the brain. The sorting procedure is, of course, the program. Hence the ideas we wish to express, as well as the sequence in which we express them, are to a very large extent predetermined by the structure of the language we are speaking. What this means is that it is very difficult for an American to say the correct things when he is speaking Turkish or Japanese. The same is of course true for Japanese and Turks who are attempting to use English.

Once the electrochemical set in the body has established something that the body wishes to communicate, it appears from the limited data available that the brain attempts to compile a message by composing one phrase at a time, though this is by no means certain. Thus having an image of the wild party shared the year before, the brain composes the phrase "the big old barn burner," and sets about to move the tongue, lips, vocal cords, etc., to produce the distinctive features which transmit this phrase to another person.

The problems encountered in speaking are different from those found in writing. In speaking, one has the problem of interference between two different language structures on a vast number of levels. In writing, one is faced only with interference on the grammatical and symbolic levels. In the first instance, that is interference in the spoken form of the language, it might be felt that when one learns a second language he drops the distinctive features, phonemes, etc., of his native language. Nothing could be farther from the truth. Look at the linguistic structure from the bottom up. Beginning on the level of the distinctive feature, Turkish utilizes lip-rounding as a distinctive feature and Japanese does not. In a conversation in which a Japanese speaker is attempting to speak Turkish, he will, even if he has studied Turkish for twenty years, often fail to utilize the lip-rounding properly and also fail to hear this distinctive feature in the speech of the Turk. As a result, a phoneme may be misidentified. The loss of a single phoneme may not be critical in a discussion, but to take a concrete example, which happened when I was working in Turkey, a friend of mine remarked once that "There are lots of rocks in Konya," or at least that was what I heard. Since this is a perfectly acceptable sentence in English, and we were both speaking English, I did not think that there was anything peculiar about it. However, it turned out later that what he had meant was "There are lots of rugs in Konya." Had it not been for a subsequent series of comments which did not relate to rocks, I would have never been wiser. What happened here? As a part of English structure, we distinguish vowels produced with the tongue low in the mouth from those produced in the middle of the mouth. Turkish does not. Hence a distinctive feature extant in English and absent in Turkish caused this speaker to produce an /a/ phoneme where he should have produced a shwa, as in the word *but*. In addition, Turkish distinctive features are such that the feature of voicing never occurs in conjunction with a stop in word-final position, hence the speaker drew out a sound /k/, instead of the voiced counterpart, i.e., /g/. The misuse of these two distinctive features caused the misidentification of two phonemes which in turn caused the misidentification of the symbol *rock* for the symbol *rug*. Once this type of symbolic misidentification has occurred, the entire communication can take on a totally different meaning. For example, if the Turk bought and paid for a thousand rugs, he would be very angry if he received in the mail a few weeks later a thousand rocks, and he would assume that the foreigner was trying to trick him. This in turn might color his entire picture of dealing with foreign people, and as a result affect his life in many unexpected ways.

As we stated in the beginning, the linguistic structure is always imbedded in a social situation. This social situation contributes many things to the process of communication. To begin with, the environment in which a given conversation takes place gives the listener a particular mental set which conditions him to hear certain words which generally occur in that context. At the same time it prevents him from hearing a large number of words which are normally not heard or used in that situation. This probably works in the following manner. As we learn our language, the words that we hear in a certain context with high frequency are stored near each other. When the sorting process begins in the brain, the social context determines the point at which the brain begins its search in the memory cells. When, in its comparisons of the input with what is stored in the memory, the brain finds a word which has a very high frequency in that situation and which makes good sense to it at the time, it identifies the word as the correct one, even if it is clearly pronounced differently. For example, if one were to say at a race track, "I just made my bed," there is a very high probability that this would be interpreted as "I just made my bet," no matter how carefully the sentence was articulated by the speaker.

To explore this situation a little further, let us look at another example. A friend of mine was standing in a hotel lobby looking out the window. Behind her she kept hearing people come up and say "skwup." For several minutes she wondered what they were saying, because they were all Americans who spoke the same language she did. After several repetitions of the event, she turned around and the instant her eyes fell on the elevator, she knew exactly that "skwup," meant "Let's go up." The full grammatical form of "Let's go up," is /letsgowəp/. The produced form was only /skwəp/. Without the social context the sentence was not identifiable by a native speaker of English. Yet, with the additional visual cue of an elevator, the listener was able to identify a sentence perfectly with exactly 50% of the phonemes present. The only vowel remaining at all was the one under primary stress. The morpheme "let" is missing entirely, and the distinctive feature of voicing is absent from the initial stop of the word *go*. This shows very clearly the way in which language and the social situation combine to transmit cues which are later interpreted by the listener to formulate the message. The most serious problem in international communication are the differential interpretations of the same cues. These interpretations are influenced, as stated in chapter II, by the life-histories of the people involved in any communication situation.

The fact that some sounds drop out and some do not is a matter of chance or whim of the individual. This is a highly structured system within the linguistic frame. The details of this procedure have not all been worked out at the present time, but some work has been done. It is clear that one of the last items to be omitted are the stressed vowels, and the first elements to be eliminated are phonemes, or indeed even morphemes, which are near 100% predictable in that particular situation. This phenomena is related to style in a very interesting way (for a discussion of this cf. Martin Joos, *The Five Clocks*) because if people know each other very well, they drop out many more sounds and words than if they do not. A formal speaker must often utilize the full forms when he is speaking in a situation where he knows little about his listeners. As a result,he must put all of the information possible into the language, relying very little on the context or past experience. If he knows listeners with different degrees of shared past experience, he must, if he wishes to be fully understood, put enough into the speech to make the point clear to the person with whom he shares the least. As a result, the amount of the full linguistic form which is omitted tells the listener to some extent how close he is to the other person, and one of the social mechanisms utilized in normal intercourse is to become less formal when we want to be even closer. The listener responds by either dropping his level, if he also wishes a close relationship, or he restores the formality, if he doesn't want to be any closer to the speaker than he already is. This is a very complicated system, and it interferes with relationships between nationals of different countries, because the system is different for each language.

In this short article I have covered very briefly the various types of elements linguists have isolated, defined and utilized in describing languages. I have attempted to show how these operate in transmitting information (or misinformation) from one person to another. The problem of international communication is complicated on all levels by what the linguist calls structural interference. For example, if speakers of one language do not utilize a particular distinctive feature, phoneme, morpheme, phrase, etc., and speakers of another language do, this difference in structure often causes miscommunication, even when both speakers are utilizing a common language, say English, which is native to neither. However, most of these problems are obviated when one utilizes the written language, because all of the phonological interference is eliminated. On the written level, the problems are basically those discussed in chapter II, i.e. the differential meanings implied by different writers when they utilize the same symbol. For example, a speaker from one country utilizes the word "man" meaning mankind, and a speaker from a middle eastern country interprets what he says as meaning "male only." This type of meaning interference can be extremely important in terms of communication between nationals of different countries, or even between representatives of different cultures in one nation.

One avenue of future research which would seem very fruitful might be to do some statistical counts on the frequencies of occurrence of various words used in international conferences. Then some sort of study might be made to indicate the widest meanings which are currently in vogue. After this has been done, an international dictionary could be prepared with at least the meanings which are arbitrarily to be used in international conferences.

Basically, what the linguists have to offer are their talents in analyzing all of the structural levels discussed in this paper. What is really needed is a thorough analysis of all levels of all languages utilized in international communications. Then these analyses should be published in such a way that the information would be easily accessible to individuals who must communicate with nationals of other countries. This certainly would not solve all the problems, but if a person is not aware that he is saying *rock* instead of *rug*, it is difficult for him to be fully effective as a communicator.

FOOTNOTES

[1] George L. Trager, *Language and Languages,* p. 10, 1972.

[2] *Ibid.*, p. 70.

[3] Noam Chomsky, *Syntactic Structures*, p. 13, 1957.

[4] Martin Joos, *Acoustic Phonetics*, p. 66, 1948.

[5] Leonard Bloomfield, *Language*, p. 79, 1933.

[6] Roman Jakobson, "Observations sur le Classement Phonologique des consonnes," in *Selected Writings of Roman Jakobson*, p. 272, 1962.

[7] Roman Jakobson, Gunner M. Fant and Morris Halle, *Preliminaries of Speech Analysis*, p. 4, 1952.

[8] Leonard Bloomfield, *Language*, pp. 161-2, 1933.

[9] Charles F. Hockett, *A Course in Modern Linguistics*, p. 123, 1960.

[10] C.F. Voegelin, A.K. Ramanujan, F.M. Voegelin, *Meaning Correlations and Selections in Morphology-Syntax Paradigms*, Bulletin of Institute of History and Philology Academia Sinica, volume XXIX, 1957.

[11] George L. Trager, *Language and Languages*, p. 49, 1972.

[12] Bernard Bloch and George L. Trager, *Outline of Linguistic Analysis*, Linguistic Society of America, Special Publications, 1942.

[13] Charles F. Hockett, *A Course in Modern Linguistics*, Macmillan Company, 1960, p. 177.

BIBLIOGRAPHY

Bloomfield, Leonard, *Language*, Henry Holt and Company (1933).

Bloomfield, Morton W. and Newmark, Leonard, *A Linguistic Introduction to the History of English*, Alfred A. Knopf (1963).

Bloch, Bernard and Trager, George L., *Outline of Linguistic Analysis*, Linguistic Society of America, Special Publications (1942).

Bram, Joseph, *Language* and *Society*, Random House (1955).

Chomsky, Noam, *Syntactic Structures,* Mouton and Co. (1957). *Aspects of the Theory of Syntax*, MIT Press (1965). *Topics in the Theory of Generative Grammar*, Mouton (1966).

Gleason, Henry A. Jr., *An Introduction to Descriptive Linguistics,* Holt, Rinehart and Winston (1955).

Harris, Zellig, *Methods in Structural Linguistics*, University of Chicago Press (1951).

Hayakawa, S.I., *Language in Thought and Action*, Harcourt Brace Jovanovich (1963).

Hockett, Charles F., *A Course in Modern Linguistics*, Macmillan (1958).

Jakobson, Roman, *Selected Writings*, Mouton (1962).

Jakobson, Roman, Gunner M. Fant and Morris Halle, *Preliminaries of Speech Analysis* (Report No. 13, Acoustic Laboratory, MIT, 1952).

Joos, Martin, *Acoustic Phonetics*, Special Publications, Linguistic Society of America (1948). *Five Clocks*, Harcourt Brace and World (1967).

Koutsoudas, A., *Writing Transformational Grammars*, McGraw-Hill (1966).

Kurath, Hans, *A Word Geography of the Eastern United States*, University of Michigan Press (1949).

Lehman, Winfred P., *Historical Linguistics*, Holt, Rinehart and Winston (1962).

Martinet, Andre, *A Functional View of Language*, The Clarendon Press (1961).

Moore, Samuel, *Historical Outlines of English Sounds and Inflections*, Revised by Albert H. Marckwardt, University of Michigan Press (1951).

Newman, Stanley, *Zuni Grammar*, University of New Mexico Press (1965).

Nida, Eugene, *Morphology*, the Descriptive Analysis of Words, University of Michigan Publications in Linguistics 2 (1949).

Pederson, Holger, *Linguistic Science in the Nineteenth Century*, Translated by J. Spargo, Indiana University Press (1962).

Pierce, Joe E., *A Statistical Study of Grammar and Lexicon in Turkish and Sahaptin (Klikitat)*, International Journal of American Linguistics, volume 29, pp. 96-103 (1963). *The Word vs. Morpheme Level of Analysis in English Grammar*, Linguistics, volume 68, pp. 29-34 (1971). *A Theory of Language, Culture and Human Behavior*, the HaPi Press (1972). *Morphemes as Sequences of Phonemes*, Linguistics, volume 80, pp. 65-67 (1972).

Pike, Kenneth L., *Phonemics*, University of Michigan Press (1947). *Intonation of American English*, University of Michigan Press (1945).

Sapir, Edward, *Language*, Harcourt Brace and Company (1921). *Selected Writings of Edward Sapir in Language, Culture and Personality*, David G. Mandelbaum, ed., University of California Press (1949).

Samarin, William J., *Field Linguistics*, Holt, Rinehart and Winston (1967).

Shannon, Claude and Warren Weaver, *The Mathematical Theory of Communication*, University of Illinois Press (1949).

Sledd, James, *A Short Introduction to English Grammar*, Scott, Foresman and Company (1959).

Sturtevant, Edgar H., *An Introduction to Linguistic Science*, Yale University Press (1947).

Trager, George L., *Language and Languages*, Chandler Publishing Company (1972).

Voegelin, C.F., Ramanujan, A.K., and Voegelin, F.M., "Typology of Density Ranges I: Introduction," *International Journal of American Linguistics*, volume 26, p. 201 (1960); and Voegelin, C.F., "Meaning Correlations and Selections in Morphology —— Syntax Paradigms, *Bulletin of Institute of History and Philology Academic Sinica* volume XXIX (1957).

Waterman, John T., *Perspectives in Linguistics* University of Chicago Press (1963).

Weinreich, Uriel, *Languages in Contact*, Publication of the Linguistic Circle of New York (1953).

Wells, Roulon, *Immediate Constituents*, Language, volume 23, pp. 81-117 (1947).

Whorf, Benjamin Lee, *Language, Thought and Reality*, John B. Carroll (ed.), MIT Press (1956).

Joe E. Pierce:

Life Histories of Individuals and Their impact on
International Communication

———————

THE CONCERN of anthropology in international communication must focus on the relationship between what has been termed language and culture (Sapir, 1949) or language in culture (Hoijer, 1954). Scholars in this field see communication failures predominantly in terms of cultural differences.

> The question of the relation between language and culture often involves a complex of issues . . . such as the degree of interdependence between language and thought, or the rest of culture, or personality, or behavior, and the relative preponderance of influence in one or the other direction.[1]

Further:

> One may look at language as making thought possible . . . as molding or restricting thought . . . as a powerful and essential means of communication . . . (or) as an artificial barrier to it.[2]

In simple English, anthropologists do not, as a rule, investigate the structures of languages, though some do. The primary concern of the anthropologist is with "metalinguistics" or "metalanguage." Metalinguistics is

> The relations of language to other patterned systems of society, or to the rest of culturally determined behavior.[3]

Hence this essay will avoid any discussion of the basic units of language in the narrowest sense, i.e. phonemes, morphemes, transforms, etc., and concentrate not on the symbol system, i.e. language, but on metalanguage.

Intercultural communication includes any attempt to transmit information or emotions between individuals from groups who do not share a common cultural heritage. This often includes international communication, though national boundaries often do not coincide with cultural boundaries. As a result, members of different cultures are sometimes citizens of the same country, e.g. Turkish and Iraki Kurds, and members of the same culture are citizens of different countries, i.e. Italians in Northern Italy and in Switzerland. Hence intercultural communication is a more inclusive concept than international communication.

Any understanding of communication, international or otherwise, must rest on the knowledge that only sound waves are transmitted from one individual to another.

> Whatever whimsical gods there be, not the least of their ironies is this, that language, which is often durable as the granite-ribbed rock, is built with air.[4]

This implies, of course, that whatever meaning a man attaches to an utterance he hears must come from within his own brain. It is imperative that those dealing with any aspect of spoken communication understand this basic fact. Information, etc., cannot be transferred from one person to another.

The field of anthropology has a history of over half a century during which a significant amount of time and energy has gone into the study of intercultural communication.

> To what extent and in what ways is a language related to the world-view of those who speak it? This question has gained prominence in American anthropology in association with the work of Benjamin Whorf and Dorothy Lee, but Whorf himself saw his work as part of a tradition formed by Boas and Sapir. In fact, interest in the question can be traced backwards through

the work of Daniel Brinton in the late nineteenth century to that of Wilhelm von Humbolt at its beginnings.[5]

The study of the relationship between language and behavior has been labeled in many ways during the past century. In the early days such research was referred to simply as studies of language and culture (Benjamin Lee Whorf, 1956) and later as studies in *Language in Culture* (Hoijer, 1954). By the mid-fifties C.F. Voegelin utlized the label *Ethnolinguistics* to cover essentially the same area, and currently, similar work is labeled *Cognitive Anthropology* (Tyler, 1969) and *Ethnoscience* (Sturtevant, 1964).

All of the above mentioned approaches appear to have one basic assumption in common, though this is not always clearly stated, and that is that the world outside the individual is composed of a vast, perhaps infinite, array of things which man can only partially perceive. Each culture classifies this vast array of things, as well as the concepts and sensations generated by these things, into a set of categories. These categories are completely arbitrary and have little or nothing to do with the nature of reality.

> Cognitive anthropology constitutes a new theoretical orientation. It focuses on *discovering* how different peoples organize and use their cultures . . . It assumes that each people has a unique system for perceiving and organizing material phenomena . . . (Traditional cultural) descriptions may tell us something about the way an anthropologist thinks about a culture, but there is little if any, reason to believe that they tell us anything about their culture.[6]

As a simple example of the arbitrariness of cultural classification systems, consider the two words blue and green in English. The range of the color spectrum which is covered by those two words, is in many languages covered by only a single term.[7] Basically, current work in this field seems to emphasize the labels which occur in a given language and represent the classes of reality (cf. Conklin, 1969). As a typical example, the Aymara have over two hundred words all of which translate into English as potato. English speakers would treat all of these two hundred classes as if they were only a single class, whereas the Aymara treat each class differently on the basis of cultural values. Many of the problems of communication are related directly to the differences between the two classification systems of two different cultures.

If the words we use represent categories of reality, and if different nationalities or different cultures categorize the world differently, then there is immediately a problem of communication. As a simple example, take the form *family* in English and *aile,* which translates into English as family from Turkish. In the former case, when an American is speaking of his family, he means his wife and children and at least part of the time his parents, and that is about all. On the other hand, when a Turk utilizes the word family, he is referring to a group of relatives that goes back in generations to his oldest living male relative and includes all of that man's male offspring with their wives, sons and unmarried daughters as well as grandsons, great-grandsons, etc., and their wives and unmarried daughters (Pierce, 1964). Hence it is easily seen that two people, one an American and the other a Turk, could talk for a long time about their families, and neither would be aware of the exact meaning of the other. This is typical of international communication. It is this basic fact of difference in classification systems which makes international communication so much more difficult than simple day to day contact with one's own people.

A sophisticated internationalist might say at this point, "but naturally when we communicate we utilize the same language, so these differences disappear, because when a student learns a second language he also learns the cultural system of classification that goes with that language." But is this true? Absolutely not! In order to understand this, we must go back and look at the entire social situation, extract the factors which contribute to communication, and then examine each factor carefully. Then and only then can we see the intricacies of the problem of international communication.

In any communication situation linguists generally identify three fundamentally different contributors to the exchange of information. The heart of these for the linguist is *language*, with all of the complexities inherent in the linguistic structure. Two facets of communication generally recognized by linguists, which are not a part of language, are *paralinguistic phenomena* and *kinesics*. The former includes such things as the tone of voice, i.e. does the man sound happy, sad, etc.; is he laughing, crying, etc. All of these qualities which are not a part of the structured system that we call language, contribute to the flow of information from the speaker to the hearer. Forcefulness, which is interpreted as anger by some, is also a part of this aspect of communication. Problems arise because paralinguistic phenomena, while not strictly speaking a part of the language, are learned, cultural behavior patterns. As a result, a voice which sounds very angry to American ears will sound sincere and heartfelt to a Middle Easterner. As a result, the American often interprets the speech of Middle Eastern diplomats as angry, when a Middle Easterner would merely interpret it as an impassioned speech. Kinesics refers to any body-movements which transmit information, such as the nods of the head which mean "yes" and "no" to Europeans. These same nods mean something quite different in the Middle East. In Turkey, for example, the side to side shaking of the head, which in Europe and America means "no," indicates that the listener does not understand what has been said. Possibly these simple examples have never shaken an international conference, but on the other hand perhaps they have; and if not, they are examples of much more subtle modes of expression, either tones of voice or body movements, which could easily disrupt any communication.

In addition to those elements listed above, there is always present in any communication situation the environment, that is, the social and political context in which a meeting occurs. One may respond with the comment that this is the same for all of the participants, and I would agree that the actual situation is the same, but each person interprets that context in terms of his own background. Thus representatives from countries even as similar as France and Belgium, not to mention such vastly different cultures as the U.S.A. and Burma, will interpret their surroundings in terms of their culture's classification system and react, not in terms of the reality of that situation, but in terms of their interpretations of that reality. Hence the social context for representatives of each country are clearly different even at the same place and the same time.

As a good example of differences in perceptions based on fundamental cultural differences, a group of Turkish students were in the U.S.A. in 1957 and were being interviewed by a newspaper reporter. The man asked if people in Turkey had washing machines and refrigerators. My answer to this question would have been a resounding "no." However, all of the students said "yes." The reporter did not pursue the question, but I wondered why the students responded the way they did, because both they and I had been in Turkey and knew the same set of facts, i.e. less than 1% of the people had such luxuries in 1957. How then could their answer have been "yes?" The Turks interpret questions much more literally than do Americans. For example, ask a Turk "didn't you go?" and he will answer "yes" if he did not, but "no" if he did. Obviously some people in Turkey have refrigerators and washing machines, therefore for them the answer to the question had to be "yes." I interpreted the question as "do most people in Turkey have such items," and of course with that interpretation the answer had to be "no." This type of differential interpretation of identical situations accounts for a very high percentage of the misunderstandings between people from different cultures.

Another factor, perhaps the most important of all in communication, is the life-history of each person who is taking part in a given discussion, i.e. the metalinguistic phenomena. Quite literally, every event that has touched a given person during his lifetime can have an impact on the decisions made by that person.

In order to understand the effect that the life-histories of individuals have on international communication, it is necessary to see briefly how a person learns the classification system utilized by his culture, and how he defines the boundaries of each class as he is enculturated into a particular society. A child at about eighteen months is just beginning to learn to speak. At somewhere near this age his vocabulary consists of a number of specific words, each generally used to label a specific object, e.g. mother, milk, etc. At some point, fairly early in the child's life, he notices that the same word is also applied to other items, i.e. another child calls its female parent "mother," and the child perhaps overgeneralizes and calls all women mother. This is a real example from some research conducted at the University of Oregon Medical School and is typical of the process of enculturation. Soon the child will call someone "mother" who is not his mother. That person will react negatively or perhaps laugh, so that the child knows perfectly well that that particular label was not appropriate for that person. With this hint, the child concludes that only some women are called mother. From that point on in the child's life his experiences help him to refine the boundaries of the class. Each time he encounters the word "mother" he notes the context in which it is used and the segment of reality that it is used to symbolize. When the word is utilized to refer to a person for which it is appropriate, communication is clear and accepted. When the child utilizes the word as a symbol for someone for whom it is not appropriate, he gets a bizarre reaction and knows that that individual is not a "mother," i.e. she is outside the class labeled by that term. This fact, and I repeat that this is a fact not a theory, has certain very important implications for all communication, but certainly for international communication, because the exact meaning of every word a person uses depends mathematically on the number of times each word has been encountered by that individual and the emotional and social context at the time of each encounter. This means that the same word can never mean exactly the same thing to any two people, since it is impossible for any two people to hear the same word in exactly the same set of situations, each with exactly the same set of emotions surrounding it, in the course of living two different lives. This is particularly true when individuals mature in different cultures, even if they have both learned English.

Another living example is appropriate at this point, because the first one was glossed over very quickly in an attempt to make the point. A girl about eighteen months old saw a dog outside her door. She asked her mother, "wazat?" which was her way of saying "what is that?" The mother responded with the word "doggie." The child repeated the word and went on about her business. A few minutes later, the family got into their car and drove out into the country. In a field near the road there was a cow, and the child pointed to the cow and repeated the word, "doggie." The mother smiled and said, "no, dear, that's a cow." One could literally see the intense concentration as the child mulled this problem over, but she merely repeated the word, "cow." Then, not much farther down the road, she spotted a horse, and pointing to it said, "cow." Again the mother smiled, nodded her head negatively and said, "no, dear, that is a horse." Again the child concentrated for a split second on this latest turn of events and repeated the word, "horse," but was obviously puzzled.

Let us attempt to reconstruct what went on in the child's mind during the learning process described above. First, she saw a small animal and was told that it was a "doggie." Based on observation of what occured, the child must have hypothesized that "four-legged animals with tails are called dogs." Then with this as an hypothesis, she set about to find a situation in which this could be tested. The first four-legged animal she saw with a tail, she called a "doggie," and was told that this was not an appropriate use of that particular word. On the basis of her experience, it was only natural for her to hypothesize that "*small* four-legged animals with tails are dogs and *large* four-legged animals with tails are cows." This she also formulated into an hypothesis, and she waited for a chance to test it. The next four-legged animal she saw was large and was called "cow." She was told that it was a "horse," i.e. her hypothesis was in error. At this point she realized that there must be a number of different categories of four-legged animals with tails, and that it was necessary for her to learn the distinctive features of each such class. Throughout the next few months, then, by careful observation, she delineated the classes, dog, cat, cow, horse, and a number of others. These words are what the linguist would call *lexical items* or *major morphemes*, and they represent the categories of reality that a particular society generally has some reason to talk about.

To relate what has been said above to the international situation, one needs only realize that every word in any language, except perhaps proper names, refers to classes of items or concepts in the real world, and that these classes have little or nothing to do with reality. The most often cited examples are the vast number of Eskimo terms for snow, all of which translate into three or four English words, the Aymara's over 200 words for potato and the Pacific Islander's proliferation of labels for palm trees, but this concept can easily be extended to all aspects of human classification. The universe includes a wide range of millions and millions of items and untold millions of concepts which each culture classifies into a small, finite number of categories.

It is perfectly clear from what has been said above that the content of a particular class of objects, e.g. cars or trucks, for each individual is determined by the life history of that individual. That is, the meaning of each word is a mathematical summation of his experience with that word. Clearly, then, the items which go into that classification are quite different in different cultures. The two categories above, i.e. car and truck, are very different in Turkish and English. The Turks do not have a word for station wagon, and station wagons are classified as trucks. As a result, when I was in Turkey, I had repeated experiences wherein total misunderstanding took place, because I drove a station wagon. I considered this vehicle to be a car, i.e. Turkish *araba* or *taksi*, but the Turks considered it to be a truck, i.e. *kamyon*. This is a simple example, but it is typical, NOT exceptional, and the logic involved can be extended to all aspects of intercultural communication.

From the example given in the paragraph above, and the increased use of automobiles in the Turkish culture, we might well predict that in the near future Turks will add a new class, i.e. station wagon, to both their linguistic set of labels and their cultural set of classes. This is a prediction which may or may not be true, because the present classification may prove to be perfectly satisfactory for all of the needs of the Turks, given their particular ways of utilizing these vehicles.[8]

Grammatical items are similar. Taking Turkish and English as examples again, there exists in each language a set of verbal structures which does not exist in the other. In English there are the so-called "perfect tenses" which have no equivalent in Turkish. One interpretation of the significance of the perfect tenses in English is the point of termination of an act. For example, if one utilizes the past perfect, "I had eaten," he means that prior to some time either expressed or implied in the conversation, he had completed the act of eating. If he utilizes the present perfect form, "I have eaten," he means that before the present time, he has completed the act of eating. If he says, "I have lived in Ankara for five years," he means that prior to the present time he has completed living in Ankara for five years. The Turkish language has no simple way of expressing these ideas, except to stretch out their equivalents in the long drawn out sentences I have given above. A Turk can say, of course, "Saat besten once aksam yemegimiz tamam oldu," *before ten o'clock I finished eating,* but his language has no simple construction such as,

"I had eaten." There is no such single grammatical category in his language, i.e. no classification system, which tends to guide his thoughts in that direction. In fact, as a result of the lack of the structural feature described above, the Turk does not think in terms of the completions of acts, which an English speaker can hardly avoid.

In Ankara there was an American who told a Turk, "I will have eaten by nine o'clock, why don't you come over then?" The Turk did not understand the perfect tense construction, though he had been speaking English for many years and could almost pass as a native speaker as far as his pronunciation was concerned. He interpreted what he heard in the only terms he could, given his particular cultural background, as "I will eat at nine o'clock." Following typical Turkish logic, he reasoned that it would take at least an hour and a half to eat, so he arrived at ten thirty. The American had waited until almost ten o'clock for the man to come, and left. As a result, the American was convinced that Turks are all unreliable, and the Turk felt that all Americans were liars. The whole problem stemmed from the fact that American culture has a grammatical structure which cannot be duplicated in Turkish, and as a result the Turk was not even able to think in terms of a category which is imperative for an English speaker. In general, Turks have more difficulty with the perfect tenses than any other single aspect of English grammar. Rarely is a Turk ever able to utilize these structures in such a way that he can communicate his desires accurately to an American, no matter how long he speaks English.

To turn the tables in the other direction, there is a set of forms in Turkish which is called the "-miş" tense, and is described in the grammar books as a past tense. However, the meaning of this tense is impossible to express simply in English, and I have never known an American who could really utilize it correctly. Generally, it appears to relieve the speaker of any responsibility for the information that he is passing on. To give an example, which I saw repeated many times in Turkey, an American is standing at a bus stop waiting for a bus. A Turk comes up and asks in Turkish the equivalent of "did the bus go?" i.e. "otobus gitmis mi?" He cannot say an equivalent for "has the bus gone?" because no such construction exists in Turkish, despite the fact that the above sentence is usually translated into

English as "has the bus gone?" The American looks about, sees no bus and responds with the Turkish sentence "gitti." A Turk, under similar circumstances, would have said, "gitmis." The difference between the two sentences is that if the first form is used, one is stating categorically that the bus is gone. If the second form is used, the speaker is saying that it appears to be so, but he really does not know. Because of the confusion between those two forms, I am sure that many Turks consider Americans to be dreadful liars, because right after an American has said, "gitti," the bus pulls up to the bus stop. The Turk wonders about the truthfulness of his informant, and the American doesn't know that anything untoward has occurred. The real meaning of the "-miş" forms is not past tense at all, but roughly, "there is no bus here. I have seen no bus, and it appears quite probable that the bus has gone, but I have no personal knowledge of this fact." The statement, "gitti," means, "I know for a fact that it went." We make no such distinction in English, because it is assumed that a person is giving the most accurate picture of whatever he saw that he can, and that all statements are probability statements. The Turk literally thinks continually in terms of whether he has heard something, whether it is highly probable, or whether he knows it to be a fact. To express the concept of a rumor a Turk duplicates the -miş as in gitmismiş, *it is rumored that he went.* The American does not think in such terms and in fact finds it almost impossible to do so. When the Turk learns English and the American learns Turkish, each carries these basic thought patterns from his own language into the new cultural situation where they are inappropriate. In anthropological parlance, this is the "interference" of the structure of the speaker's culture with the structure of the culture in which he is working.

Patterns such as that described above are not learned on a conscious level, and no speaker of any language is fully aware of what he is doing. They are learned as categories of reality by the child, as he grows up, as a part of his culture, in exactly the same manner as the young girl did earlier in establishing the categories cat, dog, cow, etc., i.e. by trial and error. By using a particular structure in hundreds of contexts and by getting feedback from the listeners each time, the child refines the category until it more or less coincides with similar categories in the minds of other members of the society. This is probably true of every category in our culture for every human being. As a result, no two individuals have the same set of categories in their respective heads, and even when two single categories appear to be the same, they usually do not include exactly the same set of real things or concepts even within a culture, and across cultural boundaries the differences are enormous.

One evening at a party in Ankara there was a rather attractive young woman from New York City as a guest, and she was generally the center of a considerable amount of attention, both because of her appearance and her constant stream of speech. Several people were impressed by the fact that it seemed that she was ordering everyone around. A number of the guests were offended by what they called "her manner," and while none of them mentioned it to her, several of them ignored her for the rest of the evening and also at subsequent social gatherings. Being both an anthropologist and a linguist, I became interested in the phenomenon, because it was very clear to me that she did not intend to order people around. If her intonation patterns were removed, her speech would seem perfectly polite and proper for the situation. Hence, what was giving everyone in the room a very bad impression of the young lady was the intonation and nothing else. It was very clear that to her these were perfectly polite. Keep in mind that everyone involved in this interchange was an American, all native speakers of English and presumably able to communicate fully with one another, yet there was an enormous gap in their communication. In different dialects of American and British English the same intonation patterns have very different meanings for the speakers. The particular intonation patterns, which were perfectly acceptable for New York City dwellers, were interpreted as domineering or commanding by the Americans who spoke different dialects. If this type of phenomenon can cause that much miscommunication within a single country, how great must it be between cultures or nationalities with totally different patterns.

A few years ago some student advisors were surprised to find that a number of their foreign students were very unhappy and felt that their American hosts were not treating them properly. This stimulated the advisors to investigate to see if they could find out exactly what it was that made the students unhappy. In exploring the problem with a group of Arabs it was discovered that they felt that Americans were unfriendly, cold and unresponsive to them as human beings. This really baffled the Americans, because they had accompanied the students from their arrival and seen them provided with almost everything that an American could imagine they would need in order to make them feel welcome and that America was indeed a very hospitable place. Despite all of this personal attention, the Arabs felt that they had been treated coldly and that no one was interested in them.

It just happened that at about the same time there were a group of Japanese students who were unhappy, and when the advisors checked carefully with them, it appeared that they had exactly the opposite complaint. They insisted that Americans were too familiar. The Americans intruded too much into their personal lives and were in general too friendly. Since both groups of students had received approximately the same kind of treatment, it became a puzzle to sort out the reasons that two groups of students, treated essentially the same way, could have such opposite interpretations of their hosts and that both interpretations could be so different from that of the hosts themselves. Clearly it had to do with cultural backgrounds.

In order to understand the phenomenon above it is necessary to look briefly at the manner in which Arabs and Japanese communicate when they are speaking with other Arabs and Japanese and the way Americans communicate when they speak to each other.[8] One major difference is the distance at which people stand when they talk (cf. Hall, Edward, 1959). Americans usually stand considerably farther apart than do Arabs and not nearly so far apart as do the Japanese. Considerable experimentation has been done by linguists on this matter and in general one finds that each culture has what it considers to be a comfortable distance at which to converse. If one stands farther back, he is felt to be cold and aloof. If he comes closer, it is assumed that he wishes to be emotionally closer. This of course causes a great many problems in international communication because these distances are very different for different cultures. An American in Turkey, who was neither an anthropologist nor a linguist, continually tried to maintain his comfortable distance when speaking with Turks. The Turks felt that he was being too unfriendly and tried to get closer. He would then back off again, and the Turk would counter by taking a step forward. It was amusing at cocktail parties to watch this performance until the Turk got the man backed into a corner, so that he could not go farther away. Then the Turk would move to a comfortable distance and continue his conversation. This utilization of what is called "personal space" is extremely important and was undoubtedly a factor in the problems of the Arabs and Japanese, since the two cultures are very different from America, but it turned out not to be the most important one in this instance.

Arab communication, when a group is conversing, is one of almost constant, penetrating eye-contact. An Arab often appears to be staring right through you when talking, and he expects you to maintain this sharp eye-contact too, because in his culture this is the normal way you feed back to the speaker that you are "in tune" with what he is saying. Americans tend, on the other hand, to shift their eyes, because "it is rude to stare." An American will in a normal, socially polite conversation, shift his gaze from one eye of his conversant to his mouth, to his other eye, away to a distant object, and then back to his face again. The more eye contact that is maintained the more intimate the situation, and this is probably true for all cultures. Americans do not maintain strong eye-contact, because this would bring them too intimately into association with their listeners, despite the fact that almost no native speaker could verbalize this fact. Hence the Arabs felt that normal eye-contact for Americans was insufficient and indicated to them that the people were not interested in what they had to say or in them as individuals. This was absolutely untrue, indicating the importance of subconscious cultural forces in any intercultural communication.

Moving now to Japan, when people converse, they almost never establish eye-contact, unless they are being *very* friendly. That is, when two people on the street are talking they stare away from the person they are talking to most of the time. Japanese, when they are talking, constantly say, "hai," "hai, hai," "hai," as the listener hears what the other person is saying. This word "hai" is translated into English as "yes," but it does not mean "yes" in any sense of the word, except "yes, I hear you, and I understand what it is that you are saying." It clearly does not mean "yes, I will comply." It is through this series of verbal utterances that the Japanese listener tells his counterpart that he hears, is with him and is interested in what he is saying, and not through eye-contact.

Looking briefly at the cultural backgrounds of the three groups, the differences in eye-contact (spelled out by the cultural system of each group) produced just exactly the type of mis-communication that one might expect. The Arab interpreted the light eye-contact, which is merely polite for Americans, as coldness. The Japanese interpreted the same phenomenon as prying and getting too close emotionally. Very little study has been done on this type of behavior patterns, and as a result we know very little about its impact on international communication, but we do know that it exists and that it causes serious problems in international relations.

To summarize briefly, the anthropologist is primarily concerned with the way cultural systems cut up reality and organize these into systems. One of the principal problems in dealing across cultural boundaries is the fact that while different cultures have classes which appear to be similar at first glance, they contain very different items, concepts or behavior patterns, and the classes often are interrelated in very different ways, e.g. a man in one culture is required to marry his brother's wife if the brother dies and in another culture the brother and the man's wife may have almost no contact. These categories are learned by the individual in any culture by a series of events in his life such that each event reinforces his categorization either positively or negatively. As a result, the system of classes of items in the minds of no two individuals is the same, even in a single culture, and they can be enormously different for people from different cultures. Meaning, all meaning, comes from inside the head of the listener in a conversation and not from the speaker. It can come from nowhere else. The only thing transmitted from one person to another is sound waves, light waves and an occasional touch. The transmitted vocal symbol elicits whatever category a given person has stored in his brain opposite that symbol and nothing else.

In addition to the confusion caused by differing categorizations of reality, there are a number of non-linguistic cultural factors usually called *paralanguage* and *kinesics* which influence the communication of ideas in any situation. These learned, patterned sound qualities and body movements are very different in different cultures and rarely are they even mentioned in language teaching and learning. To understand what is being communicated in a situation wherein a number of people are talking to each other, one must be aware of all of the physical environment, i.e. the temperature, the noise level, the objects which are visible to the conversants, as well as those that the participants know are just around the corner and could easily be seen if necessary, and the life histories of each person involved. Communication is extremely complicated, much more so than just the complexities of the language system, and as a result it is not well understood even within a culture. A great deal of research is currently needed on the non-linguistic facets of the communication situation and some of this is being done at the State University of New York in Buffalo, but presently the field is only beginning to understand the nature of these basic units or the manner in which they go together to form the cultural system. This means of course that each scholar is groping for a methodology which will make possible the "discovery" of these units in a given culture. It seems highly probable at the present time, though opinions differ considerably on this point, that all cultural units are at least similar to the linguistic unit, the phoneme. Currently, anthropologists are making detailed studies of a number of cultures, in terms of what labels they have for certain types of foods, plants, etc. It is hoped that from these studies will come the theoretical framework which will make it possible for us to tackle significant problems, such as those of misunderstanding in international communication.

One area, long neglected by anthropologists, is that of value systems. A given person in a given situation makes decisions based on his categorization of reality but also the value he places on each category. There is no valid theoretical framework and no extant methodology one can use in such research. Studies in this area must be halting gropings and, as a result, it is very difficult to secure research funds for such work, especially since they require long periods of foreign residence and substantial expenditure of foreign exchange. This is the area in which research is most needed and most neglected at the present time.

FOOTNOTES

[1] Dell Hymes, ed., *Language in Culture and Society* (New York: Harper and Row, 1964), p. 27.

[2] *Ibid.*

[3] Mario Pei, *Glossary of Linguistic Terminology* (New York: Columbia University Press, 1966), p. 160.

[4] Charlton Laird, "The Gods Who Trouble the Waters of Our Voice Stream," in *Introductory Readings on Language,* ed. by Wallace Anderson and Norman C. Stageberg (New York: Holt, Rinehart and Winston, 1962) p. 225.

[5] Dell Hymes, ed., *Language in Culture and Society* (New York: Harper and Row, 1964) p. 115.

[6] Stephen A. Tyler, *Cognitive Anthropology* (New York: Holt, Rinehart and Winston, 1969) p. 3.

[7] Cf. Hanunoo Color Categories, *Southwestern Journal of Anthropology*, 1955: pp. 339-82 for more information on this subject.

[8] Since writing this article, I found in *Hayat*, a weekly magazine from Turkey, an advertisement for station wagons, and they are now called "station wagons."

BIBLIOGRAPHY

Cherry, Colin, *On Human Communication: A Review, A Survey, and A Criticism,* John Wiley & Sons, New York, 1957.

Conklin, Harold C., "Hanunoo Color Categories," *Southwestern Journal of Anthropology,* 11: 339-44; "Lexicographical Treatment of Folk Taxonomies," in *Cognitive Anthropology*, pp. 41-66.

Hall, Edward, *The Silent Language,* The MacMillan Co., New York, 1959.

Hertzler, Joyce O., (cf. pp. 514-548 for extensive bibliography.) *A Sociology of Language*, Random House, New York, 1965.

Hoijer, Harry, ed., *Language in Culture, AAA Memoire No. 79,* University of Chicago Press, 1954.

Hymes, Dell, ed., *Language in Culture and Society*, Harper & Row, 1964.

Kroeber, A.L., *The Nature of Culture*, University of Chicago Press, Chicago, 1952.

Laird, Charlton, "The Gods Who Trouble the Waters of Our Voice Stream," in *Introductory Readings on Language*, Wallace Anderson and Norman C. Stageberg, eds., Holt, Rinehart and Winston, 1962.

Landar, Herbert, *Language and Culture*, Oxford University Press, New York, 1965.

Pei, Mario, *Glossary of Linguistic Terminology*, Columbia University Press, 1966.

Pierce, Gwendolyn, *An Exploration into the Applicability of a Psychological Technique for Anthropological Research*, The HaPi Press, Portland, Oregon, 1972.

Pierce, Joe E., *Life in a Turkish Village,* Holt, Rinehart and Winston, 1964; *Understanding the Middle East,* Tuttle and Company, Tokyo, Japan and Rutland, Vermont, 1971; *A Theory of Language, Culture and Human Behavior,* The HaPi Press, Portland, Oregon, 1972.

Sapir, Edward, *Language,* Harcourt, Brace and Company, New York, 1921; *Selected Writings of Edward Sapir,* ed. by David Mendelbaum, University of California Press, Berkeley, California, 1949.

Silva-Fuenzalida, Ismael, "Ethnolinguistics and the Study of Culture," *American Anthropologist*, 151: 446-56, 1949.

Smith, Alfred G., *Communication and Culture,* Holt, Rinehart and Winston, 1966.

Spier, Leslie, *et. al., Cognitive Anthropology*, Holt, Rinehart and Winston, New York, 1969.

Sturtevant, William C., "Studies in Ethnoscience," *American Anthropologist,* 55.3.2.99-131, 1964.

Tyler, Stephen A., *Cognitive Anthropology*, Holt, Rinehart and Winston, New York, 1969.

Whorf, Benjamin Lee, "Language and Logic,"*Technology Review,* 43: 250-52, 266-72, April, 1941; "The Relation of Habitual Thought and Behavior to Language," in *Language, Culture and*

Personality, Sapir Memorial Publishing Fund, Menasha,
Wisconsin, 1941.

Whorf, Benjamin Lee, "An American Indian Model of the Universe,"
International Journal of American Linguistics, 16: 67-72, 1950;
Language, Thought and Reality, ed. by John B. Carroll, MIT
Press and John Wiley & Sons, New York, 1956.

Margaret Schneider Stacey:

The Living Theatre of International Political Communication

PRIVATE citizens of all portions of the world are becoming the impressors and reactors to daily politically motivated international communication. Corresponding to that is the need for, and interest in, analyzing these political messages as to their weight, extent, and effect.

In this chapter three examples of category systems by which political communications might be examined are described. The first system views political communication in terms of whether it is official or private and whether it has political or non-political intent. The second system examines political communication on the basis of the levels of involvement and power. The last looks at the relationships that exist between the various sources and receivers in political communication.

The three systems selected are pertinent to this discussion since they all take into account, in varying degrees and with varying success, the bases of modern international political communication. All consider public diplomacy and mass media as important (as determinants in foreign affairs) as procedural diplomacy, heretofore the sole means of political communication between nations.

Though individual authors have refined and extended their theories, the forms chosen here seem most applicable in demonstrating how the passing of time and events do influence and often hinder analysis of this area.

The discussion includes applicable theories and prescriptions as well as consideration of the limitations and necessary adaptations of each mode of analysis. The system to be preferred is dependent upon the issue, the type and direction of involvement, and the

Weltauschauung of the investigator. To aid the process of architectonic systems, applicable theories and prescriptions, as well as extensions and limitations suspected of each mode of analysis are included. These three systems are derived from the writings of Davison, Fisher, and Lerner.

Politics, Policy, Power, Participation

Political communication, in the international sense, is concerned with the creation of policies which will affect the power relationships between sovereign states. It is an exchange of significant symbols which form policy images. These images in turn, govern international perceptions and generate the relational actions and power distributions among official and unofficial members of soverign states.

Each action of a sovereign power, each verbal and non-verbal pronouncement by a spokesman for a power is interpretable as a significant symbol which contributes to the molding of the image of the nation in the international sphere. The image presented to the beholder of the communication determines the responsive action and, eventually, the interpretation of power stances between nations.

The subtle and intricate manipulation of communication, image building and interpretation is an accelerating process. What was a determinable and understandable image of a moment, changes as swiftly as the communication causing the image changes. The number of spokesmen, the number of images, and the number of significant symbols exchanged between nations in international dialogue is so great that the analysis of international communication, at any time, between any given parties, has only limited use as a tool for prediction. Interpretation of political communication, on the international scale, has suffered from the failure to recognize these multiple influences. It has suffered from ignoring the consequence of image evolution and its impact on foreign affairs.

Heretofore, communication in international politics was regarded as a neat and easily understood phenomenon. International communication was conducted along prescribed official and legal paths. Significant symbols were employed as carefully as a Morse code but as all codes of conduct have disappeared so has this one. Images were determined, or presented, like the bidding of a hand in bridge, by set formulas, or opening a chess match by established gambits. Political tensions between nations were defined and resolved by the exchange of these delineated significant symbols. To be sure, accompanying protocol provided the means of ensuring the limits of the images. The appropriate protocol statements provided the identical interpretations of the communication for the separate spokesmen and nations.

The consequent almost aesthetic and scientific isolation of the transactions was characterized not by interpersonal communication between persons of different nationalities but between those of differing *sovereignties*. Sovereignty encompasses more than nationality. It includes supreme authority of a state over a portion of the globe.[1] Consequently, spokesmen were legally positioned persons and communication was a legal exchange. The images presented were not those of the political character of a nation but rather the image of a particular legal position in the power balance of the time. Significant symbols were not actions or words of a national with power to influence policy but, instead, they were carefully intended to be passages equally interpretable by the policy makers of all nations.

To understand more completely this transition from the age of diplomacy to the present, it is necessary to examine the changing personnel of the participants in communication, the changing concept of power, the changing definition of "policy," and the changing attitude toward the concept of politics.

From Procedural Diplomacy to Public Diplomacy

International political communication was once considered the exclusive and legitimate concern of the few: the trained diplomat, the foreign affairs officers —— the "proprietors" of the international organization. They seemed to be a group of closely linked and united cosmopolites who had created their own supranational society. Now international political communication has become the legitimate concern of everyone. Technological developments, rather than changes in politics, have brought this about. The diplomat is still the international communicator, not only behind the scenes through a press release, but also an image on the TV screen or a voice on the radio press interview, seen and heard in all parts of the world with all the concomitant effects. Through world wide interconnection the potential for a continuing global political dialogue has been created. International political communication is no longer the chatter of diplomats, the scripted and witty exchanges of international actors in traditional roles performed in the courts of the sovereigns. It has moved out of private club status and become the concern of a "world public" and of those contesting, questioning, and challenging power as well as of those who hold it.

It would be in order at this point to define the term "politics," as used in this context, as the study of the individual and the situational forces playing upon him. International politics, according to Quincy Wright, is the "art of influencing, manipulating, or controlling major groups in the world so as to advance the purpose of some against the opposition of others. The subject matter is, therefore, any international demand-response or influence relationship."[2] This collection of factors involved in the new public diplomacy includes historical and psychological elements of the individual situational forces of public opinion, material resources, organization of environment, and alliance structures. All of these play upon a decision-maker's image perception.

The decision-maker is "every man," the influences which play upon his image perception are "everything." International decision-making is not the abstract procedural approach in which a nation's policy is often believed to be determined. To understand the effect of political policy and the resulting distribution of power which forms the relationships that exist between states, one must study the manner in which a nation's spokesmen and citizens communicate information concerning that policy.

In light of these considerations, political communication could be regarded as any communication which has a political effect. From a political functional approach, the actual consequences of a political initiative or overseas program are determined not only by that policy's logic (as understood in government to government relations) but also by how the issues and policy offered are perceived by both the domestic and foreign publics.[3] When the presentations of the communication media interact with the existing knowledge, attitudes, and prejudices of the individuals receiving a political communication, the effects of that communication become apparent. This continuous image-building process is based on the integration of new information with universal concepts: learned beliefs derived culturally together with idiosyncratic perceptions of the world. Every communication item must be interpreted and translated politically by a blend of intuitive, instinctive, and culturally-derived factors from which the receivers (in the mass) derive their individual images. These images, in turn, determine action and a nation's consensus and stance. Therefore, without the influence of public opinion and consent, international politics becomes meaningless. This consent is obtained directly or indirectly, by spokesmen who constitute or envision themselves as international bargaining agents.

Sovereignty relations have been replaced by a public diplomacy which is both the cause and effect of public attitudes and opinions which influence and determine the formulation and execution of foreign politics. In other words, as stated before, the communication dimensions of international relations are greater than traditional diplomacy.[4] It is this newer, and presently more important, aspect of political communication that concerns us here. A method of describing the network of the new forms of political communication will be presented in the following pages.

Analysis Through Source and Intent Determination

International communicators must ascertain the source, official or private, and the content or intent of a statement in the international dialogue, to be able to respond in an effective manner. The first analysis system which will be described is that of Davison.[5] He bases his analysis on four categories or areas as follows.

1. The first category includes communications intended to exert a political influence abroad, such as those of the

United States Information Agency.

2.   The second category deals with official communication which is not intended, at least not primarily or obviously, to exert a political influence abroad. An example would be government sponsored sports or cultural exchanges.

3.   The third category comprises private communications which intentionally communicate to make a political impact. It includes the efforts of organizations which are intent upon improving international understanding or scholarly groups attempting to study world political problems and international political movements.

4.   The final area is that of private communication which has no political purpose. Such communication is most effective since it is least amenable or open to political control, for example, as in tourists' conversations with natives while vacationing in another country.

Political Intention versus Political Effect

Although these categories seem exhaustive, they are more useful in analyzing the extraordinary rather than the ordinary instances of political communication. The intention of a given communication, political or not, need not be related to its eventual effect. The situational forces of public opinion and information interpretation are the direct determinants of a politically oriented communication, not the intentions of the communicator. Public diplomacy may have reversed the original intent dimensions of the communication.

The motivation of international communication has changed. People visiting other nations are not there simply to see the past, the folklore and the picturesque. Many tourists, aware of existing international situations, are exhibiting greater political curiosity and are interested in learning or observing the political effect of foreign politics, power manipulations, and international reactions. Guides are becoming diplomats, tourists ambassadors.

An example of the impact of political communication on the market place is furnished in a humorous AP article by Hugh A. Mulligan. In the article, entitled "The Pushcart Armageddon Is

Really Ripe," he recounts that what to Americans is a boycott of grapes, lettuce or meat, takes on international political proportions in London. A pushcart operator commented, "The Indians won't buy Kenya peppers, the Egyptians won't touch a Jaffa orange, there is the odd chap who doesn't want a Portuguese plum or a Taswanian apple, and I'm supposed to know the situation in Cyprus just to peddle a few blasted grapefruits."[6]

Although this may be an exaggerated example, it does indicate that today non-diplomats are involved in communicating international political positions. The public at large appears to be basing more decisions as to where to go, what to do, and what to buy on the basis of international political criteria. Each decision could thus be counted as a political statement. Even if an individual is not conscious of a political situation or is internationally apolitical, his actions may still be interpreted in a political light by those who *have* taken positions.

Davison's second category explores the analysis of communication which is international or national, official or private. As it is difficult to determine what is political and what is not, it is also difficult to place a specific communication completely within one of these categories.

Today there are very few purely *intra*national events, most have at least some *inter*national aspects. Politically all of a nation's activities –– internal or external –– are at least potentially vital. Opposition leaders in small nations are as important to foreign political leaders and foreign affairs observers as the persons in power. There are few issues of political consequence arising in the world today which are not of some interest to the entire network. There are several explanations for this occurrence including the intricate and continuously changing alliance structures which provide balanced systems and relationships requiring nations to share more with each other than mere news relating to other nations.

For these same reasons it is also difficult to separate "private" from "public" in international communications. Private concerns evolve into official policies. It is more probable that official policies are regarded as mere facades to conceal private arrangements or positions. It is doubtful that a nation's foreign policy is governed solely by official statements of other nations. Furthermore, as both the number of sources and their scope of information increases, it becomes more difficult to determine whether or not a communication is the "official" or "private" position of the spokesman. The private opinions of public officials, viewed in a foreign context, can be interpreted in many ways, including its acceptance as an official policy. Conversely, a private citizen, engaged in business dealings within another country, might cite official policy of his own nation's government.

Of course, distinction between private and official communication is possible but the interpretation of such communication is the determining factor in the formation of an image and, in turn, the behavior of the receiver. It is the exceptional case where the interpreter examines both the private and official statements to compare the two points of view. Much of the time the two are merged in a stream of influences that affects the image of the source nation's events.

The need for a distinction between private and official communication is lessened by the advances in the field of communication technology. Today more information can be communicated *to* more people in more places, *from* more people in more places, within a set time, at less expense than ever before. Eight hundred million people are able to watch the same message simultaneously wherever they may be in the world. The systems of communication — satellites (Anik, the Intelsat series, etc.), microwave and cable systems — cover the globe in a matter of milliseconds.

This does not necessarily mean that effective use is made of these new facilities. Only part of the capacity for transmission of the satellite system is actually used. It becomes difficult to differentiate between private and official communication when the global exchange takes place in such a short interval. In the time it might take for a private communication to become an official one, the information (and its subject event) may no longer be of any import in the minds of the global viewers. Nevertheless, whether private or official, the communication relates to international political images and thus becomes public information.

Whether the viewers receive the communication as entertainment or subject for social conversation, it is interpreted in the light of their images of the nation of the news origin and the image of the relationship between that and the receiver's country.

Furthermore, the information that *is* broadcast always has certain international political implications. Every evening Americans listen to international broadcasts via satellite, broadcasts which cost the networks a fee of about $2,000 for every ten minutes, just to allow the Americans to learn about the politics of other nations. Why is the political information the main topic of these broadcasts? Or, more important, why is that particular international news selected instead of other items? Only a portion of the international political news gathered is ever broadcast. The who and why of this selection is an interim step between private and official communication. The relationship between the need for editing and the possibility of using news as propaganda calls for a close and objective examination of the source and the motive of the transmitting editor.

A number of questions arise. Has the editing been done to coincide with the opinions and attitudes of the society to which the message is addressed? Was the selection of news based on its political or non-political ramifications, or, perhaps, on its coincidence with the opinions and attitudes of certain official or unofficial policy makers? Have these messages been messages to fit the ears of selected audiences? Have the messages been chosen to provide the global audience with uniform images of world affairs? Is this a situation threatening free thought and choice?

Public versus Official

As with many other words in the past years, the original meaning of "propaganda" has been changed to imply an inherent dishonesty. In its original concept it was an appeal to reason and logic, presenting arguments supporting the desired point of view. Its employment in several world wars to corral public opinion on one side or the other, has demeaned it to the status of a blatant appeal to the emotions, instead of to the mind. It is, however, not the threat to freedom of thought that it is generally thought to be. The possibility of influencing the attitude and behavior of others through the systematic use of words or symbols is utilized more by, e.g. multinational companies attempting to teach hygiene in order to sell baby foods than by governments through their "Propaganda and Public Enlightenment" ministries and departments. Propaganda is limited in what it can accomplish. It is a sort of persuasion which can urge persons to do things they *already* want to do, to provide them with ammunition to support existing opinions and to create a significant effect that will help organizations rally persons to a cause or join a common effort and to provide existing organizations with information to enable them to function more effectively and efficiently. It is a type of communication which is not easily categorized. It concerns itself with varying official statements which may or may not be political in nature or subversive in political effect.[8]

National propaganda about international affairs tries mainly to communicate a favorable image of an ally or an unfavorable one of an enemy. It attempts to persuade citizens to support an existing policy. It does not so much attempt to win over as to reinforce people already committed and to gain support from the non-committed. The predominant objective is to provide significant symbols for the individual to form a clear image of an existing situation and the power of his own government in relationship to other governments. Since propaganda is a means of exerting power through communication, its effect, however negligible or minimal, will continue to be of use. Politics has always been a process of maintaining, losing, or struggling to gain or retain power – a process of retaining control and authority over others. The international political network is made up of persons attempting to gain or retain or maintain sovereignty over other people or lands. Power is the ultimate symbol in gaining prestige and maintaining image. Power creates a sense and cause for political behavior.

It is in this context that propaganda, in its function of causing people to behave in certain patterns or profess certain allegiances, becomes part of the process of creating nationalistic tendencies and national images. When coupled with cultural factors and historical traditions, it develops an image of the role of a nation in relation to the changing world situation.

The formation of images of national identity or sovereignty is not restricted solely to the official statements of policy makers but is maintained through the content and context of innumerable official and private communications from at home or abroad. The sectors of political communicators which speak internationally on power and leverage have now been joined by private individuals with political concerns as well as by officials with non-political aims. All of these admit that, at any one moment, the words of a statement may mean several different things.

In this political sense propaganda has taken many new forms, as has the communication and demonstration of power. It is no longer easy to classify a communication, intended to exert influence abroad, as political or non-political, regardless of its source -- official or private. The probabilities are high that even with more information exchanges, it remains the option of the receiver to interpret the communication as political or non-political, official or private, regardless of the source or intent. As the following section illustrates, there are third parties involved in the international "dialogue," people who are capable of their own perceptions and interpretations of what they hear or see. In this age of global communication systems, the category of private communication without political purpose must be divided into subsections determined by the power of those persons making such "non-political statements." An investigation of the levels of power in the political arena might then be a more profitable means of examining international political communication.

II.   Analysis Through Levels of Involvement

Another architechtonic system which might be more useful in understanding this complex international communication scheme is that of Lerner's four point category plan which deals with levels of involvement or power.[9] These categories are: (1) leaders, (2) participators, (3) interested persons, and (4) listeners.

Although these classifications avoid some of the problems met with Davison's system, there are several intermediate areas consisting of persons who either establish their own levels or who fluctuate between those in Lerner's disposition, and hence their communication can move from category to category. Furthermore, these areas are influential groups and, if they are not correctly identified, consideration of their power may be misunderstood and underrated. Again, as with Davison, a clean-cut distinction between categories is not possible.

The Leaders consist of a nation's elite; those persons and their advisors whose task it is to develop foreign policy and make national decisions regarding foreign relations. But who are the elite or leaders in the formulation of international policy? Are they the elected or designated leadership of a nation or are they, in actuality, an entirely other group? This point will be examined below.

The Participators, consist of industrialists and journalists who affect foreign affairs in varying ways although they are, theoretically at least, not responsible for establishing official foreign policy. Considering the many events in recent years such as the involvement of business interests in the affairs of foreign countries (Chilean copper, Rhodesian chrome, Arab oil, etc), this participatory group could readily be candidates for roles in the "elite" or "leadership" group. Industrialists are not only likely to suggest policy for their own nation's political foreign affairs but also to be involved in the policy making of other nations.

Journalists also play a more refined role than simply "participating" in foreign affairs. Journalistic efforts are directed to *digesting* events in a manner useful to the elite, to wit: a short brief — translated/interpreted. The busy state department official, unable to find the time to read all the information in the field of international relations, welcomes the condensations and summaries provided by the journals or the news programs on radio or TV. These, however, conjure up the *journalists'* images. Thus the journalist plays a very real role in influencing the behavior of the actual policy executors by his position. This position enables him to determine the content, character, and import of much of the information broadcast, not to one nation but to the world. He is, therefore, a major information "gatekeeper" and policy-making factor.

The only check on a journalist by the elite group is governmental control. In varying ways this determines what is communicated intra and internationally. Despite euphemistic terms such as "good taste" or "national security" it is still censorship of one sort or the other. Self-censorship is accepted in many nations as more "Weltansicht" than a curtailment of free speech. Policy makers often censor their own communications for fear that private conferences may become international news or to prevent other members of the elite from acquiring information. In their decision making process, as in other fields, "knowledge is power."

An act or series of acts between the levels of elite and participators requires some form of censorship or editing. As Manning has pointed out in his essays, there is often ample cause for information to be withheld.[10] Censored information is difficult to distinguish from information which has been manipulated in the name of cultural adaptation to meet the communication context of a select audience. It is virtually impossible to report a diplomatic situation publicly, no matter how accurately, without some changes which may give it a different connotation. Political communication becomes part of the situation.

The relationship between the journalist and the policy maker is a special one in this discussion since, unlike other participatory groups such as the industrialists, the journalist will not only act on the information he receives but he will pass it on to others. His principal duty is to provide explanations, justifications, exposure, or critique of an elite policy decision to the public. Working directly with the policy makers they theoretically become aware of the processes of planning or policy making, as well as the requirements of journalistic tactics and strategy. The more directly informed on the subject the journalists become, the better their reporting would be, as is shown by the work of certain state-operated presses in which the journalists are part of both the elite and the participatory levels. However, although journalists would thus be more accurate in reporting official information, they also jeopardize their freedom. However, the journalist often finds his relationship to the elite to be an indirect one.

An intermediate category exists in many nations, that of information officials or press agents who are the spokesmen of the policy makers. Their function is maintenance of contact between the policy makers and the journalists, by transmitting the information concerning a national or international decision from its source to the journalists and, hopefully, thence directly to the listeners, perhaps via the new mediums of satellite and television. The spokesmen's communiques are censored and specifically intended for the journalists —— they are "official" but convey the information to the journalists in a form which offers the latter a certain independence as to how to communicate it further.[11] Press officials are, therefore, in a sort of twilight zone —— not elite and not participatory. But this is another example of the doleful absence of trained communicators assigned to the policy formulation process and of policy makers involved in the communication process, this despite the fact that it is political communication which binds together the course of international relations and determines the images and relationships between nations.

In addition to the usual reporting, other specific symbols, slogans, and assemblies are included in the techniques for political communication intended to bring about public involvement. Particularly, there are the artistic formats: pen, canvas, poster, broadcast, film, stage —— all the practices of using art for political effect.[12] Art in politics is an important factor. It occurs largely out of awareness. However, recently it is not only unveiled but instrumental. A movie can be seen by millions and a political context will be communicated but the variables are so great, the intervening circumstances so strong, that the extent of the effect cannot be easily measured. Yet the possibility of the effect is great enough to suggest the political cause for censorship of the arts. We have heard of this —— from Plato's banning of certain musical modes as detrimental to the existence of the republic to the Soviets' view of "modern art." Art work, as a significant symbol of a nation, is important in the creation and communication of international images. The implications of art in political communication are complex when they occur within a society; they are more so when it is used as a means of universal political communication or as an international form of political expression. Politics, as the communication of power symbols, like beauty, is in the eye of the beholder. Should political art, therefore, be taken out of the context of time, place or event, to be criticized as a universal political statement? Or should it be interpreted as a cultural, national, or as an individual statement? Artists have international audiences. Few of them can escape criticism that does not include reference to political allusions (real or imagined) if these can be ascribed or discerned. Much depends upon the degree of transference or identification between, e.g., stage and reality and upon the efficacy of the symbols, signs, and images in their impact on the international situation, on public opinion toward other nations, on the power dialogue of the power relationship between nations. It is of interest, therefore, to consider how varying pieces of art will be viewed internationally and how they do or could communicate political themes affecting the political images between nations. Are policy advisors and administrators sensitive to art (in any form)?[13] Are their attitudes and conclusions affected by such art, and, if so, to what extent? Cartoons and caricatures, derogatory or lauditory ditties or airs, emotional performances —— can these be effective politically? History tells us that they can and have been. This raises the question as to the status of artists in the levels of international communicators. Are they policy makers or participators or do they deserve a level of their own? The decision seems to rest with the critics —— the journalists —— who are the final arbitors.

The power of the journalist-participator lies not only in the selection of what will be broadcast but also of the audience, the form and the amount. The quantity of information, and the pace with which it changes, outstrips his capacity to disseminate it. The selection process is largely one of chance and interest in projecting the desired image of the situations, events, policies and decisions, as well as of the nation's position in the world. Government control is, of course, also a factor. However, the image making policy leader, the information officer or artist, who goes to great lengths to develop his nation's image abroad, will be only as affective as permitted by the local journalists' coverage and the audience's interpretation of that image.

The Interested

The Audience —— those persons interested in the world beyond their community and nation —— constitutes the third of the levels.

These are either personally affected by a particular event, an emigrant or traveler, or those who support a world-wide religious or political ideological movement. They use private or official channels to make their opinions heard. They boycott, write to their elite, or to their local communication media. They demonstrate their opinions in various fashions for or against the international policy of their own nation or that of another. This vocal group of conscientious citizens has achieved increasing success in its activities and has become as influential in some cases as the elite. They often have constituted the opposition to the elite and, in time, have *become* the elite in the international affairs arena. It is generally assumed that their influence will not be immediate but, upon occasion, will affect the determination of foreign relations and the projections of international images. The youth, labor, or women's movements and their international roles are examples of groups which do not meet the relatively modest role assigned to this third group by Lerner.

The Celebrity as "Participant"

A group which does not conform to Lerner's description but which has been influential in politics consists of the individuals who are "famous" for one reason or another. These people have been made familiar to the mass public by media exposure and have thereby acquired the stature of leaders of public opinion and conveyers of international political communication. By their image of "expert" in one or more fields, they are regarded by the public also as experts in international politics.

This is true not only in the United States but also in other countries where certain cultural celebrities have become political leaders. The wide exposure through the mass media, the public desire for an "idol," and satisfaction of this desire by a cultural leader's charisma make this possible.

That people of this type do not necessarily have the background or the information to make authoritative political comments does not seem to be a matter of concern to the public. A touring performer can make public comments that reverberate within his own and visiting nation. Olympic stars become political ambassadors and athletes. Again it is difficult to determine whether or not this form of international political communication has the impact that the publicity given to it suggests. It is not at all certain that the public and, for that matter the decision makers in the elite, are able to distinguish reality from image or the actual world from a theatre presentation.

The influence of these people lies beyond their home areas and into the fields abroad. Their roles in the international flow of information or entertainment have made them international celebrities and they often epitomize some characteristics of their native lands and therefore carry with them significant symbols of their nations' images.

It is not evident in Lerner's categorization that even as these persons —— the celebrity, the involved citizen, the artist, the journalist or businessman —— might not be qualified, the elite is not necessarily either. Whether once the international decision makers were well trained in the discipline of foreign affairs, diplomacy, and law, these are not now prerequisites. We can accept this situation in areas which are recovering from revolution, developing after independence, or only learning the intricacies of foreign relations. However, according to Yost[14] this has also been true in the United States for the Kennedy, Johnson, Nixon administrations. Diplomacy is now practiced by the president's security aides. They, of course, are not necessarily the people with the most complete knowledge of the development or background of an event. For that matter, is a president?

In addition, the practice of giving ambassadorial or consular positions to political favorites rather than to those trained in foreign service continues. The implication is that foreign affair policies are created by persons who were just recently members of this third, non-elite, level —— the interested. There is also the possibility of the new elite having been a "participator," the businessman or the journalist, and then the operations seem more clouded. As administrations change in the U.S., China, Europe, any super power, the public of other nations feels hurt and fearful—how can someone unknown to them have so much control over them!

557

The University as "Participator"

If the participants in the decision making process in international affairs are *not* experts, what is the role of those persons who *are* experts in communication theory and international relations? In what category do we place them? The university is becoming increasingly active in providing a means of understanding international communication in the political sphere. Associations throughout the world, anxious to create better political understanding between nations, have provided support for many studies. However, this function of universities is limited on two fronts. First, the audience for scholars is often restricted to those colleagues who are working for or against their ideas. A journalist who has been in touch with a developing political situation or a politician sent on a fact finding mission finds it easier to make an influential political contribution to the elites and public alike than a professor who, after a study of three years, can provide results which are more precise and accurate. Although the scholar might have his grant renewed or receive a promotion, or have an article published in a scholarly journal or even the popular intellectual press, his impact on the political affairs of the world will still remain negligible unless he uses some non-scholarly channels and methods.

Of course there have been academicians serving in the national security councils, but they are not carrying out scholarly studies to make political policy nor is the information cited for an accepted policy derived from such studies. The scholar would be most useful in the area of international political communication as the source of background information, feasibility studies and the like to encode and decode international political messages more effectively. As Margaret Mead has said, the will for such investigations is universal but, not since the crisis situation of World War II, has much been done to learn more about the cultural and psychological considerations in order to communicate more effectively between nations.[15] Work in this area is increasing and results encouraging.

A second difficulty which confronts the academician in terms of international political communication is the political background of international meetings of any kind. In an informal survey by the author, of persons in the academy who attend international conferences, almost everyone said that an international meeting automatically carries with it political overtones. No matter what the theme, the meeting eventually involves power, policy and politics. This is not surprising. What *is* important is that the scholar arrives in such a situation with as little preparation as the political appointee arriving to take charge of the embassy at e.g. New Delhi. Lack of knowledge of the cultures, the value system, and the political ramifications of information and protocol of his fellow-conferees to whom he must communicate, will impede, if not prevent, the mutual understanding that is essential for the success of the conference. Western participants tend to believe that eastern bloc nations turn any communication into a political one and that any conference that calls for national delegations will eventually turn into a nationalistic "show and tell" and soon take political turns.

The cultural factors which divide persons in the international arena and particularly inhibit the conversation in the political sphere, where emotions are so close to the surface and are hidden by so much style and protocol, become profound when the conference participant finds that he is regarded as a symbol of his national identity, and, in addition to presenting scholarly contributions he must also create, project, and maintain an image that will be representative of his nation. Participants become communicators of a political line that is interpreted by the audience as an element of a total image which, in turn, will affect the relation of the members of the conference to each other.

It is this misunderstanding of cultural/political elements which interferes with achievement of goals set for the private academic meeting designed to solve international problems. With insufficient or inadequate direction from these meetings the decision makers will be even less apt to adopt the recommendations of the scholars.

The Population at Large – The Information Gap

The last level in Lerner's category system is the population at large: the masses, the apparent voice of the people who are, at least theoretically, in this nation and others, the authority for the mandate to those who form the elite and, in return, receive the dialectic of those who require the re-enforcement and backing of a popular following. These persons relate to foreign affairs almost exclusively through images created by the elite and the participators. However, to place these persons in a single category is over-simplification. In all societies there are information gaps –– the inability of segments of the population to be informed about international affairs due to inability to gain access to any channels which might supply the information. Contributing to such information gaps within the population are geographical isolation, difference in language, censorship, illiteracy, security and poverty. The better educated are more apt to have access to the communication of foreign nations and their actions. Although not as obvious or as public as the "interested" third level they are, nevertheless, more influential than persons unaware of and totally removed from the political affairs of their country. This latter group is at the same time, perhaps paradoxically, increasingly more affected and less involved due to the need for immediate action by decision makers in foreign affairs today. Again, the advance in technology, far removed from the stage coach and sailing vessels has brought this about.

The Issue Variable

It should be noted that membership in any one of the levels discussed depends upon the particular issue involved. A member of the elite determining the national policy towards, e.g., Latin America on fishing rights, may have nothing at· all to do with a similar determination towards, e.g., Russia on disarmament. An investor has no involvement with investments in certain nations in which has has no related investment. A member of the other levels may be equally apt to pass back and forth depending upon the issues. Leaders of movements attempt to discourage this and try to form coalitions of more or less permanent and constant memberships which remain involved in international concerns in general and do not limit their participation to certain issues. These attempts to build coalitions have caused a good deal of difficulaty in establishing counter-governmental movements. In some nations workers tend to avoid alliances with students, as, in our own, "hard hats" disdain social revolutionists. Calls for world revolution are not at all welcomed by political groups intent upon removing themselves from paternal control without the aid of outside groups. This is predictable considering the variables of culture and tradition of the different nations.

Social Psychological Dimensions

The levels characterized here, although useful are neither exhaustive nor mutually exclusive. While it remains true that the public is *still* not the determiner of international policy, it is also true that brainwashing of people through international propaganda via the mass media, as discussed in the first section, will not succeed in turning nations toward or away from each other.

The messages which form the interrelated patterns of acquired and shared behavior (which, in turn, create the atmosphere of international communication) are affected by several factors. These include belief system information concerning the cultures of the participants together with knowledge of the political situation, attitudes, amenability of the person to change, and emotional adherence to beliefs.

To a certain degree, policy makers —— official and unofficial, individuals or representatives, permanent or ad hoc groups —— will project their own assumptions in judging the psychological reactions to a certain course of action or in anticipating the issues to be handled by the communication media. In communication theory this is considered the relationship aspect of a message apart from the content aspect. It is the relationship aspect of international political communication that is often overlooked. Political communicators must not only consider how others will react to a statement or what the makeup of an audience might be, to ensure understanding but also consider how the receiver will relate to the sender after the communication is received. In one-to-one or nation-to-nation situations, political communication deals more directly with relationships than most other forms of international communication. The prime consideration is how nations regard others in relation to themselves.

The basic regulatory system of political communication tends to be the degree of image prestige a nation feels it has, but not necessarily does, in the world arena.[16] Nations are disparate, separated, and in opposition to natural order. Nationalism and political divisions as well as cultural influences exert pressure in this situation.

Nationalism still remains a dominant force in the world of politics and the image of nationality, as mentioned before, is still an important symbol in interpreting the communication on the international scale, be it cooperation or aggression. National feelings of sub groups within a sovereignty are presently a major cause for international tension. There still seems to be loyalty of persons to a national identity—the expansion of the family ties. Edmund Glenn described two types of nationalism which are prevalent today and are prime elements in the analysis of international political communication. One type involves loyalty to an identity with the population living within the boundaries of a national state. The second type describes a sense of cohesiveness resulting from a common experience and mutual interest. The United States, Canada and England exemplify the latter and Central and Eastern Europe, the former.[17]

III.   Relationship Categories and Internal Communication

What should be considered is the use people will make of the ideas being transmitted to them — how they will respond, how they help new organizations or existing ones, what the audience analysis is: favorable to the creators of the policy or opposing it. The objective of any individual, intent upon making his influence felt in the international political dialogue, should be the communication of an image that will gain for him the best international perspective. It is of prime importance to be able to maintain a position and to meet the challenge of opponents. The inherent basic image of persons in the international network is interpretable only as it relates to the behavior of others in political events.

New information, new events, new art, new international changes of power, tend, in varying ways, to change the image of a nation and the cycle begins again. More importantly, nations are conscious of the world's view of their relationships to others. For example, the general political image of India is not as clear as its image of its relationship toward Pakistan, or the image of the United States as its image toward the USSR. When the concept of relationship or interrelationship is mentioned, the significant symbols, the context, and the content are sharper in our minds and the message has greater meaning. International communication is structured and functions in this manner. Nations tend to communicate in terms of "the enemy of my enemy is my friend" an important syndrome in the light of the dialogue that exists in the world's conversation pit.

The significance of relationships in international political communication supersedes and complicates the levels of involvement created by Lerner and Davison. The media and developed transportation systems create interrelationships between nations which are, indeed, very personal and sensitive. With increasing close contact between people, the relationships that are built are due not to mere agreement between elites; more likely they are intricate balances of calculated arrangements and emotional ties at many levels.

A possibly more complete architectonic system would be one that introduces the importance of relationship into the systems already described by Lerner and Davison. This would create varying matrices of international political dialogue. These would describe the communications, with or without political intent, with or without political effect, with official and/or private source, official and/or private receivers, and with contexts of the communication sent and received. In pyramid fashion similar categories could be defined on the response received —— demand response of influence relationship. Each of these matrix combinations evokes another response from another matrix combination and the dialogues of international communication continues. It should be emphasized that this arrangement is flexible and that all squares of interaction occur simultaneously on each issue, to a greater or lesser degree, with different individuals involved. Such a system might also better equip the observer in his scrutiny of the flow of international communication when this occurs.

Crisis Communication

International political dialogue in crisis is a concept which can be analyzed more completely with the relationship description. More often than not international political dialogue has a crisis dimension. The more the agitation, the more the dialogue changes: one member of the conversation may dominate the other, one may capitulate to the other, the parties may compromise. They might encompass response into a compromise and go higher onto a new plateau of policy or, on the other hand, they might agree to disagree. Political communication may assume the most grim of all non-verbal communication: strategic information, strategic violence.[18]

Agitation is often caused, supplanted, or brought beyond hope of solution by the simultaneous occurrence in the international field of these crisis dialogue with many other influential conversations. The network of events surrounding (a) the situation, (b) the principals of the dialogue, and (c) the opposition to the principals, increases image effects. In addition, crisis proportions seem to be magnified as they are messaged through the press rooms and broadcast in this amplified form to the world, thus taking the discussion into the area of public diplomacy and general debate.

In public debate there is a risk of hyperbole and exaggeration. Verbally and non-verbally, there is an excess in "language." For example, almost every infringement of rights or suggestion of unfair practices has been compared to the Nazi war crimes as, in the 1972 civil war in Pakistan when both the West Pakistanis and the Bangladesh leaders accused each other of atrocities —— "the worst since Auschwitz."[19]

Excesses in language put events out of global perspective and create a situation in which worlds of dissent lose their meaning. Violence of expression, Anthony Lewis states, is not only harmful to truth but dangerous; language creates reality. By *saying* that repression is already here, we help to bring it on. Inflated rhetoric in the international political communication field will only increase the likelihood of cessation of dialogue between political parties of different nations.[20]

Hostilities in crisis, when the greatest need for international communication exists, often lead to rejection and severance of what little communication is possible under the very formalized procedures. It is, of course, psychologically dangerous to limit communication or break off contact. A vicious circle ensues in which hostility tends to rupture communication which in turn enhances antagonism and increases mutual fear and distrust. This, in turn, increases opportunities for creation of distorted images. Lack of direct channels, and time lags in communication between opponents is handled indirectly through the medium of other parties, other nations or international groups —— an unsatisfactory condition arising from all the new associated intervening variables of cultural and political elements.[21]

Misunderstanding —— Know the Receiver

Osgood has suggested that official policy maintain a strict open-ended format. That is possible if it is upheld alongside the un-official plane: (1) each unilaterally initiated act should be announced prior to public implementation, (2) each act should be part of a deliberate policy to reduce tension, (3) there should be an explicit initiation so that the other side can reciprocate.[22]

Currently there are problems associated with Osgood's prescriptive formula, the biggest being that it will most likely remain prescriptive in this day of public diplomacy. International exchange is a web of infinite dimensions and a format such as this would only arouse suspicion. Furthermore, even with public diplomacy, information is a useful device and its communication is accepted as a political tool. Obscurities or misunderstandings are the result of individuals giving, innocently or deliberately, distorted or inaccurate meanings to international statements, meanings which irritate or delude the sender and thus impede co-operative endeavors. Osgood's format is intended for learning enough to be able to resolve ideological conflict and tension involved in entering another's world. It is not applicable to situations involving the factor of trust and credence which is part of the international political communication and raises the possibility of calculated misunderstanding.

The individual prejudices that account for the biases arising from these particular instances can be detected and compensated for by timely experience or by employing a model of co-orientation.[23]

This practice will enable those in the dialogue to recognize political misunderstandings and to correct them. It is also helpful to have other background information including data, attitudes, and practices that govern the use of different types of communication channels. Even though substantially the same media is available in different societies, their use may vary, the processing of information differs, the employment of ideas changes. The type of effect is varied: whether it is intended to increase knowledge, reinforce or change attitudes, confer prestige, create bewilderment, or influence behaviors in some other way.

Furthermore, developing nations tend to also utilize differing communication mechanism depending upon (a) the educational background of the leader (not only how much but where obtained), (b) the particular culture of the nation and the culture of the presently ruling administration, (c) the form of government and the actual degree of adherence to that form, (d) the nationality of the "experts," investors, or consultants who are currently at work on development projects in that nation, and, finally, (e) the history of the nation, the imprints of the rulers of past times, colonial or otherwise. For a more complete check of influences that might account for the information patterns of political leadership in a nation, it would be useful to account for the influences of the opposition group as well.

Finally, the sender should be aware of the image in which he and his political system are held. It is hoped that despite the difficulties of orchestrating the information flow, at least the transmitted messages will be co-oriented to the receiver.

Words, Reality and Relationship Images

All the action planning proposed by so many writers on international communication seems impossible in the light of actual complex and multi-leveled realities. Politics differs from other topics of international communication because it is, at the same time, the least substantive and the most forceful. Although economics and social forces can bear upon and form the political content of a message and the context and substance, it is the political symbols that communicate power and, in turn, the consequent relationship between the communicating parties.

Frank and Weisbound, in examining verbal strategy among the super powers, suggest that words might be as important as actions in the foreign policy formulations of states and their case studies do much to suggest that perhaps words *do* speak as loudly as actions.[24] The international metaphor, the interpretation of international criticism or approval, the political compliment and the foreign condemnation in the international conversation pit —— all are couched in the various superlatives of culturally distinct statements. The worst course is silence. How much of a statement is for the purpose of image intensification or a means of structuring the images of others involved in the conversations, and how much of the message serves other purposes, intentional or not? The answers can be learned, as with misunderstandings, not only through experience but also through a functional structure approach. Nevertheless, the fact remains that words create images and it is not truths but images which govern behavior.[25]

Grant Hugo shed more light on the image and international communication theory in his book, *Appearance and Reality in International Relations*, in which he writes about misunderstandings between nations based on differently held images.[26] Only through study of the extent and type of public diplomacy in nations can various communicators become aware of the relationship images: the power arrangements, the authority allocation, the decision making process, foreign interpretations and reactions to audiences, internal reactions to internal and external leaders, self image, and desired roles.[27] One way of accomplishing this is through analysis of the opinion groups and organizations within nations.

It was natural that in time, with the increase in international communication, there would also be an increase in the number and size of groups that make use of it, incorporate it into programs, rely upon it for functioning and find themselves controlled by the governments that in some way regulate the behavior of that communication system.

International organizations in the international atmosphere, such as the France-American Society, National Council of American

Soviet Friendship, World Zionist Organization, American-Arab Association for Commerce and Industry, could be considered the most important of the non-governmental agencies which in some way affect the political complexion of the world. Without the aid, alliances, or opposition of organized groups much of the political communication would not occur.[28] Irving Janis took a new look at conflict and then suggested that fiascoes often result when decision makers are more concerned with retaining approval of groups than with the substance of the problem.[29]

The Private/Official Relationship

Another form of relationship that calls for study is that between the official and private international communicators. Domestically the relationship is important and since officials and private communicators complement each other and they thus project a stronger and more useful image abroad. The relationships of foreign governments, of one nation and the private sector of another are forged for other reasons. The Sunday *New York Times* advertising supplements inviting Americans to visit and invest in a foreign nation add another dimension of exchange to the international political dialogue. This is an attempt on the part of a nation's official government to bypass the traditional exchanges of information and go directly to the people of another nation to reach members of Lerner's second category. Investment might not be the only reason for contact. The motive could be simply to "propagandize" other nations into a more positive relationship toward that country in terms of the latter's political stability, governmental development programs, and national leaders —— all elements that bear on the success of a foreign investment.

Another form of advertising is the communication of the political views of a nation. The parties involved in a conflict try to bypass or compensate for coverage given to them in the foreign press. In these instances it is not unlikely for individual nations to enlist the aid of public relations firms to act as their spokesmen, as was the case with Biafra. More recently, Americans read of the Pakistani soldiers held as captives by India through the public relations efforts of the soldiers' wives.

A new element in international political communication is the political benefit entertainment for an international cause. While political benefit affairs are not new and those for international charities are not necessarily political, the large scale productions, at such places as Madison Square Garden, held by individuals of one nation for political causes of another and to which all levels of a foreign population can contribute, are a recent trend.

The private sector is increasingly a part not only of the national scene, (in its alternative forms of communicators for making political points), but also of the international. Individuals strike, make symbolic gestures in their life style and perform other acts of sympathy to exhibit solidarity with an international cause. Many people relate to groups in foreign countries. For example, while the Blacks in Britain have not been aroused by their own nation's politics, they have evidently identified with causes of other nations that seem more vital, making that the greater relationship.

Of course, the most frightening and dramatic form of political communication we have witnessed in this area between private and governmental sectors is the terrorist activities of the various radical movements, guerilla organizations, and religious fanatical groups that kidnap dignitaries, take hostages, and hijack airplanes to promote political objectives and to lay claim to international significance. In a communication sense, these violent crimes impress one not only as excessively cruel but also as irrational and contagious.

Society, and our government in particular, has no mechanism or methodology to combat such outbursts of political extortion. Bombs in the mail box and kidnappings of decision makers have not previously been part of international exchange in civilized countries, at least, not to this extent. However, ironically, the communication techniques of the world have made this possible, perhaps because of a belief in the consequent efficacy of the violence with wider publicity. These counter means of creating international communication networks have initiated acts that official channels have been too slow or too idiosyncratic and ego-oriented to notice.

The Official/Private Relationship

Governments are, themselves, organizations of a very complex and unwieldy structure. As with non-governmental organizations, officials may or may not communicate in a political manner. As with all organizations involved in international communication, it is important to be aware of the internal makeup of the organization and the chain of command in determining what will and will not be said. These organizations vary not only from nation to nation but also from one political era to another and from one administration to the next.

Different people in and out of foreign relations administration are called upon to speak on a particular issue. They often are contradictory in their comments, overlap in what they are trying to do, ignorant of the full picture, or uncertain as to how much they should know and say. It is another case of the blind men describing the elephant, each thinking the part he "sees" is the whole. It is estimated ten thousand messages go into and out of our state department daily.[30] But this flow somehow does not mean that these messages are the ones required or those of interest or which can possibly be assimilated and given the attention due each one with its interpreted import. Nor do officials seem to know what is occurring in other areas of government on that issue at that moment.

Opposition groups and public interests have a far easier time since they have definite questions for which they seek answers and specific points which they wish to communicate. However, the power of these groups is only as great as their ability to co-ordinate their membership in a unified communication web and to correlate information content with their messages.

Efficiency in international communication systems can best be achieved when the policy is clear both with respect to other international organizations and in relation to the manner in which governments wish to use the global connections.

People want and need to know what goes on in the world. Public opinion will be present whether or not the information that forms it is sufficient or not, true or false, complete or censored. At one time it was very useful to distinguish the type of communication flow in a closed society from that in an open society. However, as we learned from one security leak to another, ours is not the ideal open society and evidence of the existence of public opinion and public mood behind the iron curtain and other sheltered nations such as Brazil, Spain and Portugal indicates that there are no truly closed societies either.

However, open and closed aspects of societies exist in relationship situations. What is closed information in one nation might be open to a neighbor. Political considerations have caused the lack of flow of communication inside and outside nations due to fear of the repercussions when other powers acquired the information. There is no such thing as selective public communication, no matter how useful it would be. A message may have the least importance to the people to whom it is delivered. Furthermore, as the news media carries a message around the world, its final effect may be far different than the intended one. The content or topic of such a message might not coincide with the political situation, context, or audience that hears it. Such political considerations have prevented the growth of communication networks. Television networks, for example, that could prove useful, practical and economical in South America, Africa, and the Middle East have not been possible because of the political differences between the nations involved and because of a lack of interest in creating an open system.

The relationship between information systems and political systems provides an important indication of the state of the nation. The degree of journalistic freedom reflects the political stability, state of transition or degree of chaos in a country as well as the relationship between nations.[31] In this manner one can see how decreased press freedom within a nation becomes a political sign to other countries.

IV.   The Problem

The foregoing discussion was intended to bring out the difficulties involved in a strict and rigid application of general theories and principles to international political communications.

There seems to be more and more communication with less and less success in resolving the foreign affairs problems of nations. Political art is more devious and diverse, economic involvements are deeper and complex, military threat and crunch more menacing and sophisticated, and the presence of business interests more overt [32] and refined.

Political communication is obviously not an exact science. The data supply agencies are not independent and data may be restricted by political censorship or by mechanical "jamming." There are too many variables operating simultaneously. There is no assurance of the sincerity and integrity of the communications. We are dealing with human beings, senders and receivers, and their thought processes (or lack thereof) and their emotions. These vagaries of humanity cannot be reduced to a formula.

The lack of success in the study of international political communication is, in large part, due to the inability to discover or devise an architectonic system of organization that will remain valid under the ever-changing patterns of communication in this area. The cause has been ascribed to four factors.[33]

The first is the multiplicities of scholarships involved in international political communication — — so many that only a man of Renaissance calibre could cope with them. The mastering of all existing data on human behavior is an obviously impossible task and yet the only assurance for understanding such communication. The second is, as mentioned before, the interpretation of the simultaneously occurring variables without the possibility of evaluation because of the inaccessibility of the audience reactions. Thirdly, it becomes difficult to determine just what becomes political communication when this is subjected to a variety of techniques. Lastly, there is the problem of dual responsibility facing many agencies sponsoring political international communication studies, (that of dual responsibility which includes public relations work.) These "objective" groups in making these studies must also consider their need for funding through contributions and their attempts to obtain these may not be so "objective."

Summary and Conclusion

International communication is a complex web of images; mass and personal, official and private, of exchanges; direct and indirect, between nationals and internationals, about the balance of power and the relationships of power between people to people in all settings.

International communication affects all strata of society directly and indirectly. In turn, all strata of society can affect the policy of international relations, not only of just their own nation but also that of others, through apathy or by direct physical involvement. International communication occurs between governments and private parties of another as well as between or within several nations. Governments talk to the publics of other nations as well as to opposition leaders, organizations and interest groups. The bases for all international behavior are the images which are built upon the information that is blended through all of these various conflicting, overlapping, and culturally specific means of information exchange. The problems of international understanding, particularly in political terms, have no easy solution. The prescriptive ideas of various scholars, observers, and participants of the process are not apt to have any lasting effect. One-world advocates are not likely to see their objective achieved through this means. Communication, national policy and domestic restraints are indicators of the means through which nations hope to reach their goals. The area requiring much more study is that of the relationship between national policies and the effect of politically relevant behavioral acts on communications.

FOOTNOTES

[1] David Brook, *Search for Peace*, p. 91.

[2] Quincy Wright, *The Study of International Relations*, pp. 3-8 and Robert Pfaltzgraff, *Politics and the International System*, p. 2.

[3] Glen Fisher, *Public Diplomacy and the Behavioral Sciences*, p. 8.

[4] *Ibid.*, p. 9.

[5] Phillip W. Davison, *International Political Communication*, pp. 9-10.

[6] Hugh A. Mulligan, "The Pushcart Armageddon" —— AP story, 1970.

[7] Fisher, *Ibid.*, p. 12.

[8] Heinz Eulau, *The Behavioral Persuasion in Politics*.

[9] Daniel Lerner, in Arthur Hoffman, *International Communication and the New Diplomacy* p. 124.

[10] Richard Manning in Arthur Hoffman, *International Communication and the New Diplomacy*, p. 154.

[11] Harry Maynard in Arthur Hoffman, *Ibid.*, pp. 136-147.

[12] Davison, *Ibid.*, p. 164.

[13] Robert T. Bower and Laura Sharp, "The Use of Art in International Communication," *Public Opinion Quarterly*, (Spring, 1956) pp. 221-223.

[14] Charles W. Yost, "The Instruments of American Foreign Policy," *Foreign Affairs* (50 Oct., 1971) pp. 59-68.

[15] Margaret Mead in Hoffman, *Ibid.*, p. 104. For the causes of this see Davison and George in Heinz-Dietrich Fischer, John C. Merill, *International Communication, Media, Channels, Functions*, pp. 452-461.

[16] J.D. Singer, "International Influence: A Formal Model," *American Political Sciences Review* 57 (1963), pp. 420-430.

[17] Edmund S.S. Glenn, "The Two Faces of Nationalism," *Comparative Political Studies*, (October, 1970).

[18] Joseph de Rivera, *The Psychological Dimension of Foreign Policy*, pp. 279-280.

[19] Margaret L. Schneider, "When Nations Turn to Hucksters," unpublished convention paper.

[20] Anthony Lewis, "Rhetoric and Responsibility, Here and Abroad," *New York Times*, May 3, 1972.

[21] Rivera, *Ibid.*, p. 425.

[22] Charles A. Osgood, *An Alternative to War and Surrender.*

[23] Jack McLeod and Steve Chaffee, in James T. Tedischi, *The Social Influence Process,* pp. 50-100.

[24] Thomas M. Frank and Edward Weisband, *World Politics: Verbal Strategy Among the Super Powers,* p. 1971.

[25] Kenneth Boulding, *The Image,* 1956.

[26] Grant Hugo, *Appearance and Reality in International Relations,* 1971.

[27] Fisher, *Ibid.*, p. 73.

[28] Robert O'Keohane, Joseph S. Nye, Jr., *Transnational Relations and World Politics,* 1972.

[29] Irving Janis, *Victims of Group Think: A Psychological Study of Foreign Policy Decisions and Fiascoes,* 1972.

[30] Manning, *Ibid.*, p. 154.

[31] Ralph Lowenstein in Heinz-Dietrich Fischer and John Merrill, *International Communication, Media, Channels, Functions,* 1970, p. 129.

[32] Garland O. Ashley in Fischer and Merrill, *Ibid* p. 197.

[33] Davison and George, *Ibid.*, p. 461.

SELECTED BIBLIOGRAPHY

Berlin, Isaiah. "The Bent Twig: A Note on Nationalism," *Foreign Affairs*, (Oct. 1972), pp. 11-30.

Boulding, Kenneth E. *The Image.* (Ann Arbor, Mich: University of Michigan Press) 1956.

Bower, Robert T., Laura Sharp, "The Use of Art in International Communication," *Public Opinion Quarterly* (Spring, 1956), pp. 221-223.

Brook, David. *Search for Peace: A Reader in International Relations.* (New York, N.Y.: Dodd Mead and Co.) 1970.

Brown, Lester R. *World Without Borders.* (New York, N.Y.: Random House) 1972.

Buchanan, William, Hadly Cantril. *How Nations See Each Other, A Study in Public Opinion.* (Westwood, Conn.: Greenwood Press).

Cantrill, H., ed. *Tension that Cause Wars* (Urbana, Ill: University of Illinois Press) 1956.

Christiansen, B. *Attitude Toward Foreign Affairs as a Function of Personality*. (Oslo: Oslo University Press) 1956.

Cooper, Chester L. "The CIA and Decision Making," *Foreign Affairs,* (Jan. 1972), pp. 223-236.

Dahl, Robert A. *Modern Political Analysis*. (Englewood Cliffs, N.J.: Prentice Hall, Inc.) 1963.

Davison, W. Phillip. *International Political Communication*. (New York, N.Y.: Frederick A. Praeger) 1965.

Davison, W. Phillip. "Political Communication as an Instrument of Foreign Policy," *Public Opinion Quarterly*. (1963), pp. 28-36.

de Rivera, Joseph. *The Psychological Dimension of Foreign Policy*. (Columbus, Ohio: Charles E. Merrill) 1968.

Deutsch, K.W. *The Nerves of Government: Models of Political Communication and Control*. (New York, N.Y.: Free Press) 1963.

Eulau, Heinz. *The Behavioral Persuasion in Politics*. (New York, N.Y.: Random House) 1963.

Fischer, Heinz-Dietrich, John C. Merrill, eds. *International Communication Media, Channels, Functions*. (New York, N.Y.: Hastings House) 1970.

Fisher, Glen. *Public Diplomacy and the Behavioral Sciences*. (Bloomington, Ind.: Indiana University Press) 1972.

Fishman, Joshua. *Readings in the Sociology of Language*. (The Hague: Mouton Co.) 1968.

Frank, Thomas M., Edward Weisband. *World Politics: Verbal Strategy Among the Super Powers*. (New York, N.Y.: Oxford University Press) 1971.

Glenn, Edmund S. "The Two Faces of Nationalism," *Comparative Political Studies* (Oct. 1970).

Goffman, Irving. *Strategic Interaction*. (Philadephia, Penn.: University of Pennsylvania Press) 1969.

Hanrieder, W.F. "International Comparative Politics: Toward a Synthesis?" *World Politics* (April, 1968), pp. 480-493.

Hartmann, Frederick. *The New Age of American Foreign Policy* (New York, N.Y.: McMillan), 1970.

Hoffman, Arthur, ed. *International Communication and the New Diplomacy*. (Bloomington, Ind.: Indiana University Press) 1968.

Holsti, K.S. *International Politics, A Framework for Analysis.* (Englewood Cliffs, N.J.: Prentice Hall). 1961.

Holsti, O.R. "Politics and the International System: The Belief System and National Images, A Case Study," *Journal of Conflict Resolution* (June, 1962), pp. 244-252.

Holt, Claire, ed. *Culture and Politics in Indonesia.* (Ithaca, N.Y.: Cornell University Press) 1972.

Hugo, Grant. *Appearance and Reality in International Relations.* (New York, N.Y.: Columbia University Press) 1971.

Janis, Irving. *Victims of Group Think: A Psychological Study of Foreign Policy Decisions and Fiascoes.* (Boston, Mass.: Houghton Mifflin) 1972.

Jervis, R. *The Logic of Images in International Relations.* (Princeton, N.J.: Princeton University Press) 1970.

Kelman, Herbert, ed. *International Behavior: A Social Psychological Analysis.* (New York, N.Y.: Holt, Rinehart, Winston), 1964.

Kleinberg, Otto. *The Human Dimension in International Relations* (New York, N.Y.: Holt, Rinehart and Winston) 1964.

Lazarsfeld, Paul F., William H. Sewell, Harold L. Wilensky, eds. *The Uses of Sociology.* (New York, N.Y.: Basic Books) 1967.

Lewis, Anthony. "Rhetoric and Responsibility," *New York Times* (May 3, 1972).

Mulligan, Hugh A. "The Pushcart Armageddon is Really Ripe,"*Long Island Daily Press*, 1970.

North, R.C., O.R. Holt, M.G. Zaninovich, Diana Zinnia. *Content: A Handbook for the Study of International Crisis.* (Evanston, Ill.: Northwestern University Press) 1963.

O'Keohane, Robert, Josephy S. Nye, Jr., eds. *Transnational Relations and World Politics.* (Cambridge, Mass.: Harvard University Press) 1972.

Osgood, Charles. *An Alternative to War or Surrender.* (Urbana, Ill.: University of Illinois Press) 1962.

Pfallzgraff, Robert Jr., ed. *Politics and the International System.* (Philadelphia, Penn.: J.B. Lippincott Co.) 1969.

Pruitt, Dean G. "An Analysis of Responsiveness between Nations," *Journal of Conflict Resolution* (1958) pp. 265-279.

Rosenau, James H., ed. *Linkage Politics: Essays on the Convergence of National and International Systems* (New York, N.Y.: The Free Press) 1969.

Salisbury, Harrison E. "The Image and Reality in Indochina," *Foreign Affairs*, (April, 1971), pp. 381-394.

Schneider, Margaret. "When Nations Turn to Hucksters: The Rhetoric of Bangladesh," unpublished convention paper, (Dec., 1972).

Shelling, T.C. *Strategy of Conflict*. (London, Great Britain: Oxford Press) 1970.

Singer, J.D. "International Influence: A Formal Model," *American Political Science Review* (Spring, 1963), pp. 420-430.

Smith, B.L. and C. Smith, *International Communication and Public Opinion*. (Princeton, N.J.: Princeton University Press) 1956.

Tedeschi, James T. *The Social Influence Processes*. (Chicago, Ill.: Aldine-Atherton) 1972.

Thompson, Kenneth W. *Foreign Assistance: A Review from the Private Sector*. (Notre Dame, Indiana: University of Notre Dame Press) 1972.

Toma, Peter A. and Andrew Gyorgy. *Basic Issues in International Relations*, (Boston, Mass.: Allyn and Bacon, Inc.) 1967.

Wright, Quincy. *The Study of International Relations*. (New York, N.Y.: Appleton-Century-Crofts) 1955.

Yost, Charles W. "The Instruments of American Foreign Policy," *Foreign Affairs*. (Oct. 1971), pp. 59-68.

P. Terrence Hopmann

Communication and Bargaining in International Diplomacy

RECENT events in international diplomacy have underscored the fundamental importance of communication in the process of diplomatic bargaining. In October 1962, President John F. Kennedy and Premier Nikita Khrushchev engaged in both verbal and nonverbal communications to try to resolve the Cuban missile crisis before it erupted into a major war between the two nuclear superpowers. Ten years later Soviet and American leaders bargained extensively in the Strategic Arms Limitation Talks (SALT) and other arms control negotiations to try to limit the arms race, which itself made the consequences of war in the nuclear period so disastrous. These dramatic events merely highlight the general importance of the communication process in virtually all diplomatic interactions. This phenomenon has thus received considerable attention from scholars in the field of international relations, who have increasingly analyzed international diplomacy in terms of models and conceptual frameworks which include a heavy emphasis upon the communication process. In this chapter, we shall survey several of these frameworks and their application to several aspects of international diplomacy.

Four Conceptual Frameworks

Increasingly scholars studying international relations have applied models developed by communication scholars to study international diplomacy. In this section, we shall examine four such models and summarize some of the basic postulates or assumptions which have been extracted by students of international relations for application in the field of diplomatic communication.

Basic Communicative Interaction Framework

The first framework, which provides the basis for all other frameworks to be discussed herein, depicts the basic interaction pattern for a dyadic communication. The general framework is based on the writings of Shannon and Weaver (1964) and has been further explicated by many others, including Schramm (1963). The framework is diagrammed in Figure 1. There are three basic elements in the act of communication, according to this framework. First, there is a source or a sender of a message, which encodes a message, that is, converts an idea into a set of symbols to be communicated. Second, the message itself consists of a set of symbols which are conveyed through a communication channel; these symbols are in some sense independent of the semantic content assigned to them by either the source or the receiver. Third, the receiver is the recipient of the message and must decode it; that is, he must interpret the semantic content of the message in terms of his own frame of reference. As Schramm has observed, "whatever we communicate is merely a sign that stands for some meaning to the sender, and that stands to the receiver for whatever meaning he reads into it."[1] Thus, the signs in the message have "only such meaning as, by agreement and experience, we give them."

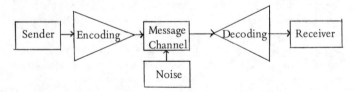

Figure 1: A Basic Model of Communicative Interactions

This model thus suggests that communication may become "distorted" when the encoding processes of the sender and the decoding processes of the receiver do not sufficiently converge. Under these conditions, especially when the shared frame of reference of the two parties is minimal, the message may mean quite different things to the sender and the receiver. Thus, in international diplomacy, the different frames of reference of individuals from different cultures, with different language backgrounds, and with different roles in the structure of the international system, may create substantial problems for the communication process, introducing considerable potential for distortion.

An additional source of distortion may be introduced by the occurrence of noise or random disturbances in the communication channels which may interfere with the transmission of the message. Noise may be counteracted by increasing redundancy, that is by increasing use of patterned symbols to overcome the random disturbance introduced by noise. Deutsch has noted that "the less the admixture of irrelevant information (or "noise"), the more efficient is a given communications channel or a given chain of command."[2] These assumptions about the sources of distortion in dyadic communication may be summarized briefly in the following postulates:

Postulate 1: The greater the gap between the shared experiences of individual senders and receivers of messages, the greater the differences in their interpretations of the same messages, and hence the greater the distortion in the process of communication.

Postulate 2: The greater the noise in a communication channel and the less the redundancy in the message, the greater the distortion in the process of communication.

Mediated Stimulus-Response Framework

Another statement of essentially this same principle, with additional implications for diplomatic communication, may be found in models based on the mediated stimulus-response paradigm of Osgood (1958). This framework treats the dyadic interaction between two actors as a sequence of stimuli and responses or mediated by internal psychological processes, as diagrammed in Figure 2. In this framework the stimulus (S) is an overt physical event or verbal act of one actor, A, which becomes an input into the decision system of another actor, B. A stimulus is thus objective and is not directly dependent upon how it is perceived or responded to by the recipient. The perception of this stimulus within actor B's decision system (r), on the other hand, evokes cognitive, affective, and evaluative responses internal to the actor. According to North this component includes: "information translation, that is, the translation of stimuli (S) into neural impulses; information transmission from the periphery of the nervous system toward the decision-making center; information integration in terms of past experience and other information 'stored' from the past; and information interpretation and the arousal of feelings about it."[3] In the literature on international relations, this component has frequently been summarized as the "definition of the situation", that is, as the subjective interpretation placed on the stimulus by the receiver.[4] The mediated stimulus (s) refers to actor B's expression of his plans, intentions, or his perceptions of his own actions toward A. In Osgood's terms, this refers to sizing up of the situation and to a process of encoding which relates self-stimulating symbolic reactions with external responses.[5] North further notes that this component includes "the selection of a response plan or hierarchy and the emotionally charged activation of it," the selection from among alternative plans and strategies of one which provides a basis for behavior, as well as "the integration of the decisions in terms of specific instrumentalities, the transmission of the decision toward the periphery of the nervous system, and the translation of the decision from the code of neural impulses into actions upon the environment."[6] Finally, the overt response (R) is the action of actor B toward actor A; it thus becomes an output from B which is transmitted as an overt behavior to A where it becomes an input. Thus the entire process is repeated within the decision system of A.

Figure 2: The Mediated Stimulus-Response Model Applied to Nation-State Interactions

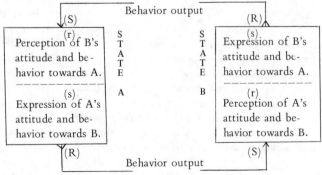

The mediated stimulus-response model, as North notes, can be applied relatively easily by analogy "in studying the nation-state (or any other organization) as a system. This appears to be a crucial consideration to the extent that state behavior (state decision-making, for example) involves individual behavior (for example, decision-making by the head of state or others)."[7] This may thus introduce into our models some elements of S-R learning theory, although, more importantly, it emphasizes an explanation for incongruity between stimulus and response in the communication behavior of actors. While a given response may often be predictable following the receipt of a particular stimulus, frequently international behavior is highly ambiguous. As Boulding has emphasized, responses are determined not by objective facts of a situation but rather by the actor's image or perception of the situation and of his response to it.[8] It is these mediated phenomena, then, which may largely account for change over time in an iterative sequence of interactions between two actors in a dyadic relationship. This assumption may be stated briefly as follows:

Postulate 3: An individual actor's response to a given verbal or nonverbal stimulus will be determined by his perceptions of the stimulus and his perceived intention in responding, as well as by the content of the stimulus itself.

Postulate 4: In a dyadic interaction, communicative interactions will be mediated and changed by perceptual processes internal to both actors.

The mediated stimulus-response framework has been applied to a general framework for analyzing international conflict and integration by North (1968). More specifically, it has been used in an anlysis of the action-reaction phenomenon between states during times of international crisis by Holsti, Brody, and North (1969) and in diplomatic negotiations on arms control by Hopmann and King (1976).

Cognitive Balance Framework

In international diplomacy, however, communications are seldom simply dyadic. That is, communication always takes place in the context of external events and in relationship to other actors, whose relationship to communicators may be quite relevant to the nature of their communication. This consideration is taken into account by Heider (1946) who suggests that an individual's communication with other individuals will be a function of his perceptions of their common attitudes towards some third person or object. The relationships within such a triad may be defined as essentially positive or negative, and balance within a triad is obtained when zero or two negative bonds connect these actors, as is the case in the four balanced triads diagrammed in Figure 3. Therefore, if actor P likes object X and he also perceives that the other actor, O, likes the same object, he will tend to engage in positive interactions (communication) with the other actor. On the other hand, if he perceives the relationship between O and X as negative, then he is likely to be negative in the communications he directs towards O. This relationship, however, does not apply to possession relationships such as those in which P and O both desire to possess X, so that they come into conflict.

Figure 3: The Cognitive Balance Model: Four Balanced Triads

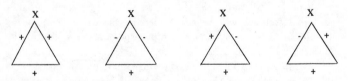

Newcomb (1955) has transformed Heider's model into a basic model of communication between two actors, A and B, about something or someone, X. The result is that the model may be based on objective attitudes of each person toward X rather than on P's perceptions of those attitudes. If A and B are interdependent and have simultaneous, joint orientations toward X, the concept of balance may be applied to their relationships. If A's and B's communications concerning X are symmetrical, that is, if there is co-orientation between them about X, then the relationship between A and B will be characterized by positive communications. Conversely, dissimilar orientations towards X by A and B will tend to produce negative communications between these two actors. Newcomb thus suggests that interdependent systems will contain

" 'strains' toward preferred states of equilibrium" or balance, so that the content of messages between A and B may be largely dependent on their joint orientations towards S.[9] This relationship applies, however, only if the following scope conditions are met: (1) the cognitive relationship must be salient for all actors involved; (2) when two or more actors are involved, the relationsip must be jointly relevant for all; and (3) all cognitive components must be interdependent and must remain intact. The basic assumption may be summarized in the following postulate:

Postulate 5: In their co-orientation toward third actors or events, actors will seek to maintain balance, so that like orientations toward the third actor or event will produce positive communications between the two and unlike orientations will produce negative communications.

This postulate has been applied to international diplomacy by several authors. Harary (1961) has used this model in an analysis of the Arab-Israeli conflict of 1956; Holsti, Hopmann and Sullivan (1973, Chapters 3 and 4) have applied it to measure consensus within NATO and the Communist bloc during the postwar period; and Hart (1974) has employed it to investigate the diplomatic interactions in the European state system in the decade of the 1870's.

Cybernetics Framework

A fourth approach has been to adopt a model based on cybernetics, emphasizing particularly information processing and feedback, resulting in adaptive behavior. The general framework for this focus is based upon Wiener's (1948) notions of entropy and information. Within this framework interactions between actors may be treated in a more dynamic fashion than is possible with any of the previous frameworks. Change over time in this framework is viewed as a probabilistic function of previous states of a system of interactions, such that each sequence of interactions leads to a series of alternatives, each with its own probabilities. Each subsequent stage in an interaction is a probabilistic or stochastic function of the preceding stage. These interactions are generally described in terms of information flows. Shannon and Weaver have described information processing as a set of interactions within which "choices are, at least from the point of view of the communications system, governed by probabilities; and in fact by probabilities which are not independent, but which, at any stage of the process, depend on the preceding choices."[10] There is uncertainty in such a system, and a change in a system of interactions may be analyzed in terms of the uncertain choices among alternatives which a system faces at any point in time. Uncertainty may be viewed as the opposite of information; a communicative act conveys information through the reduction of uncertainty about future alternative states of the system. Thus predictability or the reduction of randomness is associated with an increase in information. Garner (1962) has emphasized that notions of absolute and relative uncertainty may be used to measure the amount of information conveyed in sequences of stimuli and responses, thereby noting that this·approach may be synthesized with the mediated stimulus-response framework.

Notions of information particularly place heavy emphasis upon the concept of feedback. Feedback consists in supplying information back to decision-makers about the results of their earlier actions. The system then responds to this information about its performance and adapts its behavior to attempt to approach its intended goals more closely. Thus feedback systems, as Deutsch (1968) suggests, may reduce the randomness in a sequence of interactions, thereby reducing uncertainty. Deutsch further suggests that the efficiency of a feedback process is related to the following factors: (1) load, which refers to the "extent and speed of changes in the position of the target relative to the goal-seeking system," may detract from the effectiveness of feedback; (2) lag, that is, "the amount of time between the reception of information concerning the position of the target and the execution of the corresponding step in the goal-seeking behavior of the system," also detracts from feedback efficiency; (3) gain, which refers to the amount of change in behavior "in each corrective step taken by the system," contributes to increased effectiveness of feedback; and (4) lead, namely the ability to predict accurately the future position of moving targets from the "most recent signals received" also adds to the ability of the system to receive more accurate feedback and to adapt its behavior accordingly.[11]

In applying these concepts to international diplomacy, Burton has emphasized that a communication approach based upon the notions of systems receiving feedback and engaging in adaptive "steering" may replace power as the organizing concept for the analysis of international relations.[12] Unlike the power approach, this emphasis is not static but rather provides a means of dealing conceptually with probabilistic change and with purposive or adaptive change in systems of interaction over time. This framework has thus had a significant impact upon theories of international diplomacy, as summarized in the following postulates:

Postulate 6: The more accurate the feedback which actors receive about their performance in their environments, the less the uncertainty in the environment.

Postulate 7: The more accurate the feedback which actors receive about their performance in their environments, the greater their ability to adapt their behavior to respond to changes in their environment.

Postulate 8: The less the uncertainty in systems of interaction, the greater the ability of actors to achieve mutually acceptable joint goals and to avoid conflict.

Limitations of Communication Frameworks

All of the frameworks just described were originally developed to deal with phenomena other than international relations, so their application to international diplomacy has largely gone beyond the original scope of the theories upon which they were based. There are clearly some limitations to the application of these frameworks to international diplomacy, which restrict their usefulness. Bobrow (1972) has suggested that none of these frameworks provides an adequate basis for a rigorous *theory* of international relations, since they all lack the deductive power which such a theory requires. Specifically, he notes that the mediated stimulus-response framework only asserts relationships between the four components (S-r: s-R), without developing any derived propositions about the nature of these relationships. As such the model has served as a useful organizing device, with some theoretical suggestions implicit in its foundation in S-R learning theory, but its use has been primarily for inductive data generation rather than for the development of deductive theories. The cognitive balance models are greatly limited in their applicability by some of the scope conditions mentioned above, which are often violated in international diplomacy. Furthermore, in cases where imbalance exists, the model provides no predictions to suggest which adjustments will lead to restoration of balance. Finally, with respect to the cybernetics approach, Bobrow notes that feedback is not equivalent to communication: "Adaptation requires communication, but the reverse is not the case."[13] Similarly, information and the reduction of uncertainty are unrelated to the semantic content of communication in these theories. Thus, the cybernetics approach fails to explain all aspects of communication which may be relevant in international relations. As such, none of these approaches individually can provide the basis in communication theory for a general theory of international relations. Nevertheless, Bobrow has emphasized that communication is quite important for international relations. Bobrow defines social communication "as the transfer of meaning between persons and groups."[14] Thus, the semantic content of communication can be a crucial factor in all aspects of social interaction, including international diplomacy. As such, any theory of international diplomacy must be based in large part on considerations of this and other related aspects of the communication process, treated in dynamic terms. Here theorists of international relations, like all theorists dealing with communication, are strictly limited by the nonexistence of an adequate theory of semantics which would enable us to deal more fully with communication among nations, involving the communication of meaning from one set of decision-makers to another across national boundaries.

Methodological Developments

Along with the recent interest in the application of communication theories to the study of international diplomacy has come an interest in the development of methodologies to measure communication content in diplomatic interactions. Content analysis has been employed frequently in the analysis of diplomatic communications. Most such studies have employed computer content analysis using the General Inquirer,[15] especially the Stanford Political version of the General Inquirer.[16] The latter has been applied largely within the framework of the mediated stimulus-response model to measure the internal variables, that is r and s, which may then be related to overt behavior. The Stanford Political Dictionary rates decision-makers' perceptions of other actors, of the actions of those actors, and of themselves and their own actions along the three dimensions of Osgood's semantic differential:

1) Evaluative: Positive —— Negative
2) Potency: Strong —— Weak
3) Activity: Active —— Passive

These dimensions have been used to analyze the perceptions by Secretary of State John Foster Dulles of the Soviet Union (Holsti, 1962), of interactions leading up to the outbreak of World War I (Zinnes, 1968; Holsti, 1965; Holsti, 1972), and of interactions during the Cuban missile crisis of 1962 (Holsti, Brody, and North, 1969; Holsti, 1972). This method has also been applied to cognitive balance models to measure attitudinal consensus among alliance members in NATO and the Communist system during the postwar period (Holsti, Hopmann, and Sullivan, 1973).

Another type of content analysis instrument has been developed by Walcott and Hopmann (1975) and by Walcott, Hopmann and King (1977), based on work in small group research by Bales (1950) and in international relations by Jensen (1968). The purpose of this procedure, called Bargaining Process Analysis, is to measure bargaining behavior in verbal international negotiations. Most negotiations are assumed to be somewhat analogous to small group interactions in which verbal bargaining takes place in a mixed-motive situation. Thus traditional categories of small group analysis (positive affect, negative affect, and task behavior, i.e., questions and answers) are supplemented by characteristics of bargaining behavior of both substantive position-taking (initiations, accommodations, and retractions) and of strategic behavior (commitments, promises, and threats). This measuring instrument has been applied to studies of bargaining in small group experiments,[18] in the Eighteen Nation Disarmament Conference on the Nuclear Test Ban issue,[19] and in the Conference of the Committee on Disarmament on the negotiations leading to the Seabeds Denuclearization Treaty.[20]

Finally, scholars studying international diplomacy have been concerned with the measurement of nonverbal as well as verbal behavior and especially with the development of scales which can be employed to analyze the interrelationships between these two forms of communicative interactions. The data based on a scaling of general international interactions are generally referred to as "events data," that is, data on events in international diplomacy involving the interaction between two or more actors. Thus all events are reduced to the classical unit of "who did what to whom." Each event treated in this fashion is then scaled, either in a set of nominal categories,[21] along ordinal scales ranging from conflict to cooperation,[22] or along separate ratio scales of the degree of conflict and cooperation.[23] These kinds of data have been employed to measure overt stimuli and responses within the mediated stimulus-response framework[24] and to measure relative uncertainty within the cybernetics framework.[25]

Having now outlined some of the general theoretical and methodological applications of a communication approach in studies focusing upon various aspects of international diplomacy, we may focus in more detail upon the specific application of these approaches. We will concentrate upon two specific sets of diplomatic interactions where these theories and methods have been employed quite extensively, namely the study of crisis bargaining and of bargaining in international negotiations.

Application of Communication Framework to Aspects of International Diplomacy

Crisis Bargaining

One central focus of research involving communication models has been on bargaining in crisis situations. In times of intense crisis, such as the crises preceding the outbreak of World Wars I and II and the Korean War, the Berlin crises of 1948 and 1961, the Quemoy crisis of 1958, and the Cuban missile crisis of 1962, the ability of nations' leaders to communicate clearly, effectively, and unambiguously has been an important consideration in determining whether the crisis will escalate to a major war or if it can be resolved short of war. Therefore, research has focused very heavily upon how the communication process operates in a crisis situation and its effect upon the outcome of the crisis.

An international crisis, from the perspective of decision makers responding to the situation, has been defined by Hermann as a situation "that (1) threatens the high priority goals of the decision-making unit; (2) restricts the amount of time available for response before the situation is transformed; and (3) surprises the members of the decision-making unit when it occurs."[26] The high threat condition means that decision-makers are likely to have to operate under high stress in the crisis situation, knowing that their decisions about how to respond to the crisis may have a significant impact bearing on their ability to maintain or achieve major objectives. The fact that crises involve short decision time means that decision-makers will be under considerable time pressure to make decisions without thorough information search and a consideration of all possible alternatives. Surprise means that the decision-makers will not be able to respond routinely since they will not have anticipated the conditions giving rise to the crisis situation. In other words, the crisis situation provides considerable pressure for a decision unit, where information and communication are important, but where time and the necessity for responding to unanticipated events make more normal modes of information search, decision-making, and bargaining with other actors difficult. Finally, McClelland has defined crisis from the perspective of the international system in terms of its effects on the "stability or equilibrium of the system, or disturbance of the normal run of business conducted between actors."[27] Thus, crises not only create problems for decision-making units, but also for the structure, stability, and predictability of the inter-state interactions. The research on crisis has dealt with its impact on communication both within decision-making organizations and in interactions between nations.

Research focusing on the impact of crisis on decision-making has dealt extensively with the assertion that crises create stress for decision-makers, which affects their perceptions, internal communication, and responses. Stress has been demonstrated to have a number of significant effects on individual performance, which in turn will affect their interactions with other individuals. Milburn has summarized the findings of research about the effects of stress on individual performance as follows: "Mild stress often facilitates performance, especially if the response is uncomplicated or well learned. As stress increases, performance generally worsens; and, with very intense stress, complete disintegration of performance can occur. The more complex the task, the more likely will stress disrupt performance."[28] Stress is also likely to reduce tolerance for ambiguity, to reduce the scope of attention across time and space, and to diminish the scope of complex perceptual ability.[29] In the context of the basic model of dyadic communication, it is likely to reduce the convergence of encoding and decoding processes for actors involved in a crisis interaction, thereby leading to increased distortion in their communications and mutual perceptions.

In a series of comparative studies of the escalation of World War I in the summer of 1914 and the escalation and de-escalation of the Cuban missile crisis in 1962, Holsti (1972) and Holsti, Brody, and North (1969) have found that a number of significant distortions occur, especially in the perceptions (r) by each actor of the stimulus (S) produced by the other actor and in the communication of clear and unambiguous messages which can be interpreted similarly by sender and receiver.

First, the increased stress of a crisis has a number of potential effects on the diplomatic communication among nations involved in the crisis; a) The crisis tends to increase the volume of diplomatic communication exchanged among nations, as evidenced by increased communications among Britain, France, Russia, Germany and Austria-Hungary from June 27 through August 4, 1914. b) As crisis increases, policy makers are more likely to rely heavily on improvised or *ad hoc* means of communication rather than on normal diplomatic channels; since the regular channels may become overloaded, extra channels must be employed to speed up communication in the presence of time pressure.[30] c) As a crisis deepens the proportion of messages directed to the opposing alliance tends to decline relative to the communications which are directed to each nation's own allies.[31] Hence the lines of division between alliances tend to become more abrupt and communication-clarity between enemies tends to decline. d) As a crisis becomes more severe the increased volume of communication tends to cause communication channels to become overloaded, increasing the stress on the decision-makers.[32] Thus decision-makers may increasingly be selective in the attention which they give to incoming messages, selecting messages which reinforce their preconceived images. Furthermore, the structure of decision-making itself may break down under this communication-overload.

Second, the stress of the crisis situation is likely to exert considerable distorting effects on the perceptions by each nation's decision-makers of the behavior of the opposing nation or alliance. Basically, the crisis situation is likely to create inverted "mirror image" perceptions by each side in the conflict of each other. The decision-makers in each nation will tend to perceive that the other side has the initiative in the action and that they are merely responding at the same level of violence to actions initiated by the other side. Thus, neither side perceives that it is responsible for the escalating conflict because each side may "underperceive" the level of violence in its own response relative to an "overperception" of the level of violence in the actions of its opponent. Hence, as mediated by the internal variables in the mediated stimulus-response model, the level of overt behavior (S and R) may be characterized by increasing levels of violence while each side perceives that its response (s) is congruent with the stimulus from the other side, as perceived by itself (r). In other words, escalation may be at least partially unintended in crisis situations, as each nation responds automatically at slightly higher levels of violence while still perceiving its response to be at an identical level with the stimulus it received. When this takes place in a cyclic fashion over some period of time, levels of violence may rise dramatically even though neither side really perceives that it has taken an initiative to raise the intensity of conflict, but rather thinks that it was merely "responding in kind."

This general conclusion has been disputed by Zinnes, Zinnes, and McClure (1972) in a study employing the same data from the 1914 crisis. Using a Markov-chain model, they find that perceptions of threat generally follow after the receipt of hostile messages and that these perceptions are responded to with hostile messages; on the contrary, no hostility is perceived or expressed in the absence of the receipt of hostile messages. Zinnes, Zinnes, and McClure thus conclude that decision-makers in a crisis "do not perceive hostility when none exists, and they express hostility directly in terms of their perception of hostility. On the basis of the 1914 evidence, it does not appear that decision-makers become paranoid under the pressures of the situation."[33] Their operationalization of the variables of expression of hostility and perception of threat, however, is purely binary; therefore, this analysis does not in fact directly refute the arguments of Holsti that escalation in *intensity* of overt violence may take place as a consequence of misperception of the level of hostility received by decision-makers in a crisis situation.

Another related hypothesis which appears frequently in the literature on crisis bargaining is that, "as stress increases decision makers will tend to perceive the range of alternatives open to themselves as becoming narrower" while the "range of alternatives open to their adversaries" is expanding.[34] Holsti's test of this hypothesis in the 1914 crisis has been replicated in the laboratory, with mixed findings. In a simulated international crisis, Hermann found that search for differentiated alternative solutions to the situation was less under conditions of crisis than noncrisis.[35] In a more recent analysis, however, he has found somewhat contradictory results, namely that at high levels of threat, a decrease in the amount of time available for decision will actually produce an effort to identify a wider range of alternatives.[36] As Hermann acknowledges, however, this finding may be an artifact of shortcomings in the experimental design.[37] Indeed, there are logical reasons why this hypothesis would tend to be supported in actual crisis situations. Since, in a crisis, each side believes that the other is the initiator of action, then it also believes that the other side has available to it the alternatives which might lead to a de-escalation of the conflict. Similarly, since each side perceives that it is merely responding passively to the initiatives of the other side, then it sees that it has no alternative but to respond in kind to the provocative acts directed against it. When both sides hold these symmetrical though inverted "mirror image" perceptions of one another, crisis escalation tends to become "locked in," since each side perceives that the other has the alternatives available to it to resolve the crisis and de-escalate. When each side waits for the other to take de-escalatory initiatives, then no such initiatives are taken, and a crisis spirals until it gets out of control, resulting in war. Thus, the theory developed by Holsti suggests that mutual misperception and distorted communication between nations contributes greatly to feeding the process of crisis escalation and hence to setting off major war.

Holsti and North (1965) have further argued that states can become involved in war if they perceive themselves to be victims of injury from their enemy, even if they perceive that they are inferior in military capability to their enemy. Injury is assumed to be present when a state perceives that its own nation is primarily a target rather than an agent of hostility and when the other state is perceived as primarily an agent rather than a target of hostility. In other words, "decision makers view the policies of their nations to be friendly towards other nations, but . . . at the same time they regard that friendship to be unreciprocated."[38] This problem is particularly severe when all actors on both sides of a conflict perceive themselves to be victims of injury, as Holsti and North found to be the case for all five major powers involved in the outbreak of World War I in 1914. In this situation each perceives its cause to be just and its violent response to be "appropriate" to the injury inflicted on it by the enemy. Similarly, Siverson (1970) has found that both the Israelis and the Egyptians perceived themselves to be victims of injury in the events surrounding the Suez crisis of 1956, hence contributing to the mutual escalation of this conflict.

In a study of the Cuban missile crisis designed to parallel the study of the 1914 crisis Holsti (1972) also suggests that similar factors contributed to the initial escalation of the crisis; however, in Cuba, unlike in Europe in 1914, decision-makers were able to exercise greater control over their perceptions and extraordinary means were undertaken to improve communications during the crisis, leading eventually to the resolution of the crisis before open warfare broke out. In particular, Holsti found that in 1962 there was "a close correspondence between Soviet actions and American perceptions of the USSR."[39] While the relationship was less clear in Soviet perceptions of American actions, "in general conciliatory actions by the other side were seen as genuine efforts to delay or reverse escalation, rather than as tricks to be dismissed out of hand. Thus efforts by either party to avert a violent showdown were interpreted as such and responded to in a like manner."[40] In the Cuban missile crisis Kennedy and Khrushchev took careful efforts to communicate their intentions clearly and unambiguously, using nonverbal communications to reinforce verbal messages. They sought to avoid time pressure by carefully examining alternatives before forcing the crisis into the public arena. And they used private intermediaries and public broadcasts to convey information in a hurry when the normal diplomatic channels were overloaded or inadequate. They managed to avoid many of the problems and distortions of communications and perceptions which had contributed to the escalation of the 1914 crisis, thereby resolving the Cuban crisis before war actually broke out. Nevertheless, the Cuban crisis closely approached the point of nuclear war, and if one single important message had been distorted or misperceived it might have been sufficient to set off the first, and perhaps the only, direct conflict between the nuclear powers. As President Kennedy observed sometime later, "You can't have too many of those."

Another approach to the study of communication in crisis conditions has been taken by McClelland (1972) in a study comparing the Berlin crisis and the Taiwan-Straits-crisis. In his study of the Berlin crisis, beginning with the blockade of Berlin in the summer of 1948 and continuing through the building of the Berlin wall in the summer of 1961, McClelland (1968) found that periods of intensified crises tended to be characterized by an increase in diplomatic activity and by an increase in the variety of events. Using an information measure of relative uncertainty, he found that in both the blockade-crisis of 1948 and the Berlin-wall-crisis of 1961, higher levels of relative uncertainty were recorded in the diplomatic interactions among the nations on both sides of the conflict. This increase in uncertainty may, of course, further contribute to crisis escalation as routine patterns of diplomatic interaction are interrupted and the stable expectations upon which normal diplomatic activity are based become overrun by the increased uncertainty and loss of patterning of events. While McClelland (1972) found that the Quemoy crisis of 1958 escalated considerably more slowly, the same increasing levels of uncertainty characterized the period of crisis escalation. McClelland thus concludes that the transition from non-crisis to crisis conditions involves a " 'fanning out' rather than a 'channeling in' movement" in the variety of events, thus producing an increase in uncertainty.[41]

In short, models derived from theories of communicative interactions have been of considerable value to scholars in international relations in describing and explaining patterns of interaction in acute international crises. Especially, the identification of the differences in communication patterns between crisis- and non-crisis-periods and even more importantly between crises which escalate into overt war and those which do not, may be extremely valuable in learning how to avoid crises in the first place, and, in the event they occur, in learning how to manage them so that they can be resolved short of open hostilities.

Bargaining in Negotiations

A second aspect of diplomacy which has received considerable attention from scholars applying communications models to international relations is international negotiations. Negotiations have been defined by Iklé as "a process in which explicit proposals are put forward ostensibly for the purpose of reaching an agreement on an exchange or realization of a common interest where conflicting interests are present."[42] This definition contains several implicit assumptions about the nature of negotiations. For one thing, negotiations are possible only when two or more parties are interacting under conditions which combine elements of both conflict and cooperation, that is where there are common and conflicting interests both present. Furthermore, this definition implies that some degree of communication must be possible between nations in order to bring about an exchange and realization of common interests among them. Most theories of bargaining build on these assumptions and assume that the purpose of bargaining is to identify positions in which conflicts of interest may be resolved and common interests upgraded in such a way that no party receives an unacceptable loss and in which each party maximizes gains to the greatest extent possible within the first constraint.

The central concept in such theories is "bargaining space," the identification through verbal and non-verbal communication of a set of positions in which the minimum acceptable positions of all actors overlap. A simple model of bargaining in a conflict of interest situation for two actors is depicted in Figure 4. The vertical axis represents payoffs to each of the actors relative to no agreement;

these are represented as either gains (above the zero point) or losses (below the zero point). The horizontal axis represents solutions or outcomes on a particular issue or set of issues, which, for the purposes of this illustration, are assumed to form a continuum. We may then draw curves representing the payoffs for each actor at any point along the solution line, namely the lines A---A' and B---B'. For actor A, point *a'* represents his most preferred position and point *a* represents his minimum position, and similarly for actor B. Ikle' has noted that negotiations always involve a choice between the value of any particular agreement relative to the value of no agreement, so that agreement becomes possible only if it is valued positively by all actors relative to no agreement.[43] Therefore, a solution is possible only if some points on the line *a---a'* coincide with some points on the line *b---b'*, as is the case in Figure 4. Figure 5, on the other hand, diagrams a situation in which no agreement is possible since there is no solution available for which the gains exceed losses for both actors simultaneously.

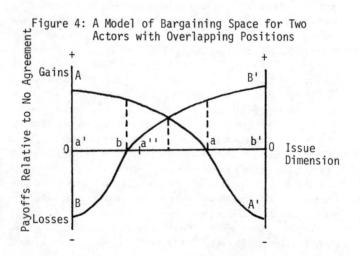

Figure 4: A Model of Bargaining Space for Two Actors with Overlapping Positions

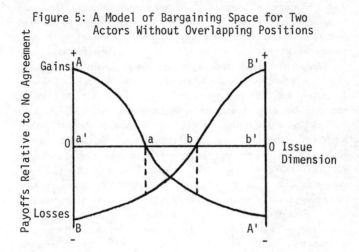

Figure 5: A Model of Bargaining Space for Two Actors Without Overlapping Positions

Therefore, the purpose of the negotiation process is for actors to communicate to one another their utilities assigned to different outcomes in order to identify issues for which bargaining space exists; this process may be referred to as the "issue definition" phase of negotiations. Once such issues have been identified, however, actors must bargain in order to reach a solution within the available bargaining space, an outcome which is by no means certain. Within the available bargaining space in Figure 4 each actor will have an incentive to maximize his payoffs, often at the expense of the other, while still securing a mutually acceptable agreement. Thus actor B will prefer to move towards the right without passing point a while A prefers to move to the left without passing point b. Here clarity of communication is important, because if actors misperceive the true minimum acceptable positions of the other, they may make miscalculations which can lead to stalemate. Uncertainty makes bargaining difficult in the absence of clear knowledge of the utilities of the other party. Thus effective communication by all actors of their utilities assigned to all particular positions is likely to enhance the probability of agreement in negotiations, especially through the reduction of uncertainty.

Actors may use a variety of strategic devices to communicate their positions on various issues, and to attempt to modify the position of other actors on the issues. We shall consider here six such devices. First, *commitments* are often used by actors to attempt to establish a firm position beyond which they will not compromise; by making a commitment they hope to persuade the other parties that the committed position represents their minimum acceptable outcome. Nevertheless, actors will use commitments frequently to try to maximize their own positions, by trying to commit themselves just inside the minimum acceptable position (as they perceive it) of the other party, thereby narrowing dramatically the range of the bargaining space. For example, A may try to commit himself to a position just to the right of point b, labelled a''. If the commitment is successful, A may convince B that agreement at this point is still preferable to no agreement for him and receive a substantial payoff. If B is not fully convinced of the credibility of A's commitment, however, he may call A's bluff and reject his proposal. Then A is forced into a choice between a compromise, with the credibility and strength of his future commitments weakened, or he may have to settle for no agreement even though he would have otherwise been willing to accept a settlement at a position farther to the right with somewhat less favorable payoffs to himself. In other words, an individual actor's decision to maximize his own gain requires the ability to convince the other actor that he is fully committed to his position and cannot compromise under any circumstances. The paradox is that this firm commitment runs "the risk of establishing an immovable position that goes beyond the ability of the other to concede, and thereby provokes the likelihood of statement or breakdown."[44]

A second device which may be employed in bargaining situations is the *threat*, which may be used by an actor to induce another participant to accept a solution favorable to himself through persuading him to modify his utilities. A threat is a communication that seeks to make the alternative of no agreement less attractive to the other party(ies). In Figure 4, if A threatens losses to B associated with no agreement, this will move the curve B---B' in a northwesterly direction, thereby widening the payoff possibilities for A and reducing the losses relative to no agreement for B in reaching a solution in the left-hand segment of the diagram. The paradox of the threat situation is that the threatener must bind himself to carry out the threat if the desired action on the part of the other actor is not carried out, or else the threat will not be credible. Yet he must also communicate to the threatened party that the threat involves some cost to himself so that the threatener would have no incentive to carry out the threat and would be likely to refrain from doing so if the desired alternative were accepted. Thus, the threat requires that the initiator must persuade the recipient that, if he responds as desired, there will be no execution of the threat; on the other hand, if he does not so respond, the threat will almost certainly be carried out.[45]

A third device for strategic communications is the *promise*, which is logically similar to the threat. A may attempt to modify B's utilities by promising B some reward associated with a particular point of agreement and which would thus increase B's gains relative to no agreement. Like the threat this would tend to shift the curve B---B' in Figure 4 in a northwesterly direction, thereby increasing B's gains for a solution which was otherwise more preferred by A, that is in the left segment of the diagram. Like the threat situation, the initiator must persuade the recipient that he will actually carry out his promises if the desired behavior ensues. He must also convince the recipient that the promise involves some loss to him so that he would not be likely to carry it out anyway.

Fourth, an *initiation* is a statement by one actor of a new position along the issue dimension line. This may have different effects, depending on whether or not it is accompanied by a commitment to that position. Assuming that it does not imply a commitment, however, it may have the effect of clarifying issues and getting bargaining under way on a particular issue, by enhancing understanding and reducing uncertainty.

Fifth, an *accommodation* refers to a movement by one actor along the issue definition line toward the preferred position of the other actor(s). This kind of a move is likely to create an impression of "flexibility," and, if perceived accurately, it is likely to create positive affect, which may spill over into more positive behaviors (in order to reduce dissonance) on the part of other actors. Of course, accommodations may also be perceived as weakness by the other actor(s), who may then seek to take advantage of the accommodating actor.

Finally, a *retraction* is a movement by one actor along the issue dimension from a previous position to a new position farther away from the position preferred by the other party(ies). In Figure 4 a retraction would involve a movement by A toward the left along the issue dimension axis. Since such a retraction is likely to reduce the gains or increase the losses relative to no agreement for B, it is likely to lead to increased negative affect by B, followed by more conflictual behaviors.

These six components of bargaining strategy may be collapsed into two broad categories for some conceptual purposes, namely "soft" and "hard" strategies. The former category includes the use of *initiations, accommodations,* and *promises,* namely *positive communications* in which one actor communicates a desire to increase the relative gains for other actors in order to enhance the prospects of agreement. The latter category includes *retractions, threats,* and *commitments,* that is those *negative communications* in which one actor indicates a desire to increase losses for the other party(ies) relative to more desired outcomes. Experimental studies of the bargaining process have frequently examined the impact that these different forms of bargaining strategy have on negotiation outcomes. For example, studies by Bixenstine and Wilson (1963) and Bixenstine, Potash, and Wilson (1963) indicate that cooperative as opposed to competitive behavior in dyadic, mixed-motive interactions is sensitive to changes in strategy. Specifically, they find that overall end-session cooperativeness is enhanced by starting with a "hard" strategy and then softening it as compared with either consistent hardness or consistent softness. Conversely, starting in a cooperative mode, then turning competitive, produces more competition than a purely competitive strategy pursued consistently. In an experimental study employing an arms control negotiation scenario, Hopmann and Walcott (1976) found that "soft" strategies were generally associated with more positive affect among negotiators and with greater levels of agreement, whereas "hard" strategies tended to produce negative affect and lower levels of agreement.

Several studies have applied this general framework to an analysis of the negotiations leading up to the Partial Nuclear Test Ban Treaty, signed in July, 1963. Jensen (1968) looked primarily at the relationships between accommodations and retractions to analyze bargaining in the test ban negotiations. He found that a good deal of the interaction was characterized by a kind of approach-avoidance conflict, as the bargaining space of the two actors was modified over time while the United States and the Soviet Union sought a solution with overlapping minimum acceptable positions. The farther the actors are away from agreement, Jensen argues, the more flexible they appear to be and the wider the bargaining space is. At this point they may make compromises with relative ease. Under these circumstances they have little to lose from concessions since there is little likelihood that they will be called upon to live by them. However, as the positions of the two sides grow closer together, the bargaining space may contract and flexibility may be reduced. At this point accommodations become more costly because there is a risk that they may have to be abided by if an actual agreement is reached. Therefore, Jensen found that, as the positions of the United States and the Soviet Union drew closer together on the test ban issue, they tended to make fewer concessions and even increased the number of retractions of previous proposals. Hence approach beyond a certain threshold led to an increase in avoidance tendencies between the negotiating parties. This dilemma was overcome, however, when the actors began to disaggregate the issue and identified a compromise solution, namely, the partial test ban, which fell within the minimum acceptable positions of both sides without maximizing the desired goals of either.

Hopmann (1972) and Hopmann and King (1976) have found that negotiations in the Eighteen Nation Disarmament Conference on the test ban issue were influenced by events in the international environment. More cooperative interactions and more positive communications between the United States and the Soviet Union tended to be associated with more positive affect, more accommodations and initiatives relative to retractions, leading to high levels of agreement. Thus, the internal behaviors of each actor were responsive to the external behaviors of the other actors. Furthermore, the internal behaviors of both actors tended to maintain consistency between attitudes and behaviors, and actions by one party tended to be responded to symmetrically by similar actions on the part of the other actor. Hopmann and King thus concluded that "negotiations may be more successful if the participating nations can reduce conflict in their general interactions and if they try to be responsive to tension-reducing or conflict-resolving behavior on the part of their negotiating partners."[46] Under these conditions, improved communications and reduced uncertainty probably enhanced the ability of the United States and the Soviet Union to reach a solution on the Partial Test Ban Treaty, thereby beginning a series of small, though important steps towards arms control after 18 years of an intensive Soviet-American arms race.

Conclusion

In conclusion, we may identify very briefly a few major tasks which must be undertaken if we wish to improve our understanding of the role of communication in international diplomacy. First, we must begin to develop more rigorous theories of the communication process which will enable us to make explanatory and predictive statements on the basis of deductively interrelated models. As noted above, none of the models of communication which have been applied to diplomacy to date have strong explanatory and predictive power in themselves. Therefore, while they often are suggestive of important and relevant insights, they are limited in their ability to provide the basis for rigorous theories of international relations. Second, in applying communication models to international diplomacy, we must confront directly the micro-macro gap discussed by Singer (1961) and others between the individual-as-actor and state-as-actor approaches to international relations. Most communication models are applicable directly only to interactions among individuals; nevertheless, diplomacy often involves the analysis of the behavior of complex decision-making organizations, composed of large scale aggregations of individual behaviors. This gap has restricted the applicability of communication models only to more individual aspects of diplomacy, such as bargaining between national leaders relatively unconstrained by their bureaucratic organizations in times of crisis and bargaining among individual negotiators in international negotiations. If models of international communication are to be applied to other aspects of diplomacy where organizational behavior is more important, then linkages between individual actors and the behavior of the decision-making units must be developed. Third, further application of communication models to various aspects of international diplomacy will have to be made simultaneously with the development of more rigorous theory in order to identify the scope conditions which limit the applicability of various generalizations based upon communications frameworks. This will enable us to develop more rigorous, though often partial, theories of important aspects of international diplomacy in which communication between individuals plays a crucial role.

FOOTNOTES

[1] Wilbur Schramm, "Communication Research in the United States," *The Science of Human Communication,* New York: Basic Books, 1963, p. 7.

[2] Karl W. Deutsch, "Communication Models and Decision Systems," James C. Charlesworth, ed., *Contemporary Political Analysis,* New York: Free Press, 1967, p. 268.

[3] Robert C. North, "The Analytical Prospects of Communications Theory," James C. Charlesworth, ed. *Contemporary Political Analysis,* New York: Free Press, 1967, p. 304.

[4] Richard C. Snyder, H.W. Bruck, and Burton Sapin, *Foreign Policy Decision Making,* New York: Free Press, 1962, pp. 65-66.

[5] Charles E. Osgood, "Behavior Theory and the Social Sciences," Roland Young, ed., *Approaches to the Study of Politics,* Evanston, Ill.: Northwestern University Press, 1958, p. 233.

[6] Op. cit., North, 1967, pp. 304-305.

[7] Robert C. North, "The Behavior of Nation-States: Problems of Conflict and Integration," Morton A. Kaplan, ed., *New Approaches to International Relations,* New York: St. Martin's Press, 1968, p. 314.

[8] Kenneth Boulding, "National Images and International Systems," *Journal of Conflict Resolution,* 1959, vol. iii, p. 120.

[9] Theodore M. Newcomb, "An Approach to the Study of Communicative Acts," E.F. Borgatta and R.F. Bales, ed., *Small Groups,* New York: Alfred Knopf, 1955, p. 149.

[10] Claude E. Shannon and Warren Weaver, *The Mathematical Theory of Communication,* Urbana, Illinois: University of Illinois Press, 1964, pp. 10-11.

[11] *Op. cit.,* Deutsch, 1967, pp. 283-284.

[12] J.W. Burton, *International Relations: A General Theory,* Cambridge, England: Cambridge University Press, 1965, pp. 146-149.

[13] Davis B. Bobrow, "Transfer of Meaning Across National Boundaries," Richard L. Merritt, ed., *Communication in International Politics,* Urbana, Illinois: University of Illinois Press, 1972, p. 55.

[14] *Ibid.,* p. 57.

[15] Philip J. Stone, *et. al., The General Inquirer: A Computer Approach to Content Analysis in the Behavioral Sciences,* Cambridge, Mass: The M.I.T. Press, 1966.

[16] Ole R. Holsti, *Content Analysis for the Social Sciences and Humanities,* Reading, Mass.: Addison-Wesley, 1969, chapter 7.

[17] Charles E. Osgood, George J. Suci and Percy H. Tannenbaum, *The Measurement of Meaning,* Urbana, Illinois: University of Illinois Press, 1959, pp. 72-73.

[18] P. Terrance Hopmann and Charles Walcott, "The Impact of International Conflict and Détente on Bargaining in Arms Control Negotiations: An Experimental Analysis," *International Interactions,* 1976, vol. 2, pp. 189-206.

[19] P. Terrance Hopmann, "Internal and External Influences on Bargaining in Arms Control Negotiations: The Partial Test Ban," Bruce M. Russet, ed., *Peace, War and Numbers,* Beverly Hills, California: Sage Publications, 1972.

[20] P. Terrance Hopmann, "Bargaining in Arms Control negotiations: The Seabeds Denuclearization Treaty," *International Organization,* Vol. 28, no.3, pp.313-344.

[21] Charles A. McClelland and Gary D. Hoggard, "Conflict Patterns in Interactions Among Nations," James N. Rosenau, ed., *International Politics and Foreign Policy,* revised edition, New York: Free Press, 1972, pp. 714-715.

[22] Lincoln E. Moses, *et. al.,* "Scaling Data on Inter-Nation Action," *Science,* May 26, 1967, pp. 1054-1059; Edward Azar, "Analysis of International Events," *Peace Research Reviews,* 1970, vol. 4, no. 1.

[23] Walter Corson, *Measuring Conflict and Cooperation Intensity in East-West Relations: A Manual and Codebook,* University of Michigan, Institute for Social Research, 1970.

[24] Ole R. Holsti, Richard A. Brody, and Robert C. North, "The Management of International Crisis: Affect and Action in American-Soviet Relations," Dean G. Pruitt and Richard C. Snyder, eds., *Theory and Research on the Causes of War,* Englewood Cliffs, N.J.: Prentice-Hall, 1969.

[25] Charles A. McClelland, "Access to Berlin: The Quantity and Variety of Events, 1948-1963," J. David Singer, ed., *Quantitative International Politics,* New York: Free Press, 1968; Charles A. McClelland, "The Beginning, Duration, and Abatement of Inter-

national Crises: Comparisons in Two Conflict Arenas," Charles F. Hermann, ed., *International Crises: Insights from Behavioral Research*, New York: Free Press, 1972.

[26] Charles F. Hermann, *Crises in Foreign Policy: A Simulation Analysis*, Indianapolis: Bobbs-Merrill, 1969, p. 29.

[27] Charles F. Hermann, "Some Issues in the Study of International Crisis," Charles F. Hermann, ed., *International Crises: Insights from Behavioral Research*, New York: Free Press, 1972, p. 7.

[28] Thomas W. Milburn, "The Management of Crisis," Charles F. Hermann, ed., *International Crises: Insights from Behavioral Research*, New York: Free Press, 1972, p. 264.

[29] Ole R. Holsti, *Crisis, Escalation, War*, Montreal: McGill-Queens University Press, 1972, p. 13.

[30] *Ibid.*, p. 95.

[31] *Ibid.*, p. 102.

[32] *Ibid.*, p. 114.

[33] Dina A. Zinnes, Joseph L. Zinnes, and Robert D. McClure, "Hostility in Diplomatic Communication: A Study of the 1914 Crisis," Charles F. Hermann, ed., *International Crises: Insights from Behavioral Research*, New York: Free Press, 1972, p. 160.

[34] *Op. cit.*, Holsti, 1972, p. 145.

[35] *Op. cit.*, Hermann, 1969, p. 168.

[36] Charles F. Hermann, "Threat, Time and Surprise: A Simulation of International Crisis," Charles F. Hermann, ed., *International Crises: Insights From Behavioral Research*, New York: Free Press, 1972, pp. 198-201.

[37] *Ibid.*, p. 210.

[38] Ole R. Holsti and Robert C. North, "The History of Human Conflict," Elton B. McNeil, ed., *The Nature of Human Conflict*, Englewood Cliffs, N.J.: Prentice-Hall, 1965, p. 163.

[39] *Op. cit.*, Holsti, 1972, p. 189.

[40] Ibid., p. 192.

[41] *Op. cit.*, McClelland, 1972, p. 93.

[42] Fred Charles Ikle, *How Nations Negotiate*, New York: Frederick A. Praeger, 1964, pp. 3-4.

[43] *Ibid.*, pp. 60-61.

[44] Thomas C. Schelling, *The Strategy of Conflict*, Cambridge, Mass.: Harvard University Press, 1960, p. 28.

[45] *Ibid.*, pp. 35-36.

[46] P. Terrence Hopmann and Timothy King, "Interactions and Perceptions in the Test Ban Negotiations," *International Studies Quarterly,* 1976, vol. 20, no. 1, p. 141.

BIBLIOGRAPHY

Azar, Edward, 1970, "Analysis of International Events," *Peace Research Reviews,* vol. 4, no. 1.

Bales, Robert F., 1950, *Interaction Process Analysis,* Cambridge, Mass.: Addison-Wesley.

Bixenstine, V.E. and Wilson, K.V., 1963, "Effects of Level of Cooperative Choice by Other Player on Choices in a Prisoner's Dilemma Game," *Journal of Abnormal and Social Psychology,* vol. 62, pp. 139-147.

Bixenstine, V.E., Potash, H.M., and Wilson, K.V., 1963, "Effects of Level of Cooperative Choice by Other Player on Choices in a Prisoner's Dilemma Game, Part II," *Journal of Abnormal and Social Psychology,* vol. 62, pp. 308-313.

Bobrow, Davis B., 1972, "Transfer of Meaning Across National Boundaries," Richard L. Merritt, ed., *Communication in International Politics,* Urbana, Illinois: University of Illinois Press.

Boulding, Kenneth E., 1959, "National Images and International Systems," *Journal of Conflict Resolution,* vol. iii, pp. 120-131.

Burton, J.W., 1965, *International Relations: A General Theory,* Cambridge, England: Cambridge University Press.

Corson, Walter, 1970, *Measuring Conflict and Cooperation Intensity in East-West Relations: A Manual and Codebook,* University of Michigan, Institute for Social Research.

Deutsch, Karl W., 1967, "Communication Models and Decision Systems," James C. Charlesworth, ed., *Contemporary Political Analysis,* New York: Free Press.

Deutsch, Karl W., 1968, *The Analysis of International Relations,* Englewood Cliffs, N.J.: Prentice-Hall.

Garner, Wendell, 1962, *Uncertainty and Structure as Psychological Concepts,* New York: John Wiley.

Harary, Frank, 1961, "A Structural Analysis of the Situation in the Middle East in 1956," *Journal of Conflict Resolution,* vol. v, pp. 167-178.

Hart, Jeffrey, 1974, "Symmetry and Polarization in the European International System, 1870-1879: A Methodological Study," *Journal of Peace Research,* vol. xi, no. 3, pp. 229-244.

Heider, Fritz, 1946, "Attitudes and Cognitive Organization," *Journal of Psychology,* vol. 21, pp. 107-112.

Hermann, Charles F., 1969, *Crisis in Foreign Policy: A Simulation Analysis,* Indianapolis: Bobbs-Merrill.

Hermann, Charles F., 1972a, "Some Issues in the Study of International Crisis," Charles F. Hermann, ed., *International Crises: Insights from Behavioral Research,* New York: Free Press.

Hermann, Charles F., 1972b: "Threat, Time, and Surprise: A Simulation of International Crisis," Charles F. Hermann, ed., *International Crises: Insights from Behavioral Research,* New York: Free Press.

Holsti, Ole R., 1962, "The Belief System and National Images: A Case Study," *Journal of Conflict Resolution,* vol. vi, pp. 244-252.

Holsti, Ole R., 1965, "The 1914 Case," *American Political Science Review,* vol. LIX, pp. 365-378.

Holsti, Ole R., 1969, *Content Analysis for the Social Sciences and Humanities,* Reading, Mass.: Addison-Wesley.

Holsti, Ole R., 1972, *Crises, Escalation, War,* Montreal: McGill-Queen's University Press.

Holsti, Ole R., Brody, Richard A., and North, Robert C., 1969: "The Management of International Crisis: Affect and Action in American-Soviet Relations," Dean G. Pruitt and Richard C. Snyder, eds., *Theory and Research on the Causes of War,* Englewood Cliffs, N.J.: Prentice-Hall.

Holsti, Ole R., Hopmann, P. Terrence, and Sullivan, John D., 1973, *Unity and Disintegration in International Alliances,* New York: John Wiley and Sons.

Holsti, Ole R., and North, Robert C., 1965, "The History of Human Conflict," Elton B. McNeil, ed., *The Nature of Human Conflict,* Englewood Cliffs, N.J.: Prentice-Hall.

Hopmann, P. Terrence, 1972, "Internal and External Influences on Bargaining in Arms Control Negotiations: The Partial Test Ban," Bruce M. Russett, ed., *Peace, War, and Numbers,* Beverly

Hills, California: Sage Publications.

Hopmann, P. Terrence, 1974: "Bargaining in Arms Control Negotiations: The Seabeds Denuclearization Treaty," *International Organization,* vol. 28, no. 3, pp. 313-344.

Hopmann, P. Terrence and King, Timothy, 1976, "Interactions and Perceptions in the Test Ban Negotiations," *International Studies Quarterly,* vol. 20, no. 1, pp. 105-142.

Hopmann, P. Terrance, and Walcott, Charles, 1976, "The Impact of International Conflict and Détente on Bargaining in Arms Control Negotiations: An Experimental Analysis," *International Interactions,* vol. 2, pp. 189-206.

Iklé, Fred Charles, 1964: *How Nations Negotiate,* New York: Frederick A. Praeger.

Jensen, Lloyd, 1968, "Approach-Avoidance Bargaining in the Test Ban Negotiations," *International Studies Quarterly,* vol. 12, pp. 152-160.

McClelland, Charles A., 1968, "Access to Berlin: The Quantity and Variety of Events, 1948-1963," J. David Singer, ed., *Quantitative International Politics,* New York: Free Press.

McClelland, Charles A., 1972: "The Beginning, Duration, and Abatement of International Crises: Comparisons in Two Conflict Arenas," Charles F. Hermann, ed., *International Crises: Insights from Behavioral Research,* New York: Free Press.

McClelland, Charles A. and Hoggard, Gary D., 1969, "Conflict Patterns in Interactions Among Nations," James N. Rosenau, ed., *International Politics and Foreign Policy,* revised edition, New York: Free Press.

Milburn, Thomas W., 1972, "The Management of Crisis," Charles F. Hermann, ed., *International Crises: Insights from Behavioral Research,* New York: Free Press.

Moses, Lincoln, E., *et. al.,* 1967, "Scaling Data on Inter-Nation Action," *Science,* May 26, 1967, pp. 1054-1059.

Newcomb, Theodore M., 1955, "An Approach to the Study of Communicative Acts," E.F. Borgatta and R.F. Bales, eds., *Small Groups,* New York: Alfred Knopf.

North, Robert C., 1967: "The Analytical Prospects of Communications Theory," James C. Charlesworth, ed., *Contemporary Political Analysis,* New York: Free Press.

North, Robert C., 1968, "The Behavior of Nation-States: Problems of Conflict and Integration," Morton A. Kaplan, ed., *New Approaches to International Relations,* New York: St. Martin's Press.

Osgood, Charles E., 1958, "Behavior Theory and the Social Sciences," Roland Young, ed., *Approaches to the Study of Politics,* Evanston, Ill.: Northwestern University Press.

Osgood, Charles E., Suci, George J., and Tannenbaum, Percy H., 1959: *The Measurement of Meaning.* Urbana, Illinois: University of Illinois Press.

Schelling, Thomas C., 1960, *The Strategy of Conflict,* Cambridge, Mass.: Harvard University Press.

Schramm, Wilbur, 1963, "Communication Research in the United States," Wilbur Schramm, ed., *The Science of Human Communication,* New York: Basic Books.

Shannon, Claude E. and Weaver, Warren, 1964, *The Mathematical Theory of Communication,* Urbana, Illinois: University of Illiniois Press.

Singer, J. David, 1961, "The Level-of-Analysis Problem in International Relations," Klaus Knorr and Sidney Verba, eds., *The International System,* Princeton, N.Y.: Princeton University Press, 1961.

Siverson, Randolph M., 1970, "International Conflict and Perceptions of Injury: The Case of the Suez Crisis," *International Studies Quarterly,* vol. 14, pp. 157-165.

Snyder, Richard C., Bruck, H.W., and Sapin, Burton, 1962, *Foreign Policy Decision Making,* New York: Free Press.

Stone, Philip J., *et. al.* 1966, *The General Inquirer: A Computer Approach to Content Analysis in the Behavioral Sciences,* Cambridge, Mass.: The M.I.T. Press.

Walcott, Charles and Hopmann, P. Terrance, 1975, "Interaction Analysis and Bargaining Behavior," *Experimental Study of Politics,* vol, iv, no. 1, pp. 1-19.

Walcott, Charles, Hopmann, P. Terrance, and King, Timothy, 1977, "The Role of Debate in Negotiation," Daniel Druckman, ed., *Negotiations: Social-Psychological Perspectives,* Beverly Hills, Ca.: Sage Publications, pp. 193-211.

Wiener, Norbert, 1948, *Cybernetics,* Cambridge, Mass.: The M.I.T. Press.

Zinnes, Dina A., 1968, "The Expression and Perception of Hostility in Prewar Crisis: 1914," J. David Singer, ed., *Quantitative International Politics,* New York: Free Press.

Zinnes, Dina A., Zinnes, Joseph L., McClure, Robert D., 1972, "Hostility in Diplomatic Communication: A Study of the 1914 Crisis." Charles F. Hermann, ed., *International Crises: Insights from Behavioral Research,* New York: Free Press.

James Magee:

Communications in International Organizations with Special Reference to the United Nations and its Agencies

---

THE international organization, like so many other of the phenomena that serve to characterize the modern world, traces its origins to the technological achievements of the nineteenth century. There is some significance, for example, in the fact that the First International Sanitary Conference was held in Paris in 1851, coinciding with London's Great Exhibition. The creation of the Austro-German Telegraphic Union had taken place two years before.

Since then, step by step with the technology that has caused the earth to shrink to a global village, the principle of international cooperation and consultation has won widening acceptance. The first health conference in Paris set the stage for joint efforts by many nations to fight disease, and helped prepare the way for today's World Health Organization. The telegraphic hook-up between two nations opened the way to the International Telecommunications Union, and a world of more than 200 million telephones, 250 million television sets, and nearly 700 million radios. While the Universal Postal Union handles the 250,000 million postal items transmitted annually between 140 countries and territories, the International Air Traffic Association provides the cooperative framework for an airline hook-up with 150,000 inter-connections.

That the international organization answered a need is clear from the steady growth in numbers of such associations. By the year 1870, a total of 34 such groupings had been established, and this had risen to a figure of over 4,000 by the end of 1976. The major groupings are inter-governmental in character, and among these the Everest is, obviously, the United Nations.

The U.N. as we know it today, is the product of political, social, philosophical, and technological processes. In the final resort, it symbolizes not only man's fear of self-destruction in a nuclear holocaust, but also the ideals cherished by many generations of the world's statesmen and thinkers. its very existence is made possible by the fact that science has virtually transformed those concepts of time and distance which once kept man —— and their quarrels —— separate from one another.

In terms of real estate, the U.N. is a glass and steel tower overlooking New York's East River, and housing the main headquarters; a slab of marble —— and more glass —— housing the headquarters in Europe at the Palais des Nations in Geneva, and regional offices in Bangkok, The Hague, Montreal, Santiago, Tokyo, and elsewhere throughout the world. It is also the umbrella for an array of specialized agencies, including the World 'Health Organization, the International Telecommunications Union, the Universal Post Union and many others, (see chart, page 653,654) with offices that stud the globe. In terms of staff, the whole U.N. "family" as it is known, groups nearly 30,000 persons in an international civil service of a kind that has evolved only in the last quarter of a century.

If the language of its Charter is to be taken as a guide, the U.N. directs its activities towards vital targets. They include the following aims:

1. To maintain international peace and security.
2. To develop friendly relations among nations based on respect for the principles of equal rights and self-determination of peoples.
3. To cooperate in solving international problems of an economic, social, cultural or humanitarian character, and in promoting respect for human rights and fundamental freedoms for all, and
4. To be a center for harmonizing the actions of nations in attaining these common ends.

Looked at in such a context, it is logical that the present Secretary-General, Mr. Kurt Waldheim, should describe the organization in the following terms: "The United Nations is, among other things, a global conference centre and the largest permanent floating diplomatic conference in the world. The process of communication is the very essence of much of the work of the U.N. One of the most important facilities which the Organization provides — and one that is largely taken for granted by its Members — is a place and a method by which all sovereign States may communicate with each other on common ground . . ."[1]

The main thrust of this essay will be towards the external aspects of U.N. communications and the related activities of affiliated or other types of international organization, because that is where the greatest quantity of material is available for study. But the discussion will also include the field of internal communications, although here the main purpose is to light up certain increasingly important targets for future research and study by other workers. The external sector relates to a period of approximately 25 years, that era which was ushered in by the uneasy peace of 1945, and during which many of the values of our materialist and industrialist society have been affected by seismic vibrations. It has also been a period during which the U.N. itself underwent radical alteration. The original member nations numbered 51, and reflected the structure of the pre-war rather than the post-war world. But within 15 years most of the colonial empires had crumbled, giving place to an emergent series of new and independent nations, and bringing membership of the U.N. to 149 by the end of last year. The U.N. therefore has been at the center of the historical process for more than a generation, and yet has not emerged with an aura of achievement in the mind of the general public. On the contrary, it is frequently seen as an ineffective and cumbersome organization, a result which points to fundamental defects in that process of communication to which Mr. Waldheim refers. In order to assess this impression, we can begin by isolating certain major elements in the process.

World Meeting Place

One of the key activities of the U.N. relates to conferences and debates, particularly those of the General Assembly and Security Council. For many professional workers today, the international conference has become a familiar ritual, and in politics and diplomacy it is almost a *sine qua non* of governmental activity. The U.N. considers that one of its most important services is the provision of a place and a methodology by which governments may communicate with each other in an atmosphere from which the notion of sovereignty has been abstracted. It is useful for the student of communications to bear in mind when looking at the workings of such international assemblies that a good deal of what takes place in public is designedly formalized. Now and again a Khruschev will enliven the proceedings, but for the most part the speechmaking, the sound and the fury represent only the tip of the iceberg. Communications is the name of the game, but unlike bilateral negotiations, the message has to be transmitted to a much wider circle at an international conference. It is a poker situation, and a Dutch commentator, Johan Kaufmann, sees it in this fashion: "It is not always sufficiently realized that although speeches and statements are an important element in conference diplomacy communications, they are by no means the only one. Visual expressions, maintaining silence when challenged, informal conversations in lobbies, in delegation offices, at luncheons, dinners and cocktail parties, information meetings, delegation press releases, all these may be as important a channel of communication as the conference statement, pronounced in plenary or committee session."[2]

It is not within the scope of the present text to delve deeper into all the communications problems presented by differences in conceptual thinking associated with ethnic and geographical origins. They exist between interlocutors not only from different continents, but also even from different racial groups in each continent, and offer rich material for other workers. What is significant for us here is that attempts to bridge such states of mind have an influence on the international conference in the sense that the overt statement has to be buttressed by the kind of activities to which Dr. Kaufmann refers. Furthermore, the "language" of the conference is also affected. All delegates are conscious of the fact that interpreters are droning steadily in the earphones of the audiences. Willy-nilly, the grinding process between nations becomes in turn a grinding process between languages. The aim is to reduce areas of possible misunderstanding and conflict, so nuances are avoided and flights of eloquence discarded. The search is for the lowest common denominator, the well-worn cliche or platitude, the bland "conferencespeak" that will transmit a basic message and no more. Another element of difficulty lies in the fact that the language a delegate uses in speaking at a conference may not be his own, so that he labors under a considerable handicap in comparison with those who, particularly if they are English or French-speaking, are linguistically "at home." Here again, we need to know more about the difficulties involved, and their relationship to conference tactics, the psychological behavior of delegations, and the construction or undermining of frameworks of agreement and dissent. However, what should be noted for overall consideration is this levelling process, which we shall see also at work in several other important sectors of communication activity, and which is of some significance in terms of impact on opinion.

The Lobby

Surrounding the U.N. are two main types of lobby — permanent and floating. The permanent lobby consists for the most part of the permanent delegations, of which there are now more than 130 in New York, and nearly 100 in Geneva. Such delegations are virtually indistinguishable from other diplomatic missions, but receive accreditation from the international organization. Throughout the year, they act as two-way contacts between their governments and the organization. One of their basic functions is to prepare for international conferences and similar debates, and assist the head of the national delegation. In addition to regular contact with the international organizations, the permanent delegations also keep in touch with each other. In this way, consensus is reached on broad positions by groups of nations before a conference even gets under way, and the behind the scenes contacts also help at times to take the sting out of looming controversies before they reach the floor of the major meeting.

When a conference is held, the pace of lobbying becomes progressively more intense. A cocktail party makes a useful facade of social exchange, but which can also serve the purpose of settling the wording of a resolution or amendment, or of bringing out the nuances in a diplomat's position. If the press are also invited, the interactions develop at a number of levels, creating and dissolving groups according to subtle but recognizable signals of gesture, eye movement and body movement, setting up defined flows of movement by groups through the room, with strategic centers of advance or withdrawal. As George Wynne, himself a former diplomat, notes: "The Geneva diplomat looks deceptively relaxed, at cocktail parties he is rarely without a drink in his hand — or an ulterior thought in his head. When he appears to be concentrating on making inroads in a trayful of canapes he is probably scribbling mental notes on a conversation just concluded with a colleague from another mission who may be engaged in the same exercise one table over . . ."[3] In New York, a diplomat attached to the Turkish Mission commented as follows: "A technician working at his home office tends to go through the rules and the books. But at the U.N. lobbying is one of the biggest aspects of the outcome of the vote and you cannot find it in any book. Most of the work here is hammered out in the corridors through bilateral and multilateral contacts and through geographic group meetings."[4]

Some of the meetings by groups on the margin of conferences are held in the officially designated lobbies and lounges at U.N. headquarters in New York and Geneva, or in a delegation office. A familiar opportunity at major meetings is often the morning or afternoon coffee break. It is used to iron out problems by direct discussion in a somewhat more relaxed and cheerful atmosphere, with cups and saucers clattering agreeably in the background. When the political influence of the U.N. was at its peak in the years after the war such contacts could turn the tide of history. For example, an elaborately casual encounter took place in the spring of 1949

between the Soviet delegate to the Security Council, Mr. Yakov
Malik, and Dr. Philip Jessup of the United States delegation, in the
delegates' lounge in New York. Over a glass of orange juice Mr. Malik
told Dr. Jessup that the USSR was ready to end the Berlin blockade
if a face-saving formula could be devised.

In addition to the communication flow through conferences
and lobby channels, the U.N. also structures information on
principles laid down by the General Assembly in 1946. Thus, the
introduction to the text of "Recommendations of the Technical
Advisory Committee on Information concerning the policies,
functions and organization of the Department of Public
Information" declares:

> "The United Nations cannot achieve the purpose for which
> it has been created unless the peoples of the world are fully
> informed of its aims and activities."

The text goes on to make clear that the emphasis on information has
a distant purpose, i.e., "to promote to the greatest possible extent an
informed understanding of the work and purposes of the United
Nations among the peoples of the world." But there are certain
hesitations about whether the U.N. should become a supranational
information center. This is clear from the instructions on
methodology. The text emphasizes that a U.N. information service
"should primarily assist and rely upon the cooperation of the
established governmental and non-governmental agencies of
information to provide the public with information on the United
Nations." The role of the information service is to supplement
existing channels of information where they prove inadequate. So we
have a dual system:

1. Press (including news agencies), radio and television
   services of governmental and non-governmental origin
   operating at U.N. headquarters in New York or at the U.N.
   in Geneva.
2. U.N. information services (written word and audio-visual)
   based either at U.N. headquarters or at the headquarters of
   specialized agencies, and at regional centers.

There are, as already noted, U.N. facilities for the press corps of accredited correspondents. These journalists, normally about 300[5] or so in New York and about 100 in Geneva, represent the main international and national news agencies, and television and radio organizations, as well as the daily, weekly and monthly press, and are in fact the main channel of information on a day-to-day basis concerning U.N. activities.

The bulk of the work of the information services in New York is related to coverage of U.N. meetings. If we exclude for a moment the audio-visual component, it seems fair to say that the main task is production of press material. A permanent staff of 12 persons of the U.N. professional grades (i.e. as distinct from clerical and administrative workers) produces press releases, and another 11 persons are taken on for additional temporary assistance during the General Assembly. Staff organization is:

1	Chief of Section
1	Chief editor
2	Editors
8	Reporters

The clerical staff number eight, and another 15 are drafted in for the period of the Assembly.

All this represents a not insignificant concentration of manpower and resources, and indicates that the activity concerned is one to which the U.N. information service attaches importance.

In terms of volume, the output is in proportion. During 1970, for example, a total of 3,450 press releases were issued totalling 17,416 pages. The breakdown of the previous four years is as follows:

	releases	pages
1969	3,515	15,061
1968	3,834	18,323
1967	3,769	16,546
1966	3,356	14,192

The minimum run for each press release is 1,200 copies, although some are produced in larger quantities to meet special needs. Of the average total production, about 650 are required for delegation distribution, 150 are sent to U.N. information centers and 400 are for correspondents at headquarters.

These releases provide summaries of debates and discussions as they take place, a valuable function in a situation where several meetings may be held simultaneously. Another group of releases includes statements by the Secretary-General, transcripts of his press conference, summaries of major economic and social reports, activities of the United Nations Development Program, signatures, ratifications, biographies, and so on. Similar material is put out in Geneva, and in addition the specialized agencies circulate releases and articles relating to their fields of interest.

Apart from day-to-day production, the information service in New York and Geneva and the units attached to the specialized agencies, handle publication of books, magazines and leaflets, and also cooperate with outside publishers and authors interested in the field of U.N. work. (Regular publications include the *U.N. Yearbook*, the FAO magazine, *Ceres*; the *U.N. Monthly Chronicle; UNESCO Courier*; the WHO magazine, *World Health*; the (lately defunct) ILO magazine, *Panorama*; and the recently established *Development Forum*, brought out by CESI.) Facilities are also made available for briefings to the press by permanent representatives, foreign ministers, heads of governments and other visiting dignitaries. As might be imagined, press conferences or briefings of this type may be held several times a week during the General Assembly, as various groups intensify lobbying activities. At regular intervals, staff members of the information service also meet the press for formal or background briefings.

In addition to the link between the press and U.N. information services via press releases, further contact is maintained by a system of briefings. This brings the press face to face not only with senior staff of the departments concerned, but can go right up through the hierarchy to the Secretary-General. On the next perimeter, briefings are held for the press when visiting officials from other agencies or offices of the U.N. are in New York or Geneva. A further outer ring of communication is added by the practice of holding briefings for the press by permanent representatives, foreign ministers, heads of government, and other top people. As might be supposed, briefings of the latter type often are prime targets for lobbying activities, and can occur almost daily during the General Assembly.

For radio broadcasting, the U.N. information service uses short-wave transmitters leased in the U.S., France, Switzerland and Italy. News bulletins are sent out once a week to all parts of the world in 17 languages, and these transmissions are rebroadcast by national stations. The weekly bulletin in a given language varies in length from five to fifteen minutes, but a few are of 30 minutes duration. Live broadcasts are made of the proceedings of the General Assembly and the Security Council, in English, French and Spanish, for transmission to Europe, Latin America, most of Africa and parts of the Middle East. Reception quality is uneven, however, and depends upon the distance from the transmitters and the intensity of ionosphere disturbances. In addition, tapes and discs are sent by air to about 130 countries for broadcast over about 1,000 radio stations.

The U.N. staff in New York is also responsible for assistance to outside television organizations and for some of the productions involved. Direct access to the main conferences and meetings is arranged via line-feeds and satellite links, and newsfilm summaries are also distributed to virtually all television stations through the two main international newsfilm agencies. The Section also makes and distributes its own documentaries by contact with subscribers.

Photography has traditionally been a strong feature of U.N. information work, and in fact, some of the magazines mentioned earlier use pictures and picture-stories very effectively. Conferences and other activities are covered regularly by photographers, and prints are made available at cost or without charge to mass media outlets. There are also occasional exhibits and displays, although much less frequently now than in former years.

The information departments in New York and other centers are supported by a system of information centers throughout the world. A 1971 estimate put the total of such centers at 15, located in 103 countries. These centers, which are sometimes combined with the offices of the Resident Representatives of the United Nations Development Programs, are intended to be microcosms of the information departments at headquarters. In addition to press releases, the information centers receive material on U.N. activities and subjects of interest from headquarters, usually in English, French or Spanish. In return the centers report press or official comment in their areas on issues of interest to the U.N. The directors of local centers are also expected to build up contacts with newsmen, opinion leaders, and representatives of power groups.

Communication between the more than 600 offices, missions and agencies within the U.N. system is usually by mail or diplomatic pouch, telex, telegram, telephone and radio. The fact that the U.N. is accorded facilities such as the mail pouch, which is usually transported by air and is not subject in normal circumstances to customs examination, is a reminder that the organization has diplomatic status vis-a-vis national governments. Another feature of the organization's status is the existence of an operational radio network. (See map.) As the links indicate, it has developed largely in response to specific peacekeeping situations. The first international telecommunications circuit was established in 1947 between New York and the U.N. mission in what was then Palestine. Messages were sent from Jerusalem to Haifa to Tangier, and then by commercial links to New York. In 1949, when a U.N. observer team was sent to Kashmir, the system was extended to Rawalpindi. At the time of the Korea crisis the system was further extended to Seoul, via Bangkok. At present a teleprinter circuit is used as the main link between New York and Geneva. From Geneva, teleprinter circuits run to Jerusalem, Cyprus, and Pakistan. Capitals in the Middle East and Asia (Cairo, Damascus, Beirut, Amman, Srinagar and New Delhi) are linked by radio. There is also an emergency Morse link between Zaire (the former Congo) and Addis Ababa.

The International "Womb"

The communications processes at work in international organizations must also be considered in human terms. Such organizations deliberately bring together men and women from many different societies and cultures, and install them in womblike structures located in, and yet separate from the visible surroundings. It is not simply a matter of setting up an office building and staffing it with administrators, planners, organizers, typists, and a tea-trolley. Very often a single group of offices may contain personnel from several different continents, with different native languages, and different systems of reference both in thinking and behavior.

Some of these differences are not at first apparent, and yet may contain the seeds of misunderstandings which can affect relationships between groups and individuals. Time, for example, is a concept which is viewed in the business world of North America in a way which can differ from the concept held by a diplomat from the Middle East. For the businessman from the U.S., time represents capital. It is vital to use it correctly, effectively, in order to maximize efficiency. He may allow himself to keep a subordinate waiting in order to emphasize the difference of status, but hardly more than 10 minutes. An Arab diplomat, on the other hand, may choose to be half an hour late for an appointment with a Western ambassador in order to draw attention to his own independence. He uses time in a different way, and values it differently. American and British personnel working together immediately experience difficulty over the correct usage of a first name or "Mr.", and often interpret the use of "sir" in two completely different ways. To the American, it is a polite form of expression between equals, or may even carry a hint of condescension. To the British colleague, it is an indication of the markedly higher social ranking of the person addressed. Put American, British, and French together, and the situation becomes even more complex. English and American typists may call one another by their first names on first acquaintance, but the French maintain much stricter protocol as a rule, and many women prefer to be addressed as "Madame" or "Mademoiselle," even by colleagues of many years standing.

There are difficulties also in relation to the handling of space or territory, within office buildings. As Edward Hall has noted:

> "Part of our overall pattern in the United States is to take a given amount of space and divide it up equally. When a new person is added, almost everyone will move his desk so that the newcomer will have his share of the space . . . It is a signal that they have acknowledged the presence of the new person

when they start rearranging the furniture . . .
> The French . . . do not divide up the space with a new
> colleague. Instead they may grudgingly give him a small desk in
> a dark corner looking towards the wall . . ."[6]

In the latter situation, an American is likely to experience a sense of
insecurity, because the signals he is receiving from the culture he is
joining are not those that he has learned to expect. In the former, it
is the French "new boy" who will feel disorientated and unsettled,
even though the group he has joined is seeking to reassure him.

In an international organization like the U.N., this sense of
uncertainty is constantly being multiplied. Stresses and pressures are
generated because the almost imperceptible codes and signals that
regulate social groups in a national context are rendered useless in a
group which may be drawn from 10, 20 or perhaps 50 different
nations. At an international conference the problem is different —
more often than not, delegates become histrionic in their national
attitudes, projecting themselves in a manner somewhat larger than
life. The Englishman emphasizes his casual empiricism, the
Frenchman is more insistent on planning, the Italian more colorful in
speech and gesture. In an international bureaucracy, however, the
opposite trend seems to emerge — the situation, the surroundings,
the people involved are elements in a different kind of play,
performed in a theatre where there is no room for spectators. Instead
of histrionics, the pressure is towards a kind of defensive shadow-
boxing, a search for protective coloring.

In a talk broadcast by the British Broadcasting Corporation in
1971, Richard Hoggart, an assistant director-general of UNESCO,
described the situation and its consequences:

> "In the nature of their jobs, staff members of international
> organizations themselves have special problems of relationships.
> They are to begin with, uprooted from more than a hundred
> different national cultures and living, most of them, in a foreign
> culture, perhaps a very foreign culture indeed. Or, if it is argued

that they do not "live in" the culture of their organization's host country (but if they have children that is difficult to avoid) let us say that they are living within an international group or professional subculture which doesn't express the national style of any one of them."[7]

That in itself returns us to the concept of the world apart, the detachment which is also so much part of the ethos of the international organization. It is a phenomenon of our time, creating itself in almost identical form wherever an international organization is set up. Those familiar with U.S. military bases in foreign countries will recognize this sense of a world apart, as will travelers at international airports, or businessmen who stay at the air-conditioned, Muzak-wired, glass-walled hotels that have sprung up in nearly every capital city today. Anthony Sampson catches the atmosphere very accurately in his book, "The New Europeans." Writing about the international world which has grown up in Brussels, a major center for the Common Market organizations, he notes that it is palpably different from the Belgian capital in which it is geographically located. "You get a glimpse of the Eurocrat's life from the notice boards: posters for national festivities, film societies, Alfa Romeos or Triumphs for sale, villas in Spain or Italy to be let, spare seats in a car driving to Rome, flats to let in the Quartier d'Europe . . . Brussels already has something of the rarefied diplomatic atmosphere of Washington (or Canberra), the same lack of roots."[8]

It would be most interesting to explore the human and social reasons that seem to make this rootless atmosphere so attractive. Personnel officers find this a problem: staff engaged by international organizations on short-term contracts have a tendency to become staff in search of long-term contracts, and prove difficult to shift. Wives and children exert pressure, because they settle down in comfortable villas and apartments, acquire friends, begin to see the world through "international" eyes. The idea of returning home loses meaning as the years go by, and for the career civil servant it is likely to mean virtual demotion and a sharp fall in living standards. A new regime may have taken over, and to go home may mean returning to face a risk of imprisonment or studied humiliation.

All this conspires to produce certain human reactions and work attitudes. "For almost all members of the staff it is a complex situation, and it can produce a whole range of unpleasant practices, such as excessive visa-hunting (that's making doubly sure that someone above you has initialled all your items of work so that, in case of unpleasant repercussions the buck has been passed); or the self-congratulatory inflation of reports after missions abroad; or the great battery of don't-rock-the-boat, *noli me tangere* attitudes which show themselves, as typically as anywhere, in the tendency to write excessively adulatory, or at least excessively guarded and on-the-one-hand-on-the-other performance reports on subordinates, or in the all-pervading marsh-gas of gossip about everything under the sun, but most often about sexual peccadillos or petty peculation (neither of which are anything like as common as the gossip implies), or in the difficulty of making jokes . . . about any aspect of the organization —— since almost all jokes might be regarded as an implied criticism of someone, somewhere, in the apparatus."[9]

Language and the Lingua Franca

If style is the man, it is inevitable that "international man" as we see him here will produce a language designed to help him keep afloat in the international world. It is a language based on English, but used for the most part by people for whom English is a foreign language. The underlying background of cultural and educational baggage becomes increasingly dense instead of lightening and clearing the way to understanding. One U.N. official, commenting on this point, drew a parallel with his own experience as a prisoner of war in a camp where men of many nations came together and developed a basic lingua franca in order to communicate. Similarly, the English used at the U.N. has become a language of the lowest common denominator, a kind of absorbent cotton wool surrounding the vogue words and "safe" phraseology of main documents. The vogue words tend to come from the universities, and in particular the sciences. "Projects" abound, with "complex implications." There are military overtones. An official quickly becomes an "officer," and instead of going on a trip, departs on "mission," "travel" becomes "duty travel." Such language reflects the influence of national bureaucracies, whose documentation offers the international civil servant a rich source of terminologies, circumlocutions, and phrases that have passed the test of frequent scanning by eyes anxious to avoid making any statement that "goes beyond the mandate." The aim is to create facades behind which work can continue — to protect rather than to explain.

U.N. officials are well aware of the defects of the language they employ. In fact, Richard Hoggart reports that a colleague of his at UNESCO put together a pseudo-document, made up of phrases taken from agency papers, a part of which reads:

> "As two-thirds of the world's population are lagging behind in the fight to secure their efficient cooperation towards possible social, economic, and cultural welfare targets, the paramount importance of the human factor in the development of these countries and its promotion in all possible ways is being increasingly recognized as a primary goal in the organization's action in favor of education, science and culture.
> In the present project great importance will therefore be attached to the implementation of research and studies aimed at exploring the high relevance of strategies of public policy in seeking developmental goals and the significance to these of behavioristic motivations and innovative patterns in different societal settings."[10]

It is a language designed to be written by computer, full of abstracts and passives, intended once again to avoid "rocking the boat," unashamedly seeking the lowest common denominator among possible languages and styles. Its aim is to maintain channels rather than to provide active communications. At times of increased political tension in the world, a diplomatic display of such gobbledegook may be the only way to avoid conflict and perhaps even disruption of the international organization, so the language serves a distinct purpose. Furthermore, it also serves a purpose within the organization, because it is used as a shock-absorber for the pressures and stresses which occur between the U.N. officials themselves as they seek to function in the non-world of the international bureaucracy.

Saturation Reached?

We have surveyed some of the principal aspects of the structure of communications in the U.N. and its specialized agencies. It is of interest to look now at how the mechanism has worked in practice, and to try to pick out some of the more salient obstacles to effective communication that have arisen. On the face of it, the world would almost seem to be saturated with information about the U.N. channels include the press, radio and television coverage of conferences and meetings, as well as background articles and documentaries; the material put out by the U.N. information and publications staff, which includes books, articles, and press releases, picture magazines, photographs and related material, and radio and television programming; material distributed by the U.N. information centers; material sent to home countries by permanent delegations and missions to the U.N.; information transmitted by representatives of member countries who attend conferences, meetings, seminars, etc. (There were over 4,000 such meetings in Geneva alone in 1971.) In 1945 the budget for U.N. information activities was just over $4 million. Since then it has risen to well over $11 million.

In spite of all this, Mr. Waldheim told the U.N. Consultative Panel on Public Information (CCPI) at a meeting in New York in September, 1972 that the U.N. "has failed to strike the imagination of the man in the street." He made it clear that not all the blame rested on the U.N. information services, noting for example, that while the membership of the organization has almost tripled, the percentage of the budget allocated to information has fallen from over 10 percent to less than five percent. Mr. Waldheim also pointed out that "in the second decade of satellite communication, the United Nations still has to send its radio and television programs to broadcasting organizations by air mail."[1]

Mr. Waldheim's observations find a counterpoint in a speech in December 1972 to the American Association for the Advancement of Science in Washington by Dr. Martin Kaplan, director of the World Health Organization's office of science and technology, in which he declared: "The United Nations idea continues to battle for its life against ignorance, indifference, provincial hostility and criticism which fails to take into account the lack of support, both financial and ideological, among the nations of its family . . ."[12]

These are observations that convey more than a hint of the disillusion felt by many persons with high ideals who are on the staff of the U.N. or its agencies. The evident public incomprehension relates in a very broad way to the total impact of the U.N. as an entity on mass opinion. A first step in analysis of the problem is to dissect out the two main types of U.N. involvement in world affairs. One major aspect is political; the other relates to economic and social development. In the political area, there has been a steady process of decline in U.N. influence. Here it is clear that today, and as matters at present stand, there is very little that the U.N. information services could do to alter the situation. At the level of high strategy, this can be viewed as the price of losing a race against time. That race was conducted by two men, Mr. Trygve Lie, first Secretary-General of the U.N., and carried on by his successor, Mr. Dag Hammarskjold. Their aim was to use the information services to appeal over the heads of governments to the public at times of crisis. Suez is one case in point, and the U.N. intervention in the Congo is another. We have seen, at the opening of this essay, that this was a possibility to which governments were very much alive, and a study of successive budget debates at the U.N. General Assemblies shows mounting pressure to reduce the financial resources available for information. Much more needs to be said about this aspect, but in summary one would conclude that the failure of the strategy and the present quasi-isolation of the U.N. from international politics are interrelated.

In economic and social development, the U.N. and its agencies have had much more room to maneuver. Mr. Tor Gjesdal, who is the former director of mass communications at UNESCO and has been closely associated with information policymaking at the U.N., points out that at the strategic level, he and others consistently advocated that the attention of the public should be directed towards the substantive nature of the work, rather than to the agency responsible.[13] If the nature of the work appeals to the public — — as is the case with the World Health Organization — — the agency shares in the "halo" effect to the extent that it is successful in coping with the problems involved. (This trend is so marked that in fact there have been suggestions that WHO should be detached from the U.N. altogether.)

Signs of Disenchantment

In spite of the success of individual agencies, however, there has been a decline in support at both governmental and public levels for U.N. development campaigns. There is ample testimony to this disenchantment in the writings of economists, politicians, and U.N. officials themselves. As the *New York Times* pointed out in an editorial in 1969, the flow of public funds from the U.S. alone began declining sharply at a time when in the view of many experts, the needs, opportunities and availability of resources for international development were never greater. Similar lack of enthusiasm was evident among other leading nations of the developed regions of the world. A cry of alarm was heard from the Canadian statesman Lester B. Pearson. A Nobelist and former chairman of the Commission for International Development, he drew attention to the weakening of the will for development aid, and titled his appeal (later printed in book form): "The Crisis of Development."[14]

In 1972 a high-ranking U.N. official, Mr. Tibor Mende, retired after a brief but brilliant career and immediately published an analysis of the situation entitlted: De L'Aide a la Recolonisation: Les Lecons d'un Echec (Aid for Recolonialization: The Lessons of a Failure).[15] The words "crisis" and "failure" sum up the views of many sectors of opinion, and the general drift of the publications which bore such titles.

Part of the difficulty can be traced to the nature of the development process. The first development campaigns began with sweeping perspectives and bold concepts. Since then, after much effort and many disappointments, it has become clear that development is a task involving long and patient efforts, with implied sacrifices on the part of both donors and recipients of aid. All this, however, also suggests further defects in communication, and the link is made in a further publication about the U.N. which appeared in 1971. Its cover says bluntly "La crise de l'information et la crise de confiance des Nations Unies (The information crisis and the confidence crisis of the United Nations)."[16]

Dams and Filters

Without making value judgments on the publications concerned, it is clear that they reflect the development of an attitude of mind which has wide support. In order, therefore, to see more clearly what kind of problems arise in U.N. informational activities, we should move closer. Study at short range indicates that what is considered in the abstract as an even flow of words along a broad channel is in reality something quite different. There are dams and filters which break up and divert the stream at strategic points. These blockages and diversions are highly significant, particularly for the impact of U.N. information efforts. We have to keep in mind, for example, that the U.N. is an organization which divides fairly neatly into "haves" and "have-nots." This division is accurately reflected in the mass media, which reach much wider audiences in the wealthy countries than in the poor ones. Press, radio and television are services that require investments of capital and skilled manpower of a kind which is scarce in the developing regions, so the weighting in regard to available outlets for U.N. material is often unevenly distributed.

This weighting in favor of the richer countries affects not only the media at grass roots level, but extends to the U.N. press corps. In terms of status in the eyes of U.N. information staff, representatives of the major news agencies come first, a long way ahead of correspondents representing individual newspapers or broadcasting organizations. If one considers volume of copy as a criterion, this is a valid assessment, because the greatest amount of daily reporting on U.N. activities is put out by staff working for Associated Press, United Press International, Reuters, Agence France Presses and Tass. But since these agencies are based in areas which lie directly within the spheres of influence of the major powers, the end result is not

always to the advantage of the U.N. Consciously or unconsciously
(and this is another line of inquiry which could be developed) the
news staff of such agencies see the world in a perspective orientated
towards the developed nations and their political struggles.
Socio-economic development and related topics are of less direct
interest. The result is summed up as follows in a recent U.N. study:
"In the present state of public information on the goals and activities
of the United Nations the news media audience perhaps receives
more than adequate information on matters in the handling of which
the world organization is particularly unsuccessful and frustrated.
This produces a rather unfavorable public image of the United
Nations, and its prestige suffers accordingly as certain very successful
constructive activities of the world organizations are at the same time
inadequately reported."[17]

The UNITAR study brings out very clearly the watershed in
news values which is created by this dichotomy in the media. The
researchers made estimates of coverage by media in the developed
and developing countries of the following topics, which were then
current:

> Political and security questions
> Cyprus
> Vietnam
> Korea
> Nuclear proliferation treaty
> Atomic weapons and radiation

The developed countries' newspapers and other outlets devoted
about one-fifth of their total coverage of all U.N. topics to this group
of questions, but the developing countries surveyed gave only about
half as much attention to such subjects. In contrast, the developing
countries devoted more interest to such issues as:

> U.N. in general
> Economic and social questions
> Health and welfare
> Human rights
> Development aid

Full details are shown in the table annexed and illustrate two very
different world views.

Elitist Trend

Furthermore, coverage of the U.N. is not evenly distributed within the media of the developed countries. There is a marked tendency, as the UNITAR inquiry shows, for coverage of U.N. matters to be found in much higher concentration in the elitist, intellectual press in the developed countries than in the mass-circulation newspapers. The researchers comment: "It would appear that the effects of bias against the United Nations or of anti-United Nations sentiment is expressed less through adverse or polemical comment than through the lack or dearth of publicity granted to United Nations affairs and events. This tendency is less evident in the prestige or elite press which is wont to discuss United Nations policies and activities . . ."[18]

Researchers working for the United Nations Association in London examined 17 British national daily and Sunday newspapers during a period of four weeks, and found the class division of U.N. news values to be very marked. During the period three of the newspapers aimed at the middle and upper social classes, i.e. *The Guardian, The Times,* and *The Daily Telegraph*, each published about eight information items a day on the U.N. and its affairs. By contrast, three other newspapers, with much larger circulations, carried only five items all told during the period, and two others carried nothing at all. The situation was somewhat complicated by the fact that the question of Southern Rhodesia was an issue both in Britain and at the U.N. at the time, and was therefore a "hard" news topic. But if this topic is excluded, the findings show that two of the other national newspapers, with much larger circulations, carried nothing at all about the U.N. during the period, and three newspapers carried only five items altogether.[19]

Furthermore, when it comes to staffing, those individual press media which are most likely to have a correspondent at the U.N. tend to be of the elitist type. These are the newspapers which (a) are most anxious to provide for their readers an information service of higher quality than the agency material, and (b) have the resources to afford such coverage. The UNITAR study showed that in the case of the "quality" press, nearly one-quarter of all information carried concerning the U.N. came from their own correspondents. In addition, a considerable amount of information about the U.N. reaches the elitist media from correspondents not based at U.N. headquarters, but working instead in contact with the specialized agencies and organs outside New York.

National Involvement

In addition to the selective factors at work in U.N. coverage, it has to be remembered that national involvement in a running story will affect (1) the interest of correspondents from that country and (2) the use made by editors of the copy they receive. In a survey of press reporting of the 18-Nation Disarmament Committee, the Stockholm International Peace Research Institute (SIPRI) showed that national considerations were very often preponderant.[20] This applied not only to the general press, but also to the elitist media. Interventions by the United Kingdom delegate received three-quarters of the space devoted to the subject in *The Times* of London, compared with some 11 percent in publications of other nations. Stockholm's *Dagens Nyheter* allocated 35 percent of the space to speeches by the Sweden delegate which in other European newspapers received only about 11 percent. It is also significant that press coverage also reflects international alignments. Whereas the press of non-aligned or non-participant countries considered speeches by the U.K. and Canadian delegates worth 20 percent of their space, the *New York Times* gave them 56 percent.

We have noted already the sense of detachment that international bureaucracies tend to acquire, and the degree to which this is reinforced by the jargon of the profession. That the ideas, aims, values, and indeed perhaps even the jargon, are able to pass through the news "screens" of the more intellectual newspapers we have just seen. Is this because they resemble the aims and values of those readers to whom such newspapers are oriented? There is a trend here which clearly reinforces a sense of elitism, of separateness, to the detriment of public communication as a whole.

An important aspect of this question is the U.N. attitude to its own information services. Earlier, in describing the scale of the information output, we noted that at the New York headquarters alone about 10 press releases are produced daily, and the manpower and budgetary resources devoted to the writing and editing of these documents is considerable. Such efforts are justified, the Secretary-General suggests in his 1972 report, because press releases are the main means of access by the U.N. to the "people of the world." Reviewing the cost of the service, he notes however, that press releases are written not only to inform the press, but also for the benefit of the U.N. secretariat and the members of delegations. That the tail has a tendency to wag the dog is made clear at a point in the report where possible ways of reducing the cost of press releases are spelled out. He concludes that the only viable way of cutting down volume and saving money would be "to evaluate U.N. meetings in strictly journalistic terms." This could be achieved by giving to each meeting "the type and extent of coverage best suited to the subject-matter involved as well as to the professional needs of the mass media concerned." It seems clear that such criteria are not at present considered paramount, and that journalistic news values are not used as a touchstone.

This impression is borne out by the UNITAR study. It confirms that the choice of topics presented in the press release, the amount of space given to each item, and the form and style of presentation are governed by factors which have very little to do with the specific needs of the news media. The report goes on:

"Naturally, the information services of the United Nations can apply only very prudent and restrained 'journalistic techniques' in order to make the information offered by them palatable and appealing to the news media; they cannot leak unauthorized information, serve up gossip, or enhance the interest of the news media in their information output by any indiscreet means. But the constraints put on the press release go beyond that. Out of regard for protocol and all sorts of bureaucratic sensibilities press releases often have to be burdened with much circumlocution and detail which in no way serves their essential purpose . . ."[21]

Apart from the somewhat loaded interpretation of "journalistic techniques," the UNITAR comment leaves us in no doubt that the press releases are seldom able to attract the interest of the media for whom they are ostensibly intended. Such a situation helps to confirm the trend to elitism, since correspondents of the "intellectual" or "quality" press are more likely to have the time and patience to sift through U.N. documentation than hard-pressed journalists working for the big-circulation dailies.

On the margin of this discussion, it is worth mentioning that according to Mr. Gjesdal, targeting of information to elite groups has always been deliberate U.N. policy. Such groups, or "cells," can act as redisseminators, the argument runs, interpreting and adapting the information to the differing socio-economic contexts that exist throughout the world. The argument is a powerful one —— although it contrasts with the high priority that virtually all U.N. and agency information services tend to accord to the international news agencies, as noted earlier.

Radio and Television: Some Constraints

We have been discussing U.N. communications so far mainly in terms of print media, so it is logical now to look at radio and television. Since the war both the latter have expanded at a much greater rate than the press. With the introduction of the transistor, the cheap, small, battery-powered radio set has spread rapidly throughout the world. Radios in Africa increased in number 10 times from 1950 to 1968, six times in Asia, and four times in Latin America. Elsewhere, radio sets have doubled, and even tripled. Television has also grown rapidly, although the major advance is still largely confined to the wealthier parts of the globe.

In theory, at least, both media could help the U.N. to reach the mass audience. Satellite casts and the establishment of such international television link-ups as Eurovision in Western Europe and Intervision in the East European countries, are producing a heightened sense of mutual awareness among the people of the world. But the budgetary and policy constraints imposed on the U.N. in this sector have so far effectively prevented the organization from taking full advantage of the electronic age. In line with the mandate already referred to, radio and television services are at present required not to go beyond "supplementing" the services of national organizations.

Given the limitations, however, the radio and television services acquit themselves creditably. For radio, broadcasting organizations in 84 states and territories report regular broadcasts of more than one U.N. program weekly. In spite of the value of this work, expenditures in this area have been reduced, in line with the overall budget reductions to which Mr. Waldheim referred in the remarks already quoted. Live television coverage from the General Assembly and the Security Council depends entirely on the willingness of stations to pay the costs involved. As a result, most broadcasts are confined to U.S. networks. It is also instructive to look at the following table of satellite transmission from New York:

Satellite Transmission

Year	Total	To Japan	To Europe	To Developing Countries
1965	5	—	5	—
1966	12	1	10	1
1967	56	3	53	—
1968	20	1	19	—
1969	18	—	17	1
1970	20	1	17	2
1971	24	4	17	3

It is clear that economic resources act as a filter, with the result that the majority of live broadcasts via satellite are received only by audiences in advanced countries, where many more earth stations are located and where broadcasting organizations are better able to afford transmission fees. This constitutes an important difficulty since part of the audience which should ideally be reached is in fact unattainable until television installations become much cheaper and simpler than they are now. (Similar considerations apply, relatively speaking, to radio broadcasting. While it is true that radio is an expanding medium in the developing countries, available receivers are still very thinly spread by comparison with the wealthier areas of the world. Such a situation is unavoidable, but still leaves vast possibilities for contact via broadcasting between the U.N. and those audiences who can be reached under present conditions.) Would it help if such audiences saw more transmissions from the General Assembly and the Security Council?[22] Once again, if judged on television news values, this would seem doubtful, since "talking heads" are seldom a major contribution to the television news program.

Behind all this, however, there is a much bigger question –– the huge gap between U.N. communications technology and that which has already been reached by member states. As Mr. Waldheim pointed out, the U.N. is still heavily dependent on the mails, an anachronistic situation in the era of McLuhan's global village. It is interesting that as far back as 1947 a proposal for a worldwide U.N. communications system was put forward by an advisory committee headed by General Frank Stoner of the U.S. One of the main points made by the committee was that the U.N. should possess its own international network of short wave radio transmitters, but the General Assembly refused to vote funds. It can be argued, and with some force, that the evolution of general communications, including air mail, telegram and telex, and the telephone, has been so rapid that for most purposes the U.N. is today well served in any case. The greater part of U.N. business is conducted by mail, and a study by UNDP in 1968 indicated that the average time required to draft a letter, have it approved, and signed, was eight days. For a telegram, preparation took five days.[23] In such a situation, the actual speed of transmission would seem to be only a marginal consideration.

The U.N., however, does not always operate in "normal" circumstances, and it has frequently been argued that its present broadcasting equipment is inadequate in terms both of political emergencies, and in relation to advances in communications technology as a whole, including satellite casting. The U.N. Secretary-General, and his senior associates concerned with peacekeeping activities, maintain that the U.N. should have its own (i.e. independent) communications systems. A study by the U.S. United Nations Association comments: "Should U.N. forces rather than observers be needed, as in Korea and the Congo, communications and all other logistical problems would increase by at least an order of magnitude. In this case, the United Nations would be obliged to rely upon communications equipment and personnel furnished by the governments supplying the U.N. forces. This could be a serious problem with 'mixed' and 'precariously balanced' forces. But the U.N. communications facilities are entirely inadequate to handle command-and-control of military forces."[24] U.N. officials also maintain that in any peacekeeping operation it is essential that the Secretary-General should be able to maintain complete impartiality, which might not be possible if he had to rely at some time on the communications facilities of a member state.

In this context, the UNA study referred to above recommended that the U.N. be given access to satellite communication for peacekeeping, disaster warning and relief, and also to assist in the work of economic and social development. U Thant, when he was Secretary-General, asked the International Telecommunications Satellite Consortium (INTELSAT) to place a limited number of channels at the disposal of the U.N. at certain times without charge for operational needs, and latest information is that such facilities may well be granted. Some hesitations have been associated with considerations of national sovereignty, but technically it is now possible to prevent "maverick" broadcasting by satellite. The idea of a U.N. satellite channel is sound, and would have many applications. The cost of such communication is steadily falling, and the U.N. could use such links not only for voice and message transmissions, but perhaps even for surveillance in sensitive areas of the world. In development work, rapid communication between agency headquarters and field units would assist decentralization. Satellites could also be used for the huge educational tasks that are waiting to be carried out in the poorer areas of the world (in fact the U.S. and India on the construction of a satellite for this purpose which can transmit to 5,000 villages.

A worldwide U.N. television service is a concept that brings us face to face with the adaptive processes that are evident within the organization as it faces the future. There are signs that new policies are emerging designed to help eliminate the defects and handicaps in

U.N. communication. One example can be seen in the efforts to develop the role of the Center for Social and Economic Information (CESI) as a kind of "commando" information unit, working with, but to some extent independently of the U.N. and its agencies. The success of the Stockholm Conference on the Environment, and the setting up of the U.N. Environment Program in Nairobi, are also highly significant pointers to the new directions in which the organization is moving. The environment involves dilemmas —— population growth, economic growth, the consequences of industrialization, the merits or demerits of science and technology, to name a few —— which are giving the term "United Nations" fresh meaning. It is at this time, when the U.N. is acquiring a role of potentially enormous significance for the quality of our lives, that communications efforts are more important than ever before.

FOOTNOTES

[1] "The Future of Communications in the Cause of Peace," speech at Columbia University, March 28, 1972.

[2] *Conference Diplomacy*, Sijthoff, Leyden and Oceana Publications, New York, 1970, pp. 162-163.

[3] *Why Geneva?* Editions Bonvent, Geneva, 1973, p. 152.

[4] *Delegates World Bulletin*, p. 66, April 9, 1973.

[5] Around this total of permanent correspondents, there floats a more shifting group of approximately another 300 to 350 "temporary" correspondents. During periods of peak news interest, the total can rise to 800, and on occasion climbs to well over 2,000.

[6] *The Silent Language,* Edward T. Hall, Fawcett Publications, 1959, p. 157.

[7] "There's No Home," Reith lecture published in *The Listener,* December 9, 1971.

[8] *The New Europeans,* Anthony Sampson, Hodder and Stoughton, London, 1968, p. 46.

[9] Hoggart, *op. cit.,* p. 795.

[10] *Op. cit.,* p. 794.

[11] Speech reported in the *Delegates World Bulletin*, New York, October, 1972.

[12] "The Role of Science in the World Health Organization," (speech reprinted as a WHO press release, February 1972.)

[13] Mr. Tor Gjesdal in a personal communication.

[14] Pall Mall Press, London 1970.

[15] *Editions Seuil*, Paris 1972.

[16] Alpha Amadou Diallo-Tayire, Editions universitaires, Fribourg, Switzerland, 1971.

[17] "The United Nations and the News Media," *UNITAR*, New York, 1972, p. 76.

[18] *Op. cit.*, p. 75.

[19] "The United Nations and the Press," Acorn Group, Newbury Park, Ilford, Essex, United Kingdom, 1967.

[20] "The ENDC and the Press," Loyal N. Gould, *SIPRI, Stockholm Papers No. 3,* Stockholm 1969.

[21] *Op. cit.*

[22] At present, continuous monitoring of both bodies is provided by U.N. cameras only for U.S. networks, who can pay for the costs involved.

[23] Some U.N. agencies have tried to meet this problem by designing forms to be filled out like a telegram which are then mailed in the ordinary way (e.g. the ILOGRAM, the Unescogram, etc.)

[24] "Space Communications: Increasing U.N. responsiveness to the problems of mankind." Report of a national policy panel established by the U.S. United Nations Association, New York, May 1971.

BIBLIOGRAPHY

Acorn Study Group. "The United Nations and the Press," Newbury Park, Ilford, Essex, England, December, 1967.

Arutyunyan. "Sovetskiy Soyuz i Organizatsiya Ob'Edinenych Natsiy."

Ash, P. "The United Nations and the periodical press, a preliminary study." *Journal of Social Psychology,* 32(2nd) (November 1950): pp. 191-205.

Austen, Warren. "A more perfect union. UN can and does reflect public opinion." *Department of State Bulletin,* 20(6 March 1949): pp. 278-281.

Basdevant, Suzanne. "Le Post de Radiodiffusion de la S.D.N. et Son Role Eventuel en Temps de Guerre," *Revenue Internationale de la Radio-electricite,* (1935).

Bass, Abraham Zishba. "Public Information Broadcasting by the United Nations: history, politics and the flow of the news." Unpublished thesis, University of Minnesota, 1969.

Benton, William. "Public opinion and world affairs." Address delivered before the Second International Conference on Public Opinion Research, Williams College, Williamstown, Mass., on 2 September 1947. *Department of State Bulletin* 17 (14 September 1947): pp. 522-526.

Boyd, Andrew, "The World from 30,000 feet," *Vista* vol. 4, no. 4 (January—February 1969).

Broadcasting Telecasting. "UN Coverage: Radio—TV Highlight Paris Meet." (26 November 1951.)

Browne, Don R. "The Limits of the Limitless Medium — International Broadcasting." *Journalism Quarterly,* no. 42 (Winter 1965)

Carnegie Endowment for International Peace. *National Studies on International Organization* — 12 books on studies in Australia, Belgium, Egypt, Federal Republic of Germany, Great Britain, Greece, Italy, Japan, Sweden, Switzerland, Turkey, and U.S.A. New York: Manhattan Publishing Company.

Carson, Saul. "This is the UN," in *Education on the Air* (Yearbook of the Institute for Education for Education by Radio and Television) 20(1950), pp. 54-71.

Chamberlin, W. "The public relations of the United Nations," *Annual Review of United Nations Affairs* (1954), pp. 209-243, 1955.

Christian Science Monitor, 41, "Britons attempt to rekindle enthusiasm of world for the United Nations." (17 May, 1949), p. 5.

Cohen, Benjamin, "The UN's Department of Public Information." *Public Opinion Quarterly* 10 (Summer 1946), pp. 145-155.

Cohen, Benjamin, "Voice of UN — The Department of Public Information." *United Nations World* (March 1947), pp. 54-57.

Cohen, Benjamin, "Public Information Activities," *Annual Review of United Nations Affairs (1950), pp. 179-190.*

Cohen, Benjamin, "America latina y las Revista interamericana de bibliografia (Washington) (1951), pp. 178-181.

Cohen, Benjamin, "Information Services," *Annual Review of United Nations Affairs* (1951), pp. 135-151.

Congaltor, A.A., and M.V. Kidton, *Public Opinion and the United Nations.* Wellington, New Zealand, Victoria University College, Department of Psychology, Publication 6, 1955.

Cory, Robert H., Jr. "Forging a public opinion policy for the United Nations," *International Organization* (May 1953), pp. 229-242.

Cory, Robert H., Jr., *Communicating Information and Ideas about the United Nations to the American People.* New York: Carnegie Endowment for International Peace; 1955.

D'Arcy, Jean. "Challenge to Cooperation," *Saturday Review* (24 October, 1970).

Davison, W. Phillips and Alexander L. George, "An Outline for the Study of International Political Communications," *Public Opinion Quarterly* 16 (1952), pp. 501-511.

Davison, W. Phillips, *International Political Communication,* New York: Praeger, 1965.

Dempsey, David, "The Publishing Scene," *Saturday Review* (13 April, 1968).

Dempsey, William C., "Communication Problems of UNESCO Television," *Journal of Communication* 6 (1956), pp. 103-107.

Deutsch, Karl W., "Political Community at the International Level: Problems of Definition and Measurement," Princeton University

Organizational Behavior Section, 1953, New York: Doubleday
Short Studies in Political Science, 1954.

Deutsch, Karl W., "Shifts in the Balance of Communication Flows: A
Problem of Measurement in International Relations," *Public
Opinion Quarterly,* vol. xx, no. 1, spring 1956, pp. 143-160.

Drexel, C. "Radio-Nations," *Wireless World* (3 August, 1934), pp.
73-74.

Dunham, Franklin, "How Can We Make Television a World-Wide
Instrument of Communication?" *Journal of Communication,* 6
(1956), pp. 47-50.

Eggington, J. "UN and the Press," *Spectator,* 210 (8 February,
1963), pp. 143-155.

Elmandjra, Mahdi, "The United Nations System: an Analysis,"
mimeographed manuscript to be published in 1972.

Everyman's United Nations. New York: United Nations, 1964.

Farace, Vincent R. "A Study of mass communication and national
development: a study of 54 variables in 109 countries."
Journalism Quarterly, 43 (Summer 1966), pp. 305-313.

Finnish National Commission for UNESCO and the Finnish
Broadcasting Company. "Report on a round table
'Communication 1980' on mass communication research and
policy, Hanko, Finland, April 9–11, 1970." Helsinki; 1970,
53pp.

Girod, Roger, "How the public is told about the results of surveys
carried out by international organizations," *International Social
Science Bulletin (UNESCO),* vol. iv, no. 4 (1952), pp. 729-739.

Gjesdal, Tor, "Mass Communication in Society," *Die Modernen
Wissenschaften und die Aufgaben der Diplomatie,* Verlag Styria,
Austria, 1963.

Gordenker, L. "UN Secretary-General and the Maintenance of
Peace," New York, N.Y.: Columbia University Press, 1967,
380pp.

Gould, Loyal N., "The ENDC and the Press," *SIPRI Stockholm
Papers,* no. 3, Uppsala, Sweden: Almquist & Wiksell, 1969.

Granitsas, Spyridon, "Downgrading of the Press continues as UN
problem," Editor and Publisher (4 July, 1970).

Granitsas, Spyridon, "UN moves Study on Codes for Freedom of
Information," Editor and Publisher (18 July 1970).

Granitsas, Spyridon, "Research Project: Is the World Getting the Message from UN?" Editor and Publisher, (15 August, 1970).

Granitsas, Spyridon, "Un Secretariat tries hard to keep secrets from press," Editor and Publisher (29 August, 1970).

Granitsas, Spyridon, "Seeds of censorship embedded at the UN," Editor and Publisher (12 September, 1970).

Granitsas, Spyridon, "Status of Press at UN hangs on a Preposition," Editor and Publisher (1 August 1970).

Granitsas, Spyridon, "UN and the Media: The Missing Date Line," Editor and Publisher (3 October 1970).

Granitsas, Spyridon, "On UN's 25th Birthday – Whole World Isn't Tuned in," Editor and Publisher (24 October 1970).

Hero, Alfred O. *Mass Media and World Affairs,* Studies in Citizen Preparation in International Relations, vol. 4, 1959, Boston: World Peace Foundation.

Hickey, Neil. "Telling the UN Story to the World," *TV Guide* (7 October 1967), pp. 14-16.

Institut Mirovoi Ekonomiki: Mezhdunarodnych Otnosheniy, Akademii Nauk SSR. "Oon. Itogi. Tendentsii. Perspektivy (K25 – Letiyu Oon)." Izdatel'stvo Mezhdunoraodnoe Otnosheniya, Moscow, 1970. Chapters 1, 4–7, 9–10, 14.

International Telecommunications Satellite Consortium. Plenipotentiary Conference on Definitive Arrangements for INTELSAT. "Utilization of the Intelsat system by the United Nations," submitted on behalf of the Secretary-General of the United Nations to Com, 1/31. (Washington, D.C.), 4 March, 1969, 22 pp.

Issraelyan, V.L., ed., "Sovetskiy Soyuzi Organizatsiya , Ob'edinennych Natsiy," Izdatel'stovNauka, Moscow, 1968, chapters 2–7, 10.

Hult, J.L. "Satellites and Technology for Communications: Shaping the Future," (P-3760) Rand Corporation (January 1968), 30pp.

Jones, Nancy C. "The Role of the United Nations in Communications Satellites," unpublished Ph.D. dissertation, University of Missouri, 1967.

Larson, Cedric, "The United Nations Department of Public Information," *Journalism Quarterly,* 27 (1950), pp. 288-296.

Lee, John, ed., *Diplomatic Persuaders: New Role of the Mass Media in International Relations.* New York: Wiley, 1968.

Lerner, Daniel and W. Schramm, eds., *Communication and Change in the Developing Countries,* Honolulu: East-West Center Press, 1967, 333pp., bibliography included.

Lewis, Dorothy, "Is Broadcasting an Effective Medium for Developing Understanding among Nations? The United Nations Radio." *Education on Air,* 21 (1951), pp. 86-90.

Lie, Trygve, *In the Cause of Peace,* New York: Macmillan, 1954, 473pp.

Lind, Lars. "UNESCO's Work in Mass Communications," *Library Quarterly,* 20 (1950), pp. 259-271.

Masaryk, Jan, "Public Opinion and the United Nations," *Free World,* vol. 12, no. 5 (December 1946), pp. 19-21.

National Opinion Research Center. *The Public Looks at the World Organization,* report no. 19, Denver, Colorado; University of Denver, 1944, 32pp.

Newsweek, "On the UN Beat," (14 October, 1968).

Paramount Pictures Corporation. "44 Miles of UN Activities recorded by Paramount," news release, (13 February 1952).

Plagge, Von R., " 'Radio-Nations': Die Radiostation des Volkerbundes," Archiv fur Funkrecht (1932), pp. 471-485.

Pool, Ithiel de Sola, "Effects of Cross-National Contact on National and International Images," *International Behavior: A Social-Psychological Analysis,* Herbert C. Kelman, ed. New York: Holt, Rinehart and Winston, 1965, pp. 104-129.

Prokf'ev, B.P. "OON — 25 Let" Izdatel'stvo Mezhdunarodnoe Otnosheniya, Moscow, 1970.

Prakash, Sarla, "United Nations Radio: A Study of Its Growth, Structure, Activities and Problems, 1952-62." Unpublished Master's thesis, Boston University, 1963.

Robinson, John P. "World Affairs Information and Mass Media Exposure," *Journalism Quarterly* (Spring 1967), pp. 23-31.

Scott, William A., "Psychological and Social Correlates of International Images," In *International Behavior: A Social-Psychological Analysis,* Herbert C. Kelman, ed. New York: Holt, Rinehart and Winston, 1965, pp. 70-103.

Schramm, Wilbur, and G.F. Winfield, "New Uses of Mass

Communication for the Promotion of Economic and Social Development," paper presented at the United Nations Conference on the Application of Science and Technology for the Benefit of the Less Developed Areas, Geneva, 1963. Washington, D.C. *U.S. Papers for the Conference,* vol. 10, 1963.

Schramm, Wilbur, ed. *One Day in the World's Press: Fourteen Great Newspapers on a Day of Crisis.* Stanford, California: Stanford University Press, 1959.

Sarnoff, David, "Freedom to Listen – A Plan for the United Nations," In his *Looking Ahead,* New York: McGraw-Hill, 1968.

Soroos, Carol Stern. "The Role of the Press in International Relations: A Review of the Literature." Unpublished manuscript, Evanston, Ill., 1969.

Szalai, Alexander, "Public Information on the United Nations: Research Project of the United Nations Institute for Training and Research," *International Organization,* vol. xxiii, no. 2 (Spring 1969), pp. 348-353.

Thant, U. "The United Nations and Some Problems of Public Understanding," address by the UN Secretary-General to news media seminar sponsored by Stanley Foundation. *UN Press Release* SG/SM/1394, 3 December, 1970.

United Nations Development Program. "Development Support Information Activities: Periodic Report by UNDP." (22 May, 1968), mimeo.

United Nations Press Release M/573. "UN Teams Up with NBC and CBS for Complete TV Coverage of UN General Assembly," (29 April 1949).

UNESCO World Communications. Paris, 1964.

United States Delegation to the United Nations. Document PC/EX/SEC/50. "Preliminary Observation concerning the Organization and Function of DPI (UN Department of Public Information)." 1945.

United States Department of State Bulletin. "Short Wave Radio Facilities made available for UN Broadcasts," 15 (27 October 1946), pp. 751-752.

United States Information Agency. "Research and Reference Service. West European Awareness and Evaluation of the UN following the Hungary and Suez Crises," Report no. 46 (May 1967), 20pp.

Ushakov, V. "Sovetskiy Soyuz v OON." Gospolitizdat, Moscow, 1960.

Wilcox, F.O. "The United Nations and Public Understanding," *Department of State Bulletin,* 36 (8 April, 1957), pp. 555-560.

Williams, Francis. *Transmitting World News,* Paris: UNESCO, 1953.

World Association for Public Opinion Research. Proceedings of Conference, 1957 in *International Social Science Bulletin,* 10 (no. 2) (1958), pp. 273-289.

Zorin, V.A. and G.I. Morozov, eds., "OON i Aktual'nye Mezhdunarodnye problemy," Isdatel'stvo Mezhdunaronoe Otnosheniya, Moscow, 1965, chapters 2-4, 8-9.

Topics and issues before the United Nations referred to in the news media of advanced and developing countries

(Percentages relate to the total number of references to all topics and issues listed.)

	Daily Press Adv. %	Daily Press Dev. %	Radio Adv. %	Radio Dev. %	Television Adv. %	Television Dev. %
(a) Topics and issues receiving markedly more coverage in advanced countries:						
Political and security questions (*)	9.3	> 5.4	4.9	> 2.0	4.3	> 3.1
International law (*)	1.5	> 0.7	2.8	> 0.3	1.7	> 0.1
Colonial and trusteeship questions (*)	0.9	> 0.5	1.1	> 0.5	0.8	> 0.4
International finance questions	1.2	> 0.9	0.9	> 0.2	1.1	> 0.7
Cyprus	0.9	> 0.4	1.8	> 0.8	0.7	1.0
Vietnam	6.6	> 3.5	4.1	> 3.6	6.8	> 3.1
Korea	0.6	> 0.5	0.4	~ 0.4	0.8	> 0.5
South West Africa (Namibia)	2.4	> 1.8	6.2	> 2.9	2.9	3.2
Southern Rhodesia	2.9	> 2.6	6.4	> 3.3	6.8	> 4.6
Nuclear proliferation treaty	4.9	> 2.9	5.1	> 2.6	3.8	> 1.7
Atomic weapons and radiation	0.9	> 0.4	1.0	> 0.5	0.8	> 0.1
Food problems, famine relief	2.3	> 1.7	1.5	> 1.1	1.8	> 1.0
Outer space	0.6	> 0.3	0.4	~ 0.4	1.0	> 0.0
All (a) together	35.0	> 21.6	36.6	> 18.6	33.3	> 19.5
(b) Topics and issues receiving markedly more coverage in developing countries						
United Nations (in general)	9.2	< 9.3	7.4	< 10.8	7.9	< 9.2
Economic and social questions (*)	6.0	< 7.2	3.0	< 5.2	3.6	2.8
Cultural and educational questions (*)	2.2	< 2.7	1.3	< 1.9	1.2	< 1.8
Health and welfare questions	1.4	< 1.9	0.6	< 1.6	0.7	< 1.3
Human rights (*)	4.5	3.9	3.1	< 4.4	3.3	< 7.3
Development and related assistance	3.1	< 8.1	2.4	< 6.9	3.9	2.8
Industrialization and labor questions	1.2	< 1.4	0.7	< 1.5	0.4	< 1.5
International trade and commerce	6.5	< 7.1	4.5	< 5.1	2.8	< 3.5
International transport and communications	0.6	< 1.0	0.4	< 0.5	0.3	< 0.6
Agriculture and fisheries	0.3	< 1.1	0.2	< 1.6	0.0	< 0.6
Middle East	17.7	< 20.5	28.1	< 30.8	32.3	< 40.0
Refugee problems	0.9	0.9	0.7	< 1.1	0.4	< 1.7
All (b) together	53.6	< 65.1	52.4	< 71.4	56.8	< 73.1

(*) Excluding special issues under a separate heading.

	Daily Press		Radio		Television	
	Adv. %	Dev. %	Adv. %	Dev. %	Adv. %	Dev. %
(c) *Topics and issues showing no marked difference in coverage*						
Science and technology	1.0	0.8	0.4	0.6	0.8	0.5
Czechoslovakia	0.6	0.2	0.3	0.1	0.4	0.6
Portuguese territories in Africa	0.5	0.3	0.9	0.8	0.3	0.5
Apartheid policies	1.9	2.0	3.0	2.6	2.3	2.5
Second Development Decade	0.1	0.1	0.1	0.1	0.0	0.0
Family planning, birth control, population	0.2	0.3	0.3	0.3	0.4	0.4
Adult education, eradication of illiteracy	0.2	0.2	0.1	0.1	0.2	0.0
Natural resources	0.5	0.5	0.6	0.5	0.4	0.5
Peaceful uses of atomic energy	0.4	0.4	0.3	0.3	0.2	0.4
Peaceful uses of seabed	0.1	0.1	0.1	0.2	0.0	0.0
Small states or territories	0.1	0.1	0.2	0.1	0.0	0.2
All together	5.6	5.0	6.3	5.7	5.0	5.6
TOTAL (including "others," indeterminate, etc.)	100.0	100.0	100.0	100.0	100.0	100.0

Source: UNITAR

THE UNITED NATIONS SYSTEM

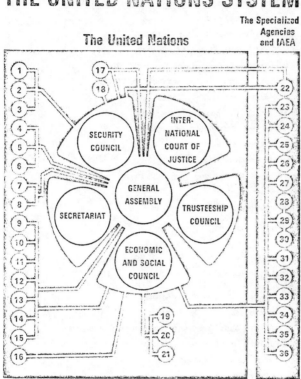

The Specialized Agencies and IAEA

The United Nations

The United Nations

1 United Nations Truce Supervision Organization in Palestine (UNTSO)

2 United Nations Military Observer Group in India and Pakistan (UNMOGIP)

3 United Nations Peace-keeping Force in Cyprus (UNFICYP)

4 Main Committees

5 Standing and Procedural Committees

6 Other Subsidiary Organs of General Assembly

7 The United Nations Relief Works Agency for Palestine Refugees in the Near East

COMMUNICATIONS IN INTERNATIONAL ORGANIZATIONS WITH SPECIAL
REFERENCE TO THE UNITED NATIONS AND ITS AGENCIES

8   United Nations Conference on Trade and Development (UNCTAD)

9   Trade and Development Board

10   United Nations Development Programme (UNDP)

11   United Nations Capital Development Fund

12   United Nations Industrial Development Organization (UNIDO)

13   United Nations Institute for Training and Research (UNITAR)

14   United Nations Children's Fund (UNICEF)

15   United Nations High Commissioner for Refugees (UNHCR)

16   Joint United Nations–FAO World Food Programme

17   Disarmament Commission

18   Military Staff Committee

19   Regional Economic Commission

20   Functional Commissions

21   Sessional, Standing and *Ad Hoc* Committees

The Specialized Agencies and IAEA

22	IAEA	International Atomic Energy Agency
23	ILO	International Labour Organisation
24	FAO	Food and Agriculture Organization of the United Nations
25	UNESCO	United Nations Educational, Scientific and Cultural Organization
26	WHO	World Health Organization
27	IMF	International Monetary Fund
28	IDA	International Development Association
29	IBRD	International Bank for Reconstruction and Development
30	IFC	International Finance Corporation
31	ICAO	International Civil Aviation Organization
32	UPU	Universal Postal Union
33	ITU	International Telecommunication Union
34	WMO	World Meteorological Organization
35	IMCO	Inter-Governmental Maritime Consultative Organization
36	GATT	General Agreement on Tariffs and Trade

SOURCE: U.N.

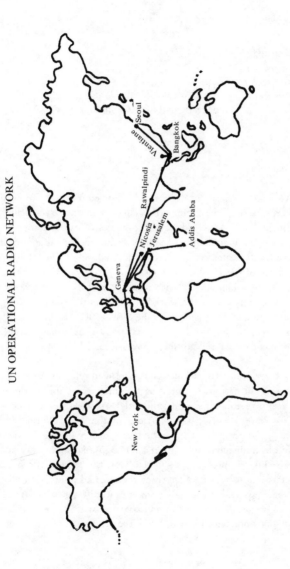

UN OPERATIONAL RADIO NETWORK

Seoul
Vientiane
Bangkok
Rawalpindi
Addis Ababa
Nicosia
Jerusalem
Geneva
New York

SOURCE: UNA — U.S.A.

655

John A. Lent:

Media Worldwide:
An Overview of Mass Communication

Introduction

THAT history repeats itself is an old axiom, and that the more things change, the more they remain the same, is another frequently heard statement. This concept of recurring-themes in history can be applied to mass communication if one looks at the sensational periods in the United States such as the yellow journalism of the 1890's, jazz journalism of the 1920's, and television's "happy talk" of the 1970's. Today's "new journalism" with its emphasis on a subjective, literary style is reminiscent of the work by Addison or Steele over 260 years ago. The muckraking periods of the early 1900's can be compared to those of today and revolutionary-reactionary trends in government-media relationships have occurred worldwide over the years.

If one wants to gain insights into the development of presses in industrialized nations centuries ago, a glimpse at Third World presses today also reveals important similarities. As was true of earlier times in the Western world, large portions of the Third World press are elitist, polemical, out of the budgetary-reach of the masses, and staffed by individuals who often came to journalism by way of other careers. Like its predecessors in the West, the Third World press also suffers from inadequate advertising revenue and production facilities. The analogy ends when one significant difference is considered, namely that when today's industrialized nations originally were granted or obtained their statehood, the printing press was essentially the only mass communication technology available. However, as the new nations of Asia, Africa, the Caribbean and Pacific are being formed in the twentieth century, they have at their disposal a variety of new technology such as radio, television, film, and satellites. These media are more pervasive, but at the same time they are also seen as more threatening to cultural and political stability, and they certainly are greater burdens because of the limited budgets of these states.

In this chapter, an effort is made to look at the development of mass communication throughout the world, primarily of printed media because they have longer histories. There will be an emphasis on recurrent traits. Additionally, recent trends and problems, representative of all mass media, are described.

Historical Perspectives

Forerunners of modern mass communication go back hundreds of years. Even before the tenth century invention of printing from movable type in China, which was a boon to the mass dissemination of messages, handwritten newsletters spread news of the royal courts or of special events. Probably the first of these was *Acta Diurna,* established by Julius Caesar in 60 B.C. It consisted of daily government announcements which were posted in the Forum. Newsletters, some handwritten, others printed, appeared infrequently in Europe after Johann Gutenberg re-invented printing from movable type for Western Europe in the mid-fifteenth century.

These publications appeared under a variety of names. They were called flysheets in Belgium and Denmark, and appeared in Denmark as early as 1542; *Cedula Novitatis* (later *Tidende*) in Norway, published as early as 1326; *flygblad* in Finland; *relation* in Austria, distributed as early as 1493, and *relaciones* in Spain. In Italy, during the Renaissance, men have known as *manatti* in Rome, *gazzettanti* in Venice and *corrieri* elsewhere, circulated handwritten newsletters, the earliest dating to 1470 in Bologna, which told of war, shipping news, travel and customs in other lands. The English had *corantos* devoted to foreign news and *diurnals* of parliamentary proceedings from at least 1621 while in the early United States there was not much evidence of such newssheets.[1] Throughout Europe, the format was similar; the newsheets usually consisted of one sheet most frequently devoted to reporting a single event. Sometimes, the newssheets were designed solely to inform members of royal-courts about lands which they governed. (Olson, 1966)

Most of Asia's first newsletters and newspapers were under royal patronage. This was the case especially in Korea, Thailand, Burma, India and Pakistan. On the Indo-Pakistan subcontinent, Muslim rulers for centuries had an efficient newsgathering-system made up of writers in various provinces who, through state-newsletters, kept the rulers fully informed. Contrary to these "only the emperor shall know" newsletters, were the *yomiuri kawaraban* circulated widely in Japan from 1610 to 1867. A *kawaraban* was an engraved clay or wooden plate used to disseminate information to the people concerning social events, national disasters, sensual matters and double suicides. Other newsletters appeared in the Philippines as early as 1637, in Indo-china in the mid-nineteenth century and in Indonesia in 1615 (Lent, 1971).

The development of printing moved at various speeds in different parts of the world after Gutenberg set up his German press in the mid-1400's. Presses were started in Italy in 1464; in Hungary and Holland during 1473; England, 1476; Sweden, 1483, and Poland, by the 1460's. Other European nations were slower in adopting printing. Russia had a press in 1553 and Norway in 1644 (Olson, 1966). As explorers from various European nations fanned out through Asia, North and South America, and much later Africa, they brought printing with them. Ironically, European colonists and missionaries brought the art of printing to most of Asia, even though next-door China had used it for centuries. Spanish friars set up the first printing press in the Philippines in 1593, 45 years before the Dayes established the first press in the United States. In parts of Latin America the Spanish developed presses during the sixteenth and seventeenth centuries. In most cases, the first presses of nearly all these nations were used to propagate Christianity through printing of the *Bible* and ecclesiastical works, and/or to support the government through issuance of decrees, announcements and gazettes.

The slowness with which printing and its by-product, newspapers, reached some nations was related to the agrarian nature of a country,[2] its cultural advancement and the leniency of its leaders. Especially in Europe, rulers had dissipated the nations' energies for centuries and in the process they had impeded cultural development. Many instances of the fear which state- and church-officials in Europe had of printing can be cited. In England, the Stationers Company was formed in 1557 to run down rebel-printers, and the Star Chamber of 1586 prescribed severe penalties for offending printers. Spanish and Portuguese printers during the same period labored under the *Autos de Fe* which imposed death penalties upon printers for minor offenses.

Even in nations with early printing presses it often took decades for newspapers to appear. Again, this was the result of the traditional and agrarian natures of these societies, and the oppressiveness of their authorities. At least 150 years elapsed from the time Sweden, Russia and Holland used their first presses and the appearance of the first newspapers in these countries. In Poland, 100 years elapsed; in the United States, 50 to 60 years. Although printing had been brought to parts of Asia in the 16th- and 17th-Centuries, the first newspapers appeared there in the late 18th- and early 19th-Centuries, some 200 to 300 years later. In the Caribbean, the time-spread between the advent of printing and the publication of the first newspapers was not so great. However, printing itself was late in penetrating that region, not arriving in the Dutch islands until 1790; the French in 1727; Spanish in 1696, and the British islands in 1717 (Lent, 1977b). Newspapers were slow in reaching Africa as well, the first being a French language paper in Egypt in 1797, followed by the *Capetown Gazette* in 1800, and the *Royal Gazette* of Sierre Leone in 1801 (Hachten, 1971; Wilcox, 1975).

The first newspapers in most regions of the world developed under authoritarian auspices. In Europe, authoritarian tendencies were the basis for the divine right of kings, the Roman Catholic Church, the political philosophies of Plato, Machiavelli's concepts, and many other ideas. In various areas of Asia, Africa, and America, because of their colonial status, presses were published under the authority of the mother country and they were used to keep colonists in touch with it rather than being developed for the nationals of those areas. Thus, colonial newspapers in most areas dwelled on foreign news, usually news of Europe. Discussing the colonial legacy of France, Spain, Belgium, Italy and England in Africa, Wilcox has written that this authoritarianism left scars on African newspapers which still have not been erased.[3]

From Elitist to Popular to Big

Newspapers were predominantly elitist in nature until the penny-press era began in the United States in the 1830's. Mock-elegant in style, these earlier papers had discussed societal matters which were irrelevant to most people, and they sold for prices which were out of the reach of the masses. With Day's *New York Sun* in 1833 appeared a new type of mass-appeal newspaper, full of simpler and more interesting writing, for the price of just one penny. In the United States other popular press movements were those of yellow journalism in the 1890's and jazz journalism in the 1920's. These periods were directly influenced by socio-cultural-economic factors such as the growth of cities, the development of large working-classes, modern technology and mass production, the rise of the common man, increased literacy, and a spirit of business-enterprise.

Similar popular presses came into existence in other areas of Europe. In England they could be noticed after 1855, and again in the 1890's, when Alfred Harmsworth in his London *Daily Mail* favored news and human-interest stories over polemics; and in France in 1863, when *La Petite Presse* ushered in *la presse à un sou*. The same trend was noticeable in Denmark in 1905 with Henrik Cavling's *Politiken,* and in Germany in the 1880's with the *anzeiger,* or advertising press. However, in at least the latter two countries, the press was not marked by the same degree of sensationalism found in newspapers published in the United States.

In a few nations of Asia a progression developed from newspapers which were used as opinion leaders and spearheads of political causes, to newspapers thought of as commercial entities. The trend was most pronounced in Japan where two contemporary newspaper giants, *Asahi* and *Mainichi,* were established during the last quarter of the 19th Century. Initially, Chinese editors in Asia did not see their newspapers as profitable businesses; Westerners introduced them to the profit motive. The popular press has taken even longer to develop in Africa and the Caribbean.

By the beginning of the 20th Century journalism in some countries had become big business, taking on the characteristics of other business structures. One-man ownership-control, consolidations, cities with only one daily newspaper, and group-operations had become commonplace, especially in the United States, through the efforts of men such as Curtis, Munsey, Hearst, and later, Newhouse, Knight, Patterson and others. The result in the United States was that the number of cities with only one daily-newspaper mushroomed from 149 to 1880 to 1,002 in 1930, and the number of cities with competing dailies went from 689 in 1910 to only 61 in 1960. In England, large press-groups such as Rothermere, Beaverbrook, Berry, Cadbury and Hulten took shape early in the 20th Century, followed later by worldwide press-empires which based their operations in London, among them those headed by Thomson, King and Murdoch. Thomson owned literally hundreds of newspapers and broadcasting-stations in all parts of the world by the 1970's.

As the new media, such as radio and television, began to compete for available advertising revenues, as wages increased and equipment and supplies became more expensive, newspapers in many nations suffered. In West Germany, for example, the number of main dailies (*hauptzeitungen*) decreased from 324 in 1963 to 143 in 1965, with a number of them in the hands of the German press-lord Axel Springer.

Asian media also have had mergers and multiple ownerships, but certainly not to the extent noticeable in the United States or England. Multiple ownerships among media have become subjects of controversy in the Philippines, India and Ceylon. However, Asia, and most of the Third World countries, have not yet had the catalysts that allow for mass-circulation newspapers and, thus, big business. Among these catalysts we can note the advent of modern technology for mass media, the appearance of media-managers who combine the skills of an imaginative editor with those of an ambitious businessman, the lowering of the prices of newspapers, and the identification of a market with resulting design of media for it (Lent, 1971).

Although most of these catalysts were available in the Socialist-world, they were used differently. The result is that the state, rather than individuals, owns all large media enterprises. The profit-motive and private-enterprise concepts thus have been deleted from the journalistic enterprises of China, the Soviet Union, Eastern Europe, Cuba, Vietnam, North Korea and Mongolia.

Political Factors

From the beginnings of printing, governments were concerned about the potential danger to them which the press represented. In most of Europe, the absolute monarchies which existed well into the 19th-Century, closely controlled publications. It has already been mentioned that similar suppression also existed in that large part of the world which for centuries was occupied or colonized by European powers. But, lest one believe that only the Third World has been afflicted by acts of oppression, it is necessary to show that the press was similarly affected, at various times, in most nations of the world. For example, the Finnish-press suffered under repressive periods of Swedish and Russian rule; the Belgian-press under Dutch oppression until independence in 1830; the Dutch under the French after 1795; the Bulgarians under Turkish rule for 478 years. With the end of these periods, usually leading to nationalism and independence, came lively journalism. There was a tremendous growth in the number of newspapers after the 1848 revolutions which swept Europe, after the American Revolution, after Norway received its independence early in the 20th Century, after Holland received its constitution in 1815, and after Italy was unified in the mid-1800's. In most instances, the press played a significant role in the drive towards revolution, nationalism, or independence.

Revolutionary desires and hopes were also the impetus for the creation of nationalist presses in various parts of Asia during the past century. Many Philippine national-heroes were journalists who led their country from under Spanish rule in the 1890's. In Malaysia, a revolutionary press appeared as early as 1904; Korea's first modern newspaper displayed nationalistic traits, and in China, during the late Manchu Dynasty, newspapers took strong political-reform stands. One Ceylonese journalist, D.R. Wijewardene, is credited with initiating and sustaining that nation's independence-movements of the 1920's and 1930's, and in Pakistan, Muslim newspapers of the 20th Century had a great deal to do with the formation of a separate Muslim nation. Elsewhere in Asia, national liberation movements, abetted by the press, developed in Burma after 1906, in Indonesia in 1908 and again after World War II, in Indo-china in the 1920's and the 1930's.

The results of these types of movements have been especially evident during the past three decades when whole continents shook off their colonial yokes. Africa, for example, had four independent nations before 1950, but between 1956-66, 35 new nations appeared. In the Caribbean and Pacific Island groups, nations received their independence primarily during the last decade, and in Asia, peoples of the Philippines, Korea, Taiwan, Pakistan, India, Indonesia, Ceylon, Malaysia, Indo-china, Burma, and other territories, have received their independence only since 1945. During the post-independence periods, a plethora of political parties developed to promote various notions of how the new states should be governed. In their wake, a strong political press also emerged. This happened in the United States in the 1780-1810 period, in Belgium after 1830, in Italy and Austria during the last quarter of the 19th Century, in the Philippines, Malaysia and other parts of Asia more recently, and now also in nearly all nations of the Caribbean area and in Africa. In many instances the political party-press died after serving its initial purposes. However, in some countries of South America, in Switzerland, Holland and Scandinavia, they have survived. The political-press is also still very much alive in the Third World, because most of this region is made up of new states.

Because a nation is independent certainly does not guarantee freedom of expression. New elites who have taken over governments and mass-media often are as oppressive as the former colonial masters, as can be frequently witnessed in the Third World. One dominant trend in the Third World, the Socialist nations and in parts of the West as well, is towards centralized governments, in the form of either the rule of a strong-union or concentration of power under one family. Ruling cliques, when they find they cannot cope with communal strife, frequently push aside constitutional guarantees by issuing emergency- or martial law-decrees. This approach is prevalent in all parts of the world. Nearly all Asian nations are going through such a phase, and the large number of military governments in Africa and Latin America represents the same trend. The lack of political stability has had deteriorating effects on many mass media. For example, in Latin America, coups have occurred in Brazil in 1964; in Argentina during 1966 and 1976; in Bolivia in 1972, and in Uruguay and Chile during 1973. About one-half of continental Latin America is currently ruled by repressive military dictatorships, which are especially evident in Brazil, Uruguay, Paraguay, Chile and Argentina, and all of which exert authoritarian controls over the media of mass communication.

Unfortunately, media typologies have neglected the Third World. The widely-used "four-theories" typology, for instance, which was developed in the cold war period of the mid-1950's when the Third World was still colonial vestiges of the First and Second Worlds, classified press systems as authoritarian, libertarian, Soviet-Communist, and social-responsibility. Authoritarian presses, evident in early European countries and in some parts of the contemporary world, are controlled by public and private groups subservient to the state; they are hindered by censorship and an inability to criticize the government. Libertarian systems, existent in Anglo-American and other Western nations since the Enlightenment, have no governmental control and emphasize freedom from restraints on contents; while Soviet-Communist presses, used by the Soviet Union and other Communist countries, are controlled by the government and the Communist Party, and stress party doctrine and government support. The social responsibility theory, which grew out of work done by the British Royal Commission on the Press and the Hutchins Commission in the United States, both in the mid-1940's, is confined to Anglo-American countries. This latter concept promotes control by organizations responsive to the public

(Siebert et. al., 1956). Now, however, a fifth theory is in order, one that results in a guided-press as found in most Third World nations. Basically, Third World-leaders explain the need for guidance of the press in this way: because Third World countries are newly-emergent, they need time to develop their institutions. During this initial period of growth, stability and unity must be sought, criticism must be minimized, and the public faith in governmental institutions and policies must be encouraged. Media must *cooperate* by stressing positive, development-inspired news, by ignoring negative societal or oppositionalist characteristics, and by supporting governmental ideologies and plans (Lent, 1976).

Pervasiveness of the Electronic Media

It often takes an anniversay-year, such as 1977 and 1978 have been for film and broadcasting, to recognize the youthfulness of some media which we now take for granted. Consider for a moment, that commercial radio only dates back to 1920, that television's success only began in the post-World War II years (although England had a regular television service in 1936), or that the talking motion picture was just 50 years old in 1977. What is striking is that in these short periods, radio, television and film have probably done more to change lifestyles around the world than the print media did in the preceding 500 years.

Part of the reason is that electronic media, especially radio, eliminate the triple barriers of illiteracy, distance, and lack of transportation. As Head wrote, referring to Africa:

> "Broadcasting uses scores of local languages, most of which never appear in print; radio and television continue to grow, while daily newspapers decline; broadcasting stations generally have large staffs and modern equipment, while most newspapers are woefully understaffed and ill-equipped."[4]

The youngest of the mass media, television, has the greatest possibility of creating the global village some prognosticators have discussed. This was evident on July 19, 1969, when 723 million people, or one-fifth of the earth's population, in 47 nations, watched man step onto the moon.[5] The growth of television has been phenomenal if one recalls that in 1950, there were only five-million receivers in the world, all concentrated in the three nations that transmitted television signals; the United States, Great Britain, and the Soviet Union. By the 1970's, the number of sets reached 357 million in over 130 nations. Only in Asia and Africa is television-viewing not a normal part of the average person's daily activity. As Varis has pointed out, although the world's television-audience is about a billion, the medium is still mainly found in the rich part of the world. Of 25,000 television transmitters in the world, 95 percent are in industrialized countries and 90 percent of the receivers are in developed nations.[6] Despite these figures, the medium is often found in isolated areas of the Third World even though it is expensive. Television is established on the Rock of Gibraltar which has a station serving 6,000 receivers; in the *kampongs* of Brunei, in color no less; and in Addis Ababa, where it is beamed from a tiny studio in six rooms of the city hall of Ethiopia's capital city.

In some Western societies, children spend more time before a television set than in their classrooms. For example, American children, before they are graduated from high school, log 15,000 hours of television viewing compared to 10,800 hours in the classroom. The average American spends six hours a day in front of his television set, compared to five for a Japanese, or four for an English viewer. The types of programs they watch are often criticized for their innaneness, conformity and violence. Public-service broadcasting-systems, such as the British Broadcasting Corporation, ARD in Germany, and Nihon Hoso Kyokai in Japan on the other hand have usually presented a more sophisticated type of programming, but usually have much smaller audiences. Each of these systems has a twenty-to-one higher ratio of documentaries and current-affairs programs than commercial television stations in the United States. Commercial television stations in the United States tend to overuse successful formats and thus doom them to early oblivion. Examples are the spate of adult Westerns and hospital-shows in the 1960's; an over-abundance of detective-, lawyer- and medical-shows in the 1970's. In the United States this may result partly from the close liaison between advertisers and producers of programs, a liaison not known in many other parts of the world. For instance in Western Europe, program-sponsorship is usually not permitted.

Commercials are used, however, in most television systems around the world. About 90 of the 130 television-countries accept them for all or part of their income. Even in Europe, where public-service broadcasting for years was financed by annual receiver license-fees, advertisements are used by two-thirds of the radio- and television-systems. Exceptions are the British Broadcasting Corporation, as well as the Belgian and Scandinavian national broadcasting media. In the Third World, Latin America is the only area where radio and television function almost exclusively as commercial and private services. Ninety-three percent of Latin American radio stations, and seventy-five percent of the television channels are private, commercial enterprises. However, ninety-five percent of the radio- and television-systems are financed by and depend upon advertising, thus including other than privately-owned media in the commercial category.

Because television-program production is too expensive for many nations, the United States, and to a lesser degree Japan, Spain, Germany, England and others, sell recorded programs to the Third World. The United States exports up to 100,000 hours of television programs annually. "Bonanza," for example, is watched weekly by 400 million people in 82 countries. The result has been that some of the nations in the Third World have accused Western nations of practicing electronic-imperialism. Sometimes, however, this type of global-broadcasting results from language, rather than political factors. For example, Spanish television has carved out a market for itself in Latin America, French television in former French colonies, and Egyptian television has tried to establish its supremacy in the Arab world, exporting 1,200 hours of programs annually. But, on the other hand, Egypt also imports 1,800 hours of television programs a year from the United States, 300 from France, and 400 from Eastern Europe. Control of broadcasting, which is the key element in describing media systems, takes various forms throughout the world. Namurois, for example, categorizes forms of control under four headings: state operated; public corporation; public interest partnership; and private enterprise. Most Communist and Third World nations employ state-operated systems, with broadcasting controlled by a government-ministry or -department,[7] while countries such as Britain, France, West Germany, Belgium and Holland have public-corporations for broadcasting which are operated autonomously under state charters. According to the Namurois typology, public-interest partnerships exist in Italy, Sweden, and Switzerland, and they are operated by legally private-corporations, with stock-interests by the state. Private-enterprise broadcasting is prevalent in the United States, Luxembourg, and among Japan's private stations. It is operated by private corporations under weak government regulations (Namurois, 1964).

Trends

Generalizing about mass media today, it might be said that the printed media in almost all nations of the world reach a much smaller audience than radio, and in many, a smaller audience than television. Outside the industrialized countries, the press hardly reaches rural people at all, but broadcasting covers the entire population. Where there exists a multiplicity of languages, there exists no press for many of the languages. All printed media have become expensive to produce and buy because of production- and newsprint-costs, and the loss of revenue to other media.

Additionally, it can be said that the number of national news-agencies is increasing, since nearly 100 nations now have their own agencies. More than half of these agencies are controlled by the state, while at least 40 are cooperatively controlled by newspapers or autonomous public corporations which in some cases have been created by the state. Five international agencies, Agence France Presse, Associated Press, United Press International, TASS, and Reuters are dominant throughout the world.

Further, it can be generalized that the majority of nations operate or directly control radio- and television-services, which are usually financed by state-funds or license-revenues, and sometimes supplemented by advertising money. Nearly all nations direct external broadcasting-services for cultural- or propaganda-purposes. Most states produce their own radio shows, although many of these consist of recordings of popular music imported from Western nations. In almost all countries of the world, there is a great deal of importation of television programs for entertainment. There is also an ever-increasing trend to use radio and television for broadcasting to schools and universities; as well as for adult-education and national-development purposes.

Europe

UNESCO, in presenting ten-year trends in the mid-1970's, reported that Europe, which has more newspapers and more circulation per 1,000 people[8] than any other region of the world, experienced a decline in the number of dailies, but an increase in circulation (UNESCO, 1975). Most European newspapers are still owned by private enterprises (some by political parties), except in Eastern Europe where the press is directed by political parties and public organizations. In the Soviet Union, the number of dailies increased from 457 in the 1960's to 639 in 1970, and the total daily-circulation reached 81 million, 25 million of which was shared by the three largest dailies. Europe continues to be the region with the largest number of long-established and highly-developed national news-agencies. All states, except four smaller ones, have agencies; 16 of them are operated by mass media-cooperatives and nine by the state. The largest agencies, Agence France Presse, Reuters, and TASS, along with United Press International and Associated Press in the United States, have been accused of practicing wire service-imperialism by transmitting their messages to Third World nations, If indeed blame is to be assigned, others must also be considered. A smaller agency, Efe in Spain, for example, sends as many as 190,000 words daily, in Spanish, to 200 daily newspapers and broadcast stations of Latin America.

The number of radio licenses and receivers per 1,000 population increased during the past decade in all but a few nations of Europe.

There are trends towards more balanced broadcasting programming in Western Europe, partly because FM, television, and satellites allow a wider range of programs for varied interests. Highly-developed television services have existed for a long time in almost all of Europe, and the number of channels and transmitters has risen during the past decade. More people are watching the medium, as evidenced by the fact that the number of receivers has increased from two to five times in most countries during the last decade, and by an even greater number in other areas. Cable-television is becoming more popular, and educational television is usually of a high quality. Western European nations telecast 2,000-7,000 hours of programs yearly, 10 to 30 percent of which are imported. Finland (40 percent), Ireland (50 percent) and Iceland (60 percent) are the largest importers of television shows. The United States provides about 50 percent of Western Europe's imports, followed by England. In Eastern Europe, 2,000 to 6,000 hours a year are telecast, 30 to 40 percent of which are imported, usually from the Soviet Union and other Eastern European nations (Paulu, 1956, 1967, 1974; Emery, 1969).

Use of satellite-technology has allowed development of such television systems as Eurovision in Western Europe, and Intervision in Eastern Europe and the Soviet Union which provide direct, efficient broadcasting to people throughout the world. European broadcasters saw the need for cooperative endeavors very early, and they joined together to form the International Broadcasting Union in 1925. By the late 1930's, IBU had 59 members and was involved in carrying out radio program exchanges. After World War II, the Cold War split the broadcasters. Those representing the Socialist nations of Europe as well as other parts of the world, formed the International Organization for Radio and Television (OIRT), while Western European broadcasters organized the European Broadcasting Union.[9]

North America

The United States has more newspapers and periodicals than any other nation in the world. American dailies are generally locally-oriented, non-competitive, and increasingly group-owned. In the ten years between 1961 and 1971, the number of dailies showed a slight increase from 1,761 to 1,763, and the number of cities with dailies increased from 1,460 to 1,500. However, in eighty-five percent of these cities, only one newspaper was published. A few cities, such as Philadelphia and New York, have as many as four dailies. But nowhere in the United States does one see a concentration of dailies such as can be found in cities like Hong Kong, Kuala Lumpur, Singapore, or even London. The number of United States dailies connected to group-ownerships has almost doubled since the 1960's, from 560 owned by 109 groups, to 900 owned by 155 chains. Cross-media ownerships are also on the increase, with 500 radio- and 200 television-stations as parts of such groups. In Canada, group-ownership of the 116 dailies is also on the increase.[10]

In Central America, the contrast in numbers of daily newspapers is bewildering. Mexico, for example, has about 200 dailies, while Belize has none and Nicaragua has four. As for news agencies, they now exist in Cuba, Mexico, the Commonwealth Caribbean, the United States, and Canada. Regional wire-agencies have been formed in the 1970's in both Central America (Agencia Centro-American de Noticias), and Commonwealth Caribbean (Caribbean News Agency).

The United States leads the world in the number of radio and television stations, transmitters and receivers: about 354 million radio receivers, and 100 million TV sets. Almost ninety-three percent of all radio-stations are privately-owned and advertising-supported, and most (2,300 stations) are affiliated to one of the four networks. United States' television has more hours of broadcasting than any other system in the world.[11] In fact, only in the United States, Canada, Japan, and Australia does television begin at the crack of dawn. In most nations, television is confined to the evening hours. Television in the United States is usually commercially-owned; 700 of the 915 stations fall in that category. Another 220 stations are non-commercial, educational channels. Cable, or Community-Antenna-Television (CATV), has grown from a system used originally in small, isolated towns to pick up better signals, to a service providing specialized programming. By the early 1970's, about six-million homes were linked to 2,700 CATV systems.

In Central America and the Caribbean, radio broadcasting is highly developed in at least Cuba, Jamaica, Mexico, Panama and Trinidad & Tobago (see Lent, 1977b for information on the latter), and television is available in most nations although the prevalance of the medium varies. Mexico has 70 television stations, which serve about seventy percent of the population, while Belize depends on television from neighboring countries. Actually, only in Canada, the United States, Mexico and Cuba is a large part of the population reached by television. Many of the programs in Spanish-speaking North America are imported, ranging from forty to eighty percent. Fifty to sixty percent of these shows emanate from the United States, while another thirty to forty percent come from Spanish-speaking countries, mainly Mexico[12] and Argentina, and ten percent from Spain, Italy and France. The English-speaking Caribbean area imports about seventy to eighty percent of its television fare, mostly from the United States and England (Lent, 1977b).

South America

Almost all of the numerous South American newspapers are privately-owned, although many have political-party ties. In the three largest nations, the number of newspapers has declined in the past decade, and in two of these, circulations are well below the 100 copies per 1,000 population range. Dailies are found in many provincial towns, as well as metropolitan areas, yet there are no dailies in the prevalent Indian languages of the continent. Only Argentina, Colombia, Chile, Venezuela and Brazil have news-agencies. In 1970, thirteen Latin-American nations formed a regional agency, LATIN. Yet, Latin America is still heavily-dependent upon information supplied by United Press International and Associated Press, and to a lesser degree, Agence France Presse. Together, these agencies provide ninety percent of all the foreign news used in the major media of the region.[13]

During the past decade, the number of radio receivers has increased in all nations, except Brazil. However, Brazil has the largest number of radio stations (1,200) of any South American Country. In most of South America, radio is the major, and often the sole source of news and entertainment. Most broadcasting is in Spanish or Portuguese, although some shows are in Indian languages. In all nations except Bolivia, television has seen a very significant growth since the 1960's, in numbers of transmitters, geographical coverage, and numbers of receivers. Yet, only in Argentina and Uruguay are there over 100 receivers per 1,000 population. About thirty to seventy percent of the television-shows are imported, mainly from the United States, but some from Argentina and Mexico.

Asia

Newspapers and magazines are published by private companies in all nations of Asia except Afghanistan, Burma, China, Iraq, North Korea, Mongolia, Vietnam, Cambodia, and Yemen. However, some presses are affiliated with or subsidized by political parties, and in most instances, government-regulations and -guidelines have had debilitating effects. In 20 nations the number of dailies and total circulations increased between the 1960's and 1970's. On the other extreme, in ten countries, the circulations remain well below 20 copies per 1,000 population.[14] The nations with the largest number of newspapers and largest circulations, China, India, and Japan, represent the varieties of press operations in Asia.

China, with over 2,000 dailies, headed by *People's Daily,* is a Communist-system based on Marxist-Leninist-Maoist doctrine which emphasizes organization of media by structure and function (Liu, 1971; Chu, 1977, 1978).

The Indian press epitomizes on the grandest of scales the types of problems faced in a less-developed country—those of production, language, literacy and circulation. Many of the 721[15] dailies suffer from lack of up-to-date equipment, trained personnel and newsprint, as well as bureaucratic entanglements. Dailies are published in 20 languages and dialects, but this represents only a fraction of the languages and dialects in use. Newspapers are expensive, costing as much as twenty-two days of a school teacher's wages for a year's subscription, and they are difficult to read for the functionally-illiterate masses. The result is low circulations. Group-ownership has been a bone of contention, since about sixty percent of the total daily-circulation is controlled by combines (Lent, 1971).

Japan's press, on the other hand, seems out-of-place in Asia. The 168 dailies, an increase of 11 since the early 1960's, are very modern, at times using technology not yet applied in Western nations. For example, as early as 1959, *Asahi*, the newspaper-giant with a circulation of nearly 12 million, transmitted its pages by radio-signals to satellite-papers a thousand miles away, and home-facsimile technology has been in use in Japan for nearly a decade. Although dailies are published in sixty cities and towns, three Tokyo papers (*Asahi, Mainichi,* and *Yomiuri*) dominate the scene, garnering nearly 25 million circulation among them.

All Middle-East- and Asian-nations, except for Thailand, Singapore, Kuwait, Saudi-Arabia and Cyprus, now have national news-agencies, although in most instances they are operated as government-press-services. Japan has two agencies, Kyoko and Jiji, that are well-known; China's New China News Agency also plays an international role. India has about thirty domestic- and feature-agencies, although the largest four were merged for control-reasons under the Gandhi-emergency in the mid-1970's.

In almost all of Asia radio is run directly by the state and is financed by license fees and some advertising. Most radio, as well as television, systems fall under the jurisdiction of a government-ministry or -bureau. The number of transmitters increased sharply in the past decade, as did the number of receivers. But, in more than half of Asia the larger part of the population is still not reached by radio, even allowing for the increasingly-widespread use of communal and school receivers. From the 1960's to the 1970's at least a dozen countries adopted television as part of the paraphernalia of modernity, or as symbols of independence. For example, the Maldives initiated color-television for an audience of ninety receivers in time for their independence-birthday in 1978. Tiny Brunei, whose only media are a government radio-station and a weekly-newspaper, set up a color television system in the mid 1970's. The number of transmitters and receivers in Asia is still relatively low, perhaps because television is such an expensive medium for developing-nations and the poverty-stricken populations. Except for China and India, Asian nations rely on imports for a large portion (thirty to seventy percent) of their television programming. More than half of these shows have been produced in the United States, followed by England. Japan television also exports to Asia but is limited by the less-than-universal nature of its language (Lent, 1978a).

Africa

Of all regions of the world, Africa has fewer daily-newspapers and lower overall circulations. For example, in nine nations no dailies exist, while in thirteen others there is only one. Ten other nations report circulations of less than twenty copies per 1,000 population. Media that do exist are concentrated in a few major cities, usually capitals. Worse yet, there was very little development from the 1960's to the 1970's. The size of the continent, with great distances between cities and inadequate transportation facilities; a multiplicity of languages, [16] few of which are spoken by a clear majority; high illiteracy rates; extensive poverty; and very oppressive governments, mitigate against the development of an active press. News-agencies have been slow to develop on the continent also. UNESCO reported a total of 27 domestic-agencies, 22 of which are run by their respective governments. Regional efforts at establishing news-agencies were made in the 1970's, but Africa still suffers from what Hachten describes as wire-service-imperialism.[17]

Radio broadcasting, which got off to a late start with wired-systems in the 1930's, is still confined to capital cities. Head reports that three-fourths of the independent-stations have transmitters in four or fewer sites. Eighteen countries have only a single transmitter location each.[18] Thus, although the number of receivers greatly increased in the past decade, radio reception in rural-areas is usually poor or non-existent. In 26 nations, for example, there are less than 50 receivers per 1,000 persons. Where provincial-radio-stations exist, they repeat centrally-produced programming, in the process creating very little indigenous content. Nation-building colors a great deal of African broadcast content, as it does in Asia. Formats for African radio-programming are primarily music, news and talk. News is usually provided by the national news-agencies, most of which are government-operated and centralized, to the extent that they receive and distribute both domestic- and foreign-news. This is a trait of Asian-agencies as well. Head pointed out that African broadcasting is heavily-involved in politics, explaining, "One-party states, military regimes, and other authoritarian forms of government manipulate the media in general, but broadcasting in particular, as conscious instruments of both internal and external policy."[19]

Television has barely touched Africa since the first system was inaugurated in Morocco in 1954. In the decade between the 1960's and 1970's, 14 nations started television-systems, bringing the total to about 25. At least 20 countries do not have television-systems. In almost all cases, television is a by-product of political independence (a characteristic of most Third World nations), or some special event, no matter how ridiculous it might appear to outsiders. For example, Uganda introduced color television in 1975 to cover Idi Amin's latest wedding. In several countries, television was specifically established as a means of promoting educational, economic, and social development. It is notably used for these purposes in Ghana, the Ivory Coast, Niger, and Senegal. Few receivers are in existence in Africa. Egypt, which has Africa's largest television-service, only has twenty receivers per 1,000 population. Forty to sixty percent of all African television-programming is imported.

Problems

Each nation in the world has mass-communication problems endemic to it which may not be universal in scope. In the United States, for example, these might include the proliferation of group- and cross-channel-ownerships, first-amendment guarantees, free-press versus fair-trial arguments, the increasingly-apparent manipulation of the public's right-to-know by advertisers, the banality of broadcasting content, or the de-emphasis of international-news coverage in most mass media. However, because of space limitations, this section will deal with problems that affect a number of nations.

One such problem relates to the big-business nature of mass media in most parts of the Western world. As newspapers and broadcasting-stations were elevated to the status of large-scale business institutions, they were accused of becoming conservative defenders of the status-quo and the military-industrial-business complex, often favoring the interest of their chief benefactors: the advertisers. Libertarian concepts, such as the "open marketplace of ideas" and the "self-righting process," became less applicable in some Western nations, since the average individual or group did not have the funds to develop or purchase media-enterprises, thus being unable to enter the media marketplace effectively. Also, individuals were not always given access to the pages of newspapers or to broadcast-airwaves to express their views, although, at least in the United States, recent events have allowed more access, especially in radio.

Increasingly, big-business-journalism is being considered culturally inappropriate and economically unfeasible by large groups of people, especially the eighty percent peasantry of the Third World. The formal media, in many regions of the world, are found to be unrelated or unintelligible to rural-people, as well as too financially taxing for poorer societies, where there is insufficient revenue available to purchase modern plants, equipment, or supplies, such as newsprint.[20] The lack of purchasing power also affects circulations and advertising. In many cases, some formal mass media have been sought by poorer nations' leaders because they are impressive paraphernalia of modernity and status symbols. Television, for example, which has become a status symbol of independence throughout the world, has been implemented irresponsibly in many nations, becoming a plaything for urban elites, while siphoning off funds from radio which is much more mass-based (Katz and Wedell, 1977).

Still other problems in regard to the Third World's capacity to produce and consume modern mass-media, are related to the multiplicity of languages in use in some nations. Polylingualism hinders the widespread use of formal media in some cultures, especially in a nation such as India, where Bombay alone has 222 mother-languages, none of which is major. Most of Africa, South- and Southeast-Asia, China, and even the small islands of the Caribbean and Pacific, have difficulties because one-language media cannot do an adequate job. In most of Eastern Europe similar problems exist, and as a result two or more languages must be based in domestic radio broadcasting. In the Soviet Union, the problem is compounded by a population which speaks 100 different languages and dialects, 67 of which are used in domestic radio and television broadcasting. All this indicates a problem which involves more than Third World countries. In other instances, technology to handle unique language scripts are either not available or not affordable. Chinese, with its thousands of characters, or Thai, with its numerous tonal marks, does not lend itself easily to mechanization; neither does Urdo, which has no type face.

Recently, there has taken place a transformation in our thinking about the communication-patterns and -needs of the rural-peoples of the world. The result has been either a down-playing of or a restructuring of the use of formal mass-media. More emphasis is being placed on using interpersonal-communication-networks and folk-media, on adapting formal mass-media to villagers' problems, on using smaller and capital-cheap media, and on re-opening ancient lines of contact between Third World nations. To provide rural people with more access to media — making them sources and actors as well as receivers — alternative media, such as audio-cassette technology, wall- and blackboard-newspapers, rural-television- and radio-projects, rural mimeographed-newspapers and folk-media, have been developed. The hope is to stop thrusting sophisticated technological-systems upon developing nations, systems that encourage them to leap across intermediate stages of development. In the process, so-called growthmania is being re-evaluated. It is no longer being taken for granted that "bigger is better" or even more efficient (Lent, 1978b).

Dramatic reversals are underway as far as the "free flow of information" between nations is concerned, which was stimulated by the United Nations and supported by many developed-nations during the past 30 years. These nations had agreed that unimpeded communication-traffic was beneficial to everyone. However, it has only been in recent years with the development of new technologies, especially satellites, that developing nations questioned that concept. They pointed out that they were literally being overwhelmed by information and cultural messages from the powerful communicator states. The Third World has argued that because this so-called free-flow is a one-way movement, their societies have become passive recipients of distorted, inadequate, and biased information. Since at least 1976, Third World nations have promoted a newspool which they hope will bring about a "balanced flow of information." At the same time, they have stated that a new information-order is needed in order to encourage and develop national-information-media. The latter proposal came out of UNESCO-thinking, which since 1971 has stated that each nation should have its own, integrated, national communication-policy to tackle problems of poverty, population, and health.

Out of all this has come the "development-communication" idea, which has swept the Third World and split press-circles elsewhere. Originally meant to report in-depth upon national development efforts, development-communication today is considered the main propaganda-technique of many developing governments, used to promote national ideologies and campaigns.

All three concepts, "unbalanced flow of information," "new information order" and "development communication," have rekindled cold-war-type fires between Western- and Socialist-nations, with the former arguing that these concepts are efforts to legitimize the authoritarianism which is rampant in the Third World. Because these concepts were either initiated or strongly supported by Socialist countries, there is suspicion among Western democracies that they are meant to deter the press-freedom goals which have already been severely affected by governments worldwide, but especially in the Third World. All this is seen as an attempt to redefine press-freedom, promulgate or alter press-levels, suspend papers, and arrest or kill journalists, restructure media to include more government-management and -ownership, levy economic sanctions, and control foreign correspondents and the images they impart of the developing world (Lent, 1977a).

FOOTNOTES

[1] In 1689, a broadsheet from Rev. Increase Mather to the governor of Massachusetts was issued, entitled *The Present State of the New English Affairs.*

[2] For example, London in 1450 was the major city of England with only 40,000 population, one-tenth of that of Paris.

[3] Dennis L. Wilcox, *Mass Media in Africa: Philosophy and Control.* New York: Praeger, 1975.

[4] Sydney W. Head, *Broadcasting in Africa: A Continental Survey of Radio and Television.* Philadelphia: Temple University Press, 1974, p. 3.

[5] Timothy Green, *The Universal Eye: World Television in the Seventies.* London: The Bodley Head, 1972, p.1.

[6] Tapio Varis, Raquel Salinas and Renny Jokelin. "International News and the New Information Order." Tampere, Finland: University of Tampere, Institute of Journalism and Mass Communication, 1977, p. 10.

[7] Head reported that in Africa, each country has one single monolithic government system; Mozambique alone does not have a government system. But, of 115 different broadcasting administrations in 58 nations, Head found in 1972 more than 40 were private, non-government radio stations. African governments own and operate broadcasting usually as part of a Ministry of Information (Head, 1974). Lent found similar patterns of strong and pervasive government control of broadcasting in Asia and the Commonwealth Caribbean (Lent, 1978a, 1977b).

[8] Eleven nations had circulation ratios of 300 copies of dailies per 1,000 population.

[9] Tapio Varis, Raquel Salinas and Renny Jokelin. "International News and the New Information Order." Tampere, Finland: University of Tampere, Institute of Journalism and Mass Communication, 1977, pp. 4-5.

[10] Only 13 of which are in French, the language of thirty percent of the population.

[11] The United States, the world's biggest exporter of television shows, imports only about two percent of its programs.

[12] Mexico is a very big exporter of programs but many are dubbed-versions of United States shows.

[13] Tapio Varis, Raquel Salinas and Renny Jokelin. "International News and the New Information Order." Tampere, Finland: University of Tampere, Institute of Journalism and Mass Communication, 1977, p. 39.

[14] Circulations are not always indicative of readership, especially in the Third World where there are secondary-audiences, because newspapers are passed from person to person.

[15] India ranks fourth after China, United States, and West Germany in numbers of dailies.

[16] Sydney W. Head, *Broadcasting in Africa: A Continental Survey of Radio and Television.* Philadelphia: Temple University Press, 1974, p. 350. In 1972, Head found polylingualism was acute in Africa. He reported 196 languages used in broadcasting, of which 173 were African. Minority-peoples demanded vernacular language-usage in broadcasting, according to Head, because of pride- and status-considerations, but also because they feared extinction of their languages.

[17] William A. Hachten, *Muffled Drums. The News Media in Africa.* Ames: Iowa State University Press, 1971, p. 86.

[18] Sydney W. Head, *Broadcasting in Africa: A Continental Survey of Radio and Television.* Philadelphia: Temple University Press, 1974, p. 10.

[19] *Ibid.,* p. 7.

[20] Newsprint is in short supply in most of the world. Only 36 countries produce newsprint, and of these, only six have surpluses to export.

BIBLIOGRAPHY

Chu, Godwin C. 1977. *Radical Change Through Communication in Mao's China.* Honolulu: University Press of Hawaii.

Chu, Godwin C. 1978. *Popular Media in China.* Honolulu: University Press of Hawaii.

Emery, Walter B. 1969. *National and International Systems of Broadcasting.* East Lansing: Michigan State University.

Green, Timothy. 1972. *The Universal Eye: World Television in the Seventies.* London: The Bodley Head.

Hachten, William A. 1971. *Muffled Drums. The News Media in Africa.* Ames: Iowa State University Press.

Head, Sydney W. 1974. *Broadcasting in Africa: A Continental Survey of Radio and Television.* Philadelphia: Temple University Press.

Katz, Elihu and George Wedell. 1977. *Broadcasting in the Third World. Promise and Performance.* Cambridge: Harvard University Press.

Lent, John A. 1971. *The Asian Newspapers' Reluctant Revolution.* Ames: Iowa State University Press.

Lent, John A. 1976. *Guided Press in Southeast Asia: National Development Versus Freedom of Expression.* Buffalo: Council on International Studies, SUNY.

Lent, John A. 1977a. "The Guiding Light." *Index on Censorship.* Sept. 10 at 17-26.

Lent, John A. 1977b. *Third World Mass Media and Their Search for Modernity: The Case of Commonwealth Caribbean, 1717-1976.* Lewisburg and London: Bucknell University Press and Associated University Presses.

Lent, John A. 1978a. *Broadcasting in Asia and the Pacific: A Continental Survey of Radio and Television.* Philadelphia and Hong Kong: Temple University Press and Heinemann Educational Books.

Lent, John A. 1978b. "Mass Media, Folk Media and Rural Masses in the Third World." Paper, International Studies Association, Washington, D.C., February 24.

Liu, Alan P.L. 1971. *Communications and National Integration in Communist China.* Berkeley: University of California Press.

Namurois, Albert. 1964. *Problems of Structure and Organization of Broadcasting in the Framework of Radio Communications.* Geneva: European Broadcasting Union.

Olson, Kenneth E. 1966. *The History Makers. The Press of Europe from Its Beginnings Through 1965.* Baton Rouge: Louisiana State University Press.

Paulu, Burton. 1956. *British Broadcasting: Radio and Television in the United Kingdom.* Minneapolis: University of Minnesota Press.

Paulu, Burton. 1967. *Radio and Television Broadcasting on the European Continent.* Minneapolis: University of Minnesota Press.

Paulu, Burton. 1974. *Radio and Television Broadcasting in Eastern Europe.* Minneapolis: University of Minnesota Press.

Schiller, Herbert. 1971. *Mass Communications and American Empire.* Boston: Beacon Press.

Siebert, Fred S., Theodore Peterson and Wilbur Schramm. 1956. *Four Theories of the Press.* Urbana: University of Illinois Press.

Tunstall, Jeremy. 1977. *The Media are American. Anglo-American Media in the World.* New York: Columbia University Press.

UNESCO 1975. *World Communications: A 200 Country Survey of Press, Radio, Television, Film.* Paris: The UNESCO Press.

Varis, Tapio, Raquel Salinas and Renny Jokelin. 1977. "International News and the New Information Order." Tampere, Finland: University of Tampere, Institute of Journalism and Mass Communication.

Wells, Alan. 1974. *Mass Communications: A World View.* Palo Alto: National Press Books.

Wilcox, Dennis L. 1975. *Mass Media in Africa: Philosophy and Control.* New York: Praeger.

J. Herbert Altschull:

Government Dialogue Through the Mass Media

GOVERNMENTS speak to one another in a variety of ways; by no means does communication between governments take place principally through official channels. Perhaps this has always been the case, but the volume of non-official communication has grown to vast proportions in the age of telegraph, telephone, radio, television and space satellite. A grim setting of Cyrus Vance's jaw can within minutes bring a frown -- or a smile -- to the lips of Leonid Brezhnev. The message has been transmitted wholly outside the machinery of official communications -- by journalists, technicians and messengers. The "message" transmitted by Vance's jaw has been "encoded" by journalists in Washington and "decoded" by journalists in Moscow for the ultimate "receiver," Brezhnev.

Modern political leaders, especially in sophisticated societies, are aware of the complications of such transmissions. The message may have been misencoded, deliberately or accidentally. But even if the message were encoded and decoded accurately, distortion remains a possibility, perhaps even a probability. Perhaps Vance was smiling inside while frowning outside, in order to deceive Brezhnev for some purpose of his own. Or perhaps Brezhnev elected to see a smile instead of a frown. In any case, "news" transmitted between nations through unofficial channels is a regular occurrence.[1] And the possibility of action based on erroneous information exists, whatever the level of political sophistication of sender and receiver. Very likely, Britain and France would have pursued a different course in the Middle East in 1956 had the governments of Eden and Mollet perceived the position of the United States differently, had they not acted on the basis of unofficial information transmitted by journalists. John Foster Dulles based a full-grown theory of international politics on his conception of "miscalculation."[2]

While the influence of journalistic reports can easily be exaggerated, one cannot dismiss the importance of news reports in international communication and indeed in decision-making. Whatever information flows along official channels in the international family, it is considerably less than the information which moves through "news" channels.

What is News?

Yet, despite the ubiquity of "news" in the communication process, no one seems to know precisely what is meant by news. In an interesting examination of this topic in 1971, Dennis J. Chase concludes that this is so because there has not developed any coherent philosophy of journalism. He cites a number of definitions, nearly all of them tautological, as "something you didn't know before, had forgotten or didn't understand," or "anything that people want to read . . . provided it does not violate the canons of good taste and the laws of libel." Chase quotes one journalism textbook as recommending a "nose for news," which is described as "of primary importance in distinguishing between news and non-news, and in establishing the importance of news."[3]

The problem, as I see it, is that news is a *dynamic* phenomenon and hence cannot be fitted into a traditional static definition. Like communication itself, news is a process.[4] One can, then, create a news model consisting of three fundamental ingredients: a phenomenon, a report and a channel of distribution. In other words, any phenomenon about which a report is distributed becomes news; when the distribution is made to the mass of the population, it becomes mass news. A phenomenon may be defined as an event, a trend (i.e., a pattern of events), or a generalization (about the events). The "events" here cited may be actual or perceived. News then remains dormant until it is reported and distributed. It is like Bishop Berkeley's tree in the forest: it has not fallen until the tumble has been reported and transmitted. News, as a dynamic process, is always capable of being changed. It is "news" one day that Israeli hostages have been freed by their abductors at the Munich Olympic games; but the next day it is news that the hostages have been slain. News is morally and ontologically neutral — it is neither true nor false, accurate nor inaccurate. It is a report about an event transmitted usually to a mass audience. This model exists in all political, social and economic systems; it is a theoretically sound model, but it is not a politically acceptable model anywhere.

Government news systems defy classification. In some societies the news media are said to be "free" and "independent," in some, it is said they are "regulated," and in others that they are "controlled." In truth, all news media are "controlled." The difference lies in the identity and nature of the controllers and in the degree of the directness of the control.[5] In Communist states, control is usually open and direct; this does not mean that there is necessarily less state control in non-Communist states. I will return to this question later, but first let us examine attitudes about news in different societies. The most influential analysis of such attitudes is *Four Theories of the Press*, written in 1956 by three of the most distinguished scholars in the field, Fred S. Siebert, Theodore B. Peterson and Wilbur Schramm.[6] The substance of this analysis has been repeated in countless subsequent books, especially in a widely-circulated book published in 1969 by William L. Rivers and Wilbur Schramm, one of the original authors, both then at Stanford University. This book, *Responsibility in Mass Communication*,[7] a heavily used textbook in schools and departments of journalism and communications, changes the word "theory" to "concept," but in general adopts the same line of reasoning about the philosophical underpinnings of journalism. While there has not been, as Chase points out, a philosophy of *news*, much has been written about philosophies of *journalism*.

It is the thesis of *Four Theories* that the earth has witnessed four philosophies of journalism, classified as "authoritarian," "libertarian," "social responsibility" and "Soviet communist." According to the authors of *Four Theories*, the authoritarian approach to communication is derived from the political philosophy of such thinkers as Plato, Machiavelli, Hobbes and Hegel and from the absolutist tradition of the Roman Church. Truth, according to these traditions, is restricted and standardized in order to safeguard thought and action; it is preserved, then, by the mechanisms of the authoritarian state.[8] Thus, in this kind of classification, most nations today –– virtually all except the United States and her allies –– approach the dissemination of news in authoritarian terms: to safeguard thought and action. The libertarian scheme, according to *Four Theories,* is derived from the ideas of the Enlightenment, drawing on Milton and Mill, Paine and Jefferson, and the worth of the individual in conflict with the state. No system today pursues the libertarian scheme, according to *Four Theories*, since its ultimate state would be anarchy.[9]

Four Theories is clear enough in contrasting these two patterns of political philosophy, although it errs in significant aspects of its analysis. On the remaining two "theories," the book is generally deficient, since it falls victim to an unrecognized cultural bias. Soviet Communist "theory" is seen as distinguished from authoritarian theory in that the news media are no longer instruments of the business system, controlled by licensing, censorship and government pressure, but are instruments of government. As *Four Theories* puts it:

> It is obvious that the Soviet media are integrated, planned, used in a way that older authoritarian media almost never were.[10]

Rivers and Schramm add:

> The older media were merely controlled; the Soviet media serve the state just as steel plants and infantry do.[11]

By definition, the "Soviet Communist Theory" is practiced only by the Soviet Union, China and those nations under their control.

By contrast, the "Social Responsibility Theory" is seen as American in origin, growing out of the reform movements of the Progressive and New Deal eras and exemplified in a special report published in 1947 by the Commission on Freedom of the Press, financed largely by a grant from *Time* magazine, under the chairmanship of Robert M. Hutchins, then chancellor of the University of Chicago, and including 12 outstanding American scholars in law, history, economics, political science and religion.[12] The Commission speaks of "social accountability" and "social responsibility;"[13] its report codifies much of the political philosophy of the 20th-Century American reformers, and urges the American press to reform itself from the excesses of "scoops and sensations" or face government intervention that would limit its freedom. In the view of the authors of *Four Theories*, clearly the goals set forth for the press in the Commission's report [14] are those which should be adopted by the news media in all parts of the planet. It escapes the authors that they are urging an "American" solution in opposition to a "Soviet" solution. It does not occur to them that a Soviet commission would likely also preach the virtues of social accountability and responsibility and reject the American scheme as authoritarian or repressive under the heel of American commerce and industry.

Four Theories asserts, for instance:

> The two systems line up almost diametrically opposite in their basic tenets, although both use words like freedom and responsibility to describe what they are doing. Our press tries to contribute to the search for truth; the Soviet press tries to convey pre-established Marxist—Leninist—Stalinist truth . . . . We bend over backward to make sure that information and ideas will compete. They bend over backward to make sure that only the line decided upon will flow through the Soviet channels.[15]

One challenge to the *Four Theories* thesis has been set forth by John C. Merrill, who maintains that the only way to guarantee the American press will be socially responsible is to empower the government to insure responsibility, a development that would put the press under direct government control.[16] Merrill argues for a pluralistic press, open to an unlimited number of conflicting ideas, but Rivers and Schramm maintain the social responsibility concept guarantees widespread access of minority opinion without government intervention.[17] There is an aura of quibbling about the issue; I shall return to the access question later.

The Question of Truth

If news is accepted as politically neutral, in accordance with the model suggested earlier, then all philosophical definitions are overlaid with value judgments and propaganda, overt or covert. After all, what is "truth" in Washington may be a "lie" in Moscow or Delhi or

Accra, and, of course, vice versa. It can be stated as an axiom that in all societies, the function of the news media is seen as reporting and disseminating the "truth." The conflict really lies in the question of "truth" and not of "news." Milton's self–righting principle has never been vetoed; Mr. Justice Holmes continues to be widely quoted about the ultimate triumph of truth in the free marketplace of ideas. Yet, modern libertarians have grown more skeptical and one hears more and more about the decline of credibility of the press, even in the United States.[18] Western writers continue to view the American press as the freest on earth, yet authorities in the Soviet Union and in much of the poorer, less industrialized world regard the American press as a tool of the great commercial forces. Indeed, Williams, Schiller and other westerners make the same argument.[19]

From the earliest days, American journalists have perceived themselves to be seekers after truth. On the other hand, Walter Lippmann has drawn the sharpest of distinctions between what appears in the newspapers and truth. "News and truth," he writes, "are not the same thing and must be clearly distinguished."[20] Students of psychology and sociology have pointed out, moreover, that journalists are citizens before they are reporters: their socialization as patriots predates their exposure to the process of gathering and disseminating news.[21] In times of war, for example, as has frequently been pointed out, truth is the first casualty.[22]

Governments at war or in crisis of course engage in elaborate efforts to justify their own actions; in the world of nation-states, reporter–patriots are not likely to publish reports which would, as the saying goes, "give aid and comfort to the enemy." Even in the dramatic challenge to authority in the publication by the *New York Times* of the Pentagon Papers, the *Times* distinguished between "news" it considered historical and reports that might do violence to national security.[23] Historically, reporters of wars have been seen by the enemy, and even by neutrals, as participants; after all, reporters in war zones have usually been placed in uniform and made reliant on military vehicles for transportation.[24]

In the United States and Western Europe, the structure of the press —— newspapers, magazines and broadcasting outlets —— is, as we have seen, pictured as rooted in libertarian philosophy, relatively free of direct government control, and committed to a program of social accountability or responsibility. But many authorities recognize that indirect controls circumscribe the press of these nations, forging a mold that conforms with the values of that society, economic, social and religious.[25] It is unthinkable to imagine a successful American newspaper espousing atheism or communism or homosexuality or even pornography. Such publications are driven underground and denied the profits or prestige of orthodox outlets. In Great Britain, the limits of ideological autonomy for the British Broadcasting Corporation has been explained by the BBC's Director General in examining its origin.[26]

> They [politicians] could see that there would be nothing but trouble if broadcasting became a party football, if it fell into the hands of unscrupulous men or groups of men of extreme views. So they settled for a compromise. Broadcasting would be subject to the ultimate control of the state, to which it owed its constitution, but it would be free from detailed control and supervision.

Capitalist societies are by no means monolithic, and conformity is a matter of degree; nonetheless, the principle is universal in capitalist societies: a free and independent press is celebrated but not practiced. One writer has characterized the American press as "aimed at protecting the physical operations of U.S. enterprises abroad as well as in fostering values and attitudes of privatism and consumerism."[27] In this writer's view, the American overseas business community manipulates not only the U.S. press in its own interests, but "enlists or subverts the mass media of the many national states in which it operates."[28]

In Communist societies, the press is not seen as free and uncontrolled. Indeed, Lenin asserted that the slogan, "freedom of the press," was designed "to deceive, corrupt and fool the exploited and oppressed masses of the people."[29] In Lenin's view, a free press was one operated under a state monopoly; it was the state which under the doctrine of democratic centralism would permit free expression until a policy was determined. Once the policy was determined, the press would serve as a conduit to win popular support. In Soviet doctrine, the journalist is seen as a political activist. "It would be bourgeois of him," Hopkins has written, "to think that he could stand aside and observe social developments."[30]

It is a barren exercise to dwell on the excesses of totalitarian control under Stalin, just as it would be fruitless to discuss the American theory in terms of the repression of the Sedition Act of 1798 or the Espionage Act of 1918. Under Stalin's successors, Soviet journalists have been given greater latitude.

Unquestionably, the degree of pluralism permitted in capitalist societies far outweighs what is allowed in Communist nations. How large a voice capitalist societies permit dissident groups is a topic which has recently attracted much attention. One scholar has argued that minority groups must be empowered by law to have access to the news media in order to make their voices heard.[31] So far, Barron and others endorsing his views have won little favor either from media owners or from the Congress or the courts.[32]

in certain respects, journalists in capitalist and Communist nations are more similar than dissimilar. In both societies, journalists are educated and mildly affluent; in their social and economic status, they tend to identify with the accepted values and standards of government leaders. In other words, their middle—class socialization makes them unconscious distributors of majoritarian goals, however they may criticize individual political leaders.[33]

Journalists in underdeveloped lands are also educated and affluent. Indeed, since there is a wider distance between the rich and the poor and only the rudest beginnings of a middle class, journalists in the underdeveloped world tend to be part of the ruling elite. In those countries, the function of the news media is seen primarily in terms of integration, and the ministries of information, especially in Africa, have used the news media as instruments to assist programs of national integration.[34] In Latin America and Asia, where industrialization and integration generally are more advanced than in Africa, the press often comes under the direct control of the ruling elite. In those countries, it is often difficult to detect a difference between the government and the commercial elite.[35] I will return to this topic later.

In all parts of the world, there seems to be a noticeable distinction between "news" generated for external or internal consumption. Governments, in their attempts to influence opinion, clearly are more interested in winning popular support at home than abroad. Many nations operate information agencies or other agencies, some frankly identifying them as ministries of propaganda, others relying on the euphemism, "public information offices." When governments speak on the record to other governments, it is through official channels. But when governments wish to speak to the public of other countries or to officials indirectly, they rely on unofficial channels. News media are viewed by governments as the most useful and acceptable of these unofficial channels. To read something in a newspaper, however, one may suspect the paper, is more assuring than to read it in a press release or a government brochure. One may question the disinterestedness of the newspaper; one will simply accept the press release as self—serving. Thus, it is clearly in the interest of a government to cloak its self—serving messages by arranging for those messages to be distributed by an "independent" press, newspaper or broadcasting outlet.[36] Awareness of the "two-step" or "multi-step" flow technique has enabled governments and sociopolitical influentials to improve persuasive techniques.

It is often said that the government and the news media are adversaries, and in truth some journalists do perceive themselves to be the watchdog of their governments, but in fact, in most instances governments and journalists are allies in the dissemination of information.[37] Euphemisms abound, and it is extraordinarily difficult to determine what is information, what is education, what is propaganda, what is news.

Global Patterns

The volume of news outlets around the world has been increasing steadily; the increase in the number of radio and television outlets is especially noticeable in the underdeveloped countries. The literacy rate is growing in all countries, and it is to be anticipated that by the end of the 20th Century, the illiteracy rate in Africa and Asia will have been substantially improved, making the communication of news a salient factor in the lives of most inhabitants of the planet. Such is not the case today.

UNESCO has set a minimum standard of "adequate communications." In 1961, it proposed the immediate target of at least 10 copies of daily newspapers for each 100 inhabitants. It also proposed the additional target of five radio receivers and two television receivers for each 100 inhabitants.[38] Clearly, much of the world is nowhere near the level of adequate communications as set forth by UNESCO. It has been estimated that to reach the standard of 10 copies of daily newspapers for each 100 persons, it would take Asia until 1992 and Africa until 2035.[39]

Obviously, then, despite the gains in the number of mass media outlets in the underdeveloped countries, the industrialized countries of North America and Europe continue to monopolize the field. For example, in 1974, the total consumption of newsprint in the world amounted to 23,200,000 metric tons; of that total, nearly half —— 11,300,000 metric tons —— was consumed in North America, mainly the United States and Canada; and consumption in Europe, exclusive of the Soviet Union, was 6,100,000 metric tons. Of the total world consumption, North America and Europe accounted for 75 percent; despite increasing literacy in other parts of the world, the share of newsprint consumption in the western world was increasing. Fifteen years earlier, in 1959, North America and Europe accounted for 72 percent of the total world consumption.[40]

Newsprint production does not necessarily reflect the impact of a government on its own citizens. As a matter of fact, there is greater diversity among the newspapers of the industrialized countries, meaning a greater opportunity for an opposing voice to be heard; the smaller the number of newspapers, the greater the opportunity for information control internally. The less industrialized lands have fewer opportunities to control readers abroad because of the presence in their countries of large numbers of correspondents from news media in the industralized world, a heavy percentage of those being representatives of the vast American, British and French news agencies, The Associated Press, United Press International, Reuters and Agence France Presse. In recent years, the less industrialized countries have engaged in sharp criticism of these news agencies and indeed have sought to limit their activities severely.[41] I will return to this subject later.

As for internal controls, many are available, not only in Asia and Africa but indeed in North America and Europe as well. In the most extreme cases, journalists who speak opposition thoughts may be imprisoned or killed. Such extremes are rarely required, even for the most ruthless of regimes. Economic pressure is a gentler method, and it is usually effective. Moreover, most journalists in underdeveloped countries are sympathetic to the objectives of the leadership, even where they may question the methods. As already pointed out, journalists are well educated and affluent; their value system is likely to be closer to that of the rulers than to that of the illiterate masses.[42]

Daily newspapers are less available in Africa, southern Asia, and Latin America than in other parts of the world, as the following table illustrates.[43]

Daily Newspapers[44]

	No. of Papers		Est. Circulation (in millions)		Circulation per 1,000 inhab.	
	1959	1974	1959	1974	1959	1974
Africa	220	232	2.9	4.4	12	12
North America	1,865	1,916	63	68	321	292
Latin America	1,065	1,206	14	22	69	70
East Asia*	280	335	40.1	65.9	282	386
Southern Asia**	1,300	1,842	10	18.2	12	15
Europe	2,020	1,812	106	117	252	248
Oceania	100	109	5	6.3	311	306
USSR	500	658	34	93.2	162	373
Total	7,350	8,110	275	395	122	129

*Includes Japan, which with 180 papers and 58 million circulation in 1974 accounts for the overwhelming bulk of the papers and circulation in East Asia. The Peoples' Republic of China, Korea and Vietnam are not included.
**Includes India, which with 822 papers and 9 million circulation in 1974 accounts for the overwhelming volume of papers and circulation in Southern Asia.

The UNESCO tabulation included 160 countries. UNESCO reported also that in 39 countries and territories, there was no daily general interest newspaper at all. There is no reliable information on how many of the newspapers can be considered "free" and "independent" in any meaningful use of those words. Again, it is to be stressed that where controls are not directly political, where there is no overt censorship, controls are exercised by economic and indirect means. All governments seek to manipulate the information published about them. The most reliable indicator of what governments *wish* to have reported about their activities comes, of course, through official press releases. These are invariably circulated by official government news agencies, the number of which has increased markedly in recent years, [45] and by radio and television outlets. Of course, government messages may be misleading; for instance, in our example involving Vance's press conference, Vance may have been pleased but may have wished to convey a message of displeasure.

Lack of resources, both in terms of machinery and in distribution channels, makes rapid growth in the number of newspapers especially difficult; in addition, illiteracy makes consumption of newspapers difficult. In this situation, radio presents a more promising outlet both for information and propaganda in the underdeveloped countries. For example, a 1960 study of four West African capitals showed that radio was the primary source of information about world affairs.[46] Radio listening, as with newspaper reading, tends to be a largely urban phenomenon. A 1966 survey showed that 60 to 65 percent of the population in West African capitals listened to the radio regularly, but that within 30 miles of the capital, the audience shrank to 15 percent of the population.[47] Language barriers are a depressing factor; there is complication enough in Africa, where tribal languages interfere with national radio or television programming. But in India, where the problem is most complex, 14 states have different official languages and 72 different languages are spoken by more than 100,000 persons.[48] National government efforts at integration are difficult, but radio does present the most efficient method available. Radio also helps distribute messages from abroad, and is an integral target of propagandists. UNESCO's breakdown of radio reception indicates a pattern similar to the pattern of newspaper consumption.[49]

Radio

	Total receivers (in millions)		Receivers per 1,000 inhabitants	
	1959	1974	1959	1974
Africa	4.2	28	18	72
North America	177	422	903	1,796
Latin America	18	65	89	206
East Asia	16	77	113	214
Southern Asia	7.5	52	9	43
Europe	91	156	216	332
Oceania	3	6	186	287
USSR	40.8	116	194	460
Total	357.5	922	159	301

The number of radio and television receivers among the have–not countries has been increasing rapidly, but even so the gap between the haves and the have–nots is substantial, especially so in the field of television: [50]

Television

	Total receivers (in millions)		Receivers per 1,000 inhabitants	
	1959	1974	1959	1974
Africa	0.04	2.7	0.2	8
North America	56.2	129.2	287	539
Latin America	2.7	24	13	81
East Asia	3.5	28.8	25	168
Southern Asia	0.1	6.9	0.1	5.4
Europe	20.3	109	48	231
Oceania	0.7	3.9	43	228
USSR	3.6	53	17	208
Total	87.14	357.5	39	131

Propaganda

Any discussion of the use by governments of the mass media must assume the primary objective of the government is one of propaganda. As Ben Bagdikian has written, "Authorities will always attempt to control information for the public good as they see it."[51] The use of information channels for propaganda is as old as the history of governments. Genghis Khan dispatched agents in advance of his armies to plant exaggerated accounts of the power of his Mongol forces.[52] With the appearance of the mass press, including broadcasting as well as print journals, governments have tended to use the media to advance national policies in three ways: (a) to insert their own material, (b) to found new media, either as overt instruments or to masquerade them as independent spokesmen and (c) to exercise censorship, either directly or under cover.[53] Much of the research into the function of propaganda in international affairs has dealt with periods of warfare or crisis. In his groundbreaking study of propaganda in wartime in 1927, Harold D. Lasswell found four principal strategic aims of propaganda in World War I: (a) to mobilize hatred against the enemy, (b) to preserve the friendship of allies, (c) to preserve the friendship and, if possible, to procure the cooperation of neutrals, and (d) to demoralize the enemy.[54] In modern times, however, propaganda has been used less for military objectives than in what can best be identified as "public relations" campaigns designed to improve the image of the nation. Journalists, especially those in the industrialized west, where competition is heavy, are susceptible to manipulation by "news management," or covert control of the flow of information through selected "leaks" and "background briefings."[55] Pressures for interpretative reporting, that is explaining what information "really means," make journalists attractive targets for the news managers,[56] who seek to carry out what one analyst of propaganda has called "the controlled dissemination of deliberately distorted notions in an effort to induce action favorable to predetermined ends of special interest groups."[57] This writer, like many others, goes on to find "something sinister" in propaganda,[58] but it is difficult to imagine any modern society, no matter how deeply devoted to ethical principles, failing to seek to manipulate public opinion on behalf of its own survival or even in support of its own version of "truth."

Inside the United States, no less than 555 agencies were registered at the beginning of 1976 as engaged in distributing propaganda on behalf of foreign principals. Most of these activities are designed to promote tourism, investment or trade.[59] Each of these agencies publishes press releases, conducts press conferences and in general attempts to manipulate the U.S. media to publicize the beneficence of the nations they represent. It is to be noted that in addition to these 555 agencies, governments in their own capitals and their embassies and consulates around the world conduct propaganda activities, usually with journalists as targets. Moreover, these nations make use of short–wave radio facilities for direct propaganda efforts, often concealing these efforts under the rubric of news broadcasts. Radio Moscow and the BBC External Services come to mind immediately, along with overt U.S. enterprises such as the Voice of America and covert activities such as Radio Free Europe. The recent development of international communication through satellites has expanded immensely the horizons of global propaganda through news channels.[60] Most governments maintain ministries of information, which are in fact propaganda agencies, although they of course publish statistical and factual information.

Governments regularly seek to use domestic journalists and manipulate foreign journalists for the purpose of communicating with other governments. For example, in Egypt, Gamal Abdel Nasser and his successor, Anwar Sadat, frequently spoke through Muhammed Hassanein Heikal, editor in chief of the largest Cairo daily, *Al Ahram*. Heikal was once described as the "anointed prophet of Nasserism" and the "grey eminence" of Sadat.[61]

Appearances are important; insofar as Heikal's function was well–known in diplomatic circles, his effectiveness was diminished. Government propaganda is more valuable if it is concealed, if it is circulated through foreign rather than domestic journalists. In London, Prime Ministers have long cultivated correspondents of the *New York Times*, recognizing that newspaper's influence in Washington. Cocktails and dinner at No. 10 Downing Street is a small price to pay for an undercover propaganda campaign. Bagdikian has put it this way:

> There are growing numbers of men who understand how
> news is generated, organized, and transmitted, and it would be

unintelligent of them if they did not use it to their own advantage.[62]

Davison predicts that an increasing volume of national resources will go into propaganda, and suggests that one of the major tasks for scholars is "to suggest ways that it [propaganda] may be more fruitfully employed in the service of international harmony in a shrinking world."[63]

In much of the world, newspapers and magazines are privately owned and operated. As already pointed out, private ownership does not free a news operation from government control or direction. The socialized journalist is usually an unwitting agent of the economic and political influentials of a nation. Even that mouthpiece for journalistic independence, the Hutchins Commission, listed as one of its five major goals for the American press "the presentation and classification of the goals and values of the society."[64] Goals and values held by dissenters and minorities, which are not part of the belief system of majoritarian journalists, are not likely to receive much attention under that banner.

Nevertheless, it is more difficult for governments to use "free" and "independent" daily newspapers for their own purposes than it is to use the broadcast media, which for the most part are under the direct control of governments. Only in North and South America has there developed a pattern of private ownership of broadcast media, but even in those countries the broadcasting outlets are invariably regulated by the government. Where outlets are regulated rather than controlled, subtlety is required for government intervention; under conditions of government control, no subtlety is necessary. In the United States, where private control is clearly the pattern, the rule set forth by the regulating body, the Federal Communications Commission, is one of fairness, in which opposing points of view must be given expression. Under such a rule, an opposition point of view may not be voiced without the balancing official dogma. In other countries, the pattern of government control is even greater. In all of Africa, and in most of Europe, Asia and Oceania, the government is in direct control of broadcasting outlets. In Europe, which is usually viewed as Libertarian, only three countries are reported as authorizing private control of broadcasting: Gibraltar, Luxembourg and Portugal, and one wonders whether anti—government opinions would find favor on Yugoslav stations. In two European countries, Britain and Switzerland, some broadcasting outlets are government controlled and some are private.[65] All government outlets which operate in foreign countries are government controlled and are for the most part unashamed propaganda outlets.

No accurate accounting of the extent of "freedom" of newspapers can be made; much government control is subtle and concealed under a series of official euphemisms. A survey of the world press in 1970 reports:

> Throughout the world — — regardless of what press theory a country might accept — — the right *to punish and to read the truth* is either denied or under constant attack. Limitations imposed on such rights are often undisguised, but they can be quite subtle.[66]

One attempt at classifying the world press in terms of freedom was undertaken in 1966 by the Freedom of Information Center at the University of Missouri. Using a 23-point factor scale, the study found 16 countries with a "high degree" of freedom, including some surprising ones, such as Guatemala, Peru and the Philippines. Predictably, in an American survey, the nations where a "high degree" of control was found contained mostly Communist nations. Of the 14 on that list, only four were not part of the Soviet sphere, Algeria, Chad, Ethiopia and Upper Volta.[67]

It is difficult to assess the effectiveness of the messages distributed by governments through the news media.[68] Indeed, it is sometimes argued that the masses of people pay little attention to public questions except those that are most dramatic, such as war or revolutionary crisis. One authority has called attention to the mounting evidence that political apathy and ignorance are "widespread among the population of all countries and may well be endemic in all societies larger than a city—state." [69] This factor does not result from moral deficiencies, he adds, but because the public affairs messages the public receive "are relatively remote and intangible."[70] Nevertheless, the dramatic messages, those of war and crisis, are of major concern.

Research: The Future

In the past 30 years, research has expanded rapidly in the field of international communications, including the role played in intergovernmental and interpersonal messages by the mass media. Some progress has been made in understanding, but not much. As pointed out earlier, there is still no clear picture of what constitutes news, and there are many ideological and socialization barriers to agreement on the quality of truth. UNESCO has been seeking since it launched its inquiries into the media in 1951 to develop greater understanding of the flow of information between and among nations, but despite the mounting stacks of reports and monographs, the barriers remain.

No issue has generated more heat at the UNESCO conferences of the 1970s than that of press freedom and the role of the press in the transmission of information between governments and the peoples of the world. While the sentiment has been universal that it is immoral for governments to use the media for propaganda purposes, there has been no agreement whatever on even the simplest of concepts.

In 1970, at the 16th General Conference of UNESCO in Paris, the delegates affirmed "the inadmissibility of using information media for propaganda on behalf of war, racialism and hatred among nations."[71] Some speakers urged UNESCO to set up a code of conduct whereby the media would be encouraged to promote accord among nations rather than discord.[72] No such resolution was passed, but UNESCO did create a panel of consultants which a year later proposed a massive research program on national, multinational and international levels. The program called for a systems approach in which analysis is made of "control, ownership, support, resources, production presentation, content, availability, exposure, consumption, use, influence and overall consequences" of the media. Of special importance was the call for "a cross–cultural comparative approach to the many relevant problem areas with . . . the general theme, 'The mass media and man's view of society.' "[73]

The proposal for new cross–cultural research was renewed at the 17th General Conference in 1972. At the same time, the delegates approved a resolution to develop a draft declaration of fundamental principles in using mass media to strengthen peace and to eliminate hate propaganda. A report was circulated indicating nine countries had in the past two years taken "positive measure" toward using the media against hate propaganda.[74] Among the countries cited for taking such measures were Argentina, Romania, the Ukraine and Syria. The disinterested analyst is likely to express some degree of skepticism about the execution of measures such as the draft statute in Syria designed to encourage the use of the media "against propaganda on behalf of war and hatred among nations."

It was at the 18th General Conference in 1974 that the most bitter dispute over press issues occurred. The central point at issue was "obstacles to the free flow of information." As has been pointed out earlier, all news media are controlled to some extent, and some delegates, primarily from Communist and underdeveloped countries, argued that the only way in which "unbiased and objective reporting" could be guaranteed was under clearly defined codes created by governments. The western countries, on the other hand, maintained that "free flow" could be achieved only if governments imposed no restraints. Some delegates argued that the main obstacles were not governments at all but lack of basic materials such as paper.[75] Finally, many delegates from Africa and Asia saw the free flow of information impeded by an imbalance of communications, since the industrialized lands, primarily the United States, could send many correspondents abroad whereas the underdeveloped nations did not have similar resources.

There then began a movement to attempt to create a new international news agency or "pool" backed by UNESCO to challenge the power of the Associated Press and United Press International. At a series of meetings over the next two years, support grew for this proposal as its backers demanded a redress of what they perceived to be an imbalance in the global flow of information. Nonaligned nations gave unanimous backing to the plan at a conference in Colombo in August, 1976, and the 19th UNESCO General Conference at Nairobi, Kenya, adopted a resolution aimed at ultimately establishing an international "news pool." The western countries went along reluctantly with the proposal advanced by Tunisia on behalf of the nonaligned countries. Clearly neither the United States nor her allies saw merit in a "more balanced and diversified exchange of news," especially after the Tunisian delegate had argued that international news agencies (meaning of course the

AP and UPI) gave a distorted picture of the Third World, concentrating on "negative aspects" of the poorer countries.[76]

Support in the west for the Tunisian resolution resulted from two factors: a desire to avoid the anger and bitterness that had characterized the Paris conference of 1974 and an effort to prevent endorsement of a stronger assault on the western stand on "free flow" prepared by the Soviet Union. The Russian draft resolution would not merely have condemned the western news agencies for presenting distorted pictures of the Third World but would have held their governments responsible. "States are responsible," the draft resolution declared, "for the activities in the international sphere of all mass media under their jurisdiction." Delegates from the United States and Western Europe managed to buy time by inducing the Conference not to vote on the Russian resolution but instead to create another commission to study the draft and report back with recommendations as to its passage.[77] A Russian delegate denounced the western powers for "blocking the will of the majority," but nevertheless did not insist on a formal vote on its proposal at the 1976 conference.[78]

It is evident from the behavior of the UNESCO delegates that all recognize that the news media play a prominent role in dialogues between governments. Each country pronounces itself in whole—hearted support of such concepts as "press freedom" and "free flow of information" through the media, yet the various power blocs mean different things by those terms, and in fact even countries within the same power blocs are not always consistent in their definitions or behaviors. Yet, despite frequently acrimonious rhetoric and the perpetual problems of nationalism and xenophobia, UNESCO delegates seem ready at each conference to support empirical cross—cultural studies.[79] The expense of such research into narrower, discrete areas is immense: the cost of the kind of global systems research proposed by UNESCO consultants is incalculable. The consultants stress "the urgent need" of such coordinated research. Who can deny the urgency?

One commentator, more modest in his aspirations but no less intense in his appeal for additional research, urges a serious study of the interaction between political systems and the media in varying societies. In his view —— and who can challenge him —— "research on the part the media play in politics has hardly begun." [80]

FOOTNOTES

[1] Bernard C. Cohen, *The Press and Foreign Policy* (Princeton, N.J.: Princeton University Press, 1963), pp. 28-30. See also Gabriel A. Almond and James S. Coleman, eds., *The Politics of the Developing Areas* (Princeton, N.J.: Princeton University Press, 1960) for an examination of the importance of news communications in underdeveloped areas, especially pp. 45-52.

[2] The question of the role of image in political decision—making has been examined frequently in the literature of political science, sociology, journalism and mass communications. For an especially interesting treatment of the topic, see Harold R. Issacs, *Scratches On Our Minds: American Images of China and India* (New York: John Day, 1958). See also Cohen, *op. cit.*; and Daniel J. Boorstin, *The Image: A Guide to Pseudo—Events in America* (New York: Harper and Row, 1964). For an examination of Dulles' views on miscalculation, see James Shepley, "How Dulles Avoided War," *Life*, vol. 40, January 16, 1956, pp. 70-72; 77-80.

[3] "The Aphilosophy of Journalism," *Quill*, vol. 59, no. 9, September, 1971, pp. 15-17. In the passage above, Chase is quoting, respectively, Turner Catledge of the *New York Times* (on a television program), and Julian Harriss and Stanley Johnson, *The Complete Reporter*, 2nd ed. (New York: Macmillan, 1965). Many other books, including Cohen, *op. cit.*, attempt to define news, but end up in the usual tautologies. For a summary of surveys and studies on the topic, see Bruce H. Westley, *News Editing,* 2nd ed. (Boston: Houghton Mifflin, 1972), pp. 314-326.

[4] J. Herbert Altschull, "What is News?", *Mass Comm Review*, December, 1974.

[5] Haluk Sahin, *Broadcasting Autonomy in Turkey 1961-1971,* unpublished dissertation, Indiana University, 1974. See especially discussion of "Ideological Autonomy," pp. 63-73.

[6] Urbana: University of Illinois Press, 1956.

[7] Revised edition, (New York: Harper and Row, 1969).

[8] *Four Theories,* p. 11.

[9] *Ibid.*, pp. 61-62.

[10] *Ibid.*, p. 141.

[11] Rivers and Schramm, *op. cit.,* p. 45.

[12] The Commission on Freedom of the Press, *A Free   and Responsible Press* (Chicago, 1947).   In addition to Hutchins, the

Commission included Zechariah Chafee, Jr., professor of law, Harvard; John M. Clark, economics, Columbia; John Dickinson, law, Pennsylvania; William E. Hocking, philosophy, Harvard; Harold D. Lasswell, law, Yale; Archibald MacLeish, former assistant secretary state; Charles E. Merriam, political science, Chicago; Reinhold Neibuhr, ethics and philosophy of religion, Union Theological Seminary; Robert Redfield, anthropology, Chicago; Beardsley Ruml, chairman, Federal Research Bank of New York; Arthur M. Schlesinger, Jr., history, Harvard; George N. Shuster, president, Hunter College.

[13] *Ibid.*, p. 126. For an interesting summary of the arguments of the Hutchins Commission and the history of press reaction, see Margaret A. Blanchard, "The Hutchins Commission, The Press and the Responsibility Concept," *Journalism Monographs,* no. 49, May, 1977.

[14] These are five in number: "a truthful, comprehensive, and intelligent account of the day's events in a context which gives them meaning" . . . . "a forum for the exchange of comment and criticism" . . . . "the projection of a representative picture of the constituent groups in the society" . . . . "the presentation and classification of the goals and values of the society" . . . . "full access to the day's intelligence," pp. 21-28.

[15] *Four Theories*, pp. 5-6.

[16] "The Press and Social Responsibility," Freedom of Information Center Publication No. 001 (Columbia, Mo.: School of Journalism, University of Missouri, 1965), p. 2. For a fuller discussion, see Merrill, *The Imperative of Freedom: A Philosophy of Journalistic Autonomy* (New York: Hastings House, 1974). Despite Merrill's criticism, he nonetheless seems to accept the *Four Theories* system of classification. See Merrill, Carter R. Bryan and Marvin Alisky, *The Foreign Press: A Survey of the World's Journalism* (Baton Rouge, La.: Louisiana State University, Press, 1970), pp. 20-23. For a variant classification system, see Raymond Williams, *Communications,* rev. ed. (London: Chato and Windus, 1969).

[17] Rivers and Schramm, *op. cit.*, pp. 56-57.

[18] See, for example, Norman E. Issacs, "The Credibility Gap and the Ombudsman," *ASNE Bulletin*, February, 1969, reprinted in

Michael C. Emergy and Ted C. Smythe, *Readings in Mass Communications* (Dubuque, Iowa: William C. Brown, 1972), pp. 77-83. The literature on press credibility is substantial.

[19] Williams, *op. cit.* Herbert L. Schiller, *Mass Communications and American Empire* (Boston: Beacon Press, 1971).

[20] *Public Opinion* (New York: Macmillan, 1922), p. 358.

[21] For a study of the self-perception of journalists engaged in reporting foreign affairs, see Cohen, *op. cit.* For an up-to-date examination of the self-perception of journalists in general, see John W.C. Johnstone, Edward J. Slawski and William W. Bowman, *The News People: A Sociological Portrait of American Journalists and Their Work* (Urbana, Ill.: University of Illinois Press, 1976). For a study of the process of political socialization, see Robert Weissberg, *Political Learning, Political Choice, and Democratic Citizenship* (Englewood Cliffs, N.J.: Prentice-Hall, 1974).

[22] Arthur Ponsonby, *Falsehood in War-time* (New York: E.P. Dutton, 1928), p. i. For a thorough examination of war correspondents, see Phillip Knightley, *The First Casualty: From the Crimea to Vietnam: The War Correspondent as Hero, Propagandist, and Myth Maker* (New York: Harcourt Brace Jovanovich, 1975).

[23] Editorial, the *New York Times*, June 16, 1971. See also Sanford J. Ungar, *The Papers and the Papers: An Account of the Legal and Political Battle over the Pentagon Papers* (New York: E.P. Dutton, 1972), p. 95.

[24] Knightley, *op. cit.* See also Joseph Gouden, *Truth is the First Casualty: The Gulf of Tonkin Affair, Illusion and Reality* (Chicago: Rand McNally, 1969), or Dale Minor, *The Information War: How the Government and the Press Manipulate, Censor, and Distort the News* (New York: Hawthorn, 1970). See also Joseph J. Mathews, *Reporting the Wars* (Minneapolis: University of Minnesota Press, 1957), p. 249: "The coming of total warfare made the matter of degree in his [the reporter's] assimilation by the military the focal question of his continued existence."

[25] Ben Bagdikian, *The Information Machines: Their Impact on Men and the Media* (New York: Harper and Row, 1971), pp. 1-27.

[26] Charles Curran, "The First Fifty Years," in *BBC Handbook 1973* (London: British Broadcasting Corporation, 1972), p. 10.

[27] Herbert I. Schiller, "Madison Avenue Imperialism," *Trans—Action*, vol. 8, nos. 5-6, March/April, 1971, p. 58.

[28] *Ibid.*, p. 53.

[29] Mark W. Hopkins, "Lenin, Stalin, Khrushchev: Three Concepts of the Press," *Journalism Quarterly* vol. 42, no. 4, Autumn, 1965, p. 4, quoting from *Lenin o Pechati* (Moscow, 1959), pp. 578-80.

[30] *Ibid.* p. 528.

[31] Jerome A. Barron, *Freedom of the Press for Whom?: The Right of Access to Mass Media* (Bloomington: Indiana University Press, 1973).

[32] See, for example, *Tornillo v. The Miami Herald*, 94 S.Ct. 2831, (1974) in which the Supreme Court rejected Barron's argument that newspapers must grant those under attack in print access to the pages of the newspaper for the right to reply.

[33] See Johnstone, Bowman and Slawski, *op. cit.*

[34] William A. Hachten, *Muffled Drums: The News Media in Africa* (Ames, Iowa: Iowa State University Press, 1971), p. 39.

[35] UNESCO, *World Communications: Press, Radio, Television, Film* (New York: UNESCO Publications Center, 1964), pp. 177-261.

[36] Everett M. Rogers (with F. Floyd Shoemaker), *Communication of Innovations: A Cross-Cultural Approach*, 2nd ed. (New York: Free Press, 1971); see, especially, Part 6, "Opinion Leadership and the Multi-Step Flow of Ideas," pp. 198-225. For the landmark work on two-step flow, see Elihu Katz and Paul F. Lazarsfeld, *Personal Influence: The Part Played by People in the Flow of Mass Communications* (New York: Free Press, 1955).

[37] See, for example, William L. Rivers, *The Adversaries: Politics and the Press* (Boston: Beacon Press, 1970). The literature on the theme is extensive.

[38] UNESCO, "Mass Media in the Developing Countries," *Reports and Papers on Mass Communication*, no. 33, 1961.

[39] Wilbur Schramm, "World Distribution of the Mass Media," in Heinz—Dietrich Fischer and John C. Merrill, eds., *International Communication: Media, Channels, Functions* (New York: Hastings, 1970), p. 157.

[40] UNESCO, *Statistical Yearbook*, 1975, pp. 677-685.

[41] No up-to-date statistical information is available on the extent of news agencies, but an interesting review, most of which remains applicable, can be found in *New Agencies: Their Structure and Operation* (UNESCO, 1953).

[42] See, for example, the statement by Manoel F. do Nascimento Brito, president of the Inter American Press Association, applauding the popularity of the government of Brazil with the people even though it was run by nonelected military men. Brito criticized "elected governments which permit certain elements to dissipate national unity and to stifle economic growth," *The Daily SIP*, vol. 1, no. 4, October 25, 1972, published during the 25th IAPA meeting in New York City. Other speakers were more hostile to their governments. German E. Ornes, editor of *El Caribe*, Santo Domingo, condemned military manager "technocrats" who, he said, stifle popular participation and "are likely to prize national power rather than the liberation of men." (*Ibid.*)

[43] UNESCO, *Statistical Yearbook, 1975*, pp. 631-639.

[44] UNESCO counts as a daily general interest newspaper one published at least four times a week and "designed to be a primary source of written information on current events connected with public affairs, international questions, politics, etc." Not all countries apply the same circulation standards, but UNESCO attempts to identify circulation as the daily average of all papers sold and all free copies distributed at home and abroad.

[45] UNESCO, *World Communications* 1964, estimates 116 news agencies in operation, including religious and other specialized groups, pp. 373-77. Most of these agencies are subject to some form of government control.

[46] United States Information Agency, "Basic Attitudes and General Communication Habits in Four West African Capitals," PMS Report No. 51, July, 1961.

[47] United States Information Agency, "Mass Media Habits in Africa," R64-66, March, 1966.

[48] Schramm, *op. cit.*, p. 155.

[49] UNESCO, *Statistical Yearbook, 1975,* pp. 699-721.

[50] *Ibid.* pp. 723-737.

[51] Bagdikian, *op. cit.*, p. 2.

[52] W. Phillips Davison, "Some Trends in International Propaganda," in *The Annuals of the American Academy of Political and Social Science* (special ed. on "Propaganda in International Affairs"), ed. L. John Martin (Philadelphia: 1971), p. 2.

[53] *Ibid.*

[54] *Propaganda Technique in the World War* (New York: Alfred A. Knopf, 1927), p. 195.

[55] The literature on news management is extensive. Among others, see Minor, *op. cit.* An outstanding analysis of propaganda, including an extensive literature review, can be found in Paul Kecskemeti, "Propaganda," in Ithiel de Sola Pool and Wilbur Schramm, eds., *Handbook of Communication*, (Chicago: Rand McNally, 1973). See also J.A.C. Brown, *Techniques of Persuasion: From Propaganda to Brainwashing* (Baltimore, Md.: Penguin Books, 1963).

[56] William O. Chittick, *State Department, Press, and Pressure Groups: A Role Analysis* (New York: Wiley, 1970).

[57] Michael Choukas, *Propaganda Comes of Age* (Washington: Public Affairs Press, 1965), p. 37.

[58] *Ibid.*, p. 280.

[59] *Report of the Attorney General to the Congress of the United States on the Administration of the Foreign Registration Act, 1938, as Amended, for the Calendar Year 1975* (Washington : Government Printing Office, 1976), mimeo.

[60] For an overview of satellite developments, see Brenda Maddox, *Beyond Babel: New Directions in Communications* (London: Andre Deutsch, 1972), especially Chapter 5, "Lament for Intelsat," pp. 82-114. See also Colin Cherry, *World Communication: Threat or Promise? A Socio–Technical Approach* (London: John Wiley, 1971).

[61] Edward R. Sheehan, "The Second Most Important Man in Egypt —— and Possibly the World's Most Powerful Journalist," *The New York Times Magazine,* August 22, 1971.

[62] Bagdikian, *op. cit.*, p. 293.

[63] Davison, *op. cit.*, p. 13.

[64] See footnote 12 above.

[65] Data on government control is from UNESCO, *Statistical Yearbook, 1971,* pp. 836-47.

[66] Merrill, Bryan and Alisky, *op. cit.,* p. 23. Italics are mine. I have called attention earlier to the central question of the difficulty in determining what is "the truth," let alone what is "news."

[67] Cited in Merrill, Bryan and Alisky, *op. cit.,* pp. 32-33. They are quoting Freedom of Information Center Publications 166, 181, and 201.

[68] See, for example, Andre Fontaine, "The Mass Media —— A Need for Greatness," in Bertram M. Gross, ed., *Social Intelligence in America's Future* (Boston: Allyn and Bacon, 1969). Fontaine asserts (p. 249): "People simply do not believe much of what the media tell them," and (p. 257): "There are large gaps in the knowledge anyone has about the impact the media have on their audiences."

[69] Herbert McClosky, "Consensus and Ideology in American Politics," *American Political Science Review,* vol. 58, no. 2, June, 1964, p. 374. Similar conclusions are drawn in John Galtung and Mari Holmboe Ruge, "The Structure of Foreign News: The Presentation of the Congo, Cuba and Cyprus Crises in Four Foreign Newspapers," *Journal of International Peace Researrch,* vol. 1, 1965, pp. 64-90.

[70] *Ibid.*

[71] UNESCO, *Records of the General Conference, Paris, 12 October to 14 November, 1970* (16th session), vol. 1, Resolutions, p. 60.

[72] For details of the proceedings, see the three-volume report on *Proceedings.* See also report of *East-West Seminar on the Role of Government Information in National Development: Papers and Proceedings* (Honolulu, 1972), especially the report by Ibrahim Sherifee, Afghanistan, who says (p. 3): "The journalist as a human with all human frailties tries to spice his statement or report with some clearly made-up phrases, a few biting words and an attempt to belittle others. I am convinced that the world press could do much in the way of allaying suspicions and mistrusts . . . "

[73] UNESCO, *Proposals for an International Programme of Communication Research* (Paris, September 10, 1971).

[74] UNESCO, *Records of the General Conference, Paris, 17 October to 21 November, 1972* (17th Session), vol. 1, Resolutions. See also UNESCO, "Report of the Meeting of Experts on Communication Policies and Planning," 17-28 July, 1972, Paris.

[75] UNESCO, *Records of the General Conference, Paris, 17 October to 23 November, 1974* (18th Session), vol. 2, Reports, pp. 125-141. See also UNESCO, "Final Report on the Meeting of Experts on Interpretations of Experience by and Through the Media," 23-26 March, 1976, Paris.

[76] UNESCO, *Records of the General Conference, Nairobi, 26 October to 30 November, 1976* (19th Session), vol. 1, Resolutions, pp. 53-54. See also *New York Times*, November 23, 1976.

[77] UNESCO 1976 Conference report, p. 53. See also *New York Times*, November 26 and 30, 1976.

[78] *Ibid.*

[79] The 1976 UNESCO report, for example, authorizes the General Director to continue implementation of the basic UNESCO program "to promote the free and balanced flow of information and the movement of persons and materials, to promote research on the role of communication in society, to further professional standards in the use of the mass media . . . "

[80] Jeremy Tunstall, ed., *Media Sociology: A Reader* (London: Constable, 1970), p. 26.

BIBLIOGRAPHY

Books

Gabriel A. Almond and James S. Coleman, eds., *The Politics of the Developing Areas* (Princeton, N.J.: Princeton University Press, 1960).

Ben Bagdikian, *The Information Machines: Their Impact on Men and the Media* (New York: Harper & Row, 1971).

Jerome A. Barron, *The Freedom of the Press for Whom?: The Right of Access to Mass Media* (Bloomington: Indiana University Press, 1973).

Daniel J. Boorstin, *The Image: A Guide to Pseudo—Events in America* (New York: Harper & Row, 1964).

J.A.C. Brown, *Techniques of Persuasion: From Propaganda to Brainwashing* (Baltimore, Md.: Penguin Books, 1963).

Colin Cherry, *World Communication: Threat or Promise? A Socio–Technical Approach* (London: John Wiley, 1971).

Michael, Choukas, *Propaganda Comes of Age* (Washington: Public Affairs Press, 1965).

Bernard C. Cohen, *The Press and Foreign Policy* (Princeton, N.J.: Princeton University Press, 1963).

Heinz–Dietrich Fischer and John C. Merrill, eds., *International Communication: Media, Channels, Functions* (New York: Hastings, 1970).

Joseph Gouden, *Truth is the First Casualty: The Gulf of Tonkin Affair, Illusion and Reality* (Chicago: Rand McNally, 1969).

William A. Hachten, *Muffled Drums: The News Media in Africa* (Ames, Iowa: Iowa State University Press, 1971).

Harold R. Isaacs, *Scratches on Our Minds: American Images of China and India* (New York: John Day, 1958).

John W.C. Johnstone, Edward J. Slawski and William W. Bowman, *The News People: A Sociological Portrait of American Journalists and Their Work* (Urbana, Ill.: University of Illinois Press, 1976).

Elihu Katz and Paul F. Lazarsfeld, *Personal Influence: The Part Played by People in the Flow of Mass Communications* (New York: Free Press, 1955).

Phillip Knightley, *The First Casualty: From the Crimea to Vietnam: The War Correspondent as Hero, Propagandist, and Myth Maker* (New York: Harcourt Brace Jovanovich, 1975).

Harold D. Lasswell, *Propaganda Technique in the World War* (New York: Alfred A. Knopf, 1927).

Walter Lippmann, *Public Opinion* (New York: Macmillan, 1922).

Brenda Maddox, *Beyond Babel: New Directions in Communications* (London: Andre Deutsch, 1972).

Joseph J. Mathews, *Reporting the Wars* (Minneapolis: University of Minnesota Press, 1957).

John C. Merrill, Carter R. Bryan and Marvin Alisky, *The Foreign Press: A Survey of the World's Journalism* (Baton Rouge: Louisiana State University Press, 1970).

John C. Merrill, *The Imperative of Freedom: A Philosophy of Journalistic Autonomy* (New York: Hastings House, 1974).

Dale Minor, *The Information War: How the Government and the Press Manipulate, Censor, and Distort the News* (New York: Hawthorn, 1970).

Hamid Mowlana, *International Communication: A Selected Bibliography* (Dubuque, Iowa: Kendall/Hunt, 1971).

Arthur Ponsonby, *Falsehood in War–time* (New York: E.P. Dutton, 1928).

Hassan Rafi–Zadeh, *International Mass Communications: Computerized Annotated Bibliography, Articles, Dissertations and Theses* (Carbondale, Ill.: Honorary Relation–Zone, International Understanding Series, 1972).

William L. Rivers, *The Adversaries: Politics and the Press* (Boston: Beacon Press, 1970).

William J. Rivers and Wilbur Schramm, *Responsibility in Mass Communications*, rev. ed. (New York: Harper & Row, 1969).

Everett M. Rogers (with F. Floyd Shoemaker), *Communication of Innovations: A Cross–Cultural Approach*, 2nd ed. (New York: Free Press, 1971).

Haluk Sahin, *Broadcasting Autonomy in Turkey 1961–1971*, unpublished dissertation, Indiana University, 1974.

Herbert J. Schiller, *Mass Communications and American Empire* (Boston: Beacon Press, 1971).

Fred S. Siebert, Theodore B. Peterson and Wilbur Schramm, *Four Theories of the Press* (Urbana: University of Illinois Press, 1956).

Jeremy Tunstall, ed., *Media Sociology: A Reader* (London: Constable, 1970).

Sanford J. Unger, *The Papers and the Papers: An Account of the Legal and Political Battle Over the Pentagon Papers* (New York: E.P. Dutton, 1972).

Robert Weissberg, *Political Learning, Political Choice, and Democratic Citizenship* (Englewood Cliffs, N.J.: Prentice–Hall, 1974).

Bruce H. Westley, *News Editing*, 2nd ed. (Boston: Houghton Mifflin, 1972).

Raymond Williams, *Communications*, rev. ed. (London: Chato and Windus, 1969).

Documents, Pamphlets, Articles

J. Herbert Altschull, "What is News?" *Mass Comm Review*, December, 1974.

Margaret A. Blanchard, "The Hutchins Commission, The Press and The Responsibility Concept," *Journalism Monographs*, no. 49, May, 1977.

Dennis J. Chase, "The Aphilosophy of Journalism," *Quill*, vol. 59, no. 9, September, 1971.

The Commission on Freedom of the Press, *A Free and Responsible Press* (Chicago: University of Chicago Press, 1947).

Charles Curran, "The First Fifty Years," in *BBC Handbook 1973* (London: British Broadcasting Corporation, 1972).

"The Daily Sip," Inter American Press Association, October 22-26, 1972.

W. Phillips Davison, "Some Trends in International Propaganda," in *The Annals of the American Academy of Political and Social Science* (special ed. on "Propaganda in International Affairs"), ed. L. John Martin (Philadelphia: 1972).

East—West Seminar on the Role of Government Information in National Development: Papers and Proceedings (Honolulu, 1972).

Andre Fontaine, "The Mass Media –– A Need for Greatness," in Bertram M. Gross, ed., *Social Intelligence in America's Future* (Boston: Allyn and Bacon, 1969).

John Galtung and Mari Holmboe Ruge, "The Structure of Foreign News: The Presentation of the Congo, Cuba and Cyprus Crises in Four Foreign Newspapers," *Journal of International Peace Research*, vol. 1, 1965.

Mark W. Hopkins, "Lenin, Stalin, Khrushchev: Three Concepts of the Press," *Journalism Quarterly*, vol. 42, no. 4, Autumn, 1965.

Norman E. Isaacs, "The Credibility Gap and the Ombudsman," *ASNE Bulletin*, February, 1969, reprinted in Michael C. Emery and Ted C. Smythe, *Readings in Mass Communications* (Dubuque, Iowa: William C. Brown, 1972).

Paul Kecskemeti, "Propaganda," in Ithiel de Sola Pool and Wilbur Schramm, eds., *Handbook of Communication,* (Chicago: Rand McNally, 1973).

Herbert McClosky, "Consensus and Ideology in American Politics," *American Political Science Review*, vol. 58, no. 2, June 1964.

John C. Merrill, "The Press and Social Responsibility," Freedom of Information Center Publication No. 001 (Columbia, Mo.: School of Journalism, University of Missouri, 1965).

New York Times.

Report of the Attorney General to the Congress of the United States on the Administration of the Foreign Registration Act, 1938, as Amended, for the Calendar Year 1975 (Washington: Government Printing Office, 1976), mimeo.

Herbert J. Schiller, "Madison Avenue Imperialism," *Trans—Action,* vol. 8, nos. 5-6, March/April, 1971.

Wilbur Schramm, "World Distribution of the Mass Media," in Heinz—Dietrich Fischer and John C. Merrill, eds., *International Communication: Media, Channels, Functions* (New York: 1970).

Edward R.F. Sheehan, "The Second Most Important Man in Egypt —— and Possibly the World's Most Powerful Journalist," *The New York Times Magazine,* August 22, 1971.

James Shepley, "How Dulles Avoided War," *Life,* vol. 40, January 16, 1956.

UNESCO, "Mass Media in the Developing Countries," *Reports and Papers on Mass Communication,* no. 33, 1961.

UNESCO, *News Agencies: Their Structure and Operation,* 1953.

UNESCO, *Proposals for an International Programme of Communication Research,* (Paris, September 10, 1971).

UNESCO, *Records of the General Conference, Paris, 12 October to 14 November 1970* (16th session), vol. 1, Resolutions.

UNESCO, *Records of the General Conference, Paris, 17 October to 21 November 1972* (17th session), vol. 1, Resolutions.

UNESCO, *Records of the General Conference, Paris, 17 October to 23 November 1974* (18th session), vol. 2, Reports.

UNESCO, *Records of the General Conference, Nairobi, 26 October to 30 November, 1976* (19th session), vol. 1, Resolutions.

UNESCO, "Report of the Meeting of Experts on Communication Policies and Planning," 17-28 July, 1972, Paris.

UNESCO, *Statistical Yearbook,* 1971, 1975.

UNESCO, *World Communications: Press, Radio, Television, Film* (New York: UNESCO Publications Center, 1964.

U.S. Information Agency, "Basic Attitudes and General Communication Habits in Four West African Capitals," PMS Report No. 51, July, 1961.

U.S. Information Agency, "Mass Media Habits in Africa," R64-66, March, 1966.

Anthony Hanley:

Intercultural International Communication

———

THE JUXTAPOSITION of ideas conveyed by the title of this book could not have been better chosen to describe the experiments and demonstrations which have been carried on continuously by the PEACESAT project since 1971. PEACESAT is the Pan Pacific Education and Communication Experiment by Satellite which was designed to bring about experiments based on multilateral and interactive communications between many different countries. The project was initiated in 1969 by John W. Bystrom, Professor of Communication at the University of Hawaii who is its Director and Principal Investigator. The experimental phase of this project began in 1971 and it has been gaining in momentum and attracting increasing world attention ever since. In 1978, it linked 16 countries across the Pacific in an intensive and daily program of communications experiments, with three additional locations planning to join the project. It continues as a working model for the world of a new type of communication between the peoples of different countries exemplifying many of the themes of this book.

Information as a Human Resource — Communication as Dissemination

PEACESAT came about because of the growth in awareness of the importance of information as a human resource and as the essential input for successful development in people, enterprises and countries alike. This is well illustrated by surveys of world information trends such as that provided by Georges Anderla in his

717

1971 O.E.C.D. report, and by the great emphasis which has been placed for years now on recurring or continuing education programs of all kinds. These are, in essence, information dissemination programs intended to enhance the personal qualities and opportunities of the citizen. In all cases communication is necessary for the provision of this information and successful communication is much assisted by feedback, responsiveness, and interaction if the information delivered is to be truly useful.

Bystrom's concept is one of an interactive and multi-way information delivery system connecting national centers at locations throughout the Pacific region, each dedicated to bringing about information exchanges between the centers. The PEACESAT plan is for the system to provide broadcast channels linking all centers at once and to make the system freely available for use by specialist groups with a need for communication. The intention is: to stimulate all types of information exchanges for educational, cultural, scientific, and national development purposes; to encourage international cooperation of all kinds; and to use the observed results from the project as a guide to its value as a future world-wide system.

PEACESAT's development has coincided with a growing interest in many areas of communications application and an appreciation of their importance. Recent advances in communication technology, coupled with falling relative costs of introducing this technology, have the potential to provide rapid development, and consequent benefits extending to many human activities and aspirations, in the following broad areas:

> Satellite radio and television systems for mass broadcasting
> Educational telecommunication networks
> Information access and exchange systems
> Computer network systems and computer conferencing
> Educational television and radio systems
> Satellite communication as an aid to development in some countries
> Teleconferencing as a partial alternative to travel
> Provision of communication facilities for isolated areas.

A communication satellite serving as a central node to make possible sets of networks of radially linked communication centers has become a feasible simplification of the technical problem of providing communication channels for all of these purposes. Access to such networks by very low cost, low powered, small earth terminals, able to provide direct satellite communication from the user's premises, is easily possible if a suitably designed communication satellite relay can be provided.

Satellite Communication Technology

Some brief comments on satellite communication technology and its implications, may be desirable as an aid to the understanding of its practical importance.

The communication satellite relay, when placed in a suitable earth orbit about the equator, at a height of about two and a half earth diameters, appears to be almost stationary above a point on the equator. At this great height about one third of the earth's surface is directly visible from the satellite. Radio frequencies which travel best along a line of sight may be used to provide communication by means of the satellite relay between all points on the earth's surface which are visible from the satellite.

The satellite equipment includes one or more transponder units, each having a radio or television receiver and re-broadcasting unit, which work on different frequencies to avoid interfering with each other's operation. The communication equipment is powered by sunlight using solar cells and has a small reserve of rechargeable battery capacity for use during the short periods when the satellite is in the earth's shadow.

The satellite's radio antenna systems are directive to provide greater sensitivity and signal power in the direction of the earth. Very highly directive spot beams, a degree or so in width and aimed at the ground terminals, are commonly used to provide large capacity communication pathways between major earth terminals at selected locations on the earth. Less highly directive global coverage beams provide smaller capacity channels accessible from any point on the earth from which the satellite is visible.

The cost of the satellite communication circuit linking any two earth stations is independent of the distance separating them. With no need for cables or radio repeater stations, the cost remains the same whether the link is between different parts of the same city or between continents. Present charges do not reflect this novel and important property of satellite communication channels because of cost-averaging over the different types of services operated by communication agencies. The trend, however, is for increasing capacity and rapidly decreasing costs.

There is a direct and complementary relationship between the characteristics of the communication satellite's transmitters and beams, and the size and cost of the earth-terminal for the service it is to provide. Accepting some oversimplification of a complex situation, it can be stated that television transmission requires a wide signal frequency channel and a good deal of power spread over it. A radio or voice transmission requires only a narrow signal frequency channel with a great deal less power. Because of this fact, hundreds of voice or radio channels can be provided within the channel frequency bandwidth, and power requirements of a single television channel.

The size of the ground-terminal antenna is a very important factor in several respects: the larger the size of the antenna the greater will be its power-multiplying property when transmitting, its sensitivity when receiving, and also the narrowness of its beam. Terminals with efficient large antennas have very narrow beams, a fraction of a degree in width, and must be pointed very precisely, often automatically by a complex control system, if their beams are to find the satellite. They are costly, precision engineering structures, and the terminals require well qualified engineers for their correct operation.

At present it is quite feasible to have reception of direct broadcast television signals by very small-antenna home terminals within areas served by a powerful satellite's regional spot beam. The up-link transmission of the television signal from the originating studio to the satellite for re-broadcast, even when sent up into the satellite's sensitive regional spot beam, requires a large ground terminal antenna and a powerful transmitter. With presently attainable satellite transmitter powers it is not possible for a global coverage beam to provide a television signal strong enough for reception by small ground terminals.

The latest technical developments in antenna design for future high-capacity satellites are directed towards the provision of global or wide area coverage by means of many overlapping, powerful spot beams. In this way the advantages of the power multiplying, sensitive, spot-beam antennas can be retained and the disadvantage of their small coverage areas overcome.

To summarize these technicalities: low-cost two-way ground terminals with small antennas and simple equipment are able to transmit and receive several voice- or radio-channels at any location within line of sight of a moderately powerful satellite providing a global coverage beam; such terminals do not require specialist engineers for their operation and can be used by ordinary, non-technical people after a little training; small ground terminals for receive-only television are feasible only within the limited areas covered by regional spot beams from a powerful satellite; two-way television ground terminals, able to transmit as well as receive, are substantial and costly installations which require specialist engineers for their operation; simple ground terminals able to transmit and receive a few voice- or radio-channels can be provided at little cost and with much less complexity than would be required for a television two-way terminal.

A New Kind of Specialist Broadcasting Service:
International, Interactive and Multiway

Satellite communication relays are now well developed, with systems in regular commercial use and they are well integrated into the world's communication networks. Working between major traffic terminals in most countries of the world, high capacity satellite links carry telephone and television circuits on a routine basis. They are one of the major benefits resulting from the development of space technology. Continuing development is in progress. NASA's latest experimental communication satellite in the Applications Technology Series, ATS-6, was designed to demonstrate, among other things, direct television broadcasts from the spacecraft to low cost community reception terminals.

We can look on these two examples as extensions of systems and services already fairly generally available: long-distance point-to-point telecommunication; and mass-broadcasting systems. Neither are novel, and their services and benefits are already well known and highly valued. The decision to use satellite relays for these communication-systems is based on the engineering and economic factors to be considered in providing communication channels capable of meeting anticipated traffic growth, and providing, economically, for the coverage of large areas.

These two examples sum up the main line of developments to date. They represent great achievements. HOWEVER, SOMETHING MORE, and of great importance is possible.

The ideal of good communication over large areas of the earth's surface is now for the first time, in reach, made realizable by the use, of communication satellites. This is a highly attractive ideal and we can justifiably have great expectations of benefits arising from its realization. There is a widespread understanding that to be able to communicate freely with our fellow-human beings, at great distances, and in other countries, is a positive thing. It is desirable in its own right as an aid to mutual understanding, and practically, as a means of mutual assistance in the form of exchanges of experience and knowledge. It is this ideal which leads to the third major application of communication satellite relays of which little has so far been heard, but which may perhaps be the application which comes closest to fulfilling our expectations. This is the use of the spacecraft as the central relay node in a radially-linked network of a large number of small earth-terminals, each having the capacity for transmission and reception. It is surprising that this third major category of application of communication satellites, which may well be of considerable importance for developing areas with poor communication, has so far received little attention.

Such networks can link all terminals on a basis of complete equality. Each terminal is able to transmit to the spacecraft and can be rebroadcast equally well to all other terminals. In addition to its important property of providing multiple point-to-point links between all terminals, this type of network can act as a multi-lateral broadcast conference network capable of providing to all countries, on a world-wide basis, services at present available only to privileged groups in some of the major developed countries of the world. A system which makes such a facility easily available for large and small communities regardless of distance and isolation, and is available to all community groups, wherever needed, would appear to be a valuable method of improving international resource sharing, cooperation and understanding. It would most certainly enhance intercultural international communication.

It is the experience of the PEACESAT project that our high expectations are confirmed: In 1978, after seven years of continuous experimental operation, the project has demonstrated that is does indeed provide all of these things, and more besides.

The Establishment of the PEACESAT Network

The establishment of the PEACESAT network has been a very substantial achievement and it is of some importance to review the experimental design, philosophy, and practical approach to the task which resulted in this success.

Bystrom's concept required a network of national centers, established, in general, at educational institutions, each dedicated to bringing about experiments in information exchange between all of the centers by means of broadcast communication channels linking all of the centers at once.

If the concept was to work and take hold it had to be the result of local acceptance and wholehearted cooperation. Since it was to be an international project it had to be designed in such a way as to prevent the exercise of centralised direct control, or a more subtle accidental dominance, national, cultural, or intellectual, by any terminal. Such dominance would only act to hinder the realization of the concept of a multiway and free-flow of information with full interaction and immediate feedback between the terminals, which was the essence of the project. The plan, therefore, was for a network of fully independent terminals, each acting as a national terminal and able to determine for itself its participation in the project exchanges.

The Pacific region was a natural choice for the project because of two fortunate coincidental factors. The first is the fact that it is a region of many territories, in great need of communication services because of isolation, and separation by vast oceanic distances. The second is the existence of the technical means to meet these needs in the form of the ATS-1 experimental satellite, launched and operated by NASA. This satellite has as a special characteristic the capacity to provide complete coverage over a very large area. ATS-1 was fitted with a high powered transponder and global coverage antenna, which had been intended for use with experiments in direct aircraft communication and weather-map facsimile-broadcasts. This spacecraft transponder was unusual in that it was suitable for use by very simple, low-cost ground terminals of little more cost or complexity than taxi radio-equipment.

The technical capacity made possible by the presence of the communication satellite was, however, only one half of the requirement for communication to take place, The other facility which was required, and of equal importance, was a network of centers actively working together. The final realization of this concept and its establishment as an operational system was a major task.

The main objective after preparing and submitting the project proposal to NASA for the use of the satellite, was to interest non-technical administrators in educational institutions in distant countries in the project. It was necessary to convince them that they, in their own territories and on their own premises, through their own efforts and at little cost, could establish and operate self-contained satellite-terminals able to link directly with others in the PEACE-SAT PROJECT. It was necessary to persuade them that sufficient benefits could come from such a project to warrant the investment of scarce resources of money, as well as time and effort. Interest had to be kindled long-distance and at first only through correspondence.

Even today, with the knowledge that the project is not only feasible but a success, it is difficult to believe that it could have been established in this way. Six years ago the expert radio engineers in most countries were so unfamiliar with the possibilities of satellite communication that they refused to believe that small ground terminals would work. The technical image of any facility necessary for satellite communication was that of a major COMSAT-style earth-terminal costing many millions of dollars. It was this preconceived idea by local experts and regulatory authorities which influenced their initial comments on the feasibility of the PEACESAT project.

Additional substantial obstacles existed to the realization and development of the project. First NASA itself, controlling the experimental access to its satellites, is a mission-oriented organization having objectives which are directed towards scientific- and technical-goals. To an organization of engineers and physical scientists, experimentation in the social uses of communication was not a particularly important goal. Thus it was not an activity that would have been expected to attract strong support or interest from that agency. 'We are not in the aid business,' was an early comment by NASA when PEACESAT began its exploration to find a more permanent access to the necessary satellite communication channel. Moreover NASA is restricted by law in the degree to which it is empowered to use its own experimental satellites for communication purposes. It is to NASA's great credit, however, that the experimental access to its ATS-1 satellite has been extended year after year, long beyond initial expectations and promises.

A second substantial obstacle for the project was the position of the national regulatory bodies which are responsible for the licensing and regulation of radio-transmissions in their territories. In most countries it is the Post and Telegraph authorities who operate communication services as a national monopoly. They tend to resist strongly any attempts to establish parallel communication systems for any special purposes. Strong legislation exists to control internal communication, and equally strong international agreements bind most countries to tight control of international communication. In these regulations there is some provision for the use of radio for scientific experimentation, but there is no provision for a project in useful communication, such as PEACESAT.

Taking these factors together, all of which presented themselves to a greater or lesser degree as each country considered the project, there was first of all a considerable degree of scepticism about the objectives of the project, its feasibility and its likely value. There was negative reaction to its technical feasibility. No regulatory provision for communication of this type existed. Competition with established communication services as well as a complicated relationship between host-institutions, local government departments and NASA also became evident. Bystrom contacted several groups in each country with a potential interest in the PEACESAT project but in all cases there was the problem of obtaining financial support for a project which was surrounded by doubts and uncertainties.

The Methodology of PEACESAT Exchanges

More important than consideration of these difficulties, which were overcome, are the achievements of the system so far. By 1978 there existed an extensive record of what had happened in six years of *daily* multi-way exchanges between the terminals. At the sixteen PEACESAT project terminals each day, and sometimes several times each day, the project had arranged for groups from the local community to assemble for friendly and structured meetings with groups at the other centers in order to deal with subjects in previously distributed, detailed agendas. A large number of specialized topics were covered in such exchanges.

The network made possible the development of flexible, rapidly responsive and effective communication between communities previously unavailable by other means. It also provided a valuable experimental framework in which many uses of international conference-communication allowing free access to common-interest community-groups in different contries and cultures, could be demonstrated and evaluated. As already indicated, the terminals are autonomous units established in a suitable host institution by local desire. Each terminal is operated and financed as a result of local interest and efforts. Each terminal is controlled by a terminal manager who acts as local experimenter, and as liaison with local groups which are invited to participate in the communication experiments.

The terminals are in fact, active centers for experiments in direct international cooperation, and the role of the terminal manager is important to the success of the project. He acts as the interface between the local community or national group and the international network as a whole. It is necessary for the terminal manager to have suitable personal characteristics as he must approach and engage the interests of many different community groups. He also needs to be aware of the resources and interests available in his community.

Experiments originate in two ways. Uses of the system which appeared likely to be of value were enumerated in the original project proposal, and they are encouraged by approaching suitable organizations and soliciting their cooperation for project studies. Another important class of system users are those who on learning of the project, come forward with proposals for trial uses which are of potential value to them. Information on the proposals for trials or studies is given to the network by the initiating terminal during 'Proposal Enquiry' periods, which are held weekly. The terminal managers then approach local groups in their communities and invite them to attend a network 'Pre-planning Meeting' to discuss the proposed trial, decide on an agenda, agree on a session chairman, and decide on a date for a working meeting.

Groups using the network sit around a table in a studio and confer with the groups at other terminals, using microphones and loudspeakers as the studio equipment. The meetings have been given the name 'exchanges' or 'exchange sessions' by Bystrom, to emphasise the mutual resource-sharing nature of the conference sessions, and also the equal status and right to communication of all terminals.

The terminal managers, because of their regular contact with each other, have a friendly and cooperative relationship. In the conduct of the exchanges this leads quickly to a friendly relationship between the groups. This is encouraged by informal introductions by the terminal managers, the use of first names, and the rapid realization of common problems and interests.

In the course of the exchanges it is usual for each new point of interest to be seized on immediately by groups from throughout the

Pacific Basin as each group sees relevance to its own problems and thus asks questions and makes comments which produce further explanations. As a result, the members of all groups benefit from each other's experiences and knowledge, and they are stimulated by learning what is done in other countries which have common problems.

A number of auxiliary devices have been used to aid the exchange of information. These have included teletypewriters, Xerox telecopiers, facsimile transmit/receive units, for the transmission of graphic material at the time of the exchange sessions, color-slide and audio-tape-cassette materials previously distributed by airmail, photographs, booklets, written materials, and overhead-projector transparencies. A Pacific map with switched indicator-lights showing the location of the transmitting terminal has been found useful as an aid to the orientation of the larger groups. In general, however, sessions proceed only with the aid of previously discussed agenda, under the control of a chairman who is selected by the participating groups.

At the New Zealand Wellington Polytechnic terminal, for example, small groups of up to a dozen people can be accommodated by using remote studios in other buildings of the Polytechnic, connected to the main terminal by cables and an inter-communication system. A carpeted and comfortably furnished small theatre and a small carpeted dining-room have been used frequently. These can accommodate groups of up to eighty people.

Conference groups at locations remote from the Polytechnic or in other New Zealand cities can use a remote terminal unit allowing microphone- and loudspeaker-systems to be used in any location to which there is access by local or long distance telephone. One example of this was a Department of Scientific and Industrial Research Conference on Remote Sensing, held at Gracefield, Lower Hutt, ten miles from the Polytechnic which was linked to other PEACESAT terminals and to the NASA Goddard Space Flight Center in Maryland, U.S.A. This was a ninety-minute exchange which included the ERTS project management group at the

NASA project headquarters.

Group meetings on aspects of neurosurgery have been conducted from the Medical Center, Clinical School, Wellington Hospital. Several New Zealand universities have been linked for series of exchanges. The largest group so far linked to the PEACESAT system was the National Education Association Convention in Chicago in 1974, where an audience of 12,000 U.S. teachers and a panel of speakers linked with representatives of teacher's organizations in Alaska and the Pacific. For this public demonstration NASA installed a small earth-terminal on the roof of the convention hall. Unfortunately this broadcast had to be terminated before completion because of an accidental transmission. Other large convention groups such as the Federation of Parent Teacher Associations have also taken part in network exchanges from remote locations in Honolulu. In instances of large group participation, particular attention is paid to arranging for interaction between the groups by providing representative panels of speakers, and by inviting questions and comments from all present.

While small groups are involved in most of the exchanges, such groups represent informed sections of the community on the special topic under discussion. Though the groups are small and specialized, the cumulative effect of the project within a community may be substantial. For example, during 1976 in Rarotonga in the Cook Group, 300 different people attended 591 exchanges for a total of 1338 attendances. The total population of this community is only about 18,000 people.

PEACESAT Exchange Activities

PEACESAT's innovations and successes seem almost endless. As of 1978, after continuing daily activity for over six years, there is available a long record of achievement. In education there have been the initial University of Hawaii credit-courses by satellite between different campuses as well as the rapid development of the University of the South Pacific's regional, satellite-linked education project based on Fiji, operating as an independent project in cooperation with PEACESAT. There also have been large numbers of exchanges between educationalists on matters of curriculum development, professional organization and teaching practice. One notable series, organized by the U.S. National Education Association, as part of its Bi-Centennial Celebration, linked teachers at many locations in the mainland United States, Alaska, Hawaii and in the Pacific Basin in a series of seminars on the common factors in multi-cultural education.

The project reports describe thousands of multiway exchange-conferences which have taken place, often as a continuing series of meetings over a period of time. Many examples of such exchange series are of considerable interest and value. They have included educational experiments of many kinds involving students, teachers, administrators, planners and parents. Health and medical experiments have included reviews of medical and surgical problems, the control of epidemics in remote areas, public health laboratory practice, and the training of health personnel. Scientific and technical exchanges range from subjects such as the ecology of atolls and problems of soil stability in New Guinea, to solar energy systems and the application of earth resources survey satellite data. Agricultural exchanges have covered many topics such as the production and marketing of papaya and the control of plant disease. Cultural exchanges are a continuing feature and a natural consequence of the PEACESAT facility as well as people's curiosity about each other. They have included regular meetings of youth leaders in music, literature, debate and poetry.

The list of exchange topics can be expanded to provide further detail of the wide range of activities encompassed by PEACESAT. Many health related exchanges have involved nursing education, the experimental transmission of X-ray photographs and ECG telemetry, discussion of traditional and modern practices in childbirth and the rearing of children, presentation of laboratory techniques for the culture and identification of pathogenic organisms, studies of water supply engineering, and dental care programs for children. There have been convincing demonstrations of the value of PEACESAT in connection with the widespread epidemic of dengue fever at many locations throughout the Pacific Basin. Virus disease specialists from Honolulu, Washington and Dunedin, New Zealand, were regularly linked with Fiji, which was at the heart of the epidemic, as well as with other Pacific Basin locations for the purpose of cooperative arrangements to control the spread of the disease, and to supply urgently needed assistance. Again, in the more recent and localised outbreak of cholera at Tarawa in the Gilbert Islands, the PEACESAT exchanges served to broadcast full information about the developing situation in Tarawa, the progress of the measures for its control, and the supply of materials for on-the-spot assistance as arranged by the national groups concerned. The PEACESAT system is ideal for this type of coordinated emergency action.

In the area of cultural exchanges again there is a long and growing list of achievements. There have been many stimulating series of exchanges between elementary, high school, and college students. One substantial series linked children from four different cultures, ranging from Alaskan Eskimos at Point Barrow to central Alaskan Indians at Beaver on the Yukon River, children in metropolitan Honolulu, and to other youngsters in Wellington, New Zealand. These meetings were preceded by detailed pre-planning between teachers and the distribution of slide and cassette background material. There have been memorable exchanges of poetry and literature, sometimes involving well-known authors, followed by discussions. Music, museum collections, debates, a detailed and highly technical series of well-attended meetings on the preservation of historic documents and cultural artifacts, and an extensive and continuing series of meetings of Pacific Basin librarians to report on, and coordinate their specialist holdings, are other examples. The South Pacific Festival of Arts held in 1976 in Rotorua, New Zealand was initially planned during a series of PEACESAT exchanges between contributing cultural groups. A major series on the effects of tourism throughout the Pacific Basin attracted participation by social scientists, hotel managers, and representatives of cultural groups.

Social and community activities are also well served. Youth groups and their leaders meet regularly. Community service-clubs jointly plan cooperative international projects. The International Planned Parenthood Federation has reviewed the Pacific situation in a series of exchanges. Organizations concerned with migrant settlement and education programs have learned much from each others' experiences with common problems arising in the transitions from simple to complex communities. Some exchanges have successfully involved French-speaking nationals from New Caledonia and the New Hebrides. The PEACESAT style of exchange is well suited to accompanying translation. Further experiments are currently being planned using this technique.

In the area of science and its applications, there also have been many instances of highly successful specialist meetings over lengthy periods. One of the earliest were the monthly exchanges between agriculture extension specialists, dealing with everything from diseases of poultry and the optimum mix of poultry feed, to economical methods of copra-drying and beef-cattle production. Groups of scientists have met together to coordinate work on their joint research reports. Fisheries management has been the basis for a joint continuing and highly topical series linked to the introduction of the 200-mile economic zone, which vastly extended the range of jurisdiction of small Pacific Basin countries. This concern led to another wide ranging series of seminars on aspects of the law-of-the-sea, given as tutorials by the University of Auckland to groups of students and administrators in other countries. In the area of space technology many Pacific Basin scientists have been exchanging information on their use of the data available in the form of multiple spectral band imagery of their countries as delivered, by NASA's remote sensing LANDSAT satellites.

Small Satellite Terminals and Multiway Communication Problems

There are encouraging signs that greater attention is now being paid to two concepts embodied in this far-sighted project: small self-contained two-way satellite terminals; and multi-way information systems. The small satellite-terminal application has recently been identified as a key consideration which should be developed in the public interest, as recommended in the 1976 U.S. Department of Commerce's report: "Lowering the Barriers to Telecommunications Growth." PEACESAT has a great deal of accumulated experience in the use of such terminals, and indeed the project has been possibly only because of the use of this direct-link satellite technology instead of complex and sometimes unreliable national switching-systems, designed for point-to-point telephone calls of short duration.

Another important development is the establishment by UNESCO of the International Commission for the Study of Communication Problems, as the result of the recognition of the fact that all is not well with the world's information systems. The inaugural address to the Commission by its first President, Dr. Sean McBride, who is the holder of both the Nobel and Lenin Peace Prizes, stated that

> "Communication is closely related to power structures. A one-way or even two-way communications system reflects and supports autocratic and paternalistic structures. A multiway information flow is indispensable for democratisation, for wider mass participation in the decision making process, as well as for mutual respect in international relations."

There is no doubt that the PEACESAT experience addresses this need in a direct and effective way.

In addition to its more general information exchange demonstrations, PEACESAT has given worthwhile operational models of relevance to current world concerns with communication. One communication objective is the provision of simple and reliable portable satellite earth-stations for use during natural disasters or emergencies of various kinds. This has been one of the objectives of a study program recommended by the International Telecommunication Union, which the PEACESAT concept fits very well. The PEACESAT network has terminals already established at many key centers, staffed with trained and experienced persons who are in daily contact with each other as a matter of course, and whose function it is to facilitate communication with specialist groups of all types within their local community. The PEACESAT network is a ready-made working system continually kept up to a state of high operational effectiveness. It is able to accept additional emergency terminals which can quickly be established in a particular disaster area, and which can immediately provide direct links to the resource centers from which aid can be expected.

The potential of the system is well illustrated by an experience during the preparation of these comments. The writer, from his office desk in the Department of Education, Wellington, New Zealand, was linked by telephone to the Polytechnic terminal as he discussed technical details of a small terminal with people at other terminals in Fiji, Honolulu, and at a small ship-borne NASA terminal, on test at sea off New York. It is suggested that readers find these locations on a globe to appreciate the full implications of this facility, provided by simple low-cost satellite earth-terminals. In the case of emergencies mentioned earlier, there were sufficient small terminals already operational at many of the locations for the value of the PEACESAT system to be demonstrated, but additional small terminals, which could have been carried by a doctor or health team, would have been desirable. Such terminals suitable for use with the PEACESAT system would cost much less than $5,000 each. What was found in all these cases was that the broadcast, fully interactive and area-wide PEACESAT conferences between specialists at all terminals, allowed a degree of dissemination and understanding of a rapidly developing emergency situation which could not have been provided by any other means. When such exchanges include decision makers in different countries, rapid action can result because of the full background of up-to-date information, instantly available, discussed by all members of the specialist groups.

Another important world concern about communication was stated in McBride's important inaugural address to the UNESCO Commission. The Commission is to pay special attention to promoting a free and balanced flow of information throughout the world, and the need to help developing countries take advantage of it. How can that be accomplished? World communication systems have slowly developed to parallel world economic and political linkages. While these may change comparatively quickly, as for example in the accelerated moves to independence by colonial territories, there are few signs that communication patterns are able to develop as quickly to suit these new situations.

Let us look at the relevance of PEACESAT's South Pacific Commission news exchange experiment to this question. This experiment, proposed by Ian Johnstone, then Radio Broadcasts Officer with the South Pacific Commission whose Headquarters is in Noumea, New Caledonia, was initiated from Fiji and has been operating for several years. Each week a news reporter from a local radio-station or newspaper attends the exchange meeting bringing a five-minute summary of local news of regional interest. Each reporter makes his contribution to the news-pool by reading his bulletin, in turn, in the usual multi-lateral broadcast-exchange manner, and gives news headlines followed by story details. At all terminals the complete exchange is recorded on tape cassettes. Each reporter leaves after an hour of such exchanges with headlines, news stories, and a back-up cassette from which excerpts can be broadcast to highlight items selected by news editors. During the exchanges the reporters have had the opportunity to raise points needing further explanation, and to discuss the background of news stories. Follow-up enquiries about particular items are not uncommon. The opportunity for direct feedback from reporters also helps them to learn what is interesting news for other countries.

The result is that small countries in the PEACESAT coverage-region, whose communication links had been directed more towards the homeland of the administering colonial power than to their regional neighbors, are now able to learn more of what their "neighbors" are doing. News-items may sometimes seem unimportant, almost of a "village" nature, but they are eagerly received by similar communities in other areas who otherwise would learn only little of each other.

Two examples will serve to point up this situation. When a shot was fired at the Governor's residence in Noumea, New Caledonia in the mid-70's, it was heard almost immediately on the other side of the world, in Paris. But it was a long-delayed wire-service echo that arrived, from Europe, weeks later in Fiji, although that island is only a few hundred miles to the east of New Caledonia. The leading PEACESAT news-exchange story which came one day from the

Honiara terminal in the Solomon Islands is another example. It covered details of a recent traditional wedding of importance on Tikopia, a small Polynesian island in the Santa Cruz Group administered by the Solomon Islands which are Melanesian islands. Tikopia has a system of sacred chiefs, and a highly complex social organization of patrilineal clans. The news item on one hand gave a detailed report of what took place during the colorful wedding practices of that culture. However, what also came through very clearly was a feeling of pride and confidence that this item was considered to be important news, and that it would be of interest to other communities. Implied in all this was a realization that the indigenous culture was of a richness that could be shared with all.

PEACESAT's Future System

The possible uses of communication systems can be arranged under three broad headings:

Two-way point-to-point services for commercial, personal and business communication.

One-way mass broadcasting systems, both commercial and public service, for entertainment, information, propaganda and education.

Two-way and multiway, non-commercial, public-service functions.

The PEACESAT project falls in the third category.

The important feature of the design of PEACESAT networks is that all terminals are equally able to transmit to all others and are able to decide for themselves whether or not to take part in a particular exchange-meeting. These properties are deliberately emphasized to give the right to the smallest and most remote community terminals to join as equals in international discussions, to let their voices be heard and their needs be understood, or if they wish, to take no part and be free of unwanted involvement. In this way it is possible to achieve effective, communication between groups and countries.

This concept is almost completely foreign to our present practices, which are tied to the concept of mass broadcasting which is capable only of the delivery of entertainment or information, suitable or not, to a passive audience, unable to contribute any local response on the basis of equality.

Despite its success PEACESAT is still little known. Where it is known and established, local communities, perhaps surprisingly, are beginning to take its existence as a matter of course. Comparatively few participants fully understand the unique nature of the communication instrument which is placed in their hands by the project, or its fragile nature as a time-limited experiment which could cease at any time.

In order to provide for PEACESAT services on a continuing basis, or to arrange for a planned medium-scale trial of an extended PEACESAT project serving both Asia and the Pacific, which would be an intermediate step, it is necessary to arrange that a replacement satellite, also accessible by small low-cost earth-terminals, be found for ATS-1. This satellite should be able to provide superior service, work on frequencies approved for satellite broadcasting, and it should be capable of providing the desired global coverage over the Asian and Pacific regions. A future service is unlikely to require more than a few channels for this purpose, but by providing these few channels many benefits can come to participating countries.

A desirable minimum terminal facility would provide simultaneous three-channel access to such a system. One channel would be the prime voice-channel, the second channel would be used for data or simultaneous graphics, including the presentation of diagrams or 'electronic blackboard' displays drawn in the course of the exchanges. The third channel would carry supervisory signalling and engineering information. All of these facilities can be provided within the bandwidth normally allocated to *one* high-quality radio-broadcast channel.

Experimental communication satellites with a capacity for community services, for example NASA's ATS-6, the Canadian CTS (now known as Hermes), and the forthcoming Japanese BSE system, have been designed with emphasis on their capacity for direct color-television broadcasts to small-antenna community and home-receivers. The wideband, high-powered signals needed for this service require that high-gain directional antennas be used with the spacecraft transponder which is thus able to provide spot-beams and restricted regional coverage only. If two-way television is to be provided with these systems, even for community-terminals, *substantial* ground-terminals are required with a resulting complexity and expense that may be anachronistic in the communities they are to serve.

Many small communities are so poor in material possessions and services that it is difficult to comprehend their status from the viewpoint of the more developed countries. Some communities may not have access to a clean water supply. Many people have no opportunity for paid employment. Educational and health budgets are at a very low level. In such circumstances expensive and eleborate technical facilities, such as two-way satellite color television systems, even if they are provided and maintained without cost to the local communities, might be considered an unsuitable and even provocative allocation of resources.

Low cost, simple, two-way voice systems which are capable of providing multi-way voice communication with a minimum of ground terminal complexity and which are able to be operated and maintained by local terminal managers are much more likely to fit into such an environment. WHEN ONE WEIGHS THE VALUE OF ADDING TELEVISION-PICTURES to such a system, against the increased spacecraft-system requirements and especially the ground-terminal *costs* and *complexity,* any benefits become questionable.

In addition there is a special value in the design of PEACESAT systems as networks of equal terminals under local control in which groups at all terminals have equal rights and facilities for communication. The PEACESAT system involves no elements of mass broadcasting and because of this is not intrusive in the society it serves. It provides and encourages ready access to good communications to those able to benefit from this.

The objective of PEACESAT has been to find by trial and demonstration the benefits of freely available purposes between specialist groups. An immediate objective, while continuing the present experiment, is to bring about an extended project which will allow PEACESAT to provide coverage to the Asian-Pacific Basin perimeter-countries, extending as far as Iran. The extended experiment is designed to link one hundred or more terminals located in the major resource-centers of these countries in a series of specialist sub-networks, as required.

The PEACESAT Consortium of nine Pacific Basin institutions actively supports this project as does PEACESAT, the Association for the Peaceful Uses of Satellites.

In conclusion it is appropriate to note that in 1978 John Bystrom received the outstanding achievement award of the University of Minnesota, in part for his achievement in the establishment of the PEACESAT project.

BIBLIOGRAPHY

Anderla, Georges. "Information in 1985," Organization for Economic Cooperation and Development, Paris, 1973.

Baker, Leigh R., "Scientific, Social and Technological Information in Papua New Guinea; Trends and Developments," *Proceedings, UNISIST Conference, Regional Information Policy and Planning in SE Asia,* Indonesia, 12-16 July, 1977.

Bystrom, J.W. "The Application of Satellites to International Interactive Service Support Communication," *Proceedings of the Royal Society of London,* vol. 345, 1975, pp. 492-510.

Bystrom, J.W. "A Satellite Communication System: Global Development and Cultural Imperialism," *New Perspectives in International Communications,* edited by J. Richstad. Honolulu: East-West Center Communications Institute, 1976, pp. 149-178.

Callison, George. "PEACESAT: Communicating by Satellite for Micronesia," *Micronesian Reporter,* Fourth Quarter, 1974.

Crombie, D.G., ed. "Lowering the Barriers to Telecommunications Growth," *U.S. Department of Commerce, Office of Telecommunications Special Publication 76-9,* Superintendent of Documents, U.S. Government Printing Office, Washington D.C.

Cutting, Alan and David Berkowitz, "PEACESAT— A Report on the Progress of an Experiment in International Educational Communication," Suva, Fiji: University of the South Pacific, 1972.

Dlabik, Peter. "?Satelliten Kommunikation-Entwichlungsland?" *Austrian Device for Development,* June 1977.

Hanley, A. "Small Earth Terminals for Satellite Communication Systems," Proceedings, New Zealand Electronics Conference, Wellington, New Zealand, 1975.

Kimble, Martin. "Missionary Efforts in Sharing Knowledge. The Ordinary Person's Satellite: A Review of the Pan Pacific Education and Communication Experiments by Satellite," *Proceedings, Slade Memorial Lecture,* National Electronics Conference, Victoria University, Wellington, New Zealand, August 18, 1977.

Kingan, Stuart. "Report on PEACESAT and other Networks Using ATS-1 in the Pacific," Asian Institute for Broadcast Development, Course on Satellite Broadcasting, Kuala Lumpur, Malaysia, July 1976.

McBride, Sean. "Communications in the Service of Mankind," The Irish Broadcasting Review, Spring 1978.

Nose, Katashi. "An Alternate Method for Phasing Crossed Yagis for Circular Polarisation," *OST,* September, 1975.

The PEACESAT Project. *Newsfile 1970-1975,* Honolulu: The PEACESAT Project, November, 1975.

PEACESAT Project (Volume 1): Early Experience. Honolulu: University of Hawaii, 1975.

PEACESAT Project (Volume 2): Social Applications. Honolulu: University of Hawaii, 1975.

PEACESAT Project (Volume 3): Networks. Honolulu: University of Hawaii, 1975.

PEACESAT Project Data Sheet.

PEACESAT Project Extended Experiment Data Sheet.

PEACESAT Project, University of Hawaii, Honolulu, Hawaii 96822.

Richstad, J. "PEACESAT: Sharing by Satellite," *Communication in the Pacific.* Honolulu: East-West Communication Institute, 1977, pp. 73-86.

John David Dupree:

The Performing Arts

SENDING the Seventh Fleet around the world is an internationally visible means of demonstrating military might. And proffering stockpiles of wheat or pork to Third World countries is considered by many to be an indicator of economic power.

But of what international import is a world-wide tour by New York's Beaux Arts Trio, Amsterdam's Concertgebouw Orchestra, or the 90-member Krasnayarsk Dance Company of Siberia? Is there such a phenomenon as "cultural power?" If not, what is the purpose of the thousands of junkets taken annually by performing artists, ensembles, and troupes ranging from gypsy dancers to opera companies?

Some see no legitimate value, since art and foreign policy are *and must be* two different things.[1] If art is made to reflect strictly political considerations, they argue, then it is no longer spontaneous and, therefore, not art.

Most artists and politicians agree, however, that cultural exchange *is* worthwhile, but disagree on what its purpose should be.

For example, one critic of the cultural exchange scene views the value of the Bolshoi Ballet or the Moiseyev Folk Dancers in furthering international understanding as follows:

> Despite the frustrations that have attended the cultural-exchange program then, there can be little doubt as to its value. Indeed, although not all of it has worked out in accordance with expectations, its larger consequences probably exceed the modest expectations with which it began. Simply in increasing the number of contacts between Russians and Americans, and in making these contacts more customary and

less strained, it has helped to open up the channels of communication. It has been associated with, and there is reason to believe it has accelerated, an important change for the better in the international atmosphere and in the posture of the Soviet Union toward the non-Communist world.[2]

Some might argue that the purpose served by international exchange in the performing arts is strictly a financial one. This type of exchange has reached multi-million dollar proportions annually, so profit alone could be enough incentive to continue the program. Many of the bookings involve between $15,000-$50,000 initial fees for performing artists, plus a percentage of the admission take above that (usually 75 percent) on a given evening. In addition, booking agents, travel agents, hotels, restaurants, and other service agencies all get a piece of the action. They, too, could advocate continuing exchange programs for purely financial reasons.

Since many of the existing programs are outside of the "business sector" of our society, however, others argue that the purpose served by international exchange of performing artists is primarily educational. University- and church-related programs would be included in this category, in addition to those conducted by groups such as Rotary International or the Austrian-American Friendship Society. Events sponsored by these groups may be the exporting of an American gospel-singing group on an African tour or the importing of a foreign-language readers' theater group from a Latin American university. In either case, these are considered to be of educational benefit rather than financial.

Finally, it can be argued that the primary purpose of exchange programs is diplomatic, to improve the relations between the publics of two or more nations. The United States government, for example, is involved quite extensively in exchange of performing artists, as is the government of the Soviet Union. By increasing understanding between the people of two countries, it is reasoned, the logistical and diplomatic problems involved in cooperation on other levels between those two governments should be minimized.

To conclude that any one of these arguments is satisfactory for explaining the utility of exchanging performing artists on an international basis is to be less than comprehensive. It is the contention in this chapter that all three factors are working simultaneously and inseparably. Therefore, we will examine the three major dimensions of the phenomenon individually: (1) government involvement; (2) public involvement (university, church, and other non-business); and (3) involvement of the business sector.

Government Involvement

U.S. participation in cultural exchange programs began as a largely defensive move in 1938.[3] The State Department's Division of Cultural Relations functioned to counter Nazi and Fascist propaganda efforts at that time. Later in the post-war (World War II) years, the Division was largely involved in a "contest or race with the Communists."[4]

By the fiscal year beginning July 1, 1955, however, the beginning of a new era was noted with a new official approach to international exchange of performing artists by the United States government. During its first year of operation, the Cultural Presentations Office of the U.S. Department of State operated on a budget of approximately $2.3 million in an attempt at world-wide coverage by American artists.[5]

A peak of $2.8 million was budgeted in fiscal 1966, during which time 37 groups and artists, comprising 827 persons, were sent to 92 countries, nearly double the 48 countries reached in the original fiscal 1955. Emphasis was now on creating a new, higher-level image of U.S. performing artists, rather than countering Communist allegations of low quality.

The impetus for this new approach began to wane in the late 1960's. Budget for this program reached an all-time low in fiscal 1970, when only $500,000 of a $1 million request was budgeted. This former figure would have been considered highly inadequate for even limited concentration in Europe alone, much less the whole world, when the program was conceived 15 years earlier. Formally published annual *Reports to the Congress and the Public* were discontinued in 1968 because the funds, and thus the program, were curtailed so much.[6]

The budget for fiscal 1972-73 was still trimmed to $800,000, which severely limited the scope of the program. Devaluation of the dollar abroad made even that amount not go as far as it usually did.

In spite of budgetary restrictions in 1972-73, many top-notch performing artists were being sent abroad by the State Department's Office of Cultural Presentations. For instance, the Fifth Dimension toured Turkey, Poland, Romania, and Czechoslovakia; the New York City Ballet performed in the Soviet Union and Poland; the Jose Limon Dance Company was sent to East Asia; and the Alwin Nikolais Dance Theater toured Latin America.

The cost involved in sending various-sized groups to foreign countries is mind-boggling, to say nothing of budget-depleting. In 1968, the estimated figure for sending a symphony orchestra on a Latin American tour was $750,000.[7] Inflation and dollar devaluation would make this more than the entire 1972-73 budget amount for the Office of Cultural Presentations. Therefore, the government-sponsored appearance of the Pittsburgh Symphony or costly productions such as *Porgy and Bess* or *Oklahoma* in even the major world capitals is virtually eliminated. As one possible consequence, many U.S. Information Service officials in Latin American and Southeast Asian countries report that second- and third-rate performers are representing the state of American artistry in their countries.[8]

Given that these exchanges do occur, what is seen as the utility of them? It is suggested by Lowry and Hooker that artist-government cooperation be handled in the following way:

> To keep artistic and political values most nearly in proper relation, government activities in the international cultural sphere should be managed directly and indirectly to:
>
> 1. Support art, the artist, and cultural activities for their own importance in society.
>
> 2. Use the strictest criteria of artistic excellence in the choice of artists and artistic groups employed;
>
> 3. Employ those talented artists and artistic groups who will in the process be assisted in their professional development.
>
> 4. Help to improve public taste.
>
> 5. Profit from the intensive and realistic advice of artists and artistic directors themselves.

6. Ensure, by means of the above principles, the moral and intellectual support of the artistic community at home and abroad.[9]

To facilitate these ideas, the Mutual Education and Cultural Exchange Act of 1961 was intended to formally "provide for the improvement and strengthening of the international relations of the United States by promoting better mutual understanding among the peoples of the world through educational and cultural exchanges."[10] Among the stipulations of the act are:

> The purpose of this Act is to enable the Government of the United States to increase mutual understanding between the people of the United States and the people of other countries by means of educational and cultural exchange; to strengthen the ties which unite us with other nations by demonstrating the educational and cultural interests, developments, and achievements of the people of the United States and other nations, and the contributions being made toward a peaceful and more fruitful life for people throughout the world; to promote international cooperation for educational and cultural advancement; and thus to assist in the development of friendly, sympathetic, and peaceful relations between the United States and the other countries of the world.[11]

Through the Act, the President of the United States is authorized to provide by grant, contract, or otherwise for students, educators, and professionals from both the U.S. and other nations to be exchanged. In addition, he is authorized to promote cultural exchanges, by financing:

> 1. Visits and interchanges between the United States and other countries of leaders, experts in fields of specialized knowledge or skill, and other influential or distinguished persons;
> 2. Tours in countries abroad by creative and performing artists from the United States, individually and in groups, representing any field of the arts, sports, or any other form of cultural attainment.

3. United States representation in international artistic, dramatic, musical, sports, and other cultural festivals, competitions, meetings, and like exhibitions and assemblies;

4. Participation by groups and individuals from other countries in nonprofit activities in the United States similar to those described in subparagraphs (2) and (3) of this paragraph, when the President determines that such participation is in the national interest.[1 2]

Allowances are also made for the President to authorize cultural centers both at home and abroad; research into educational and cultural exchange; orientation courses, language training, or other appropriate service and materials for persons traveling out of their home countries for educational and cultural purposes; plus many other programs and services to facilitate the international exchange promoted in the Act.

Because of budget limitations, however, most of the exchange of performing artists officially sponsored by the U.S. government provides for sending American artists abroad rather than bringing foreign artists to the U.S.[1 3] The "reverse flow" that exists — importing of foreign talent — is on a "private basis strictly," since Congress has never appropriated funds specifically for that purpose.[1 4] (See sections on private sector.) Occasional exceptions have been made, however minimal, when an international cultural festival is sponsored in the U.S. — for example, the Tanglewood Festival has regularly imported topnotch European performers. These exceptions, though, have usually been limited to "acting as the middle man in aiding a country in making arrangements in the United States."[1 5]

The State Department arm which is often responsible for facilitating exchange of American performing artists abroad is the United States Information Agency, or more usually, the U.S. Information Service (USIS), in most countries around the world. Logistics for performances by entire symphony orchestras or by soloists are arranged by USIS staff people located in the foreign country.

Emphasis is still on "Iron Curtain" countries, according to the Cultural Affairs Officer of USIS Mexico City, Richard B. Phillips.

"We generally don't get much support from the State Department for Latin American exchange," he said. "Performing artists and other forms of cultural exchange are sent mostly to Iron Curtain countries. With budget cutbacks in recent years, it is only occasionally that we can give some support to a group that would find it otherwise impossible to get down here.[16]

Phillips cited additional inter-cultural benefits derived from this type of international exchange.

"I see one of the primary values of cultural exchange to be that it shows people in other countries that our youngsters have severely disciplined themselves to reach a level of excellence," he said. "We have a world-wide image of being undisciplined –– going around in packs aimlessly. When these groups appear in Mexico City, I hear critics both amateur and professional saying, 'these kids are too young to be so good.' The critics just couldn't get over having that myth exploded."

Phillips estimates that between 60 and 80 American groups are brought to Mexico City each year, but most of them are brought in by private enterprise. There are several hundred programs by quality performing groups throughout the country each year, he said. In 1972-73, these included the Jerome Robbins Ballet, Betty Allen and the Utah Symphony.

The cultural exchange most frequently sponsored by the U.S. government involves musical artists.[17] Musicians, particularly at the student level, have been conspicuous in such countries as Germany and Italy, while such presentations as symphonies, musicals, and chamber music groups have been fairly limited.

Needless to say, musicians and ballet troups, which traditionally rank second in quantity, are happier about the state of exchange affairs than some other performing artists. Participation in the Theatre des Nations, which was officially launched in 1954, is the primary government-supported channel for international exchange of American dramatic artists, for instance.[18] This international approach to theater is sponsored by the national government of France, the city of Paris, and the Department of Seine. The U.S.

government still supports participation in this event, which includes cycles not only of drama, but opera and ballet as well. Occasional bursts of government support go toward sponsoring other theater arts presentations, however, such as the 1956 Latin American tour of "Teahouse of the August Moon" and the 1961 three-continent tour by the Theater Guild American Repertory Company, which cost more than $1 million.[19]

The other major way that governments are involved in international exchange of performing artists is through regulation of passports, visas, and international exchange treaties. Many governments use these regulatory powers on a regular basis for screening "undesirables" from their respective countries. For instance, the U.S. government requires performers from abroad to have an "H-2" visa if there is any money to be made by the performance.[20] This means, theoretically, that no American performer can be qualified to do the same thing. If interpreted literally, of course, this rule *could* eliminate all foreign virtuoso violinists from the U.S. as long as there were any available American virtuosos. Great Britain and Mexico are also quite strict about which performers they allow into the country and for how long.

Government involvement at this level, has created considerable controversy in the U.S. During the Vietnam War, Joan Baez and other "anti-war" performers were threatened with having passports revoked for anti-war activities overseas; during that same war, Bob Hope and other USO-supported performers were given use of U.S. government facilities on a regular basis to entertain the troops and film activities for subsequent U.S. consumption. In 1973, the power to regulate immigration was used to rule that former Beatle, John Lennon, would be expelled from the U.S. as an undesirable, since he had a 1968 marijuana conviction in England (though his wife, Yoko Ono, was allowed to stay). At the same time that legislators and congressmen were censuring anti-war activist Jane Fonda for her statements at home and abroad in 1973, the USIA continued to circulate on a world-wide basis a film on Vice-President Spiro T. Agnew which was narrated by another Hollywood performer, John Wayne.

Treaties, such as the Lacy-Zatoubin agreement, renewed at two-year intervals between the U.S. and the Soviet Union, regulate the amount of cultural, educational, and scientific exchange that takes place between the two countries. (In addition, with the USSR finally signing the International Copyright Convention in 1973, it is speculated that such things as book translations will also be regulated under this agreement.) Other similar treaties include the U.S. –– Romanian exchange agreements which are renewed on an annual basis.[21]

For nearly 20 years, the emphasis of U.S. cultural exchange programs has been on Communist countries, though the late 1960's saw a gradual change in that trend. Critics of the programs have questioned the priorities, suggesting that advanced *and* developing countries should be included in the program regardless of political leaning and that, generally, the program should be free of political influence, since art and politics *are* separate concepts. Whether these suggestions will be heeded or not remains to be seen.

Public Non-Profit Involvement

Activities of universities, churches, non-profit foundations, international friendship societies, and such civic groups as Rotary Clubs and Chambers of Commerce are involved in international exchange of performing artists on many different levels. Attempting to be comprehensive in describing these programs would be folly, but several examples will help explain the general function of this type of exchange. Though some might refer to these programs as "propaganda," the groups themselves generally consider them to be "educational."

Universities all over the country are conducting cultural exchange programs with foreign schools in an effort to broaden international understanding. The University of Kansas has exchange programs with schools in Costa Rica and Poland; the University of New Mexico reciprocates exchanges with schools in Guadalajara, Mexico, and in Ecuador.

The development of a typical university exchange program can be shown through the example of New Mexico State University, a 10,000-student southwestern university. In 1963, a State Department grant to develop a cultural exchange program with the University of Chihuahua, Mexico, was acquired by the University Cultural Program Board.[22] The board has imported such groups as the Mexican Folklorico Ballet (Mexico City) in 1972 and the Senegalese Dancers, 1973.

In addition, the university has participated in the Bi-Cultural University Alliance (BCUA) comprised of the University of Texas at El Paso, New Mexico State University, Western New Mexico University, and the University of Chihuahua. Under this program, performing artists from each of the universities travel to the others on a regular basis. For instance, the 120-member NMSU band has made several trips to Chihuahua where they stay in hotels, observe the Mexican way of life, and appear in concert.

"There is a lot to be gained for students, as well as local residents in both countries," one of the BCUA founders said.[23] "Our groups performing in Chihuahua continue to impress the Mexican people with the high caliber of their training. In some ways, our kids are an inspiration to the Mexican people — — and in others, they are inspirations to us."

Some of the American participants in this program have traveled with such groups as the Chihuahua Symphony or have been members of the international woodwind ensembles and dance troupes organized in the alliance. One of the BCUA founders, who spent 8 months in 1973 as guest lecturer/conductor at Jagielonian University, Cracow, Poland, said the benefits of this type of international cooperation continue to accrue in "ways not even imagined yet."[24]

"For students to just have to experience going through customs with their musical instruments or their oil paintings is education enough from this type of exchange," he said. "But the myths about 'foreigners' can be dispelled by traveling extensively with them or spending considerable amounts of time with them. I think in this way we've accomplished what no diplomat ever could."

Internationally-oriented church or other religious groups also engage in exchange of performing artists. The Methodist Mission Board, for instance, arranges a two-way flow of Gospel-singing groups, native dancers, and other performing groups.[25] By importing a group from a country in which the church has a mission or by taking an American group to a country where there's a church-related project, the board feels like there is mutual education taking place.

The United Nations, through UNESCO, is involved in cultural exchange. For example, in the music field, UNESCO gave the responsibility for international exchange to the International Music Council organized in 1949.[26] With emphasis on exchange of contemporary and folk music, the council has sponsored concerts, broadcasts, recordings and exchange aid for young composers. Another example of UNESCO involvement is its affiliation with the International Theater Institute established in 1948. Through the institute, there is considerable sponsorship of traveling fellowships to talented young dramatic artists each year.

Municipalities around the country are involved in various forms of exchange on an international basis. For instance, the coordinator of the Saratoga, N.Y., summer festivals engages regularly in a "straight swap" of performing artists from other countries.[27] They are flown in and flown out at the expense of the festival organizers.

Similarly, the annual Fiesta Days held in Truth or Consequences, New Mexico, by Ralph Edwards, founder of the television program of that name, utilizes international performing artists. One of the groups imported for the 1973 fiesta, for example, was the Estudiantina del Instituto Technologica de Chihauhua, conducted by Prof. Salvador Perez-Marquez. This group of student musicians has traveled extensively throughout the American southwest, as well as through northern Mexico.

A third example of the way average communities are involved in this type of exchange is Saginaw, Michigan, a town of less than 200,000 population. A city active in the "People-to-People" program, Saginaw has a "sister city" in Japan, Tokushima, with which they cooperated in building a Japanese Garden in 1971. In addition, their Community Concert Series imports such international groups as the Canadian Opera, Vienna's Johann Strauss Orchestra, and the Norwegian National Ballet. This last group from Oslo is being sponsored on its first North American tour in 1974 by His Majesty King Olaf V, Scandinavian Airlines, the Norwegian-American Steamship Line, and the Tom Wilhelmsen Foundation.[28]

Other private non-profit foundations provide opportunities for musical talent, particularly, to be extended on a regular basis. Examples of these, besides the Wilhelmsen Foundation, are the

Martha Baird Rockefeller Fund, the Guggenheim Foundation, the Rockefeller Foundation, and the American Academy in Rome which provides a place for young composers/musicians to come each year.[29]

Such groups as the Austrian-American Friendship Society and the Slovenian-American Radio Club round out the types of public efforts on various levels to cultivate international exchange of performing artists. Rotary International is involved, in addition to exchange of educational groups, students, technicians, and craftsmen, in the exchange of musicians, dance groups, and other artists to increase world understanding.[30]

Private Involvement

Importing and exporting of performing artists is big business. Therefore, it is to be expected that there are "free enterprisers," in addition to government and public service agencies, involved in this effort.

Booking agencies range from individual endeavors, such as Maurice Chalfan, a semi-retired New York agent who was the first to tour "Holiday on Ice" internationally, to Columbia Artists Management Incorporated (CAMI) and Sol Hurok Enterprises, both of New York, the two largest dealers in international performing talent.

Over the years, these groups have participated in many "firsts" which have affected international understanding. For instance, Hurok's importation of an orchestra from Turkey in 1973 marks the first time that U.S. audiences have been able to see live performances by a group that comes from a country most people do not know very much about.[31]

"Young people seeing a Turkish group or any other group either here or abroad — — are particularly impressed with the high quality of talent," according to Hurok's publicity department. "There have been instances of kids overseas being inspired to study dance in America, for instance, after seeing how accomplished some of our dance troupes are."

At Columbia Artists, barriers are also being broken down every year.[32] For instance, during the 1973-74 season, the 90-member

Krasnayarsk Dance Company of Siberia appeared in the U. S. for the first time under CAMI auspices. No conclusive studies have been conducted at this point to determine if there are other types of groups from different countries that the American people might be interested in or American groups that foreign people would like to see.

"Requests from organizations both at home and abroad largely determine how we map out the next year's offering," according to CAMI publicists. "But, of course, we are sensitive to other types of indicators among the public through informal studies conducted by staff people and friends."

The Hurok spokesmen had no comment on the issue of determining popular tastes in the field of performing artist exchange through marketing surveys, public opinion polls or other scientific means.

Summary

Millions of dollars are being spent each year on international exchange of performing artists, by countries all over the world. It is generally accepted that this is a "positive" effort on the part of any given country, though there are differences of opinion about the relative utility of this exchange in comparison to other types of international interaction, and the role the government should play in injecting its own political policies and foreign policy goals into such a program.

For many years, the Soviet Union forbade any artistic endeavor to reflect anything but "Socialist Realism," meaning the forwarding of the Communist Party cause. Nikita Khrushchev eased the pressure a bit, but other countries of the world are still debating how the line is to be drawn between diplomacy and creative exchange. The U.S. government's involvement in cultural exchange has declined since peak involvement in the late 1950's and early 1960's, but there is still a running debate on the "politics vs. art" theme.

Outside of official government channels, there is also considerable interest in international exchange of performing artists. The United Nations, non-profit foundations, universities, churches, and other "public" service groups are importing and exporting talent in their particular fields of interest. Similarly, private enterprise is involved in large-scale exchange programs.

FOOTNOTES

[1] American Assembly, *Cultural Affairs and Foreign Relations*, p. 46.

[2] Frankel, Charles, *The Neglected Aspect of Foreign Affairs: American Educational and Cultural Policy Abroad*, p. 122.

[3] American Assembly, *Cultural Affairs and Foreign Relations*, p. 48.

[4] *Ibid.*, p. 48.

[5] *Ibid., Cultural Presentations, USA, 1967-1968: A Report to the Congress and the Public*, p. iv.

[6] U.S. Department of State, Office of Cultural Presentations, interviews with Beverly Gerstein, September 6, 1972, and March 6, 1973

[7] American Assembly, *Cultural Affairs and Foreign Relations*, p. 54.

[8] *Ibid.*, p. 55.

[9] *Ibid.*, p. 46, 47.

[10] U.S. Congress, *Public Law 87-256*, p. 1.

[11] *Ibid.*, p. 1

[12] *Ibid.*, p. 2.

[13] U.S. Department of State, Office of Cultural Presentations. Interviews with Beverly Gerstein, Sept. 6, 1972, and March 6, 1973.

[14] American Assembly, *Cultural Affairs and Foreign Relations*, p. 51.

[15] *Ibid.*, p. 51, 52.

[16] U.S. Department of State, U.S. Information Service, Mexico City, D.F., Mexico. Interview with Richard B. Phillips, Cultural Affairs Officer, January 8, 1973.

[17] American Assembly, *Cultural Affairs and Foreign Relations*, p. 52.

[18] Dorian, Frederick, *Commitment to Culture*, p. 183-185.

[19] American Assembly, *Cultural Affairs, Foreign Relations*, pp. 57-58.

[20] U.S. Department of State, Office of Cultural Presentations. Interviews with Beverly Gerstein, Sept. 6, 1972, and March 6, 1973.

[21] "U.S. —— Romania Complete 1967-68 Cultural Exchange Agreement," *Department of State Bulletin* LVI (March 20, 1967), p. 31.

[22] Bi-Cultural University Alliance, Las Cruces, New Mexico: interview with John Glowacki, exchange coordinator, November 29, 1972.

[23] *Ibid.*

[24] *Ibid.*

[25] Perryman, Leonard, "The Methodist Church and Secular Mass Media in the Developing Nations," p. 35.

[26] Shuster, George N. *UNESCO: Assessment and Promise*, p. 111.

[27] Hurok Enterprises, Inc., New York, N.Y. Interviews with John Gingrich, Publicity Department, September 6, 1972 — March 5, 1973.

[28] Saginaw News, Saginaw, Michigan. Interview with Thelma McLaughlin, Head Librarian, April 16, 1973

[29] American Assembly, *Cultural Affairs, Foreign Relations*, p. 53.

[30] Rotary International, interview with Harvey C. Jacobs, former Editor of the *Rotarian* magazine, April 16, 1973

[31] Hurok Enterprises, Inc., New York, N.Y. Interviews with John Gingrich, Publicity Department, September 6, 1972 — March 5, 1973.

[32] Columbia Artists Management Inc., New York, N.Y. Interview with Hattie Clark, publicity department, March 4, 1973.

BIBLIOGRAPHY

Public Documents

U.S. Congress, *Public Law 87-256,* 87th Congress, H.R. 8666, September 21, 1961.

U.S. Department of State, Advisory Committee on the Arts, *Cultural Presentations, USA, 1964-1965: A Report to the Congress and the Public.*

U.S. Department of State, Advisory Committee on the Arts, *Cultural Presentations, USA, 1965-1966: A Report to the Congress and the Public.*

U.S. Department of State, Advisory Committee on the Arts, *Cultural Presentations, USA, 1967-1968: A Report to the Congress and the Public. (Last Report Published by the Committee.)*

Books

American Assembly, *Cultural Affairs and Foreign Relations.* Edited by Paul J. Braisted, Washington, D.C.: Columbia Books, Publishers, 1968.

Davison, W. Phillips, *International Political Communication.* Published for the Council on Foreign Relations, New York: Frederick A. Praeger, Publishers, 1965.

Dorian, Frederick, *Commitment to Culture.* Pittsburgh: University of Pittsburgh Press, 1964.

Dyer, Murray, *The Weapon on the Wall,* Baltimore: Johns Hopkins Press, 1959.

Elder, Robert Ellsworth, *The Information Machine: The United States Information Agency and American Foreign Policy,* Syracuse: Syracuse University Press, 1967.

Fischer, Heinz-Dietrich and Merrill, John C., eds., *International Communication: Media, Channels, Functions.* Studies in Public Communication, New York: Hastings House, Publishers, 1970.

Frankel, Charles, *The Neglected Aspect of Foreign Affairs: American Educational and Cultural Policy Abroad,* Washington, D.C.: The Brookings Institution, 1965.

Hoffman, Arthur S., ed., *International Communication and the New Diplomacy,* Edward R. Murrow Center of Public Diplomacy Publication, Bloomington: Indiana University Press, 1968.

Krosney, Herbert and Krosney, Mary Stewart, *Careers and Opportunities in International Service,* New York: E.P. Dutton & Co., Inc., 1965.

Laves, Walter H.C., and Thomson, Charles A., *UNESCO: Purpose, Progress, Prospects,* Bloomington: Indiana University Press, 1957.

Mowlana, Hamid, *International Communication: A Selected Bibliography.* Dubuque: Kendall/Hunt Publishing Company, 1971.

Rubin, Ronald I., *The Objectives of the U.S. Information Agency: Controversies and Analysis,* a publication of the Praeger Special

Studies in International Politics and Public Affairs, New York: Frederick A. Praeger, Publishers, 1968.

Shuster, George N., *UNESCO: Assessment and Promise*, A publication of the Council on Foreign Relations, New York: Harper and Row, Publishers, 1963.

Snyder, Harold E., *When Peoples Speak to Peoples*, Washington, D.C.: American Council on Education, 1953.

Toynbee, Arnold, *et. al. New Frontiers of Knowledge*, Washington, D.C.: Public Affairs Press, 1957.

UNESCO. *Handbook of International Exchanges*. Paris: UNESCO, 1962.

UNESCO. *Handbook of International Exchanges*. Paris: UNESCO, 1968.

U.S. Information Agency, *Catalog of Published Concert Music by American Composers*. Selected, Compiled and Prepared by the Music Branch, Information Center Service, Music Adviser, U.S. Information Agency, Washington, D.C.: U.S. Government Printing Office, 1964.

Articles and Periodicals

"Exchange Program with East Europe," *School and Society* XCV (Oct. 14, 1967), pp. 345-6.

"International Communication in the Twentieth Century," *Bulletin of Atomic Scientists* XXIV (June, 1968), pp. 53-55.

"Making Cultural Exchange a Real Exchange," *Dance Magazine* XLI (October, 1967), pp. 21-30.

"No Bolshoi," *Newsweek* LXXVI (Dec. 21, 1970), pp. 67-68.

"Our Cultural Exports: A View of the U.S. Exchange Program," *American Academy of Political and Social Science ANNALS* CCCLXXXIV (July, 1969), pp. 85-95.

"People-to-People Diplomacy: Key to World Understanding," *Department of State Bulletin* LXVII (Sept. 4, 1972), pp. 248-51.

Rowan, Carl T. "The Challenge of Cultural Communication," *International Communication*, edited by Heinz Dietrich-Fischer and John C. Merrill, New York: Hastings House, Publishers, 1970.

"University of Minnesota Band Returns from Tour of Soviet Union,"

Department of State Bulletin LX (June 23, 1969), pp. 540-542.

"U.S. — Romania Agree on 71-72 Exchange Program," *Department of State Bulletin* LXIV (January 25, 1971), pp. 126-130.

"U.S. — Romania Complete 1967-68 Cultural Exchange Agreement," *Department of State Bulletin* LVI (March 20, 1967), pp. 479-80.

"Welcome Mat: U.S. — Soviet Cultural Exchanges," *Newsweek* LXXIX (April 24, 1972), p. 36.

Unpublished Material

Columbia Artists Management Incorporated, *Artists and Attractions, 1973-1974*, New York: CAMI, 1973.

Perryman, Leonard, "The Methodist Church and Secular Mass Media in the Developing Nations," paper read for Seminar in International Communication, Chapel Hill, N.C., May 1967.

Other Sources

Bi-Cultural University Alliance, Las Cruces, New Mexico, interview with John Glowacki, exchange coordinator, November 29, 1972.

Columbia Artists Management Inc., New York, N.Y., interview with Hattie Clark, publicity department, March 4, 1973.

Hurok Enterprises, Inc., Los Angeles, Ca., interviews with Betty Ferrell, publicity department, December 22, 1972 — January 4, 1973.

Hurok Enterprises, Inc., New York, N.Y., interviews with John Gingrich, publicity department, September 6, 1972 — March 5, 1973.

Hurok Enterprises, Inc., New York, N.Y., interviews with Lee Walter, executive secretary to Sol Hurok, November 30, 1972 — March 5, 1973.

Rotary International, interview with Harvey C. Jacobs, former editor of the *Rotarian* magazine, April 16, 1973.

Saginaw News, Saginaw, Michigan, interview with Thelma McLaughlin, head librarian, April 16, 1973.

U.S. Department of State, Office of Cultural Presentations, interviews with Beverly Gerstein, September 6, 1972, and March 6, 1973.

U.S. Department of State, U.S. Information Service, Mexico City, D.F., Mexico. Interview with Richard B. Phillips, Cultural Affairs Officer, January 8, 1973.

Some concluding observations

I am sure that no author is ever completely satisfied with his or her work, and I am also certain that all editors feel some frustration as they look at a completed book like this. So much more could be said, so much more should be covered, so many more points could be validly made. Maybe that is an important experience in itself. Our culture tends to strive for "completion." We have been trained to work towards a kind of perfection which makes our work as definitive as possible, or the last word in a given field. My own hope is that none will think of anything which has been compiled or discussed in this particular book as the last or final word. Hopefully, some of it will represent the most contemporary point of view on a given subject. It is equally important that we recognize the lessons from the past, while attempting to discover experiences of human beings in the areas of intercultural and international communication which can provide us with insights beyond a given historical moment. As a result, I attempted not to be overly impressed with the latest "fad," or the most impressive contemporary innovation if it meant thoughtlessly rejecting other insights we have gained in the past. I must confess, however, that I had a specific point of view, and that I attempted to encourage all authors who participated in this effort to be cognizant of an underlying theme, or a series of interlinking themes. Thus we deal more with the role of the *individual* in communication, and an *interactive process* rather than specific episodes or individual events. This was done, because I felt we have learned in recent years that otherwise we may lose any understanding, any appreciation for the *total system* and its *interrelated parts*, as well as the highly individualized nature of human interaction.

We have seen that patterns, systems, and even specific instances of human communication are very complex. Obviously, that complexity has not caused human beings to cease communicating. Maybe the problems have not resided as much in communication, as in and among those who study human interactions. There may be an increasing need in the study of human communication to feel secure and content in the discovery of diversity. Yet our total training and cultural background have made us look for unity and agreement. As a result, we often strive to simplify admittedly complex human processes, in an attempt to come up with pseudo-scientific formulations, which we feel are acceptable under the rules or standards of natural-science methodologies.

No one can probably appreciate the richness and diversity of human interaction more than the human-communication scholar. Diversity and flexibility make human interaction and life worthwhile and excitingly creative. A lack of interaction, rigidity, and fear of the great and often disturbing variety of human experience and expression, consistently leads to closed, rather mechanical-systems, which do not only include the seed of their own destruction but which we can frequently watch decaying before our very eyes. Human beings are significantly open-, metabolic-systems, whose flexibility and ability to adjust are probably their most vital survival equipment. In the longrun that may be the most important reminder which today's communication-scholar —— as well as every practioner in the area —— can share with others in our world. Fitting human beings into existing, or developing technological or other systems, for the convenience or maintenance of those systems, may make it impossible for significantly human, spiritual- and cultural-values or -contributions, to survive. Human communication and interaction, on all levels, which encourages diversity rather than similarity or unity of response, will not only allow us to work out our own destinies, although more slowly and haltingly than some of our more impatient "leaders" would have us do, but it will certainly be more in keeping with our uniquely human qualities.

My personal thanks goes to all of the authors whose work appears in this book, for their courtesy, their encouragement, and their continued efforts to make a meaningful contribution to our understanding of intercultural and international communication.

APPENDIX

APPENDIX

REFERENCES

1. Abrams, S., & Neubauer, P.B. "Orientedness: The Person or The Thing." *The Psychoanalytic Quarterly*, 1976, vol. 45, pp. 73-99.
2. Adcock, C.J., & Webberley, M. "Primary Mental Abilities." *Journal of General Psychology*, 84(1971), pp. 229-243.
3. Adevai, G., Silverman, A.J., & McGough, W.E. "Perceptual Correlates of the Rod-and-Frame Test." *Perceptual and Motor*

Skills, 26(1968), pp. 1055-1064.

4.   Alexander, J.B., & Gudeman, H.E. "Personal and Interpersonal Measures of Field Dependence." *Perceptual and Motor Skills,* 20(1965), pp. 79-86.

5.   Alexander, S.M. "A Study of Perceptual and Verbal Differentiation Among Male College Students." (Doctoral dissertation, George Washington University, 1970). *Dissertation Abstracts International,* 31/11-B(1971), p. 6887. (University Microfilms No. 71-12, 285).

6.   Ancona, L., & Carli, R. "The Dynamics of Cinematographic Participation." *Ikon,* 76(1971), pp. 47-73.

7.   Arbuthnot, J. "Cautionary Note on Measurement of Field Independence." *Perceptual and Motor Skills,* 35(1972), pp. 479-488.

8.   Axelrod, S., & Cohen, L.D. "Senescence and Embedded-figure Performance in Vision and Touch." *Perceptual and Motor Skills,* 12(1961), pp. 283-288.

9.   Baker, E. "Perceiver Variables Involved in the Recognition of Faces." (Doctoral dissertation, University of London, 1967). Cited in 464.

10.   Barclay, A., & Cusumano, D.R. "Father Absence, Cross-sex Identity, and Field-dependent Behavior in Male Adolescents." *Child Development,* 38(1967), pp. 243-250.

11.   Bard, C. "The Relation Between Perceptual Style and Physical Activities." *International Journal of Sport Psychology,* 3(1972), pp. 107-113.

12.   Barr, H.L. "Relations Between Mode of Perception and the Tendency to Conform." (Doctoral dissertation, Yale University, 1952). *Dissertation Abstracts,* 28/11-B (1965), p. 4741. (University Microfilms No. 65-8142).

13.   Barrell, G.V., & Trippe, H.R. "Field Dependence and Physical Ability." *Perceptual and Motor Skills,* 41(1975), pp. 216-218.

14.   Barrett, G.V., & Thornton, C.L. "Cognitive Style Differences between Engineers and College Students." *Perceptual and Motor Skills,* 25(1967), pp. 789-793.

15.   Barrett, G.V., & Thornton, C.L. "Relationship Between Perceptual Style and Driver Reaction to an Emergency

Situation." *Journal of Applied Psychology,* 52(1968), pp. 169-176.

16. Barrett, G.V., Thornton, C.L., & Cabe, P.A., "Cue Conflict Related to Perceptual Style." *Journal of Applied Psychology,* 54(1970), pp. 258-264.

17. Barry, H., Child, I.L., & Bacon, M.K., "The Relation of Child Training to Subsistence Economy." *American Anthropologist,* 61(1959), pp. 51-63.

18. Bauman, G. "The Stability of the Individual's Mode of Perception and of Perception-personality Relationships." (Doctoral dissertation, New York University, 1951). *American Doctoral Dissertations,* 1951, p. 135.

19. Beasley, N.A. "The Extent of Individual Differences in the Perception of Causality." *Canadian Journal of Psychology,* 22(1968) pp. 399-407.

20. Beck, T.K.H. "An Exploratory Study of Cognitive Style Based on Perceptual Mode, Conceptual Style and Speech Code." (Doctoral dissertation, Emory University, 1975). *Dissertation Abstracts International,* 36/12:1-B(1976), p. 6349. (University Microfilms No. 76-12, 172).

21. Beckerle, G.P. "Behavioral Traits Related to Psychological Differentiation in Pre-adolescent Boys." (Doctoral dissertation, Michigan State University, 1966). *Dissertation Abstracts,* 28/01-B(1967), p. 336. (University Microfilms No. 67-7519).

22. Bell, E.G. "Inner-directed and Other-directed Attitudes." (Doctoral dissertation, Yale University, 1955). *American Doctoral Dissertations,* 1955, p. 154.

23. Berent, S. "Field-dependence and Performance on a Writing Task." *Perceptual and Motor Skills,* 38(1974), pp. 651-658.

24. Berent, S. "Field Dependence and the Central Nervous System." Summary of paper presented at 83rd Annual Convention of the American Psychological Association, Chicago, August 30, 1975.

25. Berent, S. "Rod-and-Frame Performance and Calculating Ability: A Replication." *Perceptual and Motor Skills,* 43(1976), p. 562.

26. Berent, S. "Rod-and-Frame Performance and Calculation of Serial Sevens: Brief Note." *Perceptual and Motor Skills,* 42(1976), p. 86.

27. Berent, S., Cohen, B.D., & Silverman, A.J. "Changes in Verbal and Nonverbal Learning Following a Single Left or Right Unilateral Electroconvulsive Treatment." *Biological Psychiatry,* 10(1975), pp. 95-100.

28. Berent, S., & Silverman, A.J. "Field Dependence and Differences Between Visual and Verbal Learning Tasks." *Perceptual and Motor Skills,* 36(1973), pp. 1327-1330.

29. Berger, C.R., Gardner, R.R., Clatterbuck, G.W., & Schulman, L.S. "Perceptions of Information Sequencing in Relationship Development." *Human Communication Research,* 3(1976), pp. 29-46.

30. Berry, J.W. "Ecological and Cultural Factors in Spatial Perceptual Development." *Canadian Journal of Behavioural Science,* 3(1971), pp. 324-336.

31. Berry, J.W. "Ecology, Cultural Adaptation, and Psychological Differentiation: Traditional Patterning and Acculturative Stress." In R.W. Brislin, S. Bochner, & W.J. Lonner, eds., *Cross-Cultural Perspectives on Learning.* New York: John Wiley & Sons, 1975.

32. Berry, J.W. "Independence and Conformity in Subsistence-level Societies." *Journal of Personality and Social Psychology,* 7(1967), pp. 415-418.

33. Berry, J.W. "Temne and Eskimo Perceptual Skills." *International Journal of Psychology,* 1(1966), pp. 207-229.

34. Berry, J.W., & Annis, R.C. "Ecology, Cultural and Psychological Differentiation." *International Journal of Psychology,* 9(1974), pp. 173-193.

35. Bertini, M. "Il tratto difensivo dell'isolamenta nella sua determinazione dinamica e strutturale." *Contributi Dell' Instituto di Psicologica,* 1961, Serie XXV. (Milano: Univer. Cattolica).

36. Bettinghaus, E.P. *Persuasive Communication.* New York: Holt, Rinehart and Winston, Inc., 1968.

37. Bieri, J., Bradburn, W.M., & Galinsky, M.D., "Sex Differences in Perceptual Behavior." *Journal of Personality,* 26(1958), pp. 1-12.

38.   Biggs, J.B., Fitzgerald, D., & Atkinson, S.M. "Convergent and Divergent Abilities in Children and Teachers' Ratings of Competence and Certain Classroom Behaviors." *British Journal of Educational Psychology,* 41(1971), pp. 277-286.

39.   Birnbaum, A.S.G. "Social Correlates of Field Articulation in Adolescents: the Effect Upon Productivity in the Presence of Others." (Doctoral dissertation, Hofstra University, 1975). *Dissertation Abstracts International,* 36/04-B(1975), pp. 1959-1960. (University Microfilms No. 75-23, 103).

40.   Blasi, E.R., Cross, H.A., & Hebert, J.A. "Effects of Field-dependency on Weight Comparisons." *Perceptual and Motor Skills,* 35(1972), pp. 111-114.

41.   Block, J. "A Study of Affective Responsiveness in a Lie-detection Situation." *Journal of Abnormal and Social Psychology,* 55(1957), pp. 11-15.

42.   Bloomberg, M. "Anagram Solutions of Field-independent and Field-dependent Persons." *Perceptual and Motor Skills,* 21(1965), p. 766.

43.   Bloomberg, M., & Meehan, S. "Effect of Induced Locus of Control on Change in Field Independence." *Journal of Clinical Psychology,* 31(1975), pp. 492-498.

44.   Bloomberg, M., & Soneson, S. "The Effects of Locus of Control and Field Independence-dependence on Moral Reasoning." *Journal of Genetic Psychology,* 128(1976), pp. 59-66.

45.   Bogen, J.E. "The Other Side of the Brain I: Dysgraphia and Dyscopia Following Cerebral Commissurotomy." *Bulletin of the Los Angeles Neurological Societies,* 34(1969), pp. 73-105.

46.   Bogen, J.E. "The Other Side of the Brain II: An Appositional Mind." *Bulletin of the Los Angeles Neurological Societies,* 34(1969), pp. 135-162.

47.   Bogen, J.E., DeZure, R., Ten Houten, W.D., & Marsh, J.F. "The Other Side of the Brain IV. The A/P ratio." *Bulletin of the Los Angeles Neurological Societies,* 37(1972), pp. 49-61.

48.   Bogo, N., Winget, C., & Gleser, G.C. "Ego Defenses and Perceptual Styles." *Perceptual and Motor Skills,* 30(1970), pp. 599-605.

49. Bone, R.N., & Eysenck, H.J. "Extraversion, Field-dependence, and the Stroop Test." *Perceptual and Motor Skills,* 34(1972), pp. 873-874.

50. Boschi, F., & Loprieno, M. "Comportamento in gruppo di soggetti subnormali con stile conoscitivo globale ed articolato." *Rivista di Neurobiologia,* 14(1968), pp. 1-5.

51. Boschi, F., & Loprieno, M. "Stile conoscitivo e resistenza alle pressioni di gruppo." *Rivista di Psicologia,* 62(1968), pp. 207-225.

52. Brilhart, B.L. "Relationships of Speaker-message Perception to Perceptual Field-independence." *Journal of Communication,* 20(1970), pp. 153-166.

53. Brilhart, B.L. "Speaker-message Perception and Attitude Change of Listeners as a Function of Field-independence." (Doctoral dissertation, Pennsylvania State University, 1966). *Dissertation Abstracts,* 27/05-A(1966), p. 1462. (University Microfilms No. 66-10, 454).

54. Brody, N. *Personality Research and Theory.* New York: Academic Press, 1972.

55. Broverman, D.M., Broverman, I.I., Vogel, W., Palmer, R.D., & Klaiber, E.L. "The Automatization Cognitive Style and Physical Development." *Child Development,* 35(1964), pp. 1343-1359.

56. Broverman, D.M., Klaiber, E.L., Kobayashi, Y., & Vogel, W. "Roles of Activation and Inhibition in Sex Differences in Cognitive Abilities." *Psychological Review,* 75(1968), pp. 23-50.

57. Bruce, D.K. "The Effect of Field Dependence and Anxiety on the Perception of Social Stimuli." (Doctoral dissertation, University of Utah, 1965). *Dissertation Abstracts,* 26/06-A(1965), pp. 3475-3476. (University Microfilms No. 65-12, 544).

58. Buchsbaum, M., & Fedio, P. "Hemispheric Differences in Evoked Potentials to Verbal and Nonverbal Stimuli in the Left and Right Visual Fields." *Physiology and Behavior,* 5(1970), pp. 207-210.

59. Burgoon, M. *Approaching Speech/Communication.* New York: Holt, Rinehart and Winston, Inc., 1974.

60.   Burstein, E., Vinokur, A., & Trope, Y. "Interpersonal Comparison versus Persuasive Argumentation: A More Direct Test of Alternative Explanations for Group-induced shifts in Individual Choice." *Journal of Experimental Social Psychology,* 9(1973), pp. 236-245.

61.   Bush, M., Korchin, S.J., Beall, L., & Kiritz, S. "Sex Differences in the Relationship Between Trait Anxiety and Auditory Selective Attention." *Journal of Auditory Research,* 14(1974), pp. 1-20.

62.   Campbell, S.B. "Cognitive Styles in Reflective, Impulsive, and Hyperactive Boys and their Mothers." *Perceptual and Motor Skills,* 36(1973), pp. 747-752.

63.   Campbell, S.B., & Douglas, V.I. "Cognitive Styles and Responses to the Threat of Frustration." *Canadian Journal of Behavioural Science,* 4(1972), pp. 30-42.

64.   Campbell, S.B., Douglas, V.I., & Morgenstern, G. "Cognitive Styles in Hyperactive Children and the Effect of Methylphenidate." *Journal of Child Psychology and Psychiatry,* 12(1971), pp. 55-67.

65.   Campus, N. "Transituational Consistency as a Dimension of Personality." *Journal of Personality and Social Psychology,* 29(1974), pp. 593-600.

66.   Carden, J. "Field Dependence, Anxiety and Sociometric Status in Children." (Master's thesis, University of Texas, 1958).

67.   Case, R., & Globerson, T. "Field Independence and Central Computing Space." *Child Development,* 45(1974), pp. 772-778.

68.   Cecchini, M., & Pizzamiglio, L. "Effects of Field-dependency, Social Class and Sex of Children between Ages 5 and 10." *Perceptual and Motor Skills,* 41(1975), pp. 155-164.

69.   Chapman, H.H. "Field Dependence and Communication Effectiveness." (Doctoral dissertation, University of Oklahoma, 1967). *Dissertation Abstracts,* 28/04-B(1968), p. 1692. (University Microfilms No. 67-11, 997).

70.   Clark, S.L. "Authoritarian Attitudes and Field Dependence." *Psychological Reports,* 22(1968), pp. 309-310.

71. Coates, S., Lord, M., & Jakabovics, E. "Field dependence-independence, Social-nonsocial Play and Sex Differences in Preschool Children." *Perceptual and Motor Skills.*

40(1975), pp. 195-202.

72. Cohen, B.D., Berent, S., & Silverman, A.J. "Field-dependence and Lateralization of Function in the Human Brain." *Archives of General Psychiatry,* 28(1973), pp. 165-167.

73. Cohen, B.D., Noblin, C.D., Silverman, A.J., & Penick, S.B. "Functional Asymmetry of the Human Brain." *Science,* 162(1968), pp. 475-477.

74. Cohen, B.D., & Wolfe, G. "Dream Recall and Repression: Evidence for an Alternative Hypothesis." *Journal of Consulting and Clinical Psychology,* 41(1973), pp. 349-355.

75. Cohen, S.I., Silverman, A.J., & Shmavonian, B.M. "Psychophysiological Studies in Altered Sensory Environments." *Journal of Psychosomatic Research,* 6(1962), pp. 259-281.

76. Colker, R.L. "Social Perception and Influence as a Function of Field Dependence-independence." (Doctoral dissertation, University of Pittsburgh, 1972). *Dissertation Abstracts International,* 34/01-B(1973), pp. 407-408. (University Microfilms No. 73-16, 349).

77. Comalli, P.E., Wapner, S., & Werner, H. "Perception of Verticality in Middle and Old Age." *Journal of Psychology,* 47(1959), pp. 259-266.

78. Corah, N.L. "Differentiation in Children and Their Parents." *Journal of Personality,* 33(1965), pp. 300-308.

79. Courter, R.J., Wattenmaker, R.A., & Ax, A.F. "Physiological Concomitants of Psychological Differentiation." *Psychophysiology,* 1(1965), pp. 282-290.

80. Cowan, G.A. "Response Style and Independent Perceptual Behavior." (Doctoral dissertation, Rutgers University, 1964). *Dissertation Abstracts,* 25(1964), pp. 2641-2642. (University Microfilms No. 64-10, 905).

81. Crandall, V.J., & Sinkeldam, C. "Children's Dependent and Achievement Behaviors in Social Situations and Their Perceptual Field Dependence." *Journal of Personality,* 32(1964), pp. 1-22.

82. Cronkite, G.L. *Communication and Awareness.* Menlo Park, Ca.: Cummings Publishing Company, 1975.

83.   Cronkite, G.L. "Out of the Ivory Palaces: A Proposal for Useful Research in Communication and Decision." In R.J. Kibler & L.L. Barker, eds., *Conceptual Frontiers in Speech Communication*. New York: Speech Association of America, 1969.

84.   Cronkite, G.L. & Liska, J. "A Critique of Factor Analytic Approaches to the Study of Credibility." *Communication Monographs,* 43(1976), pp. 91-107.

85.   Crutchfield, R.S., Woodworth, D.G., & Albrecht, R.E., *Perceptual Performance and the Effective Person* (WADC-TN-58-60). Lackland Air Force Base, Texas: Personnel Laboratory, Wright Air Development Center, Air Research and Development Command, April 1958. (ASTIA No. AD-151 039).

86.   Cullen, J.F., Harper, C.R., & Kidera, G.J. "Perceptual Style Differences between Airline Pilots and Engineers." *Aerospace Medicine,* 4(1969), pp. 407-408.

87.   Culver, C.M., Cohen, S.I., Silverman, A.J., & Shmavonian, B.M. "Cognitive Structuring, Field Dependence-Independence, and the Psychophysiological Response to Perceptual Isolation." In J.A. Wortis, ed., *Recent Advances in Biological Psychiatry.* New York: Plenum Press, 1964.

88.   Dargel, R., & Kirk, R.E. "Note on Relation of Anxiety of Field Dependency." *Perceptual and Motor Skills,* 37(1973), p. 218.

89.   David, O., & Glicksman, M. "Cognitive Style and the Perky Effect." *Perceptual and Motor Skills,* 42(1976), pp. 432-434.

90.   Dawson, J.L.M. "Cultural and Physiological Influences Upon Spatial-Perceptual Processes in West Africa, Part I." *International Journal of Psychology,* 2(1967), pp. 115-128.

91.   Dawson, J.L.M. "Cultural and Physiological Influences Upon Spacial-Perceptual Processes in West Africa, Part II." *International Journal of Psychology,* 2(1967), pp. 171-185.

92.   Dawson, J.L.M. "Effects of Sex Hormones on Cognitive Style in Rats and Man." *Behavior Genetics,* 2(1972), pp. 21-42.

93.   Dawson, J.L.M., Young, B.M., & Choi, P.P.C. "Developmental Influences in Pictorial Depth Perception Among Hong Kong Chinese Children." *Journal of Cross-Cultural Psychology,* 5(1974), pp. 3-22.

94.   Deever, S.G. "Ratings of Task-oriented Expectancy for Success as a Function of Internal Control and Field Independence." (Doctoral dissertation, University of Florida, 1967). *Dissertation Abstracts,* 29/01-B(1968), p. 365. (University Microfilms No. 68-9470).

95.   DeFares, P.B., & Van der Werff, J.J. "Perception and the Security-Insecurity Dimension." *Acta Psychologica,* 21(1963), pp. 68-74.

96.   DeFazio, V.J. "The Relationship Between Field Articulation, Language Abilities and Speech Perception in Male and Female College Students." (Doctoral dissertation, St. John's University, 1971). *Dissertation Abstracts International,* 32/05-B(1971), p. 2983. (University Microfilms No. 71-30, 218).

97.   DeGroot, J.C. "Emotional Climate of an Experimental Situation, Interaction Patterns, and Field Style of Subject." (Doctoral dissertation, University of Cincinnati, 1968). *Dissertation Abstracts International,* 30/02-B(1969), pp. 843-844. (University Microfilms No. 69-6333).

98.   Dengerink, H.A., O'Leary, M.R., & Kasner, K.H. "Individual Differences in Aggressive Responses to Attach: Internal-external Locus of Control and Field Dependence-independence." *Journal of Research in Personality,* 9(1975), pp. 191-199.

99.   DeRidder, J.C. *The Personality of the Urban African in South Africa.* London: Routledge & Kegan Paul, 1961.

100.   DeRussy, E.A., & Futch, E. "Field Dependence-independence as Related to College Curricula." *Perceptual and Motor Skills,* 33(1971), pp. 1235-1237.

101.   Dickstein, L.S. "Field Independence in Concept Attainment." *Perceptual and Motor Skills,* 27(1968), pp. 635-642.

102.   Dingman, R.L. "A Study of Cognitive Style Differences as a Factor of Communications in School Counseling." (Doctoral dissertation, Wayne State University, 1971). *Dissertation Abstracts International,* 32/12-A(1972), p. 6756. (University Microfilms No. 72-14, 544).

103.   DiStefano, J.J. "Interpersonal Perceptions of Field Independent and Field Dependent Teachers and Students." (Doctoral dissertation, Cornell University, 1969). *Dissertation*

Abstracts International, 31/01-A(1970), pp. 463-464. (University Microfilms No. 70-11, 225).

104.   Doktor, R.H., & Hamilton, W.F. "Cognitive Style and Acceptance of Management Science Recommendations." *Management Science,* 19(1973), pp. 884-894.

105.   Dolson, M.A. "Hospitalization, Differentiation, and Dependency." (Doctoral dissertation, University of Pittsburgh, 1973). *Dissertation Abstracts International,* 34/05-B(1973), p. 2301. (University Microfilms No. 73-27, 149).

106.   Donovan, D.M., Hague, W.H., & O'Leary, M.R. "Perceptual Differentiation and Defense Mechanisms in Alcholics." *Journal of Clinical Psychology,* 31(1975), pp. 356-359.

107.   Doob, L.W. "Behavior and Grammatical Style." *Journal of Abnormal and Social Psychology,* 56(1958), pp. 398-401.

108.   Dor-Shav, N.K. "In Search of Pre-menstrual Tension: Note on Sex-differences in Psychological Differentiation as a Function of Cyclical Physiological Changes." *Perceptual and Motor Skills,* 42(1976), pp. 1139-1142.

109.   Doyle, J.A. "Field-independence and Self-actualization." *Psychological Reports,* 36(1975), pp. 363-366.

110.   Dreyer, A.S., Hulac, V., & Rigler, D. "Differential Adjustment to Pubescence and Cognitive Style Patterns." *Developmental Psychology,* 4(1971), pp. 456-462.

111.   Dreyer, A.S., Nebelkopf, E., & Dreyer, C.A. "Note Concerning Stability of Cognitive Style Measures in Young Children." *Perceptual and Motor Skills,* 28(1969), pp. 933-934.

112.   Dronsejko, K. "Effects of CS Duration and Instructional Set on Cardiac Anticipatory Responses to Stress in Field Dependent and Independent Subjects." *Psychophysiology,* 9(1972), pp. 1-13.

113.   Dubois, T.E., & Cohen, W. "Relationship Between Measures of Psychological Differentiation and Intellectual Ability." *Perceptual and Motor Skills,* 31(1970), pp. 411-416.

114.   DuPreez, P.D. "Social Change and Field Dependence in South Africa." *Journal of Social Psychology,* 76(1968), pp. 265-266.

115.   Duval, S., & Wicklund, R. *A Theory of Objective Self-Awareness.* New York: Academic Press, 1972.

116. Duvall, N.S. ''Field Articulation and the Repression-sensitization Dimension in Perception and Memory." (Doctoral dissertation, University of North Carolina at Chapel Hill, 1969). *Dissertation Abstracts International,* 30/08-B(1970), p. 3864. (University Microfilms No. 70-3228).

117. Dyk, R.B. "An Exploratory Study of Mother-child Interaction in Infancy as Related to the Development of Differentiation." *Journal of the American Academy of Child Psychiatry,* 8(1969), pp. 657-691.

118. Dyk, R.B., & Witkin, H.A. "Family Experiences Related to the Development of Differentiation in Children." *Child Development,* 36(1965), pp. 21-55.

119. Eagle, M., Fitzgibbons, D., & Goldberger, L. "Field Dependence and Memory for Relevant and Irrelevant Incidental Material." *Perceptual and Motor Skills,* 23(1966), pp. 1035-1038.

120. Eagle, M., Goldberger, L., & Breitman, M. "Field Dependence and Memory for Social vs. Neutral and Relevant vs. Irrelevant Incidental Stimuli." *Perceptual and Motor Skills,* 29(1979), pp. 903-910.

121. Eberhard, G., & Nilsson, L. "The Rod-and-Frame Test and Emotional Maturity." *Acta Psychiatrica Scandinavica,* 43(1967), pp. 39-51.

122. Ehri, L.C., & Muzio, I.M. "Cognitive Style and Reasoning about Speed." *Journal of Educational Psychology,* 66(1974), pp. 569-571.

123. Eldersveld, S.J. "Experimental Propaganda Techniques and Voting Behavior." *American Political Science Review,* 50(1956), pp. 154-165.

124. Elkind, D., Koegler, R.R., & Go, E. "Field Independence and Concept Formation." *Perceptual and Motor Skills,* 17(1963), pp. 383-386.

125. Elliott, R. "Interrelationships Among Measures of Field dependence, Ability, and Personality Traits." *Journal of Abnormal and Social Psychology,* 63(1961), pp. 27-36.

126. Epstein, L. "The Relationship of Certain Aspects of the Body Image to the Perception of the Upright." (Doctoral dissertation,

New York University, 1958). *Dissertation Abstracts,* 22/02(1961), p. 639. (University Microfilms No. 61-2626).

127.   Evans, J.R. "Relationships of Psychological Differentiation, Emotional Distance from Reinforcing Agent, Emotional Arousal, and Responsiveness to Social Reinforcement." (Doctoral dissertation, George Peabody Teachers College, 1969). *Dissertation Abstracts International,* 31/01-B(1970), pp. 411-412. (University Microfilms No. 70-10, 902).

128.   Farley, F.H. "Field Dependence and Approval Motivation." *Journal of General Psychology,* 91(1974), pp. 153-154.

129.   Faterson, H.F., & Witkin, H.A., "Longitudinal Study of Development of the Body Concept." *Developmental Psychology,* 2(1970), pp. 429-438.

130.   Ferrell, J.G. "The Differential Performance of Lower Class, Preschool, Negro Children as a Function of Sex of *E*, Sex of *S*, Reinforcement Condition, and the Level of Field Dependence (Doctoral dissertation, University of Southern Mississippi, 1971). *Dissertation Abstracts International,* 32/05-B(1971), pp. 3028-3029. (University Microfilms No. 71-28, 831).

131.   Festinger, L., Pepitone, A., & Newcomb, T. "Some Consequences of Deindividuation in a Group." *Journal of Abnormal and Social Psychology,* 47(1952), pp. 382-389.

132.   Fiebert, M. "Cognitive Styles in the Deaf." *Perceptual and Motor Skills,* 24(1967), pp. 319-329.

133.   Fine, B.J. "Conclusion-drawing, Communicator Credibility and Anxiety as Factors in Opinion Change." *Journal of Abnormal and Social Psychology,* 54(1957), pp. 369-374.

134.   Fine, B.J. "Field-dependence-independence as 'Sensitivity' of the Nervous System: Supportive Evidence with Color and Weight Discrimination." *Perceptual and Motor Skills,* 37(1973), pp. 287-295.

135.   Fine, B.J. "Field-dependent Introvert and Neuroticism: Eysenck and Witkin United." *Psychological Reports,* 31(1972), pp. 939-956.

136. Fineman, K.R., "The Influence of Field-dependence/independence on Mothers' ability to Implement Behavior Therapy with Problem Children."

(Doctoral dissertation, University of California at Los Angeles, 1972). *Dissertation Abstracts International,* 33/07-B(1973), p. 3300. (University Microfilms No. 72-33, 917).

137.   Finley, W.W., & Clapp, R.K' "Psychological Concomitants of Response Stereotypy." *Psychophysiology,* 10(1973), pp. 205-206.

138.   Fisk, C.B. "Psychological Dependence, Perceptual Dependence and the Establishment of a Treatment Relationship Among Male Alcoholics." (Doctoral dissertation, Boston University, 1970). *Dissertation Abstracts International,* 31/05-B(1970), p. 2981. (University Microfilms No. 70-22, 385).

139.   Fitz, R.J. "The Differential Effects of Praise and Censure on Serial Learning as Dependent on Locus of Control and Field Dependency." (Doctoral dissertation, Catholic University of America, 1970). *Dissertation Abstracts International,* 31/07-B(1971), p. 4310. (University Microfilms No. 71-1457).

140.   Fitzgibbons, D.J., & Goldberger, L. "Task and Social Orientation: A Study of Field Dependency, "Arousal," and Memory for Incidental Material." *Perceptual and Motor Skills,* 32(1971), pp. 167-174.

141.   Fitzgibbons, D., Goldberger, L., & Eagle, M. "Field Dependence and Memory for Incidental Material." *Perceptual and Motor Skills,* 21(1965), pp. 743-749.

142.   Fleming, M.L., Knowlton, J.Q., Blain, B.B., Levie, W.H., & Elerian, A. *Message Design: The Temporal Dimension of Message Structure. Final Report.* Bloomington, Ind.: Indiana University Press, 1968.

143.   Fleshler, H., Ilardo, J., & Demoretcky, J. "The Influence of Field Dependence, Speaker Credibility Set, and Message Documentation on Evaluations of Speaker and Message Credibility." *Southern Speech Communication Journal,* 39(1974), pp. 389-402.

144.   Folman, R.Z. "Therapist-patient Perceptual Style, Interpersonal Attraction, Initial Interview Behavior, and Premature Termination." (Doctoral dissertation, Boston University, 1973). *Dissertation Abstracts International,*

34/04-B(1973), p. 1746. (University Microfilms No. 73-23, 482).

145. Forsberg, L.A. "The Role of Field Dependence-Field Independence in the Conservation of Mass, Weight, and Volume." (Doctoral dissertation, University of Manitoba, 1973). *Dissertation Abstracts International*, 34/11-B(1974), p. 5709. (National Library of Canada at Ottawa).

146. Freedman, N., O'Hanlon, J., Oltman, P., & Witkin, H.A. "The Imprint of Psychological Differentiation on Kinetic Behavior in Varying Communicative Contexts." *Journal of Abnormal Psychology*, 79(1972), pp. 239-258.

147. Fried, S.B. "Receptive Styles of Implicit Communication: A Look at Student Actors and Clinicians." *Perceptual and Motor Skills*, 40(1975), p. 230.

148. Galin, D. "Implications for Psychiatry of Left and Right Cerebral Specialization." *Archives of General Psychiatry*, 31(1974), pp. 572-583.

149. Galin, D., & Ornstein, R. "Lateral Specialization of Cognitive Mode: An EEG Study." *Psychophysiology*, 9(1972), pp. 412-418.

150. Gates, D.W. "Verbal Conditioning, Transfer and Operant Level "speech style" as functions of cognitive style." (Doctoral dissertation, City University of New York, 1971). *Dissertation Abstracts International*, 32/06-B(1971), p. 3634. (University Microfilms No. 71-30, 719).

151. Gazzaniga, M.S. "Recent Research on Hemispheric Lateralization of the Human Brain." *UCLA Educator*, 17(1975), pp. 9-12.

152. Gazzaniga, M.S., & Hillyard, S.A. "Language and Speech Capacity of the Right Hemisphere." *Neuropsychologia*, 9(1971), pp. 273-280.

153. Gill, N.T., Herdtner, T.J., & Lough, L. "Perceptual and Socio-economic Variables, Instruction in Body-orientation, and predicted Academic Success in Young Children." *Perceptual and Motor Skills*, 26(1968), pp. 1175-1184.

154. Glass, D.C., Lavin, D.E., Henchy, T., Gordon, A., Mayhew, P., & Donohoe, P. "Obesity and Persuasibility." *Journal of*

Personality, 37(1969), pp. 407-414.

155. Gleser, G.C., & Ihilevich, D. "An Objective Instrument for Measuring Defense Mechanisms." *Journal of Consulting and Clinical Psychology,* 33(1969), pp. 51-60.

156. Goldberger, L., & Bendich, S. "Field-dependence and Social Responsiveness as Determinants of Spontaneously Produced Words." *Perceptual and Motor Skills,* 34(1972), pp. 883-886.

157. Goldstein, G., Neuringer, C., Reiff, C., & Shelly, C.H. "Generalizability of Field Dependency in Alcoholics." *Journal of Consulting and Clinical Psychology,* 32(1968), pp. 560-564.

158. Goldstein, H.S. "Gender Identity, Stress and Psychological Differentiation in Figure-drawing choice." *Perceptual and Motor Skills,* 35(1972), pp. 127-132.

159. Goldstein, H.S., Pardes, H., Small, A.M., & Steinberg, M.D. "Psychological Differentiation and Specificity of Response." *Journal of Nervous and Mental Disease,* 151(1970), pp. 97-103.

160. Goldstein, H.S., & Peck, R. "Maternal Differentiation, Father Absence and Cognitive Differentiation in Children." *Archives of General Psychiatry,* 29(1973), pp. 370-373.

161. Goldstone, M.W. "Verbal Participation in Small Groups as a Function of Group Composition." (Doctoral dissertation, George Washington University, 1974). *Dissertation Abstracts International,* 35/04-B(1974), pp. 1910-1911. (University Microfilms No. 74-22,255).

162. Goodenough, D. R. "A Review of Individual Differences in Field Dependence as a Factor in Auto Safety." *Human Factors,* 18(1976), pp. 53-62.

163. Goodenough, D.R. "The Role of Individual Differences in Field Dependence as a Factor in Learning and Memory." *Psychological Bulletin,* 33(1976), pp. 675-694.

164. Goodenough, D.R., Gandini, E., Olkin, I., Pizzamiglio, L., Thayer, D., & Witkin, H.A. "A Study of X—Chromosome Linkage with Field Dependence and Spatial-Visualization." Unpublished study, 1974. Cited in 457.

165. Goodenough, D.R., & Karp, S.A. "Field Dependence and Intellectual Functioning." *Journal of Abnormal and Social Psychology,* 63(1961), pp. 241-246.

166. Goodenough, D.R., Witkin, H.A., Lewis, H.B., Koulack, D., & Cohen, H. "Repression, Interference, and Field Dependence as Factors in Dream Forgetting." *Journal of Abnormal Psychology,* 83(1974), pp. 32-44.

167. Gordon, B.R. "An Experimental Study of Dependence-independence in a Social and a Laboratory Setting." (Doctoral dissertation, University of Southern California, 1954). *American Doctoral Dissertations,* 1954, p. 155.

168. Gorman, B.S. "Field Dependence and Visual Maze Learning." *Perceptual and Motor Skills,* 27(1968), p. 142.

169. Greene, L.R. "Effects of Field Dependence on Affective Reactions and Compliance in Dyadic Interactions." *Journal of Personality and Social Psychology,* 34(1976), pp. 569-577.

170. Greene, L.R. "Effects of Field Independence, Physical Proximity, and Evaluative Feedback on Affective Reactions and Compliance in a Dyadic Interaction." (Doctoral dissertation, Yale University, 1973). *Dissertation Abstracts International,* 34/05-B(1973), pp. 2284-2285. (University Microfilms No. 73-26, 285).

171. Gruen, A. "A Critique and Re-Evaluation of Witkin's Perception and Perception-Personality Work." *Journal of General Psychology,* 56(1957), pp. 73-93.

172. Gruen, A. "Dancing Experience and Personality in Relation to Perception." *Psychological Monographs,* 69(1955), Whole No. 399.

173. Gruenfeld, L. W. "Cognitive Style——Field Dependence Independence as a Framework for the Study of Task and Social Orientation in Organizational Leadership." In B.M. Bass, R. Cooper, & J. A. Haas, eds. *Managing for Accomplishment.* Lexington, Mass.: D.C. Health and Company, 1970.

174. Gruenfeld, L.W., & Arbuthnot, J. "Field Independence as a Conceptual Framework for Prediction of Variability in Ratings of Others." *Perceptual and Motor Skills,* 28(1969), pp. 31-44.

175. Gruenfeld, L.W., & MacEachron, A.E. "Relationship between Age, Socio-Economic Status, and Field Independence." *Perceptual and Motor Skills,* 41(1975), pp. 449-450.

176. Gruenfeld, L.W., & Weissenberg, P. "Relationship between Supervisory Cognitive Style and Social Orientation." *Journal of Applied Psychology,* 59(1974), pp. 386-388.

177. Gruenfeld, L.W., Weissenberg, P., & Loh, W. "Achievement Values, Cognitive Style, and Social Class." *International Journal of Psychology,* 8(1973), pp. 41-49.

178. Guardo, C. "Personality, Psychological Differentiation and Personal Space." Paper presented at the Annual Meeting of the Rocky Mountain Psychological Association, Las Vegas, 1973. Cited in 464.

179. Hadley, H.D. "The Non-directive Approach to Advertising Appeals." *Journal of Applied Psychology,* 37(1953), pp. 496-498.

180. Haer, J.L. "Field Dependency in Relation to Altered States of Consciousness Produced by Sensory Overload." *Perceptual and Motor Skills,* 33(1971), pp. 192-194.

181. Harano, R.M. "Relationship of Field Dependency and Motor-Vehicle-Accident Involvement." *Perceptual and Motor Skills,* 31(1970), pp. 272-274.

182. Harley, J.P., Kalish, D.I., & Silverman, A.J. "Eye Movements and Sex Differences in Field Articulation." *Perceptual and Motor Skills,* 38(1974), pp. 615-622.

183. Harman, W.W., McKim, R.H., Mogar, R.E., Fadiman, J., & Stolaroff, M.J. "Psychedelic Agents in Creative Problem Solving, A Pilot Study." *Psychological Reports,* 19(1966), pp. 211-227.

184. Haronian, F., & Sugerman, A.A. "Field Independence and Resistance to Reversal of Perspective." *Perceptual and Motor Skills,* 22(1966), pp. 543-546.

185. Harris, A.J. "Lateral Dominance, Directional Confusion, and Reading Disability." *Journal of Psychology,* 44(1957), pp. 283-294.

186. Hart, R.P., Friedrich, G.W., & Brooks, W.D. *Public Communication.* New York: Harper & Row, Publishers, 1975.

187. Harvey, O.J., Hunt, D.E., & Schroder, H.M. *Conceptual Systems and Personality Organization.* New York: John Wiley, 1961.

188.   Hebb, D.O. *A Textbook of Psychology.* 3rd Edition. Philadelphia: Saunders, 1972.

189.   Hein, P.L., Cohen, S.I., & Shmavonian, B.M. "Perceptual Mode and Cardiac Conditioning." *Psychophysiology,* 3(1966) pp. 101-107.

190.   Heslin, R., Rotton, J., Marshall, J., & Blake, B. "Dimensions of Source Credibility and their Sensitivity to Changing Message Characteristics." *Proceedings of the Annual Convention of the American Psychological Association,* 8(1973), pp. 359-360.

191.   Hess, R.D., & Shipman, V.C. "Early Experience and the Socialization of Cognitive Modes in Children." *Child Development,* 36(1965), pp. 869-886.

192.   Hirt, M., Schroeder, H., & Kaplan, M.S. "A Failure to Provide Construct Validity for Psychological Differentiation." *Personality,* 2(1971), pp. 267-269.

193.   Holley, M. "Field-dependence-independence, Sophistication-of-body-concept, and Social Distance Selection." (Doctoral dissertation, New York University, 1972). *Dissertation Abstracts International,* 33/01-B(1972), p. 296. (University Microfilms No. 72-20, 635).

194.   Holtzman, P.D. *The Psychology of Speakers' Audiences.* Glenview, Ill.: Scott Foresman & Company, 1970.

195.   Holtzman, W.H., Swartz, J.D., & Thorpe, J.S. "Artists, Architects, and Engineers--Three Contrasting Modes of Visual Experience and their Psychological Correlates." *Journal of Personality,* 39(1971), pp. 432-449.

196.   Hovland, C.I., Lumdsdaine, A.A., & Sheffield, F.D. *Experiments in Mass Communication.* Princeton: Princeton University Press, 1949.

197.   Hovland, C.I., & Mandel, W. "An Experimental Comparison of Conclusion-drawing by the Communicator and by the Audience." *Journal of Abnormal and Social Psychology,* 47(1952), pp. 581-588.

198.   Hundleby, J.D., & Cattell, R.B. "Personality Structure in Middle Childhood and the Prediction of School Achievement and Adjustment." *Monographs of the Society for Research in Child Development,* 33(1968), Serial No. 121.

199. Hunt, D., & Randhawa, B.S. "Relationship between and among Cognitive Variables and Achievement in Computational Science." *Educational and Psychological Measurement,* 33(1973), pp. 921-928.

200. Hustmyer, F.E., & Karnes, E. "Background Autonomic Activity and 'Analytic Perception'." *Journal of Abnormal and Social Psychology,* 68(1964), pp. 467-468.

201. Ihilevich, D., & Gleser, G.C. "Relationship of Defense Mechanisms to Field Dependence-independence." *Journal of Abnormal Psychology,* 77(1971), pp. 296-302.

202. Iscoe, I., & Carden, J.A. "Field Dependence, Manifest Anxiety, and Sociometric Status in Children." *Journal of Consulting Psychology,* 25(1961), p. 184.

203. Jackson, D.N. "Independence and Resistance to Perceptual Field Forces." *Journal of Abnormal and Social Psychology,* 56(1958), pp. 279-281.

204. Jackson, D.N. "Stability in Resistance to Field Forces." (Doctoral dissertation, Purdue University, 1955). *Dissertation Abstracts,* 15(1955), p. 868. (University microfilms No. 00-11, 633).

205. James, C.D.R. "A Cognitive Style Approach to Teacher-Pupil Interaction and the Academic Performance of Black Children." (Master's thesis, Rutger's University, 1973). Cited in 464.

206. Janis, I.L., & Hovland, C.I., eds. *Personality and Persuasibility.* New Haven: Yale University Press, 1959.

207. Janov, A., & Holden, E.M. *Primal Man: The New Consciousness.* New York: Thomas Y. Crowell Company, 1975.

208. Jennings, B.S. "Some Cognitive Control Variables and Psycholinguistic Dimensions." (Doctoral dissertation, University of Florida, 1967). *Dissertation Abstracts,* 29/03-B(1968), pp. 1172-1173. (University Microfilms No. 68-13, 011).

209. Justice, M.T. "Field Dependency, Intimacy of Topic and Interpersonal Distance." (Doctoral dissertation, University of Florida, 1969). *Dissertation Abstracts International,* 31/01-B(1970), pp. 396-397. (University Microfilms No. 70-12, 243).

210. Kagan, S. "Field Dependence and Conformity of Rural Mexican and Urban Anglo-American Children." *Child*

Development, 45(1974), pp. 765-771.

211.   Kagan, S., & Zahn, G.L. "Field Dependence and the School Achievement Gap between Anglo-American and Mexican-American Children." *Journal of Educational Psychology,* 67(1975), pp. 643-650.

212.   Kangas, G.G. "An Experimental Manipulation of Expressed Values." (Doctoral dissertation, Washington State University, 1970). *Dissertation Abstracts International,* 31/08-B(1971), p. 4997. (University Microfilms No. 71-4403).

213.   Karp, S.A. "Field Dependence and Overcoming Embeddedness." *Journal of Consulting Psychology,* 27(1963), pp. 294-302.

214.   Karp, S.A., Silberman, L., & Winters, S. "Psychological Differentiation and Socioeconomic Status." *Perceptual and Motor Skills,* 28(1969), pp. 55-60.

215.   Karp, S.A., Witkin, H.A., & Goodenough, D.R. "Alcoholism and Psychological Differentiation: the Effect of Alcohol on Field Dependence." *Journal of Abnormal Psychology,* 70(1965), pp. 262-265.

216.   Kato, N. "A Fundamental Study of Rod Frame Test." *Japanese Psychological Research,* 7(1965), pp. 61-68.

217.   Katz, K.S. "Effects of Early Diet Treatment on Cognitive Abilities of Children with Phenylketonuria." (Doctoral dissertation, Rutgers University, The State University of New Jersey, 1974). *Dissertation Abstracts International,* 35/10-B(1975), p. 5116. (University Microfilms No. 75-8407).

218.   Kavanagh, M.J., & Weissenberg, F. "Relationship between Psychological Differentiation and Perceptions of Supervisory Behavior." *Proceedings of the Annual Convention of the American Psychological Association,* 8(1973), pp. 571-572.

219.   Kazelskis, R. "Field Independence and Free Recall of Nonsense Syllables;" *Perceptual and Motor Skills, 31(1970), pp.* 351-354.

220. Keiser, T. W. "Some Correlates of Perceptual Differentiation." (Doctoral dissertation, Wayne State University, 1969), *Dissertation Abstracts International,* 30/05-B(1971), p. 3007. (University Microfilms No. 71-29, 962).

221.   Kelman, H.C. & Eagly, A.H. "Attitude toward the Communicator, Perception of Communication Content, and Attitude Change." *Journal of Personality and Social Psychology,* 1(1965), pp. 63-78.

222.   Kendon, A., & Cook, M. "The Consistency of Gaze Patterns in Social Interaction." *British Journal of Psychology,* 60(1969), pp. 481-494.

223.   Keogh, B.K., Welles, M.F., & Weiss, A. *Field Dependence-Independence Problem-Solving Styles of Preschool Children. Technical Report.* Los Angeles: University of California, 1972.

224.   King, S.W. "Theory Testing: An Analysis and Extension." *Western Speech,* 27(1973), pp. 13-22.

225.   Klaiber, E.L., Broverman, D.M., & Kobayashi, Y. "The Automatization Cognitive Style, Androgens, and Monoamine Oxidase." *Psychopharmacologia,* 11(1967), pp. 320-336.

226.   Klau, L.G. "The Formation of First Impressions in Field-dependent and Field-independent Persons." (Doctoral dissertation, City University of New York, 1973). *Dissertation Abstracts International,* 33/12:1-B(1973), p. 6061. (University Microfilms No. 73-11, 355).

227.   Klein, G.S. *Perception, Motives, and Personality.* New York: Alfred A. Knopf, 1970.

228.   Kleine, P.F. "An Analysis of Cognitive and Psychological Differentiation in Perceptual and Impression Formation Tasks." (Doctoral dissertation, Washington University, 1967). *Dissertation Abstracts,* 28/10-A(1968), p. 4002. (University Microfilms No. 68-5141).

229.   Knott, J.R., Van Veen, W.J., Miller, L.H., Peters, J.F., & Cohen, S.I. "Perceptual Mode, Anxiety, Sex, and the Contingent Negative Variation." *Biological Psychiatry,* 7(1973), pp. 43-52.

230.   Konstadt, N., & Forman, E. "Field Dependence and External Directedness." *Journal of Personality and Social Psychology,* 1(1965), pp. 490-493.

231.   Koran, M.L., Snow, R.E., & McDonald, F.J. "Teacher Aptitude and Observational Learning of a Teaching Skill."

Journal of Educational Psychology, 62(1971), pp. 219-228.

232. Korner, A.F. "Individual Differences at Birth: Implications for Early Experience and Later Development." *American Journal of Orthopsychiatry,* 41(1971), pp. 608-619.

233. Kraidman, E. "Developmental Analysis of Conceptual and Perceptual Functioning under Stress and Non-stress Conditions." (Doctoral dissertation, Clark University, 1958). *Dissertation Abstracts,* 19/08(1959), pp. 2146-2147. (University Microfilms No. 58-7091).

234. Kumpf, M., & Gotz-Marchand, B. "Reduction of Cognitive Dissonance as a Function of Magnitude of Dissonance, Differentiation, and Self-esteem." *European Journal of Social Psychology,* 3(1973), pp. 255-270.

235. Lacey, J.T. "Somatic Response Patterning and Stress. Some Revisions of Activation Theory." In M.H. Appley & R. Trumball, eds., *Psychological Stress: Issues in Research.* New York: Appleton-Century-Crofts, 1967.

236. Lacey, J.T., & Lacey, B.C. "The Relationship of Resting Autonomic Activity to Motor Impulsivity." *Research Publications of the Association of Nervous and Mental Disease,* 36(1958), p. 144.

237. Ladkin, J.F., & Barker, C.L. "Psychological Differentiation in Passively-oriented Children." *Perceptual and Motor Skills,* 34(1972), pp. 703-706.

238. Laird, J.D. & Berglas, S. "Individual Differences in the Effects of Engaging in Counter-attitudinal Behavior." *Journal of Personality,* 43(1975), pp. 286-304.

239. Lapidus, L.B. "Cognitive Control, Parental Practices, and Contemporary Social Problems." *Proceedings of the Annual Convention of the American Psychological Association,* 5(1970), pp. 427-428.

240. Lawrence, G.L. "Behaviors and Attitudes of College Females Differing in Parent Identification." (Doctoral dissertation, George Peabody College for Teachers, 1968). *Dissertation Abstracts International,* 30/03-B(1969), p. 1362. (University Microfilms No. 69-13, 815).

241. Lawson, A.E. "Formal Operations and Field Independence in

a Heterogeneous Sample." *Perceptual and Motor Skills,* 42(1976), pp. 981-982.

242. League, B.J., & Jackson, D.N. "Activity and Passivity as Correlates of Field-independence." *Perceptual and Motor Skills,* 12(1961), pp. 291-298.

243. Lefcourt, H.M., Hogg, E., & Sordoni, C. "Locus of Control, Field Dependence and the Conditions Arousing Objective vs. Subjective Self-awareness." *Journal of Research in Personality,* 9(1975), pp. 21-36.

244. Lefcourt, H.M. & Siegel, J.M. "Reaction Time Performance as a Function of Field Dependence and Autonomy in Test Administration." *Journal of Abnormal Psychology,* 76(1970), pp. 475-481.

245. Lefcourt, H.M., & Telegdi, M.S. "Perceived Locus of Control and Field Dependence as Predictors of Cognitive Activity." *Journal of Consulting and Clinical Psychology,* 37(1971), pp. 53-56.

246. Lefever, M.M., & Ehri, L.C. "The Relationship between Field Independence and Sentence Disambiguation Ability." *Journal of Psycholinguistic Research,* 5(1976), pp. 99-106.

247. Lester, G. "The Rod-and-Frame Test: Some Comments on Methodology." *Perceptual and Motor Skills,* 26(1968), pp. 1307-1314.

248. Levanthal, H. "Fear: For Your Health." *Psychology Today,* 1(1967), pp. 54-58.

249. Levy, J. "Possible Basis for the Evolution of Lateral Specialization of the Human Brain." *Nature,* 224(1969), pp. 614-615.

250. Levy, J., Trevarthen, C., & Sperry, R.W. "Perception of Bilateral Chimeric Figures Following Hemispheric Deconnexion." *Brain,* 95(1972), pp. 61-78.

251. Lewis, H.B. "Shame and Guilt in Neurosis." *The Psychoanalytic Review,* 58(1971), pp. 419-438.

252. Lewis, L.H. "Acquiescence Response Set: Construct or Artifact?" *Journal of Projective Techniques and Personality Assessment,* 32(1968), pp. 578-584.

253. Lichtenstein, J.H., & Saucer, R.T. "Visual Dependency in the

Erect and Supine Positions." *Journal of Applied Psychology,* 59(1974), pp. 529-531.

254. Linton, H.B. "Dependence on External Influence: Correlates in Perception, Attitudes, and Judgment." *Journal of Abnormal and Social Psychology,* 51(1955), pp. 502-507.

255. Linton, H.B., & Graham, E. "Personality Correlates of Persuasibility." In I.L. Janis & C.I. Hovland, eds., *Personality and Persuasibility.* New Haven: Yale University Press, 1959.

256. Locascio, J.J., & Snyder, C.R. "Selective Attention to Threatening Stimuli and Field Independence as Factors in the Etiology of Paranoid Behavior." *Journal of Abnormal Psychology,* 84(1975), pp. 637-643.

257. Long, G.M. *Field Dependence-Independence: A Review of the Literature.* Pensacola, Fla.: Naval Aerospace Medical Research Laboratory, 1972. (NAMRL Monograph 19).

258. Long, G.M. "Reported Correlates of Perceptual Style: A Review of the Field Dependency-Independency Dimension." *JSAS Catalog of Selected Documents in Psychology,* 4(1974), No. 540.

259. Loo, R., & Cauthen, N.R. "Anxiety and Perceptual Articulation." *Perceptual and Motor Skills,* 43(1976), pp. 403-408.

260. Lowe, N.J.O. "A Critical Reevaluation of Witkin's Rod-and-Frame Test: Some Unresolved Questions." (Doctoral dissertation, Washington University, 1971). *Dissertation Abstracts International,* 32/02-B(1971), p. 1192. (University Microfilms No. 71-19, 821).

261. Lull, P.E. "The Effectiveness of Humor in Persuasive Speeches." *Speech Monographs,* 7(1940), pp. 26-40.

262. Lumsdaine, A.A., & Janis, I.L. "Resistance to 'Counterpropaganda' Produced by One-sided and Two-sided 'Propaganda' Presentations." *Public Opinion Quarterly,* 17(1953), pp. 311-318.

263. McAllister, L.W. "Modification of Performance on the Rod-and-Frame Test through Token Reinforcement Procedures." *Journal of Abnormal Psychology,* 75(1970), pp. 124-130.

264. McCarrey, M.W., Dayhaw, L.T., & Chagnon, G.P. "Attitude Shift, Approval Need, and Extent of Psychological Differentiation." *Journal of Social Psychology,* 84(1971), pp. 141-149.

265. McCroskey, J.C., & Wheeless, L.R. *Introduction to Human Communication.* Boston: Allyn Bacon, Inc., 1976.

266. McDavid, J. "Personality and Situational Determinants of Conformity." *Journal of Abnormal and Social Psychology,* 58(1959), pp. 241-246.

267. McFall, R.M., & Schenkein, D. "Experimenter Expectancy Effects, Need for Achievement, and Field Dependency." *Journal of Experimental Research in Personality,* 4(1970), pp. 122-128.

268. McGilligan, R.P., & Barclay, A.G. "Sex Differences and Spatial Ability Factors in Witkin's 'Differentiation' Construct." *Journal of Clinical Psychology,* 30(1974), pp. 528-532.

269. McGough, W.E., Silverman, A.J., & Bogdonoff, M.D. "Patterns of Fat Mobilization in Field Dependent and Field Independent Subjects." *Psychosomatic Medicine,* 27(1965), pp. 245-256.

270. McGuire, W.J. "The Current Status of Cognitive Consistency Theories." In S. Feldman, ed., *Cognitive Consistency.* New York: Academic Press, 1966.

271. McIntire, W.G., & Dreyer, A.S. "Relationship of Cognitive Style to Locus of Control." *Perceptual and Motor Skills,* 37(1973), pp. 553-554.

272. McKeachie, W.J. "Individual Conformity to the Attitudes of Classroom Groups." *Journal of Abnormal and Social Psychology,* 49(1954), pp. 282-289.

273. Mackenberg, E.J., Broverman, D.M., Vogel, W., & Klaiber, E.L. "Morning-to-Afternoon Changes in Cognitive Performances in the Electro-encephalogram." *Journal of Educational Psychology,* 66(1974), pp. 238-246.

274. McNett, C.W. "A Settlement Pattern Scale of Cultural Complexity." In R. Naroll & R. Cohen, eds., *A Handbook of Method in Cultural Anthropology.* New York: Natural History

Press, 1970.

275.   Marcus, E.S. "The Relationship of Psychological Differentiation to the Congruence of Temporal Patterns of Speech." (Doctoral dissertation, New York University, 1970). *Dissertation Abstracts International,* 31/04-B(1970), p. 2288. (University Microfilms No. 70-19, 016).

276.   Marcus, E.S., Welkowitz, J., Feldstein, S., & Jaffe, J. "Psychological Differentiation and the Congruence of Temporal Speech Patterns." Paper presented at the Annual Meeting of the Eastern Psychological Association, Atlantic City, April 1970.

277.   Marjerrison, G., & Keogh, R.P. "The Neurophysiology of Schizophrenia: Field Dependency and Electroencephalogram (EEG) Responses to Percepual Deprivation." *Journal of Nervous and Mental Disease,* 152(1971), pp. 390-395.

278.   Markiewicz, D. "The Effects of Humor on Persuasion." (Doctoral dissertation, Ohio State University, 1972). *Dissertation Abstracts International,* 33/08-B(1973), pp. 3986-3987. (University Microfilms No. 73-2061).

279.   Markus, E.J. "Perceptual Field Dependence Among Aged Persons." *Perceptual and Motor Skills,* 33(1971), pp. 175-178.

280.   Markus, E.J., & Nielsen, M. "Embedded-Figures Test Scores among Five Samples of Aged Persons." *Perceptual and Motor Skills,* 36(1973), pp. 455-459.

281.   Marlowe, D. "Some Psychological Correlates of Field Independence." *Journal of Consulting Psychology,* 22(1958), p. 334.

282.   Martin, P.L., & Toomey, T.C. "Perceptual Orientation and Empathy." *Journal of Consulting and Clinical Psychology,* 41(1973), p. 313.

283.   Massari, D.J. "The Relation of Reflection-Impulsivity to Field Dependence-Independence and Internal-External Control in Children." *Journal of Genetic Psychology,* 126(1975), pp. 61-67.

284.   Mausner, B., & Graham, J. "Field Dependence and Prior Reinforcement as Determinants of Social Interaction in Judgment." *Journal of Personality and Social Psychology,* 16(1970), pp. 486-493.

285. Mayo, P.R., & Bell, J.M. "A Note on the Taxonomy of Witkin's Field-independence Measures." *British Journal of Psychology*, 63(1972), pp. 255-256.

286. Mebane, D., & Johnson, D.L. "A Comparison of the Performance of Mexican Boys and Girls on Witkin's Cognitive Tasks." *Interamerican Journal of Psychology*, 4(1970), pp. 227-239.

287. Meskin, B.B., & Singer, J.L. "Daydreaming, Reflective Thought, and Laterality of Eye Movements." *Journal of Personality and Social Psychology*, 30(1974), pp. 64-71.

288. Messick, S., & Damarin, F. "Cognitive Styles and Memory for Faces." *Journal of Abnormal and Social Psychology*, 69(1964), pp. 313-318.

289. Messick, S., & Fritzky, F.J. "Dimensions of Analytic Attitude in Cognition and Personality." *Journal of Personality*, 31(1963), pp. 346-370.

290. Mihal, W.L., & Barrett, G.V. "Individual Differences in Perceptual Information Processing and Their Relation to Automobile Accident Involvement." *Journal of Applied Psychology*, 61(1976), pp. 229-233.

291. Milbourn, M.T., & Stone, V.A. "Source-message Orientation and Components of Source Credibility." *Journalism Quarterly*, 49(1972), pp. 663-668.

292. Miller, G.R. "Human Information Processing: Some Research Guidelines." In R.J. Kibler & L.L. Barker, eds., *Conceptual Frontiers in Speech Communication*. New York: Speech Association of America, 1969.

293. Milner, B. "Interhemispheric Differences in the Localization of Psychological Processes in Man." *British Medical Bulletin*, 27(1971), pp. 272-277.

294. Minard, J.G. Personal communication to Witkin, 1965. Cited in 451.

295. Minard, J.G., & Mooney, W. "Psychological Differentiation and Perceptual Defense: Studies of the Separation of Perception from Emotion." *Journal of Abnormal Psychology*, 74(1969), pp. 131-139.

296. Moore, S.F., Gleser, G.C., & Warm, J.S. "Cognitive Style in

the Organization and Articulation of Ambiguous Stimuli." *Psychonomic Science,* 21(1970), pp. 243-244.

297. Morris, L.A., & Shapiro, A.K. "MMPI Scores for Field-dependent and Field-independent Psychiatric Outpatients." *Journal of Consulting and Clinical Psychology,* 42(1974), pp. 364-369.

298. Mulgrave, N.W. "An Investigation of the Cognitive Factor Structure of Two Types of Concept-Attainment Tasks and Two Tests of Cognitive Style." (Doctoral dissertation, University of Pittsburgh, 1965). *Dissertation Abstracts,* 27/04-B(1966), p. 1283. (University Microfilms No. 66-8158).

299. Murphy, D.F. "Sensory Deprivation, Suggestion, Field Dependence, and Perceptual Regression." *Journal of Personality and Social Psychology,* 4(1966), pp. 289-294.

300. Nadeau, G.H. "Cognitive Style in Preschool Children: A Factor Analytic Study." (Doctoral dissertation, University of Minnesota, 1968). *Dissertation Abstracts,* 29/07-B(1969), p. 2623. (University Microfilms No. 68-17, 702).

301. Nash, C.S., & Nash, C.B. "Effect of Target Selection, Field Dependence, and Body Concept on ESP Performance." *Journal of Parapsychology,* 32(1968), pp. 248-257.

302. Nebelkopf, E.B., & Dreyer, A.A. "Perceptual Structuring: Cognitive Style Differences in the Perception of Ambiguous Stimuli." *Perceptual and Motor Skills,* 30(1970), pp. 635-639.

303. Nebes, R.D. "Man's so-called 'Minor' Hemisphere." *UCLA Educator,* 17(1975), pp. 13-16.

304. Nebes, R.D. "Superiority of the Minor Hemisphere in Commissurotomized Man for the Perception of the Part-whole Relations." *Cortex,* 7(1971), pp. 333-349.

305. Neufeldt, A.H., Raulston, P., & Peterson, G. "Personal Factors in Human Learning: II. Learning Ability and Subjective Stress." *Journal of General Psychology,* 88(1973), pp. 87-91.

306. Nevill, D. "Experimental Manipulation of Dependency Motivation and Its Effects on Eye Contact and Measures of Field Dependency." *Journal of Personality and Social Psychology,* 29(1974), pp. 72-79.

307. Nodelman, C. "Conservation of Substance and

Field-independence." *Graduate Research in Education and Related Disciplines*, 1(1965), pp. 3-24.

308. Norton, R.W., & Miller, L.D. "Dyadic Perception of Communication Style." *Communication Research*, 1(1975), pp. 50-67.

309. Okonji, M.O. "The Differential Effects of Rural and Urban Upbringing on the Development of Cognitive Styles." *International Journal of Psychology*, 4(1969), pp. 293-305.

310. O'Leary, M.R., Donovan, D.M., & Hague, W.H. "Interpersonal Differentiation, Locus of Control, and Cognitive Style Among Alcoholics." *Perceptual and Motor Skills*, 39(1974), pp. 997-998.

311. Oliver, R.A. "Parental Influence on Children's Cognitive Style." (Doctoral dissertation, Iowa State University, 1974). *Dissertation Abstracts International*, 35/01-B(1974), p. 485. (University Microfilms No. 74-15,443).

312. Olson, P.L. "Aspects of Driving Performance as a Function of Field Dependence." *Journal of Applied Psychology*, 59(1974), pp. 192-196.

313. Oltman, P.K., & Capobianco, F. "Field Dependence and Eye Dominance." *Perceptual and Motor Skills*, 25(1967), pp. 645-646.

314. Oltman, P.K., Goodenough, D.R., Witkin, H.A., Freedman, N., & Friedman, F. "Psychological Differentiation as a Factor in Conflict Resolution." *Journal of Personality and Social Psychology*, 32(1975), pp. 730-736.

315. Osipow, S.H. "Cognitive Styles and Educational-vocational Preferences and Selection." *Journal of Counseling Psychology*, 16(1969), pp. 534-546.

316. Otteson, J.P., & Holzman, P.S. "Cognitive Controls and Psychopathology." *Journal of Abnormal Psychology*, 85(1976), pp. 125-139.

317. Paeth, C.A. "A Likert Scaling of Student Value Statements, Field Independence–Field Dependence, and Experimentally Induced Change." (Doctoral dissertation, Oregon State University, 1973). *Dissertation Abstracts International*, 34/05-B(1973), pp. 2288-2289. (University Microfilms No. 73-25, 368).

318. Palmer, R.D. "Hand Differentiation and Psychological Functioning." *Journal of Personality,* 31(1963), pp. 445-461.

319. Pande, C.G. "Sex Differences in Field-dependence: Confirmation with Indian Sample." *Perceptual and Motor Skills,* 31(1970), p. 70.

320. Pande, C.G., & Kothari, S. "Field Dependence and the Raven's Progressive Matrices." *Psychologia*, 12(1969), pp. 49-51.

321. Parente, J.A., & O'Malley, J.J. "Training in Musical Rhythm and Field Dependence of Children." *Perceptual and Motor Skills,* 40(1975), pp. 392-394.

322. Parlee, M.B., & Rajagopal, J. "Sex Differences on the Embedded-Figures Test: A Cross-Cultural Comparison of College Students in India and in the United States." *Perceptual and Motor Skills,* 39(1974), pp. 1311-1314.

323. Paulson, S.F. "The Effects of Prestige of the Speaker and Acknowledgement of Opposing Arguments on Audience Retention and Shift of Opinion." *Speech Monographs,* 21(1954), pp. 267-271.

324. Pearce, W.B., & Brommel, B.J. "Vocalic Communication in Persuasion." *Quarterly Journal of Speech,* 58(1972), pp. 298-306.

325. Pearson, P.R. "Field Dependence and Social Desirability Response Set." *Journal of Clinical Psychology,* 28(1972), pp. 166-167.

326. Pederson, D.M. "Ego Strength and Discrepancy between Conscious and Unconscious Self-concepts." *Perceptual and Motor Skills,* 20(1965), pp. 691-692.

327. Pelto, P.J. "The Differences Between "Tight" and "Loose" Societies." *Trans-Action,* 5(1968), pp. 37-40.

328. Pemberton, C.L. "The Closure Factors Related to Temperament." *Journal of Personality,* 21(1952), pp. 159-175.

329. Perney, V.H. "Effects of Race and Sex on Field Dependence-Independence in Children." *Perceptual and Motor Skills,* 42(1976), pp. 975-980.

330. Petersen, S., & Magaro, P.A. "Reading and Field Dependence: A Pilot Study." *Journal of Reading,* 12(1969), pp. 287-294.

331. Peterson, J.M., & Sweitzer, G. "Field-independent Architecture Students." *Perceptual and Motor Skills* 36(1973), pp. 195-198.

332. Pillsbury, J.A., Meyerowitz, S., Salzman, L.F., & Satran, R. "Electroencephalographic Correlates of Perceptual Style: Field Orientation." *Psychosomatic Medicine*, 29(1967), pp. 441-449.

333. Pizzamiglio, L. "Handedness, Ear-preference, and Field-dependence." *Perceptual and Motor Skills*, 38(1974), pp. 700-702.

334. Pollack, I.W., & Kiev, A. "Spatial Orientation and Psychotherapy: An Experimental Study of Perception." *Journal of Nervous and Mental Disease*, 137(1963), pp. 93-97.

335. Pollack, M., Kahn, R.L., Karp, E., & Fink, M. "Individual Differences in the Perception of the Upright in Hospitalized Psychiatric Patients." Paper presented at the Annual Meeting of the Eastern Psychological Association, New York, 1960.

336. Quinlan, D.L. "Some Verbal Relationships between Field-dependence-independence and Relative Question Structure." (Doctoral dissertation, University of Connecticut, 1971). *Dissertation Abstracts International*, 32/05-A(1971), p. 2491. (University Microfilms No. 71-29, 899).

337. Quinlan. D.M., & Blatt, S.J. "Field Articulation and Performance Under Stress: Differential Predictions in Surgical and Psychiatric Nursing Training." *Journal of Consulting and Clinical Psychology*, 39(1972), p. 517.

338. Ramirez, M. "Cognitive Styles and Cultural Democracy in Education." *Social Science Quarterly*, 53(1973), pp. 895-904.

339. Ramirez, M., & Castaneda, A. *Cultural Democracy, Bicognitive Development, and Education*. New York: Academic Press, 1974.

340. Randolph, L.C. "A Study of the Effects of Praise, Criticism and Failure on the Problem Solving Performance of Field-dependent and Field-independent Individuals." (Doctoral dissertation, New York University, 1971). *Dissertation Abstracts International*, 32/05-B(1971), pp. 3014-3015. (University Microfilms No. 71-28, 555).

APPENDIX

341. Reckless, R., Cohen, S.I., Silverman, A.J., & Shmavonian, B.M. "Influence of Perceptual Mode and Controlled Environmental Conditions on the Response to Drugs." *Psychosomatic Medicine*, 24(1962), p. 520.
342. Reighard, P.B., & Johnson, D.T. "Effects of Birth Order and Sex on Field Independence-Dependence." *Perceptual and Motor Skills*, 37(1973), pp. 223-226.
343. Reinking, R., Goldstein, G., & Houston, B.K. "Cognitive Style, Proprioceptive Skills, Task Set, Stress, and the Rod-and-Frame Test of Field Orientation." *Journal of Personality and Social Psychology*, 30(1974), pp. 807-811.
344. Renzi, N.B. "A Study of Some Effects of Field Dependence-independence and Feedback on Performance Achievement (Doctoral dissertation, Hofstra University, 1974). *Dissertation Abstracts International,* 35/04—A,(1974), p. 2059. (University Microfilms No. 74-21, 861).
345. Reppon, J. "Field Articulation and Socio-economic and Rural-urban Variables." (Doctoral dissertation, Yeshiva University, 1966). *Dissertation Abstracts,* 28/03-B(1967), p. 1173. (University Microfilms No. 67-9945).
346. Rhodes, R.J., Carr, J.E., & Jurji, E.D. "Interpersonal Differentiation and Perceptual Field Differentiation." *Perceptual and Motor Skills,* 27(1968), pp. 172-174.
347. Riesman, D. *The Lonely Crowd.* New Haven: Yale University Press, 1950.
348. Rogalski, C.J. "Individual Differences in Verbal Behavior: Their Relationship to the Field-articulation Principle." (Doctoral dissertation, New York University, 1968). *Dissertation Abstracts International,* 30/01-B(1969), p. 389. (University Microfilms No. 69-11, 840).
349. Roodin, P.A., Broughton, A., & Vaught, G.M. "Effects of Birth Order, Sex, and Family Size on Field Dependence and Locus of Control." *Perceptual and Motor Skills,* 39(1974), pp. 671-676.
350. Rosenberg, E.S. "Some Psychological and Biological Relationships Between Masculinity and Feminity and Field

Dependence and Field Independence." (Doctoral dissertation, Northwestern University, 1975). *Dissertation Abstracts International,* 36/12:1-B(1976), p. 6453. (University Microfilms No. 76-13, 106).

351.   Rosenfeld, J.M. "Some Perceptual and Cognitive Correlates of Strong Approval Motivation." *Journal of Consulting Psychology,* 31(1967), pp. 507-512.

352.   Rosett, H.L., Nackenson, B.L., Robbins, H., & Sapirstein, M.R. "Personality and Cognitive Characteristics of Engineering Students: Implications for the Occupational Psychiatrist." *American Journal of Psychiatry,* 122(1966), pp. 1147-1152.

353.   Rosett, H.L., Robbins, H., & Watson, W.S. "Physiognomic Perception as a Cognitive Control Principle." *Perceptual and Motor Skills,* 26(1968), pp. 707-719.

354.   Rosner, S. "Consistency in Response to Group Pressures". *Journal of Abnormal and Social Psychology,* 55(1957), pp. 145-146.

355.   Rosner, S. "Studies of Group Pressure" (Doctoral dissertation, New School for Social Research, 1956). *American Doctoral Dissertations,* 1956, p. 78.

356.   Rotter, J.B. "Generalized Expectancies for Internal versus External Control of Reinforcement." *Psychological Monographs,* 80(1966), Whole No. 609.

357.   Ruble, D.N., & Nakamura, C.Y. "Task Orientation versus Social Orientation in Young Children and Their Attention to Relevant Social Cues." *Child Development,* 43(1972), pp. 471-480.

358.   Rudin, S.A., & Stagner, R. "Figure-Ground Phenomena in the Perception of Physical and Social Stimuli." *Journal of Psychology,* 45(1958), pp. 213-225.

359.   Sack, S.A., & Rice, C.E. "Selectivity, Resistance to Distraction and Shifting as Three Attentional Factors." *Psychological Reports,* 34(1974), pp. 1003-1012.

360.   Safer, J.M. "Effects of Sex and Psychological Differentiation on Responses to a Stressful Situation." (Doctoral dissertation, New School for Social Research, 1975). *Dissertation Abstracts International,* 36/06-B(1975), p. 3068. (University Microfilms No. 75-25, 458).

361. Schimek, J.G. "Cognitive Style and Defenses: A Longitudinal Study of Intellectualization and Field Independence." *Journal of Abnormal Psychology,* 73(1968), pp. 575-580.

362. Schroeder, N., Eliot, J., Greenfield, S., & Soeken, K. "Consistency of Lateral Eye Shift Related to Preschoolers' Performance on an Analytical Perceptual Task." *Perceptual and Motor Skills,* 42(1976), p. 634.

363. Schwartz, D.W., & Karp, S.A. "Field Dependence in a Geriatric Population." *Perceptual and Motor Skills,* 24(1967), pp. 495-504.

364. Schwen, T.M. "The Effect of Cognitive Styles and Instructional Sequences on Learning a Hierarchical Task." (Doctoral dissertation, Indiana University, 1970). *Dissertation Abstracts International,* 31/06-A(1970), pp. 2797-2798. (University Microfilm No. 70-23, 380).

365. Seder, J.A. "The Origin of Differences in Extent of Independence in Children: Developmental Factors in Perceptual Field Dependence." (Bachelor's thesis, Radcliffe College, 1957).

366. Seeley, O.F. "Field Dependence-independence, Internal-external Locus of Control, and Implementation of Family-planning Goals." *Psychological Reports,* 38(1976), pp. 1216-1218.

367. Selye, H. *The Stress of Life.* New York: McGraw-Hill Book Company, 1956.

368. Shelly, M.W. *Sources of Satisfaction.* Lawrence, Kansas: University of Kansas Press, 1973.

369. Shennum, W.A. "Field-dependence and Facial Expressions." *Perceptual and Motor Skills,* 43(1976), pp. 179-184.

370. Sherman, J.A. "Field Articulation, Sex, Spatial Visualization, Dependency, Practice, Laterality of the Brain and Birth Order." *Perceptual and Motor Skills,* 38(1974), pp. 1223-1235.

371. Sherman, J.A. "Problem of Sex Differences in Space Perception and Aspects of Intellectual Functioning." *Psychological Review,* 74(1967), pp. 290-299.

372. Shipman, W.G., Oken, D., & Heath, H.A. "Muscle Tension and Effort at Self Control During Anxiety." *Archives of General Psychiatry,* 23(1970), pp. 359-368.

373. Shows, W.D. "Psychological Differentiation and the *A-B* Dimension: a Dyadic Interaction Hypothesis." (Doctoral dissertation, Duke University, 1967). *Dissertation Abstracts,* 28/09-B(1968), pp. 3885-3886. (University Microfilms No. 68-2744).

374. Shulman, E. "Conformity in a Modified Asch-type Situation." (Doctoral dissertation, City University of New York, 1976). *Dissertation Abstracts International,* 36/12:1-B(1976), p. 6455. (University Microfilms No. 76-11,971).

375. Silverman, A.J. "Some Psychophysiological Aspects of Stress Responsivity." *Australian and New Zealand Journal of Psychiatry,* 3(1969), pp. 216-221.

376. Silverman, A.J., Adevai, G., & McGough, W.E. "Some Relationships between Handedness and Perception." *Journal of Psychosomatic Research,* 10(1966), pp. 151-158.

377. Silverman, A.J., Cohen, S.I., & Shmavonian, B.M. "Perceptual and Environmental Influences on Psycho-physiological Responses." In J.A. Wortis, ed.,*Recent Advances in Biological Psychiatry.* New York: Plenum Press, 1963.

378. Silverman, A.J., Cohen, S.I., Shmavonian, B.M., & Greenberg, G. "Psychophysiological Investigations in Sensory Deprivation." *Psychosomatic Medicine,* 23(1961), pp. 48-61.

379. Silverman, A.J., & McGough, W.E. "Epinephrine Response Differences in Field-dependent and Field-independent Subjects." *Biological Psychiatry,* 1(1969), pp. 185-188.

380. Silverman, A.J., McGough, W.E., & Bogdonoff, M.D. "Perceptual Correlates of the Physiological Response to Insulin " *Psychosomatic Medicine,* 29(1967), pp. 252-264.

381. Silverman, A.J., & Shmavonian, B.M. "Psychophysiological Studies in Altered Sensory Environments." *Journal of Psychosomatic Research,* 6(1962), pp. 259-281.

382. Silverman, J., Buchsbaum, M., & Stierlin, H. "Sex Differences in Perceptual Differentiation and Stimulus Intensity Control." *Journal of Personality and Social Psychology,* 25(1973), pp. 309-318.

383. Silverstone, S., & Kissin, B. "Field Dependence in Essential Hypertension and Peptic Ulcer." *Journal of Psychosomatic Research,* 12(1968), pp. 157-161.

384. Simon, W.E., & Wilde, V. "Ordinal Position of Birth, Field Dependency and Forer's Measure of Gullibility." *Perceptual and Motor Skills,* 33(1971), pp. 677-678.

385. Singer, J.L., Greenberg, S., & Antrobus, J.S. "Looking with the Mind's Eye: Experimental Studies of Ocular Motility during Daydreaming and Mental Arithmetic." *Transactions of the New York Academy of Sciences,* 33(1971), pp. 694-709.

386. Small, M.M. "Modification of Performance on the Rod-and-Frame Test." *Perceptual and Motor Skills,* 36(1973), pp. 715-720.

387. Solar, D., Bruehl, D., & Kovacs, J. "The Draw-a-Person Test: Social Conformity or Artistic Ability?" *Journal of Clinical Psychology,* 26(1970), pp. 524-525.

388. Solar, D., Davenport, G., & Bruehl, D. "Social Compliance as a Function of Field Dependence." *Perceptual and Motor Skills,* 29(1969), pp. 299-306.

389. Sousa-Poza, J.F., & Rohrberg, R. "Communicational and Interactional Aspects of Self-disclosure in Psychotherapy: Differences Related to Cognitive Style." *Psychiatry,* 39(1976), pp. 81-91.

390. Sousa-Poza, J.F., Rohrberg, R., & Shulman, E. "Field Dependence and Self-disclosure." *Perceptual and Motor Skills,* 36(1973), pp. 735-738.

391. Sperry, R.W. "The Great Cerebral Commissure." *Scientific American,* 210(1964), pp. 42-52.

392. Stafford, R.E. "Sex Differences in Spatial Visualization as Evidence of Sex-linked Inheritance." *Perceptual and Motor Skills,* 13(1961), p. 428.

393. Stansell, V., Beutler, L.E., Neville, C.W., & Johnson, D.T. "MMPI Correlates of Extreme Field Independence and Field Dependence in a Psychiatric Population." *Perceptual and Motor Skills,* 40(1975), pp. 539-544.

394. Stark, R. "An Investigation of Unilateral Cerebral Pathology with Equated Verbal and Visual-spatial Tasks." *Journal of Abnormal and Social Psychology,* 62(1961), pp. 282-287.

395. Stasz, C. "Field Independence and the Structuring of Knowledge in a Social Studies Minicourse." (Master's thesis, Rutgers University, 1974). Cited in 464.

396.   Steingart, I., Freedman, N., Grand, S., & Buchwald, C. "Personality Organization and Language Behavior: the Imprint of Psychological Differentiation on Language Behavior in Varying Communication Conditions." *Journal of Psycholinguistic Research,* 4(1975), pp. 241-255.

397.   Stone, V.A., & Hoyt, J.L. "The Emergence of Source-Message Orientation as a Communication Variable." *Communication Research,* 1(1974), pp. 89-109.

398.   Strahan, R., & Huth, H. "Relations between Embedded Figures Test Performance and Dimensions of the I-E Scale." *Journal of Personality Assessment,* 39(1975), pp. 523-524.

399.   Stuart, I.R. "Field Dependency, Authoritarianism and Perception of the Human Figure." *Journal of Social Psychology,* 66(1965), pp. 209-214.

400.   Stuart, I.R. "Perceptual Style and Reading Ability: Implications for an Instructional Approach." *Perceptual and Motor Skills,* 24(1967), pp. 135-138.

401.   Stuart, I.R., Breslow, A., Brechner, S., Ilyus, R.B., & Wolpoff, M. "The Question of Constitutional Influence on Perceptual Style." *Perceptual and Motor Skills*, 20(1965), pp. 419-420.

402.   Sugerman, A.A., & Cancro, R. "Field Dependence and Sophistication of Body Concept in Schizophrenics." *Journal of Nervous and Mental Disease,* 138(1964), pp. 119-123.

403.   Svinicki, J.G., Bundgaard, C.J., Schwensohn, C.H., & Westgor, D.J. "Physical Activity and Visual Field-dependency." *Perceptual and Motor Skills,* 39(1974), pp. 1237-1238.

404.   Sweeney, D.R., & Fine, B.J. "Pain Reactivity and Field Dependence." *Perceptual and Motor Skills,* 21(1965), pp. 757-758.

405.   Sweeney, M.A. & Cottle, W.C. "Nonverbal Acuity: a Comparison of Counselors and Noncounselors." *Journal of Counseling Psychology,* 23(1976), pp. 394-397.

406.   Taylor, D.A., & Oberlander, L. "Person-perception and Self-disclosure: Motivational Mechanisms in Interpersonal Processes." *Journal of Experimental Research in Personality,* 4(1969), pp. 14-28.

407.   Taylor, J.N. "A Comparison of Delusional and Hallucinatory Individuals Using Field Dependency as a Measure." (Doctoral

dissertation, Purdue University, 1956.) *Dissertation Abstracts,* 17/01(1957), p. 174. (University Microfilms No. 00-18, 875).

408.   Thislethwaite, D.L., & Kamenetzky, J. "Attitude Change through Refutation and Elaboration of Audience Counterarguments." *Journal of Abnormal and Social Psychology,* 51(1955), pp. 3-9.

409.   Throckmorton, R.S. "Role Playing, Social Dependence and Field Dependence: an Exploratory Study," (Doctoral dissertation, University of Nevada, 1974) *Dissertation Abstracts International,* 35/09-B(1975), p. 4712. (University Microfilms No. 75-5302).

410.   Tobacyk, J.J., Broughton, A., & Vaught, G.M. "Effects of Congruence-incongruence between Locus of Control and Field Dependence on Personality Functioning." *Journal of Consulting and Clinical Psychology,* 43(1975), pp. 81-85.

411.   Tramer, R.R., & Schludermann, E.H. "Cognitive Differentiation in a Geriatric Population." *Perceptual and Motor Skills,* 39(1974), pp. 1071-1075.

412.   Trego, R.E. "An Investigation of the Rod-and-Frame Test in Relation to Emotional Dependence and Social Cue Attentiveness." (Doctoral dissertation, Texas Christian University, 1971). *Dissertation Abstracts International,* 32/08-B(1972), p. 4910. (University Microfilms No. 72-7617).

413.   Triandis, H.C. *Attitude and Attitude Change.* New York: John Wiley & Sons, Inc., 1971.

414.   Tubbs, S.L., & Moss, S. *Human Communication: An Interpersonal Perspective.* New York: Random House, 1974.

415.   Uhlmann, F.W., & Saltz, E. "Retention of Anxiety Material as a Function of Cognitive Differentiation." *Journal of Personality and Social Psychology,* 1(1965), pp. 55-62.

416.   Vandenberg, S.G. "The Hereditary Abilities Study: Hereditary Components in a Psychological Test Battery." *American Journal of Human Genetics,* 14(1962), pp. 220-237.

417.   Vardy, M., & Greenstein, M. "Perceptual Field Dependence and Psychopathology: Replication and Critique." *Perceptual and Motor Skills,* 34(1972), pp. 635-642.

418.   Vernon, P.E. "The Distinctiveness of Field Independence." *Journal of Personality,* 40(1972), pp. 366-391.

419.   Wachtel, P.L. "Cognitive Style and Style of Adaptation." *Perceptual and Motor Skills,* 35(1972), pp. 779-785.

420.   Wachtel, P.L. "Field Dependence and Psychological Differentiation: Reexamination." *Perceptual and Motor Skills,* 35(1972), pp. 179-189.

421.   Wachtel, P.L. "Style and Capacity in Analytic Functioning." *Journal of Personality,* 36(1968), pp. 202-212.

422.   Waldrop, M.F., & Bell, R.Q. "Effects of Family Size and Density on Newborn Characteristics." *American Journal of Orthopsychiatry,* 36(1966), pp. 544-550.

423.   Wallach, M.A. "Commentary: Active-analytical vs. Passive-global Cognitive Functioning." In S. Messick & J. Ross, eds., *Measurement in Personality and Cognition.* New York: John Wiley and Sons, Inc., 1962.

424.   Wallach, M.A., Kogan, N., & Burt, R.B. "Group Risk Taking and Field Dependence-independence of Group Members." *Sociometry,* 30(1967), pp. 323-338.

425.   Ward, T. "Cognitive Processes and Learning: Reflections on a Comparative Study of 'Cognitive Style' (Witkin) in Fourteen African Societies." *Comparative Education Review,* 17(1973), pp. 1-10.

426.   Weiss, A.A., Stein, B., Atar, H., & Melnik, N. "Rorschach Test Behavior as a Function of Psychological Differentiation." *The Israel Annals of Psychiatry and Related Discplines,* 5(1967), pp. 32-42.

427.   Weiss, W. "Emotional Arousal and Attitude Change." *Psychological Reports,* 6(1960), pp. 267-280.

428.   Weissman, H.J. "Sex Differences in Perceptual Style in Junior High School in Relation to Nursery-school and Current Dependency and Sex Role Crystallization." (Doctoral dissertation, Catholic University of America, 1971). *Dissertation Abstracts International,* 32/04-B(1971), p. 2390. (University Microfilms No. 71-25, 551).

429.   Welkowitz, J. Personal communication to Witkin, 1952. Cited in 464.

430.   Welkowitz, J., & Feldstein, S. "The Relation of Experimentally Manipulated Interpersonal Perception and Psychological Differentiation to the Temporal Patterning of

Conversation." *Proceedings of the Annual Convention of the American Psychological Association,* 5(1970), pp. 387-388.

431. Wenburg, J.R., & Wilmot, W.W. *The Personal Communication Process.* New York: John Wiley & Sons, Inc., 1973.

432. Wenger, M.A. "The Measurement of Individual Differences in Autonomic Balance." *Psychosomatic Medicine,* 3(1941), pp. 427-434.

433. Wenger, M.A. "The Stability of Measurement of Autonomic Balance." *Psychosomatic Medicine,* 4(1942), pp. 94-95.

434. Wenger, M.A. "Studies of Autonomic Balance. A Summary." *Psychophysiology,* 2(1966), pp. 173-186.

435. Werner, H. "The Concept of Development from a Comparative and Organismic Point of View." In D.B. Harris, ed., *The Concept of Development: An Issue in the Study of Human Behavior.* Minneapolis: University of Minnesota Press, 1957.

436. Westbrook, M. "Judgement of Emotion: Attention versus Accuracy." *British Journal of Social and Clinical Psychology,* 13(1974), pp. 383-389.

437. White, B.O., & Kernaleguen, A.P. "Comparison of Selected Perceptual and Personality Variables among College Women Deviant and Nondeviant in their Appearance." *Perceptual and Motor Skills,* 32(1971), pp. 87-92.

438. White, B.W. "Visual and Auditory Closure." *Journal of Experimental Psychology,* 48(1954), pp. 234-240.

439. Wiggins, J.S. "Personality Structure." *Annual Review of Psychology,* 19(1968), pp. 293-350.

440. Wilner, W. "The Relationship of the Perceptual Styles of Field Dependency and Field Independency to Some Formal Features of Attitudes." (Doctoral dissertation, City University of New York, 1969). *Dissertation Abstracts International,* 30/09-A(1970), p. 4022. (University Microfilms No. 70-3402).

441. Wineman, J.H. "Cognitive Style and Reading Ability." *California Journal of Educational Research,* 22(1971), pp. 74-79.

442. Wineman, J.H. "Projected Utilization of Interpersonal Distance as a Function of Psychological Differentiation." (Doctoral dissertation, University of Utah, 1973). *Dissertation*

Abstracts International, 34/11—B(1974), pp. 5698-5699 (University Microfilms No. 74-11, 431).

443.   Winestine, M.C. "Twinship and Psychological Differentiation." *Journal of the America Academy of Child Psychiatry,* 8(1969), pp. 436-455.

444.   Witkin, H.A. "Cognitive Development and the Growth of Personality." *Acta Psychologica,* 18(1961), pp. 245-257.

445.   Witkin, H.A. "A Cognitive Style Approach to Cross-cultural Research." *International Journal of Psychology,* 2(1967), pp. 233-250.

446.   Witkin, H.A. "Cultural Influences in the Development of Cognitive Style." Paper presented at the International Congress of Psychology, Moscow, August 1966.

447.   Witkin, H.A. "Individual Differences in Ease of Perception of Embedded Figures." *Journal of Personality,* 19(1950-51), pp. 1-15.

448.   Witkin, H.A. "The Nature and Importance of Individual Differences in Perception." *Journal of Personality,* 18(1949), pp. 145-170.

449.   Witkin, H.A. "Origins of Cognitive Style." In C. Scheerer, ed., *Cognition: Theory, Research, Promise.* New York: Harper & Row, Publishers, 1964.

450.   Witkin, H.A. "Perception of Body Position and of the Position of the Visual Field." *Psychological Monographs,* 63(1949), Whole No. 302.

451.   Witkin, H.A. "Psychological Differentiation and Forms of Pathology." *Journal of Abnormal Psychology,* 70(1965), pp. 317-336.

452.   Witkin, H.A. "Psychological Self-consistency." *Transactions of the New York Academy of Sciences,* 22(1960), pp. 541-545.

453.   Witkin, H.A. "Sex Differences in Perception." *Transactions of the New York Academy of Science,* 12(1949), pp. 22-26.

454.   Witkin, H.A. "Social Influences in the Development of Cognitive Style." In D.A. Goslin, ed., *Handbook of Socialization Theory and Research.* Chicago: Rand McNally and Company, 1969.

455.   Witkin, H.A. "Some Implications of Research on Cognitive Style for Problems of Education." *Archivio di Psicologia,*

Neurologie e Psichitria, 26(1965), pp. 27-55.

456.   Witkin, H.A., & Asch, S.E. "Studies in Space Orientation. IV." Further Experiments on Perception of the Upright with Displaced Visual Fields. *Journal of Experimental Psychology,* 38(1948), pp. 762-782.

457.   Witkin, H.A., & Berry, J.W. "Psychological Differentiation in Cross-cultural Perspective." *Journal of Cross-Cultural Psychology,* 6(1975), pp. 4-87.

458.   Witkin, H.A., Birnbaum, J., Lomonaco, S., Lehr, S., & Herman, J.L. "Cognitive Patterning in Congenitally Totally Blind Children." *Child Development,* 39(1968), pp. 767-786.

459.   Witkin, H.A., Dyk, R.B., Faterson, H.F., Goodenough, D.R., & Karp, S.A. *Psychological Differentiation.* Potomac, Md.: Erlbaum, 1974. (orig. pub., 1962).

460.   Witkin, H.A., & Goodenough, D.R. "Field Dependence and Interpersonal Behavior." *ETS Research Bulletin,* RB-76-12, April 1976.

461.   Witkin, H.A., Goodenough, D.R., & Karp, S.A. "Stability of Cognitive Style from Childhood to Young Adulthood." *Journal of Personality and Social Psychology,* 7(1967), pp. 291-300.

462.   Witkin, H.A., Lewis, H.B., Hertzman, M., Machover, K., Meissner, P.B., & Wagner, S. *Personality through Perception.* Westport, Conn.: Greenwood Press, 1972. (orig. pub., 1954).

463.   Witkin, H.A., Lewis, H.B., & Weil, E. "Affective Reactions and Patient-Therapist Interactions Among More Differentiated and Less Differentiated Patients Early in Therapy." *Journal of Nervous and Mental Disease,* 146(1968), pp. 193-208.

464.   Witkin, H.A., Moore, C.A., Goodenough, D.R., & Cox, P.W. "Field-dependent and Field-independent Cognitive Styles and their Educational Implications." *ETS Research Bulletin,* RB- 75-24, June 1975.

465.   ` Witkin, H.A. & Oltman, P.K. "Cognitive Style." *International Journal of Neurology,* 6(1967), pp. 119-137.

466.   Witkin, H.A., Price-Williams, D., Bertini, M., Christiansen, B., Oltman, P., Ramirez, M., & Van Meel, J. "Social Conformity and Psychological Differentiation." *International Journal of Psychology,* 9(1974), pp. 11-29.

467. Yalom, I.D., Green, R., & Fisk, N. "Prenatal Exposure to Female Hormones: Effect on Psychosexual Development in Boys." *Archives of General Psychiatry,* 28(1973), pp. 554-561.

468. Young, H.H. "A Test of Witkin's Field-dependence Hypothesis." *Journal of Abnormal and Social Psychology,* 59(1959), pp. 188-192.

469. Zangwill, O.L. "Speech and the Minor Hemisphere." *Acta Neurologica et Psychiatrica Belgica,* 67(1967), pp. 1013-1020.

470. Zigler, E. "A Measure in Search of a Theory?" *Contemporary Psychology,* 8(1963), pp. 133-135.

471. Zigler, E. "Zigler Stands Firm." *Contemporary Psychology,* 8(1963), pp. 459-461.

472. .Zuckerman, M. "Field Dependency as a Predictor of Responses to Sensory and Social Isolation." *Perceptual and Motor Skills,* 27(1968), pp. 757-758.

473. Zytowski, D.G., Mills, D.H., & Paepe, C. "Psychological Differentiation and the Strong Vocational Interest Blank." *Journal of Counseling Psychology,* 16(1969), pp. 41-44.

INDEX